PROBLEM SOLVING SURVIVAL GUIDE
VOLUME I: CHAPTERS 1-14

INTERMEDIATE
ACCOUNTING
Fifteenth Edition

Donald E. Kieso, Ph.D., C.P.A.
KPMG Peat Marwick Emeritus Professor of Accounting
Northern Illinois University
DeKalb, Illinois

Jerry J. Weygandt, Ph.D., C.P.A.
Arthur Andersen Alumni Professor of Accounting
University of Wisconsin
Madison, Wisconsin

Terry D. Warfield, Ph.D.
Associate Professor
Director, Andersen Center for Financial Reporting and Control
University of Wisconsin
Madison, Wisconsin

CONTENTS

PREFACE: To the Student

The purpose of this problem solving tutorial is to help you to improve your success rate in solving accounting homework assignments and in answering accounting exam questions. For each chapter we provide you with:

OVERVIEW To briefly introduce the chapter topics and their importance.

LEARNING OBJECTIVES To provide you with a learning framework. Explanations of these objectives also provide you with a summary of the major points covered in the chapter.

TIPS To alert you to common pitfalls and misconceptions and to remind you of important terminology, concepts, and relationships that are relevant to answering specific questions or solving certain problems. To help you to understand the intricacies of a problematic situation and to tell you what to do in similar circumstances.

EXERCISES To provide you with a selection of problems which are representative of homework assignments which an intermediate accounting student may encounter.

MULTIPLE CHOICE To provide you with a selection of multiple-choice questions which are representative of common exam questions covering topics in the chapter.

PURPOSES To identify the essence of each question or exercise and to link them to learning objectives.

SOLUTIONS To show you the appropriate solution for each exercise and multiple-choice question presented.

EXPLANATIONS To give you the details of how selected solutions were derived and to explain why things are done as shown.

APPROACHES To coach you on the particular model, computational format, or other strategy to be used to solve particular problems. To teach you how to analyze and solve multiple-choice questions.

This book will be a welcome teaching/learning aid because it provides you with the opportunity to solve accounting problems in addition to the ones assigned by your instructor without having to rely on your teacher for solutions. Many of the exercises and questions contained herein are very similar to items in your intermediate accounting textbook; the difference is, the ones in this book are accompanied with detailed clearly-laid out solutions.

The use of the multiple choice questions in this volume and the related suggestions on how to approach them can easily increase your ability (and confidence in your ability) to deal with exam questions of this variety.

We give special thanks to Chelsea Hunt for her editorial assistance and supportive role in the completion of this workbook. We appreciate the help of Mary Ann Benson who skillfully prepared the manuscript and performed the composition of this book. We are thankful to James Hunt for his support in this project. We also thank James Emig of Villanova University for his assistance in the accuracy review of the manuscript of this new edition.

Marilyn F. Hunt
Donald E. Kieso
Jerry J. Weygandt
Terry Warfield

HOW TO STUDY ACCOUNTING

The successful study of accounting requires a different approach than most other subjects. In addition to reading a chapter, applying the material through the completion of exercises or problems is necessary to develop a true and lasting understanding of the concepts introduced in the text chapter. The study of accounting principles is a combination of theory and practice; theory describes what to do and why, and practice is the application of guidelines to actual situations. We use illustrations (practice) to demonstrate how theory works and we use theory to explain why something is done in practice. Therefore, it is impossible to separate the two in the study of accounting.

Learning accounting is a cumulative process. It is difficult to master Chapter 4 until you are thoroughly familiar with Chapters 1-3, and so on. Therefore, it is imperative that you keep up with class assignments. And because accounting is a technical subject, you must pay particular attention to terminology.

Accounting is the language of business. It is an exciting subject that provides a challenge for most business majors. Your ultimate success in life may well depend on your ability to grasp financial data. The effort you expend now will provide rewards for years to come.

We encourage you to follow the four steps for study outlined below to give yourself the best possible chance for a successful learning experience and to make the most efficient use of your time. These steps provide a system of study for each new chapter in your text.

Step 1
- Scan the learning objectives in the text.
- Scan the chapter (or chapter section) rather quickly.
- Glance over the questions at the end of the chapter.

This first step will give you an overview of the material to be mastered.

Step 2
- Read the assigned pages slowly.
- Use the marginal notes to review and to locate topics within each chapter.
- Study carefully and mark for later attention any portions not clearly understood.
- Pay particular attention to examples and illustrations.
- Try to formulate tentative answers to end-of-chapter questions.

During this phase, you will be filling in the "outline" you formed in Step 1. Most of the details will fall into place during this part of your study. The remaining steps are necessary, however, for a keen understanding of the subject.

Step 3
- Carefully read the **Overview, Learning Objectives,** and **Tips** sections of this *Problem Solving Survival Guide* volume.
- Do the **Exercises** and **Cases** in the *Problem Solving Survival Guide* that pertain to the same learning objectives as your homework assignments. Review the relevant **Illustrations** in this book.
- Do the **Multiple-Choice Type Questions** in the *Problem Solving Survival Guide* that pertain to the same study objectives as your homework assignments.
- Refer back to the sections of the chapter in the text that you marked as unclear if any. It is likely that any confusion or questions on your part will have been cleared up through your work in the *Problem Solving Survival Guide*. If a section remains unclear, carefully reread it and rework relevant pages of the *Problem Solving Survival Guide*.
- Repeat this process for each assigned topic area.

Step 4 • Write out formal answers to homework assignments in the text.

This step is crucial because you find out whether you can independently **apply** the material you have been studying to fresh situations. You may find it necessary to go back to the text and/or the *Problem Solving Survival Guide* to restudy certain sections. This is common and merely shows that the study assignments are working for you.

Additional comments pertaining to Step 3 and your usage of this *Problem Solving Survival Guide* volume are as follows:

- The **Learning Objectives** and **Tips** sections, along with **Illustrations** will aid your understanding and retention of the material. **Exercises** provide examples of application of the text material. These should be very valuable in giving you guidance in completing homework assignments which are often similar in nature and content.

- The **Approach** stated for an exercise or question is likely the most valuable feature of this *Problem Solving Survival Guide* volume because it tells you how to **think** through the situation at hand. This thought process can then be used for similar situations. It is impossible to illustrate every situation you may encounter. You can, however, handle new situations by simply applying what you know and making modifications where appropriate. Many students make the mistake of attempting to memorize their way through an accounting book. That too is an impossible feat. **Do not rely on memorization.** If this material is going to be useful to you, you must **think** about what you are reading and always be thinking of **why** things are as they are. If you know the reasoning for a particular accounting treatment, it will be much easier to remember that treatment and reconstruct it even weeks after your initial study of it.

- **Explanations** are provided for exercise and questions. These are very detailed so that you will thoroughly understand what is being done and why. These details will serve you well when you complete your homework assignments.

- Always make an honest effort to solve the exercises and answer the questions contained in this *Problem Solving Survival Guide* volume **before** you look at the solutions. Answering the questions on your own will maximize the benefits you can expect to reap from this book.

- The **Multiple-Choice Type Questions** are self-tests to give you immediate feedback on how well you understand the material. Study the **Approaches** suggested for answering these questions in the *Problem Solving Survival Guide*. Practice them when answering the multiple choice questions in the text. Apply them when taking examinations. By doing so, you will learn to calmly, methodically, and successfully process examination questions. This will definitely improve your exam scores.

- When you work an **Exercise** or **Case** in the *Problem Solving Survival Guide* or in the text, always read the instructions **before** you read all of the given data. This allows you to determine what you are to accomplish. Therefore, as you now read through the data, you can begin to process it because you can determine its significance and relevance. If you read the data before the instructions, you are likely to waste your time because you will have to reread the facts once you find out what you are to do with them. Also, more importantly, you are likely to begin to anticipate what the problem is about, which will often cause you to do things other than what is requested in the question.

Good luck and best wishes for a positive learning experience!

HOW TO APPROACH A MULTIPLE CHOICE EXAMINATION

1. Work questions in the order in which they appear on the exam. If a question looks too long or difficult and you choose to skip over it, put a big question mark in the margin to remind yourself to return to that question after others are completed. Also put a mark in the margin for any question meriting additional review at the end of the exam period.

2. Do not look at the answer choices until you have thoroughly processed the question stem (see 3 and 4 below). The wrong answers are called "distracters". The manner in which these "distractors" are developed causes them to likely mislead you or cause you to misinterpret the question if you read them too early in the process.

3. Read each question very carefully. Start with the requirement or essence of the question first (this is usually the last sentence or last phrase of the stem of the question) so that you immediately focus on the question's intent. Now as you read through the rest of the stem and encounter data, you can tell which data are relevant. Underline keywords and important facts. Be especially careful to note exception words such as **not**. Prepare intermediary solutions as you read the question. Identify pertinent information with notations in the margin of the exam. If a set of data is the basis for two or more questions, read the requirements of each of the questions **before** reading the data and before beginning to work on the first question (sometimes the questions can be worked simultaneously or you may find it easier to work them out of order).

4. Anticipate the answer before looking at the alternative solutions. Recall the applicable definition, concept, principle, rule, model, or format. If the question deals with a computation, perform the computation. Use abbreviations to describe each component of your computation; this will greatly aid you in following your work and staying on target with the question.

5. Read the answers and select the best answer choice. For computational questions, if the answer you have computed is not among the choices, check your math and the logic of your solution.

6. When you have completed all questions, review each question again to verify your choices. Reread the question requirement, scan the data, look at your selected answer, scan your work, and determine the reasonableness of your choice.

CHAPTER 1

FINANCIAL ACCOUNTING AND ACCOUNTING STANDARDS

OVERVIEW

Accounting is the language of business. As such, accountants collect and communicate economic information about business enterprises or other entities to a wide variety of persons. To be useful, financial statements must be clearly understandable and comparable so that users may compare the performance of one business with the performance of the same business for a prior period or with the performance of another similar business. Therefore, all general purpose financial statements should be prepared in accordance with the same uniform guidelines. In this chapter, we will examine the history and sources of current financial accounting standards (generally accepted accounting principles).

SUMMARY OF LEARNING OBJECTIVES

1. **Identify the major financial statements and other means of financial reporting.** Companies most frequently provide (1) the balance sheet, (2) the income statement, (3) the statement of cash flows, and (4) the statement of owners' or stockholders' equity. Financial reporting other than financial statements may take various forms. Examples include the president's letter and supplementary schedules in the corporate annual report, prospectuses, reports filed with government agencies, news releases, management's forecasts, and descriptions of an enterprise's social or environmental impact.

2. **Explain how accounting assists in the efficient use of scarce resources.** Accounting provides reliable, relevant, and timely information to managers, investors, and creditors to allow resource allocation to the most efficient enterprises. Accounting also provides measurements of efficiency (profitability) and financial soundness.

3. **Identify the objective of financial reporting.** The objective of general purpose financial reporting is to provide financial information about the reporting entity that is useful to present and potential equity investors, lenders, and other creditors in decisions about providing resources to the entity through equity investments and loans or other forms of credit. Information that is decision-useful to investors may also be helpful to other users of financial reporting who are not investors.

4. **Explain the need for accounting standards.** The accounting profession has attempted to develop a set of standards that is generally accepted and universally practiced. Without this set of standards, each company would have to develop its own standards. Readers of financial statements would have to familiarize themselves with every company's peculiar accounting and reporting practices. As a result, it would be almost impossible to prepare statements that could be compared with the statements of other companies.

5. **Identify the major policy-setting bodies and their role in the standard-setting process.** The **Securities and Exchange Commission (SEC)** is a federal agency that has broad powers to prescribe, in whatever detail it desires, the accounting standards to be employed by companies

that fall within its jurisdiction. The **American Institute of Certified Public Accountants (AICPA)** issued standards through its Committee on Accounting Procedure and Accounting Principles Board (APB). The **Financial Accounting Standards Board (FASB)** establishes and improves standards of financial accounting and reporting for the guidance and education of the public, which includes issuers, auditors, and users of financial information.

6.   **Explain the meaning of generally accepted accounting principles (GAAP) and the role of the Codification for GAAP.** Generally accepted accounting principles (GAAP) are those principles that have substantial authoritative support, such as FASB Standards, Interpretations and Staff Positions, APB Opinions and Interpretations, AICPA Accounting Research Bulletins, and other authoritative pronouncements. All these documents and others are now classified in one document referred to as the Codification. The purpose of the Codification is to simplify user access to all authoritative U.S. GAAP. The codification changes the way GAAP is documented, presented, and updated.

7.   **Describe the impact of user groups on the standard-setting process.** User groups may want particular economic events accounted for or reported in a particular way, and they fight hard to get what they want. They especially target the FASB to influence changes in the existing standards and the development of new rules. Because of the accelerated rate of change and the increased complexity of our economy, these pressures have been multiplying. GAAP is as much a product of political action as it is of careful logic or empirical findings. The International Accounting Standards Board (IASB) is working with the FASB (U.S. standard setters) toward international convergence of accounting standards.

8.   **Describe some of the challenges facing financial reporting.** Financial reports fail to provide (1) some key performance measures widely used by management, (2) forward-looking information needed by investors and creditors, (3) sufficient information about a company's soft assets (intangibles), (4) real-time financial information, and (5) easy-to-comprehend information.

9.   **Understand issues related to ethics and financial accounting.** Financial accountants are called on for moral discernment and ethical decision making. Decisions sometimes are difficult because a public consensus has not emerged to formulate a comprehensive ethical system that provides guidelines in making ethical judgments.

TIPS ON CHAPTER TOPICS

TIP: Because most business owners (stockholders of corporations) are not involved with the operation of the business, the function of measuring and reporting data to absentee owners has emerged as a critical role for accounting. This situation greatly increases the need for accounting standards.

TIP: The financial statements most frequently provided by an entity (often called the **basic financial statements** or **general purpose financial statements**) are: (1) the income statement, (2) the statement of owners' equity (or statement of stockholders' equity), (3) the balance sheet, and (4) the statement of cash flows. In addition, note disclosures are an integral part of the financial statements.

TIP: The primary focus of this textbook concerns the development of two types of financial information which are governed by generally accepted accounting principles: (1) the basic financial statements and (2) the related note disclosures.

TIP: An effective process of capital allocation is critical to a healthy economy. It promotes productivity, encourages innovation, and provides an efficient and liquid market for buying and selling securities and obtaining and granting credit. Reliable and relevant information is needed for the securities market to operate effectively.

TIP: The SEC now requires the delivery of financial reports using eXtensible Business Language (XBRL). Reporting through XBRL allows timelier reporting via the internet and allows statement users to transform accounting reports to meet their specific needs.

TIP: The terms **principles** and **standards** are used interchangeably in practice and throughout this book.

TIP: The **accrual basis of accounting** is used in preparing the basic financial statements. The accrual basis provides for (1) reporting revenues in the period they are earned (which may not be the same period in which the related cash is received), and (2) reporting expenses in the period they are incurred (which may not be the same period in which the related cash is paid). Information based on accrual accounting better indicates a company's present and continuing ability to generate favorable cash flows than does information limited to the financial effects of cash receipts and cash payments for a recent time period.

TIP: Presently, there are two sets of standards accepted for international use – GAAP and the International Financial Reporting Standards (IFRS). IFRS are issued by the London-based International Accounting Standards Board (IASB). There are many similarities between GAAP and IFRS. The IASB and the FASB are working hard to accomplish an ambitious goal which is to converge their concepts and standards.

TIP: The **Governmental Accounting Standards Board (GASB)** establishes and improves standards of financial accounting for state and local governments.

CASE 1-1

Purpose: (L.O.5) This case will identify the organizations responsible for various accounting documents.

Instructions

Presented below are a number of accounting organizations and the type of documents they have issued. Match the appropriate document to the organization involved. Note that more than one document may be issued by the same organization.

Organization

1. _____ Accounting Principles Board (APB)

2. _____ AICPA Committee on Accounting Procedure

3. _____ Financial Accounting Standards Board (FASB)

4. _____ International Accounting Standards Board (IASB)

5. _____ Accounting Standards Executive Committee of the AICPA

Document

(a) Practice Bulletins
(b) Accounting Research Bulletins
(c) Opinions
(d) Staff Positions
(e) International Financial Reporting Standards
(f) Statements of Financial Accounting Standards
(g) Technical Bulletins
(h) Statements of Position (SOP)
(i) Interpretations
(j) Industry Audit and Accounting Guides
(k) Statements of Financial Accounting Concepts

Solution to Case 1-1

1.	c, i	3.	d, f, g, i, k	5.	a, h, j
2.	b	4.	e		

CASE 1-2

Purpose: (L.O.6) This case will review the meaning of generally accepted accounting principles and their significance.

All publicly-held companies must have their annual financial statements audited by an independent CPA. In accordance with generally accepted auditing standards (which you will study in an auditing class), the auditor expresses an opinion regarding the fairness of the financial statements which are to be in conformity with generally accepted accounting principles.

Instructions
(a)   Define generally accepted accounting principles.
(b)   Identify at least six types of documents that comprise GAAP.
(c)   Explain the significance of GAAP to an auditor of financial statements.
(d)   Describe the "Codification" of GAAP and explain why it was initiated.
(e)   Describe the Codification Research System.

Solution to Case 1-2

(a)   The accounting profession has adopted a common set of standards and procedures called **generally accepted accounting principles** (often referred to as GAAP). The word "principles" refers to methods or procedures or standards. The phrase "generally accepted" means having "substantial authoritative support." A method can be considered to have substantial authoritative support if it has been approved by a rule-making body or if it has gained acceptance over time because of its universal application.

(b)   GAAP is composed of a mixture of over 2,000 documents that have developed over the last 60 years or so. The major sources of GAAP have come from the Financial Accounting Standards Board (FASB), Accounting Principles Board (APB), and Committee on Accounting Procedure (CAP). The many types of documents that comprise GAAP include the following:
a. FASB Standards, Interpretations, and Staff Bulletins
b. APB Opinions
c. AICPA Accounting Research Bulletins
d. FASB Technical Bulletins
e. AICPA Industry Audit and Accounting Guides
f. AICPA Statements of Position
g. FASB Emerging Issues Task Force Consensus Positions
h. AICPA AcSEC Practice Bulletins
i. AICPA Accounting Interpretations
j. FASB Implementation Guides (Q and A)

(c)   An enterprise shall not represent that its financial statements are presented in accordance with GAAP if its selection of accounting principles departs from GAAP and that departure has a material impact on its financial statements. Furthermore, the

AICPA's Code of Professional Conduct requires that members prepare financial statements in accordance with generally accepted accounting principles. Specifically, Rule 203 of this Code prohibits a member from expressing an opinion (upon the completion of an audit) that financial statements conform with GAAP if those statements contain a material departure from a generally accepted accounting principle.

(d)   As might be expected, the documents that comprise GAAP vary in format, completeness, and structure. In some cases, these documents are inconsistent and difficult to interpret. As a result, financial statement preparers sometimes are not sure whether they have the right GAAP; determining what is authoritative and what is not becomes difficult.

In response to these concerns, the FASB developed the **Financial Accounting Standards Board Accounting Standards Codification** (or more simply, "the Codification"). The FASB's primary goal in developing the Codification is to provide in one place all the authoritative literature related to a particular topic. This will simplify user access to all authoritative U.S. generally accepted accounting principles. The Codification changes the way GAAP is documented, presented, and updated. It explains what GAAP is and eliminates nonessential information such as redundant document summaries, basis for conclusions sections, and historical content. In short, the Codification is a major restructuring of accounting and reporting standards. Its purpose is to integrate and synthesize existing GAAP—not to create new GAAP. It creates one level of GAAP; all of the material included is considered authoritative. All other accounting literature is considered to be nonauthoritative (such as FASB Concepts Statements and textbooks). (Prior to Codification, there was a "hierarchy of GAAP" which deemed certain authoritative documents to be more authoritative then others which led to various levels of GAAP). Now there is only one level of authoritative GAAP.

The Codification includes the "essential content" of all of the documents listed in the Solution to part (b) above and relevant portions of authoritative content issued by the Securities and Exchange Commission (SEC) such as Regulation S-X and Financial Reporting Releases (FRR)/Accounting Series Releases (ASR).

The FASB currently issues accounting pronouncements through Accounting Standards Updates (Update). Updates amend the Accounting Standards Codification.

TIP: In the event that there is an accounting issue that is not addressed in the Codification, the accountant should seek support from other accounting literature. Examples of other accounting literature that is not in the Codification and therefore not authoritative include FASB Concepts Statements; AICPA Issues Papers; International Financial Reporting Standards (IFRSs) of the International Accounting Standards Board (IASB); pronouncements of other professional associations or regulatory agencies; and accounting textbooks, handbooks, and articles. (The FASB Concepts Statements would normally be more influential than other sources in this category.)

(e)   To provide easy access to the Codification, the FASB also developed the Financial Accounting Standards Board Codification Research System (CRS). CRS is an online real-time database that provides easy access to the Codification. The Codification and the related CRS provide a topically organized structure, subdivided into topics, subtopics, sections, and paragraphs, using a numerical index system.

For purposes of referencing authoritative GAAP material in your textbook, the authors will use the Codification framework. Here is an example of how the Codification framework is cited, using Intangibles as the example. The purpose of the search shown below is to determine GAAP for accounting for intangible assets other than goodwill subsequent to initial measurement.

Topic	Go to FASB ASC 350 to access Intangibles topic.
Subtopics	Go to FASB ASC 350-30 to access the General Intangibles Other Than Goodwill Subtopic of the Topic 350.
Sections	Go to FASB ASC 350-30-35 to access the Subsequent Measurement Section of the Subtopic 350-30.
Paragraph	Go to FASB ASC 350-30-35-6 to access the Intangible Assets Subject to Amortization paragraph of Section 350-30-35.

The following shows the Codification framework graphically.

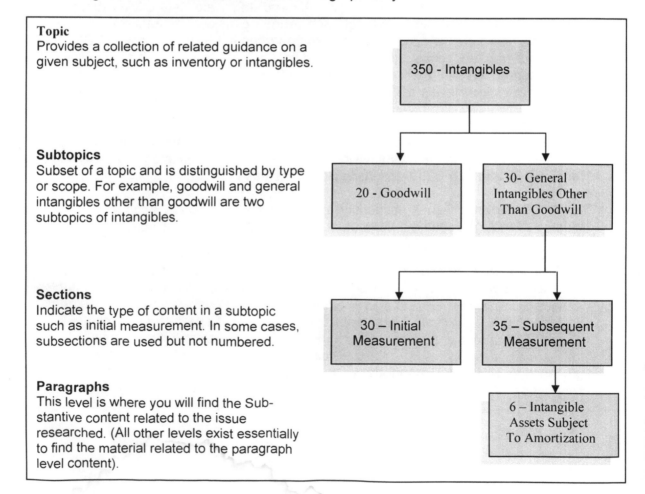

Topic
Provides a collection of related guidance on a given subject, such as inventory or intangibles.

Subtopics
Subset of a topic and is distinguished by type or scope. For example, goodwill and general intangibles other than goodwill are two subtopics of intangibles.

Sections
Indicate the type of content in a subtopic such as initial measurement. In some cases, subsections are used but not numbered.

Paragraphs
This level is where you will find the Substantive content related to the issue researched. (All other levels exist essentially to find the material related to the paragraph level content).

CASE 1-3

Purpose: (L.O.7) This case looks at the key provisions of the Sarbanes-Oxley Act.

In 2002, Congress enacted the Sarbanes-Oxley Act in response to what then were recent accounting scandals at large companies including Enron, Cendant, Sunbeam, Rite-Aid, Xerox, and WorldCom. The new law increases the resources for the SEC to combat fraud and poor reporting practices.

Instructions
Describe the six key provisions of the Sarbanes-Oxley legislation.

Solution to Case 1-3

Some of the key provisions of the Sarbanes-Oxley Act are that it:
1. Establishes an oversight board [the **Public Company Accounting Oversight Board (PCAOB)**] for accounting practices. The PCAOB has oversight and enforcement authority and establishes auditing, quality control, and independence standards and rules for auditors of public companies.

2. Implements stronger independence rules for auditors of public companies. For example, audit partners are required to rotate off clients every five years so that different partners can take responsibility for the audit. Also, the accounting firm that performs auditing services for a particular client is prohibited from offering certain types of consulting services to that same corporate client.

3. Requires CEOs, (Chief Executive Officers) and CFOs (Chief Financial Officers) of public companies to personally certify that financial statements and disclosures are accurate and complete; also requires CEOs and CFOs to forfeit bonuses and profits when there is an accounting restatement.

4. Requires audit committees of public companies to be comprised of independent members and members with financial expertise.

5. Requires codes of ethics for senior financial officers of public companies.

6. Requires public companies to attest to the effectiveness of their internal controls over financial reporting.

TIP: Internal controls are a system of checks and balances designed to prevent and detect fraud and errors.

TIP: The changes required by the Sarbanes-Oxley Act are hopefully going to help in closing the **expectations gap** – which is the gap between what the public thinks accountants **should** do and what accountants think they **can** do – but they come with a cost to society.

ANALYSIS OF MULTIPLE-CHOICE TYPE QUESTIONS

QUESTION

1. (L.O. 1) The process of identifying, measuring, analyzing, and communicating financial information needed by management to plan, evaluate, and control an organization's operations is called
   a. financial accounting.
   b. managerial accounting.
   c. tax accounting.
   d. auditing.

Approach and Explanation: Define each answer selection. Select the answer item for which your definition matches the stem of the question. **Financial accounting** is the process that culminates in the preparation of financial reports on the enterprise as a whole for use by parties both internal and external to the enterprise. (Users of these financial reports include investors, creditors, managers, unions, and government agencies.) **Managerial accounting** is the process of identifying, measuring, analyzing, and communicating financial information needed by management to plan, evaluate, and control an organization's operations. (These reports are only for the use of parties internal to the enterprise.) **Tax accounting** usually refers to tax planning, advising on tax matters, and/or preparing tax returns. **Auditing** refers to the examination of financial statements by a certified public accountant in order to express an opinion on their fairness. An auditor attests to the fairness of financial statements and their conformity to generally accepted accounting principles. (Solution = b.)

QUESTION

2. (L.O. 3) In meeting the objective of financial reporting, financial statements should provide:
   a. information about the investors in the business entity.
   b. information about the liquidation values of the resources held by the enterprise.
   c. information that is useful in assessing cash flow prospects.
   d. information that will attract new investors.

Approach and Explanation: Before you read the possible answers, mentally describe the objective of financial reporting and its emphasis. Then carefully read the suggested answers. As you read an answer choice, note whether it is a match to your description or not. The objective of financial reporting is to provide financial information about the reporting entity that is useful to present and potential equity investors, lenders and other creditors in decisions about providing resources to the entity. When making these decisions, investors and creditors are interested in assessing (1) the company's ability to generate net cash flows and (2) management's ability to protect and enhance the assets of the company, which will be used to generate future net cash inflows. (Solution = c.)

QUESTION

3. (L.O. 5) The most significant current source of generally accepted accounting principles is the:
   a. NYSE.
   b. IRS.
   c. APB.
   d. FASB.

Explanation: The mission of the Financial Accounting Standards Board (FASB) is to establish and improve standards of financial accounting and reporting. The Accounting Principles Board (APB) was the predecessor of the FASB. The New York Stock Exchange (NYSE) has nothing to do with the development of generally accepted accounting principles. The IRS (Internal Revenue Service) oversees compliance with the income tax code for the U.S. Department of the Treasury. (Solution = d.)

QUESTION
4.   (L.O. 5) Members of the Financial Accounting Standards Board are:
   a.   employed by the American Institute of Certified Public Accountants (AICPA).
   b.   part-time employees.
   c.   required to hold a CPA certificate.
   d.   independent of any other organization.

Explanation: The members of the FASB are well-paid, full-time members. The FASB is not affiliated with the AICPA; it is not associated with any single professional organization. The FASB is answerable only to the Financial Accounting Foundation. It is not necessary to be a CPA or a member of the AICPA to be a member of the FASB. FASB members must sever all ties with CPA firms, companies, or institutions. (Solution = d.)

QUESTION
5.   (L.O. 5) Which of the following pronouncements were issued by the Accounting Principles Board?
   a.   Accounting Research Bulletins
   b.   Opinions
   c.   Statements of Position
   d.   Statements of Financial Accounting Concepts

Explanation: The Accounting Principles Board issued 31 APB Opinions between the years 1962-1973. Accounting Research Bulletins (51 of them) were issued by the Committee on Accounting Procedure between 1939 and 1959. Statements of Position are issued by the AICPA (but not the APB). The FASB issues Statements on Financial Accounting Concepts (there are 7 of these to date and six of them relate to financial reporting for business enterprises). (Solution = b.)

QUESTION
6.   (L.O. 5) The body charged with the mission of establishing and improving standards of financial accounting and reporting for business enterprises is the:
   a.   Financial Accounting Foundation (FAF).
   b.   Financial Accounting Standards Board (FASB).
   c.   Financial Accounting Standards Advisory Council (FASAC).
   d.   Governmental Accounting Standards Board (GASB).

Explanation: The FASB is responsible for establishing and improving GAAP. The FAF selects the members of the FASB, and the FASAC funds their activities and generally oversees the FASB's activities (from an operational rather than from a technical standpoint). Generally, the SEC has relied on the AICPA and FASB to regulate the accounting profession and develop and enforce accounting standards. The GASB deals only with standards pertaining to state and local government reporting. (Solution = b.)

QUESTION
7.   (L.O. 5) The demise of the APB and the creation of the FAF, FASB, and FASAC are largely and most directly attributed to the:
   a.   IRS.
   b.   Great Depression.
   c.   Securities Exchange Act.
   d.   recommendations of the Wheat Committee.

Explanation: The Great Depression of the 1930s resulted in the Securities Exchange Act of 1934 which led to the formation of the Securities and Exchange Commission (SEC). These developments prompted the formation of the Committee on Accounting Procedure (CAP) which was replaced by the Accounting Principles Board (APB). When the APB needed an overhaul, it was the recommendations of the Wheat

Committee that resulted in the demise of the APB and the creation of the new standard-setting structure composed of three organizations—the Financial Accounting Foundation (FAF), the Financial Accounting Standards Board (FASB), and the Financial Accounting Standards Advisory Council (FASAC). (Solution = d.)

QUESTION
8.   (L.O. 5) The American Institute of Certified Public Accountants (AICPA) continues to be the sole entity responsible for
   a.   developing financial accounting standards.
   b.   developing auditing standards.
   c.   developing and enforcing professional ethics.
   d.   developing and grading the Certified Public Accountant (CPA) examination.

Explanation: Recently, the role of the AICPA in standard-setting has diminished. However, the AICPA continues to develop and grade the CPA examination, which is administered in all 50 states. (Solution = d.)

QUESTION
9.   (L.O. 5) The following are part of the "due process" system used by the FASB in the evolution of a typical FASB Statement of Financial Accounting Standards:
      1.   Exposure Draft
      2.   Accounting Standards Update
      3.   Public Hearing
The chronological order in which these items are released is as follows:
   a.   1, 2, 3.
   b.   1, 3, 2.
   c.   2, 3, 1.
   d.   3, 1, 2.

Explanation: The following steps are taken in the evolution of a typical FASB Statement of Financial Accounting Standards:
1.   A topic or project is identified and placed on the Board's agenda.
2.   Research and analysis are conducted by the FASB technical staff and preliminary views of pros and cons are issued.
3.   A public hearing is held on the proposed standard.
4.   The Board analyzes and evaluates the public response; The Board deliberates on the issues and prepares an **exposure draft** for release.
5.   After an exposure period for public comment, the Board evaluates all of the responses received. A committee studies the exposure draft in relation to the public responses, reevaluates its position, and revises the draft if necessary. The full Board gives the revised draft final consideration and votes on issuance of an **Accounting Standards Update**. The passage of a new FASB Accounting Standards Update requires the support of three of the five Board members. (Solution = d.)

QUESTION
10. (L.O. 5) All of the following organizations are directly involved in the development of financial accounting standards (GAAP) in the United States, **except** the:
    a.   Internal Revenue Service (IRS).
    b.   Financial Accounting Standards Board (FASB).
    c.   American Institute of Certified Public Accountants (AICPA).
    d.   Securities and Exchange Commission (SEC).

Explanation: The Internal Revenue Service (IRS) is responsible for federal income tax rules and administration. Although the IRS and its Internal Revenue Code are influences on accounting practice, they are not directly involved in the development of accounting standards (for financial statements) as are the other organizations listed. (Solution = a.)

QUESTION
11. (L.O. 7) A Brazilian corporation listed on a U.S. exchange
    a.   is permitted to use iGAAP.
    b.   must follow the accounting standards set forth by the government of Brazil.
    c.   must use U.S. GAAP.

Explanation: Presently, there are two sets of standards accepted for international use—GAAP (U.S. standards) and the International Financial Reporting Standards (IFRS). IFRS are issued by the London-based International Accounting Standards Board (IASB). U.S. companies that list overseas are still permitted to use GAAP, and foreign companies listed on U.S. exchanges are permitted to use IFRS There are many similarities between GAAP and IFRS. Already over 115 countries use IFRS, and the European Union now requires all listed companies in Europe (over 7,000 companies) to use them. It is now highly probable that the United States will adopt IFRS in the near future because the FASB recognizes the need for one set of high-quality global accounting standards. To achieve this goal, the FASB and the IASB are now working hard to find common ground related to existing and proposed standards. Both parties recognize the global markets will best be served if only one set of standards is used. For example, the FASB and the IASB formalized their commitment to the convergence of GAAP and IFRS by issuing a memorandum of understanding (often referred to as the Norwalk agreement). (Solution = a).

IFRS Insights

U.S. standards, referred to as generally accepted accounting principles (GAAP), are developed by the Financial Accounting Standards Board (FASB). International standards are referred to as International Financial Reporting Standards (IFRS) and are developed by the International Accounting Standards Board (IASB).

There are many similarities between GAAP and IFRS. Some differences between GAAP and IFAS st from the fact that the FASB and IASB have responded to different user needs. In some countries s the United Stated, the primary users of financial statements are private investors and creditors other countries, the primary users are tax authorities or central government planners.

IFRS tends to be simpler in its accounting and disclosure requirements (more "prin to comply is more detailed (more "rules-based").

The internal control standards applicable to Sarbanes-Oxley (SOX) appl listed on U.S. exchanges. There is a debate as to whether non-U.S. co with this extra layer of regulation. Do the benefits exceed the costs of

Some question whether the higher costs of SOX compliance are making the U.S. securities markets less competitive.

Most agree that there is a need for one set of international accounting standards due to the following:

a.   Multinational corporations view the entire world as their market.

b.   Mergers and acquisitions of large companies in recent years suggest even more business combinations are to occur in the future.

c.   Companies and individuals in different countries and markets are become more comfortable buying and selling goods and services from one another as communication barriers continue to topple through advances in technology.

d.   There are active financial markets of international significance. Currency, equity securities (stocks), and bonds and derivatives are traded throughout the world.

TIP: At the end of each chapter there will be a section for IFRS (International Financial Reporting Standards) Insights. Check with your professor to see if your are responsible for this section for testing purposes.

TRUE/FALSE (Circle the correct answer for each).

T F 1. International Financial Reporting Standards (IFRS) are developed by the International Accounting Standards Board (IASB).

T F 2. There are many similarities between GAAP and IFRS.

T F 3. IFRS tends to be more "rules-based" in its accounting requirements whereas GAAP tends to be simpler and more "principles-based"

T F 4. The internal control standards applicable to Sarbanes-Oxley (SOX) apply to non-U.S. companies.

Solutions:

1. T   3. F
2. T   4. F

CHAPTER 2

CONCEPTUAL FRAMEWORK
FOR FINANCIAL REPORTING

OVERVIEW

Financial statements are needed for decision making. In order to make informed decisions, a financial statement user must understand both the financial information conveyed and how it is derived. To be useful, financial statements must be clearly understandable and comparable so that users may compare the performance of one business with the performance of the same business for a prior period or with the performance of another similar business. Therefore, all general purpose financial statements should be prepared in accordance with the same uniform guidelines. In this chapter, we will examine basic accounting principles.

SUMMARY OF LEARNING OBJECTIVES

1. **Describe the usefulness of a conceptual framework.** The accounting profession needs a conceptual framework to: (1) build on and relate to an established body of concepts and objectives, (2) provide a framework for solving new and emerging practical problems, (3) increase financial statement users' understanding of and confidence in financial reporting, and (4) enhance comparability among companies' financial statements.

2. **Describe the FASB's efforts to construct a conceptual framework.** The FASB has issued seven Statements of Financial Accounting Concepts that relate to financial reporting for business enterprises. These concepts statements provide the basis for the conceptual framework. They include objectives, qualitative characteristics, and elements. In addition, measurement and recognition concepts are developed. The FASB and the IASB are now working on a joint project to develop an improved common conceptual framework that provides a sound foundation for developing future accounting standards.

3. **Understand the objective of financial reporting.** The objective of general-purpose financial reporting is to provide financial information about the reporting entity that is **useful to present and potential equity investors, lenders, and other creditors** in making decisions about providing resources to the entity. Those decisions involve buying, selling, or holding equity and debt instruments, and providing or settling loans and other forms of credit. Information that is decision-useful to capital providers may also be helpful to other users of financial reporting who are not capital providers.

4. **Identify the qualitative characteristics of accounting information.** The over-riding criterion by which accounting choices can be judged is decision usefulness—that is, providing information that is most useful for decision making. Relevance and faithful representation are the two fundamental qualities that make information decision-useful. Relevant information makes a difference in a decision by having predictive or confirmatory value and is material. Faithful

representation is characterized by completeness, neutrality, and being free from error. Enhancing qualities of useful information are (1) comparability, (2) verifiability, (3) timeliness, and (4) understandability.

5.   **Define the basic elements of financial statements.** The basic elements of financial statements are (1) assets, (2) liabilities, (3) equity, (4) investments by owners, (5) distributions to owners, (6) comprehensive income, (7) revenues, (8) expenses, (9) gains, and (10) losses. These ten elements are defined in **Illustration 2-3**.

6.   **Describe the basic assumptions of accounting.** Four basic assumptions underlying financial accounting are (1) **Economic entity:** the assumption that the activity of a business enterprise can be kept separate and distinct from its owners and any other business unit. (2) **Going concern:** the assumption that the business enterprise will have a long life. (3) **Monetary unit:** the assumption that money is the common denominator by which economic activity is conducted, and that the monetary unit provides an appropriate basis for measurement and analysis. (4) **Periodicity:** the assumption that the economic activities of an enterprise can be divided into artificial time periods.

7.   **Explain the application of the basic principles of accounting.** (1) **Measurement principle:** Existing GAAP permits the use of historical cost, fair value, and other valuation bases. Although the historical cost principle (measurement based on acquisition price) continues to be an important basis for valuation, recording and reporting of fair value information is increasing. (2) **Revenue recognition principle:** A company recognizes revenue when it satisfies its performance obligation. (3) **Expense recognition principle:** As a general rule, companies recognize expenses when the service or product actually makes its contribution to revenue (commonly referred to as *matching*). (4) **Full disclosure principle:** Companies generally provide information that is of sufficient importance to influence the judgment and decisions of an informed user.

8.   **Describe the impact that the cost constraint has on reporting accounting information.** The cost of providing the information must be weighed against the benefits that can be derived from using the information.

TIPS ON CHAPTER TOPICS

TIP: Although it can sometimes be confusing, accountants often use the terms **assumptions**, **concepts**, **principles**, **conventions**, **constraints**, and **standards** interchangeably. Regardless of the particular term used, they are all a part of GAAP (generally accepted accounting principles).

TIP: The revenue recognition principle is applied before the matching principle is applied. The revenue recognition principle gives guidance in determining what revenues to recognize in a given period. The matching principle then gives guidance as to what expenses to recognize during the period. According to the **revenue recognition principle**, revenues are to be recognized in the period the related service obligation is satisfied. (When a company agrees to perform a service or sell a product to a customer, it has a performance obligation. When the company satisfies this performance obligation, it recognizes revenue.) Per the **expense recognition principle** (or **matching principle)**, expenses are to be recognized in the same period as the revenues they helped generate.

TIP: The term **recognition** refers to the process of formally recording or incorporating an item in the accounts and thus into the body of the financial statements of an entity.

TIP: You should study **Illustration 2-2** on the hierarchy of accounting qualities until you can close your eyes and visualize that diagram. Frequently, exam questions (including CPA Examination questions) over *SFAC No. 8* can be answered by describing what is on that diagram.

TIP: Accounting assumptions underlie the more detailed accounting principles or standards. These assumptions include the economic entity assumption, the going concern assumption, the monetary unit assumption, and the periodicity assumption. They are the foundation for the basic principles which include the measurement principle, the revenue recognition principle, the expense recognition principle, and the full disclosure principle. For example, the historical cost principle (measurement based on acquisition price) and the expense recognition (matching) principle would not be appropriate if it were not for the going concern assumption. If an entity is not expected to continue in business, then plant assets would be reported on the balance sheet at their liquidation or net realizable value (estimated selling price less estimated cost of disposal) rather than at their cost, and depreciation of these assets would not be appropriate.

TIP: There are three common bases of expense recognition: (1) cause and effect, (2) systematic and rational allocation, and (3) immediate recognition. You should be able to explain and give examples for each of these. (See **Case 2-3**.)

TIP: GAAP requires that companies account for and report many assets and liabilities on the balance sheet on the basis of acquisition price; this is an application of the **historical cost principle** (measurement based on acquisition price). Cost is a reliable valuation; it is usually established by an exchange transaction between parties with conflicting interests (that is, a buyer wants to buy at the lowest price possible and a seller wants to sell at the highest price possible). However, **fair value information** may be more useful for the balance sheet for certain types of assets and liabilities and in certain industries. For example, companies report financial instruments, including derivatives, at fair value (more on this topic will be discussed in **Chapter 17**). Certain industries, such as brokerage houses and mutual funds, prepare their basic financial statements on a fair value basis.

TIP: When an asset or liability is initially recorded by a company, the historical cost for that item equals the fair value of that item. In subsequent periods, as market and economic conditions change, historical cost and fair value often diverge. As a result, fair value measures or estimates often provide more relevant information about the expected future cash flows related to the asset or liability. For example, when long-lived assets decline in value, a fair value measure determines any impairment loss (see **Chapters 11 and 12** for discussions of this topic). We presently have a "mixed attribute" system that permits the use of historical cost, fair value, and other valuation bases. Although historical cost continues to be the primary basis for valuation (due to the historical cost principle), reporting of fair value information is increasing. As you progress through the chapters of this book, watch for items and situations that call for a departure from the historical cost principle.

ILLUSTRATION 2-1
CONCEPTUAL FRAMEWORK FOR FINANCIAL REPORTING
(L.O. 2 THRU 8)

Recognition, Measurement and Disclosure Concepts

ASSUMPTIONS	PRINCIPLES	CONSTRAINT	Third Level:
1. Economic entity	1. Measurement	1. Cost	The "how"—
2. Going concern	2. Revenue recognition		implementation
3. Monetary unit	3. Expense recognition		
4. Periodicity	4. Full disclosure		

QUALITATIVE CHARACTERISTICS	ELEMENTS		
1. Fundamental qualities	1. Assets		Second Level:
A. Relevance	2. Liabilities		Bridge be-
(1) Predictive value	3. Equity		tween first and
(2) Confirmatory value	4. Investment by owners		third levels
(3) Materiality	5. Distribution to owners		
B. Faithful representation	6. Comprehensive income		
(1) Completeness	7. Revenues		
(2) Neutrality	8. Expenses		
(3) Free from error	9. Gains		
2. Enhancing qualities	10. Losses		
A. Comparability			
B. Verifiability			
C. Timeliness			
D. Understandability			

OBJECTIVE

Provide information about the reporting entity that is useful to present and potential equity investors, lenders, and other creditors in their capacity as capital providers.	First Level: The "why"— purpose of accounting.

- -

This illustration provides an overview of the FASB's conceptual framework.[1] The first level identifies the **objective of financial reporting**—that is, the purpose of financial reporting. The second level provides the **qualitative characteristics** that make accounting information useful and the **elements of financial statements** (assets, liabilities, and so on). The third level identifies the **recognition, measurement, and disclosure concepts** used in establishing and applying financial accounting standards and the specific concepts to implement the objective. These concepts include assumptions, principles, and a constraint that describe the present reporting environment.

---

[1]Adapted from William C. Norby, *The Financial Analysts Journal* (March-April, 1982), p. 22.

ILLUSTRATION 2-2
HIERARCHY OF ACCOUNTING QUALITIES (L.O. 4)

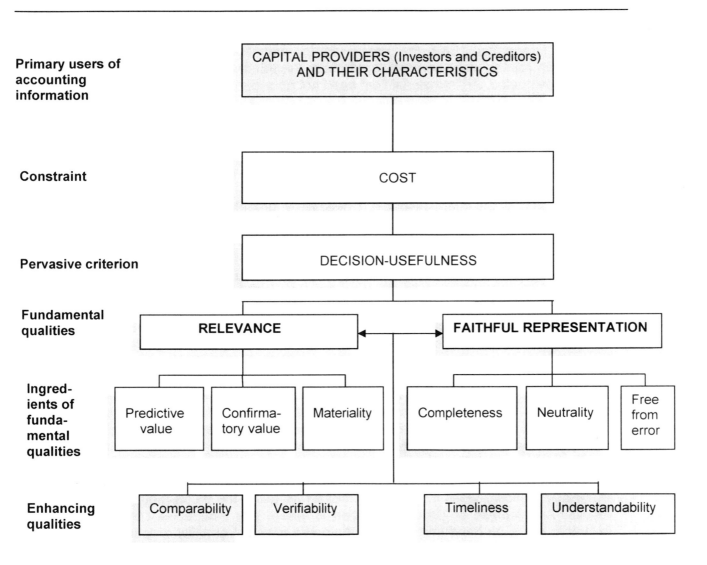

As indicated above, qualitative characteristics are either fundamental or enhancing characteristics, depending on how they affect the decision-usefulness of information. Regardless of classification, each qualitative characteristic contributes to the decision-usefulness of financial reporting information. However, providing useful financial information is limited by a pervasive constraint on financial reporting—cost should not exceed the benefits of a reporting practice.

A brief description of each fundamental and enhancing quality follows:

- **Relevance:** capable of making a difference in a decision (because the information has predictive value, confirmatory value, or both).

- **Predictive value:** helps investors to form their own expectations about the future.

- **Confirmatory value:** relevant information with confirmatory value helps users to confirm or correct prior expectations.

- **Materiality:** Is a company-specific aspect of relevance; information is material if omitting it or misstating it could influence decisions that users make on the basis of the reported financial information. Both the nature and/or magnitude of the item(s) to which the information relates must be considered; thus, the relative size and importance of an item must be evaluated. An immaterial item need not be separately disclosed.

- **Faithful representation:** numbers and descriptions match what really existed or happened. Faithful representation is necessary because a user does not have the means to evaluate the factual content of the information. Information must be complete, neutral, and free of material error.

- **Completeness:** all the information that is necessary for faithful representation is provided. An omission can cause information to be false or misleading.

- **Neutrality:** a company cannot select information to favor one set of interested parties over another. Information presented in financial statements must be unbiased.

- **Free from error:** an information item that is free from error will be a more accurate (faithful) representation of a financial item. Faithful presentation does not imply total freedom from error as estimates of various types that incorporate management's judgment are required for items such as bad debt expense and depreciation of plant assets.

- **Comparability:** information that is measured and reported in a similar manner for different companies is considered comparable and enables users to identify the real similarities and differences in economic events between companies. Consistency is a type of comparability and is present when a company applies the same accounting treatment to similar events, from period to period.

- **Verifiability:** occurs when independent measurers using the same methods, obtain similar results. An example of direct verification is where two independent auditors count the inventory items on hand and arrive at the same physical quantity amount. An example of indirect verification is where two independent auditors compute the ending inventory value by using the FIFO method. Verification here may occur by checking the quantity and costs (inputs) and recalculating the ending inventory (the output).

- **Timeliness:** having information available to decision-makers before it loses its capacity to influence decisions. Having relevant information available sooner can enhance its capacity to influence decisions.

- **Understandability:** for information to be useful, there must be a connection (linkage) between users and the decisions they make. This link, understandability, is the quality of information that lets reasonably informed users see its significance. Understandability is enhanced when information is classified, characterized, and presented clearly and concisely.

SOURCE: FASB, *Statement of Financial Accounting Concepts No. 8, Chapter 3, "Qualitative Characteristics of Useful Financial Information."*

CASE 2-1

Purpose:　(L.O. 4) This exercise is designed to review the qualitative characteristics that make accounting information useful for decision making purposes (per *SFAC No. 8).*

The qualitative characteristics that make accounting information useful for decision making are as follows:

Relevance	Neutrality
Predictive value	Free from error
Confirmatory value	Comparability
Materiality	Verifiability
Faithful representation	Timeliness
Completeness	Understandability

Instructions

Fill in the blank to identify the appropriate qualitative characteristic(s) being described in each of the statements below. A qualitative characteristic may be used more than once.

_____ 1. Two fundamental qualities that make accounting information useful for decision-making purposes.

_____ 2. Information that is capable of making a difference in a decision is said to have this fundamental quality.

_____ 3. Information that is complete and reasonably free of error and bias is said to have this fundamental quality.

_____ 4. Four enhancing qualities that are related to both relevance and faithful representation.

_____ 5. An entity is to apply the same accounting methods to similar events for successive accounting periods; that is, when an entity selects one method from a list of alternative acceptable methods, that same method is used period after period.

_____ 6. Information is measured and reported in a similar manner for different enterprises.

_____ 7. Neutrality is an ingredient of this fundamental quality of accounting information.

_____ 8. Requires that information cannot be selected to favor one set of interested parties over another.

_____   9. Predictive value is an ingredient of this fundamental quality of information.

_____   10. When information provides a basis for forecasting annual earnings for future periods, it is said to have this ingredient of a fundamental quality of accounting information.

_____   11. Quality of information that confirms or corrects users' prior expectations.

_____   12. Information must be available to decision makers before it loses its capacity to influence their decisions.

_____   13. Imperative for providing comparisons of a single firm from period to period.

_____   14. Enhancing quality being employed when companies in the same industry are using the same accounting principles.

_____   15. A company cannot suppress information just because such disclosure is embarrassing or damaging to the entity.

_____   16. The amounts and descriptions in financial statements should agree with the elements or events that these amounts and descriptions purport to represent due to this fundamental quality of information.

_____   17. Independent measurers, using the same measurement methods, obtain similar results.

_____   18. The numbers and descriptions in financial statements represent what really existed or happened.

_____   19. Requires information to be free of personal bias.

_____   20. Requires a high degree of consensus among individuals on a given measurement.

_____   21. Financial information is a tool and, like most tools, cannot be much direct help to those who are unable or unwilling to use it or who misuse it.

_____   22. Both the nature and/or magnitude of the item must be considered in determining if an item could influence decisions of a user.

_____   23. All items that are likely to influence a decision of users of financial information must be disclosed.

_____   24. An accurate representation of a financial item.

_____   25. This enhancing quality assures that there are no omissions that would cause statements to be misleading.

_____   26. Although an item such as a wastebasket may be of service for eight years, the total cost of the item may be expensed when it is purchased, because the amount is too insignificant to warrant the strict treatment of depreciation over the eight years.

_____   27. Avoid overstatement of net income, assets, and owners' equity, but do not intentionally understate them.

_____   28. Items whose amounts are very small relative to other amounts on the financial statements may be accounted for in the most expedient manner, rather than requiring strict accounting treatment under GAAP.

_____   29. Repair tools are expensed when purchased even though they may be of use for more than one period.

Solution to Case 2-1

1. Relevance and faithful representation
2. Relevance
3. Faithful representation
4. Comparability, verifiability, timeliness, and understandability
5. Comparability (consistency)
6. Comparability
7. Faithful representation
8. Neutrality
9. Relevance
10. Predictive value
11. Confirmatory value
12. Timeliness
13. Comparability (consistency)
14. Comparability
15. Neutrality (and completeness)
16. Faithful representation
17. Verifiability
18. Faithful representation
19. Neutrality
20. Verifiability
21. Understandability
22. Materiality
23. Completeness and Materiality
24. Free from error
25. Completeness
26. Materiality
27. Neutrality
28. Materiality
29. Materiality

Approach: Before beginning to fill in the twenty-nine blanks required, visualize the diagram for the hierarchy of accounting qualities (**Illustration 2-2**). Also, take a few minutes to individually consider the twelve characteristics listed and think of the key phrases involved in describing those items.

ILLUSTRATION 2-3
ELEMENTS OF FINANCIAL STATEMENTS (L.O. 5)

Assets: Probable future economic benefits obtained or controlled by a particular entity as a result of past transactions or events.

Liabilities: Probable future sacrifices of economic benefits arising from present obligations of a particular entity to transfer assets or provide services to other entities in the future as a result of past transactions or events.

Equity: Residual interest in the assets of an entity that remains after deducting its liabilities. In a business enterprise, the equity is the ownership interest.

Investments by owners: Increases in net assets of a particular enterprise resulting from transfers to it from other entities of something of value to obtain or increase ownership interests (or equity) in it. Assets are most commonly received as investments by owners, but that which is received may also include services or satisfaction or conversion of liabilities of the enterprise.

Distributions to owners: Decreases in net assets of a particular enterprise resulting from transferring assets, performing services, or incurring liabilities by the enterprise to owners. Distributions to owners decrease ownership interests (or equity) in an enterprise.

Comprehensive income: Change in equity (net assets) of an entity during a period from transactions and other events and circumstances from nonowner sources. It includes all changes in equity during a period except those resulting from investments by owners and distributions to owners.

Revenues: Inflows or other enhancements of assets of an entity or settlement of its liabilities (or a combination of both) during a period from delivering or producing goods, performing services, or other activities that constitute the entity's ongoing major or central operations.

Expenses: Outflows or other using up of assets or incurrences of liabilities (or a combination of both) during a period from delivering or producing goods, performing services, or carrying out other activities that constitute the entity's ongoing major or central operations.

Gains: Increases in equity (net assets) from peripheral or incidental transactions of an entity and from all other transactions and other events and circumstances affecting the entity during a period except those that result from revenues or investments by owners.

Losses: Decreases in equity (net assets) from peripheral or incidental transactions of an entity and from all other transactions and other events and circumstances affecting the entity during a period except those that result from expenses or distributions to owners.

ILLUSTRATION 2-4
BASIC ACCOUNTING ASSUMPTIONS, PRINCIPLES, AND CONSTRAINTS (L.O. 6, 7, and 8)

Economic entity assumption: States that economic events can be identified with a particular unit of accountability. The activities of an accounting entity can be and should be kept separate and distinct from its owners and all other accounting entities. The entity concept does not necessarily refer to a legal entity.

Going concern assumption: Assumes that the enterprise will continue in operation long enough to carry out its existing objectives and commitments. Sometimes called the **continuity assumption**, it assumes the entity will continue in operation long enough to recover the cost of its assets. This assumption serves as a basis for basic principles such as the historical cost principle. Because of this assumption, liquidation values of assets are not relevant.

Monetary unit assumption: States that only transaction data capable of being expressed in terms of money should be included in the accounting records of the economic entity. All transactions and events can be measured in terms of a common denominator—units of money. A corollary is the added assumption that the unit of measure remains constant from one period to the next (some people call the corollary the "stable dollar assumption").

Periodicity assumption: Assumes that the economic life of a business can be divided into artificial time periods. Although some companies choose to subdivide the business life into months or quarters, others report financial statements only for an annual period.

Measurement principle: Presently we have a "mixed-attribute" system that permits the use of various measurement bases. The most commonly used measurements are based on historical cost and fair value. The **historical cost principle** requires that companies account for and report many assets and liabilities on the basis of acquisition price. **Acquisition price** is measured by the fair value of the item at the date of acquisition. In addition, the cost of an asset includes all costs necessary to acquire the item and get it in the place and condition for its intended use.

Revenue recognition principle: Dictates that revenue should be recognized when the related **performance obligation** is satisfied. When a company agrees to perform a service or to sell a product to a customer, it has a performance obligation. When the company satisfies this performance obligation, it recognizes (reports) revenue. The performance obligation is considered to be satisfied when the entity has substantially accomplished what it must do to be entitled to the benefits represented by the revenues. The revenue generating process for most entities includes a number of steps. As a result, revenue is **recognized** when the "critical point" in the earnings process is reached. This critical point is different for different circumstances as the following examples illustrate. Examples are: (1) when a sale is involved, the point of sale is the critical event, (2) when long-term construction contracts are involved, progress toward completion is the critical event, (3) when products are salable in an active market at readily

ILLUSTRATION 2-4 (Continued)

determinable prices without significant additional cost, the completion of production is the critical event, and (4) when uncertainty about the collection of receivables exists for credit sales of goods and services, the receipt of cash is the critical event.

Expense recognition (or Matching principle): Dictates that expenses be matched with revenues whenever it is reasonable and practical to do so. Expenses (efforts) are recognized in the same period as the related revenue (accomplishment) is recognized. Thus, a factory worker's wages are not recognized as an expense when cash is paid or when the work is performed, or when the product is produced; they are recognized as an expense when the labor (service) or the product actually makes its contribution to the revenue generating process (which is when the related product is sold).

Full disclosure principle: Dictates that circumstances and events that make a difference to financial statement users be disclosed. An entity is to disclose through the data contained in the financial statements and the information in the notes that accompany the statements all information necessary to make the statements not misleading. To be recognized in the main body of the financial statements, an item should meet the definition of one of the basic elements, be measurable with sufficient certainty, and be relevant and reliable. The notes to financial statements generally amplify or explain the items presented in the body of the statements. Information in the notes does not have to be quantifiable, nor does it need to qualify as an element.

Cost constraint (or Cost-benefit relationship): States that the costs of providing the information must be weighed against the benefits that can be derived from using the information. In order to justify requiring a particular measurement or disclosure, the benefits perceived to be derived from it must exceed the costs perceived to be associated with the measurement or disclosure. When the perceived costs exceed the perceived benefits, a measurement or disclosure may be foregone based on its lack of practicality.

CASE 2-2

Purpose: (L.O. 6, 7, 8) This exercise will test your comprehension of the essence and significance of basic accounting assumptions, principles, and constraint.

Instructions

For each of the following statements, identify (by letter) the basic accounting assumption, principle or constraint that is **most directly** related to the given phrase. Each code letter may be used more than once.

Assumptions, Principles, and Constraint

a. Economic entity assumption
b. Going concern assumption
c. Monetary unit assumption
d. Periodicity assumption
e. Historical cost principle
f. Revenue recognition principle

g. Expense recognition (or Matching) principle
h. Full disclosure principle
i. Cost constraint (or Cost-benefit relationship)

TIP:	Before you begin to read and answer the items listed, it would be helpful to briefly think about what you know about each of the assumptions, principles, and constraints. An explanation of each appears in **Illustration 2-4**.

Statements

_____ 1. Revenue should be recognized when it is earned, which is usually at the point of sale.

_____ 2. All information necessary to ensure that the financial statements are **not** misleading should be reported.

_____ 3. This concept eliminates the "liquidation concept" in viewing business affairs.

_____ 4. Measurement of the standing and progress of entities should be made at regular intervals rather than at the end of the business's life.

_____ 5. The recorded amount of an acquired item should be the fair market value of the item at the date of acquisition.

_____ 6. There must be complete and understandable reporting on financial statements.

_____ 7. The president of a business should **not** loan his spouse the company's credit card for personal gasoline purchases.

_____ 8. Expenses should be recognized in the same period that the related revenues are recognized.

_____ 9.   This concept is often exemplified by numerous notes to the financial statements.

_____ 10.   If revenue is deferred to a future period, the related costs of generating that revenue should be deferred to the same future period.

_____ 11.   This concept includes a set of rules concerning when to recognize revenue and how to measure its amount.

_____ 12.   All transactions and events are expressed in terms of a common denominator.

_____ 13.   It is assumed that an organization will remain in business long enough to recover the cost of its assets.

_____ 14.   Changes in the purchasing power of the dollar are so small from one period to the next that they are ignored in preparing the basic financial statements.

_____ 15.   The cost of an item should be measured by the amount of the resources expended to acquire it.

_____ 16.   Accruals and deferrals are often necessary in order to report expenses in the proper time periods.

_____ 17.   Each accounting unit is considered separate and distinct from all other accounting units.

_____ 18.   An accountant assumes that a business will continue indefinitely.

_____ 19.   Assets which have appreciated in value are **not** reported at their current worth subsequent to acquisition because of this principle.

_____ 20.   Depreciation of a long-term tangible asset is based on the asset's original acquisition cost rather than the asset's current market value.

_____ 21.   In order to justify requiring a particular measurement or disclosure, the benefits perceived to be derived from it must exceed the costs expected to be associated with it.

_____ 22.   Externally acquired intangible assets are capitalized and amortized over the periods benefited.

_____ 23.   All significant postbalance sheet events are reported in the notes to the financial statements.

_____ 24.   Revenue for a retail establishment is recorded at the point of sale.

_____ 25.   All important aspects of bond indentures (contracts) are presented in the financial statements.

_____ 26.   Reporting must be done at defined time intervals. The time intervals are of equal length.

_____   27.   An allowance for doubtful (uncollectible) accounts is established.

_____   28.   A company charges its sales commission costs to expense in the same period that the sale is made.

_____   29.   When the liquidation of an enterprise looks imminent, this assumption is **inapplicable** and thus, the historical cost principle does **not** apply. Rather, assets are reported at their net realizable values.

_____   30.   The initial note to financial statements is usually a summary of significant accounting policies.

Solution to Case 2-2

1.	f	12.	c	23.	h	
2.	h	13.	b	24.	f	
3.	b	14.	c	25.	h	
4.	d	15.	e	26.	d	
5.	e	16.	g	27.	g	
6.	h	17.	a	28.	g	
7.	a	18.	b	29.	b	
8.	g	19.	e	30.	h	
9.	h	20.	e*			
10.	g	21.	i			
11.	f	22.	g			

*An argument could be made for answer "g".

CASE 2-3

Purpose: (L.O. 7) This case is designed to review three methods of matching expenses with revenues and examples of each.

An unexpired cost represents probable future benefits and hence is accounted for as an asset. An expired cost represents an expiration of benefits and hence is accounted for as an expense or a loss. There are three common bases of expense recognition (that is, guides for determining the timing of recording an expense): (1) cause and effect, (2) systematic and rational allocation, and (3) immediate recognition.

Instructions

Describe each of the three bases of expense recognition and give a few examples of each for a retail establishment.

Solution to Case 2-3

1. **Cause and effect:** When there is a direct association between the expiration of a cost and a particular revenue transaction, the expense recognition should accompany the revenue recognition; that is, the cost is expensed in the same time period that the related specific revenue is recognized.

    Examples: Cost of goods sold, sale commissions, transportation-out.

2. **Systematic and rational allocation:** This basis is used when, although a cost benefits the revenue generating process of two or more accounting periods, the cost cannot be related to particular revenue transactions. Even though a close cause-and-effect relationship between revenue and cost cannot be determined, this relationship is assumed to exist. The cost is thus initially accounted for as an asset and then allocated to the periods benefited (as an expense) in a systematic and rational manner. The allocation method used should appear reasonable to an unbiased observer and should be consistently applied from period to period.

    Examples: Depreciation of plant assets, amortization of intangibles, allocation (amortization) of prepaids (such as rent and insurance).

3. **Immediate recognition:** This basis is used when a company cannot determine a direct relationship between costs and revenue. These costs may fall in the following categories:
    (a)   Their incurrence during the period provides no discernible future benefits.
    (b)   They must be incurred each accounting period, and no build-up of expected future benefits occurs.
    (c)   By their nature, they relate to current revenues even though they cannot be directly associated with any specific revenues.
    (d)   The amount of cost to be deferred can be measured only in an arbitrary manner or great uncertainty exists regarding the realization of future benefits.
    (e)   Uncertainty exists regarding whether allocating them to current and future periods will serve any useful purpose.
    (f)   They are measures of asset costs recorded in prior periods from which no future benefits are now discernible.

Examples: Sales salaries, office salaries, utilities, repairs, advertising, accounting and legal, research and development, postage, write-off of worthless patent.

TIP:	Costs incurred by a manufacturing company are often classified into two groups: product costs and period costs. **Product costs** such as material, labor, and manufacturing overhead attach to the product and are carried into future periods (as a balance in inventory) if the product remains unsold at the end of the current period, and, therefore, the revenue recognition is deferred to the period of sale. Product costs are expensed in the period of sale in accordance with the cause and effect basis of expense recognition. **Period costs** such as officers' salaries and other administrative expenses are charged off immediately, even though benefits associated with these costs may occur in the future, because no direct relationship between cost and revenue can be determined and it is highly uncertain what, if any, benefits relate to the future.
TIP:	For a manufacturing company, depreciation of the office building is determined and expensed based on a systematic and rational allocation. On the other hand, depreciation of factory machinery is a component of manufacturing overhead; thus, it is an element of product cost. The amount of depreciation that pertains to the products produced during a period is first determined by use of the selected depreciation method. The amount of depreciation that ends up being reflected as an expense on the income statement for the same period depends on the number of products sold (not produced) during the period; it is included as a part of cost of goods sold expense.

ILLUSTRATION 2-5
FAIR VALUE BASIS (MEASUREMENT) (L.O. 7)

We presently have a "mixed-attribute" system that permits the use of various measurement bases. The most commonly used measurements are based on historical cost and fair value. Fair value may be more useful for certain types of assets and liabilities.

For example, companies report many financial instruments, including derivatives, at fair value. Also, companies in certain financial industries, such as brokerage houses and mutual funds, prepare their basic financial statements on a fair value basis. At initial acquisition, historical costs equals fair value. In subsequent periods, as market and economic conditions change, historical cost and fair value often diverge. As a result, fair value measures or estimates often provide more relevant information about the expected future cash flows related to the asset or liability. For example, when long-lived assets decline in value, a fair value measure determines any impairment loss. To increase consistency and comparability in fair value measures, the FASB established the following fair value hierarchy that provides insight into the priority of valuation techniques to use to determine fair value.

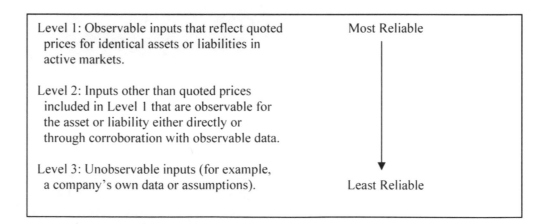

Level 1 is the most reliable because it is based on quoted prices, like a closing stock price in the *Wall Street Journal.* Level 2 is the next most reliable and would rely on evaluating similar assets or liabilities in active markets. At the least-reliable level, Level 3, much judgment is needed based on the best information available, to arrive at a relevant and reliable fair value measurement.

It is easy to arrive at fair values when markets are liquid with many traders, but fair value answers are not readily available in other situations. A great deal of expertise and sound judgment will be needed to arrive at appropriate answers. GAAP also provides guidance on estimating fair values when market-related data is not available. In general, these valuation issues relate to Level 3 fair value measurements. These measurements may be developed using expected cash flow and present value techniques discussed in **Chapter 6.**

Recently the Board has taken the additional step of giving companies the option to use fair value as the basis for measurement of financial assets and liabilities in the financial statements. The Board believes that fair value measurement for financial instruments provides more relevant and understandable information than historical cost. It considers fair value to be more relevant because it reflects the current cash equivalent value of financial instruments. As a result, companies now have the option to record fair value in their accounts for most financial instruments, including such items as receivables, investments, and debt securities.

ANALYSIS OF MULTIPLE-CHOICE TYPE QUESTIONS

QUESTION
1. (L.O. 3) The objectives of financial reporting include all of the following **except** to provide information that:
    a.   is useful to the Internal Revenue Service in allocating the tax burden to the business community.
    b.   is useful to those making investment and credit decisions.
    c.   is helpful in assessing future cash flows.
    d.   identifies the economic resources (assets), the claims to those resources (liabilities), and the changes in those resources and claims.

Explanation: Financial reporting is for the use of investors, potential investors, management, and other interested parties. It is not for the IRS. The information required to be reported to the IRS is provided by the reporting entity on tax forms and is referred to as income tax accounting as opposed to financial reporting. (Solution = a)

QUESTION
2. (L.O. 4) According to *Statement of Financial Accounting Concepts No. 8,* completeness is an ingredient of:

	Relevance	Faithful Representation
a.	Yes	Yes
b.	Yes	No
c.	No	No
d.	No	Yes

Approach and Explanation: In answering this question, read the stem and answer "Yes" (true) or "No" (false) when completing the statement with the quality of **relevance**. Then reread the stem and answer "Yes" or "No" when completing the statement with the quality of **faithful representation.** Then look for the corresponding combination of "Yes" and "No" to select your answer. In the diagram of the hierarchy of accounting qualities, completeness is linked to faithful representation and not relevance. Therefore, we want to respond "No" to the relevance column and "Yes" to the faithful representation column. (Solution = d.)

QUESTION
3. (L.O.4) According to *Statement of Financial Accounting Concepts No. 8,* which of the following is considered a constraint?
    a.   Faithful representation
    b.   Verifiability
    c.   Comparability
    d.   Costs < Benefits

Approach and Explanation: In visualizing the diagram for a hierarchy of accounting qualities (**Illustration 2-2**), it is an easy task to identify why "costs < benefits" (or benefits exceed cost) is the pervasive constraint in question and why the other selections can be eliminated in selecting the correct response. Selection "d" is correct because *SFAC No. 8* states that in order to justify requiring a particular measurement or disclosure, the benefits perceived to be derived from it must exceed the costs perceived to be associated with it. Selection "a" is incorrect because faithful representation is a fundamental quality of accounting information. Selections "b" and "c" are both enhancing qualities. (Solution = d.)

QUESTION

4.   (L.O. 4) According to *Statement of Financial Accounting Concepts No. 8,* neutrality is an ingredient of the fundamental quality of:

	Relevance	Faithful Representation
a.	Yes	Yes
b.	Yes	No
c.	No	No
d.	No	Yes

Approach and Explanation: In answering this question, read the stem and answer "Yes" (true) or "No" (false) when completing the statement with the word **relevance**. Then reread the stem and answer "Yes" or "No" when completing the statement with the phrase **faithful representation.** Then look for the corresponding combination of "Yes" and "No" to select your answer. In the diagram of the hierarchy of accounting qualities, neutrality is linked to faithful representation and not relevance. Therefore, we want to respond "No" to the relevance column and "Yes" to the faithful representation column. (Solution = d.)

QUESTION

5.   (L.O. 4) If the LIFO inventory method was used last period, it should be used for the current and following periods because of:
   a.   materiality.
   b.   verifiability.
   c.   timeliness.
   d.   comparability.

Approach and Explanation: In reading the stem of the question, cover up the answer selections. Anticipate the correct answer by attempting to complete the statement given. This process should yield the answer of "comparability." If you cannot think of the word to complete the statement, then take each answer selection and write down what each means. You should then be able to match up the question with answer selection "d."

Selection "d" is correct because consistency is a type of comparability and comparability is an enhancing quality of accounting information. To be useful, financial statements should reflect consistent application of generally accepted accounting principles. This means that a company should apply the same methods to similar accountable events from period to period. Selection "a" is incorrect because materiality refers to an ingredient of the fundamental quality of relevance whereby an item is to be given strict accounting treatment unless it is insignificant. Selection "b" is incorrect because verifiability refers to another enhancing quality (it is demonstrated when a high degree of consensus can be secured among independent measurers using the same measurement methods). Selection "c" is incorrect because timeliness is another enhancing quality which indicates that for information to be relevant and have faithful representation, it must be prepared on a timely basis. (Solution = d.)

QUESTION

6.   (L.O. 4) If a completed transaction will **not** affect any business decisions, it need **not** be separately reported in the financial statements. This guidance comes from the:
   a.   materiality quality.
   b.   periodicity assumption.
   c.   completeness quality.
   d.   full disclosure principle.

Approach and Explanation: Briefly define each of the answer selections. Choose the item for which your definition most closely agrees with the stem of the question. See **Illustration 2-2** and **Illustration 2-4**

The **materiality quality** dictates that an immaterial item need not be given strict accounting treatment; it can be given expedient treatment. An immaterial item or amount is one that does not make a difference in the decisions that are being made based on an analysis of the financial statements. The point involved here is one of relative size and importance. If the amount involved is significant when compared with other revenues and expenses, assets and liabilities, or net income of the entity, it is a material item and generally acceptable standards should be followed. If the amount is so small that it is quite unimportant when compared with other items, strict treatment is of less importance. The nature of an item may also affect the judgment of its materiality. A misclassification affecting cash has a lower threshold of materiality than the same dollar amount of a misclassification affecting plant assets. (Solution = a.)

QUESTION
7. (L.O. 4) When an entity charges the entire cost of an electric pencil sharpener to expense in the period when it was purchased even though the appliance has an estimated life of five years, we have an application of the:
   a. matching principle.
   b. materiality quality.
   c. historical cost principle.
   d. expense recognition principle.

Explanation: When an item benefits operations of more than one period, the matching principle will dictate the cost of the item be allocated (spread) systematically over the periods benefited. However, the materiality quality dictates that an immaterial item need not be given strict accounting treatment; it can be given expedient treatment. The cost of a pencil sharpener would obviously be small and thus immaterial. Consequently, the materiality quality is justification for departure from the matching principle in accounting for the cost of the pencil sharpener. (Solution = b.)

QUESTION
8. (L.O. 4) Which of the following qualitative characteristics holds that the usefulness of accounting information is magnified when the information is classified, characterized, and presented clearly and consisely?
   a. neutrality.
   b. verifiability.
   c. timeliness.
   d. understandability.

Approach and Explanation: Visualize the diagram for the hierarchy of accounting qualities (**Illustration 2-2**). Mentally review a description of each quality. For information to be useful, there must be a connection (linkage) between users of information and the decisions they make. This link, understandability, (an enhancing quality of accounting information) is the quality of information that lets reasonably informed users see its significance. Understandability is enhanced when information is classified, characterized, and presented clearly and concisely. (Solution = d.)

QUESTION
9. (L.O. 5) The term "articulation" refers to the:
   a. expression of dollar amounts in terms of a foreign currency.
   b. correction of amounts previously reported on the financial statements.
   c. interaction of the elements of financial statements.
   d. degree of preciseness of financial reports.

Approach and Explanation: Define or explain articulation before you read the answer selections. Select the answer that best fits your description. The FASB classifies the elements of financial statements into two distinct groups. The first group of three elements—assets, liabilities, and equity—describes amounts of resources and claims to resources at a **moment in time**. The other seven elements (comprehensive income and its components—revenues, expenses, gains, and losses—as well as investments by owners and distributions to owners) describe transactions, events, and circumstances that affect an enterprise during a **period of time**. The first class—assets, liabilities, and equity—is changed by elements of the second class and at any time is the cumulative result of all changes. This interaction is referred to as "articulation." That is, key figures in one statement (e.g. balance sheet) correspond to or are influenced by amounts reported in another statement (e.g. income statement). (Solution = c.)

QUESTION

10.   (L.O. 5) The calculation of comprehensive income includes which of the following?

	Operating Income	Distributions to Owners
a.	Yes	Yes
b.	Yes	No
c.	No	Yes
d.	No	No

Approach and Explanation: Define comprehensive income before reading the answer selections. Then answer "Yes" or "No" for the inclusion of each of the items in question (Operating Income and Distributions to Owners). Then look for the corresponding combination of "Yes" and "No" to select your answer. **Comprehensive income** is a change in equity (net assets) of an entity during a period from transactions and other events and circumstances from **nonowner sources.** It includes all changes in equity during a period except those resulting from investments by owners and distributions to owners. Thus it includes net income and all of its components (such as revenues, expenses, gains, and losses) and subtotals of various components of net income (such as gross profit and operating income). (Solution = b.)

QUESTION

11.   (L.O. 5) Which of the following is **false** with regard to the concept "comprehensive income"?
   a.   It is more inclusive than the traditional notion of net income.
   b.   It includes net income and all other changes in equity exclusive of owners' investments and distributions to owners.
   c.   It is an "element" in the FASB's conceptual framework.
   d.   It excludes prior period adjustments (transactions that relate to previous periods, such as corrections of errors).

Explanation: Comprehensive income includes all changes in equity during a period except those resulting from investments by owners and distributions to owners. Prior period adjustments (such as corrections of errors) are included under comprehensive income; they are excluded from the concept of net income (as it is currently applied in practice). (Solution = d.)

QUESTION

12.   (L.O. 6) The assumption that an enterprise will remain in business indefinitely and will **not** liquidate in the near future is called the:
   a.   economic entity assumption.
   b.   going concern assumption.
   c.   monetary unit assumption.
   d.   periodicity assumption.

Approach and Explanation: Read the stem (while covering up the answer selections) and attempt to complete the statement. Compare your attempt with the selections. Hopefully, you anticipated the correct answer. If your attempt does not match any of the selections given, take each selection and write down the key words in the definitions of the term. This process should lead you to the correct response.

Answer selection "b" is correct because the going concern assumption implies that an enterprise will continue in business and will not liquidate within the foreseeable future. Selection "a" is incorrect because the economic entity assumption indicates that the activities of an accounting entity should be kept separate and distinct from all other accounting entities. Selection "c" is incorrect because the monetary unit assumption indicates that all transactions and events can be measured in terms of a common denominator—units of money. Selection "d" is incorrect because the periodicity assumption indicates that the economic activities of an enterprise can be divided into equally spaced artificial time periods. (Solution = b.)

QUESTION
13. (L.O. 7) Pluto Magazine Company sells space to advertisers. The company requires an advertiser to pay for services one month before publication. Advertising revenue should be recognized when:
    a. an advertiser places an order.
    b. a bill is sent to an advertiser.
    c. the related cash is received.
    d. the related ad is published.

Approach and Explanation: Read the last sentence of the stem. We want to know the point at which revenue should be recognized. Write down what you know from the revenue recognition principle. Revenue is generally recognized when (1) realized or realizable, and (2) earned. Read the stem and think of how to apply the revenue recognition principle to the facts given. At the points when an order is placed and a bill is sent to an advertiser, revenue has neither been realized nor earned. At the point when the cash is received in advance of the publication, the revenue is realized but not earned. The revenue is earned when the related ad is published and, thus, should be recognized then. (Solution = d.)

QUESTION
14. (L.O. 7) The historical cost principle provides that:
    a. items whose costs are insignificant compared to other amounts on the financial statements may be accounted for in the most expedient manner.
    b. assets and equities be expressed in terms of a common denominator.
    c. the recorded amount of an acquired item should be the fair market value of the item.
    d. the expenses of generating revenue should be recognized in the same period that the related revenue is recognized.

Approach and Explanation: Briefly define the historical cost principle before you read the answer selections. See **Illustration 2-4**. Answer selection "a" describes the materiality quality. Selection "b" describes the monetary unit assumption. Selection "d" relates to the expense recognition principle (matching principle). (Solution = c.)

QUESTION
15. (L.O. 7) If cash is received from a customer in the current period, but the related performance obligation is **not** satisfied until a future period, the related expenses of generating the revenue should **not** be recognized until that future period. This guideline is an application of the:
    a. revenue recognition principle.
    b. full disclosure principle.
    c. matching principle.
    d. cost constraint.

Explanation: The revenue recognition principle dictates that revenue be recognized (recorded and reported) in the period the performance obligation is satisfied. The matching principle (expense recognition principle) dictates that expenses be recognized in the same period as the revenue which they helped to generate is recognized. Thus, if revenue is deferred, the related expenses should also be deferred. (Solution = c.)

QUESTION
16. (L.O. 7) The process of reporting an item in the financial statements of an enterprise is:
   a. recognition
   b. realization.
   c. allocation.
   d. incorporation.

Explanation: The term recognition refers to the process of formally recording or incorporating an item in the accounts and financial statements of an entity. An item that gets recorded in the accounts eventually gets reported in the financial statements of the enterprise. Realization is the process of converting noncash resources and rights into money and is most precisely used in accounting and financial reporting to refer to sales of assets for cash or claims to cash. The term allocation refers to the process or result of allocating (assigning costs or systematically spreading costs). The term incorporation refers to the process of establishing a business in the corporate form of organization. (Solution = a.)

QUESTION
17. (L.O. 7) Revenue is to be recognized when the related performance obligation is satisfied. This statement refers to the:
   a. revenue recognition principle.
   b. matching principle.
   c. going concern assumption.
   d. consistency quality.

Approach and Explanation: Briefly define each of the answer selections. Choose the item for which your definition most closely agrees with the stem of the question. **See Illustration 2-4 and 2-2.** The revenue recognition principle dictates that revenue be recognized (recorded and reported) in the period the related performance obligation is satisfied. The matching principle (or expense recognition principle) dictates that expenses be recognized in the same period as the revenue which they helped to generate is recognized. The going concern assumption implies that an enterprise will continue in business indefinitely. The consistency (a type of comparability) quality or characteristic dictates that for financial information to be useful, an entity is to apply the same accounting methods to similar events for successive accounting periods. (Solution = a.)

IFRS Insights

- In 2010, the IASB and the FASB completed the first phase of a jointly created conceptual framework. In this first phase, they agreed on the objective of financial reporting and a common set of desired qualitative characteristics. These were presented in the Chapter 2 discussion. The objective of this joint project is to develop a conceptual framework that leads to standards that are principles-based and internally consistent and that leads to the most useful financial reporting.

- The existing conceptual frameworks underlying GAAP and IFRS are very similar. That is, they are organized in a similar manner (objectives, elements, qualitative characteristics, etc.) There is no real need to change many aspects of the existing frameworks other than to converge different ways of discussing essentially the same concepts.
- The converged framework should be a single document, unlike the two conceptual frameworks that presently exist; it is unlikely that the basic structure related to the concepts will change.

- Both the IASB and FASB have similar measurement principles, based on historical cost and fair value. Although both GAAP and IFRS are increasing the use of fair value to report assets, at this point IFRS has adopted it more broadly. As examples, under IFRS companies can apply fair value to property, plant, and equipment; natural resources; and in some cases intangible assets. For GAAP, we still use only depreciated historical cost for these long-lived items.

- GAAP has a concept statement to guide estimation of fair value when market-related data is not available. The IASB is considering a proposal to provide expanded guidance on estimating fair values.

- The monetary unit assumption is part of each framework. However, the unit of measure will vary depending on the currency used in the country in which the company is incorporated (e.g., Chinese yuan, Japanese yen, and British pound).

- The economic entity assumption is also part of each framework although some cultural differences result in differences in its application. For example, in Japan many companies have formed alliances that are so strong that they act similar to related corporate divisions although they are not actually part of the same company.

- While the conceptual framework that underlies IFRS is very similar to that used to develop GAAP, the elements identified and their definitions are IFRS are different.

TRUE/FALSE (Circle the correct answer for each).

T   F   1.   The existing conceptual frameworks underlying GAAP and IFRS are very similar.

T   F   2.   Both the IASB and FASB have similar measurement principles, based on historical cost and fair value.

T   F   3.   Both GAAP and IFRS call for the application of current fair value to property, plant and equipment on the balance sheet.

T   F   4.   The economic entity assumption is part of the conceptual framework under GAAP but **not** under IFRS.

Solutions:

1.   T   3.   F
2.   T   4.   F

CHAPTER 3

THE ACCOUNTING INFORMATION SYSTEM

OVERVIEW

Accounting information must be accumulated and summarized before it can be communicated and analyzed. In this chapter, we will discuss the steps involved in the accounting cycle. We will emphasize the subject of adjusting entries. Throughout an accounting period, cash receipts and cash disbursements are recorded. At the end of the accounting period, adjusting entries are required so that revenues and expenses are reflected on the accrual basis of accounting. Adjusting entries are simply entries required to bring account balances up to date. The failure to record proper adjustments will cause errors on both the income statement and the balance sheet.

SUMMARY OF LEARNING OBJECTIVES

1. **Understand basic accounting terminology.** Understanding the following eleven terms helps in understanding key accounting concepts: (1) Event. (2) Transaction. (3) Account. (4) Real and Nominal accounts.(5) Ledger. (6) Journal. (7) Posting. (8) Trial Balance. (9) Adjusting entries. (10) Financial statements. (11) Closing entries.

2. **Explain double-entry rules.** The left side of an account is the debit side; the right side is the credit side. All asset and expense accounts are increased on the left or debit side and decreased on the right or credit side. Conversely, all liability and revenue accounts are increased on the right or credit side and decreased on the left or debit side. Stockholders' equity accounts, Common Stock and Retained Earnings, are increased on the credit side. The Dividends account is increased on the debit side.

3. **Identify steps in the accounting cycle.** The basic steps in the accounting cycle are (1) identifying and measuring transactions and other events, (2) journalizing (3) posting, (4) preparing an unadjusted trial balance, (5) making adjusting entries, (6) preparing an adjusted trial balance, (7) preparing financial statements, and (8) closing.

4. **Record transactions in journals, post to ledger accounts, and prepare a trial balance.** The simplest journal form chronologically lists transactions and events expressed in terms of debits and credits to particular accounts. The items entered in a general journal must be transferred to the general ledger; this procedure is called posting. Companies should prepare an unadjusted trial balance at the end of a given period after they have recorded the entries in the journal and posted them to the ledger. A trial balance is a list of all open accounts in the general ledger and their balances; it proves the equality of debits and credits after the recording and posting processes.

5. **Explain the reasons for preparing adjusting entries and identify major types of adjusting entries.** Adjustments achieve a proper recognition of revenues and expenses, so as to determine net income for the current period and to achieve an accurate statement of end-of-the period balances in assets, liabilities, and owners' equity accounts. The major types of adjusting entries are deferrals (for prepaid expenses and unearned revenues) and accruals (for accrued revenues and accrued expenses).

6. **Prepare financial statements from the adjusted trial balance.** Companies can prepare financial statements directly from the adjusted trial balance. The income statement is prepared from the revenue and expense account balances. The statement of retained earnings is prepared from the retained earnings account balance, dividends amount, and the net income (or net loss) amount. The balance sheet is prepared from the asset, liability, and equity accounts.

7. **Prepare closing entries.** In the closing process, the company transfers all of the revenue and expense account balances (income statement items) to a clearing account called Income Summary, which is used only at the end of the fiscal year. Revenues and expenses are matched in the Income Summary account and the net result of this matching represents the net income or net loss for the period. The net income or net loss amount is then transferred to an owners' equity account (Retained Earnings for a corporation and capital accounts for proprietorships and partnerships.)

8. **Prepare financial statements for a merchandising company.** The financial statements for a merchandiser differ from those for a service company as a merchandiser must account for gross profit on sales, income from operations, income before taxes, and net income. The accounting cycle for a merchandiser is performed the same as that for a service company.

*9. **Differentiate the cash basis of accounting from the accrual basis of accounting.** The cash basis of accounting records revenues when cash is received and expenses when cash is paid. The accrual basis recognizes revenue when the performance obligation is satisfied and expenses in the period incurred, without regard to the time of the receipt or payment of cash. Accrual-basis accounting is theoretically preferable because it provides information about future cash inflows and outflows associated with earnings activities as soon as a company can estimate these cash flows with an acceptable degree of certainty. Cash-basis accounting is **not** in conformity with GAAP.

   *This material is covered in **Appendix 3A** in the text.

10. **Identify adjusting entries that may be reversed. Reversing entries are most often used to reverse two types of adjusting entries: accrued revenues and accrued expenses. Adjusting entries for deferrals (prepaid expenses and unearned revenues) may also be reversed if the initial entry to record the related cash transaction is made to an expense or revenue account.

   This material is covered in **Appendix 3B in the text.

***11. **Prepare a 10-column worksheet.** The 10-column worksheet provides columns for the first (unadjusted) trial balance, adjustments, adjusted trial balance, income statement, and balance sheet. The worksheet does not replace the financial statements. Instead, it is the accountant's informal device for accumulating and sorting information needed for the financial statements. Completing the worksheet provides considerable assurance that all of the details related to the end-of-period accounting procedures and preparation of the financial statements have been properly brought together.

   ***This material is covered in **Appendix 3C** in the text.

TIPS ON CHAPTER TOPICS

TIP: This chapter is an extremely important one. A good understanding of this chapter and an ability to think and work quickly with the concepts incorporated herein are necessary for comprehending subsequent chapters. Although adjusting entries were introduced in your principles course, you are likely to discover new dimensions to this subject in your intermediate accounting course. Pay close attention when studying this chapter!

TIP: When you encounter a transaction, always analyze it in terms of its effects on the elements of the basic **accounting equation** (or **balance sheet equation**). For your analysis to be complete, it must maintain balance in the basic accounting equation. The **basic accounting equation** is as follows:

$$\text{ASSETS} = \text{LIABILITIES} + \text{OWNERS' EQUITY}$$
$$\text{or}$$
$$A = L + OE$$

Assets are economic resources. Liabilities and owners' equity are sources of resources; liabilities are creditor sources, and owners' equity represents owner sources (owner investments and undistributed profits). The basic accounting equation simply states that the total assets (resources) at a point in time equal the total liabilities plus total owners' equity (sources of resources) at the same point in time.

TIP: **An understanding of the following eleven terms is important.** (1) **Event:** a happening of consequence. An event generally is the source or cause of changes in assets, liabilities, and equity. Events may be external or internal. (2) **Transaction:** an external event involving a transfer or exchange between two or more entities. (3) **Account:** a systematic arrangement that shows the effect of transactions and other events on a specific financial item. A separate account is kept for each type of asset, liability, revenue, and expense, and for capital (owners' equity). (4) **Real and nominal accounts:** real (permanent) accounts are asset, liability, and equity accounts. They appear on the balance sheet. Nominal (temporary) accounts are revenue, expense, and dividend accounts. Except for dividends, they contain information that appears on the income statement. Nominal accounts are periodically closed; real accounts are not closed. (5) **Ledger:** the book (or computer system) containing the accounts. (6) **Journal:** the book of original entry where transactions and selected other events are initially recorded. (7) **Posting:** the process of transferring the essential facts and figures from the book of original entry to the ledger accounts. (8) **Trial balance:** a list of all open accounts in the ledger and their balances. (9) **Adjusting entries:** entries made at the end of an accounting period to bring all accounts up to date on an accrual accounting basis so that correct financial statements can be prepared. (10) **Financial statements:** statements that reflect the collection, tabulation, and final summarization of the accounting data. (11) **Closing entries:** the formal process by which all nominal accounts are reduced to zero, and the net income or net loss is determined and transferred to the appropriate owners' equity account.

TIP: **Transactions** are the economic events of an entity recorded by accountants. Some events (happenings of consequence to an entity) are not measurable in terms of money and do not get recorded in the accounting records. Hiring employees, placing an order for supplies, greeting a customer and quoting prices for products are examples of activities that do not by themselves constitute transactions.

TIP: In accordance with the **revenue recognition principle**, revenue is to be recognized (reported) in the period in which services are performed. In accordance with **the expense recognition principle (matching principle)**, the expenses incurred in generating revenues should be recognized in the same period as the revenues they helped to generate. First, the revenue recognition principle is applied to determine in what period(s) to recognize revenue. Then, the (matching) principle is applied to determine in what period(s) to recognize expense.

With the **cash basis of accounting,** a revenue item is reported in the time period when the related cash is received from the customer and an expense is recorded in the time period in which the related cash is paid. Cash basis financial statements are **not** in conformity with generally accepted accounting principles. Most companies use the **accrual basis of accounting**, whereby a revenue item is reported in the time period in which it is earned and an expense item is reported in the time period in which it is incurred.

TIP: Adjusting entries are often required so that revenues and expenses are reflected on an accrual basis of accounting (revenues recognized when earned and expenses recognized when incurred) rather than on a cash basis of accounting. Therefore, adjusting entries reflect the **accruals** and **deferrals of revenues and expenses** and also **estimated expenses. Adjusting entries** are simply entries required to bring account balances up to date before financial statements can be prepared. The failure to record proper adjustments will cause errors in both the income statement and the balance sheet.

TIP: **Deferrals** result from **cash** flows that occur **before** expense or revenue recognition. That is, cash is paid for expenses that apply to more than one accounting period or cash is received for revenue that applies to more than one accounting period. The portion of the expense that applies to future periods is deferred by reporting a prepaid expense (asset) or the portion of the revenue that applies to future periods is deferred by reporting unearned revenue (liability) on the balance sheet.

Accruals result from **cash** flows that occur **after** expense or revenue recognition. That is, cash is to be paid or received in a future accounting period for an expense incurred or a revenue earned by performing services in the current period.

TIP: Notice that **none** of the adjusting entries discussed in **Chapter 3** involves the **Cash** account. Therefore, if you are instructed to record **adjusting entries**, double check your work when it is completed. If you have used the Cash account in any adjusting entry, it is very likely in error. (The only time Cash belongs in an adjusting entry is when a bank reconciliation discloses a need to adjust the Cash account—this will be explained in **Chapter 7**—or when an error has been made that involves the Cash account, in which case a correcting entry is required.) There are, however, situations in homework assignments in which errors involving the Cash account must be corrected; in such a case, the Cash account will be involved in your **correcting** entry.

TIP: Notice that each adjusting entry discussed in this chapter involves a balance sheet account **and** an income statement account.

TIP: When preparing homework assignments, working through *The Problem Solving Survival Guide,* and answering exam questions, pay careful attention to whether a prepayment situation relates to a **cash inflow** or **cash outflow** for the entity in question. Be sure you then use the proper related account for recording the cash receipt or disbursement and correct terminology in explaining the scenario. If cash is **received** in a rental situation, the amount will be recorded (by a credit) in either an earned rent revenue account or an unearned rent revenue account, **not** in an expense or a prepaid expense account. If cash is **paid** in a rental situation, the amount will be recorded (by a debit) in either an expense or a prepaid expense account.

TIP: In an adjusting entry for an accrual (accrued revenue or accrued expense), the word "accrued" is **not** needed in either account title. If you choose to use the word "accrued" in an account title, it is appropriate to do so **only** in the balance sheet account title. For example, the entry to record accrued salaries of $1,000 is as follows:

Salaries and Wages Expense... 1,000
         Salaries and Wages Payable.......................................   1,000

The word "accrued" is not needed in either account title, but it could be used in the liability account title if desired (the account title would then be Accrued Salaries and Wages Payable). It would be wrong to insert the word "accrued" in the expense account title. Some people simply call the credit account "Accrued Salaries and Wages" (rather than "Salaries and Wages Payable") but we advise that you include the key word "Payable" and omit the unnecessary word "Accrued."

TIP: The cost of most long-lived tangible assets is allocated to expense in a systematic and rational manner. The entry to record the expiration of cost due to the consumption of benefits yielded by the asset is a debit to Depreciation Expense and a credit to Accumulated Depreciation. The amortization of intangibles is similar to depreciation.

TIP: A reduction in the net realizable value of accounts receivable or inventories is recorded in an adjusting entry by a charge to expense and a credit to a contra asset account.

TIP: An unadjusted trial balance is referred to as either "unadjusted trial balance" or simply "trial balance." An adjusted trial balance is referred to as either "adjusted trial balance" or the "adjusted trial."

TIP: Closing entries are necessary at the end of an accounting period to prepare the nominal accounts (revenues, expenses, gains, and losses) for the recording of transactions for the next accounting period. Closing entries are prepared after the nominal account balances have been used to prepare the income statement. Only nominal accounts are closed. Real accounts are never closed; their balances continue into the next accounting period. **Nominal** accounts are often called **temporary** accounts; **real** accounts are often called **permanent** accounts.

TIP: A nominal account with a credit balance is closed by a debit to that account and a credit to Income Summary. A nominal account with a debit balance is closed by a credit to that account and a debit to Income Summary. The Income Summary account is closed to an owners' equity account (Retained Earnings for a corporation) and is often called the Revenue and Expense Summary.

TIP: If a separate account is used to record owner withdrawals or owner distributions (such as Dividends or Dividends Declared for a corporation or Owner's Drawings for a proprietorship or partnership), this account is also closed at the end of the accounting period, but it is **not** closed to the Income Summary account because it is **not** a component of the net income computation. Rather, it is closed directly to Retained Earnings (for a corporation) or to Owner's Capital (for a proprietorship or partnership).

TIP: A **post-closing trial balance** contains only real accounts because the nominal accounts all have a zero balance after the closing process. A post-closing trial balance is prepared to check on the equality of debits and credits after the closing process.

***TIP: In preparing a 10-column work sheet, the debit and credit columns for every column pair must be equal before you can proceed to the next column pair. (This pertains to the first three column pairs). All five pairs of columns must balance for a work sheet to be complete.

ILLUSTRATION 3-1
DOUBLE-ENTRY (DEBIT AND CREDIT)
ACCOUNTING SYSTEM (L.O. 2)

The debit and credit rules are summarized below:

Asset Accounts	
Debit	Credit
Increase	Decrease
+	-

Liability Accounts	
Debit	Credit
Decrease	Increase
-	+

Dividends Account	
Debit	Credit
Increase	Decrease
+	-

Stockholders' Equity Accounts	
Debit	Credit
Decrease	Increase
-	+

Expense Accounts	
Debit	Credit
Increase	Decrease
+	-

↑
**Normal
Balance**

Revenue Accounts	
Debit	Credit
Decrease	Increase
-	+

↑
**Normal
Balance**

Notice that the accounts above are arranged in such a way that all of the increases ("+" signs) are on the outside and all of the decreases ("-" signs) are on the inside of this diagram.

TIP: An **account** is an individual accounting record of increases and decreases in a specific asset, liability, or stockholders' equity item. In its simplest form, an account consists of three parts: (1) the title of the account, (2) a left or debit side, and (3) a right or credit side. Because the alignment of these parts of an account resembles the letter T, it is often referred to as a **T-account.**

TIP: "Credit" does **not** mean favorable or unfavorable. In accounting, "debit and "credit" simply mean left and right, respectively. "Debit" is a term that refers to the left side of any account. Thus, the debit side of an account is always the left side. "Credit" is a word that simply refers to the right side of an account. Thus, the credit side of an account is always the right side of the account. The phrase "to debit an account" means to enter an amount on the debit (left) side of an account. Debit can be abbreviated as "Dr." and credit is abbreviated as "Cr."

TIP: A "+" indicates an increase and a "-" indicates a decrease. Therefore, a transaction which causes an increase in an asset is recorded by a debit to the related asset account; a transaction which causes a decrease in the same asset is recorded by a credit to the same account.

TIP: The normal balance of an account is the side where increases are recorded. Therefore, the normal balance of an asset account is a debit balance; the normal balance of a liability account is a credit balance.

ILLUSTRATION 3-1 (Continued)

TIP: A company's **ledger** is the book (or computer system) containing the company's accounts. Each account usually has a separate page. The **general ledger** is a collection of all the asset, liability, owners' equity, revenue, expense, and dividends accounts. A separate account should exist in the general ledger for each item that will appear on the financial statements. A **subsidiary ledger** contains the detail related to a given general ledger account.

TIP: At this stage of your study of accounting, you should be able to quickly and correctly identify the debit and credit rules for any given account. If you are slow at this process, drill on the rules until you improve. If you memorize the rules for an asset account, you can figure out the rules for all other types of accounts by knowing which rules are the opposite of the rules for assets and which are the same. Increases in assets are recorded by debits. Because liabilities and owners' equity are on the other side of the equals sign in the basic accounting equation, they must have debit and credit rules opposite of the rules for assets. Therefore, a liability or an owners' equity account is increased by a credit entry. Revenues earned increase owners' equity (retained earnings for a corporate form of organization) so the rules to record increases in revenue are the same as the rules to record increases in an owners' equity account (increases are recorded by credits). Because expenses and owners' withdrawals reduce owners' equity, they have debit/credit rules which are opposite of the rules for an owners' equity account.

TIP: In the double-entry system of accounting, for every debit there must be a credit(s) of equal amount, and vice versa.

EXERCISE 3-1

Purpose: (L.O. 2) This exercise will test your understanding of the debit and credit rules.

Instructions

For each account listed below, put a check mark (√) in the appropriate column to indicate if it is increased by an entry in the debit (left) side of the account or by an entry in the credit (right) side of the account. The first one is done for you.

		Debit	Credit
1.	Cash	√	
2.	Sales Revenue		
3.	Commissions Expense		
4.	Advertising Expense		
5.	Salaries and Wages Payable		
6.	Prepaid Insurance		
7.	Property Taxes Payable		
8.	Property Tax Expense		
9.	Dividends Declared		
10.	Interest Revenue		
11.	Salaries and Wages Expense		
12.	Commissions Revenue		
13.	Unearned Rent Revenue		
14.	Equipment		
15.	Note Payable		
16.	Building		
17.	Accounts Payable		
18.	Supplies on Hand		
19.	Accounts Receivable		
20.	Common Stock		
21.	Retained Earnings		
22.	Mortgage Payable		
23.	Loan Receivable		
24.	Bank Loan Payable		
25.	Audit Fees Incurred		
26.	Dividend Income		
27.	Fees Incurred		
28.	Fees Earned		
29.	Utilities Expense		
30.	Utilities Payable		

TIP: In essence, you are being asked to identify the normal balance of each of the accounts listed. The **normal balance** of an account is the side where increases are recorded.

Solution to Exercise 3-1

Approach: Determine the classification of the account (asset, liability, owners' equity, revenue or expense). Think about the debit and credit rules for that classification. Refer to **Illustration 3-1** and the related **TIPS** for those rules. In determining the classification of an account, look for the key words, if any, in each individual item. For example: (1) the words Revenue, Earned, or Income are often associated with a revenue account, (2) the words Expense, Incurred, or Expired are often associated with an expense account, (3) the words Receivable, Prepaid or Deferred Expense refer to types of asset accounts, and (4) the words Payable, Unearned Revenue, or Deferred Revenue refer to types of liabilities.

		Debit	Credit	Classification
1.	Cash	√		Asset
2.	Sales Revenue		√	Revenue
3.	Commissions Expense	√		Expense
4.	Advertising Expense	√		Expense
5.	Salaries and Wages Payable		√	Liability
6.	Prepaid Insurance	√		Asset
7.	Property Taxes Payable		√	Liability
8.	Property Tax Expense	√		Expense
9.	Dividends Declared	√		Owners' Equity (Owners' Withdrawals)
10.	Interest Revenue		√	Revenue
11.	Salaries and Wages Expense	√		Expense
12.	Commissions Revenue		√	Revenue
13.	Unearned Rent Revenue		√	Liability
14.	Equipment	√		Asset
15.	Note Payable		√	Liability
16.	Building	√		Asset
17.	Accounts Payable		√	Liability
18.	Supplies on Hand	√		Asset
19.	Accounts Receivable	√		Asset
20.	Common Stock		√	Owners' Equity (Owners' Investments)
21.	Retained Earnings		√	Owners' Equity (Earned Capital)
22.	Mortgage Payable		√	Liability
23.	Loan Receivable	√		Asset
24.	Bank Loan Payable		√	Liability
25.	Audit Fees Incurred	√		Expense
26.	Dividend Income		√	Revenue
27.	Fees Incurred	√		Expense
28.	Fees Earned		√	Revenue
29.	Utilities Expense	√		Expense
30.	Utilities Payable		√	Liability

EXERCISE 3-2

Purpose: (L.O. 4) This exercise will review how to record transactions in the general journal.

Transactions for the Smooth Sailing Repair Shop, Inc. for August 2014 are listed below.

1. August 1   Joan and Phillip began the business by each depositing $2,500 of personal funds in the business bank account in exchange for common stock of the newly formed corporation.
2. August 2   Joan rented space for the shop behind a strip mall and paid August rent of $800 out of the business bank account.
3. August 3   The shop purchased supplies for cash, $3,000.
4. August 4   The shop paid Cupboard News, a local newspaper, $300 for an ad appearing in the Sunday edition.
5. August 5   The shop repaired a boat for a customer. The customer paid cash of $1,300 for services rendered.
6. August 13   The shop purchased supplies for $900 by paying cash of $200 and charging the rest on account.
7. August 14   The shop repaired a boat for Zonie Kinkennon for $3,600. Phillip collected $1,000 in cash and put the rest on Zonie's account.
8. August 24   The shop collected cash of $400 from Zonie Kinkennon.
9. August 28   The shop paid $200 to Mini Maid for cleaning services for the month of August.
10. August 31   The board of directors of the corporation declared and paid a dividend of $400 in cash to its stockholders.

Instructions
(a) Explain the impact of each transaction on the elements of the basic accounting equation and translate that into debit and credit terms.
(b) Journalize the transactions listed above. Include a brief explanation with each journal entry.

SOLUTION TO EXERCISE 3-2

(a) 1.   Increase in Cash.   Debit Cash
         Increase in Common Stock.   Credit Common Stock

     2.   Increase in Rent Expense.   Debit Rent Expense
         Decrease in Cash.   Credit Cash

     3.   Increase in Supplies on Hand.   Debit Supplies on Hand
         Decrease in Cash.   Credit Cash

     4.   Increase in Advertising Expense.   Debit Advertising Expense
         Decrease in Cash.   Credit Cash

5. Increase in Cash. Increase in Service Revenue.	Debit Cash Credit Service Revenue

6. Increase in Supplies on Hand.
Decrease in Cash.
Increase in Accounts Payable.
	Debit Supplies on Hand
	    Credit Cash
	    Credit Accounts Payable

7. Increase in Cash. Increase in Accounts Receivable. Increase in Service Revenue	Debit Cash Debit Accounts Receivable Credit Service Revenue
8. Increase in Cash. Decrease in Accounts Receivable.	Debit Cash Credit Accounts Receivable
9. Increase in Cleaning Expense. Decrease in Cash.	Debit Cleaning Expense Credit Cash
10. Decrease in Retained Earnings. Decrease in Cash.	Debit Retained Earnings Credit Cash

Approach: Write down the effects of each transaction on the basic accounting equation. Think about the individual asset, liability, or stockholders' equity accounts involved. Apply the debit and credit rules to translate the effects into a journal entry. Refer to **Illustration 3-1** for the debit and credit rules for each type of account.

	GENERAL JOURNAL			J1
Date	**Account Titles and Explanations**	**Ref.**	**Debit**	**Credit**

(b)

	2014				
1. Aug.	1	Cash		5,000	
		Common Stock			5,000
		(Issued shares of stock for cash)			
2.	2	Rent Expense		800	
		Cash			800
		(Paid August rent)			
3.	3	Supplies on Hand		3,000	
		Cash			3,000
		(Purchased supplies for cash)			
4.	4	Advertising Expense		300	
		Cash			300
		(Paid Cupboard News for advertising)			
5.	5	Cash		1,300	
		Service Revenue			1,300
		(Received cash for service fees earned)			
6.	13	Supplies on Hand		900	
		Cash			200
		Accounts Payable			700
		(Purchased supplies for cash and on credit)			
7.	14	Cash		1,000	
		Accounts Receivable		2,600	
		Service Revenue			3,600
		(Performed services for customer for cash and on credit)			
8.	24	Cash		400	
		Accounts Receivable			400
		(Received cash from Zonie Kinkennon on account)			
9.	28	Cleaning Expense		200	
		Cash			200
10.	31	Retained Earnings (or Dividends Declared)		400	
		Cash			400

EXERCISE 3-3

Purpose: (L.O. 5) This exercise will provide you with examples of adjusting entries for the accrual of expenses and revenues.

The following information relates to the Yuppy Clothing Sales Company at the end of 2014. The accounting period is the calendar year. This is the company's first year of operations.

1. Employees are paid every Friday for the five-day work week ending on that day. Salaries amount to $2,400 per week. The accounting period ends on a Wednesday.
2. On October 1, 2014, Yuppy borrowed $8,000 cash by signing a note payable due in one year at 8% interest. Interest is due when the principal is paid.
3. A note for $3,000 was received from a customer in a sales transaction on May 1, 2014. The note matures in one year and bears 12% interest per annum. Interest is due when the principal is due.
4. A portion of Yuppy's parking lot is used by executives of a neighboring company. A person pays $6 per day for each day's use, and the parking fees are due by the fifth business day following the month of use. The unpaid fees at December 31, 2014 amount to $1,260.

Instructions
Using the information given above, prepare the necessary adjusting entries at December 31, 2014.

Solution to Exercise 3-3

1.	Salaries and Wages Expense	1,440	
	Salaries and Wages Payable		1,440
	($2,400 ÷ 5 = $480); ($480 x 3 = $1,440 accrued salaries)		
2.	Interest Expense	160	
	Interest Payable		160
	($8,000 x 8% x 3/12 = $160 accrued interest)		
3.	Interest Receivable	240	
	Interest Revenue		240
	($3,000 x 12% x 8/12 = $160 accrued interest)		
4.	Parking Fees Receivable	1,260	
	Parking Fees Revenue		1,260

Approach and Explanation: Write down the definitions for accrued expense and accrued revenue. Think about what is to be accomplished by each of the adjustments required in this exercise. An **accrued expense** is an expense that has been incurred but not paid. The "incurred" part results in an increase in Expense (debit) and the "not paid" part results in an increase in Payable (credit). An **accrued revenue** is a revenue that has been earned but not received. The "earned" part results in an increase in Revenue (credit) and the "not received" part results in an increase in Receivable (debit).

TIP: In an adjusting entry to record accrued salaries expenses (expense incurred, but not paid) the debit is to an expense account and the credit is to a liability account. The expense account is usually titled Salaries and Wages Expense. Possible names for the liability account include Salaries and Wages Payable and Accrued Salaries and Wages Payable.

TIP: In an adjusting entry to record accrued interest revenue (revenue earned but not received), the debit is to an asset account and the credit is to a revenue account. Possible names for that asset account are Interest Receivable and Accrued Interest Receivable. Possible names for the revenue account include Interest Revenue, Interest Income, and Interest Earned.

EXERCISE 3-4

Purpose: (L.O. 5) This exercise will provide you with examples of adjusting entries for prepaid expenses and unearned revenues (that is, for the deferral of expenses and revenues).

The following information relates to the Brittany Spears Magazine Company at the end of 2014. The accounting period is the calendar year.

1. An insurance premium of $8,000 was paid on April 1, 2014, and was charged to Prepaid Insurance. The premium covers a 24-month period beginning April 1, 2014.

2. The Office Supplies on Hand account showed a balance of $3,500 at the beginning of 2014. Supplies costing $12,000 were purchased during 2014 and debited to the asset account. Supplies of $2,200 were on hand at December 31, 2014.

3. On July 1, 2014, cash of $48,000 was received from subscribers (customers) for a 36-month subscription period beginning on that date. The receipt was recorded by a debit to Cash and a credit to Unearned Subscription Revenue.

4. At the beginning of 2014, the Unearned Advertising Revenue account had a balance of $75,000. During 2014, collections from advertisers of $800,000 were recorded by credits to Unearned Advertising Revenue. At the end of 2014, revenues received but not earned are computed to be $51,000.

Instructions
Using the information given above, prepare the necessary adjusting entries at December 31, 2014.

SOLUTION TO EXERCISE 3-4

1.	Insurance Expense	3,000	
	Prepaid Insurance		3,000
	($8,000 X 9/24 = $3,000 expired cost)		
2.	Supplies Expense	13,300	
	Office Supplies on Hand...		13,300
	($3,500 + $12,000 - $2,200 = $13,300 supplies consumed)		
3.	Unearned Subscription Revenue	8,000	
	Subscription Revenue		8,000
	($48,000 X 6/36 = $8,000 earned revenue)		
4.	Unearned Advertising Revenue	824,000	
	Advertising Revenue		824,000
	($75,000 + $800,000 - $51,000 = $824,000 earned revenue)		

Approach and Explanation: Write down the definitions for prepaid expense and unearned revenue. Think about what is to be accomplished by each of the adjustments required in this exercise. A **prepaid expense** is an expense that has been paid but not incurred. In a case where the prepayment was recorded as an increase in an asset account (such as Prepaid Expense or Supplies on Hand), the adjusting entry will record the increase in Expense (debit) and a decrease in the recorded Asset (credit) due to the consumption of the benefits yielded by the earlier prepayment. An **unearned revenue** is a revenue that has been received but not earned because the related performance obligation is not yet satisfied. In a case where the cash receipt was recorded as an increase in a liability account (such as Unearned Revenue or Deferred Revenue), the adjusting entry will record a decrease in the recorded liability Unearned Revenue (debit) and an increase in Revenue (credit) due to the earning of all or a portion of the revenue represented by the earlier cash receipt. The revenue is earned by the subsequent performance of services and thus satisfaction of the performance obligation.

It is helpful to sketch a T-account for the related asset or liability account. Enter the amounts reflected in that account before adjustment, enter the desired ending balance, and notice how the required adjustment is then obvious from facts reflected in your T-account. The T-accounts would appear as follows:

1.

2.

3.

4.

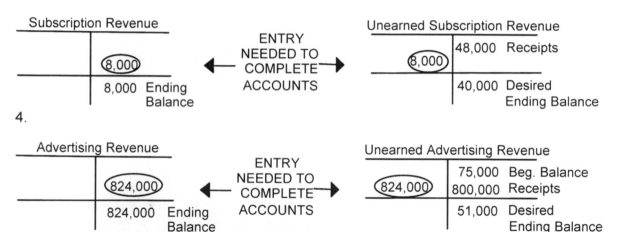

TIP: A **prepaid expense** may be called a **deferred expense**. A deferred expense is so named because the recognition of expense is being deferred (put-off) to a future period; thus, a debit is carried on the balance sheet now and will be released to the income statement in a future period when the related benefits are consumed (i.e., when the expense is incurred).

TIP: An **unearned revenue** is often called a **deferred revenue** because the recognition of revenue is being deferred to a future period; thus, a credit is carried on the balance sheet now and will be released to the income statement in a future period when the related revenue is earned by the completion of services.

TIP: An adjusting entry for prepaid insurance expense (expense paid but not incurred) involves an expense account and an asset account. The expense account is often called Insurance Expense or Expired Insurance. Possible titles for the asset account include Prepaid Insurance, Deferred Insurance Expense, Prepaid Insurance Expense, Deferred Insurance, and Unexpired Insurance.

TIP: An adjusting entry for **deferred** rent revenue (revenue collected but not earned) involves a liability account and a revenue account. Possible titles for the liability account include Unearned Rent Revenue, Unearned Rent, Deferred Rent Revenue, Rent Revenue Received in Advance, and Rental Income Collected in Advance. The use of Prepaid Rent Revenue as an account title is not appropriate because the term prepaid usually refers to the payment of cash in advance, not the receipt of cash in advance. The revenue account is often called

EXERCISE 3-5

Purpose: (L.O. 4, 5, 7) This exercise is designed to test your knowledge of what information is reflected on a trial balance, an adjusted trial balance, and a post-closing trial balance.

The following selected list of accounts are only a few taken from the trial balance at December 31, 2014 for Yasmin's Card Haven Corporation:

Account	Trial Balance Dec. 31, 2014	Adjusted Trial Balance Dec. 31, 2014	Post-Closing Trial Balance Dec. 31, 2014
Cash	$ 40,000		
Land	250,000		
Prepaid Insurance	36,000		
Insurance Expense	-0-		
Interest Expense	5,900		
Interest Payable	-0-		
Note Payable	50,000		
Rent Revenue	-0-		
Unearned Rent Revenue	24,000		
Common Stock	310,000		
Retained Earnings	79,000		

Instructions

(a)   In the Adjusted Trial Balance column, for each account, indicate if the balance of the account on the Adjusted Trial Balance is most likely to be the **SAME** amount as on the Trial Balance or a **DIFFERENT** amount. Explain the reasoning for your answers.

(b)   In the Post-closing Trial Balance column, for each account, indicate if the balance of the account on the Post-Closing Trial Balance is most likely to be the **SAME** amount as on the Adjusted Trial Balance or a **DIFFERENT** amount. Explain the reasoning for your answers.

TIP: The list of all open accounts in the general ledger and their balances is called the **trial balance.** A company may prepare a trial balance at any time. A trial balance is always prepared at the end of an accounting period as an initial step in the process of preparing financial statements. It verifies that the equality of debits and credits has been maintained during the recording and posting of transactions throughout the accounting period. The trial balance taken after all adjusting entries have been made and posted is called an **adjusted trial balance.** A trial balance taken immediately after closing entries have been made and posted is called a **post-closing** or **after-closing trial balance.**

SOLUTION TO EXERCISE 3-5

Account	Trial Balance Dec. 31, 2014	Adjusted Trial Balance Dec. 31, 2014	Post-Closing Trial Balance Dec. 31, 2014
Cash	$ 40,000	SAME	SAME
Land	250,000	SAME	SAME
Prepaid Insurance	36,000	DIFFERENT	SAME
Insurance Expense	-0-	DIFFERENT	DIFFERENT
Interest Expense	5,900	DIFFERENT	DIFFERENT
Interest Payable	-0-	DIFFERENT	SAME
Note Payable	50,000	SAME	SAME
Rent Revenue	-0-	DIFFERENT	DIFFERENT
Unearned Rent Revenue	24,000	DIFFERENT	SAME
Common Stock	310,000	SAME	SAME
Retained Earnings	79,000	SAME	DIFFERENT

Approach: Think about the types of accounts that are involved in adjusting entries. These include:

(1) Prepaid Expenses (such as Prepaid Insurance, Prepaid Rent, Supplies on Hand, and Unexpired Advertising).

(2) Unearned Revenues (such as Rent Received in Advance, Unearned Subscription Revenue, and Unearned Fees).

(3) Accrued Receivables (such as Interest Receivable, Fees Receivable, and Commission Receivable).

(4)   Accrued Payables (such as Interest Payable, Taxes Payable, and Utilities Payable).

(5)   Revenue and Expense accounts related to the foregoing four items (such as Insurance Expense, Rent Expense, Supplies Expense, Advertising Expense, Rent Revenue, Subscription Revenue, Fees Earned, Interest Revenue, Fees Revenue, Commissions Earned, Interest Expense, Taxes Expense and Utilities Expense).

(6)   Depreciation and amortization expense (such as Depreciation Expense and Amortization of Patent Expense) and the related real accounts (Accumulated Depreciation and Patents).

An account involved in an adjusting entry will have its balance changed by that entry so its balance on the Adjusted Trial will be **DIFFERENT** than its balance on the first (unadjusted) Trial Balance.

Accounts unaffected by adjusting entries will have the **SAME** balance on both the Adjusted Trial Balance and the Trial Balance.

Only accounts that are closed (temporary accounts –- revenue, expense, and dividends accounts) will have a **DIFFERENT** balance on the Post-closing Trial Balance when compared with the Adjusted Trial Balance.

Explanation: Balance sheet accounts such as Cash, Land, Investments, Note Payable, Bonds Payable, and Common Stock are rarely affected by an adjusting entry [except when an error is discovered, which requires a correcting entry, or when there is an impairment loss on an investment such as discussed in **Chapter 17** or when a bank reconciliation discloses that some minor adjustments are needed to Cash (see **Chapter 7**)].

Balance Sheet accounts such as Prepaid Insurance Expense, Interest Payable, and Unearned Rent Revenue are real accounts involved in adjusting entries; but being real accounts, they are **never** closed.

Income Statement accounts such as Insurance Expense and Rent Revenue are accounts involved in adjusting entries and are temporary so they are closed at the end of an accounting period.

EXERCISE 3-6

Purpose: (L.O. 5) This exercise will illustrate the preparation of adjusting entries from an unadjusted trial balance and additional data.

Butler's Equipment Rentals, Inc. began business in 2010. The following list of accounts and their balances represents the unadjusted trial balance of Butler's Equipment Rentals, Inc. at December 31, 2014, the end of the annual accounting period.

BUTLER'S EQUIPMENT RENTALS, INC.
Trial Balance
December 31, 2014

	Debit	Credit
Cash	$ 16,500	
Prepaid Insurance	4,320	
Supplies	13,200	
Land	62,000	
Building	50,000	
Equipment	130,000	
Accumulated Depreciation—Building		$ 10,000
Accumulated Depreciation—Equipment		52,000
Note Payable		50,000
Accounts Payable		9,310
Unearned Rent Revenue		10,200
Common Stock		30,000
Retained Earnings		60,660
Dividends	31,000	
Rent Revenue		161,960
Salaries and Wages Expense	70,600	
Interest Expense	3,500	
Miscellaneous Expense	3,010	
	$384,130	$384,130

Additional data:

1. On November 1, 2014, Butler received $10,200 rent from a lessee for a 12-month equipment lease beginning on that date and credited Unearned Rent Revenue for the entire collection.
2. Per a physical observation at December 31, 2014, Butler determines that supplies costing $2,200 were on hand at the balance sheet date. The cost of supplies is debited to an asset account when purchased.
3. Prepaid Insurance contains the premium cost of a policy that is for a 3-year term and was taken out on May 1, 2014.
4. The cost of the building is being depreciated at a rate of 5% per year.
5. The cost of the equipment is being depreciated at a rate of 10% per year.
6. The note payable bears interest at 12% per year. Interest is payable each August 1. The $50,000 principal is due in full on August 1, 2019.
7. At December 31, 2014, Butler has some equipment in the hands of renters who have used the equipment but have not yet been billed. They will make payment of $1,400 on January 2, 2015.
8. Employees are paid total salaries of $6,400 every other Friday for a two-week period ending on that payday. December 31, 2014 falls on a Wednesday. The last payday of the year is the last Friday in the year. The work week is Monday through Friday.

Instructions
(a) Prepare the year-end adjusting entries in general journal form using the information above.
(b) Prepare an adjusted trial balance at December 31, 2014.

SOLUTION TO EXERCISE 3-6

(a) 1. Unearned Rent Revenue   1,700
          Rent Revenue   1,700
          (To record rent revenue earned: $10,200 \times 2/12 = $1,700$)

    2. Supplies Expense   11,000
          Supplies...   11,000
          (To record supplies used: $13,200 - $2,200 = $11,000$)

    3. Insurance Expense   960
          Prepaid Insurance   960
          (To record insurance expired: $4,320 \times 8/36 = 960)

    4. Depreciation Expense—Building   2,500
          Accumulated Depreciation—Building   2,500
          (To record annual depreciation on building:
          $50,000 \times 5\% = $2,500$)

    5. Depreciation Expense—Equipment.................................   13,000
          Accumulated Depreciation—Equipment........................   13,000
          (To record annual depreciation on equipment:
          $130,000 \times 10\% = $13,000$)

    6. Interest Expense...   2,500
          Interest Payable   2,500
          (To record interest accrued on note:
          $50,000 \times 12\% \times 5/12 = $2,500$)

    7. Accounts Receivable (or Rent Receivable)   1,400
          Rent Revenue   1,400
          (To record accrued revenue)

    8. Salaries and Wages Expense..   1,920
          Salaries and Wages Payable   1,920
          (To record accrued salaries: $6,400 \times 3/10 = $1,920$)

Approach and Explanation: Identify each item as involving: (1) a prepaid expense, (2) an unearned revenue, (3) an accrued revenue, or (4) an accrued expense. From the facts, determine the existing account balances. Read the facts carefully to determine the desired account balances for financial statements in accordance with generally accepted accounting principles (historical cost principle, revenue recognition principle, expense recognition principle, etc.). Determine the adjusting entries necessary to bring existing account balances to the appropriate account balances.

1. On November 1, 2014, cash was received and recorded as follows:

    Cash 10,200

         Unearned Rent Revenue..   10,200

    This situation involves unearned revenue. At December 31, 2014, before adjustment, there is an Unearned Rent Revenue account with a balance of $10,200. The amount unearned at that date is $10,200 X 10/12 = $8,500. Therefore, an adjusting entry is necessary to transfer the $1,700 related to services performed from the Unearned Rent Revenue account to the Rent Revenue account.

2. This situation involves a prepaid expense. All supplies are charged to an asset account, Supplies, when purchased. Therefore, Supplies has an unadjusted balance of $13,200, which reflects the balance at the beginning of the year plus the cost of all supplies acquired during the year. Supplies on hand of $2,200 are to appear on the balance sheet. Thus, $11,000 of consumed supplies must be transferred from the asset account to an expense account in an adjusting entry.

3. This item involves a prepaid expense. The Prepaid Insurance account reflects a $4,320 balance which represents the cost of a three-year premium. That three-year period began on May 1, 2014. Therefore, eight of the total 36 months have gone by and the cost of the eight month's coverage ($960) has expired. The expired portion must be transferred from the asset account to an expense account. This will leave 28 months of coverage ($4,320 X 28/36 = $3,360 or $4,320 - $960 = $3,360) in the asset account, Prepaid Insurance, to be charged to expense in future periods.

4. This item involves a long-term prepaid expense. A long-lived tangible item such as building or equipment represents a bundle of benefits when it is acquired. These benefits are to be used up (consumed) over the course of the asset's estimated service life.

    Depreciation is a term that refers to the process of allocating the cost of a long-lived tangible asset to the periods benefited from its use. The process of depreciation is necessary to comply with the expense recognition (matching) principle. The building or equipment is used to generate revenue during the period. Consequently, a portion of the bundle of benefits represented by the asset is consumed. There is a cost associated with those consumed benefits. This cost is to be matched with the revenues it helped generate. Thus, an expense is recorded (Depreciation Expense), and an asset is reduced. It is customary, however, to make use of a contra asset account, Accumulated Depreciation, rather than to credit the asset account itself.

5. See the explanation for 4. above. Notice that a credit to Accumulated Depreciation has the same impact as a credit to the account being depreciated (Equipment, for example). Thus, total assets are reduced by the journal entry to record depreciation.

6. This situation involves an accrued expense. Interest is a function of debt balance, interest rate, and time. Interest is due and payable at the end of an interest period. The last interest payment date was August 1, 2014. Thus, interest incurred and not yet paid or payable amounts to five months worth or $2,500 ($50,000 X 12% X 5/12 = $2,500). The accrued interest is recorded by an increase to the Interest Expense account and a credit to a liability account, Interest Payable. (Note the balance before adjustment in the Interest Expense account represents seven months of interest. On August 1, 2014, an interest payment of $6,000 was made and $3,500 of that represented the interest from January 1, 2014 through July 31, 2014. The other $2,500 paid for interest would have been accrued earlier at the end of 2013.)

7. This situation involves an accrual of revenue. Services have been performed but revenue has not yet been billed or recorded or received. The "services have been performed" part is recorded in the adjusting entry by a credit to Rent Revenue. The "not received" part is recorded by a debit to Accounts Receivable or Rent Receivable. Thus, the appropriate adjusting entry increases assets and revenues earned.

8. This item involves an accrued expense. An accrued expense is an expense incurred but not yet paid. The salary for the last three work days of the year has been incurred because the employees have contributed their labor services for a period of time that has passed. The employees will not be paid until nine calendar days after the balance sheet date. The accrued expense is recorded at the balance sheet date by a debit to an expense account and a credit to a liability account.

(b)
BUTLER'S EQUIPMENT RENTALS, INC.
Adjusted Trial Balance
December 31, 2014

	Debit	Credit
Cash	$ 16,500	
* Accounts Receivable	1,400	
Prepaid Insurance	3,360	
Supplies	2,200	
Land	62,000	
Building	50,000	
Equipment	130,000	
Accumulated Depreciation—Building		$ 12,500
Accumulated Depreciation—Equipment		65,000
Note Payable		50,000
Accounts Payable		9,310
* Interest Payable		2,500
* Salaries and Wages Payable		640
Unearned Rent Revenue		8,500
Common Stock		30,000
Retained Earnings		60,660
Dividends	31,000	
Rent Revenue		165,060
Salaries and Wages Expense	71,240	
Interest Expense	6,000	
* Supplies Expense	11,000	
* Insurance Expense	960	
* Depreciation Expense—Building	2,500	
* Depreciation Expense—Equipment	13,000	
* Miscellaneous Expense	3,010	
	$404,170	$404,170

* Although these accounts are listed in a logical order on this adjusted trial balance when you consider the item's position on financial statements, account titles which are used in adjusting entries but that do **not** appear on the unadjusted trial balance are typically listed on the adjusted trial at the **end** of the listing of accounts which appeared on the unadjusted trial.

TIP: Now that the adjusted trial balance is complete, think about where the account balances are to go in the preparation of financial statements. (See the next exercise to do just that).

EXERCISE 3-7

Purpose: (L.O. 6) This exercise illustrates how the items appearing on an adjusted trial balance get reported on the financial statements.

Instructions

Using the items on the Adjusted Trial Balance at December 31, 2014 for Butler's Equipment Rentals, Inc., in the **SOLUTION TO EXERCISE 3-6**, prepare the following:

(a) Income Statement for the year ended December 31, 2014.
(b) Retained Earnings Statement for the year ended December 31, 2014.
(c) Balance Sheet (unclassified) at December 31, 2014.

SOLUTION TO EXERCISE 3-7

The solution shown here incorporates the Adjusted Trial Balance with arrows to help you to see the logical disposition of each item on the Adjusted Trial Balance as well as the "articulation" of these three basic financial statements.

BUTLER'S EQUIPMENT RENTALS, INC.
Adjusted Trial Balance
December 31, 2014

Account	Debit	Credit
Cash	$ 16,500	
Accounts Receivable	1,400	
Prepaid Insurance	3,360	
Supplies	2,200	
Land	62,000	
Building	50,000	
Equipment	130,000	
Accumulated Depreciation-- Building		$ 12,500
Accumulated Depreciation-- Equipment		65,000
Note Payable		50,000
Accounts Payable		9,310
Interest Payable		2,500
Salaries and Wages Payable		640
Unearned Rent Revenue		8,500
Common Stock		30,000
Retained Earnings		60,660
Dividends	31,000	
Rent Revenue		165,060
Salaries and Wages Expense	71,240	
Interest Expense	6,000	
Supplies Expense	11,000	
Insurance Expense	960	
Depreciation Expense-- Building	2,500	
Depreciation Expense-- Equipment	13,000	
Miscellaneous Expense	3,010	
	$404,170	$404,170

(a)

BUTLER'S EQUIPMENT RENTALS, INC.
Income Statement
For the Year Ended December 31, 2014

Revenues
Rent revenue $165,060

Expenses
Salaries and Wages expense $71,240
Interest expense 6,000
Supplies expense 11,000
Insurance expense 960
Depreciation expense-- building 2,500
Depreciation expense-- equipment 13,000
Miscellaneous expense 3,010
Total expenses 107,710
Net income .... $ 57,350

(b)

BUTLER'S EQUIPMENT RENTALS, INC.
Retained Earnings Statement
For the Year Ended December 31, 2014

Retained earnings, January 1 .... $60,660
Add: Net income 57,350
118,010
Less: Dividends 31,000
Retained earnings, December 31 .... $87,010

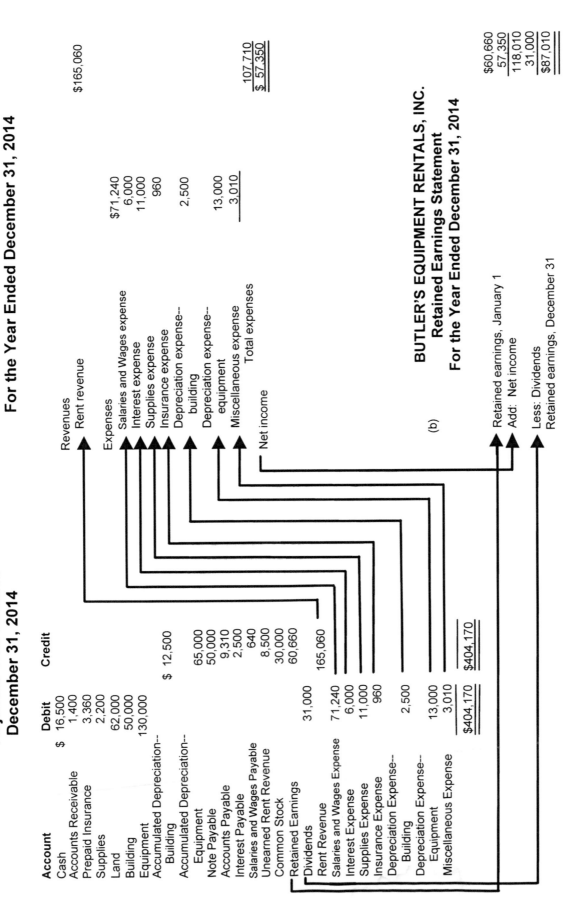

BUTLER'S EQUIPMENT RENTALS, INC.
Adjusted Trial Balance
December 31, 2014

Account	Debit	Credit
Cash	$ 16,500	
Accounts Receivable	1,400	
Prepaid Insurance	3,360	
Supplies	2,200	
Land	62,000	
Building	50,000	
Equipment	130,000	
Accumulated Depreciation—Building		$ 12,500
Accumulated Depreciation—Equipment		65,000
Note Payable		50,000
Accounts Payable		9,310
Interest Payable		2,500
Salaries and Wages Payable		640
Unearned Rent Revenue		8,500
Common Stock		30,000
Retained Earnings		60,660
Dividends	31,000	
Rent Revenue		165,060
Salaries and Wages Expense	71,240	
Interest Expense	6,000	
Supplies Expense	11,000	
Insurance Expense	960	
Depreciation Expense—Building	2,500	
Depreciation Expense—Equipment	13,000	
Miscellaneous Expense	3,010	
	$404,170	$404,170

(c)

BUTLER'S EQUIPMENT RENTALS, INC.
Balance Sheet
December 31, 2014

ASSETS

Cash		$ 16,500
Accounts receivable		1,400
Prepaid insurance		3,360
Supplies		2,200
Land		62,000
Building	$ 50,000	
Less: Accumulated depreciation	12,500	37,500
Equipment	130,000	
Less: Accumulated depreciation	65,000	65,000
Total assets		$187,960

LIABILITIES AND STOCKHOLDERS' EQUITY

Liabilities		
Note payable		$ 50,000
Accounts payable		9,310
Interest payable		2,500
Salaries and Wages payable		640
Unearned rent revenue		8,500
Total liabilities		70,950
Stockholders' equity		
Common stock		30,000
Retained earnings		87,010
Total liabilities and stockholders' equity		$187,960

Balance at Dec. 31 from Retained Earnings Statement

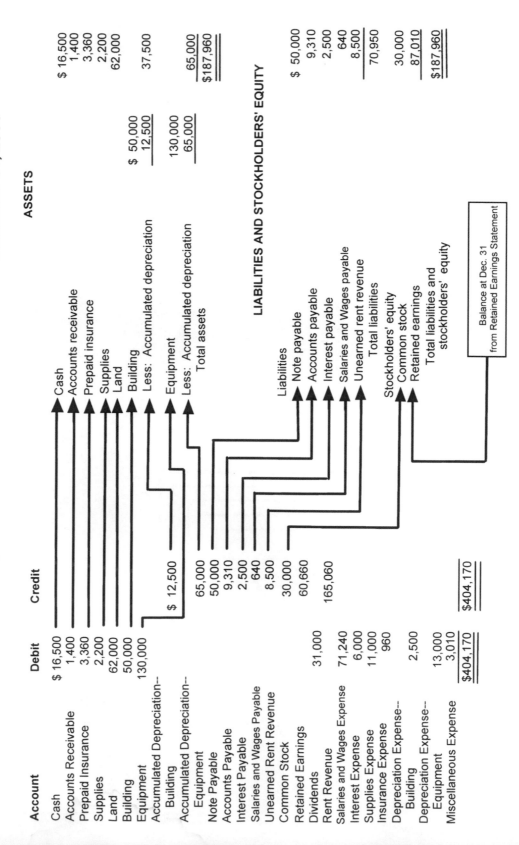

EXERCISE 3-8

Purpose: (L.O. 7) This exercise will review the preparation of closing entries.

The adjusted trial balance for the Ken and Barbie Shuck Corporation at December 31, 2014 appears as follows:

Ken and Barbie Shuck Corporation
ADJUSTED TRIAL BALANCE
December 31, 2014

	Debit	Credit
Cash	$ 4,600	
Accounts Receivable	2,200	
Supplies on Hand	2,100	
Accounts Payable		$ 700
Common Stock		5,000
Retained Earnings (January 1, 2014)		1,300
Service Revenue		4,900
Rent Expense	800	
Advertising Expense	300	
Cleaning Expense	200	
Utilities Expense	80	
Utilities Payable		80
Supplies Expense	1,700	
	$11,980	$11,980

Instructions
(a)   Prepare the appropriate closing entries at December 31, 2014.
(b)   Explain why closing entries are necessary.

Solution to Exercise 3-8

(a)   Service Revenue 4,900
         Income Summary   4,900
            (To close the revenue account
             to Income Summary)

Income Summary 3,080
      Rent Expense   800
      Advertising Expense   300
      Cleaning Expense   200
      Utilities Expense   80
      Supplies Expense   1,700
         (To close expense accounts to Income Summary)

Income Summary 1,820
      Retained Earnings   1,820
         (To close Income Summary to Retained Earnings)
         ($4,900 total revenues - $3,080 total expenses =
          $1,820 credit balance in Income Summary before closing)

(b)   The major reason closing entries are needed is that they prepare the temporary (nominal) accounts for the recording of transactions of the next accounting period. Closing entries produce a zero balance in each of the temporary accounts so that they can be used to accumulate data pertaining to the next accounting period. Because of closing entries, the revenues of 2015 are not commingled with the revenues of the prior period (2014). A second reason closing entries are needed is that the Retained Earnings account will reflect a true balance only after closing entries have been completed. Closing entries formally recognize in the ledger the transfer of net income (or loss) and dividends declared to retained earnings as indicated in the statement of retained earnings.

TIP:	The Income Summary account is used only in the closing process. Before it is closed, the balance in this account must equal the net income or net loss figure for the period.
TIP:	Where do you look for the accounts (and their amounts) to be closed? If a work sheet is used, you can use the amounts listed in the Income Statement column pair and the balance of the Dividends Declared (or Owner's Drawing) account. If a work sheet is not used, you must refer to the temporary accounts (after adjustment) in the ledger to determine the balances to be closed.

*ILLUSTRATION 3-2
CONVERSION FROM CASH BASIS ACCOUNTING TO
ACCRUAL BASIS ACCOUNTING (L.O. 9)

With the **cash basis of accounting,** a revenue item is reported in the time period when the related cash is received from the customer and an expense is recorded in the time period in which the related cash is paid. Cash basis financial statements are **not** in conformity with generally accepted accounting principles. Most companies use the **accrual basis of accounting**, whereby a revenue item is reported in the time period in which the related performance obligation is satisfied and an expense item is reported in the time period in which it is incurred.

Revenue that is earned and recognized during the period but not collected (accrued revenue) results in reporting an asset (receivable) on the balance sheet. Revenue that has been received but not earned (unearned or deferred revenue) results in reporting a liability (unearned revenue) on the balance sheet. Expense that is incurred but not paid (accrued expense) results in reporting a liability (payable) on the balance sheet. Expense that has paid but not incurred (prepaid or deferred expense) results in reporting an asset (prepaid expense).

To Convert Cash Receipts to Revenues Earned:

	Cash Received from Customers
-	Beginning Accounts Receivable
+	Ending Accounts Receivable
+	Beginning Unearned Revenues
-	Ending Unearned Revenues
=	Revenues Earned

Explanation: The balance of accounts receivable at the beginning of the period represents revenues earned in a prior period that are collected in the current period; ending accounts receivable stem from revenues earned in the current period that are not yet collected. Beginning unearned revenues represent cash collections in a prior period (not the current period) that are for revenues earned in the current period. Ending unearned revenues come from collections during the current period that are not yet recognized as earned revenues.

To Convert Cash Payments to Operating Expenses:

	Cash Paid for Operating Expenses
+	Beginning Prepaid Expenses
-	Ending Prepaid Expenses
-	Beginning Accrued Payables
+	Ending Accrued Payables
=	Operating Expenses Incurred (**Excluding** Depreciation and Bad Debt Expense)

Explanation: Beginning prepaid expenses represent amounts recognized as expense in the current period for which cash payments are not made in the current period. (The cash payments occurred in a prior period.) Ending prepaids stem from cash payments in the current period for expenses not recognized in the current period. (The expense recognition is being deferred to a future period.) Beginning accrued payables come from expenses recognized in a prior period (not the current year) that require cash payments during the current period. Ending accrued payables stem from expenses recognized during the current year that have not yet been paid.

TIP: Noncash expenses such as depreciation on plant assets, bad debt expense, amortization of intangibles, and amortization of discount on notes payable are ignored in the above format. These items would also have to be considered in computing total operating expenses incurred or in computing net income on an accrual basis.

EXERCISE 3-9

Purpose: (L.O. 5, 9) This exercise will point out the relationships that exist between cash data and accrual amounts when certain balance sheet accounts increase during the period.

Instructions

Complete each of the blanks below with one of the following, whichever is appropriate:

>   symbol for "is greater than"
<   symbol for "is less than"
or   =   symbol for "equals."

1.   On a comparative balance sheet, if an accrued receivable increased, then revenue earned _____ cash received so net income on the accrual basis _____ income on a cash basis.

2.   On a comparative balance sheet, if an unearned revenue increased, then revenue earned _____ cash received so net income on the accrual basis _____ income on a cash basis.

3.   On a comparative balance sheet, if a prepaid expense increased, then expense incurred _____ cash paid so net income on the accrual basis _____ income on a cash basis.

4.   On a comparative balance sheet, if an accrued payable increased, then expense incurred _____ cash paid so net income on the accrual basis _____ income on a cash basis.

Solution to Exercise 3-9

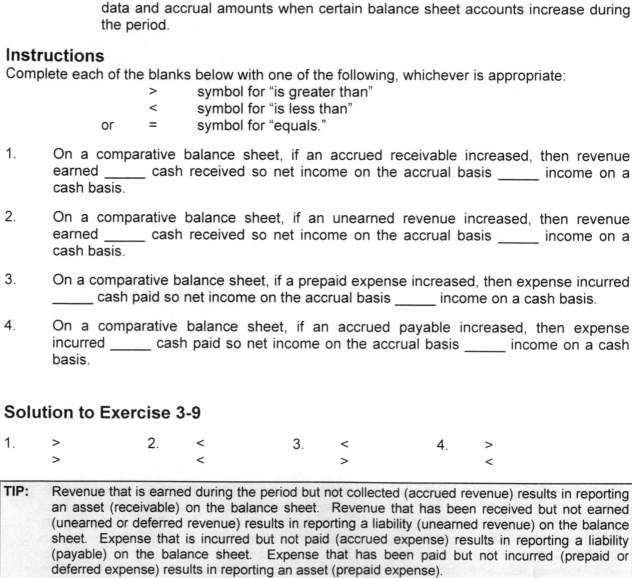

1.   >   2.   <   3.   <   4.   >
       >   <   >   <

TIP: Revenue that is earned during the period but not collected (accrued revenue) results in reporting an asset (receivable) on the balance sheet. Revenue that has been received but not earned (unearned or deferred revenue) results in reporting a liability (unearned revenue) on the balance sheet. Expense that is incurred but not paid (accrued expense) results in reporting a liability (payable) on the balance sheet. Expense that has been paid but not incurred (prepaid or deferred expense) results in reporting an asset (prepaid expense).

TIP: Notice that the signs are the **same** in the answers to 1 and 2 but the signs are **different** in the answers to 3 and 4. The reason is that **revenue** is a **positive** component of income and **expense** is a **negative** component of income.

TIP: A comparative balance sheet is a balance sheet with amounts shown for at least two different dates; for example, at the end of the current period (December 31, 2014) and at the end of the prior period (December 31, 2013). The date at the end of the prior period (end of day December 31, 2013) is the same as the date of the beginning of the current period (beginning of day January 1, 2014).

*EXERCISE 3-10

Purpose: (L.O. 9) This exercise illustrates the different results that are obtained when the accrual and the cash methods of accounting are used.

Annabell's Specialty Service Shop, a proprietorship business, conducted the following transactions during the first week in March.

1. Purchased supplies for $1,800. Paid 20% down; remaining 80% to be paid in 10 days.
2. Paid $30 for newspaper advertising to appear this week.
3. Collected $1,400 from customers on account.
4. Performed services at a $1,620 charge to customers; however, cash payment is not due until next week.
5. Paid $600 rent for the month of March.
6. Performed services for $280 cash.
7. Paid part-time sales clerk $40 wages for the week.
8. Wrote a check for $100 to the owner for her personal use.
9. Consumed supplies of $1,400.

Instructions
(a)   Compute the net income for the week, using the cash method of accounting.
(b)   Compute the net income for the week, using the accrual method of accounting.
Show your computations in good form.

Solution to Exercise 3-10

(a)   **Cash Method:**

Cash Received from Customers ($1,400 + $280)		$1,680
Less: Payment for Supplies ($1,800 x 20%)	$ 360	
Payment for Advertising	30	
Payment for Rent	600	
Payment to Employee	40	1,030
Net Income (cash method)		$ 650

> **TIP:**   Using the **cash basis** (method) of accounting, revenues are recognized (reported) in the period in which they are **received** and expenses are recognized in the period in which they are **paid**. The cash basis is **not** in accordance with generally accepted accounting principles.

(b)   **Accrual Method:**

Service Revenue ($1,620 + $280)		$ 1,900
Less: Operating Expenses		
Supplies Expense	$1,400	
Advertising Expense	30	
Rent Expense ($600 ÷ 4)	150	
Wages Expense	40	1,620
Net Income (accrual method)		$ 280

TIP: Withdrawals by owner ($100) do **not** enter into the income computations.

TIP: Using the **accrual basis** (method) of accounting, revenues are recognized in the period in which they are **earned** and expenses are recognized in the period in which they are **incurred**.

Accrual basis accounting is theoretically preferable to the cash basis because it provides information about future cash inflows and outflows associated with earnings activities as soon as a company can estimate these cash flows with an acceptable degree of certainty. That is, accrual basis accounting aids in predicting future cash flows by reporting transactions and events with cash consequences at the time the transactions and events occur, rather than when the cash is received and paid.

---

*EXERCISE 3-11

Purpose: (L.O. 9) This exercise will illustrate the conversion of cash data to accrual data.

Dr. Jeffrey Prickett, M.D., maintains the accounting records of the Holistic Center on a cash basis. During 2014, Dr. Prickett collected $305,400 from his patients and paid $91,200 in expenses. Information regarding the amount of receivables (accrued revenues), unearned revenues, payables for accrued expenses, and prepaid expenses is as follows:

	Balance at December 31, 2013	Balance at December 31, 2014
Accounts receivable	$45,000	$51,000
Unearned revenues	2,000	2,800
Accrued payables	5,200	4,980
Prepaid expenses	3,000	8,000

Instructions
(a)   Prepare a schedule to convert Dr. Prickett's cash basis income of $214,200 (excess of $305,400 cash collections over $91,200 cash disbursements) for the year 2014 to net income on an accrual basis.

(b)   Describe any items other than the above that may have to be considered in converting cash basis income to accrual basis income.

Solution to Exercise 3-11

(a)

Cash collections from patients	$305,400
Accounts receivable, beginning of year	(45,000)
Accounts receivable, end of year	51,000
Unearned revenue, beginning of year	2,000
Unearned revenue, end of year	(2,800)
Revenues earned during 2014	$310,600

Cash payments for expense items	$91,200
Accrued payables, beginning of year	(5,200)
Accrued payables, end of year	4,980
Prepaid expenses, beginning of year	3,000
Prepaid expenses, end of year	(8,000)
Expenses incurred during 2014	85,980

Revenues earned during 2014	310,600
Expenses incurred during 2014	(85,980)
Net income on accrual basis for 2014	$224,620

TIP: An alternate schedule would be as follows:

Cash basis income for 2014	$214,200
Accounts receivable, beginning of year	(45,000)
Accounts receivable end of year	51,000
Unearned revenues, beginning of year	2,000
Unearned revenues, end of year	(2,800)
Accrued payables, beginning of year	5,200
Accrued payables, end of year	(4,980)
Prepaid expenses, beginning of year	(3,000)
Prepaid expenses, end of year	8,000
Net income on accrual basis for 2014	$224,620

Notice the differences between this computation and the first solution. When converting cash basis income to net income, the balances of accounts stemming from revenue type transactions (Accounts Receivable and Unearned Revenues) are handled the same exact way as they were treated in the conversion of cash collections to revenues earned because revenues are a positive component of net income. However, when converting cash basis income to net income, the balances of accounts stemming from expense type transactions (Accrued Payable and Prepaid Expense) are handled the opposite of the way they were treated in the conversion of cash payments to expenses incurred because expenses are a negative component of net income.

Therefore, the accounts receivable balance of $45,000 at the beginning of the year is deducted from cash collections in 2014 to arrive at revenue earned in 2014 because that $45,000 was collected in 2014 but earned in a prior period. Likewise, the accounts receivable balance of $45,000 at the beginning of the year is also **deducted** from the cash basis income to arrive at net income because that $45,000 was collected in 2014 and reflected in the cash basis income of $214,200 but should not be reflected as revenue earned in the net income on an accrual basis figure.

> In comparison, the accrued payables balance of $5,200 at the beginning of the year 2014 is deducted from cash payments in 2014 to arrive at expenses incurred in 2014 because that $5,200 was paid in 2014 but incurred in a prior period. Thus, the accrued payable balance at the beginning of the year is **added** to the cash basis income figure to arrive at net income on an accrual basis because that $5,200 was paid in 2014 and reflected as a deduction in the cash basis income of $214,200 but should not be reflected as an expense incurred in the net income on an accrual basis figure. An addition is made to negate the negative number reflected in the cash basis income figure.

(b)   In addition to the items above, expense items **not** currently requiring a cash outlay such as:
● depreciation expense
● amortization of intangible assets (patents, etc.)
● amortization of discount on bonds payable would also have to be added to cash payments to arrive at expenses incurred on an accrual basis. Thus, they would reduce the net income calculation.

**EXERCISE 3-12

Purpose: (L.O. 10) This exercise will provide practice in determining which adjusting entries may be reversed.

Instructions
The following represent adjusting entries prepared for the Bent Tree Company at December 31, 2014 (end of the accounting period). The company has the policy of using reversing entries when appropriate. For each adjusting entry below, indicate if it would be appropriate to reverse it at the beginning of 2015. Indicate your answer by circling "yes" or "no."

Yes	No	1.	Deferred Advertising Expense......................	4,500	
			Advertising Expense		4,500
Yes	No	2.	Interest Expense...	800	
			Discount on Bonds Payable................		800
Yes	No	3.	Interest Receivable......................................	690	
			Interest Revenue		690
Yes	No	4.	Unearned Rental Income............................	900	
			Rental Income......................................		900
Yes	No	5.	Insurance Expense......................................	1,600	
			Prepaid Insurance...............................		1,600
Yes	No	6.	Salaries Expense...	1,100	
			Salaries Payable..................................		1,100

Solution to Exercise 3-12

1.	Yes	3.	Yes	5.	No
2.	No	4.	No	6.	Yes

> **TIP:** A **reversing entry** is an entry made at the very beginning of an accounting period that is the exact opposite of an adjusting entry made at the end of the previous period. The recording of reversing entries is an **optional** step in the accounting cycle. The **purpose** of a reversing entry is to simplify the recording of transactions in the new accounting period. The use of reversing entries does not change the amounts reported in financial statements.

Approach: Write down what the related reversing entry would look like and then (1) think about the effects that the reversing entry would have on the account balances in the accounting period that follows the one for which the adjustment was made, and (2) think about whether those effects are appropriate or not. It is appropriate to reverse an adjusting entry involving a deferral (prepaid expense or unearned revenue) **only if** the adjustment increases (rather than decreases) a balance sheet account. It is **always** appropriate to reverse an adjusting entry involving an accrual. It is **never** appropriate to reverse an adjusting entry for depreciation or amortization or bad debts.

Explanation:
1. An adjustment for a deferred expense can be reversed if the adjustment increases an asset or liability account. This adjustment increases a prepaid expense (asset) account.
2. Never reverse an adjustment for amortization of a discount or premium.
3. An accrual type adjustment can always be reversed.
4. A reversal of this entry would put back into the Unearned Rental Revenue account the amount that the adjustment indicated has been earned.
5. An adjustment for a deferral can be reversed only if it increases a balance sheet account. This adjustment decreases an asset account.
6. An accrual type adjustment can always be reversed. You can tell the adjusting entry is for an accrued expense because the debit is to an expense account and the credit is to a payable account.

**EXERCISE 3-13

Purpose: (L.O. 10) This exercise will give you practice in identifying adjusting entries that may be reversed.

Instructions
Refer to **Exercise 3-6** and the **Solution to Exercise 3-6**. Indicate the adjusting entries that can be reversed.

Solution to Exercise 3-13

Adjusting entries that may be reversed: 6, 7, 8
Adjusting entries that are **not** to be reversed: 1, 2, 3, 4, 5

Approach and Explanation: Think of the types of adjustments and whether they can be reversed. Accrual type adjusting entries can always be reversed. Therefore, items 6, 7, and 8 can be reversed. Items such as depreciation of plant assets, the recognition of bad debts, and amortization of intangibles and discounts and premiums on receivables and payables should never be reversed. Therefore, items 4 and 5 should **not** be reversed. Adjustments involving deferrals can be reversed **if** the original cash entry involved a nominal account (revenue or expense account) rather than a prepaid or unearned account (a real account) and the adjustment **increases** a prepaid expense or unearned revenue account. Therefore, items 1, 2, and 3 should **not** be reversed.

**ILLUSTRATION 3-3
SUMMARY OF ADJUSTMENT RELATIONSHIPS
AND EXPLANATIONS (L.O. 5, 10)

Type of Adjustment	Account Relationship	Reason for Adjustment	Account Balances Before Adjustment	Adjusting Entry
1. Prepaid Expense	Asset and Expense	(a) Prepaid expense initially recorded in asset account has been consumed; or,	Asset overstated Expense understated	Dr. Expense Cr. Asset
		**(b) Prepaid expense initially recorded in expense account has not been consumed.	Asset understated Expense overstated	Dr. Asset Cr. Expense
2. Unearned Revenue	Liability and Revenue	(a) Unearned revenue initially recorded in liability account has been earned; or,	Liability overstated Revenue understated	Dr. Liability Cr. Revenue
		**(b) Unearned revenue initially recorded in revenue account has not been earned.	Liability understated Revenue overstated	Dr. Revenue Cr. Liability
3. Accrued Expense	Expense and Liability	Expense incurred has not been billed nor paid nor recorded.	Expense understated Liability understated	Dr. Expense Cr. Liability
4. Accrued Revenues	Asset and Revenue	Revenue earned has not been billed nor collected nor recorded.	Asset understated Revenue understated	Dr. Asset Cr. Revenue

These situations are addressed in **Appendix 3B in the text.

Explanation:
1.   When expenses are paid for before they are incurred, the payment may either be recorded by a debit to an asset account (prepaid expense) or by a debit to an expense account. At the end of the accounting period, the accounts are adjusted as needed. If the prepayment was initially recorded by use of a prepaid (asset) account, the consumed portion is transferred to an expense account in the adjusting entry. Whereas, if the prepayment was initially recorded by use of an expense account, an adjusting entry is required only if a portion of the expense remains prepaid at the end of the accounting period (in which case the unconsumed portion is transferred to an asset account). (See **Illustration 3-4** for an example.)

2.   When revenues are received before the related services are performed, the receipt may either be recorded by a credit to a liability account (unearned revenue) or by a credit to a revenue account. At the end of the accounting period, the accounts are adjusted as needed. If the collection was initially recorded by a credit to a liability account (unearned revenue), the earned portion is transferred to a revenue account in the adjusting entry. Whereas, if the collection was initially recorded by use of a revenue account, an adjusting entry is required only if a portion of the revenue remains unearned at the end of the accounting period (in which case the unearned portion is transferred to a liability account). (See **Illustration 3-4** for an example.)

ILLUSTRATION 3-3 (Continued)

3.   Expenses are often incurred before they are paid. An expense incurred but not yet paid is called an **accrued expense**. If at the end of an accounting period this accrued expense has not been recorded (which is often the case because it usually has not been billed yet by the vendor), it must be recorded by way of an adjusting entry. Expense that accrues with the passage of time (such as interest expense) is a good example of a reason to need an accrued expense (or accrued liability) type adjusting entry.

4.   Revenues are often earned before they are collected. A revenue earned but not received is called an **accrued revenue**. If at the end of an accounting period this accrued revenue has not been recorded (which is often the case because it usually has not been billed yet), it must be recorded by way of an adjusting entry. Revenue that accrues with the passage of time (such as interest revenue) is a good example of a reason to need an accrued revenue (or accrued asset) type adjusting entry.

TIP: Examine each type of adjustment explained above and notice the logic of the resulting entry. For example, an adjustment to recognize supplies used (when the supplies were recorded in an asset account when purchased) should reduce assets and increase expenses.

TIP: Keep in mind that for accrued items (accrued revenues and accrued expenses), the related cash flow **follows** the period in which the relevant revenue or expense is recognized; whereas, with prepayment type items (unearned revenues and prepaid expenses), the related cash flow **precedes** the period in which the relevant revenue or expense is recognized.

For example, assume the accounting period is the calendar year. Consider an accrued expense such as accrued salaries at the end of 2014. An adjusting entry will be recorded at the end of 2014 so the expense will get reported on the 2014 income statement. The related cash payment to employees will take place in the following accounting period (2015, in this case). For another example, consider a prepaid expense such as the prepayment of rent in December 2014 for January 2015 occupancy. The cash payment occurs in December 2014. The expense is incurred and recognized in the following accounting period (January 2015).

**ILLUSTRATION 3-4
ALTERNATIVE TREATMENTS OF PREPAID EXPENSES
AND UNEARNED REVENUES (L.O. 5, 10)

When a company writes a check to pay for an item that affects expense in at least two different time periods (such as for an insurance premium or a license or dues), the bookkeeper may record the payment in one of two ways. Either as a prepaid expense (asset) or as an expense. The first way is used most often in introductory accounting textbooks; the second is used most often in the real world. Regardless of the way the payment is recorded, an appropriate adjusting entry will be made at the end of the accounting period so that correct balances appear on the income statement and the balance sheet. For example, a $1,200 payment is made on April 1, 2014, for a twelve-month insurance premium covering the time between April 1, 2014 and March 31, 2015. (Assume a calendar year reporting period.) A comparison of the two possible approaches appears below.

Prepayment (Cash Paid)				**Prepayment (Cash Paid)**		
Initially Debited to Asset Account			**OR**	**Initially Debited to Expense Account**		
4/1	Prepaid Insurance	1,200		4/1	Insurance Expense	1,200	
	Cash		1,200		Cash		1,200
12/31	Insurance Expense	900		12/31	Prepaid Insurance	300	
	Prepaid Insurance		900		Insurance Expense		300

After posting the entries, the accounts appear as follows:

Prepaid Insurance		
4/1	1,200	12/31 Adj.	900
12/31 Bal.	300	

| Prepaid Insurance | |
| 12/31 Adj. | 300 | |

| Insurance Expense | |
| 12/31 Adj. | 900 | |

Insurance Expense		
4/1	1,200	12/31 Adj.	300
12/31 Bal.	900	

Notice that regardless of the path, you end up at the same place—with a balance of $300 in Prepaid Insurance and a balance of $900 in Insurance Expense. That was your objective—to report balances in accordance with the accrual basis of accounting.

TIP: Reversing entries are never required. But if it is company policy to use reversing entries where appropriate, would either or both of the above adjusting entries get reversed? The adjusting entry illustrated in the left column would **not get reversed since to do so would result in reestablishing an asset amount that the adjusting entry indicated had expired. The adjusting entry illustrated in the right column **can be** reversed since a reversing entry will record $300 of insurance expense in the new accounting period (2015) which is the period we expect the remaining $300 of premium to pertain.

Illustration 3-4 (Continued)

When a company receives cash from a customer in advance of earning the related revenue by satisfying the related performance obligation, the bookkeeper may record the receipt in one of two ways. Either as an unearned revenue (liability) or as an earned revenue. The first way is used most often in introductory accounting textbooks; the second is used most often in the real world. Regardless of the way the receipt is recorded, an appropriate adjusting entry will be made at the end of the accounting period so that correct balances appear on the income statement and the balance sheet. For example, $1,200 is received on May 1, 2014, for a twelve-month magazine subscription covering the time between May 1, 2014 and April 30, 2015. (Assume a calendar year reporting period.) A comparison of the two possible approaches appears below:

Unearned Revenue (Cash Received) Initially Credited to Liability Account			OR	Unearned Revenue (Cash Received) Initially Credited to Revenue Account		
5/1	Cash	1,200		5/1	Cash	1,200
	Unearned Sub. Rev.	1,200			Subscription Revenue	1,200
12/31	Unearned Sub. Rev.	800		12/31	Subscription Revenue	400
	Subscription Revenue	800			Unearned Sub Rev.	400

After posting the entries, the accounts appear as follows:

Unearned Subscription Revenue				Unearned Subscription Revenue		
12/31 Adj.	800	5/1	1,200		12/31 Adj.	400
		12/31 Bal.	400			

Subscription Revenue				Subscription Revenue		
		12/31 Adj.	800	12/31 Adj.	400	5/1	1,200
						12/31 Bal.	800

Notice that the balances in the accounts are the same regardless of the approach used; that is, Unearned Subscription Revenue is $400, and Subscription Revenue is $800 at December 31, 2014.

**TIP: The adjusting entry illustrated in the left column would not be subject to reversal; a reversing entry can be used with the approach illustrated in the right column.

**EXERCISE 3-14

Purpose: (L.O. 5, 10) This exercise will provide you with examples of adjusting entries for:
   (1)   Prepaid expenses when cash payments are recorded in an asset (real) account.
   (2)   Prepaid expenses when cash payments are recorded in an expense (nominal) account.
   (3)   Unearned revenues when cash receipts are recorded in a liability (real) account.
   (4)   Unearned revenues when cash receipts are recorded in a revenue (nominal) account.

Thus, this exercise will review the alternative treatments of prepaid expenses and unearned revenues discussed in **Illustration 3-4**.

Each situation described below is **independent** of the others.

(1)   Office supplies are recorded in an asset account when acquired. There were $400 of supplies on hand at the beginning of the period. Cash purchases of office supplies during the period amount to $900. A count of supplies at the end of the period shows $320 worth to be on hand.

(2)   Office supplies are recorded in an expense account when acquired. There were $400 of supplies on hand at the beginning of the period. Cash purchases of office supplies during the period amount to $900. A count of supplies at the end of the period shows $320 worth to be on hand. No reversing entries are used.

(3)   Receipts from customers for magazine subscriptions are recorded as a liability when cash is collected in advance of delivery. The beginning balance in the liability account was $6,700. During the period, $54,000 was received for subscriptions. At the end of the period, it was determined that the balance of the Unearned Subscription Revenue account should be $8,000.

(4)   Receipts from customers for magazine subscriptions are recorded as revenue when cash is collected in advance of delivery. The beginning balance in the liability account was $6,700. During the period, $54,000 was received for subscriptions. At the end of the period, it was determined that the balance of the Unearned Subscription Revenue account should be $8,000. No reversing entries are used.

Instructions

For each of the **independent** situations above:
(a)   Prepare the appropriate adjusting entry in general journal form.
(b)   Indicate the amount of revenue or expense which will appear on the income statement for the period.
(c)   Indicate the balance of the applicable asset or liability account at the end of the period.
(d)   Indicate the amount of cash received or paid during the period.
(e)   Indicate the change in the applicable asset or liability account from the beginning of the period to the end of the period.

TIP:	It would be helpful to draw T-accounts for each situation. Enter the information given as it would be, or needs to be, reflected in the accounts. Solve for the adjusting entry that would be necessary to "reconcile" the facts given.

Solution to Exercise 3-14

(1) a. Office Supplies Expense 980
             Office Supplies on Hand.............................. 980
     b. Office Supplies Expense $980
     c. Office Supplies on Hand $320
     d. Cash paid $900
     e. Decrease in Office Supplies on Hand $ 80

Approach:

(2) a. Office Supplies Expense 80
             Office Supplies on Hand.............................. 80
     b. Office Supplies Expense $980
     c. Office Supplies on Hand $320
     d. Cash paid $900
     e. Decrease in Office Supplies on Hand $ 80

Approach:

TIP:	Compare situation (1) with situation (2). Notice the facts are the same **except** for the account debited for acquisitions of office supplies. The solution is then the same **except** for the adjusting entry required.

(3) a. Unearned Subscription Revenue 52,700
             Subscription Revenue.................................. 52,700
     b. Subscription Revenue $52,700
     c. Unearned Subscription Revenue $ 8,000
     d. Cash received $54,000
     e. Increase in Unearned Subscription Revenue $ 1,300

Approach:

	Subscription Revenue				Unearned Subscription Revenue	
					Beg. Bal.	6,700
		(52,700)	ENTRY NEEDED TO COMPLETE ACCOUNTS →	(52,700)	Receipts	54,000
	Ending Balance 52,700				Desired Ending Bal.	8,000

(4)   a.   Subscription Revenue 1,300
             Unearned Subscription Revenue................   1,300
      b.   Subscription Revenue $52,700
      c.   Unearned Subscription Revenue $ 8,000
      d.   Cash received $54,000
      e.   Increase in Unearned Subscription Revenue $ 1,300

Approach:

	Unearned Subscription Revenue				Subscription Revenue	
	Beg. Bal.	6,700			Receipts	54,000
		(1,300)	ENTRY NEEDED TO COMPLETE ACCOUNTS →	(1,300)		
	Desired Ending Bal.	8,000			Ending Balance	52,700

> **TIP:** Compare situation (3) with situation (4). Notice the facts are the same **except** for the account credited for receipt of revenue in advance of the period in which the revenue is earned by the performance of services. The solution is the same **except** for the adjusting entry required.
>
> **TIP:** You should be able to handle what for most students can be the most challenging situations. Refer back to the descriptions of situations (2) and (4). Redo them, assuming that reversing entries **are** used. Reversing entries are described in **Appendix 3B** in the text. Those new solutions should appear as follows.
>
> (2)   Assuming reversing entries **are** used.
>   a.   Office Supplies on Hand 320
>   Office Supplies Expense....................................   320
>   b.   Office Supplies Expense $980
>   c.   Office Supplies on Hand $320
>   d.   Cash paid $900
>   e.   Decrease in Office Supplies on Hand $ 80
>
> ## Approach:
>
> | | Office Supplies Expense | | | | Office Supplies on Hand | | |
> |---|---|---|---|---|---|---|---|
> | Reversing | 400 | | ENTRY NEEDED TO COMPLETE ACCOUNTS → | Beg. Bal. | 400 | | |
> | Acquisitions | 900 | (320) | | | (320) | Reversing | 400 |
> | Ending Bal. | 980 | | | Desired Ending Bal. | 320 | | |

(4) Assuming reversing entries **are** used.

a.	Subscription Revenue	8,000	
	Unearned Subscription Revenue.................		8,000
b.	Subscription Revenue	$52,700	
c.	Unearned Subscription Revenue	$ 8,000	
d.	Cash received	$54,000	
e.	Increase in Unearned Subscription Revenue	$ 1,300	

Approach:

Unearned Subscription Revenue			ENTRY NEEDED TO COMPLETE ACCOUNTS		Subscription Revenue	
	Beg. Bal. 6,700				Reversing	6,700
Reversing 6,700	(8,000)		← →	(8,000)	Receipts	54,000
	Desired End- ing Bal. 8,000				Ending Balance	52,700

***EXERCISE 3-15

Purpose: (L.O. 11) This exercise will allow you to quickly check your knowledge of how items are extended on a 10-column work sheet.

Instructions

The last six columns of an incomplete 10-column work sheet are illustrated below. Place an "X" in the appropriate columns to indicate the proper work sheet treatment of the balance in each of the accounts listed. (The accounts are not listed in their usual order, the work sheet is **only** partially illustrated, and the Trial Balance and Adjustments columns have been **omitted**.)

Handy Dandy Hardware
WORK SHEET
For the Year Ended December 31, 2014

Account	Adjusted Trial Balance		Income Statement		Balance Sheet	
	Debit	Credit	Debit	Credit	Debit	Credit
Advertising Expense						
Depreciation Expense						
Land						
Store Equipment						
Salaries and Wages Expense						
Mortgage Payable						
Cash						
Salaries and Wages Payable						
Prepaid Insurance						
Delivery Equipment						
Accumulated Depreciation						
Revenue Received in Advance						
Rent Expense						
Sales Revenue						
Prepaid Rent						
Dividends Declared						
Repairs Expense						
Sales Taxes Payable						
Interest Receivable						
Accounts Receivable						
Net Income						
Retained Earnings						

Solution to Exercise 3-15

Handy Dandy Hardware
WORK SHEET
For the Year Ended December 31, 2014

Account	Adjusted Trial Balance		Income Statement		Balance Sheet	
	Debit	Credit	Debit	Credit	Debit	Credit
Advertising Expense	X		X			
Depreciation Expense	X		X			
Land	X				X	
Store Equipment	X				X	
Salaries and Wages Expense	X		X			
Mortgage Payable		X				X
Cash	X				X	
Salaries and Wages Payable		X				X
Prepaid Insurance	X				X	
Delivery Equipment	X				X	
Accumulated Depreciation		X				X
Revenue Received in Advance		X				X
Rent Expense	X		X			
Sales Revenue		X		X		
Prepaid Rent	X				X	
Dividends Declared	X				X	
Repairs Expense	X		X			
Sales Taxes Payable		X				X
Interest Receivable	X				X	
Accounts Receivable	X				X	
Net Income			X			X
Retained Earnings		X				X

***TIP: The amount shown for Retained Earnings on the work sheet above is the balance of that account **before** considering dividends declared during the period (determined by the fact that a separate Dividends Declared account appears on the same work sheet) and **before** considering net income for the period.

***TIP: Every amount appearing in the Adjusted Trial Balance column pair must be extended to one of the four statement columns. Debit amounts go to a debit column further to the right and credit amounts go to a credit column further to the right of the adjusted trial balance column pair.

***TIP: When a dollar amount is added to balance the income statement column pair of columns, the same amount must be added in an opposite debit or credit column in the balance sheet column pair. This amount in a balance sheet column indicates the impact of net income (or net loss) on owners' equity.

ANALYSIS OF MULTIPLE-CHOICE TYPE QUESTIONS

QUESTION
1.   (L.O. 1) Which of the following is a nominal account?
  a.   Prepaid Insurance
  b.   Unearned Revenue
  c.   Insurance Expense
  d.   Interest Receivable

Approach and Explanation: Read the question. Before looking at the answer selections, write down the meaning of the term "nominal account." Then answer "true" or "false" as you ask whether each answer selection is a nominal account. A nominal account is an account whose balance is closed at the end of an accounting period. Revenue and expense accounts are closed; real accounts (including asset and liability accounts) are never closed. Prepaid Insurance and Interest Receivable are asset accounts. Unearned Revenue is a liability account. Insurance Expense is a nominal account. (Solution = c.)

QUESTION
2.   (L.O. 4) Which of the following errors will cause an **imbalance** in the trial balance?
  a.   Omission of a transaction in the journal.
  b.   Posting an entire journal entry twice to the ledger.
  c.   Posting a credit of $720 to Accounts Payable as a credit of $720 to Accounts Receivable.
  d.   Listing the balance of an account with a debit balance in the credit column of the trial balance.

Approach and Explanation: Analyze each error (answer selection) and write down whether or not the error will cause the trial balance to be out of balance. Look for the selection which will cause an imbalance (selection "d"). Selections "a," "b," and "c" do not cause an imbalance in the trial balance. (Solution = d.)

QUESTION
3.   (L.O. 5) Which of the following statements is associated with the accrual basis of accounting?
  a.   The timing of cash receipts and disbursements is emphasized.
  b.   A minimum amount of record keeping is required.
  c.   This method is used less frequently by businesses than the cash method of accounting.
  d.   Revenues are recognized in the period they are earned, regardless of the time period the cash is received.

Approach and Explanation: Mentally define the accrual basis of accounting. Write down the key words and phrases of your definition. Compare each answer selection with your definition and choose the one that best matches. Using the **accrual basis of accounting**, events that change a company's financial statements are recorded in the periods in which the events occur. Thus, revenues are recognized in the period in which they are earned by the satisfaction of the related performance obligation, and expenses are recognized in the period in which they are incurred, regardless of when the related cash is received or paid. Answer selections "a" and "b" refer to the cash basis of accounting which is not GAAP. (Solution = d.)

QUESTION
4.   (L.O. 5) An accrued expense is an expense that:
   a.   has been incurred but has not been paid.
   b.   has been paid but has not been incurred.
   c.   has been incurred for which payment is to be made in installments.
   d.   will never be paid.

Approach and Explanation: Write down a definition for accrued expense. Compare each answer selection with your definition and choose the best match. Expenses may be paid for in the same period in which they are incurred or they may be paid for in the period before or in the period after the one in which they are incurred. An **accrued expense** refers to an expense that has been incurred but has not yet been paid. It will be paid for in a period subsequent to the period in which it was incurred. (Solution = a.)

QUESTION
5.   (L.O. 5) In reviewing some adjusting entries, you observe an entry which contains a debit to Prepaid Insurance and a credit to Insurance Expense. The purpose of this journal entry is to record a(n):
   a.   accrued expense.
   b.   deferred expense.
   c.   expired cost.
   d.   prepaid revenue.

Approach and Explanation: Write down the entry so you can see what the entry does. Notice the entry records a prepaid expense (an asset). Then examine each answer selection one at a time. A debit to Prepaid Insurance records an increase in a prepaid expense. A prepaid expense is an expense that has been paid but has not been incurred. Another name for a prepaid expense is deferred expense. A deferred expense is an expense whose recognition is being deferred (put off) until a future period. An accrued expense is an expense incurred, but not paid. An expired cost is an expense or a loss. Prepaid revenue is a bad term for unearned revenue (or deferred revenue). (Solution = b.)

QUESTION
6.   (L.O. 5) An adjusting entry to record an accrued expense involves a debit to a(an):
   a.   expense account and a credit to a prepaid account.
   b.   expense account and a credit to Cash.
   c.   expense account and a credit to a liability account.
   d.   liability account and a credit to an expense account.

Approach and Explanation: Write down a definition for accrued expense and the types of accounts involved in an adjusting entry to accrue an expense. Find the answer selection that describes your entry.

   Dr.   Expenses
          Cr.   Liabilities

Notice the logic of the entry. An **accrued expense** is an expense incurred but not yet paid. Thus, you record the incurrence by increasing an expense account and you record the "not paid" aspect by increasing a liability account. (Solution = c.)

QUESTION
7.   (L.O. 5) The failure to properly record an adjusting entry to accrue an expense will result in an:
   a.   understatement of expenses and an understatement of liabilities.
   b.   understatement of expenses and an overstatement of liabilities.
   c.   understatement of expenses and an overstatement of assets.
   d.   overstatement of expenses and an understatement of assets.

Approach and Explanation: Write down the adjusting entry to record an accrued expense. Analyze the effects of the entry. This will help you to determine the effects of the failure to properly make that entry.

	Dr.	Expenses	xx	
	Cr.	Liabilities		xx

This entry increases expenses and liabilities. Therefore, the failure to make this entry would result in an understatement of expenses and an understatement of liabilities. (Solution = a.)

QUESTION
8.   (L.O. 5) Which of the following properly describes a deferral?
   a.   Cash is received after revenue is earned.
   b.   Cash is received before revenue is earned.
   c.   Cash is paid after expense is incurred.
   d.   Cash is paid in the same time period that an expense is incurred.

Approach and Explanation: Think about the nature of a deferral and the relative timing of revenue or expense recognition and the related cash flow. **Deferrals** result from cash flows that occur **before** expense or revenue recognition. That is, cash is paid for expenses that apply to more than one accounting period or cash is received for revenue that applies to more than one accounting period. The portion of the expense that applies to future periods is deferred by reporting a prepaid expense (asset) or the portion of the revenue that applies to future periods is deferred by reporting unearned revenue (liability) on the balance sheet.

Accruals result from cash flows that occur **after** expense or revenue recognition. That is, cash is to be paid or received in a future accounting period for an expense incurred or a revenue earned in the current period. Items a. and c. above are accrual situations. Item d. is neither an accrual or deferral situation. (Solution = b.)

QUESTION
9.   (L.O. 5) An adjusting entry to allocate a previously recorded asset to expense involves a debit to an:
   a.   asset account and a credit to Cash.
   b.   expense account and a credit to Cash.
   c.   expense account and a credit to an asset account.
   d.   asset account and a credit to an expense account.

Approach and Explanation: Write down the sketch of an adjusting entry to transfer an asset to expense. Compare each answer selection with your entry and choose the one that matches.

	Dr.	Expenses
	Cr.	Assets

(Solution = c.)

QUESTION
10. (L.O. 5) Which of the following adjusting entries will cause an increase in revenues and a decrease in liabilities?
    a. Entry to record an accrued expense.
    b. Entry to record an accrued revenue.
    c. Entry to record the consumed portion of an expense paid in advance and initially recorded as an asset.
    d. Entry to record the earned portion of revenue received in advance and initially recorded as unearned revenue.

Approach and Explanation: For each answer selection, write down the sketch of the adjusting entry described and the effects of each half of the entry. Compare the stem of the question with your analyses to determine the correct answer. (Solution = d.)

The entry to record an accrued expense:
          Dr.   Expenses
                    Cr.   Liabilities
The effects of the entry are to increase expenses and to increase liabilities.

The entry to record an accrued revenue:
          Dr.   Assets
                    Cr.   Revenues
The effects of the entry are to increase assets and to increase revenues.

The entry to record the consumed portion of a prepaid expense initially recorded as an asset is:
          Dr.   Expenses
                    Cr.   Assets
The effects of the entry are to increase expenses and to decrease assets.

The entry to record the earned portion of unearned revenue initially recorded as a liability is:
          Dr.   Liabilities
                    Cr.   Revenues
The effects of the entry are to decrease liabilities and to increase revenues.

QUESTION
11. (L.O. 5) The failure to properly record an adjusting entry to accrue a revenue item will result in an:
    a. understatement of revenues and an understatement of liabilities.
    b. overstatement of revenues and an overstatement of liabilities.
    c. overstatement of revenues and an overstatement of assets.
    d. understatement of revenues and an understatement of assets.

Approach and Explanation: Write down the adjusting entry to record an accrued revenue. Analyze the effects of the entry. This will help you to determine the effects of the failure to properly make that entry.
          Dr.   Assets   xx
                    Cr.   Revenues   xx
This entry increases assets and revenues. Therefore, the failure to make this entry would result in an understatement of assets and an understatement of revenues. (Solution = d.)

The Accounting Information System   **3-51**

QUESTION

12. (L.O. 5) The failure to properly record an adjusting entry for the expiration of insurance coverage will result in an (assume the account Prepaid Insurance was charged when the premiums were paid):
   a. overstatement of assets and an overstatement of owners' equity.
   b. understatement of assets and an understatement of owners' equity.
   c. overstatement of assets and an overstatement of liabilities.
   d. overstatement of liabilities and an understatement of owners' equity.

Approach and Explanation: Analyze the effects of the adjusting entry that should have been made:

Dr.	Insurance Expense	xx
Cr.	Prepaid Insurance	xx

This entry increases expenses which decreases net income which gets closed into Retained Earnings which is a component of owners' equity; therefore, owners' equity will be overstated by the omission of the appropriate adjusting entry. The missing adjustment also reduces assets so assets are overstated by the failure to properly adjust the accounts. (Solution = a.)

QUESTION

13. (L.O. 5) The omission of the adjusting entry to record depreciation expense will result in an:
   a. overstatement of assets and an overstatement of owners' equity.
   b. understatement of assets and an understatement of owners' equity.
   c. overstatement of assets and an overstatement of liabilities.
   d. overstatement of liabilities and an understatement of owners' equity.

Explanation: The appropriate adjusting entry records an expense (Depreciation Expense) and an increase to a contra asset account (Accumulated Depreciation). Thus, the omission of that entry will cause an understatement of expenses and an overstatement of assets. The understatement of expense causes an overstatement of net income which causes an overstatement of Retained Earnings (a component of owners' equity on the balance sheet). (Solution = a.)

QUESTION

14. (L.O. 5) An auditor is examining an adjusting entry that reduces liabilities and increases owners' equity. Which of the following adjusting entries could that be?
   a. Entry to record an accrued revenue.
   b. Entry to record the earned portion of revenue received in advance and previously recorded as Unearned Rent Revenue.
   c. Entry to record an accrued expense.
   d. Entry to record the expired portion of expense paid in advance and previously recorded as Prepaid Expense.
   e. Entry to record bad debt expense.

Explanation: The entry to record an accrued revenue increases receivables (assets) and increases revenues which increases owners' equity. The entry to record an accrued expense increases expenses (causing a decrease in owners' equity) and an increase in liabilities. The adjusting entry to record the expiration of an asset (items d and e above) will reduce assets and owners' equity. The entry to record the earning of previously recorded unearned revenue decreases liabilities and increases revenues (thus, increasing owners' equity). (Solution = b.)

QUESTION

15. (L.O. 5) The Office Supplies on Hand account had a balance at the beginning of year 3 of $1,600. Payments for acquisitions of office supplies during year 3 amounted to $10,000 and were recorded by a debit to the asset account. A physical count at the end of year 3 revealed supplies costing $1,900 were on hand. The required adjusting entry at the end of year 3 will include a debit to:

   a.   Office Supplies Expense for $300.
   b.   Office Supplies on Hand for $300.
   c.   Office Supplies Expense for $9,700.
   d.   Office Supplies on Hand for $1,900.

Approach and Explanation: Draw T-accounts. Enter the data given and solve for the adjusting entry. Compare each alternative answer to the adjusting entry you have sketched in the accounts. (Solution = c.)

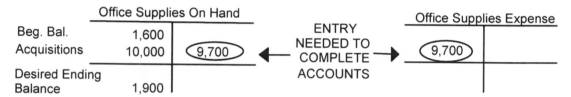

QUESTION

16. (L.O. 5) The book value of a piece of equipment is the:

   a.   original cost of the equipment.
   b.   current replacement cost of the used equipment.
   c.   current market value of the used equipment.
   d.   difference between the original cost of the equipment and its related accumulated depreciation.

Explanation: Equipment benefits the operations of several accounting periods; thus, in compliance with the matching principle, a portion of the cost of a long-lived asset should be reported as an expense during each period of the asset's useful life. Depreciation is the process of allocating the cost of an asset to expense over its useful life in a rational and systematic manner; depreciation is **not** a valuation concept. Depreciation does **not** attempt to measure the change in the fair value of the asset. The annual charge for depreciation is recorded by a debit to Depreciation Expense and a credit to Accumulated Depreciation. The Accumulated Depreciation - Office Equipment is a contra asset account and reflects the total depreciation to date. The difference between the balance in the Equipment account (the original cost of the asset) and balance in the related Accumulated Depreciation account at any given point in time represents the book value (often called carrying value or carrying amount) of the equipment. This amount will rarely equal the asset's current market value. (Solution = d.)

QUESTION

17. (L.O. 7) The purpose of recording closing entries is to:

   a.   reduce the number of nominal accounts.
   b.   enable the accountant to prepare financial statements at the end of an accounting period.
   c.   prepare revenue and expense accounts for the recording of the next period's revenues and expenses.
   d.   establish new balances in some asset and liability accounts.

Approach and Explanation: Cover up the answer selections while you read the question. Attempt to complete the statement started by the stem of the question. Think about when closing entries are made and what they do. Then go through the selections using a process of elimination approach. Closing entries clear out the balances of revenue and expense accounts so that the accounts are ready to accumulate data for a new accounting period. Selection "c" is correct. Selection "a" is incorrect; closing entries do not change the number of accounts. Selection "b" is incorrect; financial statements are prepared before closing entries are done. If closing entries were posted first, the income statement would include nothing but zero amounts. Selection "d" is incorrect, closing entries will affect only nominal accounts and owners' equity. (Solution = c.)

QUESTION
18. (L.O. 9) If ending accounts receivable exceeds the beginning accounts receivable:
   a. cash collections during the period exceed the amount of revenue earned.
   b. net income for the period is less than the amount of cash basis income.
   c. no cash was collected during the period.
   d. cash collections during the year are less than the amount of revenue earned.

Approach and Explanation: Write down a format for reconciling the amount of cash receipts to the amount of revenue earned.

Cash receipts	$
Beginning accounts receivable	( )
Ending accounts receivable	+
Revenue earned	$

Fill in what you know from the question.

Cash receipts	$ X	
Beginning accounts receivable	( )	
Ending accounts receivable	+	More than beginning receivable
Revenue earned	$	Greater than X

An increase in accounts receivable indicates that the amount of revenue earned (and recognized) exceeds the amount of cash collected. Thus, net income for the period exceeds the amount of cash basis income. (Solution = d.)

QUESTION
19. (L.O. 9) The Camphor Company made cash sales of services of $5,000 and credit sales of services of $4,200 during the month of July. The company incurred expenses of $6,000 during July of which $2,000 was paid in cash and the remainder was expected to be paid in August. Using the accrual method of accounting, net income for July amounts to:
   a. $7,200.
   b. $5,200.
   c. $3,200.
   d. $200.

Approach and Explanation: Write down the essence of the accrual method: revenues are recorded when earned and expenses are recorded when incurred. Look for the figures to fit the description. Cash sales of $5,000 plus credit sales of $4,200 equals $9,200 total revenue earned during July. Revenues earned of $9,200 minus expenses incurred of $6,000 equals net income of $3,200. (Solution = c.)

QUESTION
20. (L.O. 9) Dr. Hellinger keeps his accounting records on the cash basis. During 2014, Dr. Hellinger collected $660,000 in fees from his patients. At December 31, 2013, the good doctor had accounts receivable of $50,000 and unearned fees of $6,000. At December 31, 2014, he had accounts receivable of $68,000 and unearned fees of $4,000. The amount of fees earned on the accrual basis by Dr. Hellinger during 2014 was:
   a. $640,000.
   b. $676,000.
   c. $680,000.
   d. $724,000.
   e. None of the above. The correct answer is $_____.

Approach and Explanation: Set up a schedule to reconcile cash collections with revenue earned. Fill in the amounts given and solve.

Cash collections during 2014	$660,000
Accounts receivable, beginning of year	(50,000)
Accounts receivable, end of year	6,000
Unearned revenues, beginning of year	68,000
Unearned revenues, end of year	(4,000)
Fees earned during 2014	$680,000

Accounts receivable of $50,000 at the beginning of the year represent amounts earned last period and collected during the current year of 2014. Ending receivables of $6,000 represent amounts earned in 2014 but not collected yet. Beginning unearned revenues are part of earned revenues this current period but were not part of the current period's collections. Ending unearned revenues were collected this period but are not yet earned. (Solution = c.)

QUESTION

21. (L.O. 10) The Office Supplies on Hand account had a balance at the beginning of year 3 of $1,600. Payments for acquisitions of office supplies during year 3 amounted to $10,000 and were recorded as expense. A physical count at the end of year 3 revealed supplies costing $1,900 were on hand. Reversing entries are used by this company. The required adjusting entry at the end of year 3 will include a debit to:
   a.   Office Supplies Expense for $300.
   b.   Office Supplies on Hand for $300.
   c.   Office Supplies Expense for $9,700.
   d.   Office Supplies on Hand for $1,900.

Approach and Explanation: Draw T-accounts. Enter the data given and solve for the adjusting entry. Compare each alternative answer to the adjusting entry you have sketched in the accounts. (Solution = d.)

IFRS Insights

- As indicated in this chapter, companies must have an effective accounting system. Since the passage of the Sarbanes-Oxley Act of 2002 (SOX), companies that trade on U.S. exchanges are required to place renewed focus on their accounting systems to ensure accurate reporting.

- International companies use the same set of procedures and records to keep track of transaction data. Thus, the material in Chapter 3 dealing with the account, general rules of debit and credit, and steps in the recording process—the journal, ledger, and chart of accounts—is the same under both GAAP and IFRS.

- Transaction analysis is the same under IFRS and GAAP but, as you will see in later chapters, different standards sometimes impact how transactions are recorded.

- Rules for accounting for specific events sometimes differ across countries. For example, European companies rely less on historical cost and more on fair value than U.S. companies. Despite the differences, the double-entry accounting system is the basis of accounting systems worldwide.

- Both the FASB and IASB go beyond the basic definitions provided in your textbook for the key elements of financial statements, that is, assets, liabilities, equity, revenues, and expenses.

- A trial balance under IFRS follows the same format as shown in your textbook. As shown in the textbook, dollar signs are typically used only in the trial balance and the financial statements. The same practice is followed under IFRS, using the currency of the country in which the reporting company is headquartered.

- Internal controls are a system of checks and balances designed to prevent and detect fraud and errors. While most companies have these systems in place, many have never completely documented them nor had an independent auditor attest to their effectiveness. Both of these actions are required under SOX. Enhanced internal control standards apply only to large public companies listed on U.S. exchanges. There is continuing debate over whether foreign issuers should have to comply with this extra layer of regulation.

- As discussed in Chapter 1, IFRS is growing in acceptance around the world. For example, recent statistics indicate 40 percent of the Global Fortune 500 companies use IFRS. And the chair of the IASB predicts that IFRS adoption will grow from its current level of 115 countries to nearly 150 countries in the near future.

- Information in a company's first IFRS statements must (1) be transparent, (2) provide a suitable starting point, and (3) have a cost that does not exceed the benefits.

- The overriding principle in converting to IFRS is full retrospective application of IFRS. Retrospective application—recasting prior financial statements on the basis of IFRS—provides financial statement users with comparable information. As indicated, the objective of the conversion process is to present a set of IFRS statements as if the company always reported using IFRS.

- Upon first-time adoption of IFRS, a company must present at least one year of comparative information under IFRS.

TRUE/FALSE (Circle the correct answer for each).

T   F   1.   International companies use the same set of procedures and records to keep track of transaction data as those presented in this text.

T   F   2.   The double-entry accounting system is the basis of accounting systems worldwide.

T   F   3.   Recent statistics indicate that less than 35% of the Global Fortune 500 companies use IFRS.

T   F   4.   When a company first adopts IFRS, the company is required to have a full retrospective application of IFRS.

T   F   5.   Upon first-time adoption of IFRS, a company must present at least one year of comparative information under IFRS.

Solutions:

1.	T		4.	T
2.	T		5.	T
3.	F			

CHAPTER 4

INCOME STATEMENT AND RELATED INFORMATION

OVERVIEW

An income statement reports on the results of operations of an entity for a period of time. It is important to classify revenues, expenses, gains, and losses properly on the income statement. In this chapter, we discuss the income statement classifications and the content of the statement of retained earnings along with related disclosure issues. It is imperative that charges (debits) and credits that represent elements of income determination be properly reflected in the financial statements. Errors in the determination of income cause errors on the income statement, statement of retained earnings, and balance sheet.

SUMMARY OF LEARNING OBJECTIVES

1. **Understand the uses and limitations of an income statement.** The income statement provides investors and creditors with information that helps them predict the amount, timing and uncertainty of future cash flows. Also, the income statement helps users determine the risk (level of uncertainty) of not achieving particular cash flows. The limitations of an income statement are: (1) The income statement does not include many items that contribute to general growth and well-being of an enterprise. (2) Income numbers are often affected by the accounting methods used. (3) Income measures are subject to estimates.

    The **transaction approach** focuses on the activities that have occurred during a given period; instead of presenting only a net change in net assets, it discloses the components of the change. The transaction approach to income measurement requires the use of revenue, expense, gain, and loss accounts.

2. **Describe the content and format of the income statement.** The major elements of the income statement are as follows. (1) **Revenues:** Inflows or other enhancements of assets of an entity or settlements of its liabilities during a period from delivering or producing goods, rendering services, or other activities that constitute the entity's ongoing major or central operations. (2) **Expenses:** Outflows or other using-up of assets or incurrences of liabilities during a period from delivering or producing goods, rendering services, or carrying out other activities that constitute the entity's ongoing major or central operations. (3) **Gains:** Increases in equity (net assets) from peripheral or incidental transactions of an entity except those that result from revenues or investments by owners. (4) **Losses:** Decreases in equity (net assets) from peripheral or incidental transactions of an entity except those that result from expenses or distributions to owners.

3. **Prepare an income statement.** In a single-step income statement, just two groupings exist: revenues and expenses. Expenses are deducted from revenues to arrive at net income or net loss. The expression "single-step" is derived from the single subtraction necessary to arrive at net income. Frequently, companies report income taxes separately as the last item before net income to indicate their direct relationship to income before income taxes. A multiple-step income statement shows two further classifications: (1) a separation of operating results from those

obtained through the subordinate or nonoperating activities of the company; and (2) a classification of expenses by functions, such as merchandising or manufacturing, selling, and administration.

4.   **Explain how to report various income items.** Companies generally close irregular gains or losses or nonrecurring items to Income Summary and include them in the income statement as follows: (1) Other items of a material amount that are of an unusual or nonrecurring nature and are not considered extraordinary are separately disclosed as a component of income from continuing operations. (2) Discontinued operations of a component of a business are classified as a separate item, after continuing operations; (3) The unusual, material, nonrecurring items that are significantly different from the customary business activities are shown in a separate section for extraordinary items, below discontinued operations. If a company holds a noncontrolling interest in a subsidiary company, it must present an allocation of net income or loss that is attributable to the noncontrolling interest. Changes in accounting principle and corrections of errors are adjusted through retained earnings.

5.   **Identify where to report earnings per share information.** Because of the inherent dangers of focusing attention solely on earnings per share, the profession concluded that companies must disclose earnings per share on the face of the income statement. A company that reports a discontinued operation or an extraordinary item must report per share amounts for these line items either on the face of the income statement or in the notes to the financial statements.

6.   **Understand the reporting of accounting changes and errors.** Changes in accounting principle and corrections of errors are adjusted through retained earnings. Changes in estimates are a normal part of the accounting process. The effects of these changes are handled prospectively, with the effects recorded in income in the period of change and in future periods without adjustment to retained earnings.

7.   **Prepare a retained earnings statement.** The retained earnings statement should disclose net income (loss), dividends, adjustments due to changes in accounting principles, adjustments due to error corrections, and transfers to and restrictions of retained earnings.

8.   **Explain how to report other comprehensive income.** Companies report the components of other comprehensive income in one of two ways: (2) a single statement of comprehensive income (one statement format) or (2) in a second statement (two statement format).

TIPS ON CHAPTER TOPICS

TIP: The **income statement** or **statement of income** is often referred to as the statement of operations or the operating statement because it reports on the results of operations for a period of time. Other names include the "earnings statement," "statement of earnings," and "profit and loss statement" (or "P&L statement").

TIP: The income statement is often referred to as a link between balance sheets because it explains one major reason why the balance of owners' equity changed during the period. Owners' equity (net assets) at the beginning of the period can be reconciled with ending owners' equity as follows:

	Owners' equity at the beginning of the period
+	Additional owner investments during the period
-	Owner withdrawals during the period
±	Results of operations for the period (net income or net loss)
=	Owners' equity at the end of the period

This reconciliation of ending owner's equity with beginning owners' equity is oversimplistic in that it ignores the more complex situations discussed in this chapter such as (1) adjustments due to correction of errors in prior periods, (2) adjustments due to the effect on prior periods of a change in accounting principles, and (3) changes in accumulated other comprehensive income. The foregoing three items would also be part of this reconciliation if they were present in the situation.

TIP: A **contra revenue** item has the same effect on net income as that of an expense; it decreases net income. Contra revenue accounts include Sales Discounts and Sales Returns and Allowances.

TIP: It is often helpful to form an acronym when attempting to remember a list of items. In looking at the order of the things that can appear **after** the "Income from Continuing Operations" line on an income statement, you might come up with **DE** to help you to remember the exact order of these items:

> **D**iscontinued operations
> **E**xtraordinary items

Notice these two items appear in alphabetical order.

TIP: The income tax consequences of all items appearing above the line "Income from continuing operations before income taxes" are summarized in the line "Income taxes." Revenues cause an increase in income taxes and expenses cause a decrease in income taxes. The income tax consequences of items appearing below the "income from continuing operations" line are reported right along with the items (hence, these items are reported "net of tax"). This procedure of allocating income taxes within a period is referred to as **intraperiod tax allocation**.

TIP: An extraordinary item is reported "net of tax" by deducting the tax effect from the related gain or loss. For example, if the tax rate is 30%, an extraordinary gain of $400,000 will be reported at $280,000 net of tax. Likewise, an extraordinary loss of $400,000 will be reported at $280,000 net of tax. The gain situation increases net income, whereas the loss reduces it.

TIP: A company normally provides **comparative financial statements** for its owners. That is, financial statements for the current period are shown side by side with the company's statements for one or two (or more) immediate prior periods.

TIP: An error occurs as a result of a mathematical mistake, a mistake in the application of accounting principles, or an oversight or misuse of facts that existed at the time financial statements were prepared. When a company discovers that there was an error made in a prior period, a correction of that error entails making a proper entry(s) in the accounts and following specific reporting requirements in the preparation of financial statements. A correction for an error in the reporting of revenues or expenses in a prior period is accounted for as a **prior period adjustment** which is similar to the treatment accorded a change in accounting principle. The journal entry for a "catch-up adjustment" involves the Retained Earnings account and that amount is shown as an adjustment (**net** of the related income tax effect) to the beginning retained earnings balance on the financial statements.

If a company prepares comparative financial statements, it would restate the prior statements for the effects of the error; any effect on periods prior to the periods being shown would be reported as an adjustment to the beginning retained earnings balance for the earliest period being shown in the comparative reports.

TIP: The **restatement** of prior period financial statements means the prior statements are recast. The statements for prior periods that are being reported again (such as in comparative reports) are changed to reflect items and balances as they would have (or should have) been in a prior period under other circumstances. For example, if the prior years' reports are restated because of an error in a prior year, the restated items and amounts will reflect what would have been reported had an error not occurred. When there is a change in accounting principle (method), the retrospective application of the new accounting method is similar to restatement in that the financial statements for prior periods are redone and presented again in the current period (for comparative purposes) as if the new principle had always been used.

TIP: Net income minus preferred stock dividend requirements (i.e., income applicable to common stockholders) is divided by the weighted average of common stock shares outstanding to arrive at **earnings per share (EPS)**. This is a key ratio in financial analysis and must be disclosed on the face of the income statement. A per share amount must **always** be disclosed for "net income" on the face of the income statement. Also, a company that reports a discontinued operation or an extraordinary item must report per share amounts for these line items either on the face of the income statement or in the notes to the financial statements.

TIP: In the EPS calculation, preferred dividends are deducted from net income if they were declared; however, if the preferred stock is cumulative, the preferred dividend preference for the current period is deducted whether or not the dividends were declared. Dividends declared on common stock have no effect on the EPS calculation.

EXERCISE 4-1

Purpose: (L.O. 1) This exercise reviews the basic accounting formula (Assets = Liabilities + Owners' Equity) and the connection between the income statement and the balance sheet (which is a change in owners' equity due to the net income or net loss for the period). This exercise focuses on the capital maintenance (or change in equity) approach to income determination.

The following data were extracted from the records of Dora Loesing's Cookies, a sole proprietorship:

Total assets, beginning of the period	$100,000
Total liabilities, beginning of the period	36,000
Owner withdrawals during the period	30,000
Total assets, end of the period	108,000
Total liabilities, end of the period	38,000
Owner's contributions during the period	10,000

Instructions
Compute the amount of net income (or loss) for the period. Show computations.

Solution to Exercise 4-1

Beginning owner's equity	$ 64,000[a]
Additional owner contribution	10,000
Owner withdrawals during the period	(30,000)
Subtotal	44,000
Net income (loss) for the period	+ X
Ending owner's equity	$ 70,000[b]
Solving for X, net income =	$ 26,000

[a]$A = L + OE$
$100,000 = \$36,000 + ?$
  Beginning owner's equity = $64,000

[b]$A = L + OE$
$108,000 = \$38,000 + ?$
  Ending owner's equity = $70,000

Approach: The question asks you to solve for net income; however, no information is given regarding revenues and expenses for the period. Only balance sheet data and transactions affecting owner's equity are given. Net income (or net loss) for a period is one reason for a change in the balance of owner's equity. Write down the items that reconcile the beginning owner's equity balance with the ending owner's equity balance, enter the amounts known, compute beginning and ending owner's equity balances by use of the basic accounting equation, and then solve for the amount of net income. Recall that assets - liabilities = net assets; that is, assets - liabilities = owner's equity at a point in time.

TIP: The basic accounting equation ($A = L + OE$) is applied at a specific point in time. When you have the facts for the equation components at two different points in time for the same entity (such as amounts as of the beginning of a year and amounts as of the end of a year), you can modify the basic accounting equation to reflect that total changes in assets equals total changes in liabilities + total changes in owners' equity. Using the symbol Δ to designate change, the following equation also holds true:

$$\Delta A = \Delta L + \Delta OE$$

Reasons for changes in owners' equity include:
  (1)   additional owner investments,
  (2)   owner withdrawals, and
  (3)   results of operations (net income or net loss).

TIP: When using the **capital maintenance** (or **change in equity**) approach, the amount of owners' equity is determined at the beginning and at the end of the period (using the same valuation method). The difference between these two amounts, adjusted for owner withdrawals and additional owner investments during the same period, is the measure of net income for the period. Net income (or net loss) is the change in owners' equity for a period of time, other than from capital transactions. (The foregoing sentence ignores any changes in owners' equity due to error corrections, changes in accounting principles, and changes in accumulated other comprehensive income). Capital transactions are those that involve owners acting in their capacity of being owners of the entity. The capital maintenance approach differs from the **transaction approach** (see bottom of **Illustration 4-1**) which is prescribed by GAAP.

ILLUSTRATION 4-1
ELEMENTS OF THE INCOME STATEMENT (L.O. 2)

REVENUES. Inflows or other enhancements of assets of an entity or settlements of its liabilities during a period from delivering or producing goods, rendering services, or other activities that constitute the entity's ongoing major or central operations.

EXPENSES. Outflows or other using-up of assets or incurrences of liabilities during a period from delivering or producing goods, rendering services, or carrying out other activities that constitute the entity's ongoing major or central operations.

GAINS. Increases in equity (net assets) from peripheral or incidental transactions of an entity except those that result from revenues or investments by owners.

LOSSES. Decreases in equity (net assets) from peripheral or incidental transactions of an entity except those that result from expenses or distributions to owners.

Revenues take many forms, such as sales revenue, fees earned, dividend income, and rents earned. Expenses also take many forms, such as cost of goods sold, rent, salaries, depreciation, interest, and taxes.

Revenues and gains are similar (they both increase net income), and expenses and losses are similar (they both decrease net income). However, these terms are dissimilar in the fact that they convey significantly different information about an enterprise's performance. Revenues and expenses result from an entity's ongoing major or central operations and activities—that is, from activities such as producing or delivering goods, rendering services, lending, insuring, investing, and financing. In contrast, gains and losses result from incidental or peripheral or irregular transactions of an enterprise with other entities and from other events and circumstances affecting it. Gains and losses often arise from the sale of investments; disposal of plant assets; settlement of liabilities for an amount other than their book value; and write-offs of assets due to obsolescence, casualty, theft, or restructurings.

Revenues and expenses are commonly displayed as **gross** inflows or outflows of net assets; while gains and losses are usually displayed as **net** inflows or outflows. For example, assume a company buys an inventory item for $6,000, sells it for $10,000, and pays a sales representative a $1,000 commission. Further, the same company sells for $20,000 a plant asset with a book value (carrying value) of $15,000 and pays an outside agency $2,100 for finding the buyer. The various flows associated with the first transaction (the company's major activity or regular operations) will be reported gross on its income statement, and the various elements of the second transaction (a peripheral or incidental transaction) will be reported net. Assuming these were the only two transactions completed during the period and ignoring income taxes, the income statement would reflect the following:

Sales revenue	$ 10,000
Cost of goods sold expense	(6,000)
Gross profit	4,000
Selling expense (sales commission)	(1,000)
Income from operations	3,000
Gain on sale of plant asset	2,900[a]
Net income	$ 5,900

[a]$20,000 proceeds - $15,000 book value - $2,100 finders fee = $2,900 gain on sale.

TIP: Net income results from revenue, expense, gain, and loss transactions. These transactions are summarized in the income statement. This method of income measurement is called the **transaction approach** because it focuses on the income-related activities (broken down into completed transactions) that have occurred during the period.

ILLUSTRATION 4-2
SECTIONS OF A MULTIPLE-STEP INCOME STATEMENT (L.O. 3)

1. **OPERATING SECTION.** A report of the revenues and expenses of the company's principal operations. (This section may or may not be presented on a departmental basis.)
    (a)   **SALES OR REVENUE SECTION.** A subsection presenting sales, discounts, allowances, returns, and other related information. Its purpose is to arrive at the net amount of sales revenue.
    (b)   **COST OF GOODS SOLD SECTION.** A subsection that shows the cost of goods that were sold to produce the sales.
    (c)   **SELLING EXPENSES.** A subsection that lists expenses resulting from the company's efforts to make sales.
    (d)   **ADMINISTRATIVE OR GENERAL EXPENSES.** A subsection reporting expenses of general administration.

2. **NONOPERATING SECTION.** A report of revenues and expenses resulting from secondary or auxiliary activities of the company. In addition, special gains and losses that are infrequent or unusual, but not both, are normally reported in this section. Generally these items break down into two main subsections:
    (a)   **OTHER REVENUES AND GAINS.** A list of the revenues earned or gains incurred, generally net of related expenses, from nonoperating transactions.
    (b)   **OTHER EXPENSES AND LOSSES.** A list of the expenses or losses incurred, generally net of any related incomes, from nonoperating transactions.

3. **INCOME TAXES.** A short section reporting federal and state taxes levied on income from continuing operations.

4. **DISCONTINUED OPERATIONS.** Material gains or losses resulting from the disposal of a component of the business. (Shown net of related income tax effect.)

5. **EXTRAORDINARY ITEMS.** Unusual and infrequent material gains and losses. (Shown net of related income tax effect.)

6. **EARNINGS PER SHARE.**

EXERCISE 4-2

Purpose: (L.O. 3, 5) This exercise will allow you to contrast the multiple-step format and the single-step format for the income statement.

The accountant for Bubble Bath Products, Inc. has compiled the following information from the company's records as a basis for an income statement for the year ended December 31, 2014. (There was no change during the year in the 12,000 shares of common stock outstanding.)

Net sales	$ 970,000
Depreciation on plant assets (60% selling, 40% administrative)	70,000
Dividends declared	14,400
Rent revenue	30,000
Interest on notes payable	17,000
Market appreciation on land held as an investment	44,000
Merchandise purchases	421,000
Transportation-in—merchandise	37,000
Merchandise inventory, January 1, 2014	82,000
Merchandise inventory, December 31, 2014	81,000
Purchase returns and allowances	11,000
Wages and salaries—sales	95,000
Materials and supplies—sales	11,400
Income taxes	45,000
Wages and salaries—administrative	135,900
Other administrative expenses	46,700
Advertising expense	20,000
Express mail	6,000

Instructions
(a)   Prepare a multiple-step income statement.
(b)   Prepare a single-step income statement.

Solution to Exercise 4-2

(a)

Bubble Bath Products, Inc.
INCOME STATEMENT
For the Year Ending December 31, 2014

Sales Revenue			
Net sales revenue			$970,000
Cost of Goods Sold			
Merchandise inventory, Jan. 1		$ 82,000	
Purchases	$ 421,000		
Less purchase returns & allowances	11,000		
Net purchases	410,000		
Transportation-in	37,000	447,000	
Total merchandise available for sale		529,000	
Less merchandise inventory, Dec. 31		81,000	
Cost of goods sold			448,000
Gross profit			522,000
Operating Expenses			
Selling expenses			
Wages and salaries	95,000		
Advertising	20,000		
Materials and supplies	11,400		
Depreciation (60% x $70,000)	42,000		
Express mail	6,000	174,400	
Administrative expenses			
Wages and salaries	135,900		
Depreciation (40% x $70,000)	28,000		
Other administrative expenses	46,700	210,600	385,000
Income from operations			137,000
Other Revenues and Gains			
Rent revenue			30,000
			167,000
Other Expenses and Losses			
Interest expense			17,000
Income before taxes			150,000
Income taxes			45,000
Net income			$105,000
Earnings per share ($105,000 ÷ 12,000)			$8.75

(b)

Bubble Bath Products, Inc.
INCOME STATEMENT
For the Year Ending December 31, 2014

Revenues	
Net sales	$ 970,000
Rent revenue	30,000
Total revenue	1,000,000
Expenses	
Cost of goods sold	448,000
Selling expenses	174,400
Administrative expenses	210,600
Interest expense	17,000
Total expenses	850,000
Income before taxes	150,000
Income taxes	45,000
Net income	$ 105,000
Earnings per share	$8.75

TIP:	The nature of an entity's typical operations is critical in determining whether the results of a transaction should be classified as an operating or a nonoperating revenue, gain, expense, or loss. For example, consider rental activities. A business specializing in equipment rentals will classify rent revenue as an operating revenue. Whereas, a retail establishment that occasionally rents its temporarily idle assets to others will classify rent revenue as a nonoperating (other) revenue. For a second example, consider the sale of an investment. An investment dealer will report the revenue from a sale as an operating revenue. Whereas, a retail entity that occasionally sells an investment will report the difference between the proceeds from the sale and the investment's carrying value as a nonoperating gain or loss.
TIP:	There is no specific order in which the individual selling expenses and administrative expenses are to be listed in the multiple-step income statement. Very often, they appear in order of decreasing magnitude.
TIP:	Some accountants prefer to use a multiple-step income statement format because it discloses the amount of income from operations. Thus, by this disclosure, the difference between regular and irregular or incidental activities is highlighted. Irregular activities encompass transactions and other events that are derived from developments outside the normal operations of the business. Thus, they may not be expected to continue at the same level in future periods.
TIP:	The item "Income taxes" is sometimes called "Income tax expense." Accountants refer to it as the **tax provision** and may even use the caption "Provision for income taxes" on the income statement.

EXERCISE 4-3

Purpose: (L.O. 3, 7) This exercise will give you practice in identifying components of net income and the order of items appearing on a single-step income statement and on a retained earnings statement.

Presented below is the adjusted trial balance of the Frankie Marathon Corporation at December 31, 2014. The account titles and balances are **not** in the customary order.

Frankie Marathon Corporation
ADJUSTED TRIAL BALANCE
December 31, 2014

	Debits	Credits
Sales		$ 958,500
Notes Receivable	$ 80,000	
Investments	88,500	
Accounts Payable		51,000
Accumulated Depreciation—Equipment		31,000
Sales Discounts	10,500	
Sales Returns	17,500	
Purchase Discounts		8,000
Cash	190,000	
Accounts Receivable	95,000	
Rent Revenue		14,000
Retained Earnings		240,000
Salaries Payable		22,000
Notes Payable	75,000	
Common Stock, $15 par		300,000
Income Tax Expense	68,000	
Cash Dividends Declared	70,000	
Allowance for Doubtful Accounts		6,500
Supplies on Hand	11,000	
Freight-In	16,000	
Selling Expenses	212,000	
Administrative Expenses	114,000	
Land	65,000	
Equipment	130,000	
Inventory	79,000	
Building	104,000	
Purchases	500,000	
Dividend Income		10,000
Loss on Sale of Investment	13,000	
Interest Revenue		9,000
Interest Expense	12,500	
Bonds Payable		100,000
Gain on Sale of Land		24,500
Accumulated Depreciation—Building		26,500
Totals	$ 1,876,000	$ 1,876,000

The company uses the periodic inventory system. A physical count of inventory on December 31 resulted in an inventory amount of $100,000.

Instructions

(a) Prepare an income statement for the year ending December 31, 2014 using the single-step form. Assume that twenty thousand shares of common stock were outstanding the entire year.

(b) Prepare a retained earnings statement for the year ending December 31, 2014. Assume that the only changes in retained earnings during the current year were from net income and dividends.

Solution to Exercise 4-3

(a)

Frankie Marathon Corporation
INCOME STATEMENT
For the Year Ended December 31, 2014

Revenues
Net sales*	$ 930,500
Gain on sale of land	24,500
Rent revenue	14,000
Dividend income	10,000
Interest revenue	9,000
Total revenues	988,000

Expenses
Cost of goods sold**	487,000
Selling expenses	212,000
Administrative expenses	114,000
Loss on sale of investment	13,000
Interest expense	12,500
Total expenses	838,500
Income before taxes	149,500
Income taxes	68,000
Net income	$ 81,500

Earnings per common share ($81,500 ÷ 20,000) $ 4.08

*Net sales:
Sales			$ 958,500
Less:	Sales discounts	$ 10,500	
	Sales returns	17,500	28,000
	Net sales		$ 930,500

**Cost of goods sold:
Merchandise inventory, Jan. 1		$ 79,000
Purchases	$ 500,000	
Less purchase discounts	8,000	
Net purchases		492,000
Add freight-in		16,000
Merchandise available for sale		587,000
Less merchandise inventory, Dec. 31		100,000
Cost of merchandise sold		$ 487,000

> **TIP:** The solution presented here reports income taxes separately as the last item before net income to indicate their relationship to income before taxes. It is acceptable to list the income taxes in the expenses classification and omit the subtotal and caption for "income before taxes."

(b)

Frankie Marathon Corporation
RETAINED EARNINGS STATEMENT
For the Year Ended December 31, 2014

Balance, January 1	$240,000
Add: Net income	81,500
	321,500
Less: Cash dividends declared	70,000
Balance, December 31	$251,500

Approach:

(1)   Go through the adjusted trial balance and lightly cross through any account title that does **not** pertain to the computation of net income. With the exception of the balance of Merchandise Inventory (which is used to compute cost of goods sold when a periodic inventory system is in use), balance sheet account balances are not used in determining net income.

(2)   Compute intermediate subtotals for items such as (a) net sales, (b) cost of goods sold, (c) selling expenses, and (d) administrative expenses. Show your computations for these subtotals. (In this particular exercise, selling expenses and administrative expenses are already summarized.)

(3)   Identify revenue and gain items.

(4)   Identify expense and loss items.

(5)   Identify income taxes for the period.

(6)   Identify any discontinued operations and extraordinary items (none of these appear in this exercise).

(7)   Compute net income.

(8)   Compute earnings per share.

(9)   Identify the retained earnings balance at the beginning of the period.

(10) Include any adjustments to prior periods on the statement of retained earnings (none are identified in this exercise).

(11) Add net income for the period.

(12) Deduct dividends declared.

(13) Arrive at the retained earnings balance at the end of the period.

> **TIP:** The account balances in the adjusted trial balance that are **not** used for the solution requested are as follows: Notes Receivable, Investments, Accounts Payable, Accumulated Depreciation—Equipment, Cash, Accounts Receivable, Salaries Payable, Notes Payable, Common Stock, Allowance for Doubtful Accounts, Supplies on Hand, Land, Equipment, Building, Bonds Payable, and Accumulated Depreciation—Building.

ILLUSTRATION 4-3
TREATMENT OF IRREGULAR ITEMS (L.O. 4)

1. **DISCONTINUED OPERATIONS.** The (1) results of operations (income or loss) of a component of business that has been or will be disposed of, and (2) gain or loss on disposal of the discontinued component are reported in a separate income statement category called "Discontinued operations." This category appears **after** continuing operations but **before** extraordinary items. The gain or loss in this category is reported net of the related income tax effect.

   A component of an entity may be a reportable segment or operating segment, a reporting unit, a subsidiary, or an asset group. A segment of a business is either a separate line of business or a separate class of customer. A discontinued component of an entity comprises operations and cash flows that can be clearly distinguished operationally and for financial reporting purposes, from the rest of the entity and that will be eliminated from the ongoing operations of the entity.

2. **EXTRAORDINARY ITEMS.** Extraordinary items are reported individually in a separate category (immediately after discontinued operations, if any) net of any related income tax effect. Extraordinary items are defined as nonrecurring (infrequent) material items that differ significantly from the entity's typical business activities. In addition to being material in amount, a transaction or event must meet **both** of the following criteria to be classified as extraordinary:
   (a) **UNUSUAL NATURE.** The underlying event or transaction should possess a high degree of abnormality and be of a type clearly unrelated to, or only incidentally related to, the ordinary and typical activities of the entity, taking into account the environment in which the entity operates.
   (b) **INFREQUENCY OF OCCURRENCE.** The underlying event or transaction should be of a type that would not reasonably be expected to recur in the foreseeable future, taking into account the environment in which the entity operates.

   Examples of items that are **not** classified as extraordinary:
   (a) Writedown or writeoff of receivables, inventories, equipment leased to others, deferred research and development costs, or other intangible assets.
   (b) Gains or losses from exchange or translation of foreign currencies, including those relating to major devaluations and revaluations.
   (c) Gains or losses on disposal of a segment of a business.
   (d) Other gains or losses from sale or abandonment of property, plant, or equipment used in the business.
   (e) Effects of a strike, including those against competitors and major suppliers.
   (f) Adjustment of accruals on long-term contracts.
   (g) Gains or losses from restructurings.
   (h) Gains or losses from refunding or extinguishments of debt.

   Examples of items that **are** classified as extraordinary:
   An event or transaction that clearly meets both criteria (unusual in nature and infrequent in occurrence) and gives rise to a gain or loss from the writedown or writeoff of assets or to a gain or loss from disposal of assets and is a **direct result** of one of the following:

ILLUSTRATION 4-3 (Continued)

(a)   A **major casualty** (such as an earthquake, tornado, hurricane, flood, or hail storm).

(b)   An **expropriation** (such as the confiscation of assets by a government or the exercise of eminent domain or condemnation).

(c)   A **prohibition** under a newly enacted law or regulation.

3.   **UNUSUAL GAINS AND LOSSES.** A gain or loss that arises from a transaction that is unusual or infrequent, but not both, should be reported in the income statement as part of "income from continuing operations" (or "income before extraordinary items"). If the amount is material, it should be separately disclosed; if the amount is immaterial, it may be combined with other items on the income statement. In a multiple-step income statement, unusual gains and losses normally are classified in the "other revenues and gains" or "other expenses and losses" section, although a separate unusual items section may be displayed. Unusual gains and losses are **not** to be reported net of tax; rather, the tax consequences of these items are combined with the tax effects of all other components of income from continuing operations in the line called "income taxes."

4.   **CHANGES IN ACCOUNTING PRINCIPLE.** A change in accounting principle occurs when a company changes from one generally accepted method to another generally accepted method. Because such a change violates consistency and, therefore, reduces or destroys comparability of successive financial statements, a change in principle should only be made when the newly adopted principle is preferable (e.g., for better matching of revenues and expenses). An entity shall report a change in accounting principle through retrospective application of the new accounting principle to all prior periods. Retrospective application requires the financial statements for each individual prior period to be adjusted (recast) to reflect the application of the new principle. Any cumulative effect on periods prior to the earliest period being reported upon shall be shown as an adjustment to the opening balance of retained earnings for that period on the retained earnings statement.   That is, the effect on prior periods of using the old method is compared to the effect that would have occurred if the new method had been used for prior periods; the difference is the cumulative effect of the change on prior periods. (This subject is more thoroughly discussed in **Chapter 22**.)

5.   **CHANGES IN ACCOUNTING ESTIMATE (Normal Recurring Corrections and Adjustments).** A change from one good faith estimate to another good faith estimate because of new information or experience constitutes a change in accounting estimate. A change in an estimate will affect the amount of related revenue or expense reported in the period of change if the change affects only that period, or in the period of change (called the current period) and future periods if the change affects both. Examples are a change in the estimate of uncollectible accounts receivable (bad debts expense) and a change in the estimated service life of a plant (fixed) asset (depreciation expense). A change in estimate is **not** considered a correction of an error (prior period adjustment); therefore, it is **not** handled retroactively.

EXERCISE 4-4

Purpose: (L.O. 3, 4, 5, 6, 7) This exercise is designed to give you practice in preparing a condensed multiple-step income statement and a retained earnings statement when discontinued operations, an extraordinary item, a change in accounting principle, and a correction of an error are to be reported.

Presented below is information related to Chelsea Clinton Corp., for the year 2014.

Net sales	$ 650,000
Cost of goods sold	400,000
Selling expenses	32,000
Administrative expenses	24,000
Dividend revenue	10,000
Interest revenue	7,000
Interest expense	15,000
Write-off of goodwill due to impairment	25,000
Depreciation expense omitted in 2012	35,000
Uninsured loss due to flood (unusual and infrequent)	60,000
Dividends declared	42,000
Retained earnings at December 31, 2013	1,800,000
Effect on prior years of change in accounting principle (credit)	75,000
Loss from operations of discontinued segment of business	81,000
Gain from disposal of segment of business	100,000
Federal tax rate of 30% on all items	

Instructions
(a)   Prepare a multiple-step income statement for 2014. Assume that 50,000 shares of common stock were outstanding during 2014.
(b)   Prepare a retained earnings statement for 2014.

Solution to Exercise 4-4

(a)

Chelsea Clinton Corp.
INCOME STATEMENT
For the Year Ended December 31, 2014

Net sales		$ 650,000
Cost of goods sold		400,000
Gross profit		250,000
Operating expenses		
Selling expenses	$ 32,000	
Administrative expenses	24,000	56,000
Income from operations		194,000
Other revenues and gains		
Dividend revenue	10,000	
Interest revenue	7,000	17,000
		211,000
Other expenses and losses		
Interest expense	15,000	
Loss due to write-off of goodwill	25,000	40,000
Income before taxes and discontinued		
operations and extraordinary item		171,000
Income taxes		51,300
Income before discontinued operations and		
extraordinary item		119,700
Discontinued operations		
Loss from operations of discontinued segment of		
business (net of $24,300 income tax effect)	56,700	
Gain from disposal of segment of business		
(net of $30,000 income tax effect)	70,000	13,300
Extraordinary item		
Loss from flood (net of $18,000 income tax effect)		42,000
Net income		$ 91,000
Per share of common stock:		
Income before discontinued operations and		
extraordinary item		$2.39[a]
Discontinued operations		.27[b]
Extraordinary item (net of tax)		(.84)[c]
Net income		$1.82[d]

[a]$119,700 ÷ 50,000 shares = $2.39
[b]$13,300 ÷ 50,000 shares = .27
[c]$42,000 ÷ 50,000 shares (.84)
[d]$91,000 ÷ 50,000 shares = 1.82

TIP:	The total income taxes pertaining to 2014 for this company was $39,000. This amount resulted from a tax bill of $51,300 that relates to the tax consequences of all items reportable on the 2014 tax return **before** considering the casualty loss of $60,000, the loss of $81,000 from operations of a discontinued segment, and the $100,000 gain from disposal of a segment of business. The $81,000 loss from operations of the discontinued segment caused a reduction in taxes of $24,300 and the $100,000 gain caused an increase in taxes of $30,000. The casualty loss caused a tax savings of $18,000. Because the casualty loss is reported as an extraordinary item on the income statement, the requirement for a net-of-tax presentation calls for the $18,000 tax reduction to be reported along with the extraordinary loss. Also, net of tax presentations are required for discontinued operations, leaving income taxes of $51,300 to be matched with income before discontinued operations and before extraordinary items. The income tax effect of the accounting change involves deferred income taxes which are discussed in **Chapter 19**. The $10,500 income tax effect of the error correction would relate to an amended tax return for a prior year.
TIP:	In this case, the error correction caused a decrease in the reported amount of Retained Earnings (because it was a debit). Sometimes a correction of an error results in a credit to Retained Earnings.
TIP:	In this case, the change in accounting principle caused an increase in the reported amount of Retained Earnings (because it was a credit). Sometimes the cumulative effect of a change in accounting principle is a charge (debit) to Retained Earnings.

(b)

Chelsea Clinton Corp.
RETAINED EARNINGS STATEMENT
For the Year Ended December 31, 2014

Retained earnings, Jan. 1, 2014, as previously reported	$ 1,800,000
Less: Correction of an error in depreciation in prior period	
(net of $10,500 income tax effect)	24,500
Add: Effect on prior periods of a change in accounting principle	
(net of $22,500 income tax effect)	52,500
Adjusted balance of retained earnings at Jan. 1, 2014	1,828,000
Add: Net income	91,000
	1,919,000
Less: Dividends declared	42,000
Retained earnings, December 31, 2014	$ 1,877,000

EXERCISE 4-5

Purpose: (L.O. 4) This exercise will test your knowledge of the elements and arrangement of the major sections of the income statement.

Instructions
The following list represents captions that would appear on an income statement (single-step format) for a company reporting an extraordinary gain, an extraordinary loss, and losses from discontinued operations, as well as the results of continuing operations for the period. You are to "unscramble" the list and prepare a skeleton income statement using the captions given. (If you do not wish to write out each caption above, you may still test your knowledge by listing the appropriate letters in the correct order.)

(a)   Income before extraordinary item
(b)   Revenues
(c)   Extraordinary loss (net of tax)
(d)   Income taxes
(e)   Discontinued operations:
(f)   Extraordinary gain (net of tax)
(g)   Expenses
(h)   Loss from disposal of discontinued component of business (net of tax)
(i)   Net income
(j)   Income from continuing operations before income taxes
(k)   Loss from operations of discontinued component of business (net of tax)
(l)   Income from continuing operations

Solution to Exercise 4-5

Company Name
INCOME STATEMENT
For the Year Ended December 31, 20XX

(b)   Revenues
(g)   <u>Expenses</u>
(j)   Income from continuing operations before income taxes
(d)   <u>Income taxes</u>
(l)   Income from continuing operations
(e)   Discontinued operations:
(k)   Loss from operations of discontinued component of business (net of tax)
(h)   <u>Loss from disposal of discontinued component of business (net of tax)</u>
(a)   Income before extraordinary item
(c)   Extraordinary loss (net of tax)
(f)   <u>Extraordinary gain (net of tax)</u>
(i)   Net income

EXERCISE 4-6

Purpose: (L.O. 3, 4, 5, 6, 7) This exercise will enable you to practice identifying the proper classification for items on an income statement. It will also give you an example of how the tax effects of various items are reflected in the income statement.

Margaret Moylan had the following selected transactions and events occur during 2014. The corporation is subject to a 30% tax rate on all items. All amounts are material. The corporation is engaged in the sale of energy products. The company does not report comparative financial statements.

1.   The corporation experienced an uninsured flood loss in the amount of $60,000 during the year. A flood is unusual and infrequent in the region where the corporation resides.

2.   At the beginning of 2012, the corporation purchased an office machine for $108,000 (salvage value of $18,000) that has a useful life of six years. The bookkeeper used straight-line depreciation for 2012 and 2013, but failed to deduct the salvage value in computing the depreciable base. The same depreciation calculations were used for tax purposes.

3.   Sale of securities held as a part of Moylan's portfolio resulted in a loss of $62,200 (pretax).

4.   When its president died, the corporation realized $100,000 from an insurance policy. The cash surrender value of this policy had been carried on the books as an investment in the amount of $34,000 (the gain is nontaxable).

5.   The corporation disposed of a component of business at a loss of $140,000 before taxes.

6.   The corporation decided to change its method of inventory pricing from average cost to the FIFO method. The effect of this change on prior years would be to increase 2012 income by $64,000 and decrease 2013 income by $20,000 before taxes. The FIFO method has been used for 2014.

Instructions:
Describe how each of the items above will be reported in a multiple-step income statement for 2014. Indicate the amount that will be reported and the section of the income statement in which the amount will appear.

Solution to Exercise 4-6

1. A loss of $42,000 ($60,000 minus 30% of $60,000) will be reported in the extraordinary items section of the income statement.

2. Depreciation expense of $15,000 [($108,000 - $18,000) ÷ 6 years] will appear in the administrative expense (an operating expense) section of the 2014 income statement. The correction of an error in computing prior periods' depreciation (a prior period adjustment) will **not** appear on the income statement. Rather, a credit of $4,200 will appear on the retained earnings statement for 2014 as an adjustment to the beginning balance of retained earnings (assuming single-period rather than comparative financial statements are presented). The prior period adjustment is reported net of tax. Computations:
    $108,000 ÷ 6 = $18,000 depreciation taken in 2012.
    $108,000 ÷ 6 = $18,000 depreciation taken in 2013.
    ($108,000 - $18,000) ÷ 6 = $15,000 correct annual depreciation.
    $15,000 x 2 = $30,000 correct depreciation for 2012 & 2013.
    ($18,000 + $18,000) - $30,000 = $6,000 overstated expense in prior years.
    $6,000 - 30%($6,000) = $4,200 addition to retained earnings.

3. A loss of $62,200 will be reported in the other expenses and losses section of the income statement. It is **not** reported net of tax.

4. A gain of $66,000 ($100,000 - $34,000) will appear in the other revenues and gains section of the income statement. It is **not** reported net of tax (in this case, it had no tax effect anyway). A good caption for this item is "Gain from proceeds of life insurance policy."

5. A loss of $98,000 ($140,000 minus 30% of $140,000) will appear as a loss in the discontinued operations section of the income statement.

6. A cumulative effect on prior periods of a change in accounting principle from average cost to FIFO will appear as a $30,800 credit adjustment to retained earnings balance at the beginning of 2014 on the retained earnings statement. The 2014 income statement will report amounts based on application of the new (FIFO) method. Computations:

    $64,000 credit (increase in prior period income)
    20,000 debit (decrease in prior period income)
    44,000 credit (net catch-up adjustment needed)
    70% net of tax rate
    $30,800 credit (cumulative effect, net of tax)

ILLUSTRATION 4-4
NET INCOME AND COMPREHENSIVE INCOME (L.O. 8)

Comprehensive income includes all changes in stockholders' equity except those resulting from investments by owners and distributions to owners. Comprehensive income therefore includes all revenues, gains, expenses, and losses reported in net income. In addition, it includes gains and losses that bypass net income but are included as part of comprehensive income. These items—non owner changes in equity that bypass the income statement—are referred to as **other comprehensive income.**

An example of a gain or loss that is reported as other comprehensive income is an unrealized gain or loss on available-for-sale securities held as an investment. Excluding this type of gain or loss from net income and disclosing it separately reduces the volatility of net income due to changes in fair value yet informs the financial statement user of the gain or loss that would occur if the securities were sold at fair value. This subject is discussed further in **Chapter 17**. Other examples of other comprehensive income items are translation gains and losses on foreign currency (a subject in an advanced accounting text), excess of additional pension liability over unrecognized prior service cost (a subject of **Chapter 20**), and unrealized gains and losses on certain hedging transactions.

The FASB requires that components of other comprehensive income be reported in one of two ways: (1) a single continuous statement (**one statement approach**) referred to as the comprehensive income statement, or (2) two separate, but consecutive statements of net income and other comprehensive income (**two statement approach**) where the first statement is referred to as the income statement and the second is called the comprehensive income statement. To illustrate these two presentation formats, assume Sofia Vergara Inc. reports the following information for 2014: sales revenues, $1,600,000; cost of goods sold $1,200,000; operating expenses $180,000; and an unrealized holding gain on available-for-sale securities of $60,000. Also assume stockholders' equity at the end of 2013 comprised: common stock, $600,000; retained earnings, $100,000; and accumulated other comprehensive income, $120,000.

The first approach is to provide a combined statement. It is shown below:

Sofia Vergara Inc.
Statement of Comprehensive Income
For the Year Ended December 31, 2014

Sales revenue	$1,600,000
Cost of goods sold	1,200,000
Gross profit	400,000
Operating expenses	180,000
Net income	220,000
Other comprehensive income	
Unrealized holding gain, net of tax	60,000
Comprehensive income	$ 280,000

ILLUSTRATION 4-4 (Continued)

The combined statement has the advantage of not requiring the creation of a new financial statement. However, burying the traditional net income figure as a subtotal on the statement is a disadvantage.

The second approach is to provide information in a two income statement format. It is shown below:

Sofia Vergara Inc.
Income Statement
For the Year Ended December 31, 2014

Sales revenue	$1,600,000
Cost of goods sold	1,200,000
Gross profit	400,000
Operating expenses	180,000
Net income	$ 220,000

Sofia Vergara Inc.
Comprehensive Income Statement
For the Year Ended December 31, 2014

Net income	$220,000
Other comprehensive income	
Unrealized holding gain, net of tax	60,000
Comprehensive income	$280,000

Reporting comprehensive income in a separate statement indicates that the gains and losses identified as other comprehensive income have the same status as traditional gains and losses. In addition, the relationship of the traditional income statement to the new statement is apparent because net income is the starting point in the new statement.

ILLUSTRATION 4-4 (Continued)

In addition to a comprehensive income statement, companies also present a statement of stockholders' equity. This statement reports the changes in each stockholders' equity account and in total stockholders' equity during the year. The statement of stockholders' equity is often prepared in columnar form with columns for each account and for total stockholders' equity. A statement of stockholders' equity for Sofia Vergara Inc. is shown below:

Sofia Vergara Inc.
Statement of Stockholders' Equity
For the Year Ended December 31, 2014

	Total	Compre-hensive Income	Retained Earnings	Accumulated Other Comprehen-sive Income	Common Stock
Beginning balance	$ 820,000		$100,000	$120,000	$600,000
Issuance of stock	150,000				150,000
Net income	220,000	$220,000	220,000		
Other comprehensive income	60,000	60,000		60,000	
Ending balance	$1,250,000	$280,000	$320,000	$180,000	$750,000

The net income for a period of time is closed to Retained Earnings (a component of stockholders' equity). Other comprehensive income for a period is closed to Accumulated Other Comprehensive Income (a separate component of stockholders' equity). The accumulated other comprehensive income is reported in the stockholders' equity section of the balance sheet as follows:

Sofia Vergara Inc.
Balance Sheet (Partial)
As of December 31, 2014
(Stockholders' Equity Section)

Stockholders' equity
    Common stock $ 750,000
    Retained earnings   320,000
    Accumulated other comprehensive income   180,000
        Total stockholders' equity $1,250,000

TIP: By providing a comprehensive income statement and a stockholders' equity statement, the company reports information about all changes in net assets (owners' equity). With this information, users will be better able to understand the quality of the company's earnings. This information should help users to predict the amount, timing, and uncertainty of future cash flows.

TIP: The **statement of stockholders' equity** is often called the **statement of changes in stockholders' equity** or **stockholders' equity statement.**

TIP: Because the statement of stockholders' equity (as illustrated above) discloses **all** of the reasons for **all** changes in **all** stockholders' equity accounts (which includes Retained Earnings), most companies do **not** prepare a separate statement of retained earnings.

ILLUSTRATION 4-4 (Continued)

TIP: A company is required to display the components of other comprehensive income either (1) net of related tax effects or (2) before related tax effects with one amount shown for the aggregate amount of tax related to the total amount of other comprehensive income. Under either alternative, each component of other comprehensive income must be shown, net of related taxes, either on the face of the statement or in the notes.

TIP: A company like the The Coca-Cola Company owns substantial interests in other companies. Coca-Cola generally consolidates the financial results of these companies into its own financial statements. In these cases, Coca-Cola is referred to as the parent, and the other companies are referred to as subsidiaries. Noncontrolling interest is then the portion of equity (net assets) interest in a subsidiary **not** attributable to the parent company. When Coca-Cola prepares a consolidated income statement, GAAP requires that net income be allocated to the controlling and noncontrolling interests. This allocation is reported at the bottom of the income statement after net income. The allocation is between (1) the majority interest represented by stockholders who have the controlling interest and (2) the noncontrolling interest (referred to as the minority interest.) (Consolidated financial statements is a topic of an advanced accounting course.)

ANALYSIS OF MULTIPLE-CHOICE TYPE QUESTIONS

QUESTION
1.   (L.O. 3) In a multiple-step income statement, the excess of gross profit over operating expenses is called:
   a.   net margin.
   b.   income from operations.
   c.   net profit.
   d.   earnings.

Approach and Explanation: Visualize a multiple-step income statement. Net sales less cost of goods sold yields gross profit (sometimes called gross margin). Gross profit less operating expenses equals income from operations. From there, other revenues and gains are added, other expenses and losses are deducted, and income tax expense is deducted to arrive at net income. Another popular name for net income is earnings. Net profit would likely refer to net income. Net margin is **not** a term applied to the income statement. (Solution = b.)

QUESTION
2.   (L.O. 3) The following expenses and loss were among those incurred by Mitzer Company during 2014:

Rent for office space	$ 660,000
Loss on sale of office furniture	55,000
Interest	132,000
Accounting and legal fees	352,000
Freight-out	70,000

One-half of the rented premises is occupied by the sales department. How much of the items listed above should be classified as general and administrative expenses in Mitzer's income statement for 2014?
   a. $682,000
   b. $869,000
   c. $884,000
   d. $939,000

Approach and Explanation: For each item listed, identify where it is reported. Then collect together the ones that you identify as general and administrative (G&A) expenses.

Rent for office space:	One-half selling; one-half G&A
Loss on sale of equipment:	Other expenses and losses
Interest:	Other expenses and losses
Accounting and legal fees:	G&A expenses
Freight-out:	Selling expenses

One-half of office space (.5 x $660,000)	$330,000	
Accounting and legal fees	352,000	
General and administrative expenses	$682,000	(Solution = a.)

QUESTION
3.   (L.O. 3) Which of the following is **not** a selling expense?
   a.   Advertising expense
   b.   Office salaries expense
   c.   Freight-out
   d.   Store supplies consumed

Approach and Explanation: Take each account and determine its classification. Items "a," "c," and "d" are selling expenses because they are associated with the sales function. Office salaries are related to normal operations, but they are not related to the sales function of the business. Therefore, they are not classified as a selling expense. (Solution = b.)

QUESTION
4. (L.O. 3) The accountant for the Orion Sales Company is preparing the income statement for 2014 and the balance sheet at December 31, 2014. The January 1, 2014 merchandise inventory balance will appear:
    a. only as an asset on the balance sheet.
    b. only in the cost of goods sold section of the income statement.
    c. as a deduction in the cost of goods sold section of the income statement and as a current asset on the balance sheet.
    d. as an addition in the cost of goods sold section of the income statement and as a current asset on the balance sheet.

Explanation: The January 1, 2014 inventory amount is the beginning inventory figure. Beginning inventory is a component of the cost of goods available for sale for the period which is a component of cost of goods sold. (Solution = b.)

> **TIP:** If the question asked about the December 31, 2014 merchandise inventory balance (ending inventory) rather than the beginning inventory balance, the correct answer would have been "c" (as a deduction in computing cost of sales and as a current asset).

QUESTION
5. (L.O. 3) The following amounts relate to the current year for the Ira Company:

Beginning inventory	$ 20,000
Ending inventory	28,000
Purchases	166,000
Purchase returns	4,800
Transportation-out	6,000

The amount of cost of goods sold for the period is:
    a. $169,200.
    b. $162,800.
    c. $153,200.
    d. $147,200.

Approach and Explanation: Write down the computation model for cost of goods sold. Enter the amounts given and solve for the unknown.

$ 20,000		Beginning Inventory
+ 166,000	+	Purchases
- 4,800	-	Purchase Returns and Allowances
	-	Purchase Discounts
	+	Freight-in
181,200	=	Cost of Goods Available for Sale
- 28,000	-	Ending Inventory
$ 153,200	=	Cost of Goods Sold (Solution = c.)

> **TIP:** Transportation-out is classified as a selling expense, not a component of cost of goods sold. "Transportation-out" is often called "freight-out; "transportation-in" is another name for "freight-in."

QUESTION
6. (L.O. 4) A loss from the disposal of component of an entity should be reported in the income statement:
    a. after extraordinary items and it should be reflected net of the related income tax effect.
    b. before extraordinary items and it should be reflected net of the related income tax effect.
    c. after extraordinary items and it should not be reflected net of the related income tax effect.
    d. before extraordinary items and it should not be reflected net of the related income tax effect.

Approach and Explanation: Keep in mind the acronym **DE**. Write the items down in the proper order. Read each answer response to see if it properly describes the order in which you have listed the items.
    The correct order of the items involved in the question is as follows:
    (1)   Discontinued operations
    (2)   Extraordinary items
Both discontinued operations and extraordinary items are to be reported net of the related income tax effect. (Solution = b.)

QUESTION
7. (L.O. 4) A material loss should be presented separately as a component of income from continuing operations when it is:
    a. unusual in nature and infrequent in occurrence.
    b. unusual in nature but **not** infrequent in occurrence.
    c. an extraordinary loss.
    d. a cumulative effect of a change in accounting principle.

Approach and Explanation: Visualize an income statement and mentally identify the section that reports income from continuing operations. Read one answer at a time and determine if it correctly describes how the statement in the question stem can be completed. A material loss that is (1) unusual in nature **and** (2) infrequent in occurrence should be reported as an extraordinary item. A loss that meets one of the criteria for being classified as extraordinary, but not both, should be separately disclosed as a component of income from continuing operations. An extraordinary item is to be reported **after** (and not part of) income from continuing operations. A cumulative effect of a change in accounting principle does not affect the income statement. (Solution = b.)

QUESTION
8. (L.O. 4) During the year ended December 31, 2014, Schmelya Corporation incurred the following infrequent losses:
    1.   A factory was shut down during a major strike by employees; costs were $120,000.
    2.   A loss of $50,000 was incurred on the abandonment of computer equipment used in the business.
    3.   A restructuring charge of $75,000.
    4.   A loss of $82,000 was incurred as a result of flood damage to a warehouse.
    How much total loss should Schmelya report in the extraordinary item section of its 2014 income statement?
    a. $82,000
    b. $120,000
    c. $202,000
    d. $252,000

Approach and Explanation: It is wise to review the list of items that are classified as extraordinary items and the list of items that are not extraordinary items (see **Illustration 4-3**) until you can readily recognize items that appear in the list. In the question at hand, the first three items are on the list of items that are **not** extraordinary. Therefore, the only possible one being extraordinary is the loss from flood damage. A flood would be considered infrequent in some locations but not others. The stem of the question indicates it is deemed infrequent for Schmelya. To be classified as extraordinary, an item needs to be unusual in nature and infrequent in occurrence. However, there are certain items that do **not** constitute extraordinary items. (Solution = a.)

QUESTION
9.   (L.O. 4) Which of the following should be classified as an extraordinary item?
   a.   Loss from excess of book value of assets over amount of condemnation award.
   b.   Loss from exchange of foreign currencies.
   c.   Loss from abandonment of plant assets.
   d.   Loss from effects of a strike.

Explanation: Answer selections "b.", "c.", and "d." involve transactions that appear on the list of items that are **not** to be classified as extraordinary items on the income statement. A gain or loss from an expropriation is to be classified as an extraordinary item. When a government exercises its right to eminent domain, a condemnation award is given to the owner of the property. An excess of the asset's book value over its condemnation award results in a loss. (Solution = a.)

QUESTION
10.   (L.O. 4) When a piece of equipment is sold at a gain of $700,000 less related taxes of $280,000, and the gain is **not** considered unusual or infrequent, the income statement for the period would show these effects as:
   a.   an extraordinary item net of applicable income taxes, $420,000.
   b.   a prior period adjustment net of applicable income taxes, $420,000.
   c.   an other gain net of applicable income taxes, $420,000.
   d.   an other gain of $700,000 and an increase in income tax expense of $280,000.

Explanation: A gain or loss on the disposal of property, plant and equipment that is **not** unusual and infrequent is **not** to be classified as an extraordinary item. Therefore, a gain from such a disposal goes in the "other revenues and gains" classification. The related tax effect is reflected in the "income tax expense" figure. The only items reported net of tax are extraordinary items, discontinued operations, changes in accounting principle, and prior period adjustments. The tax effects of all other transactions are summarized in the amount captioned "income tax expense." (Solution = d.)

QUESTION
11.   (L.O. 7) A correction of an error in prior periods' income will be reported:

	In the income statement	Net of tax
a.	Yes	Yes
b.	No	No
c.	Yes	No
d.	No	Yes

Approach and Explanation: Write down what you know about the accounting for a correction of an error in computing income in a prior period. Then answer "yes" or "no" to each question posed at the top of the appropriate column. Find the combination that matches yours. A correction of an error is a prior period adjustment; it is reported net of tax as an adjustment to the beginning retained earnings balance on the statement of retained earnings in the period the error is corrected. (Solution = d.)

QUESTION

12.   (L.O. 7) The OVA Company had the following errors occur in its financial statements:

	2013	2014
Ending inventory	$12,000 Understated	$18,000 Overstated
Depreciation expense	$24,000 Overstated	$14,000 Overstated

Ignoring any related income tax effect and assuming that none of the errors were detected or corrected, by what amount will retained earnings at December 31, 2014 be misstated?
   a. $18,000 overstated.
   b. $20,000 understated.
   c. $32,000 understated.
   d. $14,000 understated.

Approach and Explanation: Explain the effects of each error separately and then combine your results. The $12,000 understatement of ending inventory for 2013 causes a $12,000 understatement of net income for 2013 and a $12,000 overstatement of net income for 2014 (because the ending inventory for 2013 is the beginning inventory for 2014); this nets to be a zero impact on the retained earnings balance at December 31, 2014.   The $24,000 overstatement of depreciation expense in 2013 causes an understatement of net income for 2013 and a corresponding $24,000 understatement of retained earnings at December 31, 2013 and at December 31, 2014.   The $18,000 overstatement of ending inventory for 2014 causes an overstatement of net income for 2014 and an $18,000 overstatement of retained earnings at December 31, 2014.   A $14,000 overstatement of depreciation expense for 2014 causes a $14,000 understatement of net income for 2014 and a $14,000 understatement of retained earnings at December 31, 2014. The net effect on retained earnings at December 31, 2014 is therefore a $24,000 understatement + an $18,000 overstatement + a $14,000 understatement which equals a $20,000 understatement. (Solution = b.)

QUESTION

13.   (L.O. 8) Comprehensive income includes all of the following **except**:
   a.   unrealized holding losses.
   b.   dividends declared and paid.
   c.   interest income.
   d.   gains on disposal of assets.

Approach and Explanation: Define comprehensive income before reading the answer selections. Then analyze each answer selection to see how it relates to the definition.   Comprehensive income includes all changes in stockholders' equity except those resulting from investments by owners and distributions to owners.   Dividends declared and paid are a distribution to owners.   Dividends received would be a component of comprehensive income. (Solution = b.)

IFRS Insights

- The income statement is a required statement for both GAAP and IFRS. In addition, the content and presentation of an IFRS income statement is similar to the one used for GAAP.

- Presentation of the income statement under GAAP follows either a single-step or multiple-step format. IFRS does not mention a single-step or multiple-step approach.

- Under GAAP, companies must report an item as extraordinary if it is unusual in nature and infrequent in occurrence. Extraordinary items are prohibited under IFRS.

- Under IFRS, companies must classify expenses by either nature or function. GAAP does not have that requirement, but the U.S. SEC requires a functional presentation either by their nature (such as cost of materials used, direct labor incurred, delivery expense, advertising expense, employee benefits, depreciation expense, and amortization expense) or their function (such as cost of goods sold, selling expenses, and administrative expenses).

  An advantage of the **nature-of-expense method** is that it is simple to apply because allocations of expense to different functions are not necessary.

  The **function-of-expense method,** however, is often viewed as more relevant because this method identifies the major cost drivers of the company and therefore helps users assess whether these amounts are appropriate for the revenue generated. A disadvantage of this method is that the allocation of costs to the varying functions may be arbitrary and therefore the expense classification becomes misleading.

- The function-of-expense method is generally used in practice although many companies believe both approaches have merit. These companies use the function-of-expense approach on the income statement but provide detail of the expenses (as in the nature-of-expense approach) in the notes to the financial statements. The IASB-FASB discussion paper on financial statement presentation also recommends the dual approach.

- IFRS identifies certain minimum items that should be presented on the income statement. GAAP has no minimum information requirements. However, the SEC rules have more rigorous presentation requirements.

- IFRS does not define key measures like income from operations. SEC regulations define many key measures and provide requirements and limitations on companies reporting non-GAAP/IFRS information.

- Both IFRS and GAAP require companies to indicate the amount of net income attributable to noncontrolling interest. They require allocation of net income or loss between two classes; (1) the majority interest represented by the shareholders who own the controlling interest, and (2) the noncontrolling interest (often referred to as the minority interest).

- GAAP and IFRS follow the same presentation guidelines for discontinued operations, but IFRS defines a discontinued operation more narrowly. Both standard-setters have indicated a willingness to develop a similar definition to be used in the joint project on financial statement presentation.

- Both GAAP and IFRS have items that are recognized in equity as part of comprehensive income but do not affect net income. Both GAAP and IFRS allow a separate comprehensive income statement or a combined statement.

- Under IFRS, revaluation of property, plant, and equipment, and intangible assets is permitted; the effects of revaluation are reported as other comprehensive income. The effect of this difference between GAAP and IFRS is that application of IFRS results in more transactions affecting equity but not net income.

- Under IFRS, companies report all revenues, gains, expenses, and losses on the income statement and, at the end of the period, close them to Income Summary. They provide useful subtotals on the income statement, such as gross profit, income from operations, income before income tax, and net income. Companies classify discontinued operations of a component of a business as a separate item in the income statement, after "Income from continuing operations." Companies present other income and expense in a separate section, before income from operations. Providing intermediate income figures helps readers evaluate earnings information in assessing the amounts, timing, and uncertainty of future cash flows.

TRUE/FALSE (Circle the correct answer for each).

T F 1. IFRS requires a multiple-step approach for presentation of the income statement.

T F 2. Like GAAP, IFRS requires that an item unusual in nature and infrequent in occurrence be classified as an extraordinary item.

T F 3. Under IFRS, companies must classify expenses by either nature or function.

T F 4. GAAP requires companies to indicate the amount of net income attributable to the non-controlling interest.

T F 5. GAAP and IFRS follow the same presentation guidelines for discontinued operations, but IFRS defines a discontinued operation more narrowly.

Solutions:

1.	F	4.	F
2.	F	5.	T
3.	T		

CHAPTER 5

BALANCE SHEET AND
STATEMENT OF CASH FLOWS

OVERVIEW

A balance sheet reports on the financial position of an entity at a point in time. A statement of cash flows reports reasons for cash receipts and cash payments during the period. In this chapter, we discuss the classifications of a balance sheet and a statement of cash flows along with related disclosure issues. It is extremely important that items are properly classified. Errors in classification will result in incorrect ratio analyses which can lead to misinterpretations of the meaning of the information conveyed. This can affect the decisions that are being made based on that information.

SUMMARY OF LEARNING OBJECTIVES

1. **Explain the uses and limitations of a balance sheet.** The balance sheet provides information about the nature and amounts of investments in a company's resources, obligations to creditors, and the owners' equity in resources. The balance sheet contributes to financial reporting by providing a basis for: (1) computing rates of return, (2) evaluating the capital structure of the enterprise, and (3) assessing the liquidity, solvency, and financial flexibility of the enterprise. Three limitations of a balance sheet are as follows: (1) The balance sheet does not reflect fair value because accountants use a historical cost basis in valuing and reporting most assets and liabilities. (2) Companies must use judgments and estimates to determine certain amounts, such as the collectibility of receivables and the useful life of long-term tangible and intangible assets. (3) The balance sheet omits many items that are of financial value to the business but cannot be recorded objectively, such as human resources, customer base, and reputation.

2. **Identify the major classifications of the balance sheet.** The general elements of the balance sheet are assets, liabilities, and equity. The major classifications of assets are current assets; long-term investments; property, plant, and equipment; intangible assets; and other assets. The major classifications of liabilities are current liabilities and long-term liabilities. The balance sheet of a corporation generally classifies owners' equity as capital stock, additional paid-in capital, and retained earnings.

3. **Prepare a classified balance sheet using the report and account formats.** The report form lists liabilities and stockholders' equity directly below assets on the same page. The account form lists assets, by sections, on the left side and liabilities and stockholders' equity, by sections, on the right side.

4. **Indicate the purpose of the statement of cash flows.** The primary purpose of a statement of cash flows is to provide relevant information about a company's cash receipts and cash payments during a period. Reporting the sources, uses, and net increase or decrease in cash enables financial statement readers to know what is happening to a company's most liquid resource.

5.   **Identify the content of the statement of cash flows.** In the statement of cash flows, companies classify the period's cash receipts and cash payments into three different activities: (1) **Operating activities** include all transactions and other events that are not defined as investing or financing activities. Operating activities generally involve producing and delivering goods and providing services. Cash flows from operating activities are generally the cash effects of transactions that enter into the determination of net income. (2) **Investing activities** include making and collecting loans and acquiring and disposing of investments (both debt and equity) and property, plant, and equipment. (3) **Financing activities** include (a) obtaining resources from owners and providing them with a return on and a return of their investment, and (b) borrowing money from creditors and repaying the amounts borrowed.

6.   **Prepare a basic statement of cash flows.** The information to prepare a statement of cash flows usually comes from comparative balance sheets, the current income statement, and selected transaction data. Companies follow four steps to prepare the statement of cash flows from these sources. (1) Determine the net cash provided by (or used in) operating activities, (2) determine the net cash provided by (or used in) investing and financing activities, (3) determine the net change (increase or decrease) in cash during the period, and (4) reconcile the net change in cash with the beginning and the ending cash balances.

7.   **Understand the usefulness of the statement of cash flows.** Creditors examine the statement of cash flows carefully because they are concerned about being paid. The amount and trend of net cash flow provided by operating activities in relation to the company's liabilities is helpful in making the assessment. Two ratios used in this regard are the current cash debt ratio and the cash debt ratio. In addition, the amount of free cash flow provides creditors and stockholders with a picture of the company's financial flexibility.

8.   **Determine which balance sheet information requires supplemental disclosure.** Four types of information normally are supplemental to account titles and amounts presented in the balance sheet: (1) **Contingencies:** Material events that have an uncertain outcome; (2) **Accounting policies:** Explanations of the valuation methods used or the basic assumptions made concerning inventory valuation, depreciation methods, investments in subsidiaries, etc.; (3) **Contractual situations:** Explanations of certain restrictions or covenants attached to specific assets or, more likely, to liabilities; (4) **Fair values:** Disclosures related to the fair value information for certain types of assets and liabilities (particularly those that relate to financial instruments).

9.   **Describe the major disclosure techniques for the balance sheet.** Companies use four methods to disclose pertinent information in the balance sheet: (1) **Parenthetical explanations:** Parenthetical information provides additional information or description following the item; (2) **Notes:** A company uses notes if it cannot conveniently show additional explanations or descriptions as parenthetical explanations; (3) **Cross reference and contra items:** Companies "cross reference" a direct relationship between an asset and a liability on the balance sheet; (4) **Supporting schedules:** Often a company uses a separate schedule to present more detailed information shown in the balance sheet, than just the single summary item shown in the balance sheet.

*10.   **Identify the major types of financial ratios and what they measure.** A ratio expresses the mathematical relationship between one quantity and another, in terms of either a percentage, a rate, or a proportion. **Liquidity ratios** measure the short-run ability to pay maturing obligations. **Activity ratios** measure the effectiveness of asset usage. **Profitability ratios** measure the success or failure of an enterprise. **Coverage ratios** measure the degree of protection for long-term creditors and investors.
    *This material is covered in **Appendix 5A** in the text.

TIPS ON CHAPTER TOPICS

TIP: It is extremely important that items are properly classified on a balance sheet. Errors in classification can result in incorrect ratio analyses (discussed in **Appendix 5A**) which may lead to misrepresentations of the meaning of the information conveyed and can effect decisions that are based on those analyses.

TIP: The balance of liabilities and the balance of owners' equity at a point in time simply serve as scorecards of the total amounts of unspecified assets which have come about from creditor sources (liabilities) and owner sources (owners' equity). Thus, you can **not** determine the amount of cash (or any other specific asset) held by an entity by looking at the balance of owners' equity or liabilities. You must look at the listing of individual assets on the balance sheet to determine the amount of cash owned.

TIP: In answering questions regarding the classification of items on a balance sheet, always assume an individual item is material in amount unless it is apparent otherwise.

TIP: Current assets are presented in the balance sheet in order of liquidity. The five major items found in the current asset classification of the balance sheet and their bases of valuation are:

Item	Basis of Valuation
Cash and cash equivalents	Fair value
Short-term investments	Fair value (generally)
Receivables	Estimated amount collectible (i.e., net realizable value)
Inventories	Lower of cost or market
Prepaid expenses	Cost

TIP: For receivables arising from unusual transactions (such as sale of property, a loan to an affiliate, or loans to employees), companies should separately classify these as long-term assets unless collection is expected within one year. If collection is expected within one year, then these receivables must be shown separately from nontrade receivables.

TIP: To classify items in financial statements, companies group those items with similar characteristics and separate items that have different characteristics. For example, companies should report separately:

1. Assets that differ in their **type or expected function** in the company's central operations or other activities. For example merchandise inventories are to be reported separately from property, plant, and equipment.

2. Assets and liabilities with **different** implications for the company's **financial flexibility.** For example, equipment owned and used in operations should be separate from leased equipment used in operations (the leased items are subject to restrictions), and land supporting the company's office facilities should be separate from land held for investment.

3. Assets and liabilities with **different general liquidity** characteristics. For example, cash is reported separately from inventories.

ILLUSTRATION 5-1
BALANCE SHEET CLASSIFICATIONS (L.O. 2)

CURRENT ASSETS: includes cash (unrestricted) and items which are expected to be converted to cash or sold or consumed within the next year or operating cycle, whichever is longer. Includes cash and cash equivalents, short-term investments, net trade receivables, short-term notes receivable, inventories, prepaid expenses, and some deferred income taxes.

LONG-TERM INVESTMENTS: includes long-term receivables, restricted funds, investments in stocks and bonds of other companies, land held for future plant site, land held for speculation, investments set aside in special funds such as a sinking fund, pension fund, or plant expansion fund, cash surrender value of life insurance, and investments in nonconsolidated subsidiaries or affiliated companies.

PROPERTY, PLANT AND EQUIPMENT: includes long-lived tangible assets (land, building, equipment, machinery, and tools) that are currently being used in operations (used to produce goods and services for customers). Two items that do not meet this criteria (because they are not currently being used in operations) but are included in property, plant and equipment are Plant Under Construction and Deposits on Equipment. Assets in this category are often referred to as plant assets or fixed assets. They are not held for resale. Leasehold improvements are often included here.

INTANGIBLE ASSETS: includes assets that lack physical substance, such as a patent, copyright, franchise, trademark, or trade names that give the holder exclusive right of use for a specified period of time. Their value to a company is generally derived from the rights or privileges granted by governmental or other authority. Also includes goodwill, licenses, customer lists, and noncompete agreements.

OTHER ASSETS: includes assets that by common practice are not classified elsewhere. Can include long-term prepaid expenses, prepaid pension cost, some long-term receivables, restricted cash or other assets in special funds, deferred income taxes, and property held for sale that is not expected to be sold within the next year.

CURRENT LIABILITIES: obligations that are due within a year and are expected to require the use of current assets or the incurrence of other current liabilities to liquidate them. Includes short-term notes payable, accounts payable, taxes payable, salaries payable, warranty obligations, deferred income taxes, current maturities of long-term debt, unearned revenues, and accrued employee benefits payable.

LONG-TERM LIABILITIES: obligations that do not meet the criteria to be classified as current liabilities. Includes long-term notes payable, lease obligations, bonds payable, deferred income taxes, mortgage payable and pension obligations.

CAPITAL STOCK: the par or stated value of shares issued or about to be issued. Includes common stock and preferred stock.

ADDITIONAL PAID-IN CAPITAL: the excess of the issuance price over the par or stated value of stock issued or about to be issued. Includes paid-in capital in excess of par from various sources including treasury stock transactions.

ILLUSTRATION 5-1 (continued)

RETAINED EARNINGS: the excess of net incomes over net losses and dividend distributions since inception of the business. An appropriation of retained earnings is a restricted portion of the total retained earnings figure.

NONCONTROLLING INTEREST (MINORITY INTEREST): the portion of the equity of subsidiaries not wholly owned by the reporting company (if applicable).

TIP: Memorize the definition of current assets. **Current assets** are cash and other assets that are expected to be converted into cash, sold, or consumed within the year or operating cycle that immediately follows the balance sheet date, whichever is longer. Think about how various examples of current assets meet this definition. Accounts receivable are current assets because they will be converted to cash shortly after the balance sheet date; inventory is a current asset because it will be sold within the year that follows the balance sheet date; prepaid insurance is a current asset because it will be consumed (used up) within the next year.

TIP: A normal **operating cycle** is the length of time required to go from cash back to cash. That is, for an entity which sells products, the operating cycle is the time required to take cash out to buy (or to manufacture) inventory then sell the inventory and receive cash (either from a cash sale or the collection of an account receivable stemming from a credit sale). Thus, the length of an entity's operating cycle depends on the nature of its business. Unless otherwise indicated, always assume the operating cycle for an entity is less than a year so that the one-year test is used as the cutoff between current and noncurrent.

TIP: Memorize the definition of current liabilities. **Current liabilities** are obligations which are expected to require the use of current assets or the incurrence of other current liabilities. A liability may be due within a year of the balance sheet and **not** be a current liability. An example is a debt due in six months that will be liquidated by use of a noncurrent asset.

TIP: In a classified balance sheet, any asset that is not classified as a current asset is a noncurrent asset. There are four noncurrent asset classifications: long-term investments; property, plant and equipment; intangible assets; and other assets.

TIP: In a classified balance sheet, liabilities are classified either as current or noncurrent liabilities. The noncurrent liabilities are usually titled "long-term liabilities" or "long-term debt."

TIP: Current assets are listed in the order of their liquidity, with the most liquid ones being listed first. Current liabilities are not listed in any prescribed order; however, notes payable (short-term) is usually listed first followed by accounts payable (and the remainder of the current liabilities are often listed in descending order of amount). Property, plant and equipment items are listed in order of length of life, with the longest life first.

TIP: "**Short-term**" is synonymous with "**current**," and "**long-term**" is synonymous with "**noncurrent**." Therefore, "short-term debt" can be used to refer to "current liabilities." Asset classifications are typically titled current and noncurrent; whereas, liability classifications are typically titled current and long-term.

TIP: All noncurrent assets (assets in classifications other than "current assets") are resources that are not expected to be converted into cash or fully consumed in operations within one year or the operating cycle, whichever is longer.

TIP: An investment may be classified as a current asset (if it is a short-term investment) or as a noncurrent asset (if it is a long-term investment). For an investment to be classified as current: (1) it should be readily marketable, and (2) there should be a lack of management intent to hold it for a long-term purpose.

TIP: A **valuation account** is an account whose balance is needed to properly value the item to which the valuation account relates. A **contra account** is a valuation account whose normal balance (debit versus credit) is opposite of the normal balance of the account to which the valuation account relates. An **adjunct account** is a valuation account whose normal balance is the same as the normal balance of the account to which it relates.

TIP: Interest on debt is due annually or more frequently (semiannually or monthly, for example). Therefore, interest accrued on long-term debt is generally classified as a current liability. Likewise, interest receivable stemming from the accrual of interest on long-term receivables is generally classified as a current asset.

TIP: A fund can consist of restricted cash or noncash assets such as stocks and bonds of other companies. Funds are reported in the long-term investment classification.

TIP: If an account title starts with "Allowance for...," then it generally is a contra balance sheet account.

TIP: If an account title starts with "Provision for...," it is generally an income statement account.

TIP: An appropriation or restriction of retained earnings is a positive component of total retained earnings. An appropriation of retained earnings refers to a portion of retained earnings which for one reason or another is restricted, which simply means it cannot be used as a basis for the declaration of dividends.

TIP: Regarding the valuation of balance sheet items, fair value information may be more useful than historical cost for valuation of certain types of assets and liabilities. This is particularly true for financial instruments (defined as cash, an ownership interest, or a contractual right to receive or obligation to deliver cash or another financial instrument where contractual rights represent assets and contractual obligations represent liabilities).

To increase consistency and comparability in the reporting of the ever expanding disclosures of fair value measures, companies follow a fair value hierarchy that provides insight into how to determine fair value. The hierarchy (depicted in **Illustration 2-5** in this book) has three levels. **Level 1** measures (the most reliable) are based on observable inputs, such as market prices for identical assets or liabilities. **Level 2** measures (less reliable) are based on market-based inputs other than those included in Level 1, such as those based on market prices for similar assets or liabilities. **Level 3** measures (least reliable) are based on unobservable inputs, such as a company's own data or assumptions.

For major groups of assets and liabilities, companies must make the following fair value disclosures: (1) the fair value measurement and (2) the fair value hierarchy level of the measurements as a whole, classified by Level 1, 2, or 3.

In addition, companies must provide significant additional disclosure related to Level 3 measurements. The disclosures related to Level 3 are substantial and must identify what assumptions the company used to generate the fair value numbers and any related income effects. Companies will want to use Level 1 and 2 measurements as much as possible. In most cases, these valuations should be very reliable, as the fair value measurements are based on market information. In contrast, a company that uses Level 3 measurements extensively must be carefully evaluated to understand the impact these valuations have on the financial statements.

Level 3 fair value measurements may be developed using expected cash flow and present value techniques, as described in Statement of Financial Accounting Concepts No. 7, "Using Cash Flow Information and Present Value in Accounting," as discussed in **Chapter 6.**

EXERCISE 5-1

Purpose: (L.O. 2) This exercise lists examples of balance sheet accounts and enables you to practice determining where they are classified.

Instructions

Indicate which balance sheet classification is the most appropriate for reporting each account listed below by selecting the abbreviation of the corresponding section.

CA	Current Assets	CL	Current Liabilities
INV	Long-term Investments	LTL	Long-term Liabilities
PPE	Property, Plant, and Equipment	CS	Capital Stock
ITG	Intangible Assets	APC	Additional Paid-in Capital
OA	Other Assets	RE	Retained Earnings

If the account is a contra account, indicate that fact by putting the abbreviation in parenthesis. If the exact classification depends on facts which are not given, indicate your answer of "depends on" by the abbreviation **DEP** and the possible classifications. If the account is reported on the income statement rather than the balance sheet, indicate that fact with an **IS**. Assume all items are material.

Classifi-cation	Account	Classifi-cation	Account
_____	1. Accounts Payable.	_____	11. Advances to Vendors.
_____	2. Accounts Receivable.	_____	12. Advertising Expense.
_____	3. Accrued Interest Receivable on Long-term Investments.	_____	13. Allowance for Bad Debts.
		_____	14. Allowance for Depreciation.
_____	4. Accrued Interest Payable.	_____	15. Allowance for Doubtful Accounts.
_____	5. Accrued Taxes Payable.		
_____	6. Accumulated Depreciation—Building.	_____	16. Allowance for Excess of Cost Over Market Value of Inventory.
_____	7. Accumulated Depreciation—Machinery.	_____	17. Allowance for Inventory Price Declines.
_____	8. Mineral Reserves.	_____	18. Allowance for Purchase Discounts.
_____	9. Advances by Customers.	_____	19. Allowance for Sales Discounts.
_____	10. Advances to Affiliates.	_____	20. Allowance for Uncollectible Accts.

Classifi-cation	Account
_____	21. Appropriation for Bond Sinking Fund.
_____	22. Appropriation for Contingencies.
_____	23. Appropriation for Future Plant Expansion.
_____	24. Appropriation for Treasury Stock Purchased.
_____	25. Bank Overdraft.
_____	26. Bond Interest Payable.
_____	27. Bond Interest Receivable.
_____	28. Bond Sinking Fund.
_____	29. Building.
_____	30. Cash.
_____	31. Cash in Preferred Stock Redemption Fund.
_____	32. Cash Surrender Value of Life Insurance.
_____	33. Certificate of Deposit.
_____	34. Common Stock.
_____	35. Construction in Process (entity's new plant under construction).
_____	36. Creditor's accounts with debit balances.
_____	37. Current Maturities of Bonds Payable (to be paid from Bond Sinking Fund).
_____	38. Current Maturities of Bonds Payable (to be paid from general cash account).

Classifi-cation	Account
_____	39. Current Portion of Mortgage Payable.
_____	40. Current Portion of Long-term Debt.
_____	41. Customers' accounts with credit balances.
_____	42. Customers' Deposits.
_____	43. Deferred Income Tax Asset.
_____	44. Deferred Income Tax Liability.
_____	45. Deferred Property Tax Expense.
_____	46. Deferred Office Supplies.
_____	47. Deferred Rental Income.
_____	48. Deferred Subscription Revenue.
_____	49. Deferred Service Contract Revenue.
_____	50. Deposits on Equipment Purchases.
_____	51. Depreciation of Equipment.
_____	52. Discount on Bonds Payable.
_____	53. Discount on Common Stock.
_____	54. Discount on Notes Payable.
_____	55. Discount on Notes Receivable.
_____	56. Dishonored Notes Receivable.
_____	57. Dividend Payable in Cash.
_____	58. Dividend Payable in Common Stock.
_____	59. Earned Rental Revenue.
_____	60. Accrued Pension Liability.

Classifi-cation	**Account**	**Classifi-cation**	**Account**
_____	61. Estimated Liability for Income Taxes.	_____	82. Leasehold Improvements.
_____	62. Estimated Liability for Warranties.	_____	83. Leasehold Costs.
_____	63. Estimated Premium Claims Outstanding.	_____	84. Loss on Sale of Marketable Securities.
_____	64. Factory Supplies.	_____	85. Machinery and Equipment.
_____	65. Finished Goods Inventory.	_____	86. Machinery and Equip. Sitting Idle.
_____	66. Furniture and Fixtures.	_____	87. Marketable Securities.
_____	67. Gain on Sale of Equipment.	_____	88. Merchandise Inventory.
_____	68. General and Administrative Expenses.	_____	89. Mortgage Payable.
_____	69. Goodwill.	_____	90. Notes Payable.
_____	70. Income Tax Payable.	_____	91. Notes Payable to Banks.
_____	71. Income Tax Refund Receivable.	_____	92. Notes Receivable.
_____	72. Income Tax Withheld (from employees).	_____	93. Notes Receivable from Officers.
_____	73. Interest Payable.	_____	94. Office Supplies on Hand.
_____	74. Interest Receivable.	_____	95. Office Supplies Prepaid.
_____	75. Interest Revenue.	_____	96. Office Supplies Expense.
_____	76. Investment in General Motors Stock.	_____	97. Office Supplies Used.
_____	77. Investment in U.S. Gov. Bonds.	_____	98. Patents.
_____	78. Investment in Unconsolidated Subsidiary.	_____	99. Petty Cash Fund.
_____	79. Land.	_____	100. Plant and Equipment.
_____	80. Land Held for Future Plant Site.	_____	101. Plant Assets No Longer Used (and now Held for Sale).
_____	81. Land Used for Parking Lot.	_____	102. Preferred Stock Redemption Fund.
		_____	103. Premium on Bonds Payable.
		_____	104. Premium on Common Stock.

Classifi-cation	Account	Classifi-cation	Account
_____	105. Prepaid Advertising.	_____	119. Store Supplies.
_____	106. Prepaid Insurance.	_____	120. Store Supplies Used.
_____	107. Prepaid Insurance Expense.	_____	121. Tools and Dies (5-year life).
_____	108. Prepaid Office Supplies.	_____	122. Tools and Dies (6-mos. life).
_____	109. Prepaid Royalty Payments.	_____	123. Treasury Stock Common (at cost).
_____	110. Prepaid Property Taxes.	_____	124. Unamortized Bond Issue Costs.
_____	111. Provision for Bad Debts.	_____	125. Unamortized Discount on Bonds Payable.
_____	112. Provision for Income Taxes.	_____	126. Unearned Rental Income.
_____	113. Rent Revenue.	_____	127. Unearned Royalties.
_____	114. Salaries Payable.	_____	128. Unearned Subscription Income.
_____	115. Sales Discounts and Allowances.	_____	129. Unexpired Insurance.
_____	116. Selling Expense Control.	_____	130. Vacation Pay Payable.
_____	117. Stock Dividends Distributable.	_____	131. Vouchers Payable.
_____	118. Stock Dividends Payable.	_____	132. Work in Process.

Solution to Exercise 5-1

Solution		Explanation and/or Comment
CL	1.	These are trade payables usually due within 30 or 60 days.
CA	2.	These are trade receivables usually due within 30 or 60 days.
CA	3.	Interest is usually due annually or more frequently.
CL	4.	A better title is simply Interest Payable (item 73).
CL	5.	A better title is simply Taxes Payable.
(PPE)	6.	This is a contra account. It is another title for item 14 (item 6 is used more frequently).
(PPE)	7.	This is a contra account and an alternative title for item 14.
PPE	8.	Tracks of natural resources are classified in PPE.
DEP: CL or LTL	9.	These advances refer to revenue amounts received in advance from customers.
DEP: CA or INV or OA	10.	These advances are loans.
DEP: CA or INV or OA	11.	These advances can be prepayments or loans.

Solution		Explanation and/or Comment
IS	12.	This is a selling expense.
(CA)	13.	This is another title for Allowance for Doubtful Accounts.
(PPE)	14.	This is another title for Accumulated Depreciation (items 6 & 7).
(CA)	15.	This is contra to Accounts Receivable.
(CA)	16.	This account arises because of the use of the lower of cost or market rule. It is contra to Inventory.
(CA)	17.	This is contra to Inventory; it is another title for item 16.
(CL)	18.	This account reflects amounts included in Accounts Payable that will not be paid because of purchase discounts to be taken.
(CA)	19.	This account reflects amounts included in Accounts Receivable that will not be collected because of sales discounts allowed.
(CA)	20.	This is another title for Allowance for Doubtful Accounts.
RE	21.	This is a restriction on retained earnings (portion of total retained earnings).
RE	22.	This is a restriction on retained earnings (portion of total retained earnings).
RE	23.	This is a restriction on retained earnings (portion of total retained earnings).
RE	24.	This is a restriction on retained earnings (portion of total retained earnings).
CL	25.	When the item exists, it is usually listed as the first item under current liabilities. It is a negative cash balance; an overdrawn bank account.
CL	26.	The interest is usually payable semi annually.
CA	27.	The interest is usually received semi annually.
INV	28.	A fund can be comprised of restricted cash or securities.
PPE	29.	This is a long-lived tangible asset used in operations.
CA	30.	This is unrestricted cash.
INV	31.	This cash is restricted for a long-term purpose.
INV or OA	32.	The assumption is that the entity will continue the insurance coverage rather than take the cash surrender value.
DEP: CA or INV	33.	Some CDs are for 90 days, 180 days, 30 months, or 60 months.
CS	34.	This reflects the par or stated value of issued shares.
PPE	35.	This is one of two exceptions to the general guidelines for items to be included in the PPE classification.
CA	36.	A creditor has been overpaid or items purchased on account have been returned for credit after payment of account has been made.
LTL	37.	This answer assumes that the Bond Sinking Fund is classified under long-term investments.
CL	38.	This item will require current assets to settle the debt.
CL	39.	"Current portion" refers to the portion that is coming due within a year of the balance sheet date.
CL	40.	Some accountants list this item first in the list of current liabilities, others list it last.
CL	41.	This arises when customers overpay or return goods after full payment is made.
DEP: CL or LTL	42.	A deposit may be an advance payment for goods and services or a security deposit.
DEP: CA or OA	43.	Deferred tax consequences of transactions reflected in the financial statements.
DEP: CL or LTL	44.	Deferred tax consequences of transactions reflected in the financial statements.

Solution		Explanation and/or Comment
CA	45.	This is another title for item 110, Prepaid Property Taxes.
CA	46.	This is another title for items 94, 95, and 108.
DEP: CL or LTL	47.	This is another title for item 126, Unearned Rental Income.
DEP: CL or LTL	48.	Some subscriptions are for one year, others are for two or more years. This is another title for item 128, Unearned Subscription Revenue.
DEP: CL or LTL	49.	A service contract often covers two or more years; revenue has been collected but not earned.
PPE	50.	This is the second of two exceptions to the general guidelines for items to be included in the PPE classification.
IS	51.	This refers to the depreciation charges for the current period.
(LTL)	52.	In the rare instance where the bonds payable are classified as current, the discount would be current also.
(CS)	53.	It is rare that common stock is sold below par.
DEP: (CL) or (LTL)	54.	A discount occurs when the effective rate exceeds the stated rate.
DEP: (CA) or (INV)	55.	A discount results when the note is issued below par.
CA	56.	A dishonored note receivable is one that has reached its maturity date and remains uncollected.
CL	57.	A dividend is usually paid approximately three to four weeks after it is declared.
CS	58.	This is a bad title for Stock Dividend Distributable. This is the same as items 117 and 118.
IS	59.	This is another title for Rent Revenue.
LTL	60.	This item will be explained in Chapter 20.
CL	61.	This is another title for Income Tax Payable.
DEP: CL or LTL	62.	Some warranties are for more than one year.
DEP: CL or LTL	63.	Premiums in this context are similar to prizes.
CA	64.	This item is similar to a prepaid expense; these supplies will be part of factory overhead (hence, work in process inventory) when used.
CA	65.	This is one of three inventory accounts for a manufacturer.
PPE	66.	These are long-lived tangible assets used in operations.
IS	67.	This is classified as Other Gains on the income statement.
IS	68.	These are Operating Expenses on the income statement.
ITG	69.	This is referred to as an unidentifiable intangible asset with an indefinite life. The only time it appears on the balance sheet at a material dollar amount is when a company has purchased the goodwill in a business acquisition.
CL	70.	This is due and will require the use of current assets within a year.
CA	71.	This item will be collected normally within 8 to 10 weeks.
CL	72.	This is payable usually within a few days.
CL	73.	This is another title for item 4 (item 73 is the preferable title).
CA	74.	Interest is normally received monthly, semiannually or annually.
IS	75.	Interest revenue is an Other Revenue item on the income statement.
CA	76.	This answer assumes there is no reason to hold the stock for a long-term purpose.
DEP: CA or INV	77.	The maturity date and management's intention will dictate the classification.
INV	78.	The fact that the investee is a subsidiary means there is an intention to hold the investee's stock for a long-term purpose.
PPE	79.	Unless otherwise indicated, this refers to land used in operations.
INV	80.	This land is not used in operations so it is PPE or possibly OA.
PPE	81.	This land is currently being used in operations.

<u>Solution</u>		<u>Explanation and/or Comment</u>
PPE	82.	Some textbooks suggest classifying Leasehold Improvements as intangible assets. Most real life companies report them as PPE.
ITG	83.	These are costs incurred in obtaining a lease.
IS	84.	Classified as an Other Expense or Loss.
PPE	85.	These are used in operations.
OA	86.	These are not being used in operations.
CA or INV	87.	This is a title often used to refer to short-term investments; it can also refer to securities (stocks and/or bonds of other entities) held for long-term purposes.
CA	88.	This is another title for Inventory for a retailer.
LTL	89.	The portion of this balance due within the next year will be reclassified and reported as a current liability.
DEP: CL or LTL	90.	These may be short-term or long-term.
DEP: CL or LTL	91.	These may be short-term or long-term.
DEP: CA or INV	92.	The maturity date will dictate if it is current or not.
DEP: CA or INV	93.	Separate disclosure must be made of related party transactions.
CA	94.	This is another title for items 46, 95, and 108.
CA	95.	This is another title for items 46, 94, and 108.
IS	96.	This is an operating expense on the income statement.
IS	97.	This is another title for Office Supplies Expense.
ITG	98.	These offer long-term rights.
CA	99.	This is one component of Cash.
PPE	100.	These are long lived tangible assets used in operations.
DEP: CA or OA	101.	Property previously used in operations and now held for sale is a current asset if the sale is expected to take place within a year; otherwise it is an Other Asset.
INV	102.	This is cash or other assets restricted for a long-term purpose.
LTL	103.	This is an adjunct type valuation account. If the related bonds payable are classified as a current liability, this valuation account will also be in current liabilities.
APC	104.	This is an adjunct type valuation account.
CA	105.	This is a prepaid expense.
CA	106.	This is another title for items 107 and 129.
CA	107.	This is another title for items 106 and 129.
CA	108.	This is another title for items 46, 94, and 95.
CA	109.	This is a prepaid expense.
CA	110.	This is another title for item 45.
IS	111.	This is another title for Uncollectible Accounts Expense or Bad Debt Expense.
IS	112.	This is another title for Income Tax expense.
IS	113.	This is classified as Other Revenue or Gains.
CL	114.	This is another title for Accrued Salaries or Accrued Salaries Payable. Salaries Payable is the preferred title.
IS	115.	This is contra to Sales Revenue.
IS	116.	A control account is an account in the general ledger for which the details appear in a subsidiary ledger.
CS	117.	This is another title for items 58 and 118. The title in item 117 is the preferred title.
CS	118.	This is another title for items 58 and 117. This is a misleading title because the word "payable" suggests a liability, which a stock dividend is not.

Solution		Explanation and/or Comment
CA	119.	This answer assumes the supplies are on hand rather than used.
IS	120.	This item refers to Store Supplies Expense.
PPE	121.	These are used in operations and have a life longer than a year.
IS	122.	The service life is so short that the benefits yielded do not extend beyond one year. Therefore, the expenditure is not capitalized.
(CS + APC + RE)	123.	When the cost method is used to account for treasury stock, the treasury stock is shown contra to the total of all other stockholder equity items.
OA	124.	This is usually called Bond Issue Costs.
(LTL)	125.	This is another title for item 52. In the rare instance where the bonds payable are classified as a current liability, the discount would be contra current liability.
DEP: CL or LTL	126.	This is another title for item 47.
DEP: CL or LTL	127.	Revenue has been received, but not earned; hence, an obligation exists to provide a service or good or a refund.
DEP: CL or LTL	128.	This is another title for item 48.
CA	129.	This is another title for items 105 and 107.
CL	130.	This is an accrued liability.
CL	131.	This is another title for Accounts Payable when a voucher system is in use.
CA	132.	This is an inventory account for a manufacturer.

Approach: For each balance sheet classification, write down a definition or description of what is to be reported in that classification. Refer to those notes as you go down the list of items to be classified. Your notes should contain the guidelines summarized in **Illustration 5-1**.

EXERCISE 5-2

Purpose: (L.O. 3) This exercise will enable you to practice identifying errors and other deficiencies in a balance sheet.

Lee Cockerell Company has decided to expand its operations. The bookkeeper recently completed the balance sheet presented below to submit to the bank in order to obtain additional funds for expansion.

Lee Cockerell Company
BALANCE SHEET
For the Year Ended 2014

Current assets	
Cash (net of bank overdraft of $15,000)	$ 180,000
Accounts receivable (net)	380,000
Inventories, at lower of FIFO cost or market	435,000
Marketable securities—at cost (fair value $110,000)	90,000
Property, plant, and equipment	
Building (net)	590,000
Office equipment (net)	180,000
Land held for future use	75,000
Intangible assets	
Franchise	90,000
Cash surrender value of life insurance	80,000
Prepaid insurance	6,000
Current liabilities	
Salaries payable	18,000
Accounts payable	85,000
Note payable, due June 30, 2016	100,000
Pension obligation	92,000
Taxes payable	40,000
Note payable, due October 1, 2015	25,000
Discount on bonds payable	50,000
Long-term liabilities	
Bonds payable, 8%, due May 1, 2018	400,000
Stockholders' equity	
Common stock, $1 par, authorized 500,000 shares,	
issued 310,000 shares	310,000
Additional paid-in capital	279,000
Retained earnings	?

Instructions

Prepare a revised balance sheet in good form. Correct any errors and weaknesses you find in the presentation above. Assume that the accumulated depreciation balance for the building is $150,000 and for the office equipment, $105,000. Marketable securities are classified as trading securities. The allowance for doubtful accounts has a balance of $20,000. The pension obligation is considered to be a long-term liability. You must solve for the balance of Retained Earnings.

Solution to Exercise 5-2

Lee Cockerell Company
BALANCE SHEET
December 31, 2014

Assets

Current Assets

Cash			$ 195,000
Trading securities, at fair value (cost is $90,000)			110,000
Accounts receivable		$ 400,000	
Less allowance for doubtful accounts		20,000	380,000
Inventories, at lower of FIFO cost or market			435,000
Prepaid insurance			6,000
Total current assets			1,126,000

Long-term Investments

Land held for future use		75,000	
Cash surrender value of life insurance		80,000	
Total long-term investments			155,000

Property, Plant, and Equipment

Building	$ 740,000		
Less accumulated depreciation—building	150,000	590,000	
Office equipment	285,000		
Less accumulated depreciation—office equipment	105,000	180,000	
Total property, plant, and equipment			770,000

Intangible Assets

Franchise			90,000
Total assets			$ 2,141,000

Liabilities and Stockholders' Equity

Current Liabilities

Bank overdraft			$ 15,000
Note payable, due October 1, 2015			25,000
Accounts payable			85,000
Taxes payable			40,000
Salaries payable			18,000
Total current liabilities			183,000

Long-term Liabilities

Note payable, due June 30, 2016		$ 100,000	
8% Bonds payable, due May 1, 2018	$ 400,000		
Less discount on bonds payable	50,000	350,000	
Pension obligation		92,000	
Total long-term liabilities			542,000
Total liabilities			725,000

Stockholders' equity

Paid-in capital

Common stock, $1 par, authorized 500,000 shares, issued and outstanding 310,000 shares	310,000		
Additional paid-in capital	279,000	589,000	
Retained earnings		827,000	
Total stockholders' equity			1,416,000
Total liabilities and stockholders' equity			$ 2,141,000

Explanation:

1. A bank overdraft in one bank account should **not** be reflected as an offset to positive cash items (such as a positive balance in another account). A bank overdraft must be reported as a current liability. (The one exception to this rule is as follows: if an account with a positive balance exists in the same bank as the overdraft, the overdraft can be reflected as an offset to the extent of that positive balance.)

2. Marketable securities in a trading portfolio are to be reported on the balance sheet at their fair value. The difference between cost and fair value has been included as an element of income and is therefore reflected in the balance of Retained Earnings at the balance sheet date. (This topic will be more fully explained in **Chapter 17**.)

3. Land held for future use is **not** to be classified in the property, plant, and equipment section because the land is not currently being used in operations.

4. Cash surrender value of life insurance is an intangible item in a legal sense (because it lacks physical substance), but it is classified as a long-term investment for accounting purposes.

5. Prepaid expenses such as prepaid insurance represent prepayments that relate to benefits that are expected to be consumed within the year that follows the balance sheet date. Hence, they are current assets.

6. A pension obligation is generally **not** expected to become due in the near future and, therefore, is not expected to require the use of current assets within a year of the balance sheet date. Hence, it is a long-term liability.

7. Discount on Bonds Payable is a contra type valuation account. A valuation account should always be reported with the account to which it relates.

8. Bonds payable are always assumed to be a long-term liability unless the facts make them appear to meet the definition for a current liability.

9. The balance of retained earnings for this exercise can be derived by determining the amount needed to cause total liabilities and stockholders' equity to equal total assets. That is, it is a "plug" figure of $827,000 in this exercise.

EXERCISE 5-3

Purpose: (L.O. 3) This exercise will enable you to practice identifying errors and other deficiencies in a balance sheet.

Presented below is a balance sheet for the Gabby Corporation.

Gabby Corporation
BALANCE SHEET
December 31, 2014

Current assets	$ 520,000	Current liabilities	$ 365,000
Investments	700,000	Long-term liabilities	920,000
Property, plant, & equipment	2,185,000	Stockholders' equity	2,690,000
Intangible assets	570,000		
	$ 3,975,000		$ 3,975,000

The following information is available:

1.   The current asset section includes: cash $120,000, accounts receivable $190,000 less $10,000 for allowance for doubtful accounts, inventories $230,000, and unearned revenue $10,000 (credit balance). Inventories are stated at their replacement cost; original cost on a FIFO basis is $200,000.

2.   The investments section includes the cash surrender value of a life insurance contract $60,000; investments in common stock, short-term $70,000 and long-term $230,000; bond sinking fund $220,000; and land upon which a new plant is being constructed $120,000. Investments are all classified as available for sale and have fair values equal to their cost.

3.   Property, plant, and equipment includes buildings $1,600,000 less accumulated depreciation $375,000; equipment $400,000 less accumulated depreciation $240,000; land $500,000; and land held for future use $300,000. The building is stated at a recent appraisal value of $1,600,000; original cost was $1,250,000.

4.   Intangible assets include a franchise $140,000, goodwill $80,000 (from the acquisition of another business), discount on bonds payable $30,000, and construction in process $320,000 (a new plant is under construction and will be ready for operations within nine months).

5.   Current liabilities include accounts payable $80,000, notes payable—short-term $110,000, notes payable—long-term $150,000, and salaries payable $25,000. It does not include any amount for loss contingencies. The company's attorney states that it is probable the company will have to pay $60,000 in 2015 due to litigation pending at the balance sheet date.

6.   Long-term liabilities are composed of 10% bonds payable (due June 1, 2020) $800,000 and pension obligation $120,000.

7.   Stockholders' equity includes preferred stock, no par or stated value, 200,000 shares authorized with 70,000 shares issued for $450,000; and common stock, $2 par value, 300,000 shares authorized with 100,000 shares issued at an average price of $10. In addition, the corporation has retained earnings of $1,240,000.

Instructions
Prepare a corrected balance sheet in good form.

Solution to Exercise 5-3

Gabby Corporation
BALANCE SHEET
December 31, 2014

Assets

Current Assets			
Cash			$ 120,000
Available-for-sale securities—at fair value			70,000
Accounts receivable		$ 190,000	
Less allowance for doubtful accounts		10,000	180,000
Inventories, at lower of FIFO cost or market			200,000
Total current assets			570,000
Investments			
Available-for-sale securities—at fair value		230,000	
Bond sinking fund		220,000	
Cash surrender value of life insurance		60,000	
Land held for future use		300,000	
Total long-term investments			810,000
Property, Plant, and Equipment			
Land		620,000	
Buildings	$ 1,250,000		
Less accumulated depreciation—building	375,000	875,000	
Construction in process		320,000	
Equipment	400,000		
Less accumulated depreciation—equip.	240,000	160,000	
Total property, plant, and equipment			1,975,000
Intangible Assets			
Franchise		140,000	
Goodwill		80,000	
Total intangible assets			220,000
Total assets			$ 3,575,000

Gabby Corporation
BALANCE SHEET
December 31, 2014
(Continued)

Liabilities and Stockholders' Equity

Current Liabilities
Notes payable			$ 110,000
Accounts payable			80,000
Estimated litigation obligation			60,000
Salaries payable			25,000
Unearned revenue			10,000
Total current liabilities			285,000

Long-term Liabilities
Notes payable		$ 150,000	
10% bonds payable, due June 1, 2022	$ 800,000		
Less discount on bonds payable	30,000	770,000	
Pension obligation		120,000	
Total long-term liabilities			1,040,000
Total liabilities			1,325,000

Stockholders' Equity
Paid-in capital
Preferred stock, no par value; 200,000 shares authorized, 70,000 issued and outstanding	450,000		
Common stock, $2 par value; 300,000 shares authorized, 100,000 issued and outstanding	200,000		
Paid-in capital in excess of par on common stock	800,000*	1,450,000	
Retained earnings		800,000**	
Total stockholders' equity			2,250,000
Total Liabilities and Stockholders' Equity			$ 3,575,000

*100,000 shares x ($10 - $2) = $800,000.

**The corrected balance for the Retained Earnings account can be reconciled with the before corrected amount as follows:

Retained Earnings, before corrections	$1,240,000
Overstatement of inventory	(30,000)
Overstatement of buildings	(350,000)
Understatement of litigation liability	(60,000)
Corrected Retained Earnings balance	$ 800,000

The errors that Gabby had on the balance sheet affected some income statement accounts (which were closed to Retained Earnings) or directly affected the Retained Earnings account.

TIP: The $620,000 reported amount for land is comprised of land $500,000 plus land upon which a new plant is being constructed $120,000.

ILLUSTRATION 5-2
OPERATING, INVESTING, AND FINANCING ACTIVITIES (L.O. 5)

DEFINITIONS:

Operating Activities: include all transactions and other events that are not defined as investing or financing activities. Operating activities generally involve producing and delivering goods and providing services. Cash flows from operating activities are generally the cash effects of transactions and other events that enter into the determination of net income.

Investing Activities: include (a) making and collecting loans; (b) acquiring and disposing of debt and equity instruments of other entities; and (c) acquiring and disposing of property, plant, and equipment and other productive assets.

Financing Activities: include (a) obtaining resources from owners and providing them with a return on and a return of their investment; and (b) borrowing money and repaying the amounts borrowed, or otherwise settling the obligation.

EXAMPLES:

Operating Activities:
   Cash inflows:
      From sales of goods or services (includes cash sales and collections on account).
      From returns on loans (interest received) and on equity securities (dividends received).
      From other transactions, such as: Amounts received to settle lawsuits, and refunds
         from suppliers.
   Cash outflows:
      To suppliers for inventory and other goods and services (includes cash purchases
         and payments on account).
      To employees for services.
      To government for taxes.
      To lenders for interest.
      To others for items such as: Payments to settle lawsuits, refunds to customers, and
         contributions to charities.
Investing Activities:
   Cash inflows:
      From sale of property, plant, and equipment.
      From sale of debt or equity securities of other entities.
      From collection of principal on loans to other entities.
   Cash outflows:
      To purchase property, plant, and equipment.[a]
      To purchase debt or equity securities of other entities.
      To make loans to other entities.

ILLUSTRATION 5-2 (Continued)

EXAMPLES:

Financing Activities:
   Cash inflows:
      From sale of equity securities (company's own stock).
      From issuance of debt instruments (bonds and notes).
   Cash outflows:
      To pay dividends to stockholders.
      To reacquire capital stock.
      To pay debt (both short-term and long-term) other than accounts payable.

[a]The cash outflows included in this category are payments at the time of purchase or soon before or after purchase to acquire property, plant, and equipment and other productive assets. Generally, only advance payments, the down payment, or other amounts paid at the time of purchase or soon before or after purchase of property, plant, and equipment and other productive assets are investing cash outflows. **Incurring directly related debt to the seller is a financing transaction and subsequent payments of principal on that debt thus are financing cash outflows.**

TIP: Cash inflows and cash outflows from operating activities are usually netted together for presentation purposes. The net cash flow provided (used) by operating activities is usually determined by taking the net income (or net loss) figure and adjusting it for the amounts necessary to reconcile the accrual basis net income to a cash basis.

EXERCISE 5-4

Purpose: (L.O. 5) The exercise enables you to practice identifying investing and financing activities.

Instructions

Place the appropriate code in the blanks to identify each of the following transactions as giving rise to an:

Code

II	inflow of cash due to an investing activity, or
IO	outflow of cash due to an investing activity, or
FI	inflow of cash due to a financing activity, or
FO	outflow of cash due to a financing activity.

_____ 1. Sell common stock to new stockholders.

_____ 2. Purchase treasury stock.

_____ 3. Borrow money from bank by issuance of short-term note.

_____ 4. Repay money borrowed from bank.

_____ 5. Purchase bonds as an investment.

_____ 6. Sell investment in real estate.

_____ 7. Loan money to an affiliate.

_____ 8. Collect on loan to affiliate.

_____ 9. Buy equipment.

_____ 10. Sell a plant asset.

_____ 11. Pay cash dividends to stockholders.

Solution to Exercise 5-4

1.	FI	4.	FO	7.	IO	10.	II
2.	FO	5.	IO	8.	II	11.	FO
3.	FI	6.	II	9.	IO		

Approach:

1.   Reconstruct journal entries for the transactions. Examine each entry to identify if there is an inflow of cash (debit to Cash) or an outflow of cash (credit to Cash).

2.   Write down the definitions for investing activities and financing activities (see below). Analyze each transaction to see if it fits one of these definitions.

   a)   **Investing activities**—include (1) making and collecting loans, (2) acquiring and disposing of investments in debt and equity instruments, and (3) acquiring and disposing of property, plant, and equipment and other productive assets.

b)   **Financing activities**—include (1) obtaining capital from owners and providing them with a return on and a return of their investment, and (2) borrowing money from creditors and repaying the amounts borrowed.

3.   Assume purchases and sales of items are for cash, unless otherwise indicated.

TIP: The journal entry to record a transaction that is an investing activity which results in a cash flow will involve: (1) Cash and (2) an asset account other than Cash, such as Investments (short-term or long-term), Land, Building, Equipment, Patent, Franchise, etc.

TIP: The journal entry to record a transaction that is a financing activity which results in a cash flow will involve: (1) Cash and (2) a liability account or an owners' equity account, such as Bonds Payable, Note Payable, Dividends Payable, Common Stock, Additional Paid-in Capital, Treasury Stock, etc.

EXERCISE 5-5

Purpose: (L.O. 6) This exercise will enable you to practice reconciling net income with net cash provided by operating activities.

The following data relate to the L. Heckenmueller Co. for 2014.

Net income	$ 75,000
Increase in accounts receivable	7,000
Decrease in prepaid expenses	3,200
Increase in accounts payable	5,000
Decrease in taxes payable	900
Gain on sale of investment	1,700
Depreciation	3,500
Loss on sale of equipment	600

Instructions
Compute the net cash provided by operating activities for 2014.

TIP: Refer to **Illustration 23-2** for guidance in reconciling net income (net loss) with net cash provided (used) by operating activities.

Solution to Exercise 5-5

Net income	$ 75,000
Increase in accounts receivable	(7,000)
Decrease in prepaid expenses	3,200
Increase in accounts payable	5,000
Decrease in taxes payable	(900)
Gain on sale of investment	(1,700)
Depreciation	3,500
Loss on sale of equipment	600
Net cash provided by operating activities	$ 77,700

Explanation:

1. Net income is a summary of all revenues earned, all expenses incurred, and all gains and losses recognized for a period. Most revenues earned during the year result in a cash inflow during the same period but there may be some cash and/or revenue flows that do not correspond. Most expenses incurred during the year result in a cash outflow during the same period but there may be some cash and/or expense flows that do not correspond.

2. An increase in accounts receivable indicates that revenues earned exceed cash collected from customers and, therefore, net income exceeds net cash provided by operating activities.

3. A decrease in prepaid expenses indicates that expenses incurred exceed cash paid and, therefore, net income is less than net cash provided by operating activities.

4. An increase in accounts payable indicates that expenses incurred exceed cash paid and, therefore, net income is less than net cash provided by operating activities.

5. A decrease in taxes payable indicates expenses incurred are less than the cash paid, and, therefore, net income is greater than net cash provided by operating activities.

6. When an investment is sold, the entire proceeds are to be displayed as an investing activity on the statement of cash flows. The gain included in net income must, therefore, be deducted from net income to arrive at the net cash provided by operating activities. If this adjustment was not made, there would be double counting for the gain amount. For example: An investment with a carrying value of $4,000 is sold for $7,000. The entire $7,000 proceeds is an investing inflow; the $7,000 includes the gain of $3,000 and a recovery of the investment's $4,000 carrying value; the $3,000 gain will be deducted from net income to arrive at the net cash from operating activities figure.

7. Depreciation is a noncash charge (debit) against income. It must be added to net income to arrive at the amount of net cash provided by operating activities.

8. A loss on the sale of equipment does not cause a cash outlay so it is added back to net income to arrive at the amount of net cash provided by operating activities. The cash proceeds from the sale of equipment are shown as a cash inflow from an investing activity.

EXERCISE 5-6

Purpose: (L.O. 6) This exercise will give you practice in preparing a statement of cash flows.

The comparative balance sheets of Spencer Corporation at the beginning and end of year 2014 appear below.

Spencer Corporation
Balance Sheets

	Dec. 31 2014	Dec. 31 2013	Inc./Dec.
ASSETS			
Cash	$10,500	$7,100	Inc. 3,400
Accounts receivable	18,000	9,400	Inc. 8,600
Prepaid expenses	2,700	3,200	Dec. 500
Investments	-0-	11,300	Dec. 11,300
Equipment	56,000	42,000	Inc. 14,000
Less: Accumulated depreciation	(10,000)	(5,000)	Inc. 5,000
Total	$77,200	$68,000	Inc. 9,200
LIABILITIES AND			
STOCKHOLDERS' EQUITY			
Accounts payable	$ 4,900	$ 4,500	Inc. 400
Unearned revenue	1,700	6,000	Dec. 4,300
Common stock	14,000	10,000	Inc. 4,000
Retained earnings	56,600	47,500	Inc. 9,100
Total	$77,200	$68,000	Inc. 9,200

During the year 2014, Spencer purchased equipment for $14,000 cash, declared and paid cash dividends of $11,200, sold investments for $19,000, and reported net income of $20,300.

Instructions
Prepare a statement of cash flows for Spencer Corporation for the year ending December 31, 2014.

TIP: The statement of cash flows summarizes all of the transactions occurring during a period that have an impact on the cash balance. The activity format is used whereby cash inflows and cash outflows are summarized by the three categories: operating, investing and financing.

TIP: Notice the increase (Inc.) in the Accumulated Depreciation account causes a **decrease** in the total assets figure.

Solution to Exercise 5-6

Spencer Corporation
Statement of Cash Flows
For the Year Ending December 31, 2014

Cash flows from operating activities:		
Net income		$20,300
Adjustments to reconcile net income		
to net cash provided by operating activities:		
Increase in accounts receivable	($8,600)	
Decrease in prepaid expenses	500	
Increase in accounts payable	400	
Decrease in unearned revenue	(4,300)	
Depreciation expense	5,000	
Gain on sale of investments	(7,700)	(14,700)
Net cash provided by operating activities		5,600
Cash flows from investing activities:		
Sale of investments	$19,000	
Purchase of equipment	(14,000)	
Net cash provided by investing activities		5,000
Cash flows from financing activities:		
Issuance of common stock	$4,000	
Payment of cash dividends	(11,200)	
Net cash used by financing activities		(7,200)
Net increase in cash		3,400
Cash at beginning of the year		7,100
Cash at end of the year		$10,500

Approach and Explanation: The net change in cash for the year can easily be determined by taking the difference between the cash balance at the end of the year ($10,500) and the cash balance at the beginning of the year ($7,100) which yields a net increase of $3,400. The reasons for that net increase of $3,400 can be found by analyzing all of the transactions that caused changes in all of the balance sheet accounts other than Cash.

The changes in Accounts Receivable, Prepaid Expenses, Accounts Payable and Unearned Revenues are all due to accruals and deferrals which help to reconcile the net income figure with the amount of net cash provided (used) by operating activities. The changes in Investments and Equipment are due to transactions which constitute investing activities. The changes in Accumulated Depreciation are usually due to the recording of depreciation expense for the current period and disposals of plant assets. The changes in nontrade liability accounts (such as Mortgage Payable, Bonds Payable, Bank Note Payable) and most changes in stockholders' equity accounts are due to transactions which constitute financing activities.

An increase of $8,600 in Accounts Receivable indicates that sales revenue (on an accrual basis) exceeded cash collections from customers by $8,600. That in turn causes net income to exceed net cash provided by operating activities, so $8,600 is deducted from net income in reconciling net income to a cash basis figure. A decrease of $500 in Prepaid Expenses indicates that expenses incurred on an accrual basis exceeded the cash payments for expenses by $500 which in turn caused net income to be less than net cash provided by operating activities. (Remember that expenses are a negative component of net income so as expenses go up, net income goes down.) An increase in Accounts Payable of $400 results from an excess of expenses incurred over cash payments for expenses which causes net income to be less than net cash from operations.

Thus, both a decrease in Prepaid Expenses of $500 and an increase in Accounts Payable of $400 are added to net income to compute a cash basis income amount. A decrease in Unearned Revenue of $4,300 reflects an excess of revenue earned over cash collections from customers this period; this means net income exceeds net cash provided by operations. Thus, the $4,300 decrease in Unearned Revenue is deducted from net income in reconciling net income to net cash provided by operating activities.

It is helpful to reconstruct the journal entry for each transaction that caused a change in the remaining balance sheet accounts. You will be able to see the impact on Cash. Assume the most common transaction caused a change in a particular account. The entries and analyses are as follows:

Cash	19,000	
Investments		11,300
Gain on Sale of Investments............................		7,700
(Sale of investments)		

There was an inflow of cash due to an investing activity—sale of investments—of $19,000. The $19,000 cash inflow represents a recovery of book value of the investment of $11,300 and a gain of $7,700. The entire $19,000 cash inflow is to be reported on the statement of cash flows as an investing activity. The gain is included in net income and net income is the starting point for determining the net cash provided by operating activities. Hence, the $7,700 gain must be deducted in determining the net cash provided by operations so as not to "double count" the $7,700 on the statement of cash flows.

Equipment..	14,000	
Cash		14,000
(Purchase of equipment)		

There was an outflow of cash due to an investing activity—purchase of property, plant, and equipment.

Depreciation Expense..	5,000	
Accumulated Depreciation..............................		5,000
(Recording of depreciation for current period)		

There was no impact on cash. There was an expense recorded but there was no cash outflow. Therefore, the amount of depreciation expense is added to net income in order to reconcile net income to net cash provided by operating activities.

Cash	4,000	
Common Stock		4,000
(Sale of common stock)		

There was an inflow of cash due to a financing activity—issuance of common stock (obtaining resources from owners).

Retained Earnings	11,200	
Cash		11,200
(Declaration and payment of cash dividends)		

There was an outflow of cash due a financing activity—payment of dividends (giving owners a return on their investment).

Income Summary	20,300	
Retained Earnings		20,300
(Net income amount is closed to Retained Earnings)		

The balance of the Income Summary account before closing is a summarized figure reflecting all revenues and all expenses; it is a summary of all transactions dealing with operations for the period. Most revenues increase cash and most expenses decrease cash so we use net income (a summary of all revenues and all expenses) as our starting point in computing cash provided by operating activities. The net income figure is then "adjusted" for the following items:
1. revenue transactions that did not bring in cash this period.
2. expense transactions that did not require a cash outlay this period.
3. revenue items of another period that produced a cash inflow this period.
4. expense items of another period that produced a cash outflow this period.

The result is the amount of net cash provided (used) by operating activities (a cash basis income figure).

> **TIP:** In **Chapter 3,** we dealt extensively with the differences between the cash basis of accounting and the accrual basis of accounting because cash data gets recorded and the financial statements have to reflect accrual basis data: thus, the need for adjusting entries. A review of **Illustration 3-2** along with **Exercise 3-9, Exercise 3-10** and **Exercise 3-11** will likely help you here in your study of the statement of cash flows.

*ILLUSTRATION 5-3
A SUMMARY OF FINANCIAL RATIOS (L.O. 10)

Ratio	Formula for Computation	Purpose or Use
I. Liquidity		
1. Current ratio	Current assets / Current liabilities	Measures short-term debt-paying ability.
2. Quick or acid-test ratio	Cash, marketable securities, and receivables (net) / Current liabilities	Measures immediate short-term liquidity.
3. Current cash debt ratio	Net cash provided by operating activities / Average current liabilities	Measures the company's ability to pay off its current liabilities out of its operations for a given year.
II. Activity		
4. Receivable turnover	Net sales / Average trade receivables (net)	Measures liquidity of receivables.
5. Inventory turnover	Cost of goods sold / Average inventory	Measures liquidity of inventory.
6. Asset turnover	Net sales / Average total assets	Measures how efficiently assets are used to generate sales.
III. Profitability		
7. Profit margin on sales	Net income / Net sales	Measures net income generated by each dollar of sales.
8. Rate of return on assets	Net income / Average total assets	Measures overall profitability of assets.
9. Rate of return on common stock equity	Net income minus preferred dividends / Average common stockholders' equity	Measures profitability of owners' investment.

ILLUSTRATION 5-3 (Continued)

Ratio	Formula for Computation	Purpose or Use
10. Earnings per share	$\dfrac{\text{Net income minus preferred dividends}}{\text{Weighted shares outstanding}}$	Measures net income earned on each share of common stock.
11. Price earnings ratio	$\dfrac{\text{Market price of stock}}{\text{Earnings per share}}$	Measures the ratio of the market price per share to earnings per share.
12. Payout ratio	$\dfrac{\text{Cash dividends}}{\text{Net income}}$	Measures percentage of earnings distributed in the form of cash dividends.
IV. Coverage 13. Debt to total assets	$\dfrac{\text{Total debt}}{\text{Total assets}}$	Measures the percentage of total assets provided by creditors.
14. Times interest earned	$\dfrac{\text{Income before interest charges and taxes}}{\text{Interest charges}}$	Measures ability to meet interest payments as they come due.
15. Cash debt coverage ratio	$\dfrac{\text{Net cash provided by operating activities}}{\text{Average total liabilities}}$	Measures a company's ability to repay its total liabilities in a given year out of its operations.
16. Book value per share	$\dfrac{\text{Common stockholders' equity}}{\text{Outstanding shares}}$	Measures the amount each share of common stock would receive if the company were liquidated at the amounts reported on the balance sheet.
17. Free cash flow	Net cash provided by operating activities minus Capital expenditures minus Dividends	Measures the amount of discretionary cash flow.

TIP: Throughout the remainder of the textbook, ratios are provided to help understand and interpret the information provided. Above, we provide you with the ratios that will be used throughout the text. You should find the chart helpful as you examine these ratios in more detail in the following chapters.

ANALYSIS OF MULTIPLE-CHOICE TYPE QUESTIONS

QUESTION

1. (L.O. 1) The amount of time that is expected to elapse until an asset is realized or otherwise converted into cash is referred to as:
   a. solvency.
   b. financial flexibility.
   c. liquidity.
   d. exchangeability.

Explanation: Liquidity describes the amount of time that is expected to elapse until an asset is realized or otherwise converted into cash or until a liability has to be paid; liquidity refers to the "nearness to cash" of assets and liabilities. Current assets are listed in the order of liquidity (with the most liquid items first) on a balance sheet. Solvency refers to the ability of an enterprise to pay its debts as they mature. Liquidity and solvency affect an entity's financial flexibility which measures the ability of an enterprise to take effective actions to alter the amounts and timing of cash flows so it can respond and adapt to financial adversity and unexpected needs and opportunities. (Solution = c.)

QUESTION

2. (L.O. 2) The Heather Miller Company has the following obligations at December 31, 2014:

I.	Accounts payable	$ 72,000
II.	Taxes payable	60,000
III.	Notes payable issued November 1, 2014, due October 31, 2015	80,000
IV.	Bonds payable issued December 1, 2005, due November 30, 2015 (to be paid by use of a sinking fund)	100,000

The amount that should be reported for total current liabilities at December 31, 2014 is:
   a. $312,000.
   b. $212,000.
   c. $132,000.
   d. $72,000.

Approach and Explanation: Write down the definition (or key phrases therein) for a current liability. (A **current liability** is an obligation which is coming due within a year of the balance sheet date and is expected to require the use of current assets or the incurrence of another current liability to liquidate it.) Analyze each of the obligations listed to see if it meets the criteria for being classified as current.

Accounts payable and taxes payable will both be due shortly after the balance sheet date and will require cash to liquidate the debts. The notes payable are due within a year of the balance sheet date and there is no evidence to indicate that assets other than current assets will be used for settlement; thus, the notes payable are a current liability. The bonds payable are coming due within a year, but they will **not** require the use of current assets to liquidate the debt because a sinking fund (restricted cash or securities classified as a long-term investment) is to be used to extinguish that debt: $72,000 + $60,000 + $80,000 = $212,000. (Solution = b.)

QUESTION

3. (L.O. 2) Land held for a future plant site should be classified in the section for:
   a. current assets.
   b. long-term investments.
   c. property, plant, and equipment.
   d. intangible assets.

Approach and Explanation: Quickly review in your mind the descriptions of what goes in each of the asset classifications. Then read each answer selection and respond **True** or **False** if the selection answers the question. The land is not being used in operations, so it doesn't belong in property, plant, and equipment. It is not lacking physical existence, so it can't be an intangible asset. The land is not expected to be converted to cash or sold or consumed within the next year, so it is not a current asset. The land properly belongs in long-term investments. (Solution = b.)

QUESTION

4.   (L.O. 2) Working capital is:
   a.   current assets less current liabilities.
   b.   total assets less total liabilities.
   c.   the same as retained earnings.
   d.   capital which has been reinvested in the business.

Explanation: The excess of total current assets over total current liabilities is referred to as working capital. Working capital represents the net amount of a company's relatively liquid resources. That is, it is the liquid buffer available to meet the financial demands of the operating cycle. (Solution = a.)

QUESTION

5.   (L.O. 2) Treasury stock is classified as a(n):
   a.   current asset.
   b.   long-term investment.
   c.   other asset.
   d.   contra stockholders' equity item.

Explanation: Treasury stock is a company's own stock that has been issued, reacquired by the corporation, but not canceled. The acquisition of treasury stock represents a contraction of owners' equity; thus it is reported as a reduction of stockholders' equity. (Solution = d.)

QUESTION

6.   (L.O. 2) Which of the following is classified as an intangible asset on a balance sheet?
   a.   Long-term receivable.
   b.   Long-term investment in stock of another enterprise.
   c.   Licenses.
   d.   Accounts Receivable.

Explanation: Intangible assets lack physical substance and usually have a high degree of uncertainty concerning their future benefits. Although receivables and investments in stock lack physical existence, they are properly classifiable elsewhere so they are **not** classified for accounting purposes as intangible assets. Accounts receivable are classified as current assets, long-term receivables and long-term investments in stock are classified as long-term investments, and licenses are classified as intangible assets. (Solution = c.)

QUESTION

7.   (L.O. 2) Which of the following should **not** be found in the long-term investment section of the balance sheet?
   a.   Land held for speculation.
   b.   Bond sinking fund.
   c.   Cash surrender value of life insurance.
   d.   Patent.

Explanation: A patent is classified as an intangible asset. Long-term investments, often referred to simply as investments, normally consist of one of four types:

1. Investments in securities, such as bonds, common stock, or long-term notes receivable.
2. Investments in tangible fixed assets not currently used in operations, such as land held for speculation or future plant site.
3. Investments set aside in special funds such as a sinking fund, pension fund, or plant expansion fund. The cash surrender value of life insurance is included here.
4. Investments in nonconsolidated subsidiaries or affiliated companies.

(Solution = d.)

QUESTION
8.   (L.O. 3) Which of the following is a contra account?
   a.   Premium on bonds payable
   b.   Unearned revenue
   c.   Patents
   d.   Accumulated depreciation

Approach and Explanation: After reading the stem and before reading the answer selections, write down the description of the term "contra account". (A **contra account** is a valuation account whose normal balance is opposite of the balance of the account to which it relates.) Then take each answer selection and answer **True** or **False** whether it meets that description. Premium on bonds payable is a valuation account, but it is an adjunct type (its normal balance is the same as the normal balance of the account to which it relates). Unearned Revenue and Patents are not valuation accounts. Accumulated Depreciation is a valuation account for property, plant, and equipment. The normal balance of the Accumulated Depreciation account is a credit and the normal balance of a property, plant, and equipment account is a debit. Hence, Accumulated Depreciation is a contra account. (Solution = d.)

QUESTION
9.   (L.O. 2) The trial balance for Keller Corp. reflected the following account balances at December 31, 2014:

Cash	$33,000
Accounts receivable (net of allowance)	72,000
Trading securities	18,000
Prepaid expenses	6,000
Patent	12,000
Land held for future business site	54,000
Inventory	90,000
Office equipment (fax, copiers, computers)	75,000
Accumulated depreciation on office equipment	45,000

The current assets total at December 31, 2014 is:
   a. $219,000
   b. $231,000
   c. $261,000
   d. $303,000

Approach and Explanation: Take each account and determine its balance sheet classification according to the guidelines in **Illustration 5-1.** Total the items to be classified as current assets. The current assets classification includes cash and items which are expected to be converted to cash or sold or consumed within the next year or operating cycle, whichever is longer. Looking at the list we find the following to be current assets:

Item	Why
$ 33,000 Cash	Cash
$ 72,000 Accounts receivable (net)	To be converted to cash in the next year.
$ 18,000 Trading securities	To be converted to cash in the next year.
$ 6,000 Prepaid expenses	To be consumed in the next year.
$ 90,000 Inventory	To be sold in the next year.
$219,000	

(Solution = a.)

QUESTION
10. (L.O.5) Which of the following should be classified as an inflow of cash in the investing section of a statement of cash flows?
   a. Cash sale of merchandise inventory
   b. Sale of delivery equipment at a loss
   c. Sale of common stock
   d. Issuance of a note payable to a bank

Approach and Explanation: Read the stem and, before reading the answer selections, write down the items that appear in the definition of investing activities. (**Investing activities** include making and collecting loans to others, acquiring and disposing of stocks and bonds of other entities, acquiring and disposing of property, plant, and equipment and other productive assets.) Think of the items included in that definition that would produce a cash inflow (collecting loans, disposing of investments and property, plant, and equipment). Look for the answer selection that fits that analysis. As you analyze each answer selection, indicate what kind of activity it represents. A cash sale of merchandise inventory is an operating activity. The sale of common stock is a financing activity. The issuance of a note payable is a financing activity. A sale of equipment is an investing activity (regardless of whether the sale is at a gain, a loss, or at book value). (Solution = b.)

QUESTION
11. (L.O. 5) An example of a cash flow from an operating activity is:
   a. payment to employees for services.
   b. payment of dividends to stockholders.
   c. receipt of proceeds from the sale of an investment.
   d. receipt of proceeds from the sale of common stock to stockholders.

Explanation: Operating activities include the cash effects of transactions that ultimately create revenues and expenses and thus enter into the determination of net income. Operating activities include collections from customers, collections of interest and dividends, payments for merchandise and other goods and services, and payments for interest and taxes. The payment of dividends is a financing activity. (The receipt of dividends is an operating activity [inflow].) The sale of an investment is an investing activity. The sale of common stock is a financing activity. (Solution = a.)

QUESTION
12. (L.O. 5) In preparing a statement of cash flows, the sale of property, plant and equipment at an amount greater than its carrying value will be classified as a(n):
   a. operating activity.
   b. investing activity.
   c. financing activity.
   d. extraordinary activity.

Approach and Explanation: Think about the nature of each of the three categories on a statement of cash flows and select the one involving disposal of plant assets:

1. operating activities—all transactions and other events that are not defined as investing, or financing activities. Cash flows from operating activities are generally the cash effects of transactions that enter into the determination of net income.
2. investing activities—include making and collecting loans, acquiring and disposing of investments (both debt and equity), and acquiring and disposing of property, plant, and equipment.
3. financing activities—include obtaining resources from owners and providing them with a return on and a return of their investment, borrowing money and repaying the amounts borrowed.

There is **no** category called "extraordinary activity" on a statement of cash flows. The fact that the asset was sold for a price exceeding the carrying value does not impact the answer because the entire proceeds from the sale are to be reported in the financing activity section. In the operating activity section, the amount of gain reflected in the net income figure is deducted from net income to arrive at "net cash provided by operating activities". (Solution = b.)

QUESTION
13. (L.O. 5) In a statement of cash flows, proceeds from the issuance of common stock should be classified as a cash inflow from:
    a.   operating activities.
    b.   investing activities.
    c.   financing activities.
    d.   lending activities.

Explanation: The issuance of common stock by a corporation is the company's way of obtaining resources from an owner (i.e., owner investment into the business). Financing activities include obtaining resources from owners. There is no category called "lending activities". (Solution = c.)

QUESTION
14. (L.O. 5) Which of the following would be classified as an investing activity on a statement of cash flows:
    a.   Issuance of bonds payable at a premium.
    b.   Purchase of land to be used in operations.
    c.   Issuance of common stock at a price equal to the par value of the stock.
    d.   Payment of dividends to stockholders.

Approach and Explanation: Think about the types of items to be included in investing activities. Investing activities include making and collecting loans, acquiring and disposing of investments (both debt and equity) and acquiring and disposing of property, plant, and equipment. Take each of the answer choices and identify where it should go on a statement of cash flows. The issuance of bonds and the issuance of stock (regardless of price) are both financing activities that usually bring an inflow of cash. The payment of dividends is a financing outflow. The purchase of land (regardless of use) is an investing outflow. (Solution = b.)

QUESTION
15. (L.O. 5) In preparing a statement of cash flows, the payment of interest to a creditor should be classified as a cash outflow due to:
    a.   operating activities.
    b.   investing activities.
    c.   financing activities.
    d.   borrowing activities.

Explanation: Borrowing money is a financing activity. Repaying amounts (the principal borrowed) is a financing activity. Paying interest on amounts borrowed is an operating activity because it is **not** included in the definition of financing activities and because the interest paid will be related to the interest incurred (interest expense) which is a transaction that enters into the determination of net income. (Solution = a.)

QUESTION
16.   (L.O. 6) Alley Cat Corporation had net income for 2014 of $5,000,000. Additional information is as follows:

Depreciation of plant assets	$2,000,000
Amortization of intangibles	$400,000
Increase in accounts receivable	$700,000
Increase in accounts payable	$900,000

Alley Cat's net cash provided by operating activities for 2014 was:
   a. $2,800,000.
   b. $7,200,000.
   c. $7,400,000.
   d. $7,600,000.

Explanation: The depreciation and amortization amounts are items that reduce net income but do not cause a decrease in cash during the current period. The increase in accounts receivable indicates that sales revenue earned for the period exceeded the cash collections from customers, and therefore net income exceeded the net cash provided by operating activities. The increase in accounts payable indicates that expenses incurred exceeded cash payments for expense type items which caused net income to be less than net cash provided by operating activities. The solution is as follows:

Net income	$5,000,000
Depreciation of plant assets	2,000,000
Amortization of intangibles	400,000
Increase in accounts receivable	(700,000)
Increase in accounts payable	900,000
Net cash provided by operating activities	$7,600,000

(Solution = d.)

QUESTION
17.   (L.O. 6) Net cash flow from operating activities for 2014 for Graham Corporation was $75,000. The following items are reported on the financial statements for 2014:

Depreciation and amortization	5,000
Cash dividends paid on common stock	3,000
Increase in accrued receivables	6,000

Based only on the information above, Graham's net income for 2014 was:
   a. $64,000.
   b. $66,000.
   c. $74,000.
   d. $76,000.

Approach and Explanation: Write down the format for the reconciliation of net income to net cash flow from operating activities. Fill in the information given. Solve for the unknown.

Net income	$ X
Depreciation and amortization	5,000
Increase in accrued receivables	(6,000)
Net cash flow from operating activities	$ 75,000

Solving for X, net income = $76,000. Cash dividends paid on common stock have no effect on this computation because cash dividends paid is not a component of net income and not an operating activity. Cash dividends paid is classified as a financing activity. (Solution = d.)

QUESTION

18.   (L.O. 7) Free cash flow is:
   a.   net cash provided by operating activities minus capital expenditures and dividends.
   b.   net cash provided by operating activities minus retirement of debt and purchases of treasury stock.
   c.   the amount of cash obtained from donations.
   d.   the amount of net cash increase during the period.

Explanation: One method of examining a company's financial flexibility is to develop a free cash flow analysis. This analysis starts with net cash provided by operating activities and ends with free cash flow which is calculated as net cash provided by operating activities less capital expenditures and dividends. Free cash flow is the amount of discretionary cash flow a company has for purchasing additional investments, retiring its debt, purchasing treasury stock, or simply adding to its liquidity. This measure indicates a company's level of financial flexibility. (Solution = a.)

QUESTION

19.   (L.O. 7) Net cash provided by operating activities divided by average total liabilities equals the:
   a.   Current cash debt coverage ratio.
   b.   Cash debt coverage ratio.
   c.   Free cash flow.
   d.   Current ratio.

Approach and Explanation: Visualize the computation of each ratio or computation referenced in the answer selections. The current cash debt coverage ratio equals net cash provided by operating activities provided by average current liabilities. The cash debt coverage ratio is computed by net cash provided by operating activities divided by average total liabilities. Free cash flow is calculated as net cash provided by operating activities less capital expenditures and dividends. The current ratio is current assets divided by current liabilities. (Solution = b.)

QUESTION

*20.   (L.O. 10) Activity ratios measure the effectiveness of asset usage. One of the activity ratios is the:
   a.   inventory turnover ratio.
   b.   current ratio.
   c.   acid-test ratio.
   d.   rate of return on assets.

Explanation: The activity ratios include the (1) receivable turnover ratio, (2) inventory turnover ratio, and (3) asset turnover ratio. The current ratio and acid-test (or quick) ratio are both liquidity ratios. The rate of return on assets ratio is a profitability ratio. (Solution = a.)

QUESTION

*21.   (L.O. 10) The current ratio is 3:1 for the Hamstock Company at a balance sheet date. What is the impact on that ratio of a collection of accounts receivable?
   a.   Current ratio is increased.
   b.   Current ratio is decreased.
   c.   Current ratio is unaffected.
   d.   Cannot be determined.

Approach and Explanation: Reconstruct the journal entry for the transaction. Analyze the effect of the debit portion of the entry on each element of the ratio and then analyze the effect of the credit portion of the entry on each element of the ratio. The entry to record the collection of accounts receivable involves a debit to Cash and a credit to Accounts Receivable. There is no change in the total amount of current assets. There is no change in the total amount of current liabilities. Thus, there is no change in the current ratio which is current assets divided by current liabilities. (Solution = c.)

IFRS Insights

- As in GAAP, the balance sheet and the statement of cash flows are required statements for IFRS. In addition, the content and presentation of an IFRS balance sheet and cash flow statement are similar to those used for GAAP. In general, the disclosure requirements related to the balance sheet and the statement of cash flows are much more extensive and detailed in the United States.

- IFRS recommends but does not require the use of the title "statement of financial position" rather than balance sheet.

- IFRS requires a classified statement of financial position except in very limited situations, IFRS follows the same guidelines as this textbook for distinguishing between current and noncurrent assets and liabilities. However, under GAAP, public companies must follow SEC regulations, which require specific line items. In addition, specific GAAP standards mandate certain forms of reporting this information.

- Under IFRS, current assets are usually listed in the reverse order of liquidity. For example, under GAAP cash is listed first, but under IFRS it is listed last.

- IFRS has many differences in terminology. For example, in the investment category of the statement of financial position, stock is called shares, and in the equity section common stock is called share capital—ordinary.

- Both IFRS and GAAP require disclosures about (1) accounting policies followed, (2) judgments that management has made in the process of applying the entity's accounting policies, and (3) the key assumptions and estimation uncertainty that could result in a material adjustment to the carrying amounts of assets and liabilities within the next financial year. Comparative prior period information must be presented and financial statements must be prepared annually.

- Both IFRS and GAAP require presentation of the noncontrolling interest in the equity section of the balance sheet.

- Use of the term "reserve" is discouraged in GAAP, but there is no such prohibition in IFRS.

- With IFRS, the statement of financial position accounts are **classified.** That is, a statement of financial position groups together similar items to arrive at significant subtotals. Furthermore, the material is arranged so that important relationships are shown. The IASB indicates that the parts and subsections of financial statements are more informative than the whole. Therefore, the IASB discourages the reporting of summary accounts alone (total assets, net assets, total liabilities, etc.).

  Companies should report and classify individual items in sufficient detail to permit users to assess the amounts, timing, and uncertainty of future cash flows. Such classification also makes it easier for users to evaluate the company's liquidity and financial flexibility, profitability, and risk. Companies then further divide these items into several sub-classifications.

- For IFRS, the statement of financial position is usually presented in "report form" format. Some companies use other statement of financial position formats. For example, companies sometimes deduct current liabilities from current assets to arrive at working capital. Or, they deduct all liabilities from all assets. Some companies report the subtotal *net assets,* which equals total assets minus total liabilities.

- Using IFRS, the **equity** (also referred to as **shareholders' equity**) section is one of the most difficult sections to prepare and understand. This is due to the complexity of ordinary and preference share agreements and the various restrictions on equity imposed by corporation laws, liability agreements, and boards of directors. Companies usually divide the section into six parts:

  1. **Share Capital.** The par or stated value of shares issued. It includes ordinary shares (sometimes referred to as *common shares*) and preference shares (sometimes referred to as *preferred shares*).

  2. **Share Premium.** The excess of amounts paid-in over the par or stated value.

  3. **Retained Earnings.** The corporation's undistributed earnings.

  4. **Accumulated Other Comprehensive Income.** The aggregate amount of the other comprehensive income items.

  5. **Treasury Shares**. Generally, the amount related to ordinary shares repurchased.

  6. **Noncontrolling Interest** (Minority Interest). A portion of the equity of subsidiaries not owned by the reporting company.

- Using IFRS, for ordinary shares, companies must disclose the par value and the authorized, issued, and outstanding share amounts. The same holds true for preference shares. A company usually presents the share premium (for both ordinary and preference shares) in one amount, although subtotals are informative if the sources of additional capital are varied and material.

- Under IFRS, the retained earnings amount may be divided between the **unappropriated** (the amount that is usually available for dividend distribution) and **restricted** (e.g., by bond indentures or other loan agreements) amounts. In addition, companies show any shares reacquired (treasury shares) as a reduction of equity.

- For IFRS, accumulated other comprehensive income (sometimes referred to as *reserves* or *other reserves*) includes such items as unrealized gains and losses on non-trading equity investments and unrealized gains and losses on certain derivative transactions. Non-controlling interest, sometimes referred to as minority interest, is also shown as a separate item (where applicable) as a part of equity.

- Many companies reporting under IFRS often use the term "reserve" as an all-inclusive catch-all for items such as retained earnings, share premium, and accumulated other comprehensive income. Under GAAP, the term "reserve" is discouraged.

- GAAP and IFRS differ in the IFRS provision for balance sheet revaluations of property, plant, and equipment. Under the *revaluation model*, revaluations are recorded and reported as part of equity. To illustrate, Nelson Company uses IFRS and has property and equipment on an historical cost basis of €2,000,000. At the end of the year, Nelson appraises its property and equipment and determines it had a revaluation increase of €243,000. Nelson records this revaluation under IFRS with an increase to property and equipment as well as a valuation reserve in equity (an increase in equity in this case). A note to the financial statements explains the change in the revaluation equity account from one period to the next.

- The FASB and the IASB are working on a project to converge their standards related to financial statement presentation. A key feature of the proposed framework is that each of the statements will be organized, in the same format, to separate an entity's financing activities from its operating and investing activities and, further, to separate financing activities into transactions with owners and creditors. Thus, the same classifications used in the statement of financial position would also be used in the statement of comprehensive income and the statement of cash flows. The project has three phases.

TRUE/FALSE (Circle the correct answer for each).

T F 1. In comparing GAAP with IFRS, in general, the disclosure requirements related to the balance sheet and the statement of cash flows are much more extensive and detailed in the United States.

T F 2. The IFRS requires the use of the title "balance sheet" rather than "statement of financial condition."

T F 3. Under IFRS, cash is listed last in the current assets section.

T F 4. Use of the term "reserve" is discouraged in IFRS but there is no such prohibition in GAAP.

T F 5. Under IFRS revaluations of property, plant and equipment are recorded and reported as part of equity. GAAP does **not** follow the same revaluation model.

T F 6. Companies that use IFRS may report noncurrent assets before current assets and equity before liabilities in using the "report form" format for the statement of financial position.

Solutions:

1.	T	4.	F
2.	F	5.	T
3.	T	6.	T

CHAPTER 6

ACCOUNTING AND THE
TIME VALUE OF MONEY

OVERVIEW

Due to the time value of money, a certain sum today is not equal to the same sum at a future point in time. We must consider the compound interest factor for the time between two given dates in order to determine what amount in the future is equivalent to a given sum today or what amount today is equivalent to a given sum in the future. We compound the dollar amount forward in time in the former case and discount the dollar amount from the future to the present time in the latter case. In this chapter we discuss both of these procedures for a single sum and the appropriate procedures for compounding and discounting annuities. Interest tables appear at the end of this chapter.

SUMMARY OF LEARNING OBJECTIVES

1. **Identify accounting topics where the time value of money is relevant.** Some of the applications of present-value-based measurements to accounting topics are: (1) notes, (2) leases, (3) pensions and other postretirement benefits, (4) long-term assets, (5) stock-based compensation (6) business combinations, (7) disclosures, (8) installment contracts, (9) sinking funds, and (10) environmental liabilities.

2. **Distinguish between simple and compound interest.** Interest is a payment for the use of money. It is the excess cash received or repaid over and above the amount lent (invested) or borrowed (principal). Simple interest is interest that is computed on the amount of the principal only. It is the return on (or growth of) the principal for one time period. Simple interest is commonly expressed as follows:

$$\text{Interest} = p \times i \times n$$

where: p = principal
i = rate of interest for a single period
n = number of periods

Compound interest is computed on principal **and** on any interest earned to date on that principal that has not been paid or withdrawn.

3. **Use appropriate compound interest tables.** In order to identify which of the five compound interest tables to use, determine whether you are solving for (1) the future value of a single sum, (2) the present value of a single sum, (3) the future value of a series of sums (an annuity), or (4) the present value of a series of sums (an annuity). In addition, when a series of equal payments or receipts that occur at equal intervals of time (an annuity) is involved, identify whether these sums are received or paid (1) at the **beginning** of each period (annuity due) or (2) at the **end** of each period (ordinary annuity).

4.   **Identify variables fundamental to solving interest problems.** The following four variables are fundamental to all compound interest problems: (1) **Rate of interest:** unless otherwise stated, an annual rate that must be adjusted to reflect the length of the compounding period if less than a year. (2) **Number of time periods:** the number of compounding periods (a period may be equal to or less than a year). (3) **Future value:** the value at a future date of a given sum or sums invested assuming compound interest. (4) **Present value:** the value now (present time) of a future sum or sums discounted back to the present assuming compound interest.

5.   **Solve future and present value of 1 problems.** The future value (or future amount) of a single sum is the value at a future point in time of a given amount to be deposited (or invested) today using compound interest. The present value of a single sum is the current worth of a given future sum. In determining the future value, we move forward in time using a process of accumulation; in determining present value, we move backward in time using a process of discounting. The present value is always a smaller amount than a known future amount because interest will be earned and accumulated on the present value to the future date.

6.   **Solve future value of ordinary and annuity due problems.** The future value of an annuity is the future value (accumulated total) of a series of equal deposits at regular intervals at compound interest. Both deposits and interest increase the accumulation. Thus, the future value of an annuity is the sum of all the rents plus the accumulated compound interest on them.

7.   **Solve present value of ordinary and annuity due problems.** The present value of an annuity is the present value (worth) of a series of equal rents due in the future, all discounted at compound interest; in other words, it is the sum when invested today at compound interest that will permit a series of equal withdrawals at regular intervals.

8.   **Solve present value problems related to deferred annuities and bonds**. Deferred annuities are annuities in which rents begin after a specified number of periods. The future value of a deferred annuity is computed the same as the future value of an annuity not deferred. To find the present value of a deferred annuity, compute the present value of an ordinary annuity of 1 as if the rents had occurred for the entire period, and then subtract the present value of rents not received during the deferral period. The current market value of bonds is the combined present values of the interest annuity and the principal amount. The preferred procedure for amortization of bond discount or premium is the effective interest method, which (1) computes bond interest expense using the effective interest method (this is done by multiplying the carrying value of he bonds at the beginning of the period by the effective interest rate), (2) computes the cash amount of bond interest (this is done by multiplying the face amount of the bonds by the stated interest rate), and (3) compares those two items to determine the amount of amortization.

9.   **Apply expected cash flows to present value measurement.** The expected cash flow approach uses a range of cash flows and the probabilities of those cash flows to provide the most likely estimate of expected cash flows. The proper interest rate used to discount the cash flows is the risk-free rate of return.

TIPS ON CHAPTER TOPICS

TIP: Tables for future value and present value factors appear at the end of this chapter.

TIP: The **future value of 1** (a single sum) is often referred to as the **future amount of 1**, and the **future value of an annuity** is often called the **future amount of an annuity**.

TIP: Anytime you have a present value or a future value problem to solve, it is wise to draw a time diagram (or time line). This picture will help you to determine:
1.   if you are given present value or future value data or both.
2.   if you are dealing with a single sum or an annuity situation.
3.   what you are to solve for—present value, future value, n (number of periods), i (interest rate) or rent.

TIP: Future value involves finding the value at a future date of a given amount today; that is, finding the amount a given sum today will accumulate to be at a future date. Present value involves finding the value today of a given amount specified at future date; that is, finding the amount which if invested today at a specified rate would grow to be that given amount.

TIP: The present value of a single sum is based on three variables: (1) the dollar amount to be received or paid (future value), (2) the length of time until the amount is received or paid (number of periods), and (3) the interest rate (the discount rate). The process of determining the present value is referred to as discounting the future value. The relationship of these fundamental variables is depicted in the following diagram.

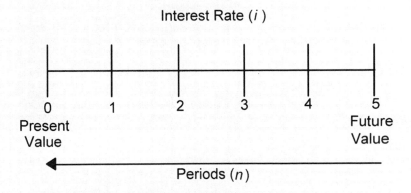

Unless otherwise indicated, an interest rate is stated on an annual basis. To convert an annual interest rate into a compounding period interest rate, divide the annual rate by the number of compounding periods per year. The total number of periods is determined by multiplying the number of years involved by the number of compounding periods per year.

TIP: The **interest rate** is often referred to as the **discount rate** in computing present value. The **higher** the discount rate (interest rate) is, the **lower** the present value will be

TIP: One payment (or receipt) involved in an annuity is called a **rent.**

TIP: The factor for the "present value of 1" is the reciprocal (inverse) of the factor for the "future value of 1." Thus, if you are given the factor from the Future Value of 1 Table for $n = 3$, $i = 8\%$ which is 1.25971, you can compute the factor for the "present value of 1" for $n = 3$, $i = 8\%$ by dividing 1 by 1.25971. This division yields a factor of .79383, which does agree with the factor for $n = 3$, $i = 8\%$ in the Present Value of 1 Table.

TIP: The factor for the present value of an ordinary annuity of 1 for *n* periods is the sum of factors for the present value of 1 for each of the *n* periods. For example, the factor for the present value of an ordinary annuity of 1 for *n* = 3, *i* = 8% (which is 2.57710) is equal to sum of the factors from the 8% column of the Present Value of 1 Table for *n* = 1, *n* = 2, *n* = 3 (.92593 + .85734 + .79383 = 2.57710).

TIP: The factor for the future value of an ordinary annuity of 1 for *n* = 3, *i* = 8% is 3.24640. It reflects interest on the first rent for two periods, interest on the second rent for one period, and no interest on the third rent. The factor for the future value of an annuity due of 1 for *n* = 3, *i* = 8% is 3.50611. It reflects interest on the first rent for three periods, interest on the second rent for two periods, and interest for one period on the third rent. Thus, for a given *n* and *i*, the factor for an annuity due is greater than the factor for an ordinary annuity.

TIP: Referring to the TIP immediately above, we can see that the future value of an annuity due factor can be found by multiplying the future value of an ordinary annuity factor by 1 plus the interest rate. Likewise, the present value of an annuity due factor can be found by multiplying the present value of an ordinary annuity factor by 1 plus the interest rate.

TIP: A deferred annuity is an annuity in which the rents begin after a specified number of periods. A deferred annuity does not begin to produce rents until two or more periods have expired.

TIP: A factor for the present value or the future value of an annuity reflects one rent per period. Therefore, if an annuity involves a delay before the rents begin, the factor for *n* must be adjusted before the problem can be solved.

TIP: Any present value or future value problem is an application (or variation) of one or more of the following formulas: (parentheses indicate multiplication)

Future Value of an Amount = Present Value (Future Value of 1 Factor)
Present Value of an Amount = Future Value (Present Value of 1 Factor)
Future Value of an Annuity = Rent (Future Value of an Annuity Factor)
Present Value of an Annuity = Rent (Present Value of an Annuity Factor)

Future value and present value tables appear at
the end of this chapter in this volume.

ILLUSTRATION 6-1
PRESENT VALUE-BASED ACCOUNTING MEASUREMENTS
(L.O. 1)

Financial reporting uses different measurements in different situations—historical cost for equipment, net realizable value for inventories, fair value for investments. As was discussed in **Chapter 2,** the FASB increasingly is requiring the use of fair values in the measurement of assets and liabilities. According to the FASB's recent guidance on fair value measurements, the most useful fair value measures are based on market prices in active markets. Within the fair value hierarchy these are referred to as Level 1. Recall that Level 1 fair value measures are the most reliable because they are based on quoted prices, such as a closing stock price in the Wall Street Journal.

However, for many assets and liabilities, market-based fair value information is not readily available. In these cases, fair value can be estimated based on the expected future cash flows related to the asset or liability. Such fair value estimates are generally considered Level 3 (least reliable) in the fair value hierarchy because they are based on unobservable inputs, such as a company's own data or assumptions related to the expected future cash flows associated with the asset or liability. As discussed in the fair value guidance, present value techniques are used to convert expected cash flows into present values, which represent an estimate of fair value.

Because of the increased use of present values in this and other contexts, it is important to understand present value techniques. Some of the applications of present value-based measurements to accounting topics are listed below. Many of these will be discussed in detail in the following chapters.

1. **Notes.** Valuing noncurrent receivables and payables that carry no stated interest rate or a lower than market interest rate.

2. **Leases.** Valuing assets and obligations to be capitalized under long-term leases and measuring the amount of the lease payments and annual leasehold amortization.

3. **Pensions and Other Postretirement Benefits**. Measuring service cost components of employers' postretirement benefits expense and postretirement benefits obligation.

4. **Long-term assets.** Evaluating alternative long-term investments by discounting future cash flows. Determining the value of assets acquired under deferred payment contracts. Measuring impairments of assets.

5. **Stock-based compensation.** Determining the fair value of employee services in compensatory stock-option plans.

6. **Business combinations.** Determining the value of receivables, payables, liabilities, accruals, and commitments acquired or assumed in a "purchase."

7. **Disclosures.** Measuring the value of future cash flows from oil and gas reserves for disclosure in supplementary information.

8. **Installment contracts.** Measuring periodic payments on long-term purchase contracts.

9. **Sinking funds.** Determining the contributions necessary to accumulate a fund for debt retirements.

10. **Environmental liabilities.** Determining the fair value of future obligations for asset retirements.

TIP: In addition to accounting and business applications, compound interest, annuity, and present value concepts apply to personal finance and investment decisions. In purchasing a home or car, planning for retirement, and evaluating alternative investments, you will need to understand time value of money concepts.

ILLUSTRATION 6-2
FUNDAMENTAL CONCEPTS UNDERLYING
FUTURE VALUE AND PRESENT VALUE PROBLEMS (L.O. 2, 3, 4)

---

1. **Simple Interest.** Interest on principal only, regardless of interest that may have accrued in the past.

2. **Compound Interest.** Interest accrues on the unpaid interest of past periods as well as on the principal.

3. **Rate of Interest.** Interest is usually expressed as an annual rate. When the interest period is shorter than one year, the interest rate for the shorter period must be determined.

4. **Annuity.** A series of payments or receipts (called rents) that occur at equal intervals of time.
   Types of annuities:
   a. **Ordinary Annuity.** Each rent is payable (receivable) at the end of the period.
   b. **Annuity Due.** Each rent is payable (receivable) at the beginning of the period.

5. **Future Value.** Value at a later date of a single sum that is invested at compound interest.
   a. **Future Value of 1** (or value of a single sum). The future value of $1.00 (or a single given sum), *FV*, at the end of *n* periods at *i* compound interest rate (Table 1).
   b. **Future Value of an Annuity.** The future value of a series of rents invested at compound interest; in other words, the accumulated total that results from a series of equal deposits at regular intervals invested at compound interest. Both deposits and interest increase the accumulation.
      1. **Future Value of an Ordinary Annuity.** The future value on the date of the last rent.
      2. **Future Value of an Annuity Due.** The future value one period after the date of the last rent. When an annuity due table is not available, use Table 3 with the following formula:

ILLUSTRATION 6-2 (Continued)

$$\begin{array}{lcl} \text{Value of annuity due of 1} & & \text{(Value of ordinary annuity for} \\ \text{for } n \text{ rents} & = & n \text{ rents) X (1 + interest rate)} \end{array}$$

6. **Present Value.** The value at an earlier date (usually now) of a given future sum discounted at compound interest.

   a. **Present Value of 1** (or present value of a single sum). The present value (worth) of $1.00 (or a given sum), due n periods hence, discounted at i compound interest (Table 2).

   b. **Present Value of an Annuity.** The present value (worth) of a series of rents discounted at compound interest; in other words, it is the sum when invested at compound interest that will permit a series of equal withdrawals at regular intervals.

      1. **Present Value of an Ordinary Annuity.** The value now of $1.00 to be received or paid at the end of each period (rents) for n periods, discounted at i compound interest (Table 4).

      2. **Present Value of an Annuity Due.** The value now of $1.00 to be received or paid at the beginning of each period (rents) for the n periods, discounted at i compound interest (Table 5). To use Table 4 for an annuity due, apply this formula:

$$\begin{array}{lcl} \text{Present value of annuity due} & & \text{(Present value of an ordinary annuity} \\ \text{of 1 for } n \text{ rents} & = & \text{of } n \text{ rents) X (1 + interest rate).} \end{array}$$

Future value and present value tables appear at
the end of this chapter in this volume.

ILLUSTRATION 6-3
STEPS IN SOLVING FUTURE VALUE AND
PRESENT VALUE PROBLEMS (L.O. 5, 6, 7)

Step 1:   Classify the problem into one of six types:
   a. Future value of a single sum.
   b. Present value of a single sum.
   c. Future value of an ordinary annuity.
   d. Present value of an ordinary annuity.
   e. Future value of an annuity due.
   f. Present value of an annuity due.

Step 2:   Determine n, the number of compounding periods, and i, the interest rate per period.
   a. Draw a time diagram. This is helpful when the number of periods or number of rents must be figured out from the dates given in the problem.
   b. If interest is compounded more than once a year:
      1) To find n: **multiply** the number of years by the number of compounding periods per year.
      2) To find i: **divide** the annual interest rate by the number of compounding periods per year.

Step 3:   Use n and i (if known) to choose the proper interest factor from the interest table indicated in Step 1.

Step 4:   Solve for the missing quantity. A summary of the possibilities appears in **Illustration 6-5**. Abbreviations used in that summary are explained at the end of the summary.

TIP: After determining expected cash flows, a company must use the proper interest rate to discount the cash flows. That interest rate for this purpose has three components: (1) **Pure Rate of Interest (2%-4%).** This would be the amount a lender would charge if there were no possibilities of default and no expectation of inflation. (2) **Expected Inflation Rate of Interest (0%- ?).** Lenders recognize that in an inflationary economy, they are being paid back with less valuable dollars. As a result, they increase their interest rate to compensate for this loss in purchasing power. When inflationary expectations are high, interest rates are high. (3) **Credit Risk Rate of Interest (0%-5%).** The government has little or no credit risk (i.e., risk of nonpayment) when it issues bonds. A business enterprise, however, depending upon its financial stability, profitability, etc., can have a low or high credit risk.

TIP: Many situations require that a business estimate expected future cash flows. The FASB takes the position that after computing the expected cash flows, a company should discount those cash flows by the **risk-free rate of return.** That rate is defined as the **pure rate of return plus the expected inflation rate.** Any credit risk is already incorporated in the determination of the probability of receipt or payment used in the computation of the expected cash flow. Therefore, the rate used to discount the resulting expected cash flows should consider **only** the pure rate of interest along with the inflation rate.

ILLUSTRATION 6-4
STEPS IN SOLVING FUTURE VALUE AND
PRESENT VALUE PROBLEMS ILLUSTRATED (L.O. 5, 6, 7)

The steps in solving future value and present value problems (listed in **Illustration A-3** are illustrated below and on the following pages:

1. **If $10,000 is deposited in the bank today at 8% interest compounded annually, what will be the balance in 5 years?**

    Step 1: This is a future value of a single sum problem.
    Step 2: $n = 5$; $i = 8\%$

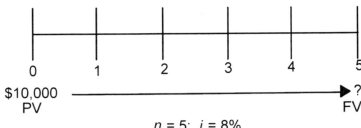

$$n = 5; \quad i = 8\%$$

    Step 3: The interest factor from Table 1 is 1.46933.
    Step 4: Future Value = Present Value x $FVF_{n,i}$
             Future Value = $10,000 x 1.46933
             Future Value = $14,693.30

2. **A company needs $100,000 to retire debt when the debt matures two years from now. What amount must be deposited on January 1, 2014 at 8% interest compounded quarterly in order to accumulate the desired sum by January 1, 2016?**

    Step 1: This is a present value of a single sum problem.
    Step 2: It is 2 years from 1/1/14 to 1/1/16. The annual interest rate is 8%. $n = 2 \times 4 = 8$; $i = 8\% \div 4 = 2\%$.

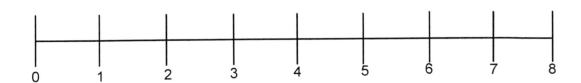

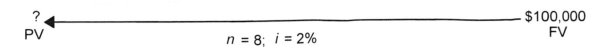

$$n = 8; \quad i = 2\%$$

    Step 3: The interest factor from Table 2 is .85349.
    Step 4: Present Value = Future Value x $PVF_{n,i}$
             Present Value = $100,000 x .85349
             Present Value = $85,349.00

ILLUSTRATION 6-4 (Continued)

3.   **If $71,178 can be invested now, what annual interest rate must be earned in order to accumulate $100,000 three years from now?**

Step 1:   This can be solved either as a future value or as a present value of a single sum problem. This solution illustrates the present value approach.
Step 2: $n = 3$; i must be solved for.

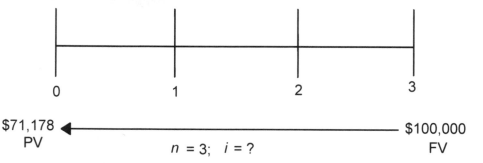

$71,178
PV

$100,000
FV

$n = 3$; $i = ?$

Step 3: i must be solved for.
Step 4:   Present Value = Future Value x $PVF_{n,i}$
$71,178 = $100,000 x $PVF_{n,i}$
$71,178 ÷ $100,000 = $PVF_{n,i}$
.71178 = $PVF_{n,i}$
Refer to Table 2 in the 3 period row.
    $i = 12\%$

4.   **If $1,000 is deposited into an account at the end of every year for six years, what will be the balance in the account after the sixth deposit if all amounts on deposit earn 6% interest?**

Step 1:   This is a future value of an ordinary annuity problem.
Step 2: $n = 6$; $i = 6\%$

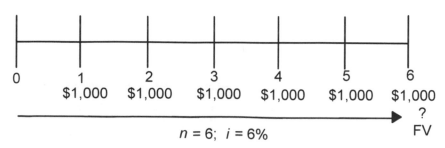

0   1   2   3   4   5   6
$1,000 $1,000 $1,000 $1,000 $1,000 $1,000
?
FV

$n = 6$; $i = 6\%$

Step 3:   The interest factor from Table 3 is 6.97532.
Step 4:   Future Value of an Ordinary Annuity = Rent x $FVF\text{-}OA_{n,i}$
Future Value of an Ordinary Annuity = $1,000 x 6.97532
Future Value of an Ordinary Annuity = $6,975.32

ILLUSTRATION 6-4 (Continued)

5. What amount must be deposited at 10% in an account on January 1, 2014 if it is desired to make equal annual withdrawals of $10,000 each, beginning on January 1, 2015 and ending on January 1, 2018?

    Step 1: This is a present value of an ordinary annuity problem.
    Step 2: The time diagram shows 4 withdrawals. $n = 4$; $i = 10\%$

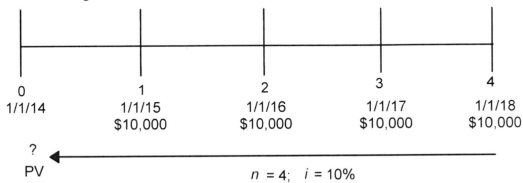

    Step 3: The interest factor from Table 4 is 3.16986.
    Step 4: Present Value of an Ordinary Annuity = Rent x PVF-OA$_{n,i}$
             Present Value of an Ordinary Annuity = $10,000 x 3.16986
             Present Value of an Ordinary Annuity = $31,698.60

6. Beginning today, six annual deposits of $1,000 each will be made into an account paying 6%. What will be the balance in the account one year after the sixth deposit is made?

    Step 1: This is a future value of an annuity due problem.
    Step 2: $n = 6$; $i = 6\%$.

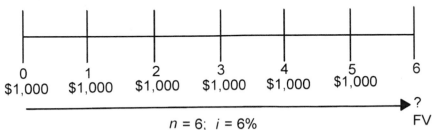

    Step 3: Table 3 with factors for future value of an ordinary annuity (FVF-OA$_{n,i}$) can be used to derive the factor needed here for future value of an annuity due (FVF-AD$_{n,i}$). The process is as follows:

FVF-OA for $n = 6$, $i = 6\%$	6.97532
Multiplied by $1 + i$	1.06
FVF-AD for $n = 6$, $i = 6\%$	7.39384

    Step 4: Future Value of an Annuity Due = Rent x FVF-AD$_{n,i}$
             Future Value of Annuity Due = $1,000 x 7.39384
             Future Value of Annuity Due = $7,393.84

ILLUSTRATION 6-4 (Continued)

> **TIP:** Compare the results of this problem with those of **Problem 4** above. The solution to problem 4 can be multiplied by (1 + *i*) to get the answer to number 6.
> Proof: $6,975.32 x 1.06 = $7,393.84.
> Although both situations use the same number of equal rents and the same interest rate, the interest is earned on all of the deposits for one period more under the annuity due situation.

7.   **What is the present value of four annual payments of $10,000 each if interest is 10% and the first payment is made today?**

Step 1:   This is a present value of an annuity due problem.
Step 2:   *n* = 4; *i* = 10%.

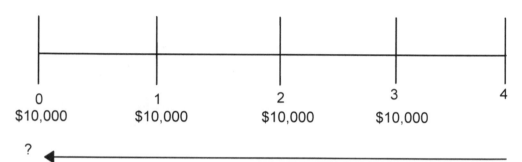

Step 3:   The interest factor from Table 5 is 3.48685.
This factor can also be derived by using the present value of an ordinary annuity table (Table 4) as follows:

PVF-OA for *n* = 4, *i* = 10%	3.16986
Multiplied by 1 + *i*	1.10
PVF-AD for *n* = 4, *i* = 10%	3.48685

Step 4:   Present Value of an Annuity Due = Rent x PVF-AD$_{n,i}$
Present Value of an Annuity Due = $10,000 x 3.48685
Present Value of an Annuity Due = **$34,868.50**

> **TIP:** Compare the results of this problem with those of **Problem 5** above. The solution to problem 5 can be multiplied by (1 + *i*) to get the answer to number 7.
> Proof: $31,698.60 x 1.10 = $34,868.46
> (Difference of $.04 is due to the rounding of the factors.)
> Although both situations use the same number of equal rents and the same interest rate, the discounting is done on all of the deposits for one period less under the annuity due situation.

ILLUSTRATION 6-4 (Continued)

8. **What amount must be deposited at the end of each year in an account paying 8% interest if it is desired to have $10,000 at the end of the fifth year?**

Step 1:   This is a future value of an ordinary annuity problem.
Step 2: $n = 5$; $i = 8\%$.

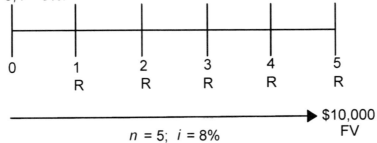

Step 3:   The interest factor from Table 3 is 5.86660.
Step 4:   Future Value of an Ordinary Annuity = Rent x FVF-OA$_{n,i}$
$10,000 = Rent x 5.86660
$10,000 ÷ 5.86660 = Rent
Rent = $1,704.56

TIP: You can prove this solution by: $1,704.56 x 5.86660 = $9,999.97
The difference of $.03 is due to rounding.

ILLUSTRATION 6-5
SUMMARY OF SIX TYPES OF FUTURE VALUE
AND PRESENT VALUE PROBLEMS (L.O. 5, 6, 7)

1.   Future Value of a Single Sum

    a.   Future Value   = Present Value x $FVF_{n,i}$

    b. $FVF_{n,i}$ = $\dfrac{\text{Future Value}}{\text{Present Value}}$

        (1) "*I*" unknown and "*n*" known, or   Trace solved factor to Table 1.
        (2) "*n*" unknown and "*I*" known   Trace solved factor to Table 1.

TIP: The present value amount is sometimes called the **principal.**

2.   Present Value of a Single Sum

    a.   Present Value   = Future Value x $PVF_{n,i}$

    b. $PVF_{n,i}$ = $\dfrac{\text{Present Value}}{\text{Future Value}}$

        (1) "*i*" unknown and "*n*" known, or   Trace solved factor to Table 2.
        (2) "*n*" unknown and "*i*" known   Trace solved factor to Table 2.

3.   Future Value of an Ordinary Annuity

    a.   Future Value of an Ordinary Annuity   = Rent x $FVF\text{-}OA_{n,i}$

    b.   Rent   = $\dfrac{\text{Future Value of an Ordinary Annuity}}{FVF\text{-}OA_{n,i}}$

    c. $FVF\text{-}OA_{n,i}$ = $\dfrac{\text{Future Value of an Ordinary Annuity}}{\text{Rent}}$

        (1) "*i*" unknown and "*n*" known, or   Trace solved factor to Table 3.
        (2) "*n*" unknown and "*i*" known   Trace solved factor to Table 3.

4.   Present Value of an Ordinary Annuity

    a.   Present Value of an Ordinary Annuity   = Rent x $PVF\text{-}OA_{n,i}$

    b.   Rent   = $\dfrac{\text{Present Value of an Ordinary Annuity}}{PVF\text{-}OA_{n,i}}$

    c. $PVF\text{-}OA_{n,i}$ = $\dfrac{\text{Present Value of an Ordinary Annuity}}{\text{Rent}}$

        (1) "*i*" unknown and "*n*" known, or   Trace solved factor to Table 4.
        (2) "*n*" unknown and "*i*" known   Trace solved factor to Table 4.

ILLUSTRATION 6-5 (Continued)

5. Future Value of an Annuity Due

a. Future Value of an Annuity Due $\quad = \quad$ Rent x $FVF\text{-}AD_{n,i}$

b. Rent $\qquad\qquad = \quad \dfrac{\text{Future Value of an Annuity Due}}{FVF\text{-}AD_{n,i}}$

> **TIP:** There is no table in this book for Future Value of an Annuity Due, so ordinary annuity factors must be modified as follows:
>
> $FVF\text{-}AD_{n,i} = FVF\text{-}OA_{n,i} \times (1 + i)$ **OR** $FVF\text{-}AD_{n,i} = FVF\text{-}OA_{n+1,i} - 1.00000$

6. Present Value of an Annuity Due

a. Present Value of an Annuity Due $\quad = \quad$ Rent x $PVF\text{-}AD_{n,i}$

b. Rent $\qquad\qquad = \quad \dfrac{\text{Present Value of an Annuity Due}}{PVF\text{-}AD_{n,i}}$

c. $PVF\text{-}AD_{n,i}$ $\qquad\qquad = \quad \dfrac{\text{Present Value of an Annuity Due}}{\text{Rent}}$

    (1) "i" unknown and "n" known, or $\qquad$ Trace solved factor to Table 5.
    (2) "n" unknown and "i" known $\qquad\quad$ Trace solved factor to Table 5.

> **TIP:** Factors for the present value of an annuity due can be derived by adjusting factors from the Table for Present Value of an Ordinary Annuity as follows:
>
> $PVF\text{-}AD_{n,i} = PVF\text{-}OA_{n,i} \times (1 + i)$ **OR** $PVF\text{-}AD_{n,i} = PVF\text{-}OA_{n-1,i} + 1.00000$

Abbreviations:

i	=	Interest Rate
n	=	Number of Periods or Rents
$FVF_{n,i}$	=	Future Value of 1 Factor for n periods at i interest
$PVF_{n,i}$	=	Present Value of 1 Factor for n periods at i interest
$FVF\text{-}OA_{n,i}$	=	Future Amount of an Ordinary Annuity of 1 Factor for n periods at i interest
$PVF\text{-}OA_{n,i}$	=	Present Value of an Ordinary Annuity of 1 Factor for n periods at i interest
$FVF\text{-}AD_{n,i}$	=	Future Amount of an Annuity Due of 1 Factor for n periods at i interest
$PVF\text{-}AD_{n,i}$	=	Present Value of an Annuity Due of 1 Factor for n periods at i interest

EXERCISE 6-1

Purpose: (L.O. 3) This exercise will test your knowledge of the applicability of the five compound interest tables discussed in this chapter.

Instructions

For each independent situation below, (1) indicate which table you would need to use in order to locate the appropriate factor to solve for the figure requested, and (2) indicate if you divide (D) or multiply (M) by that factor to solve for the figure requested. Use the appropriate numerals and letters to indicate your answer for each.

I.	Future Value of 1
II.	Present Value of 1
III.	Future Value of an Ordinary Annuity of 1
IV.	Present Value of an Ordinary Annuity of 1
V.	Present Value of an Annuity Due of 1

> **TIP:**   There are two approaches to solving problems involving present value or future value of a single sum; there is only one approach available for solving annuity problems.

(1)   (2)

_____ _____   1. $1,000 is put on deposit today to earn 6% interest, compounded annually. How much will be on deposit at the end of 8 years?

_____ _____   2.   What amount today is equivalent to receiving $600 at the end of every year for 6 years, assuming interest is compounded annually at the rate of 5%?

_____ _____   3.   If you wish to be able to withdraw the sum of $8,000 at the end of 12 years, how much do you have to deposit today, assuming interest is compounded annually at the rate of 6%?

_____ _____   4.   If $400 is put in a savings account at the end of every year for 5 years, how much will be accumulated in the account if all amounts that remain on deposit earn 6% interest, compounded annually?

_____ _____   5.   What amount today is equivalent to receiving $1,000 ten years from now if interest of 7% is compounded annually?

_____ _____   6.   What amount today is equivalent to receiving $1,000 at the end of each year for ten years if interest of 7% is compounded annually?

_____ _____   7.   How much must be deposited today to allow for the withdrawal of $1,000 at the end of each year for ten years if interest of 7% is compounded annually?

_____ _____   8.   What is the present value of $500 due in 8 years at 6% compounded interest?

_____ _____   9.   What is the future value of an ordinary annuity of $100 per period for 6

_____ _____ 10. How much money must be deposited today to be able to withdraw $700 at the end of 7 years, assuming 7% compounded interest?

_____ _____ 11. How much money must be deposited today to be able to withdraw $700 at the beginning of each of 7 years, assuming 7% compounded interest?

_____ _____ 12. What is the discounted value of $700 due in 7 years at a 7% compounded interest rate?

_____ _____ 13. What is the future value of $700 put on deposit now for 7 years at 7% compounded interest?

_____ _____ 14. What is the future value in seven years of $700 put on deposit at the end of each of 7 years if all amounts on deposit earn 7% compound interest?

_____ _____ 15. How much can be withdrawn at the end of 5 years if $1,000 is deposited now at a 6% compound interest rate?

_____ _____ 16. What amount can be withdrawn at the end of each period for five years if $1,000 is deposited now and all amounts on deposit earn 6% interest compounded annually?

_____ _____ 17. If a debt of $5,000 is to be repaid in five equal beginning-of-year installments, what is the amount of each installment if interest at 7% is charged on the unpaid balance?

_____ _____ 18. What amount must be deposited at the end of each of four years to accumulate a fund of $7,000 at the end of the fourth year, assuming interest at a rate of 6% compounded annually?

Solution to Exercise 6-1

1.	I	M	or	II	D
2.	IV	M			
3.	II	M	or	I	D
4.	III	M			
5.	II	M	or	I	D
6.	IV	M			
7.	IV	M			
8.	II	M	or	I	D
9.	III	M			
10.	II	M	or	I	D
11.	V	M			
12.	II	M	or	I	D
13.	I	M	or	II	D
14.	III	M			
15.	I	M	or	II	D
16.	IV	D			
17.	V	D			
18.	III	D			

Approach and Explanation: Draw a time diagram and place each fact given in the appropriate position on the diagram. Determine what is to be solved for in the question. Think about the content of each of the five compound interest tables included at the end of this chapter. Review the use of the interest factors as summarized in **Illustration 6-5**. The titles and the contents of the five interest tables are as follows:

1. **Future Value of 1 Table.** Contains the amount to which $1 will accumulate if deposited now at a specified rate of interest and left for a specified number of periods (Table 1).

2. **Present Value of 1 Table.** Contains the amount that must be deposited now at a specified rate of interest to equal $1 at the end of a specified number of periods (Table 2).

3. **Future Value of an Ordinary Annuity of 1 Table.** Contains the amount to which periodic rents of $1 will accumulate if the payments (rents) are invested at the **end** of each period at a specified rate of interest for a specified number of periods (Table 3).

4. **Present Value of an Ordinary Annuity of 1 Table.** Contains the amount that must be deposited now at a specified rate of interest to permit withdrawals of $1 at the **end** of regular periodic intervals for the specified number of periods (Table 4).

5. **Present Value of an Annuity Due of 1 Table.** Contains the amount that must be deposited now at a specified rate of interest to permit withdrawals of $1 at the **beginning** of regular periodic intervals for the specified number of periods (Table 5).

EXERCISE 6-2

Purpose: (L.O. 5, 6, 7) This exercise will illustrate some key concepts such as (1) the more frequently interest is compounded, the more interest will accumulate; (2) the greater the interest rate, the lower the present value will be; and (3) there is more interest reflected in an annuity due situation than in an ordinary annuity situation.

Instructions

Answer each of the questions below following the steps outlined in **Illustration 6-3**. Interest tables are included at the end of this chapter. Use the appropriate factors where needed.

There are a wide variety of situations in which present value and/or future value concepts must be applied. A few of them are illustrated in the questions that follow.

1. If $1,000 is put on deposit today to earn 6% interest, how much will be on deposit at the end of 10 years if interest is compounded annually?

2. If $1,000 is put on deposit today to earn 6% interest, how much will be on deposit at the end of 10 years if interest is compounded semiannually?

3. In comparing questions 1 and 2, which answer would you expect to be the larger? Why?

4. What is the value today of $1,000 due 10 years in the future if the time value of money is 6% and interest is compounded once annually?

5. What is the value today of $1,000 due 10 years in the future if the time value of money is 6% and interest is compounded semiannually?

6. In comparing questions 4 and 5, which answer would you expect to be the larger? Why?

7. What is the present value of $1,000 due in 10 years if interest is compounded annually at 10%?

8. What is the present value of $1,000 due in 10 years if interest is compounded annually at 8%?

9. In comparing questions 7 and 8, which answer would you expect to be the larger? Why?

10. If $1,000 is deposited at the end of each year for 10 years and all amounts on deposit draw 6% interest compounded annually, how much will be on deposit at the end of 10 years?

11.   If $1,000 is deposited at the beginning of each year for 10 years and all amounts on deposit draw 6% interest compounded annually, how much will be on deposit at the end of 10 years?

12.   In comparing questions 10 and 11, which answer would you expect to be the larger? Why?

Solution to Exercise 6-2

1.   (1)   This is a future value of a single sum problem.
      (2) $n = 10$; $i = 6\%$.

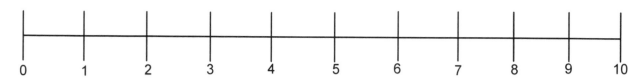

      (3)   The interest factor from Table 1 is 1.79085.
      (4)   Future Value = Present Value x $FVF_{n,i}$
             Future Value = $1,000 x 1.79085
             Future Value = $1,790.85

2.   (1)   This is a future value of a single sum problem.
      (2) $n = 10 \times 2 = 20$; $i = 6\% \div 2 = 3\%$

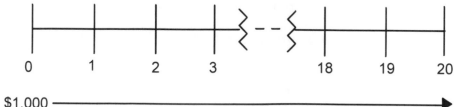

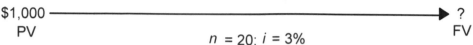

      (3)   The interest factor from Table 1 is 1.80611.
      (4)   Future Value = Present Value x $FVF_{n,i}$
             Future Value = $1,000 x 1.80611
             Future Value = $1,806.11

3.   We would expect the answer to **Question 2** to be a little larger than the answer to question 1 because the interest is compounded more frequently in question 2 which means there will be a larger amount of accumulated interest by the end of year 10 in this scenario.

4.   (1)   This is a present value of a single sum problem.
      (2) $n = 10$; $i = 6\%$.

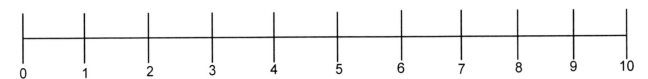

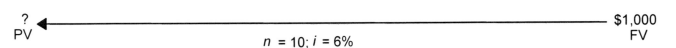

      (3)   The interest factor from Table 2 is .55839.
      (4)   Present Value = Future Value x $PVF_{n,i}$
             Present Value = $1,000 x .55839
             Present Value = <u>$558.39</u>

5.   (1)   This is a present value of single sum problem.
      (2) $n = 10 \times 2 = 20$; $i = 6\% \div 2 = 3\%$

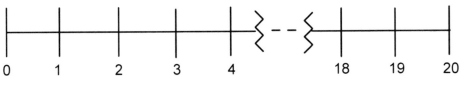

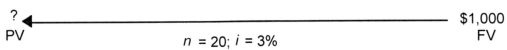

      (3)   The interest factor from Table 2 is .55368.
      (4)   Present Value = Future Value x $PVF_{n,i}$
             Present Value = $1,000 x .55368
             Present Value = <u>$553.68</u>

6.   We would expect the answer to **Question 4** to be the larger because the more frequently that interest is compounded, the more the total interest will be. The greater the interest, the less the present value. Thus, the answer to question 5 has more interest reflected and a lesser present value figure.

7. (1)   This is a present value of a single-sum problem.
    (2) $n = 10$; $i = 10\%$

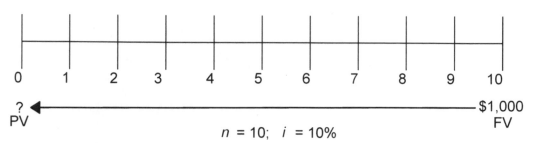

    (3)   The interest factor from Table 2 is .38554.
    (4)   Present Value = Future Value x $PVF_{n,i}$
           Present Value = $1,000 x .38554
           Present Value = $\underline{\$385.54}$

8. (1)   This is a present value of a single-sum problem.
    (2) $n = 10$; $i = 8\%$

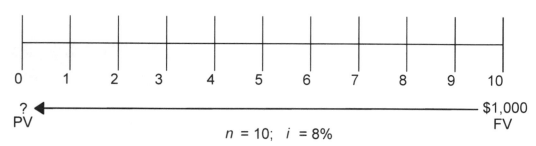

    (3)   The interest factor from Table 2 is .46319.
    (4)   Present Value = Future Value x $PVF_{n,i}$
           Present Value = $1,000 x .46319
           Present Value = $\underline{\$463.19}$

9.   We would expect the answer to **Question 8** to be the larger because the smaller the
      discount rate, the larger the present value. This is the case because the interest amount
      is smaller. The less the interest, the greater the present value figure.

10.   (1)   This is a future value of an ordinary annuity problem.
        (2) $n = 10$; $i = 6\%$

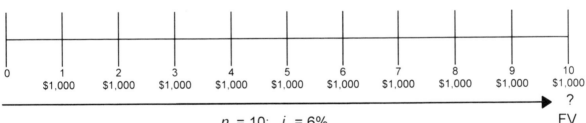

        (3)   The interest factor from Table 3 is 13.18079.
        (4)   Future Value of an Ordinary Annuity = Rent x FVF-OA$_{n,i}$
                Future Value of an Ordinary Annuity = $1,000 x 13.18079
                Future Value of an Ordinary Annuity = $13,180.79

11.   (1)   This is a future value of an annuity due problem.
        (2) $n = 10$; $i = 6\%$

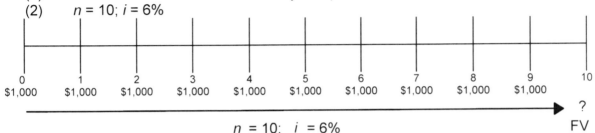

        (3)   The interest factor can be derived as follows:
                FVF-OA for $n = 10$, $i = 6\%$ (Table 3)   13.18079
                Multiply by $(1 + i)$ x   1.06
                FVF-AD for $n = 10$, i = 6%   13.97164
        (4)   Future Value of an Annuity Due = Rent x FVF-AD$_{n,i}$
                Future Value of an Annuity Due = $1,000 x 13.97164
                Future Value of an Annuity Due = $13,971.64

12.   We would expect the answer to **Question 11** to be the larger because there is one more
        interest period reflected in the annuity due arrangement. The number of rents are the
        same, the interest rate is the same, but the rents begin earlier in the annuity due setup
        so there is one more interest period reflected.

TIP: In computing the **future amount** of an **ordinary annuity**, the number of compounding periods is
        one less than the number of rents. In computing the **future amount** of an **annuity due**, the
        number of compounding periods is the **same** as the number of rents. On the other hand, in
        computing the **present value** of an **ordinary annuity**, the final rent is discounted back the **same**
        number of periods that there are rents. In computing the **present value** of an **annuity due**, there
        is **one less** discount period than there are rents.

EXERCISE 6-3

Purpose: (L.O. 5, 6) This exercise will exemplify a situation that requires a two-part solution.

Judson Green borrowed $90,000 on May 1, 2014. This amount plus accrued interest at 12% compounded semiannually is to be repaid in total on May 1, 2024. To retire this debt, Judson plans to contribute to a debt retirement fund four equal amounts starting on May 1, 2020 and continuing for the next three years. The fund is expected to earn 10% per annum.

Instructions
How much must be contributed each year by Judson Green to provide a fund sufficient to retire the debt on May 1, 2024?

Solution to Exercise 6-3

Amount to be repaid on May 1, 2024:
Time diagram:

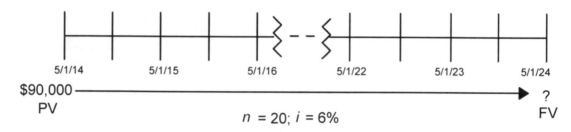

Future Value = $90,000 x $FVF_{n,i}$
Future Value = $90,000 x 3.20714
Future Value =   <u>$288,642.60</u>

Amount of annual contribution to retirement fund:
Time diagram:

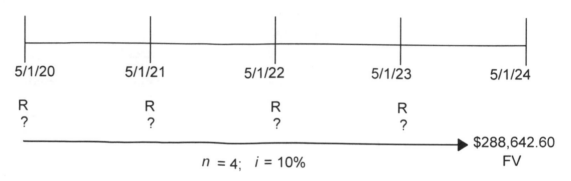

R = rent; FV = future value

Future value of ordinary annuity of 1 for 4 periods at 10%   4.64100
Multiplied by $(1 + i)$ x   1.10
Future value of annuity due of 1 for 4 periods at 10%   5.10510
Future value of an annuity due = Rent x FVF-AD$_{n,i}$
$288,642.60 = Rent x 5.10510
$288,642.60 ÷ 5.10510 = Rent
Rent = $56,540.05

Approach: First solve for the future value of a single sum. This future amount is $288,642.60. Then solve for the rent reflected in the future value of an annuity due. The rent is $56,540.05. The solution to the first part establishes the future value of an annuity due for which the rent must be determined in the second part of the problem.

EXERCISE 6-4

Purpose: (L.O. 5, 6, 7) This exercise will illustrate how to solve present value problems that require the computation of the rent in an annuity or the number of periods or the interest rate.

Instructions
Using the appropriate interest table, provide the solution to each of the following four questions by computing the unknowns.

(a)   Jimmy Gunshanan has $5,000 to invest today at 5% to pay a debt of $7,387. How many years will it take him to accumulate enough to liquidate the debt if interest is compounded once annually?

(b)   Jimmy's friend Nathan has a $6,312.40 debt that he wishes to repay four years from today. He intends to invest $5,000.00 for four years and use the accumulated funds to liquidate the debt. What rate of interest will he need to earn annually in order to accumulate enough to pay the debt if interest is compounded annually?

(c)   Patricia McKiernan wishes to accumulate $35,000 to use for a trip around the world. She plans to gather the designated sum by depositing payments into an account at Sun Bank which pays 4% interest, compounded annually. What is the amount of each payment that Patricia must make at the end of each of six years to accumulate a fund balance of $35,000 by the end of the sixth year?

(d)   Your sister is twenty years old today and she wishes to accumulate $900,000 by her fifty-fifth birthday so she can retire to her summer place on Lake Tahoe. She wishes to accumulate the $900,000 by making annual deposits on her twentieth through her fifty-fourth birthdays. What annual deposit must your sister make if the fund will earn 8% interest compounded annually?

Solution to Exercise 6-4

(a)   Time diagram:

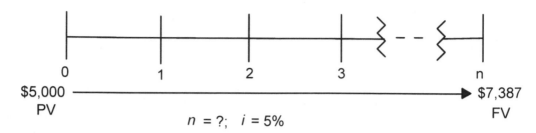

$$0 \qquad 1 \qquad 2 \qquad 3 \qquad\qquad n$$

$5,000 ——————————————————→ $7,387
PV   FV

$$n = ?; \quad i = 5\%$$

Future Value Approach   **OR**   *Present Value Approach*

Future value = Present value x $FVF_{n,i}$ Present value = Future value x $PVF_{n,i}$

$7,387.00 = $5,000 x $FVF_{n,i}$ $5,000.00 = $7,387 x $PVF_{n,i}$

1.4774 = FV factor for i = 5%, n = ?   .67686 = PV factor for i = 5%, n = ?

By reference to Table 1, 1.47746 is   By reference to Table 2, .67684 is
  the FV factor for i = 5%, n = 8   the PV factor for i = 5%, n = 8

n = 8 years n = 8 years

(b)   Time diagram:

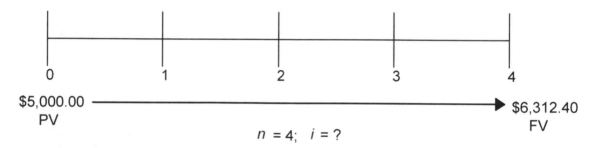

$$0 \qquad 1 \qquad 2 \qquad 3 \qquad 4$$

$5,000.00 ——————————————————→ $6,312.40
PV   FV

$$n = 4; \quad i = ?$$

Future Value Approach   **OR**   *Present Value Approach*

Future value = Present value x $FVF_{n,i}$ Present value = Future value x $PVF_{n,i}$

$6,312.40 = $5,000.00 x $FVF_{n,i}$ $5,000.00 = $6,312.40 x $PVF_{n,i}$

1.26248 = FV factor for n = 4, i = ?   .79209 = PV factor for n = 4, i = ?

By reference to Table 1, 1.26248 is   By reference to Table 2, .79209 is the
  the FV factor for n = 4, i = 6%.   PV factor for n = 4, i = 6%.

i = 6% i = 6%

(c)   Time diagram:

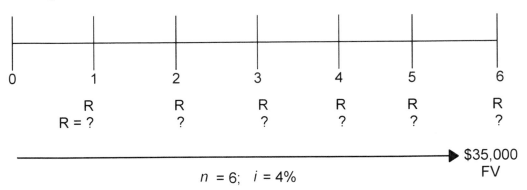

$n = 6$; $i = 4\%$

Future Value = Rent x FVF-OA$_{n,i}$
$35,000 = Rent x 6.63298
$35,000 ÷ 6.63298 = Rent
$5,276.66 = Rent

(d)   Time diagram:

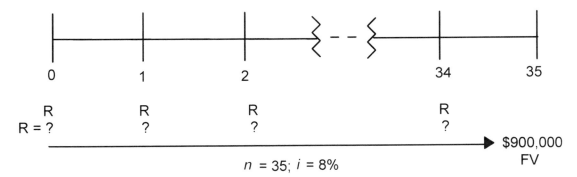

$n = 35$; $i = 8\%$

Future value of an ordinary annuity due of 1 for 35 periods at 8%	172.31680
Multiplied by $(1 + i)$	x 1.08
Future value of annuity due of 1 for 35 periods at 8%	186.10214

Future value of annuity due = Rent x FVF-AD$n,i$
$900,000 = Rent x 186.10214
$900,000 ÷ 186.10214 = Rent
$4,836.05 = Rent

EXERCISE 6-5

Purpose: (L.O. 8) This exercise will illustrate a situation that involves the present value of an annuity along with the present value of a single sum.

Your client, E-Trader, Inc., has acquired Doogle in a business combination that is to be accounted at fair market value. Along with the assets and business of Doogle, E-Trader assumed an outstanding debenture bond issue having a principal amount of $5,000,000 with interest payable semiannually at a stated rate of 6%. Doogle received $5,800,000 in proceeds from the issuance five years ago. The bonds are currently 20 years from maturity. Equivalent securities command an 8% rate of interest with interest paid semiannually.

Instructions
Your client requests your advice regarding the amount to record as the fair value (present value) of the acquired bond issue.

Solution to Exercise 6-5

Time diagram:

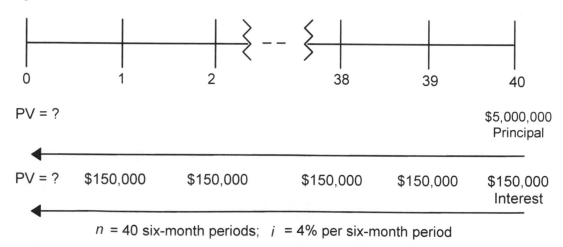

n = 40 six-month periods; i = 4% per six-month period

Present value of the principal = $5,000,000 x .20829	$ 1,041,450.00
Present value of the interest payments = $150,000 x 19.79277	2,968,915.50
Total present value of bond liability	$ 4,010,365.50

Approach and Explanation: Draw a time diagram and enter all future cash flows where they belong. The fair value of the bond liability being acquired by E-Trader is determined by discounting all of the future cash flows related to the bond issue back to the present date using the current market rate of interest (4% per six-month interest period). The face amount of the bonds ($5,000,000) is a single sum due in 20 years (40 semiannual periods). The interest payments constitute an ordinary annuity for forty semiannual periods. Each interest payment is computed by multiplying the stated rate (3% per interest period) by the face amount of the bonds ($5,000,000).

EXERCISE 6-6

Purpose: (L.O. 9) This exercise will apply the expected cash flow approach.

Ozzie Electronics sells high-end plasma TVs and offers a 3-year warranty on all new TVs sold. Ozzie has entered into an agreement with Electronic Service Labs to provide all warranty services on the 95 TVs sold in 2013. The controller for Ozzie estimates the following expected warranty cash outflow associated with the TVs sold in 2013.

	Cash Flow Estimate	Probability Assessment
2014	$20,000	20%
	30,000	60%
	40,000	20%
2015	$25,000	30%
	30,000	50%
	45,000	20%
2016	$30,000	20%
	45,000	40%
	60,000	40%

Instructions

Determine the fair value of the warranty liability for the sales made in 2013. Use expected cash flow and present value techniques. Use an annual discount rate of 6%.

Solution to Exercise 6-6

	Cash Flow Estimate	X	Probability Assessment	= Expected Cash Flow		
2014	$20,000		20%	$ 4,000		
	30,000		60%	18,000		
	40,000		20%	8,000	X PV Factor, n = 1, I = 6%	Present Value
				$30,000	.94340	$28,302.00
2015	$25,000		30%	$ 7,500		
	30,000		50%	15,000		
	45,000		20%	9,000	X PV Factor, n = 2, I = 6%	Present Value
				$31,500	.89000	$28,035.00
2016	$30,000		20%	$ 6,000		
	45,000		40%	18,000		
	60,000		40%	24,000	X PV Factor, n = 3, I = 6%	Present Value
				$48,000	.83962	$40,301.76
				Total Estimated Liability		$96,638.76

ILLUSTRATION 6-6
USING FINANCIAL CALCULATORS

Once you have mastered the underlying concepts in this chapter, you will find it extremely beneficial to learn how to solve time value of money problems by using a financial calculator. A business professional uses a financial calculator rather than the tables used in this chapter because most business applications involve an interest rate or time periods not provided in the interest tables. For example, most real life problems involve interest compounded monthly or daily. Thus a 6% annual rate compounded monthly for 5 years requires our calculations to use a .5% rate (not provided in the tables) for 60 periods (not provided in the tables). The most common keys used to solve time value of money problems are:

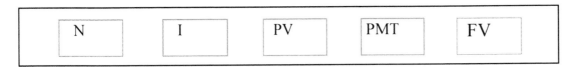

where

N	=	number of periods
I	=	interest rate per period (some calculators use I/YR or i)
PV	=	present value (occurs at the beginning of the first period)
PMT	=	payment (all payments are equal, and none are skipped)
FV	=	future value (occurs at the end of the last period)

On many calculators, these keys are actual buttons on the face of the calculator, on others, they appear on the display after the user accesses a present value menu.

In solving time value of money problems, you generally know (or are given) three of four variables and will solve for the remaining variable. The fifth key (the key not used) is given a value of zero to ensure that this variable is not used in the computation.

To illustrate the use of a financial calculator, let's assume that you want to know the future value of $10,000 invested to earn 8%, compounded annually for 5 years.

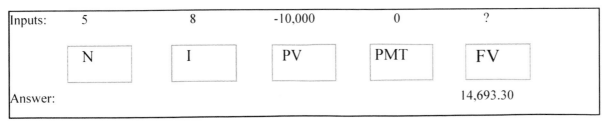

The diagram shows you the information (inputs) to enter into the calculator, N = 5, I = 8, PV = -10,000, and PMT is not used (or PMT = 0) because a series of payments did not occur in the problem. You press FV for the answer and the future value is $14,693.30. This is the same answer you would get using compound interest tables ($10,000 X 1.46933 = $14693.30).

The use of plus and minus signs in time value of money problems with a financial calculator can be confusing. Most financial calculators are programmed so that the positive and negative cash flows in any problem offset each other. In the future value problem above, we identified the $10,000 initial investment as a negative (outflow); the answer 14,693.30 was shown as a positive, reflecting a cash inflow. If the 10,000 were entered as a positive, then the final answer would have been reported as a negative (-14,693.30) If you understand what is required in a problem, you should be able to interpret a positive or negative amount in determining the solution to a problem.

In the problem above, we assumed that compounding occurs once a year. Some financial calculators have a default setting, which assumes that compounding occurs 12 times a year. You must determine what default period has been programmed into your calculator and change it as necessary to arrive at the proper compounding period.

Most financial calculators store and calculate using 12 decimal places. As a result, because compound interest tables generally have factors only up to 5 decimal places, a slight difference in the final answer can result. In most time value of money problems, the final answer will not include more than two decimal points.

To illustrate the future value of an ordinary annuity, assume that you are asked to determine the future value of six $1,000 deposits made at the end of each of the next 6 years, each of which earns interest at 6%, compounded annually. The setup is as follows:

Inputs:	6	6	0	-1,000	?
	N	I	PV	PMT	FV
Answer:					6,975.32

In this case, you enter N = 6, I = 6, PV = 0, PMT = -1,000, and then press FV to arrive at the answer 6,975.32. The $1,000 payments are shown as negatives because the deposits represent cash outflows that will accumulate with interest to the amount to be received (cash inflow) at the end of 6 years.

Recall that in any annuity problem you must determine whether the periodic payments occur at the beginning or the end of the period. If the first payment occurs at the beginning of the period, most financial calculators have a key marked "Begin" (or "Due") that you press to switch from the end-of-period payment mode (for an ordinary annuity) to beginning-of-period payment mode (for an annuity due). For most calculators, the word BEGIN is displayed to indicate that the calculator is set for an annuity due problem. (Some calculators use DUE).

With a financial calculator you can solve for any interest rate or for any number of periods in a time value of money problem. For example, assume you are financing a car with a 3-year loan. The loan has a 9.5% nominal annual interest rate, compounded monthly. The price of the car is $6,000, and you want to determine the monthly payments, assuming that the payments start one month after the purchase.

Inputs:	36	9.5	6,000	?	0
	N	I	PV	PMT	FV
Answer:				-192.20	

By entering N = 36 (12 x 3), I = 9.5, PV = 6,000, FV = 0, and then pressing PMT, you can determine that the monthly payments will be $192.20. Note that the payment key is usually programmed for 12 payments per year. Thus, you must change the default (compounding period) if the payments are different than monthly.

ANALYSIS OF MULTIPLE-CHOICE TYPE QUESTIONS

QUESTION
1. (L.O. 3, 7) A grandfather wishes to set up a fund today that will allow his grandson to withdraw $5,000 from the fund at the beginning of each year for four years to pay for college expenses. The first withdrawal is to occur later today. How should grandpa compute the required investment if the fund is to earn 6% interest compounded annually and the fund is to be exhausted by his last withdrawal?

   a. $5,000 multiplied by the factor for the present value of an annuity due of 1 where $n = 4$, $i = 6\%$.
   b. $5,000 divided by the factor for the present value of an annuity due of 1 where $n = 4$, $i = 6\%$.
   c. $5,000 multiplied by the factor for the future amount of an annuity due of 1 where $n = 4$, $i = 6\%$.
   d. $5,000 divided by the factor for the future amount of an annuity due of 1 where $n = 4$, $i = 6\%$.

Approach and Explanation: Follow the steps in solving future value and present value problems:
1. This is a present value of an annuity due problem.
2. Time diagram:

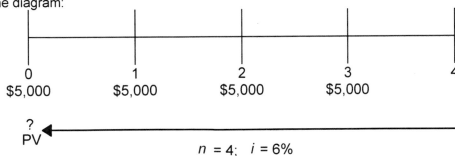

3. The factor for present value of annuity due for $n = 4$, $i = 6\%$ can be found in Table 5; it can also be derived by multiplying the factor for $n = 4$, $i = 6\%$ from the table for present value of an ordinary annuity times $1 + i$.
4. Present Value of an Annuity Due = Rent x Present Value of an Annuity Due Factor.
Therefore, the present value of the annuity due equals $5,000 multiplied by the factor for present value of an annuity due for $n = 4$, $i = 6\%$. (Solution = a.)

Questions 2 and 3 use the following present value table. Given below are the present value factors for $1.00 discounted at 9% for one to five periods.

Periods	Present Value of $1 *i* = 9%
1	.91743
2	.84168
3	.77218
4	.70843
5	.64993

QUESTION

2.   (L.O. 3, 5) What amount should be deposited in a bank account today if a balance of $1,000 is desired four years from today and the prevailing interest rate is 9%?

   a. $1,000 x .91743 x 4
   b. $1,000 x .70843
   c. $1,000 ÷ .70843
   d. $1,000 x (.91743 + .84168 + .77218 + .70843)

Approach and Explanation: Follow the steps in solving future value and present value problems:

1.   This is a present value of a single sum problem.
2.   Time diagram:

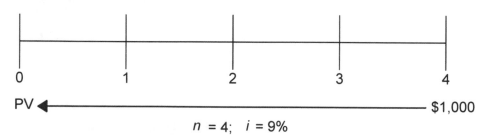

0   1   2   3   4

PV ◄———————————————————————————— $1,000

n = 4;   *i* = 9%

3.   The present value factor is .70843 for *n* = 4, *i* = 9%.
4.   Present Value = Future Value x PV Factor
      Present Value = $1,000 x .70843   (Solution = b.)

QUESTION

3.   (L.O. 3, 5) If $1,000 is deposited today to earn 9% interest compounded annually, how much will be on deposit at the end of three years?

   a. $1,000 x .77218
   b. $1,000 ÷ .77218
   c.   ($1,000 ÷ .91743) x 3
   d.   ($1,000 ÷ .77218) x 3

Approach and Explanation:

1. This is a future value of a single sum problem.
2. Time diagram:

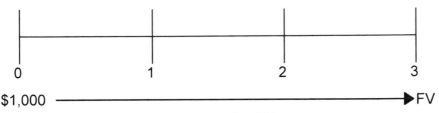

$n = 3; \quad i = 9\%$

3. The future value factor is not given; however, for a single sum, the future value factor is the inverse of the present value factor. Therefore, 1.00000 divided by the present value factor for $n = 3$, $i = 9\%$ equals the future value factor for $n = 3$, $i = 9\%$.
4. Future Value = Present Value x FV Factor
   Future Value = $1,000 x (1 ÷ .77218)
   Future Value = $1,000 ÷ .77218 (Solution = b.)

> **TIP:** By looking at the time diagram, you can reason out that the amount on deposit at the end of three years should be greater than $1,000 but less than $1,500 (three years of 9% simple interest would give a balance of $1,270 and the compounding process would yield a little higher figure). In looking at the alternative answers, you can see that selection "a" will yield a result that is less than $1,000; selection "b" will give a result close to $1,300; selection "c" will give a result close to $3,200; and selection "d" will yield a result that is close to $3,900. Therefore, a reasonableness test would show that answer selection "b" must be the correct choice.

QUESTION

4. (L.O. 4) In the time diagram below, which concept is being depicted?

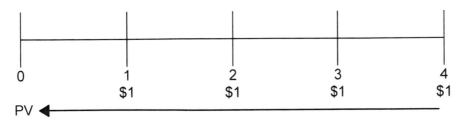

   a. Present value of an ordinary annuity
   b. Present value of an annuity due
   c. Future value of an ordinary annuity
   d. Future value of an annuity due

Explanation: It is an annuity since there is a series of equal periodic payments or receipts. The annuity is an ordinary one because the payments are due at the **end** (not the beginning) of each period. The arrow is drawn so that it is headed back to the present rather than forward to the future. Thus, we have a present value problem. (Solution = a.)

QUESTION

5. (L.O. 6) If the interest rate is 10%, the factor for the future value of annuity due of 1 for $n = 5$, $i = $ 10% is equal to the factor for the future value of an ordinary annuity of 1 for $n = 5$, $i = 10\%$:
   a. plus 1.10.
   b. minus 1.10.
   c. multiplied by 1.10.
   d. divided by 1.10.

Explanation: All amounts involved in an annuity due come in exactly one period earlier than for an ordinary annuity. Therefore, all of the rents and accumulated interest are allowed to generate interest for one more period in the annuity due case. (Solution = c.)

QUESTION

6.   (L.O. 7) A grandmother is setting up a savings account to help fund her granddaughter's college expenses. She is putting $40,000 in an account today that will earn 6% interest compounded annually. How much may Josey, the granddaughter, withdraw at the beginning of each of four years of college if her first withdrawal is to be one year from today and her last withdrawal is to exhaust the fund? The answer would be determined by which one of the following?

a. $40,000 multiplied by the factor for the present value of an ordinary annuity of 1 where n = 4, i = 6%.

b. $40,000 divided by the factor for the present value of an ordinary annuity of 1 where n = 4, i = 6%.

c. $40,000 multiplied by the factor for the future amount of an ordinary annuity of 1 where n = 4, i = 6%.

d. $40,000 divided by the factor for the future amount of an ordinary annuity of 1 where n = 4, i = 6%.

Approach and Explanation: Follow the steps in solving future value and present value problems.

1.   This is a present value of an ordinary annuity problem although by the wording of the question it could easily be confused with an annuity due situation. There are four rents and the first one is to be received a year from today.

2.   Time diagram:

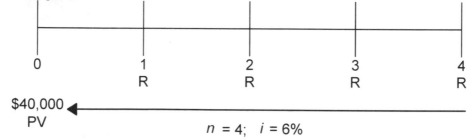

3.   The factor for present value of an ordinary annuity for n = 4, i = 6% would be obtained from Table 4.

4.   Present Value of an Ordinary Annuity = Rent x Present Value of an Ordinary Annuity Factor. The Rent would be determined by dividing both sides of the equation by the factor. Therefore, the rent would equal the $40,000 divided by the factor for the present value of an ordinary annuity of 1. (Solution = b.)

QUESTION

7.   (L.O. 4) On December 1, 2014, Michael Hess Company sold some machinery to Shawn Keling Company. The two companies entered into an installment sales contract at a predetermined interest rate. The contract required four equal annual payments with the first payment due on December 1, 2014, the date of the sale. What present value concept is appropriate for this situation?

a.   Future amount of an annuity of 1 for four periods

b.   Future amount of 1 for four periods

c.   Present value of an ordinary annuity of 1 for four periods

d.   Present value of an annuity due of 1 for four periods.

Explanation: There is a series of equal payments due at the first of each period (year) because the first payment is due at the date of the sale (December 1, 2014); hence, this is an annuity due. The relevant amount to solve for would be the present value of the annuity; this present value would be involved in the determination of the sale (or purchase) price of the machinery. (Solution = d.)

QUESTION

8. (L.O. 4) On May 1, 2014, a company purchased a new machine that it does **not** have to pay for until May 1, 2016. The total payment on May 1, 2016 will include both principal and accumulated interest. Assuming interest is computed at a 10% rate compounded annually, the total payment due will be the price of the machine multiplied by what time value of money factor?
   a. Future value of 1
   b. Future value of an ordinary annuity of 1
   c. Present value of 1
   d. Present value of an ordinary annuity of 1

Explanation: The total payment due will be the price today (present value) plus the interest that will accumulate in two years. In computing the future value of a given amount today, the given amount is multiplied by a future value of 1 factor. (Solution = a.)

QUESTION

9. (L.O. 3) A series of equal receipts at equal intervals of time when each receipt is received at the beginning of each time period is called an:
   a. ordinary annuity.
   b. annuity in arrears.
   c. annuity due.
   d. unearned receipt.

Explanation: A series of equal receipts or payments at equal intervals is called an annuity. An ordinary annuity is an annuity where the rents (receipts or payments) occur at the **end** of each period; another name for an **ordinary annuity** is an **annuity in arrears**. An annuity due is one where the first rent occurs at the **beginning** of the first period; another name for an **annuity due** is an **annuity in advance**. (Solution = c.)

QUESTION

10. (L.O. 5) Which of the following statements is true?
    a. The higher the discount rate, the higher the present value.
    b. The process of accumulating interest on interest is referred to as discounting.
    c. If money is worth 10% compounded annually, $1,100 due one year from today is equivalent to $1,000 today.
    d. If a single sum is due on December 31, 2017, the present value of that sum decreases as the date draws closer to December 31, 2017.

Explanation: Selection "a" is false because the higher the discount rate the lower the present value. Selection "b" is false because the process of accumulating interest on interest is referred to as compounding; discounting refers to the process of computing present value. Selection "d" is false because the present value of a single sum increases over time due to the time value of money (accumulation of interest). Selection "c" is correct because 10% of $1,000 is $100 interest; $1,000 today plus interest of $100 for one year means $1,100 one year from today is equivalent to $1,000 today if money is worth 10%. (Solution = c.)

QUESTION

11. (L.O. 8) Jake Co. has outstanding a 7% 10-year bond issue with a face value of $200,000. The bond was originally sold to yield a 6% annual interest rate. Jake uses the effective interest method. On December 31, 2013, the carrying amount of the bond was $210,000. What amount of unamortized premium should Jake report in its December 31, 2014 balance sheet?
   a. $9,000.
   b. $8,600.
   c. $7,900.
   d. $2,100.

Explanation: The carrying value at the beginning of the period ($210,000) is multiplied by the yield (effective) rate (6%) to determine interest expense for the period ($210,000 x 6% = $12,600). The face value ($200,000) is multiplied by the stated rate (7%) to determine the cash amount of interest for the period ($200,000 x 7% = $14,000). The difference between the interest expense of $12,600 and the amount of interest to be paid in cash of $14,000 is the amount of premium amortization for the period of $1,400. The unamortized premium is therefore $10,000 minus $1,400 = $8,600. (Solution = b.)

QUESTION

12. (L.O. 9) The interest rate to be used in performing an expected cash flow application is the
   a. pure rate of return.
   b. expected inflation rate.
   c. risk-free rate.
   d. credit risk rate of interest.

Explanation: The **pure rate of interest** (2% - 4%) is the amount a lender would charge if there are no possibilities of default and no expectation of inflation. The **expected inflation rate** is the estimated rate to compensate for loss of purchasing power in an inflationary economy. The **credit risk rate of interest** is a rate reflecting an enterprise's financial stability and profitability. The **risk-free rate of return** is defined as the pure rate of return plus the expected inflation rate. The FASB notes that the expected cash flow framework adjusts for credit risk because it incorporates the probability of receipt or payment into the computation of expected cash flows. Therefore, the rate used to discount the expected cash flows should consider only the pure rate of interest and the inflation rate. (Solution = c.)

IFRS Insights

- The time value of money concept is universal and applied the same, regardless of whether a company follows GAAP or IFRS.

Table 1 FUTURE VALUE OF 1 (FUTURE VALUE OF A SINGLE SUM)

$$FVF_{n.i} = (1 + i)^n$$

(n) Periods	2%	2-1/2%	3%	4%	5%	6%
1	1.02000	1.02500	1.03000	1.04000	1.05000	1.06000
2	1.04040	1.05063	1.06090	1.08160	1.10250	1.12360
3	1.06121	1.07689	1.09273	1.12486	1.15763	1.19102
4	1.08243	1.10381	1.12551	1.16986	1.21551	1.26248
5	1.10408	1.13141	1.15927	1.21665	1.27628	1.33823
6	1.12616	1.15969	1.19405	1.26532	1.34010	1.41852
7	1.14869	1.18869	1.22987	1.31593	1.40710	1.50363
8	1.17166	1.21840	1.26677	1.36857	1.47746	1.59385
9	1.19509	1.24886	1.30477	1.42331	1.55133	1.68948
10	1.21899	1.28008	1.34392	1.48024	1.62889	1.79085
11	1.24337	1.31209	1.38423	1.53945	1.71034	1.89830
12	1.26824	1.34489	1.42576	1.60103	1.79586	2.01220
13	1.29361	1.37851	1.46853	1.66507	1.88565	2.13293
14	1.31948	1.41297	1.51259	1.73168	1.97993	2.26090
15	1.34587	1.44830	1.55797	1.80094	2.07893	2.39656
16	1.37279	1.48451	1.60471	1.87298	2.18287	2.54035
17	1.40024	1.52162	1.65285	1.94790	2.29202	2.69277
18	1.42825	1.55966	1.70243	2.02582	2.40662	2.85434
19	1.45681	1.59865	1.75351	2.10685	2.52695	3.02560
20	1.48595	1.63862	1.80611	2.19112	2.65330	3.20714
21	1.51567	1.67958	1.86029	2.27877	2.78596	3.39956
22	1.54598	1.72157	1.91610	2.36992	2.92526	3.60354
23	1.57690	1.76461	1.97359	2.46472	3.07152	3.81975
24	1.60844	1.80873	2.03279	2.56330	3.22510	4.04893
25	1.64061	1.85394	2.09378	2.66584	3.38635	4.29187
26	1.67342	1.90029	2.15659	2.77247	3.55567	4.54938
27	1.70689	1.94780	2.22129	2.88337	3.73346	4.82235
28	1.74102	1.99650	2.28793	2.99870	3.92013	5.11169
29	1.77584	2.04641	2.35657	3.11865	4.11614	5.41839
30	1.81136	2.09757	2.42726	3.24340	4.32194	5.74349
31	1.84759	2.15001	2.50008	3.37313	4.53804	6.08810
32	1.88454	2.20376	2.57508	3.50806	4.76494	6.45339
33	1.92223	2.25885	2.65234	3.64838	5.00319	6.84059
34	1.96068	2.31532	2.73191	3.79432	5.25335	7.25103
35	1.99989	2.37321	2.81386	3.94609	5.51602	7.68609
36	2.03989	2.43254	2.89828	4.10393	5.79182	8.14725
37	2.08069	2.49335	2.98523	4.26809	6.08141	8.63609
38	2.12230	2.55568	3.07478	4.43881	6.38548	9.15425
39	2.16474	2.61957	3.16703	4.61637	6.70475	9.70351
40	2.20804	2.68506	3.26204	4.80102	7.03999	10.28572

8%	9%	10%	11%	12%	15%	(n) Periods
1.08000	1.09000	1.10000	1.11000	1.12000	1.15000	1
1.16640	1.18810	1.21000	1.23210	1.25440	1.32250	2
1.25971	1.29503	1.33100	1.36763	1.40493	1.52088	3
1.36049	1.41158	1.46410	1.51807	1.57352	1.74901	4
1.46933	1.53862	1.61051	1.68506	1.76234	2.01136	5
1.58687	1.67710	1.77156	1.87041	1.97382	2.31306	6
1.71382	1.82804	1.94872	2.07616	2.21068	2.66002	7
1.85093	1.99256	2.14359	2.30454	2.47596	3.05902	8
1.99900	2.17189	2.35795	2.55803	2.77308	3.51788	9
2.15892	2.36736	2.59374	2.83942	3.10585	4.04556	10
2.33164	2.58043	2.85312	3.15176	3.47855	4.65239	11
2.51817	2.81267	3.13843	3.49845	3.89598	5.35025	12
2.71962	3.06581	3.45227	3.88328	4.36349	6.15279	13
2.93719	3.34173	3.79750	4.31044	4.88711	7.07571	14
3.17217	3.64248	4.17725	4.78459	5.47357	8.13706	15
3.42594	3.97031	4.59497	5.31089	6.13039	9.35762	16
3.70002	4.32763	5.05447	5.89509	6.86604	10.76126	17
3.99602	4.71712	5.55992	6.54355	7.68997	12.37545	18
4.31570	5.14166	6.11591	7.26334	8.61276	14.23177	19
4.66096	5.60441	6.72750	8.06231	9.64629	16.36654	20
5.03383	6.10881	7.40025	8.94917	10.80385	18.82152	21
5.43654	6.65860	8.14028	9.93357	12.10031	21.64475	22
5.87146	7.25787	8.95430	11.02627	13.55235	24.89146	23
6.34118	7.91108	9.84973	12.23916	15.17863	28.62518	24
6.84847	8.62308	10.83471	13.58546	17.00000	32.91895	25
7.39635	9.39916	11.91818	15.07986	19.04007	37.85680	26
7.98806	10.24508	13.10999	16.73865	21.32488	43.53532	27
8.62711	11.16714	14.42099	18.57990	23.88387	50.06561	28
9.31727	12.17218	15.86309	20.62369	26.74993	57.57545	29
10.06266	13.26768	17.44940	22.89230	29.95992	66.21177	30
10.86767	14.46177	19.19434	25.41045	33.55511	76.14354	31
11.73708	15.76333	21.11378	28.20560	37.58173	87.56507	32
12.67605	17.18203	23.22515	31.30821	42.09153	100.69983	33
13.69013	18.72841	25.54767	34.75212	47.14252	115.80480	34
14.78534	20.41397	28.10244	38.57485	52.79962	133.17552	35
15.96817	22.25123	30.91268	42.81808	59.13557	153.15185	36
17.24563	24.25384	34.00395	47.52807	66.23184	176.12463	37
18.62528	26.43668	37.40434	52.75616	74.17966	202.54332	38
20.11530	28.81598	41.14479	58.55934	83.08122	232.92482	39
21.72452	31.40942	45.25926	65.00087	93.05097	267.86355	40

Table 2 PRESENT VALUE OF 1 (PRESENT VALUE OF A SINGLE SUM)

$$PVF_{n,i} = \frac{1}{(1 + i)^n} = (1 + i)^{-n}$$

(n) Periods	2%	2-1/2%	3%	4%	5%	6%
1	.98039	.97561	.97087	.96154	.95238	.94340
2	.96117	.95181	.94260	.92456	.90703	.89000
3	.94232	.92860	.91514	.88900	.86384	.83962
4	.92385	.90595	.88949	.85480	.82270	.79209
5	.90573	.88385	.86261	.82193	.78353	.74726
6	.88797	.86230	.83748	.79031	.74622	.70496
7	.87056	.84127	.81309	.75992	.71068	.66506
8	.85349	.82075	.78941	.73069	.67684	.62741
9	.83676	.80073	.76642	.70259	.64461	.59190
10	.82035	.78120	.74409	.67556	.61391	.55839
11	.80426	.76214	.72242	.64958	.58468	.52679
12	.78849	.74356	.70138	.62460	.55684	.49697
13	.77303	.72542	.68095	.60057	.53032	.46884
14	.75788	.70773	.66112	.57748	.50507	.44230
15	.74301	.69047	.64186	.55526	.48102	.41727
16	.72845	.67362	.62317	.53391	.45811	.39365
17	.71416	.65720	.60502	.51337	.43630	.37136
18	.70016	.64117	.58739	.49363	.41552	.35034
19	.68643	.62553	.57029	.47464	.39573	.33051
20	.67297	.61027	.55368	.45639	.37689	.31180
21	.65978	.59539	.53755	.43883	.35894	.29416
22	.64684	.58086	.52189	.42196	.34185	.27751
23	.63416	.56670	.50669	.40573	.32557	.26180
24	.62172	.55288	.49193	.39012	.31007	.24698
25	.60593	.53939	.47761	.37512	.29530	.23300
26	.59758	.52623	.46369	.36069	.28124	.21981
27	.58586	.51340	.45019	.34682	.26785	.20737
28	.57437	.50088	.43708	.33348	.25509	.19563
29	.56311	.48866	.42435	.32065	.24295	.18456
30	.55207	.47674	.41199	.30832	.23138	.17411
31	.54125	.46511	.39999	.29646	.22036	.16425
32	.53063	.45377	.38834	.28506	.20987	.15496
33	.52023	.44270	.37703	.27409	.19987	.14619
34	.51003	.43191	.36604	.26355	.19035	.13791
35	.50003	.42137	.35538	.25342	.18129	.13011
36	.49022	.41109	.34503	.24367	.17266	.12274
37	.48061	.40107	.33498	.23430	.16444	.11579
38	.47119	.39128	.32523	.22529	.15661	.10924
39	.46195	.38174	.31575	.21662	.14915	.10306
40	.45289	.37243	.30656	.20829	.14205	.09722

8%	9%	10%	11%	12%	15%	(n) Periods
.92593	.91743	.90909	.90090	.89286	.86957	1
.85734	.84168	.82645	.81162	.79719	.75614	2
.79383	.77218	.75132	.73119	.71178	.65752	3
.73503	.70843	.68301	.65873	.63552	.57175	4
.68058	.64993	.62092	.59345	.56743	.49718	5
.63017	.59627	.56447	.53464	.50663	.43233	6
.58349	.54703	.51316	.48166	.45235	.37594	7
.54027	.50187	.46651	.43393	.40388	.32690	8
.50025	.46043	.42410	.39092	.36061	.28426	9
.46319	.42241	.38554	.35218	.32197	.24719	10
.42888	.38753	.35049	.31728	.28748	.21494	11
.39711	.35554	.31863	.28584	.25668	.18691	12
.36770	.32618	.28966	.25751	.22917	.16253	13
.34046	.29925	.26333	.23199	.20462	.14133	14
.31524	.27454	.23939	.20900	.18270	.12289	15
.29189	.25187	.21763	.18829	.16312	.10687	16
.27027	.23107	.19785	.16963	.14564	.09293	17
.25025	.21199	.17986	.15282	.13004	.08081	18
.23171	.19449	.16351	.13768	.11611	.07027	19
.21455	.17843	.14864	.12403	.10367	.06110	20
.19866	.16370	.13513	.11174	.09256	.05313	21
.18394	.15018	.12285	.10067	.08264	.04620	22
.17032	.13778	.11168	.09069	.07379	.04017	23
.15770	.12641	.10153	.08170	.06588	.03493	24
.14602	.11597	.09230	.07361	.05882	.03038	25
.13520	.10639	.08391	.06631	.05252	.02642	26
.12519	.09761	.07628	.05974	.04689	.02297	27
.11591	.08955	.06934	.05382	.04187	.01997	28
.10733	.08216	.06304	.04849	.03738	.01737	29
.09938	.07537	.05731	.04368	.03338	.01510	30
.09202	.06915	.05210	.03935	.02980	.01313	31
.08520	.06344	.04736	.03545	.02661	.01142	32
.07889	.05820	.04306	.03194	.02376	.00993	33
.07305	.05340	.03914	.02878	.02121	.00864	34
.06763	.04899	.03558	.02592	.01894	.00751	35
.06262	.04494	.03235	.02335	.01691	.00653	36
.05799	.04123	.02941	.02104	.01510	.00568	37
.05369	.03783	.02674	.01896	.01348	.00494	38
.04971	.03470	.02430	.01708	.01204	.00429	39
.04603	.03184	.02210	.01538	.01075	.00373	40

Table 3 FUTURE VALUE OF AN ORDINARY ANNUITY OF 1

$$FVF\text{-}OA_{n,i}= \frac{(1+i)^n - 1}{i}$$

(n) Periods	2%	2-1/2%	3%	4%	5%	6%
1	1.00000	1.00000	1.00000	1.00000	1.00000	1.00000
2	2.02000	2.02500	2.03000	2.04000	2.05000	2.06000
3	3.06040	3.07563	3.09090	3.12160	3.15250	3.18360
4	4.12161	4.15252	4.18363	4.24646	4.31013	4.37462
5	5.20404	5.25633	5.30914	5.41632	5.52563	5.63709
6	6.30812	6.38774	6.46841	6.63298	6.80191	6.97532
7	7.43428	7.54743	7.66246	7.89829	8.14201	8.39384
8	8.58297	8.73612	8.89234	9.21423	9.54911	9.89747
9	9.75463	9.95452	10.15911	10.58280	11.02656	11.49132
10	10.94972	11.20338	11.46338	12.00611	12.57789	13.18079
11	12.16872	12.48347	12.80780	13.48635	14.20679	14.97164
12	13.41209	13.79555	14.19203	15.02581	15.91713	16.86994
13	14.68033	15.14044	15.61779	16.62684	17.71298	18.88214
14	15.97394	16.51895	17.08632	18.29191	19.59863	21.01507
15	17.29342	17.93193	18.59891	20.02359	21.57856	23.27597
16	18.63929	19.38022	20.15688	21.82453	23.65749	25.67253
17	20.01207	20.86473	21.76159	23.69751	25.84037	28.21288
18	21.41231	22.38635	23.41444	25.64541	28.13238	30.90565
19	22.84056	23.94601	25.11687	27.67123	30.53900	33.75999
20	24.29737	25.54466	26.87037	29.77808	33.06595	36.78559
21	25.78332	27.18327	28.67649	31.96920	35.71925	39.99273
22	27.29898	28.86286	30.53678	34.24797	38.50521	43.39229
23	28.84496	30.58443	32.45288	36.61789	41.43048	46.99583
24	30.42186	32.34904	34.42647	39.08260	44.50200	50.81558
25	32.03030	34.15776	36.45926	41.64591	47.72710	54.86451
26	33.67091	36.01171	38.55304	44.31174	51.11345	59.15638
27	35.34432	37.91200	40.70963	47.08421	54.66913	63.70577
28	37.05121	39.85980	42.93092	49.96758	58.40258	68.52811
29	38.79223	41.85630	45.21885	52.96629	62.32271	73.63980
30	40.56808	43.90270	47.57542	56.08494	66.43885	79.05819
31	42.37944	46.00027	50.00268	59.32834	70.76079	84.80168
32	44.22703	48.15028	52.50276	62.70147	75.29883	90.88978
33	46.11157	50.35403	55.07784	66.20953	80.06377	97.34316
34	48.03380	52.61289	57.73018	69.85791	85.06696	104.18376
35	49.99448	54.92821	60.46208	73.65222	90.32031	111.43478
36	51.99437	57.30141	63.27594	77.59831	95.83632	119.12087
37	54.03425	59.73395	66.17422	81.70225	101.62814	127.26812
38	56.11494	62.22730	69.15945	85.97034	107.70955	135.90421
39	58.23724	64.78298	72.23423	90.40915	114.09502	145.05846
40	60.40198	67.40255	75.40126	95.02552	120.79977	154.76197

8%	9%	10%	11%	12%	15%	(n) Periods
1.00000	1.00000	1.00000	1.00000	1.00000	1.00000	1
2.08000	2.09000	2.10000	2.11000	2.12000	2.15000	2
3.24640	3.27810	3.31000	3.34210	3.37440	3.47250	3
4.50611	4.57313	4.64100	4.70973	4.77933	4.99338	4
5.86660	5.98471	6.10510	6.22780	6.35285	6.74238	5
7.33592	7.52334	7.71561	7.91286	8.11519	8.75374	6
8.92280	9.20044	9.48717	9.78327	10.08901	11.06680	7
10.63663	11.02847	11.43589	11.85943	12.29969	13.72682	8
12.48756	13.02104	13.57948	14.16397	14.77566	16.78584	9
14.48656	15.19293	15.93743	16.72201	17.54874	20.30372	10
16.64549	17.56029	18.53117	19.56143	20.65458	24.34928	11
18.97713	20.14072	21.38428	22.71319	24.13313	29.00167	12
21.49530	22.95339	24.52271	26.21164	28.02911	34.35192	13
24.21492	26.01919	27.97498	30.09492	32.39260	40.50471	14
27.15211	29.36092	31.77248	34.40536	37.27972	47.58041	15
30.32428	33.00340	35.94973	39.18995	42.75328	55.71747	16
33.75023	36.97371	40.54470	44.50084	48.88367	65.07509	17
37.45024	41.30134	45.59917	50.39593	55.74972	75.83636	18
41.44626	46.01846	51.15909	56.93949	63.43968	88.21181	19
45.76196	51.16012	57.27500	64.20283	72.05244	102.44358	20
50.42292	56.76453	64.00250	72.26514	81.69874	118.81012	21
55.45676	62.87334	71.40275	81.21431	92.50258	137.63164	22
60.89330	69.53194	79.54302	91.14788	104.60289	159.27638	23
66.76476	76.78981	88.49733	102.17415	118.15524	184.16784	24
73.10594	84.70090	98.34706	114.41331	133.33387	212.79302	25
79.95442	93.32398	109.18177	127.99877	150.33393	245.71197	26
87.35077	102.72314	121.09994	143.07864	169.37401	283.56877	27
95.33883	112.96822	134.20994	159.81729	190.69889	327.10408	28
103.96594	124.13536	148.63093	178.39719	214.58275	377.16969	29
113.28231	136.30754	164.49402	199.02088	241.33268	434.74515	30
123.34587	149.57522	181.94343	221.91317	271.29261	500.95692	31
134.21354	164.03699	201.13777	247.32362	304.84772	577.10046	32
145.95062	179.80032	222.25154	275.52922	342.42945	644.66553	33
158.62667	196.98234	245.47670	306.83744	384.52098	765.36535	34
172.31680	215.71076	271.02437	341.58955	431.66350	881.17016	35
187.10215	236.12472	299.12681	380.16441	484.46312	1014.34568	36
203.07032	258.37595	330.03949	422.98249	543.59869	1167.49753	37
220.31595	282.62978	364.04343	470.51056	609.83053	1343.62216	38
238.94122	309.06646	401.44778	523.26673	684.01020	1546.16549	39
259.05652	337.88245	442.59256	581.82607	767.09142	1779.09031	40

Table 4 PRESENT VALUE OF AN ORDINARY ANNUITY OF 1

$$PVF\text{-}OA_{n,i} = \frac{1 - \dfrac{1}{(1+i)^n}}{i}$$

(n) Periods	2%	2-1/2%	3%	4%	5%	6%
1	.98039	.97561	.97087	.96154	.95238	.94340
2	1.94156	1.92742	1.91347	1.88609	1.85941	1.83339
3	2.88388	2.85602	2.82861	2.77509	2.72325	2.67301
4	3.80773	3.76197	3.71710	3.62990	3.54595	3.46511
5	4.71346	4.64583	4.57971	4.45182	4.32948	4.21236
6	5.60143	5.50813	5.41719	5.24214	5.07569	4.91732
7	6.47199	6.34939	6.23028	6.00205	5.78637	5.58238
8	7.32548	7.17014	7.01969	6.73274	6.46321	6.20979
9	8.16224	7.97087	7.78611	7.43533	7.10782	6.80169
10	8.98259	8.75206	8.53020	8.11090	7.72173	7.36009
11	9.78685	9.51421	9.25262	8.76048	8.30641	7.88687
12	10.57534	10.25776	9.95400	9.38507	8.86325	8.38384
13	11.34837	10.98319	10.63496	9.98565	9.39357	8.85268
14	12.10625	11.69091	11.29607	10.56312	9.89864	9.29498
15	12.84926	12.38138	11.93794	11.11839	10.37966	9.71225
16	13.57771	13.05500	12.56110	11.65230	10.83777	10.10590
17	14.29187	13.71220	13.16612	12.16567	11.27407	10.47726
18	14.99203	14.35336	13.75351	12.65930	11.68959	10.82760
19	15.67846	14.97889	14.32380	13.13394	12.08532	11.15812
20	16.35143	15.58916	14.87747	13.59033	12.46221	11.46992
21	17.01121	16.18455	15.41502	14.02916	12.82115	11.76408
22	17.65805	16.76541	15.93692	14.45112	13.16300	12.04158
23	18.29220	17.33211	16.44361	14.85684	13.48857	12.30338
24	18.91393	17.88499	16.93554	15.24696	13.79864	12.55036
25	19.52346	18.42438	17.41315	15.62208	14.09394	12.78336
26	20.12104	18.95061	17.87684	15.98277	14.37519	13.00317
27	20.70690	19.46401	18.32703	16.32959	14.64303	13.21053
28	21.28127	19.96489	18.76411	16.66306	14.89813	13.40616
29	21.84438	20.45355	19.18845	16.98371	15.14107	13.59072
30	22.39646	20.93029	19.60044	17.29203	15.37245	13.76483
31	22.93770	21.39541	20.00043	17.58849	15.59281	13.92909
32	23.46833	21.84918	20.38877	17.87355	15.80268	14.08404
33	23.98856	22.29188	20.76579	18.14765	16.00255	14.23023
34	24.49859	22.72379	21.13184	18.41120	16.19290	14.36814
35	24.99862	23.14516	21.48722	18.66461	16.37419	14.49825
36	25.48884	23.55625	21.83225	18.90828	16.54685	14.62099
37	25.96945	23.95732	22.16724	19.14258	16.71129	14.73678
38	26.44064	24.34860	22.49246	19.36786	16.86789	14.84602
39	26.90259	24.73034	22.80822	19.58448	17.01704	14.94907
40	27.35548	25.10278	23.11477	19.79277	17.15909	15.04630

8%	9%	10%	11%	12%	15%	(n) Periods
.92593	.91743	.90909	.90090	.89286	.86957	1
1.78326	1.75911	1.73554	1.71252	1.69005	1.62571	2
2.57710	2.53130	2.48685	2.44371	2.40183	2.28323	3
3.31213	3.23972	3.16986	3.10245	3.03735	2.85498	4
3.99271	3.88965	3.79079	3.69590	3.60478	3.35216	5
4.62288	4.48592	4.35526	4.23054	4.11141	3.78448	6
5.20637	5.03295	4.86842	4.71220	4.56376	4.16042	7
5.74664	5.53482	5.33493	5.14612	4.96764	4.48732	8
6.24689	5.99525	5.75902	5.53705	5.32825	4.77158	9
6.71008	6.41766	6.14457	5.88923	5.65022	5.01877	10
7.13896	6.80519	6.49506	6.20652	5.93770	5.23371	11
7.53608	7.16073	6.81369	6.49236	6.19437	5.42062	12
7.90378	7.48690	7.10336	6.74987	6.42355	5.58315	13
8.24424	7.78615	7.36669	6.98187	6.62817	5.72448	14
8.55948	8.06069	7.60608	7.19087	6.81086	5.84737	15
8.85137	8.31256	7.82371	7.37916	6.97399	5.95424	16
9.12164	8.54363	8.02155	7.54879	7.11963	6.04716	17
9.37189	8.75563	8.20141	7.70162	7.24967	6.12797	18
9.60360	8.95012	8.36492	7.83929	7.36578	6.19823	19
9.81815	9.12855	8.51356	7.96333	7.46944	6.25933	20
10.01680	9.29224	8.64869	8.07507	7.56200	6.31246	21
10.20074	9.44243	8.77154	8.17574	7.64465	6.35866	22
10.37106	9.58021	8.88322	8.26643	7.71843	6.39884	23
10.52876	9.70661	8.98474	8.34814	7.78432	6.43377	24
10.67478	9.82258	9.07704	8.42174	7.84314	6.46415	25
10.80998	9.92897	9.16095	8.48806	7.89566	6.49056	26
10.93516	10.02658	9.23722	8.54780	7.94255	6.51353	27
11.05108	10.11613	9.30657	8.60162	7.98442	6.53351	28
11.15841	10.19828	9.36961	8.65011	8.02181	6.55088	29
11.25778	10.27365	9.42691	8.69379	8.05518	6.56598	30
11.34980	10.34280	9.47901	8.73315	8.08499	6.57911	31
11.43500	10.40624	9.52638	8.76860	8.11159	6.59053	32
11.51389	10.46444	9.56943	8.80054	8.13535	6.60046	33
11.58693	10.51784	9.60858	8.82932	8.15656	6.60910	34
11.65457	10.56682	9.64416	8.85524	8.17550	6.61661	35
11.71719	10.61176	9.67651	8.87859	8.19241	6.62314	36
11.77518	10.65299	9.70592	8.89963	8.20751	6.62882	37
11.82887	10.69082	9.73265	8.91859	8.22099	6.63375	38
11.87858	10.72552	9.75697	8.93567	8.23303	6.63805	39
11.92461	10.75736	9.77905	8.95105	8.24378	6.64178	40

Table 5 PRESENT VALUE OF AN ANNUITY DUE OF 1

$$\text{PVF-AD}_{n,i} = 1 + \frac{1 - \dfrac{1}{(1+i)^{n-1}}}{i}$$

(n) Periods	2%	2-1/2%	3%	4%	5%	6%
1	1.00000	1.00000	1.00000	1.00000	1.00000	1.00000
2	1.98039	1.97561	1.97087	1.96154	1.95238	1.94340
3	2.94156	2.92742	2.91347	2.88609	2.85941	2.83339
4	3.88388	3.85602	3.82861	3.77509	3.72325	3.67301
5	4.80773	4.76197	4.71710	4.62990	4.54595	4.46511
6	5.71346	5.64583	5.57971	5.45182	5.32948	5.21236
7	6.60143	6.50813	6.41719	6.24214	6.07569	5.91732
8	7.47199	7.34939	7.23028	7.00205	6.78637	6.58238
9	8.32548	8.17014	8.01969	7.73274	7.46321	7.20979
10	9.16224	8.97087	8.78611	8.43533	8.10782	7.80169
11	9.98259	9.75206	9.53020	9.11090	8.72173	8.36009
12	10.78685	10.51421	10.25262	9.76048	9.30641	8.88687
13	11.57534	11.25776	10.95400	10.38507	9.86325	9.38384
14	12.34837	11.98319	11.63496	10.98565	10.39357	9.85268
15	13.10625	12.69091	12.29607	11.56312	10.89864	10.29498
16	13.84926	13.38138	12.93794	12.11839	11.37966	10.71225
17	14.57771	14.05500	13.56110	12.65230	11.83777	11.10590
18	15.29187	14.71220	14.16612	13.16567	12.27407	11.47726
19	15.99203	15.35336	14.75351	13.65930	12.68959	11.82760
20	16.67846	15.97889	15.32380	14.13394	13.08532	12.15812
21	17.35143	16.58916	15.87747	14.59033	13.46221	12.46992
22	18.01121	17.18455	16.41502	15.02916	13.82115	12.76408
23	18.65805	17.76541	16.93692	15.45112	14.16300	13.04158
24	19.29220	18.33211	17.44361	15.85684	14.48857	13.30338
25	19.91393	18.88499	17.93554	16.24696	14.79864	13.55036
26	20.52346	19.42438	18.41315	16.62208	15.09394	13.78336
27	21.12104	19.95061	18.87684	16.98277	15.37519	14.00317
28	21.70690	20.46401	19.32703	17.32959	15.64303	14.21053
29	22.28127	20.96489	19.76411	17.66306	15.89813	14.40616
30	22.84438	21.45355	20.18845	17.98371	16.14107	14.59072
31	23.39646	21.93029	20.60044	18.29203	16.37245	14.76483
32	23.93770	22.39541	21.00043	18.58849	16.59281	14.92909
33	24.46833	22.84918	21.38877	18.87355	16.80268	15.08404
34	24.98856	23.29188	21.76579	19.14765	17.00255	15.23023
35	25.49859	23.72379	22.13184	19.41120	17.19290	15.36814
36	25.99862	24.14516	22.48722	19.66461	17.37419	15.49825
37	26.48884	24.55625	22.83225	19.90828	17.54685	15.62099
38	26.96945	24.95732	23.16724	20.14258	17.71129	15.73678
39	27.44064	25.34860	23.49246	20.36786	17.86789	15.84602
40	27.90259	25.73034	23.80822	20.58448	18.01704	15.94907

8%	9%	10%	11%	12%	15%	(n) Periods
1.00000	1.00000	1.00000	1.00000	1.00000	1.00000	1
1.92593	1.91743	1.90909	1.90090	1.89286	1.86957	2
2.78326	2.75911	2.73554	2.71252	2.69005	2.62571	3
3.57710	3.53130	3.48685	3.44371	3.40183	3.28323	4
4.31213	4.23972	4.16986	4.10245	4.03735	3.85498	5
4.99271	4.88965	4.79079	4.69590	4.60478	4.35216	6
5.62288	5.48592	5.35526	5.23054	5.11141	4.78448	7
6.20637	6.03295	5.86842	5.71220	5.56376	5.16042	8
6.74664	6.53482	6.33493	6.14612	5.96764	5.48732	9
7.24689	6.99525	6.75902	6.53705	6.32825	5.77158	10
7.71008	7.41766	7.14457	6.88923	6.65022	6.01877	11
8.13896	7.80519	7.49506	7.20652	6.93770	6.23371	12
8.53608	8.16073	7.18369	7.49236	7.19437	6.42062	13
8.90378	8.48690	8.10336	7.74987	7.42355	6.58315	14
9.24424	8.78615	8.36669	7.98187	7.62817	6.72448	15
9.55948	9.06069	8.60608	8.19087	7.81086	6.84737	16
9.85137	9.31256	8.82371	8.37916	7.97399	6.95424	17
10.12164	9.54363	9.02155	8.54879	8.11963	7.04716	18
10.37189	9.75563	9.20141	8.70162	8.24967	7.12797	19
10.60360	9.95012	9.36492	8.83929	8.36578	7.19823	20
10.81815	10.12855	9.51356	8.96333	8.46944	7.25933	21
11.01680	10.29224	9.64869	9.07507	8.56200	7.31246	22
11.20074	10.44243	9.77154	9.17574	8.64465	7.35866	23
11.37106	10.58021	9.88322	9.26643	8.71843	7.39884	24
11.52876	10.70661	9.98474	9.34814	8.78432	7.43377	25
11.67478	10.82258	10.07704	9.42174	8.84314	7.46415	26
11.80998	10.92897	10.16095	9.48806	8.89566	7.49056	27
11.93518	11.02658	10.23722	9.54780	8.94255	7.51353	28
12.05108	11.11613	10.30657	9.60162	8.98442	7.53351	29
12.15841	11.19828	10.36961	9.65011	9.02181	7.55088	30
12.25778	11.27365	10.42691	9.69379	9.05518	7.56598	31
12.34980	11.34280	10.47901	9.73315	9.08499	7.57911	32
12.43500	11.40624	10.52638	9.76860	9.11159	7.59053	33
12.51389	11.46444	10.56943	9.80054	9.13535	7.60046	34
12.58693	11.51784	10.60858	9.82932	9.15656	7.60910	35
12.65457	11.56682	10.64416	9.85524	9.17550	7.61661	36
12.71719	11.61176	10.67651	9.87859	9.19241	7.62314	37
12.77518	11.65299	10.70592	9.89963	9.20751	7.62882	38
12.82887	11.69082	10.73265	9.91859	9.22099	7.63375	39
12.87858	11.72552	10.75697	9.93567	9.23303	7.63805	40

CHAPTER 7

CASH AND RECEIVABLES

OVERVIEW

In previous chapters, you learned the basic formats for general purpose financial statements. In this chapter you begin your in-depth study of accounting for items appearing on the balance sheet: (1) what is to be included in an item classification, (2) rules for determining the dollar amount to be reported, (3) disclosure requirements, (4) special accounting procedures which may be required and, (5) related internal control procedures. In this chapter, you will learn what is to be included under the cash caption on the balance sheet. Also, the methods of accounting for accounts receivable and notes receivable are discussed. Some key internal controls which should be employed for business activities involving cash are discussed in the first appendix to this chapter.

Many businesses grant credit to customers. They know that, when making sales "on account," a risk exists because some accounts will never be collected. However, the cost of these bad debts is more than offset by the profit from the extra sales made due to the attraction of granting credit. The collections department may make many attempts to collect an account before "writing-off" a bad debtor. Frequently, an account is deemed to be uncollectible a year or more after the date of the credit sale. In this chapter, we will discuss the allowance method of accounting for bad debts. The allowance method permits the accountant to estimate the amount of bad debt expense that should be matched with current revenues rather than waiting to book expense at the time of an actual write-off of an individual receivable.

SUMMARY OF LEARNING OBJECTIVES

1. **Identify items considered cash.** To be reported as "cash," an asset must be readily available for the payment of current obligations and free from contractual restrictions that limit its use in satisfying debts. Cash consists of coin, currency, and available funds on deposit at the bank. Negotiable instruments such as money orders, certified checks, cashier's checks, personal checks, and bank drafts are also viewed as cash. Savings accounts are usually classified as cash.

2. **Indicate how to report cash and related items.** Companies report cash as a current asset in the balance sheet. The reporting of other related items are as follows: (1) **Restricted cash:** The SEC recommends that companies state separately legally restricted deposits held as compensating balances against short-term borrowing among the "Cash and cash equivalent items" in Current Assets. Restricted deposits held against long-term borrowing arrangements should be separately classified as noncurrent assets in either the Investments or Other Assets sections. (2) **Bank overdrafts:** Companies should report overdrafts separately in the Current Liabilities section of the balance sheet. These items are sometimes included with accounts payable. If material, these overdrafts should be separately disclosed either on the face of the balance sheet or in the related notes. (3) **Cash equivalents:** Companies often report this item together with cash as "Cash and cash equivalents."

3.   **Define receivables and identify the different types of receivables.** Receivables are claims held against customers and others for money, goods, or services. The receivables are classified into three types: (1) current or noncurrent, (2) trade or nontrade, and (3) accounts receivable or notes receivable.

4.   **Explain accounting issues related to the recognition of accounts receivable.** Two issues that may complicate the measurement of accounts receivable are the: (1) availability of discounts (trade and cash discounts) and (2) length of time between the sale and the payment due dates (the interest element). Ideally, companies should measure receivables in terms of their present value—that is, the discounted value of the cash to be received in the future. The profession specifically excludes from the present value considerations receivables arising from normal business transactions that are due in customary trade terms within approximately one year.

5.   **Explain accounting issues related to the valuation of accounts receivable.** Companies value and report short-term receivables at net realizable value—the net amount expected to be received in cash, which is not necessarily the amount legally receivable. Determining net realizable value requires estimating uncollectible receivables.

6.   **Explain accounting issues related to the recognition and valuation of notes receivable.** Companies record short-term notes at face value and long-term notes receivable at the present value of the cash they expect to collect. When the interest stated on an interest-bearing note is equal to the effective (market) rate of interest, the note is recorded at face value. When the stated rate differs from the effective rate and the note is exchanged for something other than cash, a company records either a discount or premium. Like accounts receivable, short-term notes receivable are recorded and reported at their net realizable value. The same is also true of long-term receivables. Special issues relate to uncollectibles and impairments.

7.   **Explain the fair value option.** Companies have the option to record receivables at fair value. Once the fair value option is chosen, the receivable is reported on the balance sheet at fair value. The change during the period in fair value is recorded as an unrealized gain or loss which is reported as a component of net income.

8.   **Explain accounting issues related to disposition of accounts and notes receivable.** To accelerate the receipt of cash from receivables, the owner may transfer the receivables to another company for cash. The transfer of receivables to a third party for cash may be accomplished in one of two ways (1) **Secured borrowing:** A creditor often requires that the debtor designate or pledge receivables as security for a loan. (2) **Sales (factoring) of receivables:** Factors are finance companies or banks that buy receivables from businesses and then collect the remittances directly from the customers. In many cases, transferors may have some continuing involvement with the receivables sold. Companies use a financial components approach to record this type of transaction.

9.   **Describe how to report and analyze receivables.** Companies should report receivables with appropriate offset of valuation accounts against receivables, classify receivables as current or noncurrent, identify pledged or designated receivables, and disclose the credit risk inherent in the receivables. Analysts assess receivables based on receivables turnover and the days outstanding.

*10.   **Explain common techniques employed to control cash.** The common techniques employed to control cash are: (1) **Using bank accounts:** a company can vary the number and location of banks and the types of accounts to obtain desired control objectives. (2) **The imprest petty cash system:** It may be impractical to require small amounts of various expenses to be paid by check, yet some control over them is important. (3) **Physical protection of cash balances:** Adequate control of receipts and disbursements is a part of the protection of cash balances.

Every effort should be made to minimize the cash on hand in the office. (4) **Reconciliation of bank balances:** Cash on deposit is not available for count and is proved by preparing a bank reconciliation.

*This material is covered in **Appendix 7A** in the text.

**11. Describe the accounting for a loan impairment. A creditor bases an impairment loan loss on the difference between the present value of the future cash flows (using the historical effective-interest rate) and the carrying amount of the note.

This material is covered in **Appendix 7B in the text.

TIPS ON CHAPTER TOPICS

TIP: Trade accounts receivable result from the sale of products or services to customers. Nontrade accounts receivable (amounts that are due from nontrade customers who do not buy goods or services in the normal course of the company's main business activity) should be listed separately from the trade accounts receivable balance on the balance sheet.

TIP: In the event that a customer's account has a credit balance on the balance sheet date, it should be classified as a current liability and not offset against other accounts receivable with debit balances.

TIP: The net realizable value of accounts receivable is the amount of the receivables expected to be ultimately converted to cash.

TIP: Whenever you want to analyze the effect of (1) recording bad debt expense, (2) writing off an individual customer's account receivable, and/or (3) the collection of an account receivable that was previously written off, write down the related journal entry(ies) and analyze each debit and credit separately. (See **Illustration 7-1** for examples.)

TIP: Given a $1,000 receivable to be collected three years from today, that receivable has a value today (present value) that is less than $1,000 due to the time value of money (i.e. interest). The present value of the $1,000 due in three years is the amount of money that, if invested today at a specified interest rate, would grow to be $1,000 at the end of a three-year period. The higher the interest rate, the lower the present value. Present value concepts are used in this chapter in accounting for notes receivable. If you need to review these concepts and applications, consult **Chapter 6** of your book.

TIP: There are two methods of accounting for bad debts; they are:
1. **Direct Write-Off Method:** No entry is made until a specific account has definitely been established as uncollectible. Then the loss is recorded by crediting Accounts Receivable and debiting Bad Debt Expense.
2. **Allowance Method:** An estimate is made of the expected uncollectible accounts from all sales made on account or from the total of outstanding receivables. This estimate is entered as an expense and an indirect reduction in accounts receivable (via an increase in the allowance account) in the period in which the sale is recorded.

The direct write-off method is not a generally accepted method for an entity having a material amount of bad debts because it fails to properly match bad debt expense with the related revenue (in the period the credit sale was recognized) and it overstates Accounts Receivable as to their net realizable value. The direct write-off method may be used for an entity whose bad debts amount to an immaterial sum.

> **TIP:** A note receivable is considered to be **impaired** when it is probable that the creditor will be unable to collect all amounts due (both principal and interest) according to the contractual terms of the loan. In that case, the present value of the expected future cash flows is determined by discounting those flows at the historical effective rate. This present value amount is deducted from the carrying amount of the receivable to measure the loss.

EXERCISE 7-1

Purpose: (L.O. 1) This exercise will review the items which are included in the "Cash" caption on a balance sheet.

In auditing the balance sheet at December 31, 2014 for the Maxwell Vermillion Company, you find the following:

		Cash	Not in Cash
(a)	Coins and currency for change funds.		
(b)	Coins and currency which are from the current day's receipts which have not yet been deposited in the bank.		
(c)	Petty cash.		
(d)	General checking account at First Union Bank.		
(e)	General checking account at Sun Trust Bank.		
(f)	Unused stamps.		
(g)	Deposit in transit.		
(h)	Customer's NSF check (returned with bank statement).		
(i)	Postdated checks from customers.		
(j)	Certificate of deposit—60 day CD purchased on December 1, 2014.		
(k)	Certificate of deposit—matures in 6 months.		
(l)	100 shares of General Motors stock (intention is to sell in one year or less).		
(m)	Cash to be used to retire long-term debt.		
(n)	Travel advances made to executives for business purposes.		
(o)	Cash advance to executive for personal reasons.		
(p)	Money market fund that provides checking account privileges.		
(q)	Commercial paper with maturity of 270 days.		
(r)	Treasury bills with 182-day maturity.		
(s)	Treasury Bills with a 91-day maturity.		
(t)	Commercial paper with original maturity of 30 days.		
(u)	Money on deposit in Bank of America, held as compensating balances against a short-term bank obligation and other short-term borrowing arrangements.		
(v)	Money on deposit in Wells Fargo Bank, held as compensating balances against a long-term loan from the bank and other long-term borrowing arrangements.		
(w)	Cash fund restricted for the payment of an existing obligation classified as a current liability.		
(x)	Bank overdraft.		
(y)	Money market savings certificate with original maturity of 48 months, intended to be held until maturity.		

Instructions

Select the items from the list above that should be included in the "Cash" caption on the balance sheet as of December 31, 2014. For any item not included in "Cash", indicate the proper classification.

Solution to Exercise 7-1

Items to be **included** as "Cash" on the balance sheet include:

(a)   Coins and currency for change funds.
(b)   Coins and currency which are from the current day's receipts which have not yet been deposited in the bank—this is said to be "cash on hand" or could be considered a "deposit in transit" in preparing a bank reconciliation (see **Appendix 7A**).
(c)   Petty cash—included in "Cash" because this fund is used to meet current operating expenses and to liquidate current liabilities.
(d)   General checking account at First Union Bank—the amount included should be the "adjusted cash balance" per a bank reconciliation (see **Appendix 7A**).
(e)   General checking account at Sun Trust Bank—the amount included should be the "adjusted cash balance" per a bank reconciliation (see **Appendix 7A**).
(g)   Deposit in transit—this amount is already reflected in the "balance per books" and will be reflected in the "adjusted cash balance" per the bank reconciliation (see **Appendix 7A**).
(p)   Money market fund that provides checking account privileges.

Items to be **excluded** from "Cash" include:

(f)   Unused stamps—report as a Prepaid Expense (such as Office Supplies on Hand).
(h)   Customer's NSF check—classify in Accounts Receivable.
(i)   Postdated checks from customers—classify in Accounts Receivable.
(j)   Certificate of deposit—60 day—original maturity date was 3 months or less—classify as cash equivalents (which are often combined with "Cash").
(k)   Certificate of deposit—original maturity date not 3 months or less—classify as Short-term Investment.
(l)   100 shares of General Motors Stock—classify as Short-term Investment because there is a lack of intent to hold for a long-term purpose and is readily marketable.
(m)   Cash to be used to retire long-term debt—classify as Long-term Investment (assuming the related debt is classified as long-term).
(n)   Travel advances made to executives for business purposes—classify in Prepaid Expenses.
(o)   Cash advance to executive for personal reasons—classify as a receivable (will later be collected from employee or deducted from employee's paycheck).
(q)   Commercial paper—report as a Short-term Investment.
(r)   Treasury bills with 182-day maturity—report as a Short-term Investment.
(s)   Treasury bills with a 91-day maturity—classify as cash equivalents (which are often combined with "Cash").
(t)   Commercial paper with original maturity of 30 days—classify as cash equivalents (which are often combined with "Cash").

(u)   Deposit maintained as compensating balances against short-term borrowing arrangement—separate from other cash and classify with cash and cash equivalents in current assets.

(v)   Deposit maintained as compensating balances against long-term borrowing arrangement—report as noncurrent asset either in the Investments or Other Assets section of the balance sheet.

(w)   Restricted funds for payment of obligation classified as current liability—classify in Current Assets but report separately from regular cash items.

(x)   Bank overdraft—classify in Current Liabilities. (This answer assumes there is no right of offset.)

(y)   Money market savings certificates with original maturity of 48 months, intended to be held until maturity—report as long-term Investment.

TIP: Items (j), (s) and (t) are cash equivalents. Most entities include cash equivalents with cash; others report them as temporary (short-term) investments (immediately following cash in the current asset section of the balance sheet).

Explanation: Cash, the most liquid of assets, is the standard medium of exchange and the basis for measuring and accounting for all other items. To be included in the Cash caption under current assets, the cash must be readily available for current obligations, and it must be free of from any contractual restriction that limits its use in satisfying debts. Cash in a fund that is restricted for some long-term purpose (such as for future plant expansion) is classified as a long-term investment.

Cash consists of coin, currency, and available funds on deposit at the bank. Negotiable instruments such as money orders, certified checks, cashier's checks, personal checks, and bank drafts are also viewed as cash. Savings accounts are usually classified as cash, although the bank has the legal right to demand notice before withdrawal. But, because prior notice is rarely demanded by banks, savings accounts are considered cash.

Money market funds, money market savings certificates, certificates of deposit (CDs), and similar types of deposits and "short-term paper" that provide small investors with an opportunity to earn high rates of interest are more appropriately classified as temporary investments than as cash.   The reason is that these securities usually contain restrictions or penalties on their conversion to cash.   Money market funds that provide checking account privileges, however, are usually classified as cash.

TIP: Cash is often combined with cash equivalents and reported by the caption "cash and cash equivalents." **Cash equivalents** are short-term highly liquid investments that are both (a) readily convertible to known amounts of cash, and (b) so near their maturity that they present insignificant risk of changes in interest rates. Generally only investments with original maturities of (three) months or less qualify under these definitions. Examples of cash equivalents are Treasury bills, commercial paper, and money market funds.

TIP: An entity that has cash in an amount that exceeds its immediate needs will usually temporarily invest the excess cash. A variety of "short-term paper" is available for investment. For example, **certificates of deposit** (CDs) represent formal evidence of indebtedness, issued by a bank, subject to withdrawal under the specific terms of the instrument. Issued in $10,000 and $100,000 denominations, they generally mature in 30 to 360 days and generally pay interest at the short-term interest rate in effect at the date of issuance. Some banks have CDs that have a 3- or 5-year term. In **money market funds**, a variation of the mutual fund, the yield is determined by the mix of Treasury bills, and commercial paper making up the fund's portfolio. Most money market funds require an initial minimum investment of $5,000; many allow withdrawal by check or wire transfer. **Treasury bills** are U.S. government obligations generally having 91- and 182-day maturities; they are sold in $10,000 denominations at weekly government auctions. **Commercial paper** is a short-term note (30 to 270 days) issued by corporations with good credit ratings. Issued in $5,000 and $10,000 denominations, these notes generally yield a higher rate than Treasury bills.

TIP: Banks and other lending institutions often require customers to whom they lend money to maintain minimum cash balances in checking or savings accounts. These minimum balances, called **compensating balances,** are defined by the SEC as: "that portion of any demand deposit (or any time deposit or certificate of deposit) maintained by a corporation which constitutes support for existing borrowing arrangements of the corporation with a lending institution. The SEC recommends that **legally restricted deposits** held as compensating balances against **short-term** borrowing arrangements be stated separately among the "cash and cash equivalent items" in current assets. Restricted deposits held as compensating **balances against long-term** borrowing arrangements should be separately classified as noncurrent assets in either Investments or Other Assets sections, using a caption such as "Cash on Deposit Maintained as Compensating Balance."

EXERCISE 7-2

Purpose: (L.O. 2) This exercise will require you to properly classify items qualifying as "cash" and to properly report a bank overdraft.

The Skogsberg Corporation had the following items at a balance sheet date:

Checking account at Sun Trust Bank	$ 12,400
Checking account at Bank of America	10,500
Checking account at First Union Bank	(3,000)
Checking account at Republic Bank	5,100
Postdated check from customer	600
Savings account at Sun Trust Bank	32,000
Money market fund at Sun Trust (with checking privileges)	40,000
Deposit at telephone company (required for service)	1,000
NSF check received from customer (reflected as a positive amount in a bank balance above)	210
Change fund	450
Cash from customer not yet deposited in bank	1,750

Instructions:

(a)   Compute the amount to be reported with the "Cash" caption in current assets at the balance sheet date.

(b)   Indicate the proper reporting for items that are **not** included in your answer to part (a).

SOLUTION TO EXERCISE 7-2

(a)
Checking account at Sun Trust Bank	$ 12,400
Checking account at Bank of America	10,500
Checking account at Republic Bank	5,100
Savings account at Sun Trust Bank	32,000
Money market fund at Sun Trust	40,000
NSF check from customer	(210)
Change fund	450
Receipts to be deposited (Cash on Hand)	1,750
Total Cash	$101,990

(b)   (1)   The overdraft of $3,000 at First Union Bank is classified as a current liability. The only time a bank overdraft is used to offset positive balances in other bank accounts (that is, reflected in the Cash caption) is when the overdraft occurs in an account that is in the same bank as other accounts with positive balances that equal or exceed the amount of overdraft (that is, when a legal right of offset is assumed to exist).

(2)   The postdated check from customer for $600 is classified as a receivable in current assets.

(3)   The $1,000 deposit at the telephone company is classified as an other asset (if the deposit is to remain beyond one year from the balance sheet date) or as a separate item in current assets usually listed after prepaid expenses (if the deposit is to be returned or applied to the telephone bill within the next year).

(4)   The NSF check from a customer for $210 should be reclassified to the receivables section of current assets.

ILLUSTRATION 7-1
ENTRIES FOR THE ALLOWANCE METHOD (L.O. 5)

Journal Entry			Effect on Net Income	Effect on Working Capital	Effect on Allowance Account	Effect on Net Receivables
Entry to record bad debt expense, $1,000			Decrease $1,000	No effect	No effect	No effect
Bad Debt Expense	1,000		Decrease $1,000	No effect	No effect	No effect
Allowance for Doubtful Accounts		1,000	No effect	Decrease $1,000	Increase $1,000	Decrease $1,000
Net effect of entry			Decrease $1,000	Decrease $1,000	Increase $1,000	Decrease $1,000
Entry to write-off a customer's account, $200				Increase $200	Decrease $200	Increase $200
Allowance for Doubtful Accounts	200		No effect	Increase $200	Decrease $200	Increase $200
Accounts Receivable		200	No effect	Decrease $200	No effect	Decrease $200
Net effect of entry			No effect	No effect	Decrease $200	No effect
Entries to record collection of account receivable previously written off, $120				Increase $120		Increase $120
Accounts Receivable	120		No effect	Increase $120	No effect	Increase $120
Allowance for Doubtful Accounts		120	No effect	Decrease $120	Increase $120	Decrease $120
Cash	120		No effect	Increase $120	No effect	No effect
Accounts Receivable		120	No effect	Decrease $120	No effect	Decrease $120
Net effect of entries			No effect	No effect	Increase $120	Decrease $120

TIP: Be careful to distinguish the entry to write-off a customer account from the entry to record bad debt expense. The journal entry to record the estimated bad debt expense for a period and to adjust the corresponding allowance for doubtful accounts involves a debit to Bad Debt Expense and a credit to Allowance for Doubtful Accounts. The entry to write off an individual customer's account (an actual bad debt) involves a debit to Allowance for Doubtful Accounts and a credit to Accounts Receivable.

TIP: Two entries are necessary to record the recovery of an account that was previously written off:
1. An entry to record the reinstatement of the account receivable (debit Accounts Receivable and credit Allowance for Doubtful Accounts). This is simply a reverse of the write-off entry.
2. An entry to record the collection of the receivable (debit Cash and credit Accounts Receivable).

TIP: Allowance for Doubtful Accounts is often called Allowance for Uncollectible Accounts. (Both of these account titles start with "Allowance for" which typically indicates a contra type balance sheet account.) Reserve for Bad Debts is a frequently used but objectionable title for the allowance account.

TIP: Bad Dept Expense is often called Uncollectible Accounts Expense **or** Doubtful Accounts Expense. Provision for Bad Debts is another name for the Bad Debt Expense account.

ILLUSTRATION 7-1 (Continued)

TIP: Notice that the entry to record bad debts reduces current assets and reduces net income. The entry to record the write-off of an individual account has **no** net effect on the amount of current assets nor does it affect income. It merely reduces Accounts Receivable and the Allowance for Doubtful Accounts account (which is a contra item) so the entry has no **net** effect on the net realizable value of accounts receivable. Thus, it is the entry to record the bad debt expense that impacts **both** the income statement and the balance sheet.

TIP: The normal balance of the Allowance for Doubtful Accounts is a credit. Therefore, a debit balance in this account indicates an abnormal balance. It is **not** uncommon to have a debit balance in the allowance account before adjusting entries are prepared because individual accounts may be written off at various times during a period and the entry to adjust the allowance account is prepared at the end of the period before financial statements are prepared. After adjustment, the allowance account will have a credit balance.

TIP: When it is time to prepare the adjusting entry for bad debts (at the end of an accounting period), the existing balance in the Allowance for Doubtful Accounts account (that is, the balance before adjustment) is **NOT** considered in determining the amount of the adjusting entry **IF** the percentage-of-sales approach is used. However, the balance in the allowance account before adjustment **IS** used in determining the amount of the adjusting entry when the aging analysis approach (one method of estimating the net realizable value of existing receivables) is used to implement the allowance method of accounting for bad debts. The application of these two guidelines is illustrated by the **Solution to Exercise 7-3** (entries 1 and 2).

TIP: When using the allowance method and estimating bad debt expense as a percentage of credit sales for the period, the amount of bad debt expense is simply calculated and recorded; a by-product of this approach is the increasing of the allowance account. When using the allowance method and estimating the net realizable value of accounts receivable (such as by an aging analysis), the amount of uncollectible accounts calculated represents the new ending balance of the allowance account. The adjusting entry records the amount necessary to increase (or decrease) the current allowance account balance to equal the newly computed one. A by-product of this approach is the increasing of bad debt expense for the period.

TIP: Sales Discounts Forfeited is classified as an "Other Revenue" item on the income statement.

TIP: Theoretically, the net method is better in that the receivable is stated closer to its realizable value, and the net sales figure measures the revenue earned from the sale. As a practical matter, however, the net method is seldom used because it requires additional analysis and bookkeeping. For example, the net method requires adjusting entries to record sales discounts forfeited on accounts receivable that have passed the discount period.

TIP: An estimate of uncollectible accounts must be made for long-term receivables in the same manner as is done for short-term trade accounts receivable (that is, use the allowance method to account for bad debts).

TIP: Specific long-term receivables such as loans that are identified as impaired must receive an impairment evaluation. An **impairment loss** is calculated by the difference between the investment in the loan (generally the principal plus accrued interest) and the expected future cash flows discounted at the loan's historical effective interest rate. When using the historical effective interest rate, the value of the investment will change only if some of the legally contracted cash flows are reduced. A company recognizes a loss in this case because the future cash flows have changed. The company ignores interest rate changes caused by current economic events that affect the fair value of the loan. An impairment loss is recorded by a debt to Bad Debt Expense and a credit to Allowance for Doubtful Accounts.

CASE 7-1

Purpose: (L.O. 5) This exercise will identify the two approaches of applying the allowance method of accounting for uncollectible accounts receivable.

Howell's Department Store offers a store credit card for the convenience of its customers. Even though the store follows up on delinquent accounts, past experience indicates that a predictable amount of credit sales will ultimately result in uncollectible accounts. Because bad debts are a material amount, Howell uses the allowance method of accounting for uncollectible accounts.

Instructions
(a) Describe the two methods available for determining the amount of the adjusting entry to record bad debt expense and to adjust the allowance account. Also discuss the emphasis of each method.
(b) Explain why the direct write-off method is not a generally accepted accounting method for Howell's Department Store.

Solution Case 7-1

(a) When using the allowance method of accounting for bad debts, there are two methods available for determining the amount of the adjusting entry to record bad debt expense and to adjust the allowance account. They are:
(1) **The percentage of sales basis:** This method focuses on estimating bad debt expense. The average percentage relationship between actual bad debt losses and net credit sales (or total credit sales) of the period is used to determine the amount of expense for the period. This method focuses on the matching of current bad debt expense with revenues of the current period and thus emphasizes the income statement. The amount of bad debt expense is simply calculated and recorded **without** regard to the existing balance in the allowance account; a by-product of this approach is the increase in the allowance account.

(2) **The percentage of receivables basis:** This method focuses on estimating the cash (net) realizable value of the current receivables and thus emphasizes the balance sheet. It only incidentally measures bad debt expense; the expense reported may not be the best figure to match with the amount of credit sales of the current period. The existing balance in the allowance account (that is, the balance before adjustment) is a factor in determining the required adjusting entry because this method focuses on increasing the allowance balance to an appropriate figure. If this method is to be used, the **aging** technique is preferable to the use of a

simple percentage times total accounts receivable. An aging analysis takes into consideration the age of a receivable. The older the age, the lower the probability of collection.

> **TIP:** Very often, an entity may use the percentage-of-sales method to account for bad debts for interim periods and then use the aging method to adjust the allowance account at year-end for annual reporting purposes.

(b)   Under the direct write-off method, bad debt losses are not estimated and no allowance account is used. No entry regarding bad debts is made until a specific account has definitely been established as uncollectible. Then the loss is recorded by a debit to Bad Debt Expense and a credit to Accounts Receivable. (Under the direct write-off method, if an account previously written off is recovered in the future, the amount collected is debited to cash and credited to a revenue account titled Uncollectible Accounts Recovered.)

When the direct write-off method is used, Accounts Receivable will be reported at its gross amount and bad debts expense is often recorded in a period different from the period in which the revenue was recorded. Thus, no attempt is made to match bad debt expense to sales revenues in the income statement or to show the cash (net) realizable value of the accounts receivable in the balance sheet. Consequently, unless bad debt losses are insignificant, the direct write-off method is **not** acceptable for financial reporting purposes. Howell's bad debts are material (significant) in amount. The direct write-off method is, however, used for tax purposes.

EXERCISE 7-3

Purpose: (L.O. 5, 8) This exercise will require you to record: (1) the adjusting entry to recognize bad debt expense and adjust the Allowance for Doubtful Accounts account, and (2) the transfer of accounts receivable with recourse.

The trial balance before adjustment at December 31, 2014 for the G & H Wood Company shows the following balances:

	Dr.	Cr.
Accounts Receivable	$ 90,000	
Allowance for Doubtful Accounts	2,120	
Sales (all on credit)		$ 500,000
Sales Returns and Allowances	7,600	

Instructions

Using the data above, give the journal entries required to record each of the following cases (each situation is **independent**):

1.   The company estimates bad debts to be 1.5% of net credit sales.
2.   G & H Wood Company performs an aging analysis at December 31, 2014 which indicates an estimate of $6,000 of uncollectible accounts.
3.   The company wants to maintain the Allowance for Doubtful Accounts at 4% of gross accounts receivable.
4.   To obtain additional cash, G & H Wood Company factors, without recourse, $20,000 of accounts receivable with Fleetwood Finance. The finance charge is 10% of the amount factored.

Solution to Exercise 7-3

1.   Bad Debt Expense [($500,000 - $7,600) x 1.5%]....................   7,386
          Allowance for Doubtful Accounts....................................   7,386

Explanation: The percentage of net credit sales approach to applying the allowance method of accounting for bad debts focuses on determining an appropriate expense figure. The existing balance in the allowance account is **not** relevant in the computation.

2.   Bad Debt Expense   8,120
          Allowance for Doubtful Accounts
          ($6,000 + $2,120)...   8,120

Explanation: An aging analysis provides the best estimate of the net realizable value of accounts receivable. By using the results of the aging to adjust the allowance account, the amount reported for net receivables on the balance sheet is the net realizable value of accounts receivable. It is important to notice that the balance of the allowance account before adjustment is a determinant in the adjustment required. The following T-account reflects the facts used to determine the necessary adjustment:

Allowance for Doubtful Accounts			
Unadjusted balance	2,120	Adjustment needed	8,120
		Desired balance at 12/31/14	6,000

3.   Bad Debt Expense 5,720
          Allowance for Doubtful Accounts
              [($90,000 x 4%) + $2,120] 5,720

Explanation: This entry is to adjust the allowance account. A by-product of the entry is the recognition of uncollectible accounts expense. Because an appropriate balance for the valuation account is determined to be a percentage of the receivable balance at the balance sheet date, the existing balance ($2,120 debit) in the allowance account **must** be considered in computing the necessary adjustment.

4.   Cash 18,000
       Loss on Sale of Receivables ($20,000 x 10%) 2,000
          Accounts Receivable 20,000

Explanation: The factoring of accounts receivable without recourse is accounted for as a sale of accounts receivable; hence, the receivables are removed from the accounts, cash is recorded, and a loss is recognized for the excess of the face value of the receivables over the proceeds received.

EXERCISE 7-4

Purpose: (L.O. 6) This exercise will illustrate the accounting for a situation involving the exchange of a noncash asset or service for a promissory note where the fair value of the asset or service is known.

General Host's annual accounting period ends on December 31. On July 1, 2014, General Host Company sold land having a fair market value of $700,000 in exchange for a four-year noninterest-bearing promissory note in the face amount of $1,101,460. The land is carried on General Host Company's books at a cost of $620,000.

Instructions
(a)   Prepare the journal entry that should be recorded by General Host company for the sale of the land in exchange for the note.
(b)   Prepare the amortization schedule for the note receivable accepted in the transaction.
(c)   Prepare the necessary journal entries at December 31, 2014 and December 31, 2015 that relate to the note receivable.

Solution to Exercise 7-4

(a) Timeline:

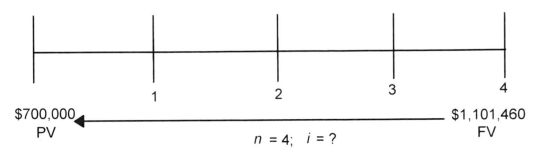

7/1/14	Notes Receivable	1,101,460.00	
	Discount on Notes Receivable..................		401,460.00
	Land...		620,000.00
	Gain on Sale of Land		
	($700,000 - $620,000)		80,000.00

The exchange price is equal to the fair market value of the property (which is $700,000).
The interest rate implicit in this price is therefore calculated by:

$700,000 = $1,101,460 \times$ PV Factor
$700,000 \div $1,101,460 = .63552$
By reference to Table 2 (Present Value of 1 Table) at end of **Chapter 6**,
.63552 is the PV factor for $n = 4$, $i = 12\%$.

(b)   **Amortization Schedule for Note**

Date	0% Stated Interest	12% Effective Interest	Amortization of Discount	PV Balance
7/01/14				$ 700,000.00
6/30/15	$0	$ 84,000.00[a]	$ 84,000.00	784,000.00
6/30/16	0	94,080.00	94,080.00	878,080.00
6/30/17	0	105,369.60	105,369.60	983,449.60
6/30/18	0	118,010.40[1]	118,010.40	1,101,460.00
Totals	$0	$401,460.00	$ 401,460.00	

[a]$700,000.00 x 12% = $84,000.00.
[1]Includes rounding error of $3.55.

TIP:	In most exercises, we round to the nearest dollar. When working assignments dealing with interest, it is helpful to round to the nearest penny. That way you can more readily determine if any "plug" figure at the end of an amortization schedule is due to a rounding error (rounding difference) or an error of greater consequence.

(c)	12/31/14	Discount on Notes Receivable	42,000.00	
		Interest Revenue		42,000.00
		(1/2 x $84,000 = $42,000)		

| 12/31/15 | Discount on Notes Receivable .... | 89,040.00 | |
| | Interest Revenue .... | | 89,040.00 |

(1/2 x $84,000 = $42,000;
1/2 x $94,080 = $47,040;
$42,000 + $47,040 = $89,040)

Explanation: When a note is received in exchange for property, goods, or services in a bargained transaction entered into at arms length, the stated interest rate is assumed to be fair and is thus used to compute interest revenue unless:

1.   No interest rate is stated, or
2.   The stated interest rate is unreasonable, or
3.   The face amount of the note is materially different from the current cash sales price for the same or similar items or from the current market value of the debt instrument.

In these circumstances, the present value of the note is measured by the fair value of the property, goods, or services. General Host received a note in exchange for land, and the fair value of the land was known to be $700,000; thus, the fair value of the land was used to establish the present value of the note and the rate implicit in the note was then computed to be 12%. (See **Exercise 7-5** for an example of a situation where the fair value of the property, goods, or services exchanged for a note is not known.)

EXERCISE 7-5

Purpose: (L.O. 6) This exercise will illustrate the accounting for a situation involving the exchange of a noncash asset or service for a promissory note where the fair value of the asset or service is **not** known.

Fairmont Company's annual accounting period ends on December 31. On July 1, 2014, Fairmont Company rendered services in exchange for a 3%, 8-year promissory note having a face value of $300,000 with interest payable annually. Fairmont Company recently had to pay 8% interest for money that it borrowed from Arizona National Bank. The customer in this transaction has a credit rating that requires them to borrow money at 12% interest.

Instructions
(a)   Prepare the journal entry that should be recorded by Fairmont Company for the sale of the services in exchange for the note.
(b)   Prepare the amortization schedule for the note receivable accepted in the transaction.
(c)   Prepare the necessary journal entries at December 31, 2014, June 30, 2015, and December 31, 2015 that relate to the note receivable. Assume the customer makes the scheduled interest payments on time. Also, assume amortization is recorded only at year-end. Fairmont does not use reversing entries.

Solution to Exercise 7-5

(a)   Timeline:

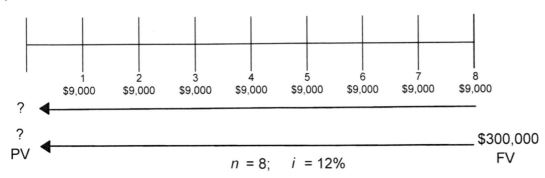

1	2	3	4	5	6	7	8
$9,000	$9,000	$9,000	$9,000	$9,000	$9,000	$9,000	$9,000

?

?
PV $300,000
FV

$n = 8;\quad i = 12\%$

7/1/14	Notes Receivable	300,000.00	
	Discount on Notes Receivable		134,127.24
	Service Revenue		165,872.76

Use the market rate of interest to compute the present value of the note which is then used to establish the exchange price in the transaction. The market rate of interest should be the rate the borrower normally would have to pay to borrow money for similar activities.

	Computation of the present value of the note:	
	Maturity value	$300,000.00
	Present value of $300,000 due in 8 years at 12% ($300,000 x .40388)	$121,164.00
	Present value of $9,000 payable annually for 8 years at 12% ($9,000 x 4.96764)	44,708.76
	Present value of the note and interest	(165,872.76)
	Discount on note receivable	$134,127.24

(b)   **Amortization Schedule for Note**

Date	3% Stated Interest	12% Effective Interest	Amortization of Discount	PV Balance
7/01/14				$ 165,872.76
6/30/15	$ 9,000.00[a]	$ 19,904.73[b]	$ 10,904.73[c]	176,777.49[d]
6/30/16	9,000.00	21,213.30	12,213.30	188,990.79
6/30/17	9,000.00	22,678.89	13,678.89	202,669.68
6/30/18	9,000.00	24,320.36	15,320.36	217,990.04
6/30/19	9,000.00	26,158.80	17,158.80	235,148.84
6/30/20	9,000.00	28,217.86	19,217.86	254,366.70
6/30/21	9,000.00	30,524.00	21,524.00	275,890.70
6/30/22	9,000.00	33,109.30[1]	24,109.30	300,000.00
Totals	$72,000.00	$206,127.24	$ 134,127.24	

[a]$300,000.00 face value x 3% stated interest rate = $9,000.00 stated interest.
[b]$165,872.76 present value x 12% effective-interest rate = $19,904.73 effective interest.
[c]$19,904.73 effective interest - $9,000.00 stated interest = $10,904.73 discount amortization.

ᵈ$165,872.76 PV balance 7/01/14 + $10,904.73 discount amortization for 12 months = $176,777.49 PV balance 6/30/15.
¹Includes rounding error of $2.42.

(c)	12/31/14	Interest Receivable..	4,500.00	
		Discount on Notes Receivable	5,452.37	
		Interest Revenue		9,952.37
		(1/2 x $9,000 = $4,500;		
		1/2 x $19,904.73 = $9,952.37)		
	6/30/15	Cash...	9,000.00	
		Interest Revenue		4,500.00
		Interest Receivable..		4,500.00
	12/31/15	Interest Receivable..	4,500.00ᵃ	
		Discount on Notes Receivable	11,559.01ᵇ	
		Interest Revenue		16,059.01ᶜ

      ᵃ1/2 x $9,000.00 = $4,500.00 interest receivable at 12/31/15.
      ᵇ1/2 x $19,904.73 = $9,952.36 interest earned 1/1/15 thru 6/30/15;
        1/2 x $21,213.30 = $10,606.65 interest earned 7/1/15 thru 12/31/15;
        $9,952.36 + $10,606.65 = $20,559.01 total interest earned in 2015;
        $20,559.01 effective interest for 2015 - $9,000.00 stated interest for
        2015 = $11,559.01 discount amortization for 2015.
      ᶜ$20,559.01 total interest for 2015 - $4,500.00 balance in Interest
        Revenue account before adjustment = $16,059.01 interest to record
        at 12/31/15.

Explanation: When a note is received in exchange for property, goods, or services in a bargained transaction entered into at arms length, the stated interest rate is assumed to be fair and is thus used to compute interest revenue unless:

1.   No interest rate is stated, or
2.   The stated interest rate is unreasonable, or
3.   The face amount of the note is materially different from the current cash sales price for the same or similar items or from the current market value of the debt instrument.

In these circumstances, the present value of the note is measured by the fair value of the property, goods, or services. If the fair value of the property, goods, or services is not readily determinable, the market value of the note is used to establish the present value of the note. If the note has no ready market, the present value of the note is approximated by discounting all of the related future cash receipts (for interest and principal) on the note at the market rate of interest. This rate is referred to as an imputed rate and should be equal to the borrower's incremental borrowing rate (that is, the rate of interest the maker of the note would currently have to pay if it borrowed money from another source for this same purpose) Fairmont received a note in exchange for services. No information was given about the fair value of the services or the market value of the note. Thus, the borrower's incremental borrowing rate of 12% was used to impute interest and determine the note's present value.

ILLUSTRATION 7-2
FAIR VALUE MEASUREMENT OF NOTES RECEIVABLE (L.O. 7)

Like accounts receivable, companies record and report **short-term notes receivable** at their net realizable value. This involves estimating the amount of uncollectibles by using either a percentage of sales revenue or an analysis of the receivables.

Because the value of **long-term notes receivables** can change significantly over time from its original cost, the FASB allows a company to choose the **fair value** option for receivables whereby the receivables are reported at fair value and the related unrealized **holding gain or loss** (which is the net change in fair value of the receivable from one period to another, exclusive of interest revenue recognized but not recorded) is reported as part of net income. As a result, the company reports the receivable on the balance sheet at fair value each reporting date and it reports the change in fair value each period as part of net income for the period.

The company must be consistent with its method of choice for long-term receivables. That is, if it elects the fair value option (at the time the financial instrument is originally recognized) then it must continue with that method for that receivable. However, if it does not elect the fair value option for a given financial instrument at the date of recognition, it may not use this option on that specific instrument in subsequent periods.

For example, assume Noreniel Company has notes receivable with a carrying amount of $700,000 at December 31, 2014. The company has elected to use the fair value measurement for these receivables. This is the first valuation for these receivables. The fair value of these receivables is $780,000 at December 31, 2014 and $735,000 at December 31, 2015. Having elected to use the fair value option, Noreniel Company must value these receivables at fair value in all subsequent periods in which it holds these receivables. Thus, the following journal entries would be recorded:

At December 31, 2014

Fair Value Adjustment – Notes Receivable	80,000	
Unrealized holding Gain or Loss – Income		80,000
($780,000 - $700,000 = $80,000)		

At December 31, 2015

Unrealized Holding Gain or Loss – Income	45,000	
Fair Value Adjustment – Notes Receivable		45,000
($780,000 - $735,000= $45,000)		

Thus the asset would be reported at $780,000 on December 31, 2014 and $735,000 at December 31, 2015. An unrealized holding gain would increase the net income figure for the year ending December 31, 2014 and an unrealized holding loss would decrease net income reported for the year ending December 31, 2015.

> **TIP:** One of the main reasons a note receivable may have a fair value that is significantly different than its carrying amount (adjusted historical cost) is the fact that the current relevant interest rate often differs from the stated interest rate in the note (which was the current rate at the date the note originated.)

ILLUSTRATION 7-3
ACCOUNTING FOR TRANSFERS OF RECEIVABLES (L.O. 8)

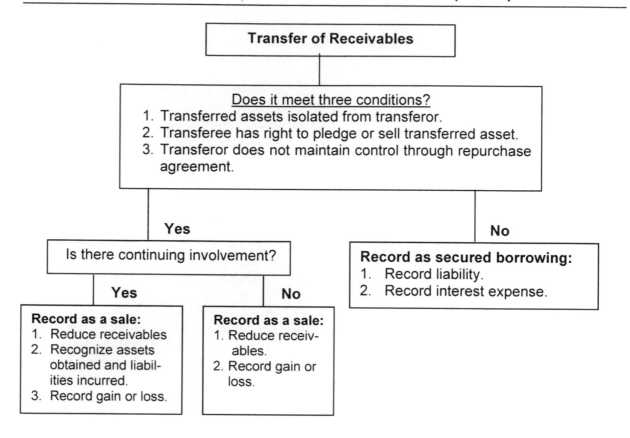

| TIP: | If there is continuing involvement in a sale transaction, the assets obtained and liabilities incurred must be recorded at fair value. |

EXERCISE 7-6

Purpose: (L.O. 8) This exercise will help you to compare two possible ways of structuring a sale of accounts receivable (1) without recourse, or (2) with recourse.

Jedd Hale Corporation factors $90,000 of accounts receivable with Klein-Seay Financing, Inc. Klein-Seay Financing will collect the receivables. The receivable records are transferred to Klein-Seay Financing on August 15, 2014. Klein-Seay Financing assesses a finance charge of 4% of the amount of accounts receivable and also retains an amount equal to 6% of accounts receivable to cover probable adjustments.

Instructions

(a)   Explain the conditions that must be met for a transfer of receivables with recourse to be accounted for as a sale.
(b)   Explain when the financial components approach is used in accounting for a transfer of accounts receivable.
(c)   Prepare the journal entry for both Jedd Hale Corporation and Klein-Seay Financing to record the transfer of accounts receivable on August 15, 2014 assuming the receivables are sold without recourse.
(d)   Prepare the journal entry for both Jedd Hale Corporation and Klein-Seay Financing to record the transfer of accounts receivable on August 15, 2014 assuming the receivables are sold with recourse and the conditions required for sale accounting are met. Further, assume the recourse obligation has a fair value of $2,000.

Solution to Exercise 7-6

(a)   The FASB concluded that a sale occurs only if the seller surrenders control of the receivables to the buyer. The following three conditions must be met before a sale can be recorded:
1.   The transferred asset has been isolated from the transferor (put beyond reach of the transferor and its creditors).
2.   The transferees have obtained the right to pledge or exchange either the transferred assets or beneficial interests in the transferred assets.
3.   The transferor does not maintain effective control over the transferred assets through an agreement to repurchase or redeem them before their maturity.

If the three conditions are met, a sale occurs. Otherwise, the transferor should record the transfer as a secured borrowing. If sale accounting is appropriate, it is still necessary to consider assets obtained and liabilities incurred in the transaction. If there is continuing involvement in a sale transaction, the assets obtained and liabilities incurred must be recorded at fair value.

(b)   A **financial components approach** is used to account for a transfer of accounts receivable with recourse whenever the transfer arrangement meets the conditions necessary for the transfer to be accounted for as a sale (see answer (a) above). If receivables are sold (factored) with recourse, the seller guarantees payment to the purchaser in the event the debtor fails to pay. Under the financial components approach, each party to the sale recognizes the assets and liabilities that it controls after the sale and no longer recognizes the assets and liabilities that were sold or extinguished.

(c)   Sale of receivables without recourse:

Jedd Hale Corp.			**Klein-Seay Financing**		
Cash	81,000		Accounts Receivable	90,000	
Due from Factor	5,400*		Due to Jedd Hale		5,400
Loss on Sale of Re-			Financing Revenue		3,600
ceivables	3,600**		Cash		81,000
Accounts Receivable		90,000			

*$90,000 X 6% = $5,400
**$90,000 X 4% = $3,600

TIP: The factor's profit will be the difference between the financing revenue of $3,600 and the amount of any uncollectible receivables.

(d)   Sale of receivables with recourse:

Jedd Hale Corp.			**Klein-Seay Financing**		
Cash	81,000		Accounts Receivable	90,000	
Due from Factor	5,400		Due to Jedd Hale		5,400
Loss on Sale of Re-			Financing Revenue		3,600
ceivables	5,600*		Cash		81,000
Accounts Receivable		90,000			
Recourse Liability		2,000			

*Cash received	$81,000
Due from factor	5,400
Subtotal	86,400
Resource obligation	(2,000)
Net proceeds expected	$84,400
Carrying (book) value	$90,000
Net proceeds	(84,400)
Loss on sale of receivables	$ 5,600

TIP: In this case, a liability of $2,000 is recorded by Jedd Hale to indicate the probable payment to Klein-Seay Financing for uncollectible receivables. If all the receivables are collected, Jedd Hale would eliminate its recourse liability and increase net income. Klein-Seay Financing's profit is the financing revenue of $3,600 because it will have no bad debts related to these receivables.

EXERCISE 7-7

Purpose: (L.O. 8) This exercise will illustrate the computations and entries involved in accounting for the transfer of receivables that is treated as a secured borrowing transaction.

Nijjar Winery transfers $350,000 of its accounts receivable to Monrovia Bank as collateral for a $250,000 note on September 1, 2014. Nijjar will continue to collect the accounts receivable; the account debtors are not notified of the arrangement. Monrovia Bank assesses a finance charge of 1% of the accounts receivable and interest on the note of 12%. Settlement by Nijjar Winery to the bank is made monthly for all cash collected on the receivables.

Instructions

Prepare the journal entries for both Nijjar Winery and Monrovia Bank to record the following:
(a) Transfer of accounts receivable and issuance of the note on September 1, 2014.
(b) Collection in September of $220,000 of the transferred accounts receivable less cash discounts of $3,000. In addition, sales returns of $7,000 were processed.
(c) Remittance by Nijjar of September collections plus accrued interest to the bank on October 1.
(d) Collection in October of the balance of the transferred accounts receivable less $1,000 written off as uncollectible.
(e) Remittance by Nijjar of the balance due of $33,000 ($250,000 - $217,000) on the note plus interest on November 1.

Solution to Exercise 7-7

(a)

Nijjar Winery			**Monrovia Bank**		
Cash	246,500		Notes Receivable	250,000	
Finance Charge	3,500*		Finance Revenue		3,500*
Notes Payable		250,000	Cash		246,500

*1% X $350,000 = $3,500

(b)

			(No Entry)
Cash	217,000		
Sales Discounts	3,000		
Sales Returns	7,000		
Accounts Receivable		227,000*	

*$220,000 + $7,000 = $227,000

(c)

Nijjar Winery			Monrovia Bank		
Interest Expense	2,500*		Cash	219,500	
Notes Payable	217,000		Interest Revenue		2,500*
Cash		219,500	Notes Receivable		217,000

*$250,000 X .12 X 1/12 = $2,500

(d)

Cash	122,000		(No Entry)	
Allowance for Doubtful				
Accounts	1,000			
Accounts Receivable		123,000*		

*$350,000 - $227,000 = $123,000

(e)

Interest Expense	330*		Cash	33,330	
Notes Payable	33,000		Interest Revenue		330*
Cash		33,330	Notes Receivable		33,000

*$33,000 X .12 X 1/12

TIP: Receivables are often used as collateral in a borrowing transaction. A creditor often requires that the debtor designate or pledge receivables as security for the loan. The debtor continues to collect the accounts receivable; the account debtors are not notified of the arrangement. If the loan is not paid when due, the creditor has the right to convert the collateral to cash—that is, to collect the receivables. (If the receivables are transferred to the transferee for custodial purposes, the custodial arrangement is often referred to as a **pledge**.) **Factors** are finance companies or banks that buy receivables from businesses for a fee and then collect remittances directly from the customers. This exercise **(Exercise 7-7)** illustrates a borrowing transaction whereas **Exercise 7-6** illustrates a sales transaction.

TIP: A recent phenomenon in the sale (transfer) of receivables is **securitization. Securitization** takes a pool of assets such as credit card receivables, mortgage receivables, or car loan receivables, and sells shares in these pools of interest and principal payments. How does this differ from factoring? Factoring usually involves the sale to only one company, fees are high, the quality of receivables is low, and the seller afterward does not service the receivables. In a securitization, many investors are involved, margins are tight, the receivables are of higher quality, and the seller usually continues to service the receivables. In either a factoring or a securitization transaction, a company sells receivables on either a **without recourse** or a **with recourse basis.**

*ILLUSTRATION 7-4
TWO FORMATS FOR BANK RECONCILIATIONS (L.O. 10)

First One:
    Balance per bank
- Add positive items per books not on bank's records.
- Deduct negative items per books not on bank's records.
- Add or deduct, whichever is applicable, bank error in recording receipts or disbursements.

    Correct cash balance

    Balance per books
- Add positive items per bank not on books.
- Deduct negative items per bank not on books.
- Add or deduct, whichever is applicable, depositor error in recording receipts or disbursements.

    Correct cash balance

Second One:
    Balance per bank
- Add positive items per books not on bank's records.
- Deduct negative items per books not on bank's records.
- Add or deduct, whichever is applicable, bank error in recording receipts or disbursements.
- Deduct positive items per bank not on books.
- Add negative items per bank not on books.
- Add or deduct, whichever is applicable, depositor error in recording receipts or disbursements.

    Balance per books

Examples of reconciling items:
    Positive item per books not on bank's records:
        Deposit in transit
    Negative item per books not on bank's records:
        Outstanding check
    Positive item per bank not on books:
        Note collected by bank
        Interest paid by bank to depositor on account balance
    Negative item per bank not on books:
        Bank service charge
        Customer's NSF check returned by bank
        Note paid by bank
        Automatic payments made by bank for depositor
    Error by bank:
        In recording receipt
        In recording disbursement
    Error by depositor:
        In recording receipt
        In recording disbursement

ILLUSTRATION 7-4 (Continued)

TIP: The objective of a bank reconciliation is to explain all reasons why the bank balance differs from the book balance and to identify errors and omissions in the bank's records and in the book records. In the context of a bank reconciliation, "per bank" refers to the records of the bank pertaining to the depositor's account and "per books" refers to the depositor's records of the same bank account.

TIP: If you have a checking account, look at the back of your bank statement. A bank often includes a form to assist you in reconciling your bank account. Very often that form reconciles the cash balance per bank to the cash balance per books rather than reconciling both the bank cash balance and the book cash balance to the correct (adjusted) cash balance.

TIP: A depositor's checking account is a liability on the bank's books, so a bank debit memo decreases the depositor's cash balance and a bank credit memo increases the depositor's cash balance. On the bank statement, debits appear as a result of checks that have cleared during the month or bank debit memos for items such as bank service charges (BSC). Credits on the bank statement represent deposits or bank credit memos.

TIP: The "Balance per bank" caption on a bank reconciliation is often replaced with "Balance per bank statement," and "Balance per books" is often titled "Balance per ledger."

TIP: The "Correct cash balance" caption on a bank reconciliation is often replaced with "Adjusted cash balance." The adjusted cash balance as determined by the bank reconciliation will be the amount used to report for cash on the balance sheet. (The Cash account in the general ledger often includes cash on hand and cash in the bank, although separate ledger accounts such as Cash in Bank and Cash on Hand may be used. The balance of this account and any other unrestricted cash accounts, such as the Petty Cash account, are added together to report cash on the balance sheet.)

TIP: Some items in a bank reconciliation will require adjustments either on the depositor's books or in the bank's records, while the others will not. When the balance per bank to correct cash balance format is used in preparing a single-column bank reconciliation, all of the reconciling items appearing in the lower half of the reconciliation (balance per books to correct cash balance) require adjustment on the depositor's books. All of the reconciling items appearing in the upper half of the reconciliation **except** for deposits in transit and outstanding checks require adjustment on the bank's books.

TIP: Unless otherwise indicated, an NSF check is assumed to be a customer's NSF check; that is, an NSF check is considered to be from a customer of the depositor, rather than a depositor's NSF check.

TIP: Beginning cash balance **per bank** plus total receipts for the month **per bank** minus total disbursements for the month **per bank** equals ending cash balance **per bank.** Total deposits or receipts per bank for a month include all deposits made by the depositor during the month plus any bank credit memos (such as for interest credited by the bank or a customer's note receivable collected by the bank). Total checks paid or disbursements per bank for a month include all the depositor's checks which cleared the banking system during the month plus any bank debit memos originating during the month (such as for bank service charges or a customer's NSF check).

TIP: Beginning cash balance **per books** plus total receipts for the month **per books** minus total disbursements for the month **per books** equals ending cash balance **per books.**

*EXERCISE 7-8

Purpose: (L.O. 10) This exercise will help you review situations that give rise to reconciling items on a bank reconciliation and identify those which require adjusting entries on the depositor's books.

A sketch of the bank reconciliation at July 31, 2014 for the Ace Electric Company and a list of possible reconciling items appear below.

Ace Electric Co.
BANK RECONCILIATION
July 31, 2014

Balance per bank statement, July 31			$X,XXX
A. Add:		$XXX	
		XXX	X,XXX
			X,XXX
B. Deduct:			X,XXX
Correct cash balance, July 31			$X,XXX
Balance per books, July 31			$ X,XXX
C. Add:		$XXX	
		XXX	X,XXX
			X,XXX
D. Deduct:		XXX	
		XXX	
		XXX	
		XXX	X,XXX
Correct cash balance, July 31			$X,XXX

_____   1.   Deposits of July 30 amounting to $1,482 have not reached the bank as of July 31.

_____   2.   A customer's check for $40 that was deposited on July 20 was returned NSF by the bank; return has not been recorded by Ace.

_____   3.   Bank service charge for July amounts to $3.

_____   4.   Included with the bank statement was check No. 422 for $702 as payment of an account payable. In comparing the check with the cash disbursement records, it was discovered that the check was incorrectly entered in the cash disbursements journal for $720.

_____   5.   Outstanding checks at July 31 amount to $1,927.

_____   6.   The bank improperly charged a check of the Ace Plumbing Co. for $25 to Ace Electric Co.'s account.

_____   7.   The bank charged $8 during July for printing checks.

_____ 8.   During July, the bank collected a customer's note receivable for the Ace Electric Co.; face amount $1,000, interest $20, and the bank charged a $2 collection fee. This transaction has not been recorded by Ace.

_____ 9.   A check written by Ace in June for $180 cleared the bank during July.

_____ 10. Deposits of June 30 for $1,200 were recorded by the company on June 30 but were not recorded by the bank until July 2.

Instructions

(a)   Indicate how each of the 10 items listed above would be handled on the bank reconciliation by placing the proper code letter (A, B, C, D) in the space provided. The applicable code letters appear in the sketch of the bank reconciliation. Use the code "NR" for any item which is not a reconciling item on July 31.

(b)   Assume that the July 31 balance per bank statement was $4,332. Complete the bank reconciliation using the items given and answer the questions that follow:

1.   What is the adjusted (correct) cash balance at July 31? $_____

2.   What is the balance per books **before** adjustment at July 31?

3.   What reconciling items require an adjusting entry on Ace Electric Company's books? (Identify by item numbers.)

4.   What item(s) requires a special entry on the bank's records to correct an error(s)?

Solution to Exercise 7-8

(a)   1.   A   6.   A
      2.   D   7.   D
      3.   D   8.   C, C, D
      4.   C   9.   NR
      5.   B   10. NR

> **TIP:** Items 9 and 10 would have been reconciling items of cash balances on the June 30 bank reconciliation (the prior month).

(b)   1. $3,912* ($4,332 + $1,482 + $25 - $1,927 = $3,912)
      2. $2,927* [X + $18 + $1,020 - $40 - $3 - $8 - $2 = $3,912 (answer to question 1)]
           X = $2,927
      3.   2; 3; 4; 7; 8
      4.   6

*See the completed bank reconciliation on the following page.

Approach to part (b) 2: You can compute the correct cash balance by completing the top half of the bank reconciliation (balance per bank to correct cash balance). The correct cash balance can then be entered on the last line of the bottom half of the reconciliation and used along with certain reconciling items to "work backwards" to compute the $2,927 cash balance per books before adjustment.

Ace Electric Co.
BANK RECONCILIATION
July 31, 2014

Balance per bank statement, July 31		$ 4,332
Add: Deposits in transit on July 31	$1,482	
Check improperly charged by bank	25	1,507
		5,839
Deduct: Checks outstanding as of July 31		1,927
Correct cash balance at July 31		$3,912
Balance per books, July 31		$2,927
Add: Error in recording check No. 422	$ 18	
Collection of customer's note receivable and		
interest by bank	1,020	1,038
		3,965
Deduct: Customer's NSF check	40	
Bank service charge for July	3	
Cost of printing checks	8	
Bank collection fee	2	53
Correct cash balance at July 31		$3,912

TIP: The required adjusting entries on the depositor's books would be:

Cash..	18	
Accounts Payable...		18
(To correct error in recording check No. 422)		
Cash..	1,020	
Note Receivable...		1,000
Interest Revenue...		20
(To record collection of note receivable by bank)		
Accounts Receivable	40	
Cash		40
(To record customer's NSF check)		
Miscellaneous Expense	13	
Cash		13
(To record bank service charges:		
[$3 + $8 + $2 = $13])		

TIP: The above entries can be combined into one compound entry.

TIP: Keep in mind that deposits in transit and outstanding checks are reconciling items but do **not** require adjusting entries on either the bank's books or the depositor's books.

TIP: Note that a transportation error (reversing the order of numbers such as $702 and $720) will cause a difference divisible by 9.

*EXERCISE 7-9

Purpose: (L.O. 10) This exercise reviews the journal entries involved with establishing and maintaining a petty cash fund.

The Kirmani Corporation makes most expenditures by check. The following transactions relate to an imprest fund established by the Kirmani Corporation to handle small expenditures on an expedient basis.

Transactions

May	4	Wrote a $100 check to establish the petty cash fund.
	6	Paid taxi $2 to deliver papers to a branch office.
	6	Purchased stamps, $13.
	8	Paid $15 for advertising posters.
	12	Paid $6 for mail received with "postage due."
	12	Paid $8 for coffee supplies.
	13	Paid $17 for office supplies.
	14	Paid bus charges of $18 to ship goods to a customer.
	15	Counted the remaining coins and currency in the fund, $20. Wrote a check to replenish the fund.

Instructions

(a)   Record the transactions in general journal form.
(b)   Answer the questions that follow:

1.   How much coin and currency should have been in the petty cash box at the end of the day on May 12? $_____

2.   How much coin and currency should have been in the petty cash box on May 15 before replenishment? $_____

3.   What was the balance in the Petty Cash ledger account on May 12? $_____

4.   What was the balance in the Petty Cash ledger account at the end of the day, May 15? $_____

TIP: In order to answer the last two questions, it would be helpful to post the journal entries to a T-account for Petty Cash.

Solution to Exercise 7-9

(a) May 4   Petty Cash.. 100

         Cash 100

              (To establish a petty cash fund)

    May 15   Miscellaneous Expense ($2 + $8) 10

         Postage Expense ($13 + $6) 19

         Advertising Expense 15

         Office Supplies 17

         Transportation-out 18

         Cash Over and Short 1

              Cash 80

              (To replenish the petty cash fund)

(b) 1. There should have been $56 in coin and currency in the fund at the end of the day on May 12. ($100 - $2 - $13 - $15 - $6 - $8 = $56)

    2. There should have been $21 in coin and currency in the fund on May 15 before replenishment. ($100 - $2 - $13 - $15 - $6 - $8 - $17 - $18 = $21)

TIP:	Because only $20 was found in the fund at that date, there was a shortage of $1, which must be recorded by a debit to the Cash Over and Short account.

    3. $100
    4. $100

TIP:	The balance of the Petty Cash account changes **only** when the fund is established or the size of the fund is increased or decreased. The Petty Cash account balance is **not** affected by expenditures from the fund nor replenishments. (No journal entry is made at the time an expenditure is made. Expenditures from the fund are accounted for at the date of replenishment.)
TIP:	Petty Cash is not normally reported separately on the balance sheet. The balance of the Petty Cash account is generally lumped together with all other cash items when a balance sheet is prepared.

ANALYSIS OF MULTIPLE-CHOICE TYPE QUESTIONS

QUESTION
1.   (L.O. 1) Which of the following items should **not** be included in the Cash caption on the balance sheet?
      a.   Coins and currency in the cash register
      b.   Checks from other parties presently in the cash register
      c.   Amounts on deposit in checking account at the bank
      d.   Postage stamps on hand

Explanation: Cash on hand, cash in banks, and petty cash are often combined and reported simply as Cash. Undeposited checks from other parties is a component of cash on hand. Postage stamps on hand are classified as a prepaid expense. (Solution = d.)

QUESTION
2.   (L.O. 2) The SEC recommends that legally restricted deposits held at a bank as compensating balances against long-term borrowing arrangements should be:
      a.   used to reduce the amount reported as long-term debt on the balance sheet.
      b.   reported separately among the "cash and cash equivalent items" in Current Assets on the balance sheet.
      c.   separately classified as noncurrent assets in either the Investments or Other Assets sections of the balance sheet.
      d.   used to reduce the amount reported as short-term debt on the balance sheet.

Explanation: The SEC recommends that legally restricted deposits held as compensating balances against short-term borrowing arrangements be stated separately among the "cash and cash equivalent items" in Current Assets. Restricted deposits held as compensating balances against long-term borrowing arrangements should be separately classified as noncurrent assets in either the Investments or Other Assets sections, using a caption such as "Cash on Deposit Maintained as Compensating Balance." To use the asset balance to directly reduce a debt (answer selections "a" and "d" would be "offsetting assets against liabilities" which violates a rule against offsetting or setoff. Only in rare circumstances is it permissable to offset assets and liabilities.) (Solution = c.)

QUESTION
3.   (L.O. 4) Trade discounts are
      a.   not recorded in the accounts; rather they are a means of computing a price.
      b.   used to avoid frequent changes in catalogues.
      c.   used to quote different prices for different quantities purchased.
      d.   all of the above.

Explanation: Customers are often quoted prices on the basis of list or catalogue prices that may be subject to a trade or quantity discount. Such trade discounts are used to avoid the need for frequent changes in catalogues, to quote different prices for different quantities purchased, or to hide the true invoice price from competitors. Trade discounts are not recorded in the accounts. They are used to compute the sales (or purchase) price of an item which is recorded in the accounts. Thus an item with a list price of $800 subject to a trade discount of 30% has a selling (or purchase) price of $560 which is recorded in the accounts. (Solution = d.)

TIP: A chain discount occurs when a list price is subject to several trade discounts. When a chain discount is offered, the amount of each trade discount is determined by multiplying (1) the list price of the merchandise **less** the amount of prior trade discounts by (2) the trade discount percentage.

QUESTION
4.   (L.O. 5) Gatorland recorded uncollectible accounts expense of $30,000 and wrote off accounts receivable of $25,000 during the year. The net effect of these two transactions on working capital was a decrease of:
a. $55,000.
b. $30,000.
c. $25,000.
d. $5,000.

Approach and Explanation: Reconstruct both entries referred to in the question. Then analyze each debit and each credit separately as to its effect on working capital (total current assets minus total current liabilities). (Refer to **Illustration 7-1**.)

			Effect on Working Capital
Uncollectible Accounts Expense	30,000		None
Allow. for Uncollectible Accounts		30,000	Decrease 30,000
Allowance for Uncollectible Accounts	25,000		Increase 25,000
Accounts Receivable		25,000	Decrease 25,000
Net Effect			Decrease 30,000
			(Solution = b.)

QUESTION
5.   (L.O. 5) Chelser Corporation performed an analysis and an aging of its accounts receivable at December 31, 2014, which disclosed the following:

Accounts receivable balance	$ 100,000
Allowance for uncollectible accounts balance	5,000
Accounts deemed uncollectible	7,400

The net realizable value of the accounts receivable at December 31 is:
a. $87,600.
b. $92,600.
c. $95,000.
d. $97,600.

Approach and Explanation: Read the last sentence of the question: "The net realizable value of the accounts receivable at December 31 is..." Underline "net realizable value of accounts receivable." Write down the definition of net realizable value of accounts receivable—amount of accounts receivable ultimately expected to be converted into cash. Read the details of the question. If an aging shows $7,400 of the $100,000 accounts are deemed uncollectible, then the remaining $92,600 are expected to be converted into cash. (Because the balance of the allowance account does not agree with the amount of uncollectibles per the aging, the allowance for uncollectible accounts balance must be the unadjusted balance or the percentage of sales method is being used to determine the amount to record as bad debt expense.) (Solution = b.)

QUESTION

6.   (L.O. 5) The following data are available for 2014:

Sales, cash	$ 200,000
Sales, credit	500,000
Accounts Receivable, January 1	80,000
Accounts Receivable, December 31	72,000
Allowance for Doubtful Accounts, January 1	4,000
Accounts written off during 2014	4,600

The journal entry to record bad debt expense for the period and to adjust the allowance account is to be based on an estimate of 1% of credit sales. The entry to record the uncollectible accounts expense for 2014 would include a debit to the Bad Debt Expense account for:

a. $7,200.
b. $5,600.
c. $4,400.
d. $5,000.

Approach and Explanation: Think about the emphasis of the entry when the percentage-of-sales basis is used. This method emphasizes the income statement. Therefore, 1% times credit sales equals bad debt expense ($500,000 x 1% = $5,000). The balance of the allowance account before adjustment does **not** affect this computation or entry. (Solution = d.)

QUESTION

7.   (L.O. 5) The following data are available for 2014:

Sales, cash	$ 200,000
Sales, credit	500,000
Accounts Receivable, January 1	80,000
Accounts Receivable, December 31	72,000
Allowance for Doubtful Accounts, January 1	4,000
Accounts written off during 2014	4,600

The journal entry to record bad debt expense for the period and to adjust the allowance account is to be based on an aging analysis of accounts receivable. The aging analysis of accounts receivable at December 31, 2014, reveals that $5,200 of existing accounts receivable are estimated to be uncollectible. The entry to record the uncollectible accounts expense for 2014 will involve a debit to the Bad Debt Expense account for:

a. $9,800.
b. $5,800.
c. $5,200.
d. $4,600.

Approach and Explanation: An aging analysis is performed to determine the best figure to represent the cash (net) realizable value of the accounts receivable in the balance sheet. Thus, $5,200 is the desired balance for the allowance account at the reporting date. Determine the existing balance in the allowance account and the adjusting entry needed to arrive at the desired ending balance.

Allowance for Doubtful Accounts

Write-offs, 2014	4,600	Balance, 1/1/14	4,000	**Entry**
Balance before adjustment	600	Adjustment needed	X	**←Needed.**
		Desired balance at 12/31/14	5,200	

Solving for X: $X - \$600 = \$5,200$
                            $X = \$5,200 + \$600$
                            $X = \underline{\$5,800}$ (Solution = b.)

QUESTION
8.   (L.O. 5) The following data are available for 2014:

Allowance for Doubtful Accounts, January 1	$ 41,000
Writeoffs of accounts receivable during the year	35,000
Net credit sales for the year	1,300,000

Bad debts are estimated to be 3% of net credit sales. The balance of the allowance account after adjustment should be:
   a. $4,000.
   b. $39,000.
   c. $45,000.
   d. $80,000.

Approach and Explanation: Draw a T-account. Enter the data given and solve for the amount requested.

Allowance for Doubtful Accounts			
		41,000	Beginning Balance
Writeoffs	35,000	39,000	Expense = 3% X $1,300,000
		45,000	Ending Balance

(Solution = c.)

QUESTION
9.   (L.O. 6) On January 1, 2014 West Park Co. exchanged equipment for a $480,000 zero-interest-bearing note due on January 1, 2017 from Chamberlain's Health Products. Chamberlain's incremental borrowing rate at January 1, 2014 was 10%. The present value of $1 discounted at 10% for three periods is $0.75. The amount of interest revenue that should be included in West Park's income statement for the year 2015 is:
   a. $0.
   b. $36,000.
   c. $39,600.
   d. $48,000.

Explanation: The note received in exchange for equipment is an arms' length transaction and the stated interest rate is unreasonable in relation to the market rate of interest. The fair value of the equipment is not available information. Therefore, the present value of the note is to be approximated by discounting all of the future cash receipts related to the note, and the discounting is done using the market rate of interest (borrower's incremental borrowing rate). The face amount of $480,000 is discounted back three periods to yield a present value balance at January 1, 2014 of $360,000 ($480,000 X .75 = $360,000). The effective interest method is used to determine the amount of interest to report each period.

Present Value Balance   X   Interest Rate Per   X   Time   =   Interest
at Beginning of Period   Period

$360,000 X 10% X 12/12 = $36,000 Interest for 2014

The interest for 2015 (the second year) would be computed as follows:

$360,000	Present value, January 1, 2014
+ 36,000	Interest for 2014
396,000	Present value, December 31, 2014
(0)	Payment
396,000	Present value (carrying value), January 1, 2015
X 10%	Effective or yield rate of interest
$ 39,600	Interest for 2015 (the second year)

(Solution = c.)

QUESTION

10. (L.O. 7) Marzella Corporation has elected to use the fair value measurement for its notes receivables (newly acquired in 2013). The carrying amount of these receivables is $460,000 at December 31, 2013 and $425,000 at December 31, 2014. The fair value of these receivables is $500,000 at December 31, 2013 and $435,000 at December 31, 2014. Which of the following is a true statement regarding the financial statements prepared at December 31, 2014?

   a. A valuation account with a debit balance of $65,000 will be reported on the balance sheet.
   b. An unrealized holding gain will increase the net income figure for the year 2014.
   c. An unrealized holding loss of $10,000 will be reported on the income statement for 2014.
   d. An unrealized holding loss of $30,000 will be reported on the income statement for 2014.

Approach and Explanation: Prepare the journal entries for the facts given and analyze the impact of those entries on the financial statements. Because the notes receivables originated in 2013, there was no Fair Value Adjustment account balance at the beginning of 2013. Thus the entry to establish the $40,000 debit balance necessary at the end of 2013 is:

At December 31, 2013

Fair Value Adjustment—Notes Receivable	40,000	
Unrealized Holding Gain or Loss—Income		40,000
($500,000 F.V. - $460,000 C.V. = $40,000)		

The receivables get reported at the fair value of $500,000 on the balance sheet and a holding gain of $40,000 is on the income statement for 2013.

At December 31, 2014

Unrealized Holding Gain or Loss—Income	30,000	
Fair Value Adjustment—Notes Receivable		30,000
($435,000 - $425,000 = $10,000 balance needed)		
($40,000 existing debit balance - $10,000 desired		
debit balance = $30,000 adjustment needed)		

The receivables get reported at the fair value of $435,000 on the balance sheet and a holding loss of $30,000 is on the income statement for the year 2014. The amount going to the income statement is simply whatever is needed in the adjusting entry to bring the valuation account (Fair Value Adjustment) to its desired balance in order to report the receivables at their fair value (carrying value of $425,000 in the Notes Receivable account + $10,000 debit balance in the Fair Value Adjustment account = $435,000). (Solution = d.)

QUESTION

11. (L.O. 8) A company has a large amount of accounts receivable and a ready need for cash. The company may accelerate the receipt of cash from customers' accounts receivable thru:

	Factoring	Assignment
a.	Yes	Yes
b.	Yes	No
c.	No	Yes
d.	No	No

Explanation: The company can transfer accounts receivable to a third party for cash by the assignment or factoring (sale) of the accounts receivable. (Solution = a.)

QUESTION
12.   (L.O. 9) The accounts receivable turnover ratio measures the:
   a.   number of times the average balance of accounts receivable is collected during the period.
   b.   percentage of accounts receivable turnover over to a collection agency during the period.
   c.   percentage of accounts receivable arising during certain seasons.
   d.   number of times the average balance of inventory is sold during the period.

Approach and Explanation: Write down the components of the **accounts receivable turnover ratio.** Think about why it is computed. The computation is as follows:

$$\text{Accounts Receivable Turnover Ratio} = \frac{\text{Net Sales}}{\text{Average trade receivables (net)}}$$

Because cash sales do not go through the Accounts Receivable account, only net credit sales belong in the numerator; however, very often that information is not available. The accounts receivable ratio measures the number of times, on average, the accounts receivable balance was collected during the period. This ratio is used to assess the liquidity of the receivables. This ratio can be divided into 365 days to obtain the **average days to collect accounts receivable.** (Solution = a.)

QUESTION
*13.   (L.O. 10) The term "outstanding checks" refers to:
   a.   checks that have been lost in the mail or for some other reason have been misplaced.
   b.   depositor checks which have been processed by the bank but have not yet been recorded by the depositor.
   c.   customer checks which have been returned by the bank because the customer's bank would not honor them.
   d.   depositor checks which have not yet cleared the banking system.

Explanation: There is a lag time between the date a check is issued and the date the check clears the banking system. During the time between these two dates, the checks are referred to as "outstanding checks." Checks written by the enterprise but not mailed until **after** the balance sheet date should not be included with outstanding checks. Rather, they should be added back to the cash balance and reported as accounts payable. (Solution = d.)

QUESTION
*14.   (L.O.10) The following information pertains to Cruiser Co. at December 31, 2014:

Bank statement balance	$20,000
Checkbook balance	28,200
Deposit in transit	10,000
Outstanding checks	2,000
Bank service charges for December	200

In Cruiser's balance sheet at December 31, 2014, cash should be reported as:
   a. $18,000.
   b. $20,000.
   c. $28,000.
   d. $30,000.

Approach and Explanation: When a question relates to data used in a bank reconciliation, you should sketch out the format for a bank reconciliation, put in the information given, and solve for the unknown piece.

Balance per bank statement	$ 20,000
Deposit in transit	10,000
Outstanding checks	(2,000)
Correct cash balance	$ 28,000
Balance per books	$ 28,200
Bank service charges	(200)
Correct cash balance	$ 28,000

In this particular question, the completion of either the top half or the bottom half of the reconciliation using the bank-to-correct balance method would be enough to solve for the answer requested. (Solution = c.)

QUESTION

*15.   (L.O. 10) The following data relate to the bank account of Springfield Cleaners:

Cash balance, September 30, 2014 per bank	$ 10,000
Cash balance, October 31, 2014 per bank	21,500
Checks paid during October by bank	5,900
Checks written during October per books	6,800
Cash balance, October 31, 2014 per books	22,200
Bank service charges for October, not recorded on books	100
Deposits per books for October	19,000

The amount of deposits recorded by the bank in October is:
a. $19,000.
b. $17,500.
c. $11,500.
d. $5,700.

Approach and Explanation: Think about how deposits recorded by the bank affect the cash balance per bank and other items that cause that balance to change. Plug in the figures given and solve for the unknown.

Balance per bank, September 30	$ 10,000
Deposits per bank during October	X
Bank credit memoranda	-0-
Checks paid by bank during October	(5,900)
Bank service charge for October and other bank debit memoranda	(100)
Balance per bank, October 31	$ 21,500

Solving for X:
$10,000 + X - $5,900 - $100 = $21,500
X = $21,500 - $10,000 + $5,900 + $100
X = $17,500 (Solution = b.)

QUESTION
*16.   (L.O. 10) The following information pertains to Tommy-Jer Corporation at December 31, 2014:

Balance per bank	$ 10,000
Deposit in transit	3,000
Outstanding checks	8,000
Bank service charges for December	200
Bank erroneously charged Tommy-Jer's account for Sonny-Ber's check written for $700. As of Dec. 31, the bank had not corrected this error	700

Tommy-Jer's cash balance per ledger (books) before adjustment at December 31, 2014 is:
a. $14,100.
b. $5,900.
c. $5,500.
d. $4,100.

Approach and Explanation: The balance per books (before adjustment) can easily be computed by putting the data into the format for a bank reconciliation. Either format (balance per bank to balance per books or balance per bank to correct balance) can be used. Each approach is illustrated below: (Solution = b.)

Balance per bank statement	$ 10,000
Deposit in transit	3,000
Outstanding checks	(8,000)
Bank service charges	200
Bank error in charge for check	700
Balance per ledger	$ 5,900

Balance per bank statement	$ 10,000
Deposit in transit	3,000
Outstanding checks	(8,000)
Bank error in charge for check	700
Correct cash balance	$ 5,700

Balance per books (ledger)	$ X
Bank service charge	(200)
Correct cash balance	$ 5,700

X = $5,900

IFRS Insights

- The basic accounting and reporting issues related to recognition and measurement of receivables, such as the use of allowance accounts, how to record discounts, use of the allowance method to account for bad debts, and factoring, are similar for both IFRS and GAAP.

- The accounting and reporting related to cash is essentially the same under both IFRS and GAAP. In addition, the definition used for cash equivalents is the same. One difference is that, in general, IFRS classifies bank overdrafts as cash, whereas GAAP reports overdrafts as liabilities.

- Like GAAP, cash and receivables are generally reported in the current assets section of the balance sheet under IFRS. However, companies may report cash and receivables as the last items in current assets under IFRS. Under GAAP, current assets are reported in order of liquidity.

- IFRS requires that loans and receivables be accounted for at amortized cost, adjusted for allowances for doubtful accounts. IFRS sometimes refers to these allowances as **provisions.** The entry to record the allowance would be:

Bad Debt Expense	xxxxx	
Provision for Doubtful Accounts		xxxxx

- Although IFRS implies that receivables with different characteristics should be reported separately, there is no standard that mandates this segregation. GAAP has explicit guidance in this area.

- The fair value option is similar under GAAP and IFRS but not identical. The international standard related to the fair value option is subject to certain qualifying criteria **not** in the U.S. standard. In addition, there is some difference in the financial instruments covered.

- IFRS and GAAP differ in the criteria used to account for transfers of receivables. IFRS is a combination of an approach focused on risks and rewards and loss of control. GAAP uses loss of control as the primary criterion. In addition, IFRS generally permits partial transfers; GAAP does not.

- IFRS provides detailed guidelines to assess whether receivables should be considered uncollectible (often referred to as *impaired*). GAAP does not identify a specific approach. Under IFRS, companies assess their receivables for impairment each reporting period and start the impairment assessment by considering whether objective evidence indicates that one or more loss events have occurred. Examples of possible loss events are:

  - Significant financial problems of the customer.
  - Payment defaults.
  - Renegotiation of terms of the receivable due to financial difficulty of the customer.

- Measurable decrease in estimated future cash flows from a group of receivables since initial recognition, although the decrease cannot yet be identified with individual assets in the group.

A receivable is considered impaired when a loss event indicates a negative impact on the estimated future cash flows to be received from the customer. The IASB requires that the impairment assessment should be performed as follows:

1. Receivables that are individually significant are considered for impairment separately, if impaired, the company recognizes it. Receivables that are not individually significant may also be assessed individually, but it is not necessary to do so.

2. Any receivable individually assessed that is not considered impaired is included with a group of assets with similar credit-risk characteristics and collectively assessed for impairment.

3. Any receivables **not individually assessed are collectively assessed** for impairment.

- The accounting for loan impairments is similar between GAAP and IFRS. Subsequent to recording an impairment, events or economic conditions may change such that the extent of the impairment loss decreases (e.g., due to an impairment in the debtor's credit rating.) Under IFRS, some or all of the previously recognized impairment loss shall be reversed either directly, with a debit to Accounts Receivable, or by debiting the allowance account and crediting Bad Debt Expense. Such reversals of impairment losses are **not** allowed under GAAP.

- The question of recording fair values for financial instruments will continue to be an important issue to resolve as the Boards work toward convergence. Both the IASB and the FASB have indicated that they believe that financial statements would be more transparent and understandable if companies recorded and reported all financial instruments at fair value. That said, in *IFRS 9,* which was issued in 2009, the IASB created a split model, where some financial instruments are recorded at fair value, but other financial assets, such as loans and receivables, can be accounted for at amortized cost if certain criteria are met.

TRUE/FALSE (Circle the correct answer for each).

T   F   1. A company using IFRS will classify a bank overdraft as cash (which will decrease the total amount reported as cash and cash equivalents).

T   F   2. IFRS allows for classifying cash and receivables as the last items in current assets.

T   F   3. The accounting for loan impairments is similar between GAAP and IFRS.

T   F   4. Under GAAP, some or all of a previously recognized impairment loss on receivables shall be reversed either directly, with a debit to Accounts Receivable, or by debiting the allowance account and crediting Bad Debt Expense.

T   F   5. Both the IASB and the FASB have indicated that they believe that all financial instruments should be reported at fair value.

Solutions:

1.	T		4.	F
2.	T		5.	T
3.	T			

CHAPTER 8

VALUATION OF INVENTORIES: A COST-BASIS APPROACH

OVERVIEW

In accounting, the term inventory refers to a stock of goods held for sale in the ordinary course of business or goods that will be used or consumed in the production of goods to be sold. A number of questions regarding inventory are addressed in this chapter; these include: (1) How does a periodic inventory system differ from a perpetual system? (2) What goods should be included in inventory? (3) What costs are included in inventory? (4) How will the selection of a particular cost flow assumption affect the income statement and balance sheet? (5) How do you compute the various layers of inventory when the dollar-value LIFO method is used?

SUMMARY OF LEARNING OBJECTIVES

1. **Identify major classifications of inventory.** Only one inventory account, Inventory, appears in the financial statements of a merchandising concern. A manufacturer normally has three inventory accounts: Raw Materials, Work in Process, and Finished Goods. Companies report the cost assigned to goods and materials on hand but not yet placed into production as raw materials inventory. They report the cost of the raw materials on which production has been started but not completed, plus the direct labor cost applied specifically to this material and a ratable share of manufacturing overhead costs, as work in process inventory. Finally, they report the costs identified with the completed but unsold units on hand at the end of the fiscal period are reported as finished goods inventory.

2. **Distinguish between the perpetual and periodic inventory systems.** A perpetual inventory system maintains a continuous record of changes in inventory in the Inventory account. That is, a company records all purchases and sales (issues) of goods directly in the Inventory account as they occur. Under a periodic inventory system, companies determine the quantity of inventory on hand only periodically. A company debits a Purchases account for purchases and the Inventory account remains unchanged during the period. A company determines cost of goods sold at the end of the period by subtracting ending inventory from cost of goods available for sale. A company ascertains ending inventory by physical count.

3. **Determine the goods included in inventory and the effects of inventory errors on the financial statements.** Companies record purchases of inventory when they obtain legal title to the goods (generally when they receive the goods). Shipping terms must be evaluated to determine when legal title passes, and careful consideration must be made for cost of goods sold on consignment and sales with buy-back agreements and high rates of return. *If a company misstates ending inventory:* (1) inventory and retained earnings will be misstated in the balance sheet, which leads to miscalculation of working capital and the current ratio, and (2) cost of goods sold and net income will be misstated in the income statement. *If a company misstates purchases (and related accounts payable) and ending inventory by the same amount:* (1) inventory and accounts payable will be misstated in the balance sheet, which leads to miscalculation of the current ratio. (2) cost of goods sold and net income will **not** be misstated in

the income statement (even though purchases and ending inventory are both misstated in the income statement).

4.   **Understand the items to include as inventory cost.** Product costs are those costs directly associated with the acquisition of goods and the conversion of such goods to a salable condition; hence they are properly included in the cost of inventory items in the Inventory account. Such charges include purchases, freight charges on goods purchased, other direct costs of acquisition, labor, and other production costs incurred in processing the goods up to the time of sale. Manufacturing overhead costs are also allocated to inventory. **Manufacturing overhead costs** include indirect material, indirect labor, and such items as depreciation, taxes, insurance, heat, and electricity incurred in the manufacturing process. Selling, administrative and interest costs are generally not included as inventory costs; they are period costs and thereby charged to expense in the period incurred.

5.   **Describe and compare the cost flow assumptions used in accounting for inventories.** (1) **Average-cost** prices items in inventory on the basis of the average cost of all similar goods available during the period. (2) **First-in, first-out (FIFO)** assumes that costs are used in the order in which the related goods were purchased. The cost of inventory on hand at a balance sheet date must therefore represent the most recent purchase prices. (3) **Last-in, first-out (LIFO)** matches the cost of the last goods purchased against revenue.

6.   **Explain the significance and use of a LIFO reserve.** The difference between the inventory method used for internal reporting purposes and LIFO is referred to as Allowance to Reduce Inventory to LIFO or the LIFO reserve. The change in the LIFO reserve is referred to as the LIFO Effect. Companies should disclose either the LIFO reserve or the replacement cost of the inventory in the financial statements.

7.   **Understand the effect of LIFO liquidations.** LIFO liquidations match costs from preceding periods against sales revenues reported in current dollars. This distorts net income and results in increased taxable income in the current period. LIFO liquidations can occur frequently when using a specific goods LIFO approach.

8.   **Explain the dollar-value LIFO method.** An important feature of the dollar-value LIFO method is that companies determine and measure increases and decreases in a pool in terms of total dollar value, not the physical quantity of specific goods in the inventory pool.

9.   **Identify the major advantages and disadvantages of LIFO.** The major advantages of LIFO are the following: (1) It matches recent costs against current revenues to provide a better measure of current earnings. (2) As long as the price level increases and inventory quantities do not decrease, a deferral of income tax occurs in LIFO. (3) Because of the deferral of income tax, cash flow improves. Major disadvantages are: (1) reduced earnings, (2) inventory is stated in terms of old costs which may be far below current costs, (3) the cost flow does **not** approximate the physical flow of the items except in unique situations, and (4) involuntary liquidation issues.

10.   **Understand why companies select given inventory methods.** Companies ordinarily prefer LIFO in the following circumstances: (1) if selling prices and revenues have been increasing faster than costs; and (2) if a company has a fairly constant "base stock" (which is typical in companies dealing with refining, chemicals, and glass.) Conversely, LIFO would probably not be appropriate in the following circumstances: (1) if sales prices tend to lag behind changes in costs; (2) if specific identification is traditional such as in the sales of automobiles, farm equipment, art, and antique jewelry; and (3) when unit costs tend to decrease as production increases, thereby nullifying the tax benefit that LIFO might provide.

TIPS ON CHAPTER TOPICS

TIP: The term inventory (or merchandise inventory) is the label given to goods held by a merchandise firm (either wholesale or retail) when goods have been acquired for resale. The terms raw materials, work in process, and finished goods refer to inventories of a manufacturing entity.

TIP: The cost of an inventory item includes all costs necessary to acquire the item and bring it to the location and condition for its intended use. This cost would include the item's purchase price, transportation-in, and any special handling charges. However, transportation-out is **not** included in the cost of inventory; it is classified as a selling expense on the income statement for the period in which the expense was incurred.

TIP: The transportation terms designate the point at which title passes. F.o.b. shipping point (or seller) means the title passes to the buyer when it leaves the seller's dock. F.o.b. destination (or buyer) means the title passes to the buyer when it arrives at the buyer's dock. Assuming that Palmer Company in Bay Hill, Florida sells to Tiger Woods in Orlando, Florida, the following shows synonymous terms:

f.o.b. shipping point	**f.o.b. destination**
or f.o.b. seller	or f.o.b. buyer
or f.o.b. Bay Hill, Florida	or f.o.b. Orlando, Florida

TIP: FIFO (first-in, first-out) means the cost of the first items put into inventory are used to price the first items out to cost of goods sold. Thus, the earliest acquisition prices are used to price cost of goods sold for the period, and the latest (most current) acquisition prices are used to price items in the ending inventory. LIFO (last-in, first-out) uses the most recent costs to price the units sold during the period, and it uses the oldest prices to cost the items in the ending inventory. Thus, in a period of rising prices, the method that will yield the lowest net income on the income statement and the lowest ending inventory on the balance sheet is the LIFO method.

TIP: The cost of the ending inventory determined by using the average-cost method is an amount between the cost of the ending inventory determined by using the LIFO method and the cost of the ending inventory determined by using the FIFO method. It uses a weighted-average cost.

TIP: When working a problem which requires the computation of either ending inventory or cost of goods sold, remember that the total of the ending inventory and the cost of goods sold should equal the total cost of goods available for sale during the period (beginning inventory plus the net cost of purchases).

TIP: Sales revenue represents the **selling prices** of goods sold, whereas cost of goods sold expense represents the **cost** of items sold.

TIP: The inventory pricing method selected by an entity does **not** have to correspond to the actual physical flow of goods. Thus, a company **can** use the LIFO method to determine the cost of ending inventory even though the first goods purchased are the first to be sold. (It is rare to find a company whose inventory has an actual physical flow of last-in; first-out. Examples would include piles of coal, sand, gravel, some feed bins, and the like.)

ILLUSTRATION 8-1
PERPETUAL VS. PERIODIC INVENTORY SYSTEMS (L.O. 2)

Features of a Perpetual System

1. Purchases of merchandise for resale are debited to Inventory rather than to Purchases.
2. Freight-in, Purchase Returns and Allowances, and Purchase Discounts are recorded in the Inventory account rather than in separate accounts.
3. Cost of goods sold is recognized for each sale by debiting the Cost of Goods Sold account, and crediting the Inventory account.
4. Inventory is a control account that is supported by a subsidiary ledger of individual inventory records. The subsidiary records show the quantity and cost of each type of inventory on hand. At any point during the accounting period (assuming all postings are up to date), the balance of the Inventory account reflects the cost of the items that should be on hand at that point in time.

Features of a Periodic System

1. Purchases of merchandise for resale are debited to a Purchases account.
2. The Freight-in, Purchase Returns and Allowances, and Purchase Discounts accounts are separate accounts which are used to record information about inventory acquisitions during the accounting period.
3. Cost of goods sold is recognized only at the end of the accounting period when the (1) ending inventory amount (determined by physical count, pricing, and extensions) is recorded in the Inventory account, (2) the Purchases, Freight-in, Purchase Returns and Allowances, and Purchase Discounts account balances are closed to the Income Summary account, and (3) the beginning inventory amount is transferred from the Inventory account to the Income Summary account.
4. There is no subsidiary ledger for inventory. All during the accounting period, the Inventory account reflects the cost of the inventory items on hand at the beginning of the period (beginning inventory). The Inventory account is **not** updated for acquisitions and withdrawals of inventory during the period; it is updated only at the end of the period to reflect the cost of the items on hand at the balance sheet date.

TIP: When a company uses a perpetual system, it must periodically do a physical count to verify the accuracy of the perpetual records. When a difference exists between the perpetual inventory balance and the physical inventory count, the company needs to record an adjusting entry. For example, assume the Inventory account reflects a balance of $58,000 when the physical count shows only $54,000 of goods on hand. The entry to record the difference is:

Inventory Over and Short	4,000	
Inventory		4,000

The over and short balance is normally included in cost of goods sold on the income statement, however, sometimes it is reported in the "Other expenses and losses" or "Other revenues and gains" section of the income statement.

ILLUSTRATION 8-1 (Continued)

EXAMPLE	
PERPETUAL SYSTEM	**PERIODIC SYSTEM**
1. There are 8 units in beginning inventory at a cost of $2,000 each.	
The Inventory account shows the inventory on hand at $16,000.	The Inventory account shows the inventory on hand at $16,000.
2. Purchase 12 items on account at $2,000 each.	

Inventory 24,000
    Accounts Payable   24,000
	Purchases 24,000
	    Accounts Payable 24,000

3. Return one defective item for $2,000 credit.	

Accounts Payable 2,000
    Inventory   2,000
	Accounts Payable 2,000
	    Purchase Returns
	    & Allowances 2,000

4. Sell 15 items on account for $3,000 each.	

Accounts Receivable 45,000
    Sales   45,000
 	
Cost of Goods Sold 30,000
    Inventory   30,000
	Accounts Receivable 45,000
	    Sales 45,000

5. End of period entries for inventory-related accounts (4 units on hand at $2,000 each).	

No entries are necessary:
The Inventory account shows the ending balance as $8,000 ($16,000 + $24,000 − $2,000 − $30,000)
	Inventory (ending, by physical count) 8,000
	Purchase Returns & Allowances 2,000
	Cost of Goods Sold 30,000
	    Purchases 24,000
	    Inventory (beginning) 16,000

ILLUSTRATION 8-2
RECORDING PURCHASES DISCOUNTS—GROSS AND NET METHODS (L.O. 4)

A vendor may offer a discount for payment of items purchased within a specific time frame. The following illustrates the two methods of accounting for purchase discounts:

Gross Method			Net Method		
Purchase cost $40,000, terms 2/10, net 30:					
Purchases	40,000		Purchases	39,200	
Accounts Payable		40,000	Accounts Payable		39,200
Invoices of $16,000 are paid within discount period:					
Accounts Payable	16,000		Accounts Payable	15,680	
Purchase Discounts		320	Cash		15,680
Cash		15,680			
Invoices of $24,000 are paid after discount period:					
Accounts Payable	24,000		Accounts Payable	23,520	
Cash		24,000	Purchase Discounts Lost	480	
			Cash		24,000

> **TIP:** If a company uses the net method, it considers purchase discounts lost as a financial expense and reports it in the "Other expenses and losses" section of the income statement. This treatment is considered better for two reasons: (1) It provides a correct reporting of the cost of the asset and related liability. (2) It can measure management inefficiency by holding management responsible for discounts not taken.
>
> **TIP:** As you learned in an earlier chapter, if a company uses the gross method, it reports purchases discounts contra to purchases (i.e., as a reduction of inventory cost).
>
> **TIP:** The net method is more in alignment with the historical cost principle in that the fair value of the item(s) received (cash equivalent price of the purchase) is the purchase price net of any discount allowed.

EXERCISE 8-1

Purpose: (L.O. 4) This exercise will give you practice in identifying the items that should be included as inventory cost.

Instructions
Indicate which of the items listed below would typically be reported as inventory in the financial statements by placing a "X" in the corresponding blank. If an item should **not** be included in the cost of inventory, indicate how it should be reported in the financial statements. The reporting period ends on December 31.

_____ 1. Raw materials on hand **not** yet placed into production by a manufacturing firm.

_____ 2. Raw materials on which a manufacturing firm has started production, but which are **not** completely processed.

_____ 3. Factory labor costs incurred on goods completed but still unsold by a manufacturer.

_____ 4. Factory supplies on hand.

_____ 5. Costs identified with units completed by a manufacturing firm, but **not** yet sold.

_____ 6. Goods out on consignment at another company's store.

_____ 7. Goods held on consignment from another company.

_____ 8. Goods purchased f.o.b. shipping point that are in transit at December 31.

_____ 9. Goods purchased f.o.b. destination that are in transit at December 31.

_____ 10. Goods sold f.o.b. shipping point that are in transit at December 31.

_____ 11. Goods sold f.o.b. destination that are in transit at December 31.

_____ 12. Goods sold on an installment basis.

_____ 13. Costs incurred to advertise goods held for resale.

_____ 14. Interest costs incurred to finance activities associated with making goods ready for sale; the goods are routinely manufactured items.

_____ 15. Interest costs on assets produced as discrete projects (such as ships or real estate) for sale.

_____ 16. Cost of sales brochures on hand.

_____ 17. Investments in stocks and bonds that will likely be sold within the next year.

_____ 18. Office supplies on hand.

_____ 19.   Freight charges on goods purchased for resale.

_____ 20.   Supplies purchased for use in the delivery and sales functions of the enterprise.

Solution to Exercise 8-1

Items to be included in inventory: 1, 2, 3, 4, 5, 6, 8, 11, 15, and 19.

The following items would **not** be reported as inventory:

7.   Goods held on consignment from others are not reported in the financial statements because they are not owned by the reporting entity.

9.   Goods purchased f.o.b. destination that are in transit at December 31 are still the property of the vendor; title will not pass until they are received by the reporting entity.

10. Goods sold f.o.b. shipping point that are in transit at December 31 are no longer the property of the seller; title passed at the date they were shipped which was before year-end. Thus, the sale should be recorded and cost of the items sold should be reported as cost of goods sold in the financial statements.

12. Goods sold on an installment basis are accounted for as merchandise sold; therefore, the cost of those goods is reflected in cost of goods sold expense on the income statement.

13. Costs incurred to advertise goods held for resale are classified as advertising expense on the income statement.

14. Interest costs incurred for inventories that are routinely manufactured are expensed as incurred and are reflected as interest expense in the income statement. According to a FASB standard, these costs are **not** to be capitalized. (The word "capitalized" in this case means accounted for as a component of the cost of the asset, inventory). The FASB's standard on this subject states that companies should capitalize interest costs related to assets constructed for internal use or assets produced as discrete projects (such as ships or real estate projects) for sale or lease. (Such discrete projects should take considerable time to complete, entail substantial expenditures, and be likely to involve significant amounts of interest cost.)

16. The cost of sales brochures on hand represents a cost of advertising. If this is considered to relate to sales of future periods, it will currently be an unexpired cost and reflected as a prepaid expense in the current asset section of the balance sheet. If there is doubt about these brochures being used in the future to generate sales, the cost should be reported as advertising expense on the income statement.

17. Investments in stocks and bonds that will likely be sold within the next year are classified as short-term investments in the current asset section of the balance sheet.

18. Office supplies on hand are reported as a prepaid expense in the current asset section of the balance sheet. When these supplies are later consumed, their cost will be reported as office expense in the general and administrative classification on the income statement.

20. Supplies purchased for use in the delivery and sales functions of the enterprise should be reported as selling expense on the income statement.

Explanation: Inventory is the label given to assets that are to be sold in the normal course of business or to assets to be incorporated (directly or indirectly) into goods that are manufactured and then sold. The cost of inventory includes all costs necessary to acquire (or manufacture) goods and to bring them to the location and condition for sale to customers.

1. Raw materials on hand are reported as Raw Materials Inventory. They will be reclassified as Work in Process Inventory when the materials are put into the manufacturing process and will become part of the cost of Finished Goods Inventory when the related goods have completed the manufacturing process. The cost of the finished goods will be charged to cost of goods sold expense in a later period when the goods are sold.

2. Raw materials on which production has begun but has not been completed are called Work-in Process Inventory on the balance sheet.

3. Factory labor costs are costs necessary for a manufacturer to manufacture an inventory item. For completed goods, the related factory labor costs are classified as Finished Goods Inventory on the balance sheet.

4. Factory supplies are indirect materials, i.e., materials that are necessary in the production process but are not directly incorporated in the products; they simply facilitate production. Indirect materials on hand are reported as a part of a company's inventories since they ultimately will be consumed in the production process. Examples of factory supplies include oils and fuels for factory equipment, and cleaning supplies for factory equipment.

5. Costs identified with goods completed but not yet sold by a manufacturer are reflected as Finished Goods Inventory on the balance sheet.

6. Goods out on consignment at another company's store are merchandise owned by the entity but in the possession of others. The consignor retains title and includes the goods in inventory until the merchandise is sold by the consignee.

8. Goods purchased f.o.b. shipping point that are in transit at the balance sheet date are to be included in the inventory of the buyer even though the buyer hasn't received them yet. When the terms of sale are f.o.b. shipping point, title passes to the buyer with the loading of goods at the point of shipment.

11. Goods sold f.o.b. destination that are in transit at the balance sheet date are to be included in the inventory of the seller even though the seller no longer has possession of the merchandise. When terms of the sale are f.o.b. destination, legal title does not pass until the goods are received by the buyer. Therefore, the seller does not record

a sale and the related withdrawal of inventory until the buyer receives the merchandise.

15. Interest costs related to assets produced as discrete projects for sale (such as ships or real estate) should be capitalized, that is, included as part of the cost of the asset.

19. Freight charges on goods purchased for resale or to be included in the manufacturing of items for resale are to be included as the cost of inventory. They are part of the costs necessary to acquire goods and get them to the location of their intended use.

TIP: Sometimes it is difficult to determine the exact time of legal passage of title for goods. The following summary of rules may be helpful.

<u>General Rule</u>
Inventory is buyer's when received, except:
FOB shipping point — Buyer's at time of delivery to common carrier
Consignment goods — Seller's, not buyer's
Sales with buybacks — Seller's, not buyer's
Sales with high rates of returns — Buyer's, if you can estimate returns
Sales on installments — Buyer's, if you can estimate collectibility

TIP: Costs incurred by a manufacturing company are often classified into two groups: product costs and period costs. **Product costs** such as material, labor, and manufacturing overhead attach to the product and are carried into future periods (as a balance in inventory) if the product remains unsold at the end of the current period, and, therefore, the revenue recognition is deferred to the period of sale. Product costs are thus expensed in the period the related product is sold. **Period costs** such as officers' salaries and other administrative expenses, advertising and other selling expenses, and interest expense (a financing cost) are charged to (expensed in) the period incurred.

TIP: Depreciation for the current period of the office building and any showroom facilities for a manufacturing company is charged to the current period. It is **not** a product cost. Depreciation on the office building relates to the general administration of the business (operating expense). Depreciation of showroom facilities relates to the sales function (operating expense) and thus is not a cost of manufacturing the product.

TIP: Depreciation of factory machinery is a component of manufacturing overhead; thus, it is an element of product cost. The amount of depreciation that pertains to the products produced during a period is first determined by use of the selected depreciation method. The amount of depreciation that ends up being reflected as an expense on the income statement for the same period depends on the number of products sold (not produced) during the period; it is included as part of cost of goods sold expense.

TIP: The amount of depreciation of factory related items for the period that pertains to the products that were produced during the current period but that remain unsold at the end of the period is reflected as part of Finished Goods Inventory at the end of the period. The amount of depreciation for the period that pertains to the goods that were partially processed during the current period and that remain in process at the end of the period is reflected as part of Work in Process Inventory at the end of the period.

EXERCISE 8-2

Purpose: (L.O. 3) This exercise will enable you to practice identifying the effects of inventory errors on the financial statements.

The net income per books of Wacky Wicks Company was determined without knowledge of the errors indicated.

Year	Net Income Per Books	Error in Ending Inventory	
2011	$ 150,000	Overstated	$ 9,000
2012	156,000	Overstated	21,000
2013	162,000	Understated	33,000
2014	168,000	No error	

Instructions
Compute the correct net income figure for each of the four years after taking into account the inventory errors.

Solution to Exercise 8-2

Year	Net Income Per Books	Add Over-statement Jan. 1	Deduct Under-statement Jan. 1	Deduct Over-statement Dec. 31	Add Under-statement Dec. 31	Corrected Net Income
2011	$ 150,000			$ 9,000		$ 141,000
2012	156,000	$ 9,000		21,000		144,000
2013	162,000	21,000			$ 33,000	216,000
2014	168,000		$ 33,000			135,000

Approach and Explanation: When more than one error affects a given year (such as in 2012), analyze each error separately then combine the effects of each analysis to get the net impact of the errors. The beginning inventory for 2012 (ending inventory for 2011) was overstated by $9,000. Therefore, cost of goods sold was overstated by $9,000, and net income for 2012 was understated by $9,000. The ending inventory for 2012 was overstated by $21,000. Therefore, cost of goods sold was understated, and net income for 2012 was overstated by $21,000. An understatement in net income of $9,000 and an overstatement of $21,000 in 2012 net to an overstatement of $12,000 for the net income figure reported for 2012. This overstatement of $12,000, combined with the $156,000 amount reported, yields a corrected net income figure of $144,000 for 2012.

Another way of analyzing the effects of an individual error is illustrated below for the $21,000 overstatement of inventory at the end of 2012.

		Effect on 2012		Effect on 2013	
	Beginning inventory			Overstated	$21,000
+	Cost of goods purchased				
=	Cost of goods available for sale			Overstated	21,000
-	Ending inventory	Overstated	$21,000		
=	Cost of goods sold	Understated	21,000	Overstated	21,000
	Sales				
-	Cost of goods sold	Understated	21,000	Overstated	21,000
=	Gross profit	Overstated	21,000	Understated	21,000
-	Operating expenses				
=	Net income	Overstated	21,000	Understated	21,000

Thus, the previously computed net income figure for 2012 must be reduced by $21,000 to correct for this error. Also, the net income figure for 2013 must be increased by $21,000 to correct for the same error.

> **TIP:** An understatement in ending inventory of year 1 will cause an understatement in net income for year 1 and an overstatement in net income for year 2. Thus, retained earnings and working capital at the end of year 1 are understated. However, assuming no more errors are committed at the end of year 2, retained earnings and working capital are **not** affected at the end of year 2.

EXERCISE 8-3

Purpose: (L.O. 5, 9) This exercise reviews the characteristics and the effects of using various pricing methods to determine inventory costs.

Instructions

Answer each of the following questions by inserting one of these abbreviations in the space provided:

SI	(specific identification)	FIFO	(first-in-first-out)
WA	(weighted-average)	LIFO	(last-in-first-out)

_____   1.   Which inventory cost method **best** matches current costs with current revenues on the income statement?

_____   2.   Which inventory cost method yields the most realistic amount for inventory, compared to replacement cost, on the balance sheet?

_____   3.   Which method results in the most exact ending inventory valuation when inventory items of the same type are **not** homogenous?

_____   4.   Which method is based on the assumption that inventory flow is "mixed" and therefore "mixes" all acquisition prices?

During a period of **rising prices**, which method yields the:

_____   5.   lowest net income figure?

_____   6.   lowest amount for inventory on the balance sheet?

_____   7.   lowest cost of goods sold figure?

_____   8.   lowest owners' equity figure?

_____   9.   lowest income tax bill for the current year?

During a period of **declining prices**, which method yields the:

_____   10.   lowest net income figure?

_____   11.   lowest amount for inventory on the balance sheet?

_____   12.   lowest cost of goods sold figure?

_____   13.   lowest owners' equity figure?

_____   14.   best cash flow?

Solution to Exercise 8-3

1. LIFO	4. WA	7. FIFO	10. FIFO	13. FIFO
2. FIFO	5. LIFO	8. LIFO	11. FIFO	14. FIFO
3. SI	6. LIFO	9. LIFO	12. LIFO	

Approach: Write down a description of the weighted-average, FIFO, and LIFO cost flow assumptions. Note the relative effects of these methods on the income statement and the balance sheet in a period of rising prices.

TIP: **Inventory pricing method** is a synonymous term for **inventory costing method**.

TIP: **FIFO (first-in, first-out)** means the cost of the first items put into inventory are used to price the first items out to cost of goods sold. Thus, the earliest acquisition prices are used to price cost of goods sold for the period, and the latest (most current) acquisition prices are used to price items in the ending inventory. **LIFO (last-in, first-out)** uses the most recent costs to price the units sold during the period, and it uses the oldest prices to cost the items in ending inventory. Thus, in a period of rising prices, the method that will yield the lowest net income on the income statement **and** the lowest ending inventory on the balance sheet is the LIFO method. Because LIFO yields the lowest taxable income under these conditions, it also improves cash flow due to the lower amount of cash required to be paid for income taxes in the current period.

> **TIP:** Some corporations prefer to use the LIFO method for purposes of determining taxable income on the entity's tax return because, in periods of inflation, LIFO yields a lower taxable income figure than other inventory costing methods (and therefore the best cash flow situation). LIFO is said to defer holding gains; therefore, the payment of related income taxes is deferred also. For example, assume two inventory items are purchased for $50. One is sold for $75 and the other is held for a while. In the meantime, the supplier raises his price to $60. One more item is purchased to keep the inventory quantity at two. Then the old item is sold at a new selling price of $90. There is a $10 gain experienced because an item was purchased at $50 and held while prices (both acquisition and selling) increased. Using the FIFO method, that holding gain will be recognized in the current period as a part of the gross profit figure [sales of $165 ($75 + $90) minus cost of goods sold of $100 ($50 + $50) = gross profit of $65 ($25 + $40)]. Whereas if the LIFO method is used, that holding gain is deferred to a future period when the LIFO base is liquidated. Thus, the gross profit would only amount to $55 under LIFO [sales of $165 ($75 + $90) minus cost of goods sold of $110 ($50 + $60) = gross profit of $55 ($25 + $30)]. The difference between $65 gross profit under FIFO and $55 gross profit under LIFO is the $10 deferral of holding gain under LIFO.

EXERCISE 8-4

Purpose: (L.O. 2, 5) This exercise will allow you to practice performing calculations to determine inventory cost under each of three costing (pricing) methods, using both the periodic and the perpetual systems.

The Griggs Company is a multi-product firm. Presented below is information concerning one of their products, Infusion-39:

Date	Transaction	Quantity	Cost
1/1	Beginning inventory	1,000	$12
2/4	Purchase	2,000	18
2/20	Sale	2,500	
4/2	Purchase	3,000	22
11/4	Sale	2,000	

Instructions

Compute the cost of the ending inventory, assuming Griggs uses:
(a)   Periodic system, FIFO cost method.
(b)   Perpetual system, FIFO cost method.
(c)   Periodic system, LIFO cost method.
(d)   Perpetual system, LIFO cost method.
(e)   Periodic system, average-cost method.
(f)   Perpetual system, moving-average-cost method.

Solution to Exercise 8-4

(a) **Periodic-FIFO:**

	Units
Beginning inventory	1,000
Purchases (2,000 + 3,000)	5,000
Units available for sale	6,000
Sold (2,500 + 2,000)	4,500
Goods on hand (assumed)	1,500

1,500 units x $22 = $33,000

(b) **Perpetual-FIFO:** Same as periodic: $33,000

> **TIP:** The use of FIFO with a perpetual system always yields the same results as the use of FIFO with a periodic system. The same does **not** hold true with the LIFO or average cost methods.

(c) **Periodic-LIFO:**

1,000 units x $12	=	$12,000
500 units x $18	=	9,000
1,500 units	=	$21,000

(d) **Perpetual-LIFO:**

Date	Purchased	Sold	Balance
1/1			1,000 x $12 = $12,000
2/4	2,000 x $18 = $36,000		(2,000 x $18) + (1,000 x $12) = $48,000
2/20		(2,000 x $18) + (500 x $12) = $42,000	500 x $12 = $6,000
4/2	3,000 x $22 = $66,000		(3,000 x $22) + (500 x $12) = $72,000
11/4		2,000 x $22 = $44,000	(1,000 x $22) + (500 x $12) = $28,000

(e) **Periodic-average:**

1,000 x $12	=	$ 12,000
2,000 x $18	=	36,000
3,000 x $22	=	66,000
6,000		$114,000

$114,000 ÷ 6,000 = $19 each

1,500 Units
x $19
$28,500

(f)   **Perpetual-average:**

Date	Purchased	Sold	Balance
1/1			1,000 x $12 = $12,000
2/4	2,000 x $18 = $36,000		3,000 x $16[a] = $48,000
2/20		2,500 x $16 = $40,000	500 x $16 = $ 8,000
4/2	3,000 x $22 = $66,000		3,500 x $21.14[b] = $73,990
11/4		2,000 x $21.14 = $42,280	1,500 x $21.14 = $31,710

[a]
$$
\begin{array}{lr}
1,000 \times \$12 = & \$12,000 \\
\underline{2,000} \times \$18 = & \underline{36,000} \\
3,000 & \underline{\$48,000}
\end{array}
$$

$$\$48,000 \div 3,000 = \$16.00$$

[b]
$$
\begin{array}{lr}
500 \times \$16 = & \$\ 8,000 \\
\underline{3,000} \times \$22 = & \underline{66,000} \\
3,500 & \underline{\$74,000}
\end{array}
$$

$$\$74,000 \div 3,500 = \$21.14$$

TIP:	When using the average-cost method and a perpetual system, a new average unit cost must be computed **only** after each new purchase; a sale will **not** affect the average unit cost. The average-cost method applied to a perpetual system is often called the **moving-average** method. In any case, the average cost is a weighted-average cost.
TIP:	Examine your solution to the exercise above and judge the reasonableness of your answers. What do you expect the relationship of the answers to be for the periodic system?
	(1) Because the trend of the acquisition costs was upward, the ending inventory computed under LIFO should be lower than the ending inventory figure computed under FIFO.
	(2) The cost of the ending inventory determined by using the average method should be between the amount of the ending inventory determined by using the LIFO method and the amount of the ending inventory determined by using the FIFO method.

EXERCISE 8-5

Purpose: (L.O. 4) This exercise will enable you to practice determining how to handle goods in transit and other items necessary for proper inventory valuation.

Jennifer Laudermilch Company, a supplier of artworks, provided the following information for the year ended December 31, 2014.

Inventory at December 31, 2014 (at cost, based on a physical count of goods in Laudermilch's warehouse on 12/31/14)	$ 820,000
Accounts payable at December 31, 2014	460,000
Net sales (sales less sales returns)	7,000,000

The Company has hired you to advise their bookkeeper on a list of items relating to goods in transit, consigned goods, and other issues. The list of items is as follows:

_____ 1. Laudermilch received goods costing $32,000 on January 2, 2015. The goods had been shipped f.o.b. shipping point on December 27, 2014, by Geoffrey Harrill Company.

_____ 2. Laudermilch received goods costing $41,000 on January 4, 2015. The goods had been shipped f.o.b. destination on December 28, 2014 by Nanula Company.

_____ 3. Laudermilch sold goods costing $18,000 to O'Toole Company on December 29, 2014. The goods were picked up by the common carrier on that same date and shipped f.o.b. shipping point. They were expected to arrive at the buyer's business as early as January 3, 2015. An invoice for $29,000 was recorded and mailed on December 29.

_____ 4. Laudermilch sold goods costing $30,000 to Matheson Company on December 31, 2014. The goods were picked up by the common carrier on that same date and shipped f.o.b. destination. They were expected to arrive at the buyer's store as early as January 2, 2015. These goods were billed to the customer for $45,000 on December 31 and were not included in the physical count at December 31, 2014.

_____ 5. Laudermilch is the consignor for a collection of prints. The prints are hanging in the showroom of The Dizzy Decorator. They cost Laudermilch $62,000 and are priced to sell at $95,000. They were not included in the physical count.

_____ 6. Laudermilch is the consignee for some goods from Asian Collectibles. They cost the consignor $50,000 and are priced to sell for $76,000 with Laudermilch to get a commission of 10%. They were included in the ending inventory at the selling price.

_____ 7. Included in the physical count were goods billed to a customer f.o.b. shipping point on December 31, 2014. These items had a cost of $24,000 and were billed at $38,000. The shipment was on Laudermilch's loading dock waiting to be picked up by the common carrier and was included in the physical count at December 31, 2014.

_____ 8. Goods received from a vendor on December 26, 2014 were included in the physical count. However, the related $44,000 vendor invoice was not included in accounts payable at December 31, 2014 because the accounts payable copy of the receiving report was lost. These goods are marked to sell for $65,000.

Instructions

(a)   Indicate which of the items listed above should be included as part of ending inventory cost in the December 31, 2014 balance sheet by placing an "x" in the corresponding blank before the item.

(b)   Using the format shown below, prepare a schedule of adjustments as of December 31, 2014 to the initial amounts per Laudermilch's accounting records. Show separately the effect, if any, of each of the eight transactions on the December 31, 2014 amounts. If the transactions would have no effect on the initial amount shown, state NONE.

Adjustments increase (or decrease)	Inventory	Accounts Payable	Net Sales
Initial Amounts	$ 820,000	$ 460,000	$ 7,000,000
1.			
2.			
3.			
4.			
5.			
6.			
7.			
8.			
Total Adjustments	$_____	$_____	$_____
Adjusted Amounts	$_____	$_____	$_____

Solution to Exercise 8-5

(a)   **Items to be included in inventory:** 1, 4, and 5.

(b)

Adjustments increase (or decrease)	Inventory	Accounts Payable	Net Sales
Initial Amounts	$ 820,000	$ 460,000	$ 7,000,000
1.	32,000	32,000	None
2.	None	None	None
3.	None	None	None
4.	30,000	None	(45,000)
5.	62,000	None	None
6.	(76,000)	None	None
7.	None	None	(38,000)
8.	None	44,000	None
Total Adjustments	48,000	76,000	(83,000)
Adjusted Amounts	$ 868,000	$ 536,000	$6,917,000

Explanation:

1.   When the terms of the purchase are f.o.b. shipping point, ownership of the goods passes to the buyer when the public carrier accepts the goods from the seller. Therefore, title passed to Laudermilch on December 27, 2014, but the goods were not physically present to be included in the physical count at December 31, 2014. The balance sheet at December 31, 2014, should reflect these goods as inventory and the related account payable.

2.   These goods would not have been included in the physical count at December 31, 2014, and are not to be included in the inventory at that date. Title did not pass to Laudermilch until the goods were received on January 4, 2015.

3.   With shipping terms of f.o.b. shipping point, title passed to the customer (O'Toole) when the goods were picked up by the common carrier on December 29, 2014. Therefore, the goods are properly excluded from the ending inventory, and the sale has been properly recorded in 2014.

4.   With shipping terms of f.o.b. destination, title did not pass to Matheson (the buyer) until the goods were received by the buyer, which had to be sometime in 2015. Therefore, the sale was improperly recorded in 2014. The goods were not on the premises late December 31, 2014, so were excluded from the physical count. However, their cost should be included in ending inventory to be reported on the balance sheet.

5.   Under a consignment arrangement, the holder of the goods (called the **consignee**) does not own the goods. Ownership remains with the shipper of the goods (called the **consignor**) until the goods are sold to a customer. Laudermilch, the consignor, should

include merchandise held by the consignee as part of its inventory. The goods were not in Laudermilch's warehouse when the physical count was taken; however, they should be included as part of the inventory balance at December 31, 2014.

6.   Laudermilch does not own the goods which it holds on consignment. Therefore, these goods should be excluded from its inventory; they should be included in the inventory of Asian Collectibles.

7.   The $24,000 of goods on the loading dock were properly included in the physical count because they had not been released to the common carrier by the end of the day, December 31, 2014. However, the sale was improperly recorded; therefore, an adjustment is needed to reduce sales by the billing price of $38,000.

8.   The $44,000 of goods received on December 26, 2014 were properly included in the physical count of inventory; $44,000 must be added to accounts payable since the invoice was not included in the December 31, 2014 accounts payable balance.

> **TIP:**   Errors in accounting for goods in transit can affect the analysis of financial statements. For example, the failure to include inventory goods in transit that were shipped by the vendor f.o.b. shipping point will cause the current ratio to be misstated. Inventory and Accounts Payable will be understated by the same amount causing the current ratio to be overstated (assuming total current assets exceed total current liabilities). When this understatement of ending inventory and accounts payable is intentional, it is referred to as "window dressing" of the current ratio. You may be able to think of other ways a company might cause "window dressing" of the current ratio.

EXERCISE 8-6

Purpose: (L.O. 5) This exercise will illustrate the effect on net income when the LIFO cost method rather than the FIFO cost method is used in a period of rising prices. It also requires you to examine the effect of both the beginning inventory and the ending inventory on the net income computation.

Using the FIFO cost method, Rasulo Company had a beginning inventory of $24,000, ending inventory of $30,000, and net income of $80,000. If Rasulo had used the LIFO cost method, the beginning inventory would have been $20,000 and the ending inventory would have been $23,000.

Instructions
Compute what net income would have been if the LIFO cost method had been used.

Solution to Exercise 8-6

Using LIFO:
Beginning inventory would have been less by $4,000; therefore,
Cost of goods sold would have been less by $4,000 and
Net income would have been more by $4,000, and
Ending inventory would have been less by $7,000; therefore,
Cost of goods sold would have been more by $7,000 and
Net income would have been less by $7,000, therefore:

Net income using FIFO	$ 80,000
Decrease in beginning inventory using LIFO	4,000
Decrease in ending inventory using LIFO	(7,000)
Net income using LIFO	$ 77,000

CASE 8-1

Purpose: (L.O. 6) This case will discuss the nature and use of a LIFO reserve. Many companies use LIFO for tax and external reporting purposes, but maintain a FIFO, average cost, or standard cost system for internal reporting purposes.

Instructions

(a)   State a few reasons why a company may use LIFO for external reporting and FIFO for internal reporting purposes.

(b)   Explain what a LIFO reserve is and how it works.

Solution to Case 8-1

(a)   An entity may choose to use LIFO for tax purposes and for general purpose financial statements published for external users while using the FIFO inventory costing method for internal reports for several reasons such as:

1.   Companies often base their pricing decisions on a FIFO, average, or standard cost assumption, rather than a LIFO basis.

2.   Record keeping on some basis other than LIFO is easier because the LIFO assumption usually does not approximate the physical flow of the product.

3.   Profit-sharing and other bonus arrangements often depend on a non-LIFO inventory assumption.

4.   The use of a pure LIFO system is troublesome for interim periods, for which estimates must be made of year-end quantities and prices.

TIP: Many entities prefer to use the LIFO method for tax purposes because in periods of increasing prices, LIFO results in a lower taxable income figure for the current period thereby deferring the payment of income taxes.

TIP: A company can use one inventory cost method for financial reporting purposes and a different method for income tax reporting purposes. However, in the tax law, there is what we call the **LIFO conformity rule.** This rule requires that if a company uses LIFO for tax purposes, it must also use LIFO for reporting in the general purpose financial statements (although neither tax law nor GAAP requires a company to pool its inventories in the same manner for book and tax purposes). Even though this rule exists, a company often overcomes this disadvantage by providing supplemental disclosures in the notes to the financial statements. These supplemental disclosures often include non-LIFO income numbers as well as non-LIFO inventory numbers so that readers can more readily make meaningful interpretations of the statements and better comparisons with statements of other companies that do not use LIFO.

(b)   A **LIFO reserve** is the difference between the ending inventory amount derived by the inventory method used for internal reporting purposes (FIFO, for example) and the ending inventory amount derived by the use of the LIFO method employed for external reporting purposes. This difference is often recorded in an account called Allowance to Reduce Inventory to LIFO. The change in the balance of this account from one period to the next is called the **LIFO effect**. For example, assume the Sullivan Company uses FIFO for internal reports and LIFO for external reports. At January 1, 2014, the Allowance to Reduce Inventory to LIFO account balance was $45,000. At the end of 2014, the inventory balance is $460,000 under FIFO and $400,000 under LIFO. The LIFO effect for 2014 is $15,000 and is recorded as follows:

Cost of Goods Sold	15,000	
Allowance to Reduce Inventory to LIFO....		15,000

The Allowance to Reduce Inventory to LIFO balance of $60,000 would be deducted from the $460,000 Inventory account balance on the balance sheet to ensure that the inventory is stated on a LIFO basis at year-end. Either the amount of the LIFO reserve or the replacement cost of the inventory should be disclosed in the financial statements or the accompanying notes.

EXERCISE 8-7

Purpose: (L.O. 8) This exercise illustrates the use of the dollar-value LIFO method. It shows how a decrease in the ending inventory in terms of base prices from one year to the next affects the calculations and then what happens when an increase in the ending inventory at base prices occurs.

Presented below is information related to Tina Argentine Company.

Date	Ending Inventory (End of Year Prices)	Price Index (Percentage)
December 31, 2009	$ 160,000	100
December 31, 2010	231,000	105
December 31, 2011	216,000	120
December 31, 2012	247,000	130
December 31, 2013	308,000	140
December 31, 2014	348,000	145

Instructions

Compute the ending inventory for Tina Argentine Company for 2009 through 2014 using the dollar-value LIFO method.

Solution to Exercise 8-7

	Current $		Price Index (Percentage)		Base-Year $	Change
2009	$ 160,000	÷	100	=	$ 160,000	—
2010	231,000	÷	105	=	220,000	$+60,000
2011	216,000	÷	120	=	180,000	(40,000)
2012	247,000	÷	130	=	190,000	+10,000
2013	308,000	÷	140	=	220,000	+30,000
2014	348,000	÷	145	=	240,000	+20,000

Ending Inventory—Dollar Value LIFO:

2009 $ 160,000

2010	$160,000 @ 100 =	$160,000
	60,000 @ 105 =	63,000
		$223,000

2011	$160,000 @ 100 =	$160,000
	20,000 @ 105 =	21,000
		$181,000

2012	$160,000 @ 100 =	$160,000
	20,000 @ 105 =	21,000
	10,000 @ 130 =	13,000
		$194,000

2013	$160,000 @ 100 =	$160,000
	20,000 @ 105 =	21,000
	10,000 @ 130 =	13,000
	30,000 @ 140 =	42,000
		$236,000

2014	$160,000 @ 100 =	$160,000
	20,000 @ 105 =	21,000
	10,000 @ 130 =	13,000
	30,000 @ 140 =	42,000
	20,000 @ 145 =	29,000
		$265,000

Approach and Explanation: (1) The ending inventory must first be converted from current dollars to base-year dollars. This is done by dividing the ending inventory at current prices by the current price index. (2) Next, the ending inventory at base-year prices is apportioned into layers, according to individual years in which the inventory was acquired. (3) Each layer is then priced using the index of the year in which it was acquired in order to obtain the inventory at dollar-value LIFO cost.

TIP: When using the dollar-value LIFO method, you must determine the layers of inventory in terms of base prices. Then each of those layers must be priced in terms of the price level of the period in which each particular layer was added.

TIP: When performing the computations for the dollar-value LIFO method, watch that the results are what you would expect them to be. For instance, most companies experience a trend of increasing prices. Therefore, in converting the ending inventory at current cost to base prices, you would expect the ending inventory at base prices to be an amount that is less than the ending inventory at current cost.

TIP: Whenever a layer, or a portion thereof, is eliminated (such as is the case in 2011 above), it is gone forever and cannot be restored. Notice how in 2012, when there is again an increase in inventory, the newly added layer for 2012 is priced at the index of the year in which that layer was added (2012) and **not** at the index of the portion of the 2010 layer that was eliminated in 2011. This process is consistent with the last costs into inventory being the first costs out (LIFO); thus, inventory is valued at the earliest purchase prices.

TIP: When using the dollar-value LIFO method, a current price index may be given, or you may have to solve for it. For instance, if prices increased over the current year by 8%, the current price index would be 108. Using another example, if ending inventory is given as $128,800 at current cost and $115,000 at base prices, the current price index is 112 ($128,800 ÷ $115,000 = 1.12, which is 112 percent). This approach is generally referred to as the **double-extension method** because the value of the units in inventory is extended at both base year prices and current year prices.

ANALYSIS OF MULTIPLE-CHOICE TYPE QUESTIONS

QUESTION

1.   (L.O. 4) At December 31, 2014, a physical count of merchandise inventory belonging to Rhoda Corp. showed $1,000,000 to be on hand. The $1,000,000 was calculated before any potential necessary adjustments related to the following:

- Excluded from the $1,000,000 was $80,000 of goods shipped f.o.b. shipping point by a vendor to Rhoda on December 30, 2014 and received on January 3, 2015.
- Excluded from the $1,000,000 was $72,000 of goods shipped f.o.b. destination to Rhoda on December 30, 2014 and received on January 3, 2015.
- Excluded from the $1,000,000 was $95,000 of goods shipped f.o.b. destination by Rhoda to a customer on December 28, 2014. The customer received the goods on January 4, 2015.

The correct amount to report for inventory on Rhoda's balance sheet at December 31, 2014 is:
a. $1,072,000.
b. $1,095,000.
c. $1,175,000.
d. $1,247,000.

Explanation:
(1)   The $80,000 should be added to the $1,000,000 because f.o.b. shipping point means the title transferred to Rhoda when the goods left the seller's dock on December 30, 2014.
(2)   The $72,000 is properly excluded from the ending inventory because title did not pass to Rhoda until Rhoda received the goods on January 3, 2015.
(3)   The $95,000 should be added to the $1,000,000 because the goods belong to Rhoda until they are received by the customer (in 2015).

$1,000,000
+   80,000
+   95,000
$1,175,000   Amount to report for ending inventory at December 31, 2014.

(Solution = c.)

QUESTION

2.   (L.O. 2) The following amounts relate to the current year for the Dan Harrier Company:

Beginning inventory	$ 40,000
Ending inventory	56,000
Purchases	332,000
Purchase returns	9,600
Freight-out	12,000

The amount of cost of goods sold for the period is:
a. $338,400.
b. $325,600.
c. $306,400.
d. $294,400.

Approach and Explanation: Write down the computation model for cost of goods sold. Enter the amounts given and solve for the unknown.

	$ 40,000		Beginning Inventory
+	332,000	+	Purchases
-	9,600	-	Purchase Returns and Allowances
	0	-	Purchase Discounts
	0	+	Freight-in
	362,400	=	Cost of Goods Available for Sale
-	56,000	-	Ending Inventory
	$306,400	=	Cost of Goods Sold

(Solution = c.)

TIP:	Freight-out is classified as a selling expense, not a component of cost of goods sold. Freight-out is not a cost necessary to get the inventory item to the place and condition for sale; it is a cost incurred in the selling function.

QUESTION

3. (L.O. 2) The accountant for the Orion Sales Company is preparing the income statement for 2014 and the balance sheet at December 31, 2014. Orion uses the periodic inventory system. The January 1, 2014 merchandise inventory balance will appear:
    a. only as an asset on the balance sheet.
    b. only in the cost of goods sold section of the income statement.
    c. as a deduction in the cost of goods sold section of the income statement and as a current asset on the balance sheet.
    d. as an addition in the cost of goods sold section of the income statement and as a current asset on the balance sheet.

Explanation: The January 1, 2014 inventory amount is the beginning inventory figure. Beginning inventory is a component of the cost of goods available for sale for the period which is a component of cost of goods sold. (Solution = b.)

TIP:	If the question asked about the December 31, 2014 merchandise inventory balance (ending inventory) rather than the beginning inventory balance, the correct answer would have been "c" (as a deduction in computing cost of sales and as a current asset).

QUESTION

4. (L.O. 3) Knight Publishing sells textbooks to United College Bookstores with an agreement that United may return for full credit any books not sold. When should United record the books sent to Knight as sold?
    a. When Knight ships the books to United.
    b. When Knight can reasonably estimate the amount of returns.
    c. When the return period ends.
    d. When United sells the books to students.

Explanation: When the publisher can reasonably estimate the amount of returns, it should consider the goods sold but establish a return liability for the amount of estimated returns. (Solution = b.)

QUESTION

5. (L.O. 3) If the beginning inventory for 2013 is overstated, the effects of this error on cost of goods sold for 2013, net income for 2013, and assets at December 31, 2014, respectively are:
    a. overstatement, understatement, overstatement.
    b. overstatement, understatement, no effect.
    c. understatement, overstatement, overstatement.
    d. understatement, overstatement, no effect.

Approach and Explanation: For questions dealing with inventory errors, assume a periodic system unless otherwise indicated. Write down the components of the cost of goods sold computation and analyze the resulting effects on net income.

		2013	**2014**
	Beginning inventory	Overstated	No effect
+	Cost of goods purchased		↓
=	Cost of goods available for sale	Overstated	
-	Ending inventory		
=	Cost of goods sold	Overstated	
	Net income	Understated	

The inventory at the end of 2013 and the inventory at the end of 2014 are both apparently free of error because the inventory at a balance sheet date is determined by a physical count and pricing process. Assume there are no errors in this process unless otherwise indicated. (Solution = b.)

TIP: The fact that the inventory at the beginning of 2013 was in error indicates that the inventory at the end of 2012 was in error because the ending inventory of one period is the beginning inventory of the next period.

TIP: When analyzing a question like this one, it is often helpful to create an example with numbers.

QUESTION

6. (L.O.3) If beginning inventory is understated by $7,000, and ending inventory is overstated by $3,000, net income for the period will be:
   a. overstated by $10,000.
   b. overstated by $4,000.
   c. understated by $4,000.
   d. understated by $10,000.

Approach and Explanation: Each error's effect on net income should be determined separately. The effect on net income is dependent on the effect on the computation of cost of goods sold (which is an expense affecting net income). The effects are then combined to compute the **total** effect on net income for the period. (Solution = a.)

	First Error	**Second Error**	**Total Effect**
Beg. Inventory	Understated $7,000		Understated $7,000
+ Purchases			
= Goods Available	Understated $7,000		Understated $7,000
- Ending Inventory		Overstated $3,000	Overstated $3,000
= Cost of Goods Sold	Understated $7,000	Understated $3,000	Understated $10,000
Net Income	Overstated $7,000	Overstated $3,000	Overstated $10,000

QUESTION

7. (L.O. 5, 9) Which inventory costing method most closely approximates current cost for each of the following:

	Ending Inventory	Cost of Goods Sold
a.	FIFO	FIFO
b.	FIFO	LIFO
c.	LIFO	FIFO
d.	LIFO	LIFO

Approach and Explanation: Write down which inventory method (LIFO or FIFO) reports current cost for ending inventory and which uses current cost to price cost of goods sold and then look for your answer combination. FIFO uses the first cost in as the first cost out, so the last (most current) costs are used to price the ending inventory. Therefore, FIFO is the answer for the first column. In contrast, LIFO uses the last cost in (current cost) as the first cost out (to cost of goods sold), so LIFO reflects the most current costs experienced in cost of goods sold. Therefore, LIFO is the answer for the second column. Answer "b" is the determined combination. (Solution = b.)

QUESTION

8. (L.O.4) Dr. Dong Company purchased goods with a list price of $50,000, subject to trade discounts of 20% and 10%, with a 2% cash discount allowed if payment is made within 10 days of receipt. Dr. Dong uses the gross method of recording purchases. Dr. Dong should record the cost of this merchandise as:
    a. $34,000.
    b. $35,000.
    c. $36,000.
    d. $50,000.
    e.   None of the above.

Explanation: Trade discounts are not recorded in the accounts; they are means of computing a sales (purchase) price. Using the gross method of recording purchases, the cash discount allowed does not affect the amount recorded in the Purchases account; the cash discount allowed will be recorded if it is taken and will be recorded as a credit to Purchase Discounts. (Solution = c.)

Computations:	
List price	$ 50,000
First trade discount ($50,000 x 20%)	(10,000)
Subtotal	40,000
Second trade discount ($40,000 x 10%)	(4,000)
Purchase price	$ 36,000

> **TIP:** A chain discount occurs when a list price is subject to several trade discounts. When a chain discount is offered, the amount of each trade discount is determined by multiplying (1) the list price of the merchandise **less** the amount of prior trade discounts by (2) the trade discount percentage.

QUESTION

9. (L.O. 4) Grennan Retail Company incurred the following costs in 2014:
    Freight-in on purchases
    Interest on loan to acquire inventory
    Selling costs

    Should the above items be included or excluded in determining Grennan's inventory valuation for its balance sheet?

	Freight-in	Interest	Selling Costs
a.	Include	Include	Include
b.	Include	Include	Exclude
c.	Include	Exclude	Exclude
d.	Exclude	Exclude	Exclude

Explanation: Freight-in is a product cost. The cost of inventory should include all costs necessary to get the inventory in the place and condition for its intended purpose (resale). Freight-in is necessary to get the merchandise to the location for resale. Interest costs should not be capitalized for inventories that are acquired by a merchandiser (because the goods do not require a period of time to ready them for sale) or inventories that are routinely manufactured or otherwise produced in large quantities on a repetitive basis. Therefore, the interest on this inventory is a period cost. Selling expenses are treated as a period cost. (Solution = c.)

QUESTION

10.   (L.O. 5) For 2014, Selma Co. had beginning inventory of $75,000, ending inventory of $90,000 and net income of $120,000, using the LIFO inventory method. If the FIFO method had been used, beginning inventory would have been $85,000, ending inventory would have been $105,000 and net income would have been:
   a. $125,000.
   b. $115,000.
   c. $145,000.
   d. $95,000.

Approach and Explanation: Develop the answer by analyzing the effects on the cost of goods sold computation and resulting effects on net income. (Solution = a.)

	LIFO	FIFO	Effect on Cost of Goods Sold		Effect on Net Income	
Beginning Inventory	$ 75,000	$ 85,000	Increase	$10,000	Decrease	$10,000
+ Purchases						
= Goods Available						
- Ending Inventory	90,000	105,000	Decrease	15,000	Increase	15,000
= Cost of Goods Sold						
Net Income	120,000	?	Decrease	5,000	Increase	5,000

Net income using LIFO	$ 120,000
Increase in net income	5,000
Net income using FIFO	$ 125,000

QUESTION

11.   (L.O. 2, 5) The following facts pertain to the cost of one product carried in the merchandise inventory of the Herara Store:

Inventory on hand, January 1	200 units @ $20 =	$ 4,000
Purchase, March 18	600 units @ $24 =	14,400
Purchase, July 20	800 units @ $26 =	20,800
Purchase, October 31	400 units @ $30 =	12,000

A physical count of the inventory on December 31 reveals that 500 units are on hand. If the FIFO cost method is used with a periodic inventory system, the inventory should be reported on the balance sheet at:
   a. $40,000.
   b. $36,600.
   c. $14,600.
   d. $11,200.
   e.   None of the above.

Approach and Explanation: Think about what FIFO stands for: the first cost is in the first out to cost of goods sold. Therefore, ending inventory is comprised of the latest costs experienced. (Solution = c.)

400 units @ $30 =		$ 12,000
100 units @ $26 =		2,600
Ending inventory at FIFO		$ 14,600

QUESTION

12. (L.O. 2, 5) Refer to the data in **Question 11** above. If the average costing method is used, the cost of goods sold for the year amounts to:
  a. $38,400.
  b. $37,500.
  c. $12,800.
  d. $12,500.

Approach and Explanation: Read the question carefully. Notice it asks for the cost of goods sold and not for the ending inventory as you might expect.

Total cost of all units available for sale:	
Beginning inventory	$ 4,000
Purchases ($14,400 + $20,800 + $12,000)	47,200
Cost of goods available for sale	$ 51,200

$51,200	Cost of goods available for sale
÷ 2,000[1]	Units available for sale
= $25.60	Average unit cost

$25.60 Average unit cost x 500 units =	$12,800 Ending inventory
$25.60 Average unit cost x 1,500[2] units =	$38,400 Cost of goods sold

[1]200 + 600 + 800 + 400 = 2,000 units available for sale.
[2]2,000 units available - 500 units in ending inventory = 1,500 units sold.
(Solution = a.)

QUESTION

13. (L.O. 5) Refer to the data in **Question 11** above. If the LIFO costing method is used, the cost of goods sold for the year amounts to:
  a. $40,000.
  b. $36,600.
  c. $14,600.
  d. $11,200.

Approach and Explanation: Notice the question asks for the cost of goods sold rather than the cost of the ending inventory. You may approach the solution one of two ways: You may cost the items sold or compute the cost of the ending inventory and deduct that cost from the cost of goods available for sale. Using the first of these two approaches, think of what LIFO stands for: the last cost in is the first cost out to cost of goods sold. (Solution = a.)

Units available	2,000
Units on hand at end of period	(500)
Units sold	1,500

400 units @ $30 =	12,000
800 units @ $26 =	20,800
300 units @ $24 =	7,200
1,500 units =	40,000 Cost of goods sold

TIP:	The cost of the ending inventory using LIFO would be:		
	200 units @ $20	=	$ 4,000
	300 units @ $24	=	7,200
	500 units	=	$ 11,200 Ending inventory

QUESTION

14. (L.O. 5) In a period of rising prices, which inventory flow assumption will result in the lowest amount of income tax expense?
    a. FIFO
    b. LIFO
    c. Average-cost
    d. Income tax expense will be the same under all cost flow assumptions.

Explanation: Income taxes are determined by applying a tax rate to the amount of taxable income for the period. The inventory cost flow assumption yielding the highest cost of goods sold expense will yield the lowest income before tax figure. On a tax return, the cost of goods sold figure is a deduction in arriving at taxable income. The lower the taxable income, the lower the taxes due (thus, the lower the income tax expense) and the less cash required to pay taxes. In a period of rising prices, LIFO charges the highest costs experienced to cost of goods sold expense, yielding the lowest taxable income figure. (Solution = b.)

QUESTION

15. (L.O. 5) In a period of rising prices, which of the following inventory cost flow methods will yield the largest reported amount for cost of goods sold?
    a. Specific identification.
    b. FIFO.
    c. LIFO.
    d. Average-cost.

Explanation: In a period of rising prices, the most recent purchase prices are the highest ones experienced by the entity. Using LIFO, the latest costs (the highest ones, in this instance) are used to price cost of goods sold and the earliest ones are used to price ending inventory. FIFO would give the lowest cost of goods sold in a period of rising prices. The results of the average-cost method would fall between the results of the LIFO and FIFO methods. The specific identification method would likely yield a cost of goods sold figure similar to FIFO (but not more than LIFO) because specific identification would use the cost of the specific items sold to price the cost of the goods sold, and the specific items sold usually follow a first-in, first-out physical flow. (Solution = c.)

QUESTION

16. (L.O. 8) McGraty Corp. uses dollar-value LIFO. Its inventory was $500,000 in terms of base-year prices at December 31, 2014. At December 31, 2015, McGraty's inventory was $600,000 at base-year prices and $660,000 at current cost. McGraty's inventory at December 31, 2015, using dollar-value LIFO, is:
    a. $660,000.
    b. $610,000.
    c. $600,000.
    d. $550,000.

Approach and Explanation: Set up the problem as you normally would a dollar-value LIFO problem, even though the data given is not what you might expect.

Date	Ending Inventory @ Current Costs	÷ Price Index (Percentage)	= Ending Inventory @ Base Prices	Dollar-Value LIFO Cost
12/31/14			$500,000	$500,000
12/31/15	$660,000	?	600,000	?

Normally you are told the index and are then able to divide the inventory at current cost by the index to get the inventory at base-year prices. Here, you need to solve for the index by dividing $660,000 by $600,000 which gives you 1.10; so the index, in percentage terms, is 110. The ending inventory at dollar-value LIFO therefore is: (Solution = b.)

Base-Year $	%		Dollar-Value LIFO Cost
$500,000 x	100	=	$ 500,000
$100,000 x	110	=	110,000
			$ 610,000

IFRS Insights

IFRS Insights related to inventory are presented in **Chapter 9.**

CHAPTER 9

INVENTORIES:
ADDITIONAL VALUATION ISSUES

OVERVIEW

Sometimes a business is faced with the situation where impairments in the value of its inventory are so great relative to selling prices that items cannot be sold at a normal profit. In compliance with a conservative approach, any impairments in value should be recognized in the current period and the inventory should be reported at the lower-of-cost-or-market (LCM) on the balance sheet. By following the LCM rule, the impairment is recognized in the period in which it occurs, rather than in the later period of disposal of the inventory. Accounting for declines in inventory value is discussed in this chapter.

Sometimes a business may need to estimate the cost of inventory on hand at a certain date. Two estimation techniques—the gross profit and the retail method of inventory estimation—are discussed in this chapter. Although the conventional retail method yields results which are to approximate a lower-of-average-cost-or-market valuation for the inventory, the retail method also can be used to approximate FIFO cost, lower of FIFO cost or market, weighted-average cost, LIFO cost, etc. The conventional retail method and the LIFO retail method are discussed in this chapter.

SUMMARY OF LEARNING OBJECTIVES

1. **Describe and apply the lower of cost or market rule.** If inventory declines in value below its original cost for whatever reason, a company should write down the inventory to reflect this loss. The general rule is to abandon the historical cost principle when the future utility (revenue-producing ability) of the asset drops below its original cost.

2. **Explain when companies value inventories at net realizable value.** Companies value inventory at net realizable value when (1) there is a controlled market with a quoted price applicable to all quantities, (2) no significant costs of disposal are involved, and (3) the cost figures are too difficult to obtain.

3. **Explain when companies use the relative sales value method to value inventories.** When a company purchases a group of varying units at a single lump-sum price—a so-called basket purchase—the company may allocate the total purchase price to the individual items on the basis of relative sales value.

4.   **Discuss accounting issues related to purchase commitments.** Accounting for purchase commitments is controversial. Some argue that a company should report purchase commitment contracts as assets and liabilities at the time the contract is signed. Others believe that the present recognition at the delivery date is most appropriate. The FASB neither excludes nor recommends the recording of assets and liabilities for purchase commitments, but it notes that if companies recorded such contracts at the time of commitment, the nature of the loss and the valuation account should be reported when the price falls.

5.   **Determine ending inventory by applying the gross profit method.** Companies follow these steps to determine ending inventory by applying the gross profit method: (1) Compute the gross profit percentage on selling price. (2) Compute gross profit by multiplying net sales by the gross profit percentage. (3) Compute cost of goods sold by subtracting gross profit from net sales. (4) Compute ending inventory by subtracting cost of goods sold from total goods available for sale.

6.   **Determine ending inventory by applying the retail method.** Companies follow these steps to determine ending inventory by the conventional retail method: (1) To estimate inventory at retail, deduct the sales for the period from the retail value of the goods available for sale. (2) To find the ratio of cost to retail for all goods passing through a department or firm, divide the total goods available for sale at cost by the total goods available for sale at retail. (3) To convert the inventory valued at retail to approximate a lower of cost or market figure, apply the cost-to-retail ratio.

7.   **Explain how to report and analyze inventory.** Accounting standards require financial statement disclosure of: (1) the composition of the inventory (in the balance sheet or in a separate schedule in the notes), (2) significant or unusual inventory financing arrangements, and (3) inventory costing methods employed (which may differ for different elements of inventory). Accounting standards also require the consistent application of costing methods from one period to another. Common ratios used in the management and evaluation of inventory levels are inventory turnover and average days to sell the inventory.

*8.   **Determine ending inventory by applying the LIFO retail methods.** The application of LIFO retail is made under two assumptions: stable prices and fluctuating prices. **Procedures under stable prices:** (a) Because the LIFO method is a cost method, both the markups and the markdowns must be considered in obtaining the proper cost-to-retail percentage. (b) Since the LIFO method is concerned primarily with the additional layer (or the amount that should be subtracted from the previous layer), the beginning inventory is excluded from the cost-to-retail percentage used to price a newly added layer. (c) The markups and markdowns apply only to the goods purchased during the current period and not to the beginning inventory. **Procedures under fluctuating prices:** The steps are the same as for stable prices except that in computing the LIFO inventory under a dollar-value LIFO approach, the dollar increase in inventory is found and deflated to beginning-of-the-year prices to determine whether actual increases or decreases in quantity have occurred. If quantities increase, this increase is priced at the new index to compute the new layer. If quantities decrease, the decrease is subtracted from the most recent layers to the extent necessary.

    *This material is discussed in **Appendix 9A** of the text.

TIPS ON CHAPTER TOPICS

TIP: As used in the phrase "lower of cost or market," the term **market** refers to the market in which the entity buys (not the market in which it sells). Thus, market means current replacement cost (by purchase or by reproduction) except that: (1) market should not exceed the net realizable value (ceiling) and (2) market should not be less than the net realizable value reduced by an allowance for an approximately normal profit margin (floor).

TIP: The **net realizable value of inventory** is the net amount of cash expected to ultimately be received from the sale of the inventory. Thus, the net realizable value of inventory is the estimated selling price in the ordinary course of business less reasonably predictable costs of completion and disposal.

TIP: When there have been price declines in inventory items, a company abandons the historical cost principle. A departure from cost is justified because a company should charge a loss of utility against revenues in the period in which the loss occurs, not in the period of sale. Use of the lower-of-cost-or-market method for price declines is a **conservative approach** to inventory valuation. That is, when doubt exists about the value of an asset, a company should choose the lower amount.

TIP: If the utility of an inventory item declines prior to the period of sale (disposal), that loss of utility should be recognized in the period of decline rather than the period of disposal. Thus, if an inventory item has become obsolete, the amount of write down determined by the LCM rule should be recognized as a loss in the period of the decline in utility.

TIP: The **conventional retail method** is used to approximate a lower-of-average-cost-or-market figure for inventory valuation. There are other versions of the retail method. In each application, an amount of inventory expressed in terms of retail prices is converted to a cost or to a lower-of-cost-or-market amount by multiplying the retail figure by a ratio. The components of the ratio vary depending on which version of the retail method is desired.

EXERCISE 9-1

Purpose: (L.O. 1) This exercise reviews the steps involved in the determination of the lower-of-cost-or-market (LCM) valuation for inventory.

The Richard G. Long Company handles ten different inventory items. The normal profit on each item is 25% of the selling price.

Instructions
From the information below, complete the blanks to calculate the value to be used for the inventory figure for financial statements if the LCM rule is applied to individual items.

| Item | No. of Units on Hand | Cost | Per Unit | | | | | | | | |
			Replace-ment Cost	Expected Selling Price	Expected Cost to Sell	Ceil-ing	Floor	Market	LCM	Item Total
1	100	$7.00	$ 7.50	$ 10.00	$ 1.00					
2	10	7.00	6.25	10.00	1.00					
3	50	7.00	9.25	10.00	1.00					
4	10	9.50	9.25	10.00	1.00					
5	20	5.00	6.25	10.00	1.00					
6	100	8.00	7.25	10.00	1.00					
7	30	12.00	11.50	16.00	1.00					
8	10	16.00	15.50	16.00	1.00					
9	20	14.00	11.00	20.00	2.00					
10	10	17.00	16.00	20.00	2.00					
					Grand Total					

Solution to Exercise 9-1

| Item | Per Unit | | | | # of Units | Item Total |
	Ceiling	Floor	Market	LCM		
1	$ 9.00	$ 6.50	$ 7.50	$ 7.00	100	$ 700.00
2	9.00	6.50	6.50	6.50	10	65.00
3	9.00	6.50	9.00	7.00	50	350.00
4	9.00	6.50	9.00	9.00	10	90.00
5	9.00	6.50	6.50	5.00	20	100.00
6	9.00	6.50	7.25	7.25	100	725.00
7	15.00	11.00	11.50	11.50	30	345.00
8	15.00	11.00	15.00	15.00	10	150.00
9	18.00	13.00	13.00	13.00	20	260.00
10	18.00	13.00	16.00	16.00	10	160.00
				Grand	Total	$ 2,945.00

Approach and Explanation: Write down the two steps involved in determining the lower of cost or market and perform the steps in order for each of the items:

Step 1: Find market. Market is the middle value of replacement cost, ceiling, and floor. For example:

	Item 1	Item 2	Item 3	Item 4	Item 5
Estimated selling price	$10.00	$10.00	$10.00	$10.00	$10.00
- Cost to complete and dispose	1.00	1.00	1.00	1.00	1.00
= Net realizable value (ceiling)	9.00	9.00	9.00	9.00	9.00
- Normal profit margin	2.50*	2.50	2.50	2.50	2.50
= Floor	$ 6.50	$ 6.50	$ 6.50	$ 6.50	$ 6.50

*$10.00 x 25% = $2.50.

Ceiling	$ 9.00	$ 9.00	$ 9.00	$ 9.00	$ 9.00
Floor	6.50	6.50	6.50	6.50	6.50
Replacement cost	7.50	6.25	9.25	9.25	6.25
Middle of these three values	7.50	6.50	9.00	9.00	6.50

Step 2: Compare cost with market and choose the lower.

Cost	$ 7.00	$ 7.00	$ 7.00	$ 9.50	$ 5.00
Market (from Step 1)	7.50	6.50	9.00	9.00	6.50
Lower of cost or market	7.00	6.50	7.00	9.00	5.00

TIP: There are two simple steps to follow in order to apply the **lower of cost or market rule** to an inventory item. Be sure to follow them in order:

Step 1: Find market: List the replacement cost, net realizable value (ceiling), and the net realizable value less a normal profit margin (floor) and choose the **middle** value of these three amounts. Thus:

(a) market is replacement cost if the replacement cost is in the range between the "ceiling" value and the "floor" value.

(b) market is the "ceiling" value if the replacement cost is equal to or above the ceiling.

(c) market is the "floor" value if the replacement cost is equal to or below the floor.

Step 2:   Compare market (as determined in Step 1) **with cost and chose the lower** of the two. This choice is the amount at which the inventory is to be reported on the balance sheet.

EXERCISE 9-2

Purpose: (L.O. 1) This exercise will illustrate the effects of the failure to properly apply the LCM rule.

Bava uses the lower-of-cost-or-market rule to value its inventory. At December 31, 2014, the following facts pertain to Product X-17.

Original cost	$420
Replacement cost	365
Expected selling price	400
Estimated selling expenses	50
Normal profit	25% of selling price
Quantity in ending inventory	100 units

The accountant for Bava used the replacement cost value ($365) to value Product X-17 at December 31, 2014.

Instructions

Answer the following questions:

1.   Is $365 the correct unit value for Product X-17 for balance sheet reporting at December 31, 2014? Explain.
2.   If $365 is not the correct value, explain the effect of the misstatement on the following: (a) income statement for the year ending December 31, 2014, (b) balance sheet at December 31, 2014, (c) income statement for the year ending December 31, 2015, and (d) balance sheet at December 31, 2015. Assume that all of Product X-17 on hand at December 31, 2014 was sold during 2015.

Solution to Exercise 9-2

1. $365 is **not** the correct value for Product X-17 at December 31, 2014.

Explanation: The ceiling value of $350 should have been used for the market figure (replacement cost of $365 exceeds the ceiling value of $350) and the ceiling is lower than original cost ($420); hence, $350 is the correct unit value for ending inventory at December 31, 2014.

Computations:

Expected selling price	$ 400
Estimated selling expenses	(50)
Ceiling	350
Normal profit ($400 x 25%)	(100)
Floor	$ 250
Ceiling	$ 350
Floor	250
Replacement cost	365
Middle of these three values	$ 350
Cost	$ 420
Market	350
Lower of cost or market	$ 350

2.   (a)   Net income for 2014 is overstated by $1,500.
     (b)   Assets are overstated by $1,500 and owners' equity is overstated by $1,500 at December 31, 2014.
     (c)   Net income for 2015 is understated by $1,500.
     (d)   No effect on the balance sheet at December 31, 2015.

Explanation:
(a) $365 - $350 = $15.
      $15 x 100 = $1,500.
      The error will cause an overstatement of ending inventory which results in an understatement of cost of goods sold expense which causes an overstatement in net income for 2014 in the amount of $1,500.

(b)   Ending inventory is overstated by $1,500, so assets at December 31, 2014 are overstated by $1,500. Owners' equity at December 31, 2014 is also overstated by $1,500 because net income for 2014 (which is overstated by $1,500) is closed into owners' equity at the end of the accounting period.

> **TIP:** Visualize the basic accounting equation. This error will maintain balance in the basic accounting equation. If assets are overstated, then something else in the equation must be effected to keep the equation in balance. In this case, it is an overstatement of owners' equity because the error affects income (and that effect flows into owners' equity).

(c)   The inventory is all sold in 2015. Bava's accountant is using $365 as the carrying value for each of the 100 units when the correct unit value should be $350. This will cause net income for the year ending December 31, 2015 to be understated by $1,500 because cost of goods sold will be overstated by $1,500.

(d)   The inventory in question is no longer on hand at December 31, 2015, so there is no effect on assets at that date. The $1,500 understatement in income for 2015 is closed into owners' equity which has a balance that is overstated by $1,500 at the beginning of 2015; thus, the owners' equity balance at December 31, 2015 is correct.

TIP: The application of the lower-of-cost-or market rule incorporates only losses in value that occur in the normal course of business from such causes as style changes, shift in demand, or regular shop wear. A company should reduce damaged or deteriorated goods to net realizable value.

CASE 9-1

Purpose: (L.O. 1, 6) This case addresses three inventory topics: (1) inventoriable costs, (2) the LCM rule, and (3) the retail method.

Toastie Corporation, a retailer of small kitchen appliances, purchases its inventories from various suppliers.

Instructions

(a)   1.   Explain what costs will be inventoriable for Toastie.

       2.   Explain why Toastie's administrative costs would or would not be inventoriable.

(b)   1.   Toastie uses the lower of cost or market rule for its inventory. What is the theoretical justification for this rule?

       2.   The original cost of the inventory is above the replacement cost which is above the net realizable value of the inventory. Explain what amount should be used to value the inventory and why.

       3.   Explain and illustrate the journal entry that should be made to record an excess of cost over market when the LCM method is used along with a perpetual inventory system.

(c)   Toastie currently uses the average-cost method to determine the cost of its inventory. To simplify the procedures involved in counting and pricing its ending inventory, Toastie Corporation is considering the use of the conventional retail method. How should Toastie treat the beginning inventory and net markups in calculating the cost ratio to use to determine the ending inventory? Explain why.

Solution to Case 9-1

(a)   1.   Toastie's inventoriable costs should include all costs incurred to get the appliances ready for sale to the customer. It includes not only the purchase price of the goods but also the other associated costs incurred for the appliances up to the time they are ready for sale to the customer, for example, transportation-in.

     2.   Administrative costs are assumed to expire with the passage of time and not to attach to the product. Furthermore, administrative costs do not relate directly to inventories, but are incurred for the benefit of all functions of the business. Thus, administrative costs should be treated as period costs, not as product costs; that is, they are not inventoriable.

(b)   1.   The lower of cost or market rule is used for valuing inventories because the decline in the utility of the inventories below their cost should be recognized as a loss in (and matched with) the period in which the decline took place. Also, it is a conservative approach to inventory valuation.

     2.   The net realizable value should be used to value the inventory because market is less than cost. In this instance, "market" is the ceiling (net realizable value) because replacement cost > ceiling > floor and "market" is the middle value. This indicates that there has been a decline in the utility of the inventory. The inventory should be written down and a loss recorded. The inventory should never be valued at more than net realizable value. Apparently, not only will Toastie Corporation fail to realize a profit when it sells the inventory, it will not even recover its original cost.

TIP: The ceiling and floor values exist so as to reject the use of replacement cost as a market figure in the use of the lower-of-cost-or market rule where the replacement is not an appropriate figure for the valuation of an item in ending inventory. If the replacement cost of an item exceeds its net realizable value, a company should not report inventory at replacement cost; the company can receive only the estimated selling price less cost of disposal. Thus, anything more than the net realizable value figure will overstate the inventory item. The floor establishes a value below which a company should not price inventory, regardless of replacement cost. It makes no sense to value inventory below its net realizable value less a normal profit margin. This minimum amount (floor) measures what the company can receive for the inventory and still earn a normal profit. To value the inventory below the floor amount will understate the inventory.

     3.   There are two methods of recording the write down of the inventory from cost to market with a perpetual system. The **cost-of-goods-sold method** buries the loss in the cost of goods sold amount. The **loss method** is preferable because it clearly discloses the loss resulting from the market decline of inventory prices.

Cost-of-Goods-Sold Method	**Loss Method**
Cost of Goods Sold	Loss Due to Market Decline of Inventory
Inventory	Allowance to Reduce Inventory to Market

TIP: The Allowance to Reduce Inventory to Market account is reported on the balance sheet as a contra Inventory item. Thus a credit to it has the same effect as a credit to Inventory but keeps subsidiary inventory ledgers and records in correspondence with the control account (for a perpetual system) without changing prices. For homework purposes, use an allowance account to record market adjustments, unless otherwise instructed.

(c)   Toastie's beginning inventory at cost and at retail would be included in the calculation of the cost-to-retail ratio because the conventional retail method approximates a lower of **average** cost or market valuation. An average-cost method reflects all costs experienced (both from the beginning inventory and from purchases) in the ending inventory calculation. Net markups would be included in the calculation of the cost ratio. This procedure reduces the cost ratio because there is a larger denominator for the cost ratio calculation. Thus, a conservative approach for balance sheet valuation is being followed and a lower of cost or market valuation is approximated.

EXERCISE 9-3

Purpose: (L.O. 3) This exercise will demonstrate the use of the relative sales value method to value inventories.

Rhile Jones Corporation purchased a tract of unimproved land on Lake Sybelia for $1,000,000. Costs of subdividing and readying the land for residential lots amounted to $140,000. The lots are of two sizes and some are lakefront, so they vary in market prices as follows:

Type	No. of Lots	Sales Price per Lot
1	10	$ 60,000
2	15	80,000
3	6	100,000

Lots remaining unsold at December 31, 2014 were as follows:

Type	No. of Lots
1	4
2	9
3	2

Instructions
Compute the value to be reported for the inventory of lots on hand on the December 31, 2014 balance sheet.

Solution to Exercise 9-3

Type	# of Lots	Sales Price per Lot	Total Sales Price	Relative Sales Price	Total Cost	Cost Allocated to Lots	Cost per Lot
1	10	$ 60,000	$ 600,000	6/24	$1,140,000	$ 285,000	$ 28,500
2	15	80,000	1,200,000	12/24	1,140,000	570,000	38,000
3	6	100,000	600,000	6/24	1,140,000	285,000	47,500
			$2,400,000			$1,140,000	

Ending Inventory:

Type	Lots Left	Cost per Lot	Total
1	4	$ 28,500	$114,000
2	9	38,000	342,000
3	2	47,500	95,000
			$551,000

Explanation: When a group of varying units is purchased (acquired) at a single lump sum price (often called a basket purchase), the total cost is allocated to the various items based on their relative sales (market) values. (The petroleum industry widely uses the relative sales value method to value (at cost) the many products and by-products from a barrel of crude oil.)

EXERCISE 9-4

Purpose: (L.O. 5) This exercise will illustrate the use of the gross profit method of inventory estimation when: (1) gross profit is expressed as a percentage of cost, and (2) gross profit is expressed as a percentage of selling price.

Tim McInnes requires an estimate of the cost of goods lost by fire on April 2. Merchandise on hand on January 1 was $38,000. Purchases since January 1 were $72,000; freight-in, $3,400; and purchase returns and allowances, $2,400. Sales totaled $100,000 to April 2. Goods costing $7,700 were left undamaged by the fire; all other goods were destroyed.

Instructions
(a)   Compute the cost of goods destroyed, assuming that the gross profit is 25% of cost.
(b)   Compute the cost of goods destroyed, assuming that the gross profit is 25% of sales.

Solution to Exercise 9-4

(a)   (1)   Gross profit is 25% of cost.
Gross profit = 25% ÷ (100% + 25%) = 20% of sales.
Gross profit = 20% of sales.

(2)

Net sales	$100,000
Gross profit %	20%
Estimated gross profit	$20,000

(3)

Net sales	$100,000
Estimated gross profit	(20,000)
Estimated cost of goods sold	$ 80,000

(4)

Merchandise on hand, January 1		$38,000
Purchases	$72,000	
Purchase returns & allowances	(2,400)	
Net purchases	69,600	
Freight-in	3,400	73,000
Total merchandise available for sale		111,000
Estimated cost of goods sold		(80,000)
Estimated ending inventory on April 2		31,000
Undamaged goods		(7,700)
Estimated fire loss		$23,300

(b) (1) Gross profit is 25% of sales.

	(2)	Net sales	$100,000
		Gross profit %	25%
		Estimated gross profit $25,000	$ 25,000

	(3)	Net sales	$100,000
		Estimated gross profit	(25,000)
		Estimated cost of goods sold	$ 75,000

	(4)	Total merchandise available for sale [see part (a) (4) above]	$111,000
		Estimated cost of goods sold	(75,000)
		Estimated ending inventory on April 12	36,000
		Undamaged goods	(7,700)
		Estimated fire loss	$28,300

TIP: It is important to understand that inventory is accounted for in terms of the **cost** of goods acquired, and the Sales account reflects the **selling prices** of goods that have been sold during the period. Therefore, the profit element must be removed from the sales amount to arrive at the estimated cost of the goods sold amount.

Approach: Use these steps to perform the calculations:

(1) **Compute the gross profit percentage on selling price.**
In part (a), this must be computed; in part (b), it is a given piece of information.

(2) **Compute estimated gross profit** by multiplying net sales by the gross profit percentage. **Caution:** *The gross margin percentage used here must be stated* in terms of *selling price.*

(3) **Compute estimated cost of goods sold** by subtracting gross profit from net sales.

(4) **Compute estimated ending inventory** on hand at the end of the period by subtracting cost of goods sold from total goods available for sale.

(5) **Determine the estimated loss** from fire by deducting the cost of the undamaged goods from the estimated cost of inventory on hand at April 2, (Step 4).

TIP: **Gross profit** is synonymous with **gross margin.**

TIP: The gross profit percentage (expressed as a percentage of selling price) and the cost of goods sold percentage (also expressed as a percentage of selling price) are complements; that is, they sum to 100%. When the gross profit method of inventory estimation is used and the gross margin is expressed in terms of cost, the gross margin must first be expressed in terms of selling price before you can proceed with the computations. One method of conversion is to memorize and use the following formula:

$$\frac{\text{Gross margin on}}{\text{Selling price}} = \frac{\text{Percentage markup on cost}}{100\% + \text{Percentage markup on cost}}$$

> Another approach to deriving this formula is shown below. It uses the familiar formula: Sales (S) – Cost of Goods Sold (CGS) = Gross Profit (GP).
>
> Example: If GP = 25% of cost, then cost of goods sold is 100%.
>   Putting this much information into our formula above: S – 100% = 25%.
>   Therefore S = 125%
>   Expressing GP as a percentage of S we get: 25% + 125% = 20%.
>   Thus, gross profit = 20% of sales

TIP: Gross profit on selling price will always be less than gross profit expressed as a percentage of cost.

TIP: The terms **gross margin percentage**, **gross profit percentage, rate of gross profit,** and **percentage markup** are thought of to be synonymous, although companies more commonly use the term **markup** in referring to a relationship to cost and then use the term **gross profit** in referring to a relationship to sales.

TIP: The gross profit (gross margin) method only provides an **estimate** of inventory cost. This method is deficient in that it uses past percentages in determining the markup and the markup is usually not uniform for all items in inventory. The method is normally unacceptable for financial reporting purposes (except for interim reports). The method is useful in estimating inventory when the inventory has been destroyed and for verifying the reasonableness of inventory amounts determined by other methods.

ILLUSTRATION 9-1
WHAT IS INCLUDED IN A CONVENTIONAL RETAIL INVENTORY COMPUTATION? (L.O. 6)

	Cost	Retail
Beginning inventory	$ 500	$ 1,000
Purchases	18,000	34,000
Purchase returns	(1,800)	(3,000)
Purchase discounts	(440)	
Purchase allowances	(460)	
Freight-in	2,000	
Goods available for sale	17,800	32,000
Markups		2,100
Markup cancellations		(700)
Subtotals	17,800	33,400
Markdowns		(1,110)
Markdown cancellations		300
Subtotals	17,800	32,590
Sales (gross)		(28,000)
Employee discounts		(1,070)
Sales returns		520
Estimated normal shrinkage		(840)
Ending inventory at retail		$ 3,200

Cost-to-retail ratio $= \dfrac{\$17,800}{33,400} = 53.3\%$

Ending inventory at lower of average cost or market = 53.3% X $3,200 = $1,706

TIP: Notice there is an amount in both the cost column and retail column for purchase returns because when an item is returned to a vendor by an enterprise, the item is physically removed from the shelves (inventory); thus, both the item's cost and retail price are no longer relevant to the computation. However, for purchase discounts and purchase allowances, an amount appears only in the cost column because the vendor reduces the cost of an inventory item, but the inventory item remains in inventory to be sold.

Payment of freight on purchases increases the cost of acquiring an inventory item but no new retail price is added to inventory; the original retail price of the inventory item was chosen to recover the purchase price plus freight plus a profit. Markups, related markup cancellations, markdowns, and related markdown cancellations all pertain to retail prices, not to cost. A merchandiser may increase or decrease the selling (retail) prices while holding merchandise, but that has no impact on the price paid to the wholesale vendor (cost) for the item.

Sales reduce the amount of retail goods on hand; hence sales are deducted in the retail column. Sales returns cause a return of merchandise to the shelves; hence, they are reflected as an addition in the retail column. When sales are recorded gross, companies do **not** use the sales discounts amount in the retail inventory calculations. The gross sales amount is the true reduction in retail prices from the shelves. Normal shrinkage is deducted from the amount of goods available at retail before applying a cost-to-retail ratio to compute ending inventory at

ILLUSTRATION 9-1 (cont.)

cost; therefore, the cost of ending inventory is effectively reduced because of estimated shrinkage. Typically employees are allowed an employee discount and the sales price is recorded net of it. Thus, employee discounts are deducted from the retail column in the same way as sales because they reduce the amount recorded for sales but they eliminate retail prices available for sale.

TIP: The following concepts apply to the **retail inventory method:**

Markup or markon: The difference between cost and original retail (sales price). Such as an item is purchased for $25 and is priced to sell for $45: the markup is $20.

Additional markup: The amount by which a selling price is marked above the original retail price. For example, the retail price is raised to $48 while it is being held for sale: the additional markup is $3. (It is confusing, but many retailers refer to the "additional markup" simply as "markup". Usually by context you can tell if an amount of "markup" is truly the (original) "markup" or "additional markup." Homework assignments or examinations may use either term.

Markup cancellation: The amount by which an additional markup is reduced or cancelled. For example, the item above is marked from a retail price of $48 to $46 while it is still held for sale: the (additional) markup cancellation is $2.

Markdown: The excess of the original retail price over a new lowered retail price. For example, if the item above is now marked from $46 to $40, there has been a(n) (additional) markup cancellation of $1 and a markdown of $5.

Markdown cancellation: A reduction in a markdown. For example, the item above is now marked from $40 to $44 while still being held for sale: there is a markdown cancellation of $4.

Net additional markup: Additional markups less additional markup cancellations.

New markdowns: Markdowns less markdown cancellations.

TIP: The conventional retail method **includes** net markups (often called net additional markups) but **excludes** net markdowns from the **ratio computation**. The reason for this is that a lower-of-cost-or-market valuation is desired when the conventional retail method is used. (Net markdowns would also be included in the ratio if a straight average cost value rather than a lower-of-average-cost-or-market valuation were desired.) The omission of the net markdowns from the ratio computation results in a higher denominator and therefore a lower resulting ratio than what would be derived if the net markdowns were to be included in the ratio computation. When there have been markdowns, any related writedowns in inventory should be reflected in the current income statement (from a conservative point of view). This is accomplished by reporting the inventory at a lower value which means more of the cost of goods available for sale goes to the income statement as cost of goods sold expense.

TIP: In using the conventional retail method, the net markdowns are **omitted** from the ratio computation, but they must be **included** in determining the estimated ending inventory at retail.

TIP: The retail inventory method can be used only if sufficient information is accumulated and maintained. Purchases are recorded in the accounts at cost. Although not recorded in the accounts, the retail value of purchases and the changes in that value (markups, markup cancellations, markdowns, and markdown cancellations) must be recorded in supplemental records for use in inventory calculations utilizing the retail inventory method.

ILLUSTRATION 9-2
HOW TO COMPUTE AND APPLY THE COST/RETAIL RATIO
FOR THE RETAIL METHOD (L.O. 6, *8)

Method (Basis)	Cost/Retail Ratio	How to Compute Ending Inventory
1. Conventional (Lower of Average Cost or Market).	(Beginning inventory at cost + net cost of purchases) ÷ (beginning inventory at retail + net purchases at retail + net markups).	Ending inventory at retail x ratio.
2. Average Cost	(Beginning inventory at cost + net cost of purchases) ÷ (beginning inventory at retail + net purchases at retail + net markups – net markdowns)	Ending inventory at retail x ratio
*3. LIFO Cost (ignoring change in price level).		
a. If ending inventory at retail is higher than beginning inventory at retail (added layer).	(Net cost of purchases) ÷ (net purchases at retail + net markups - net markdowns).	(Beginning inventory at cost) + (added layer at retail x ratio).
b. If ending inventory at retail is less than beginning inventory at retail.	Beginning inventory at cost ÷ beginning inventory at retail.	Ending inventory at retail x ratio.

*This material is covered in **Appendix 8A** in the text.

*EXERCISE 9-5

Purpose: (L.O. 6, *8) This exercise illustrates two variations of the retail inventory method. It will provide an opportunity to compare and contrast these two approaches.

The records of Nancy Klintworth's Baubles report the following data for the month of May.

Sales	$ 79,000
Sales returns	1,000
Markups	10,000
Markup cancellations	1,500
Markdowns	9,300
Markdown cancellations	2,800
Freight on purchases	2,400
Purchases (at cost)	48,000
Purchases (at sales price)	88,000
Purchase returns (at cost)	2,000
Purchase returns (at sales price)	3,000
Beginning inventory (at cost)	30,000
Beginning inventory (at sales price)	46,500

Instructions
(a)   Compute the ending inventory by the conventional retail inventory method.
*(b)   Compute the ending inventory using the retail method to approximate a LIFO cost figure (assuming stable prices).

   *This material is covered in **Appendix 8A** in the text.

Solution to Exercise 9-5

	Cost		Retail
Beginning inventory	$ 30,000		$ 46,500
Purchases	48,000		88,000
Purchase returns	(2,000)		(3,000)
Freight on purchase	2,400		
Goods available for sale	78,400		131,500
Net markups:			
Markups		$ 10,000	
Markup cancellations		(1,500)	8,500
	78,400		140,000
Net markdowns:			
Markdowns		9,300	
Markdown cancellations		(2,800)	(6,500)
	$ 78,400		133,500
Net sales ($79,000 - $1,000)			(78,000)
Ending inventory, at retail			$ 55,500

(a)   Cost-to-retail ratio = $78,400 ÷ $140,000 = 56%
      Ending inventory at lower of average cost or market = 56% x $55,500 = $31,080

(b)   Cost-to-retail ratio = $48,400ª ÷ 87,000ᵇ = 55.63%

	Retail	Ratio	LIFO Cost
Beginning inventory layer	$ 46,500		$ 30,000
Layer added in May	9,000ᶜ	55.63%	5,007
Ending inventory	$ 55,500		$ 35,007

ª$78,400 - $30,000 = $48,400   Net cost of purchases.
ᵇ$133,500 - $46,500 = $87,000   Retail value of purchases plus net markups less net markdowns.
ᶜ$55,500 - $46,500 = $9,000   Excess of ending inventory at retail over beginning inventory at retail.

Approach and Explanation:
(a)   Step 1: **Compute the ending inventory at retail.** This is done by determining the retail value of goods available for sale, adjusting that figure for net markups and net markdowns, and deducting the retail value of goods no longer on hand (sales, estimated theft, etc.).

      Step 2: **Compute the cost-to-retail ratio.** The conventional retail method approximates an average cost amount so both beginning inventory and net purchases information is used in the ratio. The conventional retail method is to approximate a lower-of-cost-or-market value so the net markups are included but the net markdowns are excluded from the ratio computation.

      Step 3: **Determine the ending inventory at an approximate lower-of-average-cost-or-market value.** Apply the appropriate cost-to-retail ratio (Step 2) to the total ending inventory at retail (Step 1).

(b)   Step 1: **Compute the ending inventory at retail.** This is done the same way as Step 1 in Part (a) above.

      Step 2: **Compute the cost-to-retail ratio.** When the LIFO method is used, ending inventory is priced in layers. If the ending inventory at retail is higher than the beginning inventory at retail, a new inventory layer was added during the period [Part (b) assumes stable prices] and the beginning inventory is intact. Therefore, the ending inventory is composed of the beginning inventory layer(s) and a new layer. A cost-to-retail ratio is needed to cost the new layer. Because the layer added came from purchases of the current period, beginning inventory information is **not** included in this ratio. Because LIFO cost rather than a lower-of-cost-or-market valuation is desired, both the net markups and net markdowns are reflected in the ratio computation.

      Step 3: **Determine the ending inventory at an approximate LIFO cost (assuming stable prices).** Determine the cost of each layer in the ending inventory. Because a new layer was added in May, the beginning inventory layer is still intact at the end of the period ($46,500 at retail and

$30,000 at LIFO cost). The ratio for the added layer (55.63% as determined in Step 2) is used to convert the $9,000 increase in inventory during the period at retail prices to a LIFO cost amount.

TIP:	If the ending inventory at retail had been equal to or less than the beginning inventory at retail figure ($46,500), then a different ratio would be needed. That ratio would be one which expresses the relationship of the cost of the beginning inventory ($30,000) to the retail value of the beginning inventory ($46,500). The ending inventory at retail would have been multiplied by that ratio (64.516%) to determine the LIFO cost of the ending inventory. Assuming an ending inventory at retail of $40,000, the ending inventory at LIFO cost would be $25,806.
TIP:	If prices had not been stable, additional procedures would have been required to eliminate the effects of price-level changes in order to measure the real increases in inventory, not the dollar increase.
TIP:	Compare the steps for each variation of the retail method utilized in this exercise. Notice that **Step 1** is the **same** for each of the two scenarios and, therefore, yields the same results ($55,500 ending inventory at retail). Notice that Step 3 always applies a ratio to this $55,500 (or a portion thereof). The differences between these two scenarios then stem from the appropriate ratio (Step 2) to be applied in each case and the layers that may exist in a LIFO situation. Look at each scenario and think through the logic of the ratio calculation as explained in this solution. This process should make it easier to recall how to handle similar situations as you encounter them. **Illustration 9-2** will help to summarize and compare these variations on the use of the retail method.

*EXERCISE 9-6

Purpose: (L.O. *8) This exercise will illustrate the use of the dollar-value LIFO retail method when there is: (a) a decrease in inventory and (b) an increase in inventory.

You assemble the following information for Henrietta's Department Store, which computes its inventory under the dollar-value LIFO retail method.

	Cost	**Retail**
Inventory on January 1, 2014	$ 227,200	$ 320,000
Purchases	340,400	460,000
Increase in price level for year		8%

Instructions

(a)   Compute the cost of the inventory on December 31, 2014, assuming that the ending inventory at retail is $286,200.

(b)   Compute the cost of the inventory on December 31, 2014, assuming that the ending inventory at retail is $351,000.

Solution to Exercise 9-6

(a)   Ending inventory at current retail prices $ 286,200
      Ending inventory at base retail prices ($286,200 ÷ 1.08)   265,000

This calculation reveals that the inventory quantity has declined below the beginning level (compare $265,000 with $320,000); the ending inventory is merely a portion of the beginning inventory. Therefore, the cost-to-retail ratio reflected in the beginning inventory layer is used to price the ending inventory.

   $227,200 ÷ $320,000 = 71% Cost-to-retail ratio for beginning inventory

   $265,000 x 71% = $ 188,150

Approach and Explanation:

Step 1:   **Deflate the $286,200 ending inventory at current retail prices to base retail prices of $265,000.** The ending inventory at current retail prices is reduced to base retail prices by dividing the $286,200 by the ending price level index (108%). The price level increased 8% during the year so assigning an index of 100 (base) to the beginning of the year would mean the index at the end of the year would be 108% (8% higher than 100).

Step 2:   **Determine whether a real increase or a decrease has occurred in inventory.** This is done by comparing the ending inventory at base retail prices ($265,000) with the beginning inventory at base retail prices ($320,000).

Step 3:   **Determine the ending inventory at dollar-value LIFO.** The ending inventory is merely a portion of the beginning inventory layer. The ending inventory at base retail prices is then converted to a cost figure by using the appropriate cost-to-retail ratio which is the ratio reflected in the beginning inventory.

(b)   Ending inventory at current retail prices $ 351,000

Ending inventory at base retail prices ($351,000 ÷ 1.08)   325,000
Beginning inventory at base retail prices   320,000
Layer added—at base prices   5,000

Ending Inventory:	**Retail at Base Price**	**Dollar-Value LIFO**
Beginning inventory	$ 320,000	$ 227,200
Additional layer	5,000	3,996*
Ending inventory	$ 325,000	$ 231,196

   *The $5,000 layer at base prices must be restored to the price level of the period in which it was added: $5,000 x 1.08 = $5,400 and then the cost-to-retail ratio for items purchased during the current year must be applied to that $5,400: $5,400 x 74%** = $3,996.
   **The cost-to-retail ratio for items purchased during 2014 is computed as follows: $340,400 ÷ $460,000 = 74%.

Approach and Explanation:
Step 1:   **Deflate the $351,000 ending inventory at current retail prices to base retail prices of $325,000.** This is done by dividing the $351,000 by 108%.
Step 2:   **Determine whether a real increase or a decrease has occurred in inventory.** This is done by comparing the ending inventory at base retail prices ($325,000) with the beginning inventory at base retail prices ($320,000). A real increase of $5,000 in terms of base retail prices has occurred.
Step 3:   **Determine the ending inventory at dollar-value LIFO.** The ending inventory is composed of two layers—the beginning inventory layer and a layer added during 2014. The cost of the beginning inventory layer is carried over from last period. The added layer must first be priced in terms of current retail prices (multiply $5,000 x 1.08) because the layer was added in 2014 and then that result ($5,400) is converted to a cost figure by multiplying it by the appropriate cost-to-retail ratio (74%). The appropriate cost-to-retail ratio is the relationship of cost to retail of the purchases made in 2014.

ANALYSIS OF MULTIPLE-CHOICE TYPE QUESTIONS

QUESTION

1. (L.O. 1) Crosby Co. is just beginning its first year of operations. Crosby intends to use either the perpetual moving average method or the periodic weighted average method, and to apply the lower of cost or market rule either to individual items or to the total inventory. Prices of most inventory items are expected to increase throughout 2014, although the prices of a few items are expected to decrease. What inventory system should Crosby Co. select if it wants to minimize the inventory carrying amount at the end of the first year?

	Inventory Method	Cost or Market Application
a.	Perpetual	Individual items
b.	Perpetual	Total inventory
c.	Periodic	Individual items
d.	Periodic	Total inventory

Approach and Explanation: Think about the results of using the perpetual moving average method versus the results of using the periodic weighted average method. In a period of rising prices, the periodic weighted average method will yield the lower ending inventory figure (the ending weighted average unit cost for the perpetual system will be higher than the weighted average unit cost for the period for the periodic system). Then think about the results of applying the lower-of-cost-or-market rule to individual items versus the results of applying it to the total inventory. The individual item approach gives the most conservative valuation for balance sheet purposes. When categories or total inventory is used, situations caused by products whose replacement cost is higher than original cost are allowed to offset situations where replacement cost is lower than original cost. When an item-by-item approach is used, all possible declines in utility are recognized and not offset by inventory items whose replacement cost exceeds original cost. Combine the results of these analyses to get the final answer. (Solution = c.)

QUESTION

2. (L.O. 1) Peachy Products has an item in inventory with a cost of $85. Current replacement cost is $75. The expected selling price is $100, estimated selling costs are $18, and the normal profit is $5. Using the lower-of-cost-or-market rule, the item should be included in the inventory at:
    a. $75.
    b. $77.
    c. $82.
    d. $85.

Approach and Explanation: Write down the two steps in determining LCM and follow them:
(1)   Find market: Three possibilities:
                        Ceiling ($100 - $18) = $82
                        Floor ($82 - $5) = $77
                        Replacement cost = $75
        Choose the middle value of these three: $77 = market
(2)   Compare market with cost and choose the lower.
        Market of $77 versus cost of $85. Lower = $77   (Solution = b.)

QUESTION

3. (L.O. 1) In applying the lower-of-cost-or-market rule to inventories at December 31, 2014, Xavier Corporation wrote the inventory down from $500,000 to $420,000. Using the loss method of recording inventory at market, this writedown should be reported:
   a. as a prior period adjustment of $80,000.
   b. as an operating expense in 2014.
   c. as an extraordinary item on the 2014 income statement.
   d. as a part of cost of goods sold expense.
   e. immediately after cost of goods sold or immediately after gross profit on the 2014 income statement.

Explanation: Using the loss method of recording inventory at market when the market is lower than cost, the $80,000 loss will be shown separately from cost of goods sold (below cost of goods sold) in the income statement; it is **not** an extraordinary item. The cost-of-goods-sold method of adjusting inventory to market would include the $80,000 reduction in value as an unidentifiable part of cost of goods sold. (Solution = e.)

QUESTION

4. (L.O. 4) In 2014, Lucas Manufacturing signed a noncancelable contract with a supplier to purchase raw materials in 2015 for $700,000. Before the December 31, 2014 balance sheet date, the market price for these materials dropped to $510,000. The journal entry to record this situation at December 31, 2014 will result in a credit that should be reported:
   a. as a valuation account to Inventory on the balance sheet.
   b. as a current liability.
   c. as an appropriation of retained earnings.
   d. on the income statement.

Approach and Explanation: Draft the entry referred to in the question. Think about the classification of each account in the entry. Focus on the credit part addressed in the stem of the question. The journal entry is:

Unrealized Holding Loss on Purchase Commitments	190,000	
Estimated Liability on Purchase Commitments		190,000

The loss would be reported on the income statement under Other Expenses and Losses. The liability is reported as a current liability because the contract is to be executed within the year that immediately follows the balance sheet date. (Solution = b.)

This entry is in alignment with a conservative approach to financial reporting. The entry is made because the noncancelable contract price is greater than the market price and the buyer expects that losses will occur when the purchase is effected. The buyer should recognize losses in the period during which such declines in market prices take place related to purchase commitments. When Lucas purchases the materials in the next accounting period, Purchases (or Inventory) will be debited for $510,000, Estimated Liability on Purchase Commitments will be debited for $190,000, and Cash will be credited for $700,000.

QUESTION

5. (L.O. 5) The following information pertains to the Godfrey Company for the six months ended June 30 of the current year:

Merchandise inventory, January 1	$ 700,000
Purchases	5,000,000
Freight-in	400,000
Sales	6,000,000

Gross profit is normally 25% of sales. What is the estimated amount of inventory on hand at June 30?
   a. $100,000
   b. $1,600,000
   c. $2,100,000
   d. $4,600,000

Approach and Explanation: Use the following steps to solve a gross profit inventory method question:

(1)   **Compute the gross profit percentage on selling price:**
Gross profit is 25% of cost (given).

TIP:	This problem was simple because the gross profit percentage given in the problem is stated in terms of sales. When the gross margin percentage is expressed in terms of cost (such as in cases where a "markup" percentage is given), that percentage must first be converted to the equivalent percentage of selling price before the other computations can be performed.

(2)   **Compute estimated gross** profit by multiplying net sales by the gross profit percentage.

Sales	$6,000,000
Gross profit percentage	25%
Estimated gross profit	$1,500,000

(3)   **Compute estimated cost of goods sold** by subtracting gross profit from net sales.

Sales	$6,000,000
Estimated gross profit	(1,500,000)
Estimated cost of goods sold	$4,500,000

(4)   **Compute estimated ending inventory** by subtracting cost of goods available for sale.

Beginning inventory	$ 700,000
Purchases	5,000,000
Freight-in	400,000
Cost of goods available for sale	6,100,000
Estimated cost of goods sold	(4,500,000)
Estimated ending inventory	$1,600,000

(Solution = b.)

QUESTION
6.   (L.O. 5) The cost of goods available for sale for 2014 for Storey Corporation was $2,700,000. The gross profit rate was 20% of sales. Sales for the year amounted to $2,400,000. The ending inventory is estimated to be:
a. $0.
b. $480,000.
c. $540,000.
d. $780,000.

Explanation: <u>Step 1</u>:   Compute the gross profit percentage on selling price:
Gross profit is 20% of sales.

<u>Step 2</u>:   Compute estimated gross profit:

Sales	$2,400,000
Gross profit percentage	X 20%
Estimated gross profit	$ 480,000

<u>Step 3</u>:   Compute estimated cost of goods sold:

Sales	$2,400,000
Estimated gross profit	(480,000)
Estimated cost of goods sold	$1,920,000

<u>Step 4</u>:   Compute estimated ending inventory:

Cost of goods available for sale	$2,700,000
Estimated cost of goods sold	(1,920,000)
Estimated ending inventory (at cost)	$ 780,000

(Solution = d.)

QUESTION

7.   (L.O. 5) If gross profit is 25% of cost, then gross profit as a percentage of sales equals:
   a.   80%.
   b.   75%.
   c.   33 2/3%.
   d.   20%.

Explanation: Sales (S) - Cost of Goods Sold (CGS) = Gross Profit (GP)
   If GP = 25% of cost, then cost of goods sold = 100%.
   S - 100% = 25%.
   S = 125%.
   Expressing gross profit (GP) as a percentage of sales (S) we get:
       25% ÷ 125% = 20%.
   Thus, gross profit = 20% of sales.

(Solution = d.)

QUESTION

8.   (L.O. 6) A company uses the retail method to estimate ending inventory for interim reporting purposes. If the retail method is used to approximate a lower-of-average-cost-or-market valuation, which of the following describes the proper treatment of net markups and net markdowns in the cost-to-retail ratio calculation?

	Net Markups	Net Markdowns
a.	Include	Include
b.	Include	Exclude
c.	Exclude	Include
d.	Exclude	Exclude

Approach and Explanation: First notice that the lower-of-average-cost-or-market approach to the retail method is often referred to as the conventional retail method. Recall that using a lower-of-cost-or-market figure is an application of the principle of conservatism. Also recall that the retail method involves multiplying the ending inventory at retail by a ratio. The lower the ratio, the lower the computed inventory value. Including the net markups (increases in retail prices) but excluding the net markdowns (decreases in retail prices) gives the highest denominator possible for the ratio calculation which yields the lowest ratio possible. (Note: Net markups are often called net additional markups.) (Solution = b.)

QUESTION

9.   (L.O. 6) The following data relate to the merchandise inventory of the Hofma Company:

Beginning inventory at cost	$ 13,800
Beginning inventory at selling price	20,000
Purchases at cost	31,000
Purchases at selling price	50,000

What is the cost to retail ratio?
a.   156%.
b.   145%.
c.   69%.
d.   64%.

Explanation:

Ratio	=	Cost ÷ Retail
Ratio	=	($13,800 + $31,000) ÷ ($20,000 + $50,000)
Ratio	=	$44,800 ÷ $70,000
Ratio	=	64% (Solution = d.)

QUESTION

10.   (L.O. 6) The Ruffier Department Store uses the conventional retail inventory method. The following information is available at December 31, 2014:

	Cost	Retail
Beginning inventory	$ 37,800	$ 60,000
Purchases	200,000	290,000
Freight-in	7,200	
Sales		275,000

What is the estimated cost of the ending inventory?
a. $47,250.
b. $52,500.
c. $53,586.
d. $192,500.

Computations:	Cost	Retail
Beginning inventory	$ 37,800	$ 60,000
Purchases	200,000	290,000
Freight-in	7,200	
Cost of goods available for sale	$ 245,000	350,000
Sales		(275,000)
		$ 75,000

Step 1: Ending inventory at retail
Step 2: Cost to retail ratio = $245,000 ÷ $350,000 = 70%
Step 3: Estimated cost of ending inventory = $75,000 x 70% = $ 52,500

Approach and Explanation: Think about how the conventional retail method of inventory estimation works. An estimate of the ending inventory at retail is made by deducting sales from the retail value of goods available for sale, and the ending inventory at retail is converted to a cost value by applying an appropriate ratio which is an expression of the relationship between inventory cost and its retail value. Apply the following steps to compute the amount required:

Step 1: **Compute the ending inventory at retail.** Deduct net sales from the retail price of all of the goods available for sale during the period. Arrive at $75,000.

Step 2: **Compute the cost to retail ratio.** Divide the cost of the goods available for sale ($245,000) by the retail value of those same goods ($350,000). Arrive at 70%.

Step 3: **Determine the estimated cost of the ending inventory.** Apply the cost to retail ratio (70%) to the ending inventory at retail ($75,000). Arrive at $52,500. (Solution = b.)

QUESTION

11. (L.O. 7) Which of the following statements is **false** regarding an assumption of inventory cost flow?

    a.   The cost flow assumption need not correspond to the actual physical flow of goods.

    b.   The assumption selected may be changed each accounting period.

    c.   The FIFO assumption uses the earliest acquired prices to cost the items sold during a period.

    d.   The LIFO assumption uses the earliest acquired prices to cost the items on hand at the end of an accounting period.

Explanation: Once a method is selected from acceptable alternative methods, the entity must consistently apply that method for successive periods. The reason for this **consistency concept** is that **comparability** of financial statements is reduced or lost if methods are changed from period to period. However, an entity may change a method if it becomes evident that another method is more appropriate. (Solution = b.)

QUESTION

12. (L.O. 8) The Billy Dial Department Store uses a calendar year and the LIFO retail inventory method (assuming stable prices). The following information is available at December 31 of the current year:

	Cost	Retail
Beginning inventory	$ 37,200	$ 60,000
Purchases	200,000	290,000
Freight-in	4,000	
Net markups		30,000
Net markdowns		20,000
Sales		285,000

What is the ending inventory at LIFO cost?

    a. $46,763.

    b. $47,400.

    c. $47,603.

    d. $50,250.

Computations:	Cost	Retail
Beginning inventory	$ 37,200	$ 60,000
Purchases	200,000	290,000
Freight-in	4,000	
Goods available for sale	241,200	350,000
Net markups		30,000
Subtotals	$ 241,200	380,000
Net markdowns		(20,000)
Sales		(285,000)
Ending inventory at retail		$ 75,000

Ending inventory:	Retail	Ratio	Cost
Beginning layer	$ 60,000		$ 37,200
Added layer	15,000	68%*	10,200
Ending inventory	$ 75,000		$ 47,400

*$204,000ª ÷ $300,000ᵇ = 68%

ª$200,000 + $4,000 = $204,000
ᵇ$290,000 Purchases + $30,000 Markups - $20,000 Markdowns = $300,000

Approach and Explanation: Think about how LIFO works. If the ending inventory is greater than the beginning inventory, the ending inventory is comprised of the beginning inventory plus a new layer; if the ending inventory is less than the beginning inventory, the ending inventory is comprised of a remaining portion of the beginning inventory layer. Think about how the retail method of inventory estimation works. An estimate of the ending inventory at retail is made by deducting sales from the retail value of goods available for sale and the ending inventory at retail is converted to a cost or to a lower-of-cost-or-market value by applying an appropriate ratio which is an expression of the relationship between inventory cost and its retail value. Apply the following steps to compute the amount required:

Step 1: **Compute the ending inventory at retail.** Arrive at $75,000.
Step 2: **Compute the cost-to-retail ratio.** Comparing ending inventory at retail ($75,000) with beginning inventory at retail ($60,000) indicates a layer was added during the current year. Therefore, a ratio is needed to cost the layer which was added during the current year. The ratio for the new layer should exclude the beginning inventory. The ratio should include both net markups and net markdowns to approximate a cost (rather than a LCM valuation).
Step 3: **Determine the ending inventory at an approximate LIFO cost.** Use the beginning layer ($37,200 at LIFO cost) and apply the purchases' cost-to-retail ratio (68%) to the added layer at retail ($15,000). (Solution = b.)

QUESTION
13. (L.O. 7) The inventory turnover ratio is a measure of the liquidity of the inventory. This ratio is computed by dividing:
   a. the cost of goods sold by 365 days.
   b. the cost of goods sold by the average amount of inventory on hand.
   c. net credit sales by the average amount of inventory on hand.
   d. 365 days by the cost of goods sold.

Approach and Explanation: Write down the formula to compute the inventory turnover ratio. Think about the logic of each of the computation's components. The formula is as follows:

$$\frac{\text{Inventory}}{\text{Turnover ratio}} = \frac{\text{Cost of Goods Sold}}{\text{Average Inventory}}$$

The cost of goods sold figure is a cost figure whereas net credit sales is a figure reflecting the selling prices of items sold. The cost of an inventory item is reflected in the Inventory account until such time when the item is sold; then, the cost is transferred to the Cost of Goods Sold account. If an item is sold on credit, the selling price of the item is recorded in the Accounts Receivable account. Hence, the accounts receivable turnover ratio uses net credit sales and average accounts receivable balance; whereas, the inventory turnover ratio uses cost of goods sold and the average inventory balance for its computation. A variant of the inventory turnover ratio is the **average days to sell inventory.** (Solution = b.)

QUESTION

14.   (L.O. 7) The average days to sell inventory is computed by dividing:
       a.   365 days by the inventory turnover ratio.
       b.   the inventory turnover ratio by 365 days.
       c.   net sales by the inventory turnover ratio.
       d.   365 days by cost of goods sold.

Explanation: The **average days to sell inventory** is a variant of the inventory turnover ratio. It is computed by dividing 365 days by the inventory turnover ratio. It measures the average number of days an item remains in inventory before it is sold. (Solution = a.)

IFRS Insights

- IFRS and GAAP account for inventory acquisitions at historical cost and evaluate inventory for lower-of-cost-or-market subsequent to acquisition.

- Who owns the goods—goods in transit, consigned goods, special sales agreements—as well as the costs to include in inventory are essentially accounted for the same under IFRS and GAAP.

- The requirements for accounting for and reporting inventories are more principles-based under IFRS. That is, GAAP provides more detailed guidelines in inventory accounting.

- A major difference between IFRS and GAAP relates to the LIFO cost flow assumption. GAAP permits the use of LIFO for inventory valuation. IFRS prohibits its use. **FIFO and average-cost are the only two acceptable cost flow assumptions permitted under IFRS.** Both sets of standards permit specific identification where appropriate.

- In the lower-of-cost-or-market test for inventory valuation, IFRS defines market as net realizable value. GAAP, on the other hand, defines market as replacement cost subject to the constraints of net realizable value (the ceiling) and net realizable value less a normal markup (the floor). **IFRS does not use a ceiling or a floor to determine market.**

- Under GAAP, if inventory is written down under the lower-of-cost-or-market valuation, the new basis is now considered its cost. As a result, the inventory may **not** be written back up to its original cost in a subsequent period. Under IFRS, the write-down may be reversed in a subsequent period up to the amount of the previous write-down. Both the write-down and any subsequent reversal should be reported on the income statement.

- IFRS requires both biological assets and agricultural produce at the point of harvest to be reported to net realizable value. GAAP does not require companies to account for all biological assets in the same way. Furthermore, these assets generally are **not** reported at net realizable value. Disclosure requirements also differ between the two sets of standards.

TRUE/FALSE (Circle the correct answer for each).

T F 1. A major difference between IFRS and GAAP relates to the LIFO cost flow assumption. GAAP permits the use of LIFO for inventory valuation and IFRS prohibits its use.

T F 2. Both IFRS and GAAP define market as replacement cost subject to the constraints of net realizable value (the ceiling) and net realizable value reduced by a normal markup (the floor).

T F 3. If inventory is written down under the lower-of-cost-or-market valuation using IFRS, the writedown may be reversed in a subsequent period up to the amount of the previous writedown.

T F 4. IFRS requires both biological assets and agricultural products at the point of harvest to be reported at net realizable value.

T F 5. Under GAAP, biological assets generally are reported at net realizable value.

Solutions:

1.	T	4.	T
2.	F	5.	F
3.	T		

CHAPTER 10

ACQUISITION AND DISPOSITION OF PROPERTY, PLANT, AND EQUIPMENT

OVERVIEW

Assets that have physical existence and that are expected to be used in revenue-generating operations for more than one year or operating cycle, whichever is longer, are classified as long-term tangible assets. Some problems may arise in determining the acquisition cost of a fixed asset, such as: the initial acquisition may be the result of several expenditures, a plant asset may be obtained in exchange for the issuance of stock, one fixed asset may be exchanged for another fixed asset, a plant asset may be obtained on a deferred payment plan, or additional expenditures may be involved subsequent to acquisition. These and other issues and their related accounting procedures are examined in this chapter.

SUMMARY OF LEARNING OBJECTIVES

1. **Describe property, plant, and equipment.** The major characteristics of property, plant, and equipment are: (1) They are acquired for use in operations and not for resale. (2) They are long-term in nature and usually subject to depreciation. and (3) They possess physical substance.

2. **Identify the costs included in the initial valuation of land, buildings, and equipment.** The costs included in the initial valuation of property, plant, and equipment at acquisition are as follows:

    Cost of land: Includes all expenditures made to acquire land and to ready it for use. Land costs typically include (1) the purchase price; (2) closing costs, such as title to the land, attorney's fees, and recording fees; (3) costs incurred in getting the land in condition for its intended use, such as grading, filling, draining, and clearing; (4) assumption of any liens, mortgages or encumbrances on the property; and (5) any additional land improvements that have an indefinite life.

    Cost of buildings: Includes all expenditures related directly to their acquisition or construction. Costs related to constructed assets include (1) materials, labor, overhead costs, and avoidable interest cost incurred during construction and (2) professional fees and building permits.

    Cost of equipment: Includes (1) the purchase price, (2) freight and handling charges incurred, (3) insurance on the equipment while in transit, (4) cost of special foundations if required, (5) assembling and installation costs, and (6) costs of conducting trial runs.

3. **Describe the accounting problems associated with self-constructed assets.** The assignment of indirect costs of manufacturing creates special problems because companies cannot trace these costs directly to work and material orders related to the fixed assets constructed. Companies might handle these costs in one of two ways: (1) Assign no fixed overhead to the cost of the constructed asset, or (2) assign a portion of all overhead to the construction process. Companies use the second method extensively in practice.

4. **Describe the accounting problems associated with interest capitalization.** Only avoidable actual interest (with modifications) incurred during the acquisition period should be capitalized.

and therefore companies should defer (capitalize) interest cost. Once construction is completed, the asset is ready for its intended use and revenues can be earned. Any interest cost incurred in purchasing an asset that is ready for its intended use should be expensed.

5.   **Understand accounting issues related to acquiring and valuing plant assets.** The following issues relate to acquiring and valuing plant assets: (1) *Cash discounts:* Whether taken or not, they are generally considered a reduction in the cost of the asset. The real cost of the asset is the cash or cash equivalent price of the asset. (2) *Deferred-payment contracts:* Companies account for assets purchased on long-term credit contracts at the present value of the consideration exchanged between the contracting parties. (3) *Lump sum purchase:* Allocate the total cost among the various assets on the basis of their relative fair values. (4) *Issuance of stock:* If the stock is being actively traded, the market value of the stock issued is a fair indication of the cost of the property acquired; if the market value of the capital stock exchanged is not determinable, establish the fair value of the property and use it as the basis for recording the asset and issuance of the common stock. (5) *Exchanges of nonmonetary assets:* The accounting for exchanges of nonmonetary assets depends on whether the exchange has commercial substance. See **Illustration 10-1** for a summary of how to account for exchanges of nonmonetary assets. (6) *Contributions:* A contribution is a nonreciprocal transfer. A nonreciprocal transfer is to be recorded at the fair value of the asset involved. In general, contributions received are to be recorded by a credit to a revenue account. Contributions given are recorded by a debit to Contribution Expense.

6.   **Describe the accounting treatment for costs incurred subsequent to acquisition.** **Illustration 10-2** summarizes how to account for costs subsequent to acquisition.

7.   **Describe the accounting treatment for the disposal of property, plant, and equipment.** Regardless of the time of disposal, companies take depreciation up to the date of disposition and then remove all accounts related to the retired asset. Gains or losses on the retirement of plant assets should be shown in the income statement along with other items that arise from customary business activities. If an asset is scrapped or abandoned without any cash recovery, a loss should be recognized equal to the asset's book value. If scrap value or insurance proceeds exist, the gain or loss that occurs is the difference between the proceeds and the asset's book value. Gains or losses on involuntary conversions, if unusual and infrequent, may be reported as extraordinary items.

TIPS ON CHAPTER TOPICS

TIP: **Property, plant, and equipment** is a classification that is often referred to as **fixed assets** or **plant assets**. Included in this section should be long-lived tangible assets that are currently being used in operations to generate goods and services for customers. Two exceptions to this guideline are: (1) Construction of Plant in Process, and (2) Deposits on Machinery. In each of these cases, the asset is not yet being used in operations but an expenditure has been made which is to be classified in the Property, Plant, and Equipment section of the balance sheet. Idle fixed assets are to be classified as Investments or as Other Assets and plant assets no longer used and held for sale are to be classified either as Current Assets or Other Assets, depending on whether they are expected to be sold within the next year or not. Land held by a land developer is classified as Inventory.

TIP: In determining the **cost of a plant asset,** keep in mind the same guideline we had for inventory. The cost includes all costs necessary to get the item to the location and condition for its intended use.

TIP: In determining the cost of a plant asset, keep in mind the historical cost principle. **Cost** is measured by the cash or cash equivalent price of obtaining the asset. When cash is given to acquire an asset, it is a relatively simple matter to determine the asset's cost. However, when a noncash asset is given in exchange or when a deferred payment plan is involved, more thought is required to determine the asset's cost. Pay close attention to these areas as they are often the subjects from which discriminating exam questions are derived.

TIP: Ordinarily companies account for the exchange of nonmonetary assets on the basis of the fair value of the asset given up or the fair value of the asset received, whichever is more clearly evident. When one noncash asset is exchanged for another noncash asset, it is important to determine if the exchange has commercial substance. An exchange has **commercial substance** if the future cash flows change significantly as a result of the transaction. That is, if the company is in the same economic position as before the exchange, the exchange lacks commercial substance. If the asset exchange lacks commercial substance **and** if a gain is experienced on the disposal of the old asset, then we are to depart from the historical cost principle in determining the cost of the new asset; the entire gain or a portion of the gain (depending on whether boot is received) is to be deferred.

TIP: In the context of accounting for property, plant, and equipment, the term **"capitalize"** means to record and carry forward into one or more periods expenditures from which benefits or proceeds will be realized; thus, a balance sheet account is debited.

TIP: In accounting for the many expenditures related to the operation and maintenance of property, plant, and equipment, the accountant must determine whether to record these individual expenditures by a debit to the income statement or by a debit to the balance sheet. In making this determination, keep in mind that expenditures benefiting the company for more than the current accounting period should be capitalized in order to properly match expenses with revenues (through the process of depreciation) over successive accounting periods; expenditures for items that do not yield benefits beyond the current accounting period should be expensed.

TIP: In the context of the topic of property, plant, and equipment, the term **carrying value** refers to the amount derived by deducting the balance in the Accumulated Depreciation account from the balance in the related asset account. Synonymous terms are: **book value**, net asset value, undepreciated value, and **carrying amount**. Book value may be very different from fair value. Fair value is often referred to as fair market value or market value. The computation of book value is **not** affected by the estimated residual value or salvage value.

TIP: The net cost (cost less scrap proceeds) of tearing down an old building should be charged (debited) to the Land account if the building was someone else's old building and recently acquired along with the land as a site to be used for another structure. (The cost is charged to Land because it was necessary to get the land in the condition for its intended purpose—to provide space upon which to erect a new building.) The cost of tearing down an old building should be charged to Loss on Disposal of Building if the building has been used in the entity's operations and is now demolished to make way for another building or an alternative use of the land. Therefore, the cost of tearing down an old building is **never** charged to the Building account.

TIP: A **nonreciprocal transfer** (transfer of assets in one direction) of a nonmonetary asset is to be recorded at the fair value of the asset at the date of transfer. Property donated to an entity is an example of this type of transaction and results in a credit to Contribution Revenue. Some companies subscribe to the approach whereby a donation from a government entity is recorded by a credit to Donated Capital (Additional Paid-in Capital). The party making the donation records an expense (Contribution Expense) in the amount of the fair value of the asset given.

TIP: Sometimes a company will promise to donate (pledge) some type of asset in the future. If the promise is **unconditional** (such as when the passage of time is what triggers the gifting), the company should report the contribution expense and the related payable immediately, using the fair value of the related asset to measure the amount. If the promise is **conditional,** the company recognizes expense when it transfers the asset.

TIP: In cases where land is held as an investment (such as land held for speculation or land held for future plant site), the related property taxes, insurance, and other direct costs incurred while holding the land are often capitalized until such time the investment begins to generate revenue. Such costs are no longer capitalized once the asset begins to generate revenue.

TIP: Property, plant and equipment assets are usually carried on the books at undepreciated cost. The use of fair value to measure property, plant and equipment is usually unacceptable as it would require the recognition of gains or losses prior to disposition of the assets. However, if the fair value of the property is less than its carrying amount, the asset may be written down. These situations occur when the asset is impaired (discussed in **Chapter 11**) or where the asset is being held for sale. A long-lived asset classified as held for sale should be measured at the lower of its carrying amount or fair value less cost estimated to sell it. A long-lived asset is not depreciated if it is classified as held for sale; this is because such assets are not being used to generate revenues.

CASE 10-1

Purpose: (L.O. 2, 6) This case will review the costs to be capitalized for property, plant, and equipment.

Property, plant, and equipment generally represents a large portion of the total assets of a company. Accounting for the acquisition and usage of such assets is, therefore, an important part of the financial reporting process.

Instructions

(a)   Distinguish between an expense and a capitalized expenditure. Explain why its distinction is important.

(b)   Identify at least six costs that should be capitalized as the cost of land. Assume that land with an existing building is acquired for cash and that the existing building is to be removed immediately in order to provide space for a new building on that site.

(c)   Identify at least five costs that should be capitalized as the cost of a building.

(d)   Identify at least six costs that should be capitalized when equipment is acquired for cash.

(e)   Describe the factors that determine whether expenditures relating to property, plant, and equipment already in use should be capitalized.

(AICPA Adapted)

Solution to Case 10-1

(a)   A **capitalized expenditure** (or **capital expenditure**) is expected to yield benefits either in all future accounting periods (acquisition of land) or in a limited number of accounting periods (acquisition of buildings and equipment). Capitalized expenditures are recorded as assets, and, if related to assets of limited life, amortized over the periods which will be benefited. An **expense** is an expenditure for which the benefits are **not** expected to extend beyond the current period. Hence, it benefits only the current period (recorded as an expense) or it benefits no period at all (recorded as a loss).

The distinction between expenses and capitalized expenditures is of significance because it involves the timing of the recognition of expense and, consequently, the determination of periodic earnings. This distinction also affects the costs reflected in the asset accounts which will be recovered from future periods' revenues.

If an expense item is improperly capitalized, net income of the current period is overstated, assets are overstated, and future earnings are understated for all the periods to which the improperly capitalized cost is amortized. If the cost is not amortized, future earnings will not be affected, but assets and retained earnings will continue to be overstated for as long as the cost remains on the books. If a nonamortizable capital expenditure is improperly expensed, current earnings are understated and assets and retained earnings are understated for all foreseeable periods in the future. If an amortizable capital expenditure is improperly expensed, net income of the current period is understated, assets and retained earnings are understated, and net income is overstated for all future periods to which the cost should have been amortized.

(b)   The cost of land may include:
- (1)   purchase price.
- (2)   survey fees.
- (3)   title search fees.
- (4)   escrow fees.
- (5)   delinquent property taxes assumed by buyer.
- (6)   broker's commission.
- (7)   legal fees.
- (8)   recording fee.
- (9)   unpaid interest assumed by buyer.
- (10)   cost of clearing, grading, landscaping, and subdividing (less salvage).
- (11)   cost of removing old building (less salvage).
- (12)   special assessments such as lighting or sewers if they are permanent in nature.
- (13)   landscaping of permanent nature.
- (14)   any other cost necessary to acquire the land and get it in the condition necessary for its intended purpose.

> **TIP:**   Typically, the cost of land includes the cost of elements that occur prior to excavation for a new building. Costs related to the foundation of the building are elements of building cost.

(c)   The cost of a building may include:
- (1)   purchase price or construction costs (including an allocation of overhead if self-constructed).
- (2)   excavation fees.
- (3)   architectural fees.
- (4)   building permit fee.
- (5)   cost of insurance during construction (if paid by property owner).
- (6)   property taxes during construction.
- (7)   interest during construction (only interest actually incurred).
- (8)   cost of temporary buildings.
- (9)   any other cost necessary to acquire the building and get it in the location and condition for its intended purpose.

(d)   The cost of equipment may include:
- (1)   purchase price (less discounts allowed).
- (2)   sales tax.
- (3)   installation charges.
- (4)   freight charges during transit.
- (5)   insurance during transit.
- (6)   cost of labor and materials for test runs.
- (7)   cost of special platforms.
- (8)   ownership search.
- (9)   ownership registration.
- (10)   breaking-in costs.
- (11)   other costs necessary to acquire the equipment and get it to the location and condition for its intended use.

(e)   The factors that determine whether expenditures relating to property, plant, and equipment already in use should be capitalized are as follows:
    (1)   Expenditures are material.
    (2)   They are nonrecurring in nature.
    (3)   They benefit future periods in some way such as by doing one of the following:
        a.   They extend the useful life of a plant asset.
        b.   They enhance the quality or quantity of existing services.
        c.   They add new asset services.
        d.   They reduce future operating costs of existing assets.
        e.   They are required to meet environmental concerns and regulations.

Approach:
1.   Scan all requirements before you begin on the first question. Sometimes the latter requirements will help you to see more clearly what is really being requested in the earlier requirements. Sometimes the solution to one requirement appears to overlap with the solution to another part of the question.
2.   Prepare a key word outline before you begin writing detailed answers. This outline should very briefly list the concepts you want to cover in your paragraph(s). This outline will help you to organize your thoughts before you begin writing sentences.

EXERCISE 10-1

Purpose: (L.O. 2, 6) This exercise will help you identify which expenditures related to property, plant, and equipment should be capitalized and which should be expensed.

> **TIP:**   Remember that expenditures which benefit the company for more than the current accounting period should be capitalized in order to properly match expenses with revenues over successive accounting periods. Expenditures for items that do not yield benefits beyond the current accounting period should be expensed.

Instructions
Assume all amounts are material. For each of the following independent items, indicate by use of the appropriate letter if it should be:

        C = Capitalized   or   E = Expensed

_____   1.   Invoice price of drill press.

_____   2.   Sales tax on computer.

_____   3.   Costs of permanent partitions constructed in an existing office building.

_____   4.   Installation charges for new conveyer system.

_____   5.   Costs of trees and shrubs planted in front of office building.

_____   6.   Costs of surveying new land site.

_____   7.   Costs of major overhaul of delivery truck.

_____   8.   Costs of building new counters for show room.

_____   9.   Costs of powders, soaps, and wax for office floors.

_____   10.   Cost of janitorial services for office and show room.

_____   11.   Costs of carpets in a new office building.

_____   12.   Costs of annual termite inspection of warehouse.

_____   13.   Insurance charged for new equipment while in transit.

_____   14.   Property taxes on land used for parking lot.

_____   15.   Cost of a fan installed to help cool old factory machine.

_____   16.   Cost of exterminator's services.

_____   17.   Costs of major redecorating of executives' offices.

_____   18.   Cost of fertilizers for shrubs and trees.

_____   19.   Cost of labor services for self-constructed machine.

_____   20.   Costs of materials used and labor services expended during trial runs of new machine.

Solution to Exercise 10-1

1.	C	6.	C	11.	C	16.	E
2.	C	7.	C	12.	E	17.	C
3.	C	8.	C	13.	C	18.	E*
4.	C	9.	E*	14.	E	19.	C
5.	C	10.	E	15.	C	20.	C

*This answer assumes the products were consumed during the current period. Material amounts of unused supplies on hand at the balance sheet date should be reported as a prepaid expense.

TIP: As used in this chapter, the term **capital expenditure** refers to one which is expected to benefit more than one period; hence, it is initially recorded as an asset and should be expensed over the periods benefited. An **expenditure** for which there is **no** benefit to any period beyond the current period, should be recorded by a debit to either an expense account or to a loss account in the period incurred.

EXERCISE 10-2

Purpose: (L.O. 2) This exercise will give you practice in identifying expenditures to be capitalized.

Hughes Supply Company, a newly formed corporation, incurred the following expenditures related to Land, to Buildings, and to Machinery and Equipment.

Cash paid for land and dilapidated building thereon		$ 300,000
Removal of old building	$ 60,000	
Less salvage	16,500	43,500
Surveying before construction to determine best		
position for building		1,110
Interest on short-term loans during construction		22,200
Excavation before construction for basement		57,000
Fee for title search charged by abstract company		1,560
Architect's fees		8,400
Machinery purchased (subject to 2% cash discount,		
which was not taken)		165,000
Freight on machinery purchased		4,020
Storage charges on machinery, necessitated by noncompletion		
of building when machinery was delivered on schedule		6,540
New building constructed (building construction took 8 months		
from date of purchase of land and old building)		1,500,000
Assessment by city for sewers (a one-time assessment)		4,800
Transportation charges for delivery of machinery from storage		
to new building		1,860
Installation of machinery		6,000
Trees, shrubs, and other landscaping after completion of building		
(permanent in nature)		16,200

Instructions
(a)   Identify the amounts that should be debited to Land.
(b)   Identify the amounts that should be debited to Buildings.
(c)   Identify the amounts that should be debited to Machinery and Equipment.
(d)   Indicate how the costs above **not** debited to Land, Buildings, or Machinery and Equipment should be recorded.

Solution to Exercise 10-2

	(a) Land	(b) Bldgs.	(c) M&E	(d) Other
Cash paid for land & old bldg.	$300,000			
Removal of old building ($60,000 - $16,500)	43,500			
Surveying before construction		$ 1,110		
Interest on loans during construction		22,200		
Excavation before construction		57,000		
Abstract fees for title search	1,560			
Architect's fees		8,400		
Machinery purchased			$161,700	$ 3,300 Misc. Exp. (Int. Exp.)
Freight on machinery			4,020	
Storage charges caused by noncompletion of building				6,540 Misc. Exp. (Loss)
New building construction		1,500,000		
Assessment by city	4,800			
Transportation charges— machinery				1,860 Misc. Exp. (Loss)
Installation—machinery			6,000	
Landscaping	16,200			
Totals	$366,060	$1,588,710	$171,720	$11,700

> **TIP:** The purchase price of the machine is the **cash equivalent price** at the date of acquisition which is the $165,000 reduced by the 2% cash discount allowed ($3,300), whether or not the discount is taken. The additional outlay of $3,300 is due to extending the time for payment which is equivalent to interest (time value of money). The cost of the machine does **not** include the $6,540 storage charges and $1,860 transportation charges out of storage because these costs were not planned costs necessary to get the equipment to the location intended for use; rather they were caused by the lack of completing the building on schedule (hence, account for these costs as a loss or miscellaneous expense).

CASE 10-2

Purpose: (L.O. 5) This case will review the rules for determining a plant asset's cost when the asset is acquired on a deferred payment plan or in a nonmonetary exchange.

A company often acquires property, plant, and equipment by means other than immediate cash payment.

Instructions
(a) Explain how to determine a plant asset's cost if it is acquired on a deferred payment plan.
(b) Explain how to determine a plant asset's cost if it is acquired in exchange for a nonmonetary asset when the transaction has commercial substance.
(c) Explain how to determine a machine's cost if it is acquired in exchange for a similar machine, a small cash payment is made, and the transaction lacks commercial substance.

Solution to Case 10-2

(a)   A plant asset acquired on a deferred-payment plan should be recorded at an equivalent cash price excluding interest. If a fair rate of interest is not stated in the sales contract, an imputed interest rate should be determined. The asset should then be recorded at the contract's present value, which is computed by discounting the payments at the stated or imputed interest rate. The interest portion (stated or imputed) of the contract price should be charged to interest expense over the life of the contract.

(b)   An exchange has commercial substance when the future cash flows (timing and amounts) generated by the new asset are expected to differ significantly from the future flows expected to be generated by the old asset if it were retained. When the exchange has commercial substance, a plant asset acquired in exchange for another nonmonetary asset should be recorded at the fair value (cash equivalent value) of the consideration given or the fair value of the consideration received, whichever is more clearly determinable. This is an application of the historical cost principle. Any gain or loss on the exchange of the old asset should be recognized. (An exchange has commercial substance if the future cash flows change materially as a result of the transaction.)

(c)   In an exchange lacking commercial substance, when exchanging an old machine and paying cash for a new machine, the new machine should be recorded at the amount of monetary consideration (cash) paid plus the undepreciated cost of the nonmonetary asset (old machine) surrendered if there is no indicated loss. If a loss is indicated, it should be recognized. This would reduce the recorded amount of the new machine. An experienced loss is indicated when the old asset's market value is less than its carrying value at the date of exchange; a gain is indicated if the asset's market value exceeds its carrying value. No experienced gain, however, should be recognized by the party paying monetary consideration in an exchange lacking commercial substance.

> **TIP:** In an exchange lacking commercial substance, when cash is paid in an exchange of similar assets and the market value of the asset to be exchanged is less than its book value (an experienced loss), the historical cost principle is followed in determining the cost of the new asset. Additionally, the loss on the old asset is recognized in total. When cash is paid in an exchange of similar assets and the market value of the asset to be exchanged is greater than its book value (a gain), there is a departure from the historical cost principle in determining the cost of the new asset and the gain is **not** recognized.
>
> **TIP:** Nonmonetary assets are items whose price in terms of the monetary unit may change over time. Monetary assets (which include cash and short- or long-term accounts and notes receivable) are fixed in terms of units of currency by contract or otherwise.

EXERCISE 10-3

Purpose: (L.O. 4) This exercise will provide an example of the capitalization of interest cost incurred during construction.

Marvel Company engaged Invention Company to construct a special purpose machine to be used in its factory. The following data pertain:

1.   The contract was signed by Marvel on August 30, 2014. Construction was begun immediately and was completed on December 1, 2014.
2.   To aid in the financing of this construction, Marvel borrowed $600,000 from Bank of Okahumpa on August 30, 2014 by signing a $600,000 note due in 3 years. The note bears an interest rate of 12% and interest is payable each August 30.
3.   Marvel paid Invention $200,000 on August 30, 2014, and invested the remainder of the note's proceeds ($400,000) in 5% government securities until December 1.
4.   On December 1, Marvel made the final $400,000 payment to Invention.
5.   Aside from the note payable to the Bank of Okahumpa, Marvel's only outstanding liability at December 31, 2014 is a $60,000, 9%, 5-year note payable dated January 1, 2012, on which interest is payable each December 31.

Instructions

(a)   Calculate the weighted-average accumulated expenditures, interest revenue, avoidable interest, total interest incurred, and interest cost to be capitalized during 2014. Round all computations to the nearest dollar.

(b)   Prepare the journal entries needed on the books of Marvel Company at each of the following dates: August 30, 2014; December 1, 2014; and December 31, 2014.

Solution to Exercise 10-3

(a)   **Computation of Weighted-Average Accumulated Expenditures:**

Expenditures			Capitalization		Weighted-Average
Date	Amount	x	Period	=	Accumulated Expenditures
August 30	$200,000		3/12		$50,000
December 1	400,000		0		0
					$50,000

Interest Revenue: $400,000 x 5% x 3/12 = $5,000

Avoidable Interest:

	Weighted-Average				
	Accumulated Expenditures	x	Interest Rate	=	Avoidable Interest
	$50,000		12%		$6,000

Total Interest Incurred:

$600,000 x 12% x 4/12	=	$ 24,000	
$60,000 x 9%	=	5,400	
		$ 29,400	

Interest to be capitalized: $6,000

(b)	8/30	Cash	600,000	
		Notes Payable		600,000
		Machine...	200,000	
		Short-term Investments	400,000	
		Cash.		600,000
	12/1	Cash	405,000	
		Interest Revenue		
		($400,000 x 5% x 3/12)............................		5,000
		Short-term Investments		400,000
		Machine...	400,000	
		Cash.		400,000
	12/31	Machine [computed in part (a)]............................	6,000	
		Interest Expense ($29,400 - $6,000).....................	23,400	
		Cash ($60,000 x 9%)...................................		5,400
		Interest Payable		
		($600,000 x 12% x 4/12).............................		24,000

Explanation: Paragraphs 6 and 7 of *SFAS No. 34* state:

"The historical cost of acquiring an asset includes the costs necessarily incurred to bring it to the condition and location for its intended use. If an asset requires a period of time in which to carry out the activities necessary to bring it to that condition and location, the interest cost incurred during that period as a result of expenditures for the asset is a part of the historical cost of acquiring the asset. The objectives of capitalizing interest are (a) to obtain a measure of acquisition cost that more closely reflects the enterprise's total investment in the asset and (b) to charge a cost that relates to the acquisition of a resource that will benefit future periods against the revenues of the periods benefited."

Examples of assets that qualify for interest capitalization are: (1) assets that an enterprise constructs for its own use (such as facilities), and (2) assets intended for sale or lease that are constructed as discrete projects (such as ships or real estate projects). Interest cannot be capitalized for inventories that are routinely manufactured or otherwise produced in large quantities on a repetitive basis. Marvel's machine is a qualifying asset.

The amount to be capitalized is that portion of the interest cost incurred during the asset's acquisition period that theoretically could have been avoided (for example, by avoiding additional borrowings or by using the funds expended for the asset to repay existing borrowings) if expenditures for the asset had not been made.

Avoidable interest is determined by applying an appropriate interest rate(s) to the weighted-average amount of accumulated expenditures for the asset during the period. The appropriate rate is that rate associated with a specific new borrowing, if any. If average accumulated expenditures for the asset exceed the amount of a specific new borrowing associated with the asset, the capitalization rate to be applied to such excess shall be a weighted average of the rates applicable to other borrowings of the enterprise.

(Alternatively, the FASB does allow that the interest rate to be used may rely exclusively on an average rate of all borrowings, if desired.)

The weighted-average amount of accumulated expenditures for the asset represents the average investment tied up in the qualifying asset during the period. For Marvel, a $200,000 balance in Machine for the three-month capitalization period (date of expenditures to the date the asset is ready for use) means an equivalent (average) investment of $50,000 on an annual basis. Marvel uses only the 12% rate applicable to the specific new borrowing to compute the avoidable interest because the specific borrowing ($600,000) exceeds the weighted-average accumulated expenditures.

The amount of interest to be capitalized is not to exceed the actual interest costs incurred. Thus, Marvel compares its avoidable interest of $6,000 and its actual interest incurred of $29,400 and chooses the lower amount to capitalize. Any interest amounts earned on funds borrowed which are temporarily in excess of the company's needs are to be reported as interest revenue rather than be used to offset the amount of interest to be capitalized. Thus, Marvel will report $5,000 as interest revenue and that $5,000 will not affect the amount of interest to be capitalized.

EXERCISE 10-4

Purpose: (L.O. 5) This exercise will give you practice in accounting for the acquisition of a plant asset on a deferred payment plan.

Starstruck, Inc. purchased a computer network on December 31, 2014 for $200,000, paying $50,000 down and agreeing to pay the balance in five equal installments of $30,000 payable each December 31 beginning in 2015. An assumed interest rate of 10% is implicit in the purchase price and is the market rate of interest.

Instructions (Round to the nearest cent)
(a)   Prepare the journal entry(ies) at the date of purchase.
(b)   Prepare an amortization schedule for the installment agreement.
(c)   Prepare the journal entry(ies) at December 31, 2015, to record the cash payment and the applicable interest expense (assume the effective interest method is employed).
(d)   Prepare the journal entry(ies) at December 31, 2016, to record the cash payment and the applicable interest expense (assume the effective interest method is employed).

Solution to Exercise 10-4

(a)   Time diagram:

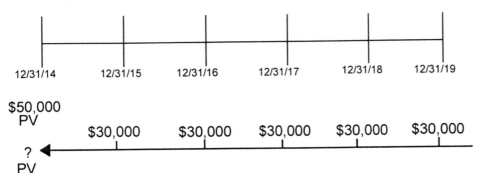

Entry:

Equipment	163,723.70*	
Discount on Notes Payable	36,276.30	
Cash.		50,000.00
Notes Payable ($30,000 x 5)		150,000.00

*PV of a $30,000 ordinary annuity @ 10% for 5 years

($30,000 x 3.79079)	$ 113,723.70
Down payment	50,000.00
Capitalized value of equipment	$ 163,723.70

(b)

Date	Cash Payment	10% Interest Expense	Reduction of Principal	Liability Balance
12/31/14				$113,723.70
12/31/15	$ 30,000.00	$ 11,372.37	$ 18,627.63	95,096.07
12/31/16	30,000.00	9,509.61	20,490.39	74,605.68
12/31/17	30,000.00	7,460.57	22,539.43	52,066.25
12/31/18	30,000.00	5,206.63	24,793.37	27,272.88
12/31/19	30,000.00	2,727.12*	27,272.88	-0-
Totals	$ 150,000.00	$ 36,276.30	$113,723.70	

*This is a plug figure, which includes a rounding error of $0.17.

(c)
December 31, 2015

Notes Payable	30,000.00	
Interest Expense (see schedule)	11,372.37	
Cash.		30,000.00
Discount on Notes Payable		11,372.37

(d)

December 31, 2016

Notes Payable	30,000.00	
Interest Expense (see schedule)..	9,509.61	
Cash.		30,000.00
Discount on Notes Payable		9,509.61

TIP: For each entry in (c) and (d), two entries could replace the one compound entry. For example, the two equivalent entries for (c) would be:

Notes Payable	30,000.00	
Cash		30,000.00
Interest Expense	11,372.37	
Discount on Notes Payable		11,372.37

TIP: When a deferred payment plan is involved in the acquisition of a noncash asset, pay careful attention to whether a fair rate of interest is stated in the agreement. When an unreasonably low stated interest rate is present, interest must be imputed so that the effective amount of interest reported reflects the market rate of interest.

EXERCISE 10-5

Purpose: (L.O. 5) This exercise reviews the computations involved in a lump-sum purchase of plant assets.

The Eliason Company paid $750,000 cash for a package of plant assets. The package consisted of the following:

	Seller's Book Value	Market Value
Land	$ 60,000	$ 300,000
Building	120,000	400,000
Equipment	220,000	250,000
Tools	100,000	50,000
Total	$ 500,000	$ 1,000,000

Instructions
(a) Prepare the journal entry for Eliason to record the acquisition of these assets on the company's books.
(b) Why must you allocate the total cost to separate accounts for the individual assets? Why can't you simply use "Plant Assets" as an account and record the total cost to that account? Explain.

Solution to Exercise 10-5

(a)	Land	225,000	
	Building	300,000	
	Equipment..	187,500	
	Tools	37,500	
	Cash...		750,000

Approach and Explanation: The total cost ($750,000) is to be allocated to the individual assets based on the relative market values of these assets. The formula that can be used to accomplish this objective is as follows:

$$\frac{\text{Market Value of One Item in Group}}{\text{Market Value of All items in Group}} \times \begin{array}{c}\text{Amount to be}\\\text{Allocated}\end{array} = \begin{array}{c}\text{Amount to be Assigned to}\\\text{Item Designated in the}\\\text{Numerator}\end{array}$$

Land:	($300,000 ÷ $1,000,000) x $750,000 =	$225,000
Building:	($400,000 ÷ $1,000,000) x $750,000 =	$300,000
Equipment:	($250,000 ÷ $1,000,000) x $750,000 =	$187,500
Tools:	($50,000 ÷ $1,000,000) x $750,000 =	$37,500

> **TIP:** Sum the four answers obtained by using the formula. They should total to the amount you set out to allocate ($750,000, in this case).

(b) The total cost must be allocated to the individual assets because land is not subject to the process of depreciation, and the depreciable assets normally are subject to different service lives and maybe even different depreciation methods.

> **TIP:** There are several areas in accounting which utilize the formula to allocate a single sum between two or more items based on the relative fair market values of the items involved. That formula is as follows:
>
> $$\frac{\begin{array}{c}\text{Market Value}\\\text{of One Item in Group}\end{array}}{\text{Market Value of All Items in Group}} \times \begin{array}{c}\text{Amount to be}\\\text{Allocated}\end{array} = \begin{array}{c}\text{Amount to be Assigned to}\\\text{Item Designated in the}\\\text{Numerator}\end{array}$$
>
> This formula is used in **Chapter 10** to allocate one lump-sum amount of cost to the individual assets acquired in a **lump sum purchase** (often called a **basket purchase**). The formula will also be used in volume two of this book in **Chapter 15** to allocate the proceeds from the issuance of several classes of securities, in **Chapter 16** to allocate the proceeds from the issuance of bonds with detachable warrants, and in **Chapter 17** to allocate the cost of an investment. The formula is also useful in the managerial accounting arena such as in the case where there are joint costs to be allocated to joint products. The same formula was used in **Chapter 9** to allocate the cost of certain inventory items to units based on their relative sales values.

ILLUSTRATION 10-1
SUMMARY OF REQUIREMENTS FOR RECOGNIZING GAINS AND LOSSES ON EXCHANGES OF NONMONETARY ASSETS (L.O. 5)

1. Compute the total gain or loss experienced on the transaction, which is equal to the difference between the fair value of the asset given up and the book value of the asset given up. An excess of fair value over book value indicates an experienced gain; an excess of book value over fair value indicates an experienced loss.

2. If a loss is computed in 1, always recognize the entire loss.

3. If a gain is computed in 1,
    (a)   and the exchange has commercial substance, the entire gain is recognized.
    (b)   and the exchange lacks commercial substance,
       (1)   and no cash is involved, no gain is recognized.
       (2)   and some cash is given, no gain is recognized.
       (3)   and some cash is received, the following portion of the gain is recognized:

$$\frac{\text{Cash Received (Boot)}}{\text{Cash Received (Boot)} + \text{Fair Value of Other Assets Received}} \times \text{Total Gain Experienced}$$

TIP: An exchange has commercial substance if the future cash flows (timing and amounts) are expected to change significantly because of the transaction.

TIP: When cash is received in a nonmonetary exchange where a gain on the old asset is evident, the amount of cash received can affect the portion of the gain to be recognized. If the amount of cash received is 25% or more of the total fair value of the exchange, the **entire** gain is to be recognized.

TIP: "Boot" is a term used to describe monetary consideration (such as cash or a receivable which is a claim for cash) given or received in an exchange of nonmonetary assets. When boot is **received** in an exchange that lacks commercial substance, a portion of the fair value of the old asset exchanged is converted to a more liquid asset and a **proportionate** amount of the gain is recognized by the party receiving the boot if a gain has been experienced.

TIP: A conservative approach to financial reporting requires **all losses to be recognized** rather than deferred to future periods. Also if a loss on the old asset was not recorded, the new asset would be recorded at an amount in excess of its fair value (cash equivalent price) which would overstate assets.

TIP: A trade-in allowance is usually not a good estimate of the fair value of a used asset because it often includes a price concession off of the list price of the new asset.

TIP: The rules stated here for recognition of gain or loss pertain to reporting on general purpose financial statements. These rules differ from the treatment called for on an income tax return.

TIP: The rules above can also be summarized by the type of exchange as follows:

Type of Exchange	Accounting Rule
Exchange has commercial substance	Recognize gains immediately
	Recognize losses immediately
Exchange lacks commercial substance—no cash (boot) received	Defer gains
	Recognize losses immediately
Exchange lacks commercial substance—cash (boot) is received	Recognize partial gain
	Recognize losses immediately

Note: If cash is 25% or more of the fair value of the exchange, recognize the entire gain because **both** parties should consider the transaction a monetary exchange and thereby rely solely on fair value for the asset measurements.

TIP: Often the party receiving boot is a dealer and therefore, the asset they are giving up is considered to be inventory. As a result, the dealer records sales revenue and related cost of goods sold. The used machine is received by the dealer and is recorded at fair value. This type of transaction almost always has commercial substance to the dealer.

EXERCISE 10-6

Purpose: (L.O. 5) This exercise will allow you to practice recording the exchange of nonmonetary assets.

Thien Le Company exchanged equipment used in its manufacturing operations plus $15,000 in cash for similar equipment used in the operations of Peggy Gunshanan Company. The following information pertains to the exchange:

	Thien Le Co.	Peggy Gunshanan Co.
Equipment (cost)	$ 84,000	$ 84,000
Accumulated depreciation	66,000	30,000
Fair value of equipment	31,500	46,500
Cash given up	15,000	

Instructions

(a)   Prepare the journal entries to record the exchange on the books of both companies assuming the exchange lacks commercial substance.

(b)   Prepare the journal entries to record the exchange on the books of both companies assuming the fair value of Thien Le Co.'s old asset is $16,500 (rather than $31,500) and the fair value of Peggy Gunshanan's old equipment is $31,500 (rather than $46,500). Assume the exchange lacks commercial substance.

(c)   Prepare the journal entries to record the exchange on the books of both companies, assuming the fair value of Thien Le Co.'s old asset is $46,500 (rather than $31,500) and the fair value of Peggy Gunshanan's old equipment is $61,500 (rather than $46,500). Assume the exchange lacks commercial substance.

Solution to Exercise 10-6

(a)   **Thien Le Company:**

Equipment (New)	33,000	
Accumulated Depreciation	66,000	
Equipment (Old)		84,000
Cash		15,000

Computation of book value:

Cost of old asset	$ 84,000
Accumulated depreciation	(66,000)
Book value of old asset	$ 18,000

Computation of gain:

Fair value of equipment given	$ 31,500
Book value of equipment given	(18,000)
Gain experienced on old asset	$ 13,500

Valuation of new equipment:

Book value of equipment given	$18,000
Boot given	15,000
Cost of new equipment	$33,000

Fair value of equipment received	$46,500	
Gain deferred	(13,500)	
Cost of new equipment	$33,000	

Peggy Gunshanan Company:

Cash	15,000	
Equipment (New)	31,500	
Accumulated Depreciation	30,000	
Loss on Disposal of Plant Asset.	7,500	
Equipment (Old)		84,000

Computation of book value:

Cost of old asset	$84,000
Accumulated depreciation	(30,000)
Book value of old asset	$54,000

Computation of loss:

Fair value of equipment given	$ 46,500
Book value of equipment given	(54,000)
Loss experienced on old asset	$ (7,500)

Valuation of new equipment:

Book value of equipment given	$54,000
Loss recognized on disposal	(7,500)
Fair value of equipment given	46,500
Boot received	(15,000)
Cost of new equipment	$31,500

Approach and Explanation: Refer to **Illustration 10-1** which summarizes the rules for recognizing gains and losses experienced on exchanges of nonmonetary assets.

Thien Le has experienced a gain of $13,500 on the old asset. It is an exchange of similar productive assets in an exchange that lacks commercial substance. Boot is given; therefore, the gain is not recognized. Rather than crediting a gain, the gain is reflected in the cost of the new asset by reducing what otherwise would have been recorded as the new asset's cost. Thus, the gain is deferred and there is a departure from the historical cost principle in determining the cost of the new asset.

Peggy Gunshanan has experienced a loss. A loss is always recognized, regardless of whether the exchange has or lacks commercial substance and regardless of whether boot is given or received. (Think about the conservatism constraint here to help you to remember this.) The historical cost principle is followed in determining the amount to record for the equipment received.

> **TIP:** The parties will bargain so that the total fair value given equals the total fair value received. Therefore, since Peggy Gunshanan is giving up equipment worth $46,500, but Thien Le's equipment is only worth $31,500, Thien Le is also giving $15,000 cash to Peggy Gunshanan.

(b)   **Thien Le Company:**

Equipment (New)	31,500	
Accumulated Depreciation	66,000	
Loss on Disposal of Plant Asset...........................	1,500	
Equipment (Old)		84,000
Cash.		15,000

Computation of loss:

Fair value of equipment given	$16,500
Book value of equipment given	(18,000)
Loss experienced on old asset	$ (1,500)

Valuation of new equipment:

Book value of equipment given	$18,000
Loss recognized on disposal	(1,500)
Boot given	15,000
Cost of new equipment	$31,500

OR

Fair value of equipment given	$16,500
Boot given	15,000
Cost of new equipment	$31,500

Peggy Gunshanan Company:

Cash	15,000	
Equipment (New)	16,500	
Accumulated Depreciation	30,000	
Loss on Disposal of Plant Asset...........................	22,500	
Equipment (Old)		84,000

Computation of loss:

Fair value of equipment given	$ 31,500
Book value of equipment given	(54,000)
Loss experienced on old asset	$ (22,500)

Valuation of new equipment:

Book value of equipment given	$ 54,000
Loss recognized on disposal	(22,500)
Fair value of equipment given	31,500
Boot received	(15,000)
Cost of new equipment	$16,500

Explanation: Both Thien Le and Peggy Gunshanan experienced losses on the disposal of their old plant assets. A loss is always to be recognized (because of conservatism). The historical cost principle is followed in determining the cost of the new plant asset.

(c)   **Thien Le Company:**

Equipment (New)	33,000	
Accumulated Depreciation	66,000	
Equipment (Old)		84,000
Cash.		15,000

Computation of gain:

Fair value of equipment given	$46,500
Book value of equipment given	(18,000)
Gain experienced on old asset	$ 28,500

Valuation of new equipment:

Book value of equipment given	$18,000
Boot given	15,000
Cost of new equipment	$33,000

OR

Fair value of equipment given	$46,500
Gain deferred	(28,500)
Boot given	15,000
Cost of new equipment	$33,000

Peggy Gunshanan Company:

Cash	15,000	
Equipment (New)	40,830	
Accumulated Depreciation	30,000	
Equipment (Old)		84,000
Gain on Disposal of Plant Asset.............................		1,830

Computation of gain experienced:

Fair value of equipment given	$61,500
Book value of equipment given	(54,000)
Gain experienced on old asset	$ 7,500

Computation of gain recognized:
   [$15,000 ÷ ($15,000 + $46,500)] x $7,500 = $1,830

TIP:	The cash received is less than 25% of the total fair value of the exchange [$15,000 ÷ ($15,000 + $46,500) = 24.39% which is less than 25%]. Thus, only a portion of the gain is recognized on Peggy Gunshanan's books.

Valuation of new equipment:

Book value of equipment given	$54,000
Fair value of boot received	(15,000)
Gain recognized	1,830
Cost of new equipment	$40,830

OR

Fair value of equipment given	$61,500
Boot received	(15,000)
Gain deferred ($7,500 - $1,830)	(5,670)
Cost of new equipment	$40,830

Explanation: Thien Le's entire gain is deferred (**not** recognized currently) because Thien Le is giving boot in an exchange of nonmonetary assets in an exchange that lacks commercial substance. The "gain" serves to reduce the recorded value of the new asset. Peggy Gunshanan's gain is partially recognized because boot is being **received** in an exchange of similar productive assets in an exchange that lacks commercial substance. The portion of the gain recognized is determined by a ratio of the boot received to the total fair value of the consideration received. The portion of the gain experienced but not recognized reduces what otherwise would have been recorded as the cost of the new equipment.

ILLUSTRATION 10-2
EXPENDITURES SUBSEQUENT TO ACQUISITION (L.O. 6)

A plant asset often requires expenditures subsequent to acquisition. Generally, four major types of expenditures may be incurred relative to existing plant assets; they are as follows:

- **Additions.** Increase or extension of existing assets.
- **Improvements and Replacements.** Substitution of an improved asset for an existing one.
- **Rearrangement and Reinstallation.** Movement of assets from one location to another.
- **Repairs.** Expenditures that maintain assets in condition for operation.

Costs that are incurred subsequent to acquisition are to be capitalized (by a debit to an asset account or to an accumulated depreciation account, depending on the circumstances) if they are material, nonrecurring in nature, and benefit future periods in some manner such as by doing one or more of the following:

a.   They extend the useful life of a plant asset.
b.   They enhance the quality or quantity of existing services.
c.   They add new asset services.
d.   They reduce future operating costs of existing assets.
e.   They are required to meet governmental regulations (such as for environmental reasons).
f.   They facilitate future production.

The accounting treatment appropriate for various costs incurred subsequent to the acquisition of capitalized assets is summarized as follows:

ILLUSTRATION 10-2 (Continued)

Type of Expenditure	Normal Accounting Treatment
Additions	Capitalize cost of addition to asset account.
Improvements and Replacements	(a) **Carrying value of old asset known:** Remove cost of and accumulated depreciation on old asset, recognizing any gain or loss. Capitalize cost of improvement/replacement. (b) **Carrying value of old asset unknown:** 1. If the asset's useful life is extended, debit accumulated depreciation for cost of improvement/replacement. 2. If the quantity or quality of the asset's productivity is increased, capitalize cost of improvement/replacement to asset account.
Rearrangement and Reinstallation	(a) If original installation cost is **known**, account for cost of rearrangement/reinstallation as a replacement (carrying value known). (b) If original installation cost is **unknown** and rearrangement/reinstallation cost is **material** in amount and benefits future periods, capitalize as an asset. (c) If original installation cost is **unknown** and rearrangement/reinstallation cost is **not material or future benefit is questionable**, expense the cost when incurred.
Repairs	(a) **Ordinary:** Expense cost of repairs when incurred. (b) **Major:** As appropriate, treat as an addition, improvement, or replacement.

> **TIP:** Does an expenditure increase future service potential of the asset? If so, capitalize the expenditure. Does an expenditure merely maintain the existing level of service? If so, expense the expenditure in the period incurred.

CASE 10-3

Purpose: (L.O. 6) This case will provide a few examples of the accounting for costs subsequent to the acquisition of fixed assets.

Hardent Resources Group has been in its plant facility for twenty years. Although the plant is quite functional, numerous repair costs are incurred to maintain it in sound working order. The company's plant asset book value is currently $750,000, as indicated below:

Original cost	$ 1,350,000
Accumulated depreciation	(600,000)
Book value	$ 750,000

During the current year, the following expenditures were made involving the plant facility:
(a)   The entire plant was repainted at a cost of $26,000.
(b)   The roof was an asbestos cement slate; for safety purposes, it was removed and replaced with a new and better quality roof at a cost of $62,000. Book value of the old roof was $31,000.
(c)   Because of increased demands for its product, the company increased its plant capacity by building a new addition at a cost of $315,000.
(d)   The plumbing system was completely updated at a cost of $53,000. The cost of the old plumbing system was not known. It is estimated that the useful life of the building will not change as a result of this updating.
(e)   A series of major repairs were made at a cost of $50,000, because parts of the wood structure were rotting. The cost of the old wood structure was not known. These extensive repairs are estimated to increase the useful life of the building.

Instructions

Indicate how each of these transactions would be recorded in the accounting records.

Solution to Case 10-3

(a)   Expenditures that do not increase the service benefits of the asset are expensed. Painting costs are considered ordinary repairs because they maintain the existing condition of the asset or restore it to normal operating efficiency.

(b)   The approach to follow is to remove the old book value of the roof and substitute the cost of the new roof. It is assumed that the expenditure increases the future service potential of the asset. Recognize a loss equal to the book value of the old roof removed.

(c)   Any addition to plant assets is capitalized because a new asset has been created. This addition increases the service potential of the plant.

(d)   Conceptually the book value of the old plumbing system should be removed. However, in practice, it is often difficult if not impossible to determine this amount. In this case, one of two approaches is followed. One approach is to capitalize the cost of the replacement on the theory that sufficient depreciation was taken on the item to reduce the carrying amount to almost zero. A second approach is to debit accumulated depreciation on the theory that the replacement extends the useful life of the asset and thereby recaptures some or all of the past depreciation. In our present situation, the problem specifically states that the useful life is not extended and therefore debiting accumulated depreciation is inappropriate. Thus, this expenditure should be added to the cost of the plant facility.

(e)   See discussion in (d) above. In this case, because the useful life of the asset has increased, a debit to accumulated depreciation would appear to be the most appropriate treatment.

EXERCISE 10-7

Purpose: (L.O. 7) This exercise will (1) illustrate several different ways in which you may dispose of property, and (2) discuss the appropriate accounting procedures for each.

Presented below is a schedule of property dispositions for Friedlander Co.

Schedule of Property Dispositions

	Cost	Accumulated Depreciation	Cash Proceeds	Fair Market Value	Nature of Disposition
Land	$ 80,000		$ 64,000	$ 64,000	Condemnation
Building	30,000	—	7,200	—	Demolition
Warehouse	130,000	—	148,000	148,000	Destruction by fire
Machine	16,000	$22,000	3,600	14,400	Trade-in
Furniture	20,000	6,400	—	5,600	Contribution
Automobile	16,000	15,700	5,920	5,920	Sale
		6,920			

The following additional information is available:

• **Land.** On January 7, a condemnation award was received as consideration for unimproved land held primarily as an investment, and on April 7, another parcel of unimproved land to be held as an investment was purchased at a cost of $70,000.

• **Building.** On May 4, land and building were purchased at a total cost of $150,000, of which 20% was allocated to the building on the corporate books. The real estate was acquired with the intention of demolishing the building, and this was accomplished during the month of August. Cash proceeds received in August represent the net proceeds from demolition of the building.

- **Warehouse.** On January 2, the warehouse was destroyed by fire. The warehouse was purchased several years ago and had been depreciated $22,000. On June 15, part of the insurance proceeds was used to purchase a replacement warehouse at a cost of $130,000.

- **Machine.** On October 31, the machine was exchanged for another similar machine having a fair market value of $10,800 and cash of $3,600 was received. The exchange lacked commercial substance.

- **Furniture.** On July 2, furniture was contributed to a qualified charitable organization. No other contributions were made or pledged during the year.

- **Automobile.** On December 31, the automobile was sold to Dee Dee Burgess, a stockholder.

Instructions

Indicate how these items would be reported on the income statement of Friedlander Co.

(AICPA adapted)

Solution to Exercise 10-7

The following accounting treatment appears appropriate for these items:

- **Land.** The loss on the condemnation of the land of $16,000 ($80,000 - $64,000) should be reported as an extraordinary item on the income statement. A condemnation comes about from a government unit exercising its right of eminent domain. *Eminent domain* is defined as "expropriation of assets by a government." Expropriation of assets was given as an example of an extraordinary item in *APB Opinion 30*. The $70,000 land purchase has no income statement effect.

- **Building.** There is no recognized gain or loss on the demolition of the building. The entire purchase cost ($30,000), decreased by the demolition proceeds ($7,200), is allocated to land.

- **Warehouse.** The gain on the destruction of the warehouse should be reported in the "other revenues and gains" section of the income statement. A fire can happen in any environment; therefore, it is not an extraordinary item. The gain is computed as follows:

Insurance proceeds		$148,000
Cost	$130,000	
Accumulated depreciation	(22,000)	(108,000)
Realized gain		$ 40,000

Some contend that a portion of this gain should be deferred because the proceeds are reinvested in similar assets. Deferral of the gain in this situation is not permitted under GAAP.

- **Machine.** The recognized gain on the exchange would be computed as follows:

Fair market value of old machine		$14,400
Cost	$16,000	
Accumulated depreciation	(6,400)	(9,600)
Total gain experienced		$ 4,800

Total gain recognized = $4,800 x [$3,600 ÷ ($3,600 + $10,800)] = <u>$1,200</u>

This gain would probably be reported in the "other revenues and gains" section. It might be considered an unusual item, but it would usually not be infrequent. The cost of the new machine would be capitalized at $7,200:

Carrying value of old asset	
($16,000 - $6,400)	$9,600
Boot received	(3,600)
Gain recognized	1,200
Cost of new machine	$7,200

OR

Fair market value of new machine		$10,800
Gain experienced	$4,800	
Gain recognized	(1,200)	
Gain deferred		(3,600)
Cost of new machine		$ 7,200

- **Furniture.** The contribution of the furniture to a charitable organization would be reported as a contribution expense of $5,600 with a related gain on disposition of furniture of $1,300 [$5,600 - ($20,000 - $15,700)]. The contribution expense and the related gain may be netted, if desired, for reporting purposes. The net effect is a decrease in net income of $4,300.

- **Automobile.** The loss on sale of the automobile of $3,160 [$5,920 - ($16,000 - $6,920)] should probably be reported in the "other expenses and losses" section. This is a related party transaction; such transactions require special disclosure.

TIP: The receipt of the condemnation award (January 7) represents an **involuntary conversion of nonmonetary assets to monetary assets**. Any gain or loss related to the transaction shall be recognized even though the enterprise reinvests or is obligated to reinvest the monetary assets in replacement nonmonetary assets. The receipt of insurance proceeds due to the destruction of the warehouse is also an involuntary conversion of nonmonetary assets to monetary assets. The conditions surrounding a condemnation are usually unusual and infrequent and thus cause the related gain or loss to be classified as an **extraordinary item**.

TIP:	The sale of property, plant, and equipment for cash should be accounted for as follows:
	(1) The carrying value at the date of the sale (cost of the property, plant, and equipment less the accumulated depreciation) should be removed from the accounts.
	(2) The excess of cash from the sale over the carrying value removed is accounted for as a gain on the sale, while the excess of carrying value removed over cash from the sale is accounted for as a loss on the sale.
TIP:	When a plant asset is disposed of, the accumulated depreciation must be updated before the gain or loss can be computed. The discussions above assume that updating has taken place.

ANALYSIS OF MULTIPLE-CHOICE TYPE QUESTIONS

QUESTION

1.   (L.O. 2) Jacobson Manufacturing Company purchased a machine for $65,000 on January 2, 2014. At the date of purchase, Jacobson incurred the following additional costs:

Loss on sale of old machine	$ 2,000
Freight-in	900
Installation cost	1,500
Breaking-in costs	650

The amount to record for the acquisition cost of the new machine is:
a. $65,000.
b. $67,400.
c. $68,050.
d. $69,400.

Approach and Explanation: Apply the guideline: The cost of a plant asset includes all costs required to get the item to the location and condition for its intended purpose.

Purchase price	$ 65,000
Freight-in	900
Installation cost	1,500
Breaking-in costs	650
Total acquisition cost	$ 68,050

The loss on sale of the old machine should be charged to an income statement account so it will not impact the new asset's value. (Solution = c.)

QUESTION

2.   (L.O. 2) Buena Vista Hotel purchases Embassy Hotel with the intention of demolishing the Embassy Hotel and building a new high-rise hotel on the site. The cost of the Embassy Hotel should be:
a.   capitalized as part of the cost of the land.
b.   capitalized as part of the cost of the new hotel.
c.   written off as a loss when it is torn down.
d.   depreciated over the life of the new hotel structure.

Explanation: The cost of the land should include all costs necessary to acquire it and prepare it for its intended use by the buyer—which is to provide a site for a new building. (Solution = a.)

QUESTION
3. (L.O. 2) The Jupiter Company purchased a parcel of land to be used as the site of a new office complex.   The following data pertain to the purchase of the land and the beginning of construction for the new building:

Purchase price of land	$200,000
Attorney's fees for land transaction	1,000
Title insurance cost	2,000
Survey fees to determine the boundaries of the lot	800
Excavation costs for the building's foundation	8,000
Costs of clearing and grading the land	1,400

The total acquisition cost of the land is:
a. $213,200.
b. $205,200.
c. $203,800.
d. $202,400.
e. $200,000.

Approach and Explanation: Think about how the cost of land is determined: an asset's cost includes all costs necessary to acquire the asset and get it to the location and condition for its intended purpose. When land has been purchased for the purpose of constructing a building, all costs incurred up to the excavation for the new building are considered land costs. Think of the common components of land cost (refer to the listing in the **Solution to Case 10-1).** The cost is computed as follows:

Purchase price	$200,000
Attorney's fees	1,000
Title insurance	2,000
Survey fees	800
Costs of clearing and grading	1,400
Total cost of land	$205,200

The $8,000 excavation costs for the building's foundation should be charged (debited) to the Building account. (Solution = b.)

QUESTION
4. (L.O. 2) The Venus Company hired an architect to design plans and a construction firm to build a new office building on a parcel of land it owns. The following data relates to the building:

Price paid to the construction firm	$320,000
Architect fees	18,000
Permit fees	1,200
Property taxes during the construction period	800
Insurance premium for first year of operations	3,000
Property taxes during the first year of operations	6,000

The total acquisition cost of the new building is:
a. $349,000.
b. $340,000.
c. $338,000.
d. $320,000.

Approach and Explanation: Think about how the cost of a building is determined: an asset's cost includes all costs necessary to acquire the asset and get it to the location and condition for its intended purpose. Think of the common components of building cost (refer to the listing in the **Solution to Case 10-1).** The cost is computed as follows:

Price paid to construction firm	$320,000	
Architect fees	18,000	
Permit fees	1,200	
Property taxes during construction	800	
Total cost of building	$340,000	(Solution = b.)

QUESTION

5.   (L.O. 2)   The Patty Company purchased a piece of office equipment to be used in operations. The following expenditures and other data relate to the equipment:

Invoice price excluding sales tax	$12,000
Sales tax	600
Delivery charges	200
Installation costs	300
Cost of a special platform	400
Cost of supplies used in testing	80
Insurance premium for first year of use	60

The total acquisition cost of this piece of equipment is:
a. $13,640.
b. $13,580.
c. $13,100.
d. $12,700.

Approach and Explanation: Apply the cost principle: the cost of equipment includes all costs necessary to acquire the equipment, transport it to the place where it will be used, and prepare it for use. Thus, all costs related to equipment incurred prior to use in regular operations are charged to the Equipment account.   Recurring costs (such as for insurance and maintenance) incurred after the equipment is ready for use should be expensed in the period incurred.   Refer to the list of common elements of equipment cost in the **Solution to Case 10-1.**   The cost of the equipment is determined as follows:

Invoice price	$12,000	
Sales tax	600	
Delivery charges	200	
Installation costs	300	
Costs of special platform	400	
Costs of supplies used in testing	80	
	$13,580	(Solution = b.)

QUESTION

6.   (L.O. 3) A manufacturing company decides to build its own factory equipment. The cost of self-constructed plant assets may include which of the following:

	Materials	Labor	Mfg. Overhead
a.	Yes	Yes	Yes
b.	Yes	Yes	No
c.	Yes	No	No
d.	No	Yes	No

Explanation: In addition to the materials and labor used to build a plant asset, the manufacturer should assign a pro rata portion of the manufacturing overhead to obtain the asset's cost. However, the asset should not be recorded for more than its fair value (the total amount that would be charged by an outside independent producer). (Solution = a.)

QUESTION

7.   (L.O. 4) Herndon Inc. has a fiscal year ending October 31. On November 1, 2013, Herndon borrowed $20,000,000 at 15% to finance construction of a new plant. Repayments of the loan are to commence the month following completion of the plant. During the year ending October 31, 2014, expenditures for the partially completed structure totaled $12,000,000. These expenditures were incurred evenly through the year. Interest earned on the unexpended portion of the loan amounted to $800,000 for the year. What amount of interest should be capitalized as of October 31, 2014?

   a. $0.
   b. $100,000.
   c. $900,000.
   d. $2,200,000.

Explanation: The situation is one which qualifies for the capitalization of interest. The following steps should help to compute the amount:

   (1)   **Find the weighted-average accumulated expenditures** for the period:

Total expenditures at beginning of the period	$ 0
Total expenditures at end of the period	12,000,000
Sum	$ 12,000,000

   $12,000,000 ÷ 2 = average of $6,000,000

   (2)   **Determine the interest rate to use.** Because the amount of a specific borrowing ($20,000,000) exceeds the weighted-average accumulated expenditures ($6,000,000), use the interest rate for that specific borrowing (15%).

   (3)   **Compute the avoidable interest** by multiplying the appropriate interest rate (15% from Step 2) by the weighted-average accumulated expenditures ($6,000,000 from Step 1).

   $6,000,000 x 15% = $900,000 Avoidable interest

   (4)   **Determine the amount of interest to capitalize** by selecting the lower of the actual interest incurred (15% x $20,000,000 = $3,000,000) or the amount of avoidable interest ($900,000 from Step 3). The lower in this case is the $900,000 avoidable interest. (Solution = c.)

> **TIP:**   The interest earned ($800,000) is to be reported as revenue on the income statement and should not be used to offset the interest to be capitalized.

QUESTION

8.   (L.O. 5) A large plot of land was donated by the City of Moberly to the Dupont Corporation to entice the company to build a plant and provide new jobs in the community. The land should be recorded on Dupont's books at:

   a.   the cost of the attorney's fees involved in handling the transaction.
   b.   the value assigned by Dupont's board of directors.
   c.   the land's market value.
   d.   no more than one dollar because the land was obtained for no cost.

Explanation: A donation (contribution) is a **nonreciprocal transfer** (value goes in only one direction rather than in both directions as happens in an exchange transaction). A nonreciprocal transfer is to be recorded at the fair value of the property, goods, or services involved. Although contributions received are normally credited to revenue, a donation from a governmental entity to a for-profit entity to entice the business to its community is sometimes credited to Donated Capital (an element of additional paid-in capital on the balance sheet). Contributions of property from governmental entities are excluded from the scope of the FASB's guidance on contributions which in general requires contributions received to be recognized as revenue.   The authors of your text believe all donations received should be recorded by credits to revenue. (Solution = c.)

QUESTION

9.   (L.O. 5) The Holstrum Corporation intends to acquire some plant assets from Bailey Corporation by issuing common stock in exchange. The cost of the assets should be measured by:
   a.   the par value of the stock.
   b.   the market value of the stock.
   c.   the book value of the stock.
   d.   Bailey's carrying value of the assets.

Explanation: Cost is measured by the fair market value (cash equivalent) of the consideration given (the stock in this case), or the fair market value of the consideration received (the plant assets in this case), whichever is the more objectively determinable. If the market value of the common stock is not determinable, the fair market value of the plant assets should be used. (Solution = b.)

TIP: If treasury stock is used to acquire a new plant asset, the same rule applies: record the asset at the fair value (market value) of the treasury stock or at the fair value of the asset, whichever is the more objectively determinable.

QUESTION

10.   (L.O. 5) In January 2014, Barbie Company entered into a contract to acquire a new machine for its factory. The machine, which had a cash price of $300,000, was acquired in exchange for the following:

Down payment	$ 30,000
Note payable in 24 equal monthly installments	240,000
500 shares of Barbie common stock, with	
an agreed value of $100 per share	50,000
Total	$ 320,000

Prior to the machine's use, installation costs of $8,000 were incurred. The amount to record for the acquisition cost of the machine is:
   a. $300,000.
   b. $308,000.
   c. $320,000.
   d. $328,000.

Approach and Explanation: Any time you have a question regarding the acquisition cost of a plant asset, write down (or mentally review) the two rules regarding asset cost: (1) Cost is measured by the fair market value (cash equivalent) of the consideration given or the fair market value of the consideration received, whichever is the more clearly evident; and (2) An asset's cost includes all costs necessary to get it to the location and condition for its intended purpose. Then apply the rules to the situation given.

The cash equivalent of the machine acquired is $300,000 (cash price). The cash equivalent of the consideration given is the cash down payment of $30,000 plus the fair value of the stock ($50,000) plus the present value of the note payable (something less than $240,000). Because no information is given about the market value of the note or the appropriate interest rate for the note, but the cash equivalent price is given for the asset received, the more objectively determinable figure is the $300,000. The $8,000 installation cost must be added to get the total acquisition cost. (Solution = b.)

QUESTION
11.   (L.O. 5) Two home builders agree to exchange tracts of land that each holds for purposes of development. An appraiser was hired and the following information is available:

	Batson	Beamer
Book value of land	$ 50,000	$ 72,000
Fair value of land	80,000	100,000
Cash paid	20,000	

The future cash flows are **not** expected to change materially for either party. In recording this exchange should a gain be recognized by Batson, Beamer, or both parties?

	Batson	Beamer
a.	Yes	Yes
b.	Yes	No
c.	No	Yes
d.	No	No

Approach and Explanation:
(1)   **Determine if the exchange has commercial substance.** One tract of land for another to use for the same purpose where the future cash flows are not expected to change materially for either party is an exchange that **lacks** commercial substance.
(2)   **Determine if a gain or loss is experienced.** Fair value exceeds book value for both parties so both have experienced a gain.
(3)   **Determine if boot is given or received.** Batson is giving boot; Beamer is receiving boot.
(4)   **Write down the rules for recognition of gain in an exchange lacking commercial substance.** The party giving boot (Batson) is not to recognize any gain. The party receiving boot is to recognize a portion of the gain experienced. In this case, the receipt of cash by Beamer represents a partial sale of the land, thus converting a portion of the old asset's fair value to cash. (Solution = c.)

QUESTION
12.   (L.O. 5) Refer to the facts of **Question 11**. The amount to be recorded by Batson for the acquisition cost of the new tract of land is:
    a. $50,000.
    b. $70,000.
    c. $72,000.
    d. $80,000.
    e. $100,000.

Approach and Explanation: When boot is given in an exchange lacking commercial substance, no gain is to be recognized. The cost of the new asset is equal to the recorded value (book value) of the old asset, reduced for any impairment (minus any loss recognized), plus the boot given. There was no loss in this case; therefore, $50,000 book value + $20,000 boot = $70,000 cost. A journal entry approach can also be used (the debit to the new asset account is a plug figure): (Solution = b.)

Land (New)...	70,000	**Plug last.**
Land (Old)	50,000	**Do second.**
Cash.......................................	20,000	**Do first.**

The cost of the new tract of land can also be determined as follows:

Fair market value of asset given	$ 80,000
Cash given	20,000
Cost of new before deferral of gain on old	100,000
Gain on old to be deferred	(30,000)a
Cost of new asset	$ 70,000 (Solution = b.)

aFair market value of old asset	$80,000
Book value of old asset	(50,000)
Gain on old asset experienced but not recognized	$30,000

QUESTION

13. (L.O. 5) The King-Kong Corporation exchanges one plant asset for a similar plant asset and gives cash in the exchange. The exchange is **not** expected to cause a material change in the future cash flows for either entity. If a gain on the disposal of the old asset is indicated, the gain will:
    a.   be reported in the Other Revenues and Gains section of the income statement.
    b.   effectively reduce the amount to be recorded as the cost of the new asset.
    c.   effectively increase the amount to be recorded as the cost of the new asset.
    d.   be credited directly to the owner's capital account.

Explanation: The payer of cash in an exchange of nonmonetary assets in an exchange lacking commercial substance is **not** to recognize any gain on the disposal of the old asset. The gain is deferred by way of reduction (credit) to the cost of the new asset received in the exchange. The gain is thus spread over future periods by way of lower depreciation charges (because of a lower cost figure for the new asset). (Solution = b.)

QUESTION

14. (L.O. 7) A van has an original cost of $42,000 and accumulated depreciation of $11,000. It is sold for $27,000 cash. The journal entry to record the sale will include a:
    a.   debit to Loss on Disposal of Plant Assets for $4,000.
    b.   credit to Gain on Disposal of Plant Assets for $4,000.
    c.   credit to Vans for $27,000.
    d.   debit to Loss on Disposal of Plant Assets for $15,000.

Approach and Explanation: Prepare the journal entry to record the sale. Begin with the cash received so debit Cash. Remove the old asset from the books; credit Vans for $42,000 and debit Accumulated Depreciation for $11,000. Examine the entry and determine what is needed to balance the entry; a debit balancing figure represents a loss or a credit balancing figure represents a gain.

In this case, a debit of $4,000 is needed to balance; hence, a loss of $4,000 is recorded. (Solution = a.)

Cash	27,000	
Accumulated Depreciation—Vans	11,000	
Loss on Disposal of Plant Assets	4,000	
Vans		42,000

QUESTION
15.   (L.O. 6) In accounting for plant assets, which of the following outlays made subsequent to acquisition should be fully expensed in the period the expenditure is made?
   a.   Expenditure made to increase the efficiency or effectiveness of an existing asset.
   b.   Expenditure made to extend the useful life of an existing asset beyond the time frame originally anticipated.
   c.   Expenditure made to maintain an existing asset so that it can function in the manner intended.
   d.   Expenditure made to add new asset services.

Explanation: If an expenditure benefits future periods, it should be capitalized (debited to a balance sheet account); if the expenditure does not yield benefits to a future period, it should be recorded by a debit to an income statement account. An expenditure made to maintain an existing asset in good working condition does not provide any benefits other than those that were in potential when the original asset was acquired; hence, it should be expensed. Answer selections "a," "b," and "d" all represent future economic benefits; hence, they should be debited to an asset account or to an accumulated depreciation account, depending on whether or not an asset's life is increased by the expenditure subsequent to acquisition. (Solution = c.)

IFRS Insights

IFRS Insights related to property, plant, and equipment are presented in **Chapter 11.**

CHAPTER 11

DEPRECIATION, IMPAIRMENTS, AND DEPLETION

OVERVIEW

Expenses arise from the cost of goods or services that are consumed in the process of generating revenue. When a long-term tangible asset is acquired, it actually represents a bundle of future asset services. The total cost of these services equals the acquisition cost of the asset **minus** the asset's expected (estimated) market value at the end of its useful life. As a productive asset is used, services (benefits) are consumed; therefore, a portion of the original asset cost should be charged to expense in order to comply with the matching principle. The process of allocating (expensing) the cost of long-term tangible assets over the accounting periods during which the asset is used is called **depreciation**. The process of allocating the costs of natural resources to inventory (and later to cost of goods sold) is called **depletion**. Depreciation and depletion are discussed in this chapter.

SUMMARY OF LEARNING OBJECTIVES

1. **Explain the concept of depreciation.** Depreciation is the accounting process of allocating the cost of long-lived tangible assets to expense in a systematic and rational manner to those periods expected to benefit from the use of the asset.

2. **Identify the factors involved in the depreciation process.** Three factors involved in the depreciation process are (1) determining the depreciation base for the asset, (2) estimating the service life, and (3) selecting a method of cost apportionment (depreciation).

3. **Compare activity, straight-line, and decreasing-charge methods of depreciation.** (1) *Activity method:* Assumes that depreciation is a function of use or productivity instead of the passage of time. The life of the asset is considered in terms of either the output it provides, or an input measure such as the number of hours it works. (2) *Straight-line method:* Considers depreciation a function of time instead of a function of usage. The straight-line procedure is often the most conceptually appropriate when a decline in usefulness is constant from period to period. (3) *Decreasing-charge method:* Provides for a higher depreciation charge in the earlier years and lower charges in later periods. The main justification for this approach is that the asset is the most productive and suffers the greatest loss of services in its earlier years.

4. **Explain special depreciation methods.** Two special depreciation methods are as follows: (1) *Group and composite methods:* The term "group" refers to a collection of assets that are similar in nature; "composite" refers to a collection of assets that are dissimilar in nature. The group method is frequently used where the assets are fairly homogeneous (similar in nature) and have approximately the same useful lives. The composite approach may be used when the assets are heterogeneous (dissimilar) and have different lives. (2) *Hybrid or combination methods:* These methods may combine straight-line/activity approaches.

5. **Explain the accounting issues related to asset impairment.** The process to determine an impairment loss is as follows. (1) Review events and changes in circumstances for possible impairment. (2) If events or changes suggest impairment, determine if the sum of the expected future net cash flows from the long-lived asset is less than the carrying amount of the asset. If less, measure the impairment loss. (3) The impairment loss is the amount by which the carrying

impairment loss, the reduced carrying amount of the long-lived asset is now considered its new cost basis. An impairment loss may not be restored for an asset held for use. If the company expects to dispose of the asset, it should report the impaired asset at the lower-of-cost-or-net realizable value. It is not depreciated. An impaired asset held for disposal can be continuously revalued and written up or down in future periods as long as the write-up is never greater than the carrying amount before impairment.

6.   **Explain the accounting procedures for depletion of natural resources.** To account for depletion of natural resources, companies: (1) establish the depletion base, and (2) write off resource cost. Four factors are involved in establishing the depletion base: (a) Acquisition costs, (b) Exploration costs, (c) Development costs, and (d) Restoration costs. To write off resource cost, companies normally compute depletion on the units-of-production method. Thus, depletion is a function of the number of units withdrawn during the period. To obtain a cost per unit of product, the total cost of the natural resource less salvage value is divided by the number of units estimated to be in the resource deposit. To compute depletion, this cost per unit is multiplied by the number of units extracted.

7.   **Explain how to report property, plant, and equipment and natural resources.** The basis of valuation for property, plant, and equipment and for natural resources should be disclosed along with pledges, liens, and other commitments related to these assets. Companies should not offset any liability secured by property, plant, and equipment or by natural resources against these assets, but should report it in the liabilities section. Property, plant, and equipment not currently employed as producing assets in the business should be segregated from assets used in operations. When assets are depreciated, a valuation account normally called Accumulated Depreciation is credited. When assets are depleted, an accumulated depletion account may be used or the depletion may be credited directly to the natural resource account. Companies engaged in significant oil and gas producing activities must provide significant additional disclosures about these activities. Analysis may be performed to evaluate the asset turnover ratio, profit margin on sales, and the rate of return on assets.

*8.   **Describe income tax methods of depreciation.** Congress enacted a Modified Accelerated Cost Recovery System (MACRS) in the Tax Reform Act of 1986. It applies to depreciable assets placed in service in 1987 and later. The computation of depreciation under MACRS differs from the computation under GAAP in three respects: (1) a mandated tax life, which is generally shorter than the economic life; (2) cost recovery on an accelerated basis; and (3) an assigned salvage value of zero.

      *This material is covered in **Appendix 11A** in the text.

TIPS ON CHAPTER TOPICS

TIP: **Residual value** is often referred to as **salvage value**, and sometimes it is called estimated **scrap value**.

TIP: Residual value is used in the computation of depreciation for the early years of life of an asset whenever the straight-line method or the sum-of-the-years'-digits method or an activity method is used. Salvage value is **not** a factor in determining depreciation for the early years of life if a declining-balance method is used; however, salvage value can affect the amount computed for depreciation in the last year(s) of an asset's life. An asset should **not** be depreciated below its salvage value.

TIP: The **activity method** is often called the **variable charge** approach or the **units of output** or the **units of production method**.

TIP: The **declining-balance depreciation method** applies a constant rate to a declining book value to calculate depreciation. The rate used is often twice the straight-line rate, in which case the method is then referred to as the **200% declining-balance method** or the **double declining-balance method**. Sometimes the rate is one and one-half times the straight-line rate, in which case the method is called the **150% declining-balance method**.

TIP: The **book value** of a plant asset is determined by deducting the balance of accumulated depreciation from the balance of the related asset account. The balance in the related asset account is generally the asset's original cost. Thus, the estimated residual value does not directly affect the book value computation. Book value is often called **carrying value**, **carrying amount**, **net asset value**, or **undepreciated value**. An asset's book value at a given date may be far different than its market (fair) value at the same date.

TIP: **Depreciable cost** or **depreciation base** is a term that refers to the total amount to be depreciated over the life of the asset. It is determined by deducting the estimated residual value from the cost of the asset.

TIP: When an asset being depreciated by a group or composite depreciation method is disposed of, no gain or loss is recorded; the difference between the original cost of the asset and the proceeds from disposal is charged to Accumulated Depreciation.

TIP: Companies can use either the full-cost approach or the successful-efforts approach to account for exploration costs in the oil and gas industry.

Those who favor the **full-cost concept** argue that the cost of drilling a dry hole is a cost needed to find the commercially profitable wells and therefore should be capitalized. Those who favor the successful-efforts concept believe that companies should capitalize only the costs of successful projects (i.e., only the costs directly related to a successful project) gets charged to that project; any remaining costs are treated as period charges (expenses).

TIP: Fair-value information is required for supplemental disclosures for gas and oil producers. Revenue recognition accounting (RRA) has been suggested for those companies but is not a generally accepted method. Under RRA, as soon as a company discovers oil, it would report the value of the oil on the balance sheet and in the income statement. Thus, RRA is a fair-value approach, in contrast to full-costing and successful-efforts concepts which are historical cost approaches.

CASE 11-1

Purpose: (L.O. 1, 2) This case examines the process of matching the cost of fixed assets with the revenues which the assets help to generate.

Plant assets provide services for two or more periods. There is a cost to the services consumed; this cost should be matched with the periods benefited.

Instructions
(a)   Briefly define depreciation as used in accounting.
(b)   Identify the factors that are relevant in determining the annual depreciation and explain whether these factors are determined objectively or whether they are based on judgment.

(AICPA Adapted)

Solution to Case 11-1

(a)   Depreciation is the accounting process of allocating an asset's historical cost (recorded amount) to the accounting periods benefited by the use of the asset. It is a process of cost allocation, not valuation. Depreciation is not intended to provide funds for an asset's replacement; it is merely an application of the matching principle.

(b)   The factors relevant in determining the annual depreciation for a depreciable asset are the initial recorded amount (acquisition cost and any subsequent capitalized costs), estimated salvage value, estimated useful life, and deprecation method.

Assets are typically recorded at their acquisition cost, which is in most cases objectively determinable. But cost assignments in other cases—"basket purchases" and selection of an implicit interest rate in asset acquisition under deferred-payment plans—may be quite subjective and involve considerable judgment.

The salvage value is an estimate of an amount potentially realizable when the asset is retired from service. It is initially a judgment factor and is affected by the length of the asset's useful life to the enterprise.

The useful life is also a judgment factor. It involves selecting the "unit" of measure of service life and estimating the number of such units embodied in the asset. Such units may be measured in terms of time periods or in terms of activity (for example, years or machine hours). When selecting the life, one should select the lower (shorter) of the physical life or the economic life to the user. Physical life involves wear and tear and casualties; economic life involves such things as technological obsolescence and inadequacy.

Selecting the depreciation method is generally a judgment decision; but, a method may be inherent in the definition adopted for the units of service life, as discussed earlier. For example, if such units are machine hours, the method is a function of the number of machine hours used during each period. A method should be selected that will best measure the portion of services expiring each period. Once a method is selected, it may be applied by using a predetermined, objectively derived formula.

EXERCISE 11-1

Purpose: (L.O. 3) This exercise will give you practice in computing depreciation for three successive periods for three commonly used methods.

Hudspeth Company purchases equipment on January 1, Year 1, at a cost of $645,000. The asset is expected to have a service life of 12 years and a salvage value of $60,000.

Instructions

(a) Compute the amount of depreciation for each of Years 1 through 3 using the straight-line depreciation method.

(b) Compute the amount of depreciation for each of Years 1 through 3 using the sum-of-the-years'-digits method.

(c) Compute the amount of depreciation for each of Years 1 through 3 using the double-declining balance method. (In performing your calculations, round the constant percentage to the nearest one-hundredth of a percentage point and round final answers to the nearest dollar.)

Solution to Exercise 11-1

(a) $\dfrac{\$645,000 - \$60,000}{12} = \underline{\$48,750}$ Depreciation for each of Years 1 through 3 using the straight - line method.

(b) $\dfrac{12 \times 13}{2} = 78$

12/78 x ($645,000 - $60,000) =	$90,000	depreciation Year 1
11/78 x ($645,000 - $60,000) =	$82,500	depreciation Year 2
10/78 x ($645,000 - $60,000) =	$75,000	depreciation Year 3

(c) $\dfrac{100\%}{12} \times 2 = 16.67\%$

$645,000 x 16.67% =	$107,522	depreciation Year 1
($645,000 - $107,522) x 16.67% =	$ 89,598	depreciation Year 2
($645,000 - $107,522 - $89,598) x 16.67% =	$ 74,662	depreciation Year 3

EXERCISE 11-2

Purpose: (L.O. 3) This exercise will provide an illustration of the computations for depreciation of partial periods using three common methods.

Kalidas Company purchased a new plant asset on April 1, 2014, at a cost of $345,000. It was estimated to have a service life of 20 years and a salvage value of $30,000. Kalidas uses the calendar year as its accounting period.

Instructions (Round all final answers to the nearest dollar.)

(a)   Compute the amount of depreciation for this asset for 2014 and 2015 using the straight-line method.

(b)   Compute the amount of depreciation for this asset for 2014 and 2015 using the sum-of-the-years'-digits method.

(c)   Compute the amount of depreciation for this asset for 2014 and 2015 using the double-declining balance method.

Solution to Exercise 11-2

(a) $\dfrac{\$345,000 - \$30,000}{20 \text{ years}} \times 9/12 = \underline{\$11,813}$ depreciation for 2014

$\dfrac{\$345,000 - \$30,000}{20 \text{ years}} = \underline{\$15,750}$ depreciation for 2015

Approach and Explanation: Write down and apply the formula for straight-line depreciation. Multiply the annual depreciation amount by the portion of the asset's first year of service that falls in the given accounting period.

$$\frac{\text{Cost} - \text{Salvage Value}}{\text{Estimated Service LIfe}} = \text{Depreciation Charge}$$

(b) $\dfrac{20\ (20 + 1)}{2} = 210$

$9/12 \times 20/210 \times (\$345,000 - \$30,000) \quad = \quad \underline{\$22,500}$ depreciation for 2014

$3/12 \times 20/210 \times (\$345,000 - \$30,000) \quad = \quad \$\ 7,500$
$+\ 9/12 \times 19/210 \times (\$345,000 - \$30,000) \quad = \quad \underline{\ \ 21,375}$
$\underline{\$28,875}$ depreciation for 2015

Approach and Explanation: Write down and apply the formula for sum-of-the-years'-digits depreciation. Apportion the depreciation for the given asset year between the two accounting periods involved. The first nine months of the asset's first year of life fall in the 2014 calendar year. The last three months of the asset's first year of life and the first nine months of the asset's second year of life fall in the 2015 calendar year. There is no shortcut to the two-part computation of depreciation for 2015, as illustrated above.

Formula: $\dfrac{n\ (n + 1)}{2} = \text{Sum of the Years}$

$\dfrac{\text{No. of Years Remaining at Beginning of Asset Year}}{\text{Sum of the Years}} \times (\text{Cost} - \text{Salvage Value}) = \text{Depreciation for Full Asset Year}$

(c)   Straight-line rate $\dfrac{100\%}{20}$ = 5%;   5% x 2 = 10%

10% x $345,000 = $34,500 depreciation for asset's first year
10% x ($345,000 - $34,500) = $31,050 depreciation for asset's second year

9/12 x $34,500 = $25,875 depreciation for 2014

3/12 x $34,500 =	$ 8,625	
+ 9/12 x $31,050 =	23,288	
	$ 31,913	depreciation for 2015

Approach and Explanation: Write down and apply the formula for the declining balance method. Apportion the depreciation for a given **asset year** between the two accounting periods involved.

$$\text{Constant Percentage} \times \begin{array}{c}\text{Book Value}\\\text{at Beginning}\\\text{of Asset Year}\end{array} = \text{Depreciation for Asset Year}$$

An alternative approach is as follows:
   After the first partial year, calculate depreciation for a full **accounting year** by multiplying the constant percentage by the book value of the asset at the beginning of the accounting period.
          Thus, the computation for 2015 would be as follows:
              10% x ($345,000 - $25,875) = $31,913.

EXERCISE 11-3

Purpose: (L.O. 3) This exercise is designed to test your ability to solve for missing data by applying your knowledge regarding depreciation computations.

Dunlap Company acquired a plant asset at the beginning of Year 1. The asset has an estimated service life of 5 years. An employee has prepared depreciation schedules for this asset using three different methods to compare the results of using one method with the results of using other methods. You are to assume that the following schedules have been correctly prepared for this asset using (1) the straight-line (SL) method, (2) the sum-of-the-years'-digits (SYD) method, and (3) the double-declining balance (DDB) method (switching to the straight-line method after the mid-life of the asset).

Year	Straight-line	Sum-of-the-Years'-Digits	Double-declining Balance
1	$ 6,000	$ 10,000	$ 14,400
2	6,000	8,000	8,640
3	6,000	6,000	5,184
4	6,000	4,000	888
5	6,000	2,000	888
Total	$ 30,000	$ 30,000	$ 30,000

Instructions

Answer the following questions:

(a)   What is the cost of the asset being depreciated?

(b)   What amount, if any, was used in the depreciation calculations for the salvage value of this asset?

(c)   Which method will produce the highest charge to income in Year 1?

(d)   Which method will produce the highest charge to income in Year 4?

(e)   Which method will produce the highest book value for the asset at the end of Year 3?

(f)   If the asset is sold at the end of Year 3, which method would yield the highest gain (or lowest loss) on disposal of the asset?

Solution to Exercise 11-3

(a)   If there is any salvage value and the amount is unknown (as is the case here), the cost would have to be determined by looking at the data for the double-declining balance method.

$$100\% \div 5 = 20\%; \quad 20\% \times 2 = 40\%$$
$$\text{Cost} \times 40\% = \$14,400; \quad \$14,400 \div .40 = \underline{\$36,000} \text{ cost of asset}$$

Approach: Write down the formula for each of the depreciation methods mentioned. Fill in the data given for Year 1. Examine what remains to be solved.

(Cost - Salvage Value) ÷ Estimated Service Life = St.-line Depreciation
(Cost - Salvage Value) ÷ 5 = $6,000

(# of Years Remaining at Beginning of Asset Year ÷ Sum of the Years)
   x (Cost - Salvage Value) = SYD Depreciation
5 ÷ 15 x (Cost - Salvage Value) = $10,000

Constant Percentage x Cost = DDB Depreciation
40% x Cost = $14,400

There are two variables (cost and salvage value) unknown for each of the first two methods, and there is no way to solve for either of them. However, cost can easily be determined for the third method (DDB). Once you solve for cost, it is a simple matter to solve for salvage value.

(b) $36,000 cost (answer a) - $30,000 total depreciation = $6,000 salvage value

Approach: The difference between the answer to part (a) and the total depreciation per the schedule ($30,000) is the salvage value used.

(c)   The highest charge to income for Year 1 will be yielded by the double-declining balance method.

Approach: Examine the depreciation schedules. Notice the method that results in the highest depreciation amount for Year 1.

(d)   The highest charge to income for Year 4 will be yielded by the straight-line method.

Approach: Examine the depreciation schedules given. Notice the method that results in the highest depreciation amount for Year 4.

(e)   The method to yield the highest book value at the end of Year 3 would be the method that yields the lowest accumulated depreciation at the end of Year 3 which is the straight-line method. Computations:

SL   = $36,000 - ($6,000 + $6,000 + $6,000)
        = $18,000 book value at the end of Year 3.
SYD   = $36,000 - ($10,000 + $8,000 + $6,000)
        = $12,000 book value at the end of Year 3.
DDB   = $36,000 - ($14,400 + $8,640 + $5,184)
        = $7,776 book value at the end of Year 3.

Approach: Write down the formula to compute book value: Cost - Accumulated Depreciation = Book Value. To obtain a high book value, you need a low accumulated depreciation. Examine the depreciation schedules to determine the method that would yield the lowest total depreciation for the first three years.

(f)   The method that will yield the highest gain (or lowest loss) if the asset is sold at the end of Year 3 is the method which will yield the lowest book value at the end of Year 3. In this case, it is the double-declining balance method.

Approach: Write down the formula to compute gain or loss on disposal: Selling Price - Book Value = Gain (Loss). To obtain a high gain, you need a low book value. Examine the formula for book value. To get a low book value, you need high depreciation charges. Use the depreciation schedules to determine the method that would yield the highest accumulated depreciation balance at the end of three years.

EXERCISE 11-4

Purpose: (L.O. 4) This exercise will enable you to practice working with the composite method for computing depreciation.

Presented below is information related to the Lori Demro Corporation (all assets are acquired at the beginning of Year 1):

Asset	Cost	Estimated Scrap	Estimated Life (in years)
A	$60,750	$8,250	10
B	50,400	7,200	9
C	54,000	4,800	8
D	28,500	2,250	7
E	35,250	3,750	6

Instructions

(a)   Compute the rate of depreciation per year to be applied to the plant assets under the composite method.
(b)   Compute the composite life.
(c)   Prepare the adjusting entry necessary at the end of the year to record depreciation for Year 1.
(d)   Prepare the entry at the end of Year 6 to record the sale of fixed asset D for cash of $7,500. It was used for 6 years, and depreciation was recorded under the composite method.

Solution to Exercise 11-4

(a)

Asset	Cost	Estimated Scrap	Depreciable Cost	Estimated Life	Depreciation Per Year
A	$ 60,750	$ 8,250	$ 52,500	10	$ 5,250
B	50,400	7,200	43,200	9	4,800
C	54,000	4,800	49,200	8	6,150
D	28,500	2,250	26,250	7	3,750
E	35,250	3,750	31,500	6	5,250
	$228,900	$26,250	$202,650		$25,200

Composite rate = $25,200 ÷ $228,900; or <u>11.009%</u>

Approach and Explanation: Steps to compute the composite rate:

1.   Compute what would be the amount of annual straight-line depreciation for each asset by dividing each asset's **depreciable cost** by its estimated service life. Sum these amounts ($25,200).

2.   Compute the composite rate by dividing the total depreciation per year (results of Step 1—$25,200) by the amount of **original cost** ($228,900).

(b)   Composite life = $202,650 ÷ $25,200; or <u>8.04 years</u>

Approach and Explanation: Compute the composite life by dividing the total depreciable cost ($202,650) by the total annual depreciation charge ($25,200).

(c)

End of Year 1

Depreciation Expense on Plant Assets..............................	25,200	
Accumulated Deprecation on Plant Assets		25,200
($228,900 x 11.009% = $25,200)		

Approach and Explanation: Compute the depreciation for any given year by multiplying the balance in the asset account by the composite rate (results of Step 2). The balance in the asset account will change over time due to the acquisition of new assets and the disposal of old assets.

(d)

End of Year 6

Cash	7,500	
Accumulated Depreciation on Plant Assets	21,000	
Plant Assets		28,500

Approach and Explanation: When using the group or composite method, no gain or loss on disposition of a specific asset is recorded. The difference between the proceeds (if any) on disposal and the original cost of the asset is debited (or credited) to the Accumulated Depreciation account. Thus, if an asset is retired before, or after, the average service of the group is reached, the resulting gain or loss is buried in the Accumulated Depreciation account.

EXERCISE 11-5

Purpose: (L.O. 4) This exercise will provide you with an illustration of how to account for a change in the estimated service life and salvage value of a plant asset due to an expenditure subsequent to acquisition.

The Russell Company purchased a machine on January 1, 2004 for $105,000. The machine was being depreciated using the straight-line method over an estimated life span of 20 years, with a $15,000 salvage value. At the beginning of 2014, when the machine had been in use for 10 years, the company paid $25,000 to overhaul the machine. As a result of this improvement, the company estimated that the useful life of the machine would be extended an additional 5 years and the salvage value would be reduced to $10,000.

Instructions
Compute the depreciation charge for 2014.

Solution to Exercise 11-5

Cost	$ 105,000
Accumulated depreciation at 1/1/14	(45,000)[a]
Book value at 1/1/14	60,000
Additional expenditure capitalized	25,000
Revised book value	85,000
Current estimate of salvage value	(10,000)
Remaining depreciable cost at 1/1/14	75,000
Remaining years of useful life at 1/1/14	÷ 15[b]
Depreciation expense for 2014	$ 5,000

[a]Cost	$105,000
Original estimate of salvage value	(15,000)
Original depreciable cost	90,000
Original service life in years	÷ 20
Original depreciation per year	4,500
Number of years used	x 10
Accumulated depreciation at 1/1/14	$ 45,000

[b]Original estimate of life in years	20
Number of years used	(10)
Additional years	5
Remaining years of useful life at 1/1/14	15

> **TIP:** A change in the estimated useful life and/or salvage value of an existing depreciable asset is to be accounted for prospectively (in current and/or future periods). Therefore, the book value at the beginning of the period of change, less the current estimate of salvage value, is to be allocated over the remaining periods of life, using the appropriate depreciation method. The book value at the beginning of the period of change is calculated using the original estimates of service life and salvage value.
>
> **TIP:** The $25,000 cost of overhaul is capitalized in this case because the cost benefits future periods by extending the useful life of the machine.

Approach: Whenever you have a situation that involves a change in the estimated service life and/or salvage value of a depreciable asset, use the format shown above to compute the remaining depreciable cost and allocate that amount over the remaining useful life using the given depreciation method.

EXERCISE 11-6

Purpose: (L.O. 3) This exercise will allow you to practice using various depreciation methods and it will also give you the opportunity to compare the results of using one method to the results of using another method.

On January 1, 2014, Irish Company, a machine-tool manufacturer, acquires a piece of new industrial equipment for $1,000,000. The new equipment has a useful life of five years and the salvage value is estimated to be $100,000. Irish estimates that the new equipment can produce a total of 40,000 units and expects it to produce 10,000 units in its first year. Production is then estimated to decline by 1,000 units per year over the remaining useful life of the equipment.
    The following depreciation methods may be used:
   • Double declining-balance
   • Straight-line
   • Sum-of-the-years'-digits
   • Units-of-output

Instructions
(a)   Identify which depreciation method would result in the maximization of profits for financial statement reporting for the **three**-year period ending December 31, 2016. Prepare a schedule showing the amount of accumulated depreciation at December 31, 2016, under the method selected. Show supporting computations in good form. Ignore present value and income tax considerations in your answer.
(b)   Identify which depreciation method would result in the minimization of profits for the **three**-year period ending December 31, 2016. Prepare a schedule showing the amount of accumulated depreciation at December 31, 2016, under the method selected. Show supporting computations in good form. Ignore present value and income tax considerations in your answer.

(AICPA Adapted)

Solution to Exercise 11-6

(a) The straight-line method of depreciation would result in the maximization of profits for financial statement reporting for the three-year period ending December 31, 2016.

Irish Company
ACCUMULATED DEPRECIATION USING STRAIGHT-LINE METHOD
December 31, 2016

(Cost - Salvage Value) ÷ Estimated Service Life

($1,000,000 - $100,000) ÷ 5 years = $180,000

Year	Depreciation Expense	Accumulated Depreciation
2014	$ 180,000	$ 180,000
2015	180,000	360,000
2016	180,000	540,000
	$ 540,000	

(b) The double declining balance method of depreciation would result in the minimization of profits for the three-year period ending December 31, 2016.

Irish Company
ACCUMULATED DEPRECIATION USING
DOUBLE DECLINING-BALANCE METHOD
December 31, 2016

Straight-line rate is 5 years, or 20%. Double declining-balance rate is 40% (20% x 2). Ignore salvage value.

Year	Book Value at Beginning of Year	Depreciation Expense	Accumulated Depreciation
2014	$1,000,000	$400,000	$400,000
2015	600,000	240,000	640,000
2016	360,000	144,000	784,000
		$784,000	

Other supporting computations:

Irish Company
ACCUMULATED DEPRECIATION USING
SUM-OF-THE-YEARS'-DIGITS METHOD
December 31, 2016

$[n \times (n + 1)] \div 2 = [5 \times (5 + 1)] \div 2 = 15$

5/15 X ($1,000,000 - $100,000) = $300,000
4/15 x ($1,000,000 - $100,000) = $240,000
3/15 X ($1,000,000 - $100,000) = $180,000

Year	Depreciation Expense	Accumulated Depreciation
2014	$ 300,000	$ 300,000
2015	240,000	540,000
2016	180,000	720,000
	$ 720,000	

Irish Company
ACCUMULATED DEPRECIATION USING
UNITS-OF-OUTPUT METHOD
December 31, 2016

(Cost - Salvage Value) ÷ Total Units of Output =
($1,000,000 - $100,000) ÷ 40,000 =
$22.50 Depreciation per Unit

10,000 x $22.50 = $225,000
9,000 x $22.50 = $202,500
8,000 x $22.50 = $180,000

Year	Depreciation Expense	Accumulated Depreciation
2014	$ 225,000	$ 225,000
2015	202,500	427,500
2016	180,000	607,500
	$ 607,500	

EXERCISE 11-7

Purpose: (L.O. 6) This exercise will give you practice in computing depletion.

During 2014, Alston Corporation acquired a mineral mine for $2,700,000, of which $450,000 is attributable to the land value after the mineral has been removed. Engineers estimate that 15 million units of mineral can be recovered from this mine. During 2014, 1,200,000 units were extracted and 800,000 units were sold.

Instructions
Compute the depletion for 2014.

Solution to Exercise 11-7

($2,700,000 - $450,000) ÷ 15,000,000 = $.15

$.15 x 1,200,000 = $180,000 Depletion for 2014

Approach and Explanation: Write down the formula to compute depletion, enter the data given, and solve.

$$\frac{\text{Acquisition Cost } + \text{ Costs to Explore and Develop} - \text{ Residual Value of Land } + \text{ Costs to Restore Land to Alternative Use}}{\text{Number of Units to be Extracted}} = \frac{\text{Depletion Cost Per}}{\text{Recoverable Unit}}$$

Depletion Cost Per Recoverable Unit	x	Units Extracted During Period	=	Depletion for the Period

> **TIP:** The depletion charge for the period is the amount to be removed from the property, plant, and equipment classification ($180,000 in this case). It is based on the units **extracted** from the earth during the period. The portion of this $180,000 which gets to the income statement is dependent upon the number of units **sold**. When the number of units extracted exceed the number sold, as in this exercise, a portion of the depletion costs gets reported in the Inventory account on the balance sheet. (In this case $120,000 would be included in cost of goods sold on the income statement and $60,000 would be included in ending inventory on the balance sheet.)

> **TIP:** Depletion for the units extracted during the period is recorded by a debit to Inventory and a credit to the natural resource account or to an Accumulated Depletion account (a contra asset account). The depletion pertaining to the units sold during the period is debited to Cost of Goods Sold and credited to Inventory. The depletion pertaining to the units sold during the period is debited to Cost of Goods Sold and credited to Inventory.

ILLUSTRATION 11-1
ACCOUNTING FOR IMPAIRMENTS (L.O. 5)

A summary of the key concepts in accounting for impairments is presented below:

A **recoverability test** is used to determine whether an impairment has occurred: If the sum of the expected future net undiscounted cash flows (from the use of the asset and its eventual disposition) is less than the carrying amount of the asset, the asset has been impaired.

If the recoverability test indicates that an impairment has occurred, a loss is computed. The impairment loss is the amount by which the carrying amount of the asset exceeds its fair value. The fair value of an asset is measured by its market value (if an active market exists) or by the present value of expected future net cash flows (if an active market does not exist). If an asset is to be disposed of instead of held for use, the asset's net realizable value (fair value less cost to sell) is used as a measure of the net cash flows that will be received from this asset.

Subsequent to recognizing the loss from impairment, the following guidelines are to be followed:

1. If the asset is to be held for use, it will be depreciated based on the new cost basis.
2. If the asset is to be sold, no more depreciation is taken once the asset is no longer used.
3. Restoration of the impairment loss is not permitted for an asset which is held for use.
4. Restoration of the impairment loss is allowed for an asset held for sale. Because assets held for disposal will be recovered through sale rather than through use in operations, they are continually revalued. Each period they are reported at the lower of cost or net realizable value. Thus, an asset held for disposal can be written up or down in future periods, as long as the write-up does not produce a new carrying value greater than the carrying amount of the asset before an adjustment was made to reflect a decision to dispose of the asset.

> **TIP:** Losses or gains related to impaired assets should be reported as part of income from continuing operations. Thus, they are **not** classified as extraordinary items.

> **TIP:** International accounting standards permit write-ups for subsequent recoveries of impairments back up to the original amount before the impairment. U.S. GAAP prohibits those write-ups, except for assets to be disposed of.

ANALYSIS OF MULTIPLE-CHOICE TYPE QUESTIONS

QUESTION
1.   (L.O. 2) The term "depreciable cost," or "depreciable base," as it is used in accounting, refers to:
   a.   the total amount to be charged (debited) to expense over an asset's useful life.
   b.   cost of the asset less the related depreciation recorded to date.
   c.   the estimated market value of the asset at the end of its useful life.
   d.   the acquisition cost of the asset.

Approach and Explanation: Write down a definition of depreciable cost **before** you read any of the answer selections. **Depreciable cost** or **depreciable base** is the total amount of asset cost that can be expensed over the life of the asset; thus, it is original cost less estimated residual (salvage) value. Answer selection "b" describes the term book value. Answer selection "c" describes salvage value or residual value. Selection "d" represents the total cost of the asset. (Solution = a.)

QUESTION
2.   (L.O. 2) A machine is purchased by the Dunnagin Company for $18,000. Dunnagin pays $6,000 in cash and gives a note payable for $12,000 that is payable in installments over a four-year period. Dunnagin estimates that the machine could physically last for 12 years, even though Dunnagin expects to use it in its business for only 9 years. The period of time to be used by Dunnagin for depreciation purposes is:
   a.   4 years.
   b.   5 years.
   c.   9 years.
   d.   12 years.

Approach and Explanation: Think about the objective of the depreciation process—to allocate an asset's cost to the periods benefited. The asset should be depreciated over its useful life, which is the length of time the asset will be of service to the entity using it. (Solution = c.)

QUESTION
3.   (L.O. 3) A machine with an estimated service life of five years and an expected salvage value of $5,000 was purchased on January 1, 2014 for $50,000. The amount to be recorded for depreciation for 2014, 2015, and 2016, respectively, using the sum-of-the-years'-digits method will be:
   a. $20,000; $12,000; $7,200.
   b. $16,667; $13,333; $10,000.
   c. $15,000; $12,000; $9,000.
   d. $15,000; $8,000; $4,400.

Approach and Explanation: Write down the formula to compute SYD depreciation. Enter the data given and solve.

$$\frac{n\,(n+1)}{2} = \text{Sum of the Years} \qquad\qquad \frac{5\,(6)}{2} = 15$$

$$\frac{\text{\# of Years Life Remaining at Beginning of Asset Year}}{\text{Sum of the Years}} \times (\text{Cost} - \text{Salvage Value}) = \text{Depreciation for Full Asset Year}$$

2014: ($50,000 - $5,000) x 5/15 =	$ 15,000	
2015: ($50,000 - $5,000) x 4/15 =	$ 12,000	
2016: ($50,000 - $5,000) x 3/15 =	$ 9,000	(Solution = c.)

QUESTION

4. (L.O. 3) A machine with an estimated service life of five years and an expected salvage value of $5,000 was purchased on January 1, 2014, for $50,000. The amount to be recorded for depreciation for years 2014, 2015, and 2016, respectively, using the 200% declining-balance method will be:
   a. $20,000; $12,000; $7,200.
   b. $18,000; $10,800; $6,480.
   c. $16,667; $13,333; $10,000.
   d. $10,000; $8,000; $6,400.

Approach and Explanation: Write down the formula for the declining-balance method. Enter the data given and solve.

Book Value at Beginning of Year x Constant Percentage = Depreciation

Constant Percentage = 2 x (100% ÷ Life) = 2 x (100% ÷ 5) = 40%

2014: $50,000 x 40% =	$20,000
2015: ($50,000 - $20,000) x 40% =	$12,000
2016: ($50,000 - $20,000 - $12,000) x 40% =	$ 7,200

(Solution = a.)

QUESTION

5. (L.O. 3) Salvage (residual) value may or may not be used in computing depreciation expense in the early years of an asset's life. Net income is understated if, in the first year, estimated salvage value is **excluded** from the depreciation computation when using the:

	Units of Output Method	Sum-of-the-Years'-Digits Method
a.	Yes	Yes
b.	No	No
c.	No	Yes
d.	Yes	No

Approach and Explanation: Before looking at the methods addressed directly in the question, think about how salvage value affects the depreciation computation under various methods. In considering the common depreciation methods such as straight-line, activity methods, sum-of-the-years'-digits, and declining-balance methods, the declining-balance methods are the only methods that do not use the residual value in computing depreciation in the early years of the asset's life. However, the residual value may affect the computations with the declining-balance method in the latter years of the asset's life because the asset should not be depreciated below its residual value. The units-of-output method is an activity method. (Solution = a.)

QUESTION

6. (L.O. 3, 7) A machine was purchased for $8,000,000 on January 1, 2014. It has an estimated useful life of 8 years and a residual value of $800,000. Depreciation is being computed using the sum-of-the-years'-digits method. What amount should be shown for this machine, net of accumulated depreciation, in the company's December 31, 2015 balance sheet?
   a. $4,200,000
   b. $5,000,000
   c. $6,300,000
   d. $6,600,000

Approach and Explanation: Write down the formula to compute book value and the formula to compute

solve. Be careful that you don't get so involved with the computation for depreciation that you lose sight of the question—and that is, to compute the book value of the equipment. It would be helpful to underline the middle of the last sentence of the stem of the question in order to keep your focus on what is being asked.

Cost - Accumulated Depreciation = Book Value

$$\frac{\text{No. of Years Remaining Life}}{\text{Sum of the Years}} \times (\text{Cost} - \text{Salvage Value}) = \text{Depreciation Charge}$$

$$\frac{n\ (n\ +\ 1)}{2} = \text{Sum of the Years} \qquad\qquad \frac{8\ (8\ +\ 1)}{2} = 36$$

8/36 x ($8,000,000 - $800,000) = $1,600,000 depreciation for 2014.
7/36 x ($8,000,000 - $800,000) = $1,400,000 depreciation for 2015.

Depreciation for 2014	$ 1,600,000
Depreciation for 2015	1,400,000
Accumulated depreciation at 12/31/15	$ 3,000,000

Cost	$ 8,000,000
Accumulated depreciation	(3,000,000)
Book value at 12/31/15	$ 5,000,000 (Solution = b.)

QUESTION

7. (L.O. 3, 4) Tammy Corporation purchased a machine on July 1, 2014 for $900,000. The machine has an estimated life of five years and a salvage value of $120,000. The machine is being depreciated by the 150% declining-balance method. What amount of depreciation should be recorded for the year ended December 31, 2015?
    a. $229,500
    b. $198,900
    c. $189,000
    d. $163,800

Approach and Explanation: Write down the formula to use for the declining-balance approach. (Notice the facts indicate there is a partial period for the first year (2014) and the question asks for the depreciation for the 2015 reporting period.) Compute the rate that is 150% of the straight-line rate. Apply the formula to the facts given. Remember that salvage value is not used with this method in computing depreciation in the early years of the asset's life.

Constant Percentage x Book Value at Beginning of the Year = Depreciation

$$\frac{100\%}{\text{Life}} = \frac{100\%}{5\ \text{years}} = 20\% \qquad 20\% \times 150\% = 30\% \text{ constant percentage}$$

30% x $900,000 = $270,000 First year of life
30% x (900,000 - $270,000) = $189,000 Second year of life
   1/2 x $270,000 = $135,000 for 2014
   (1/2 x $270,000) + (1/2 x $189,000) = $229,500 for 2015
OR
   30% x ($900,000 - $135,000) = $229,500 for 2015   (Solution = a.)

QUESTION

8.   (L.O. 3, 4) A plant asset with a five-year estimated useful life and no salvage value is sold during the second year of the asset's life. How would the use of the straight-line method of depreciation instead of an accelerated depreciation method affect the amount of gain or loss on the sale of the plant asset?

	Gain	Loss
a.	Increase	Decrease
b.	Decrease	Increase
c.	No Effect	Increase
d.	No Effect	No Effect

Approach and Explanation: An accelerated method would result in more accumulated depreciation and, therefore, a lower book value. In contrast, the straight-line method results in less accumulated depreciation and a higher book value. This means a lower gain or a higher loss is computed if the asset is sold and the straight-line method is in use. One way you can prove this to yourself is to make up a set of facts (cost, service life, accelerated method to use) and assume the asset is sold for a given amount at the end of the second year. Compare that gain or loss with the gain or loss that would result if the straight-line method is used. (Solution = b.)

QUESTION

9.   (L.O. 4) Roberts Truck Rental uses the group depreciation method for its fleet of trucks. When it retires one of its trucks and receives cash from a salvage company, the carrying value of property, plant, and equipment will be decreased by the:

   a.   original cost of the truck.
   b.   original cost of the truck less the cash proceeds.
   c.   cash proceeds received.
   d.   cash proceeds received and original cost of the truck.

Approach and Explanation: Write down the journal entry to record the disposal of the truck and analyze its effect. Remember that no gain or loss is recorded on the disposal when the group or composite method is used.

Cash	....	Proceeds
Accumulated Depreciation	....	**Plug**
Truck	....	Original Cost

In analyzing the entry's net effect on the book value (carrying amount) of property, plant, and equipment we find the following: (1) The decrease in Truck will reduce PP&E by the truck's original cost. (2) The debit to Accumulated Depreciation will increase PP&E by the excess of the truck's original cost over the proceeds from disposal. (3) Therefore, the net effect is to decrease PP&E by the amount of the cash proceeds from the sale. (Solution = c.)

QUESTION

10.   (L.O. 4) Which of the following uses a straight-line depreciation calculation?

	Group Depreciation	Composite Depreciation
a.	Yes	Yes
b.	Yes	No
c.	No	Yes
d.	No	No

Explanation: Both the group and composite depreciation methods use a straight-line method calculation. Both methods perform one calculation for a group of assets. The group method is used for a collection of similar assets; whereas, the composite method is used for a group of dissimilar assets. Each method involves the computation of a total depreciable cost for all the assets included in one asset account and of an estimated weighted-average useful life. (Solution = a.)

QUESTION

11.   (L.O. 4) The Schoen Company purchased a piece of equipment at the beginning of 2004 for $60,000. The equipment was being depreciated using the straight-line method over an estimated life of 20 years, with no salvage value. At the beginning of 2014, when the equipment had been in use for 10 years, the company paid $10,000 to overhaul the equipment. As a result of this improvement, the company estimates that the useful life of the equipment will be extended an additional five years. What should be the depreciation expense for this equipment in 2014?

   a. $2,000
   b. $2,667
   c. $3,000
   d. $1,867

Approach and Explanation: Write down the model or format to compute depreciation whenever there has been a change in the estimated service life and/or salvage value. Fill in the data of the case at hand and solve.

Cost	$ 60,000
Accumulated depreciation at 1/1/14	(30,000)^a
Book value (before overhaul) at 1/1/14	30,000
Additional expenditure capitalized (if any)	10,000
Revised book value (after overhaul)	40,000
Current estimate of salvage value	0
Remaining depreciable cost at 1/1/14	40,000
Remaining years of useful life at 1/1/14	÷ 15^b
Depreciation expense for 2014	$ 2,667
	(Solution = b.)

^{a}Cost	$ 60,000
Original estimate of salvage	(0)
Original depreciable cost	60,000
Original service life in years	÷ 20
Original depreciation per year	3,000
Number of years used	x 10
Accumulated depreciation at 1/1/14	$ 30,000

^{b}Original estimate of life in years	20
Number of years used	(10)
Additional years	5
Remaining years of useful life at 1/1/14	15

TIP:	Be careful when computing the length of time between two dates. The length of time between the beginning of 2004 and the beginning of 2014 is 10 years; whereas, the length of time between the end of 2004 and the beginning of 2014 is nine years. It is a common mistake to deduct one year from the other (2014 - 2004 = 10 years). As you can see from the foregoing, that will not always work. It is wise to write down the years that fall between the two dates and then count those years on your list. For example, the length of time between the end of 2011 and the beginning of 2014 is two years and is determined as follows:	
	2012	1
	2013	2

QUESTION

12.   (L.O. 5) As the result of certain changes in circumstances indicating that the carrying amount of plant assets may not be recoverable, Timberlake Company reviewed the assets at the end of 2014 for impairment. The company estimates that it will receive net future cash inflows of $85,000 (undiscounted) as a result of continuing to hold and use these assets. The fair value of the assets at December 31, 2014 is estimated to be $75,000. The assets were acquired two years ago at a cost of $500,000 and have been depreciated using the straight-line method and a five-year service life. The loss from impairment to be reported at the end of 2014 is:

    a. $0.
    b. $215,000.
    c. $225,000.
    d. $300,000.

Explanation: The carrying amount of the asset at the end of 2014 is $300,000 [$500,000 cost less (2 years X $500,000 X 20%)], but the recoverable amount is only $85,000. Thus, the test for recognition of an impairment loss has been met according to GAAP. The impairment loss is measured by the excess of the carrying amount ($300,000) over the fair value ($75,000). Therefore, Timberlake should recognize a loss of $225,000 ($300,000 - $75,000 = $225,000). (Solution = c.)

QUESTION

13.   (L.O. 7) The book value of a plant asset is:

    a.   the fair market value of the asset at a balance sheet date.
    b.   the asset's acquisition cost less the total related depreciation recorded to date.
    c.   equal to the balance of the related accumulated depreciation account.
    d.   the assessed value of the asset for property tax purposes.

Approach and Explanation: Write down the definition for the term book value: **book value** is the asset's original cost (acquisition cost) less accumulated depreciation. Look for the answer selection that agrees with your definition. (Solution = b.)

QUESTION

14.   (L.O. 7) The rate of return on assets (ROA) can be computed by which of the following computations?

1. $\dfrac{\text{Net income}}{\text{Net sales}}$

2. $\dfrac{\text{Net sales}}{\text{Average total assets}}$

3.   Profit margin on sales x Asset turnover

4. $\dfrac{\text{Net income}}{\text{Average total assets}}$

    a.   Formula 1.
    b.   Formula 2.
    c.   Formula 3.
    d.   Formula 4.
    e.   Formula 3 or 4.

Explanation: Formula 1 above measures the rate of return on sales (**profit margin on sales ratio**). Formula 2 computes the **asset turnover ratio**. Formula 3 is one of two ways to compute the **rate of return on total assets**; Formula 4 is the second of two ways to compute the **rate of return on total assets.** (Solution = e.)

IFRS Insights

* GAAP adheres to many of the same principles of IFRS in the accounting for property, plant, and equipment. Major differences relate to use of component depreciation, impairments, and revaluations.

* The definition of property, plant, and equipment is essentially the same under GAAP and IFRS.

* Under both GAAP and IFRS, changes in depreciation method and changes in useful life are treated in current and future periods. Prior periods are **not** affected.

* The accounting for plant asset disposals is the same under GAAP and IFRS.

* The accounting for the initial costs to acquire natural resources is similar under GAAP and IFRS.

* Under both GAAP and IFRS, interest costs incurred during construction must be capitalized. Recently, IFRS converged to GAAP.

* The accounting for exchanges of nonmonetary assets has recently converged between IFRS and GAAP. GAAP now requires that gains on exchanges of nonmonetary assets be recognized if the exchange has commercial substance .This is the same framework used in IFRS.

* IFRS also views depreciation as allocation of cost over an asset's life. GAAP permits the same depreciation methods (straight-line, diminishing-balance, units-of-production) as IFRS.

* IFRS requires component depreciation. Under GAAP, component depreciation is permitted but is rarely used.

* Under IFRS, companies can use either the historical cost model or the revaluation model. GAAP does **not** permit revaluations of property, plant, and equipment or mineral resources.

* In testing for impairments of long-lived assets, GAAP uses a two-step model to test for impairments. As long as future undiscounted cash flows exceed the carrying amount of the asset, no impairment is recorded. The IFRS impairment test is stricter. However, unlike GAAP, reversals of impairment losses are permitted. The amount of the recovery of the loss is limited to the carrying amount that would result if the impairment had not occurred. That is, any loss recovery resulting in a carrying value for the asset that exceeds its historical cost is **not** permitted.

TRUE/FALSE (Circle the correct answer for each).

T F 1. Interest costs incurred during construction must be capitalized for both GAAP and IFRS.

T F 2. The accounting for plant asset disposals is the same under GAAP and IFRS.

T F 3. In accounting for an exchange of nonmonetary assets, neither GAAP nor IFRS permits a gain to be recognized.

T F 4. IFRS requires component depreciation. Component depreciation is prohibited by GAAP.

T F 5. Reversals of impairment losses for assets to be held for use are permitted by IFRS and prohibited by GAAP.

Solutions:

1.	T	4.	F
2.	T	5.	T
3.	F		

CHAPTER 12

INTANGIBLE ASSETS

OVERVIEW

The balance sheet classification for intangible assets is used to report assets which lack physical existence and are not financial instruments. For instance (1) bank deposits and accounts receivable both are intangible by a legal definition but are financial instruments and are properly classified as current assets for accounting purposes, and (2) investment in stock (or bonds) is intangible in nature but is a financial instrument and should be classified as either a current asset or a long-term investment for accounting purposes. Assets such as patents, trademarks, copyrights, franchises, trade names, subscription lists, licenses, and goodwill are intangible in nature and are classified in the Intangible Assets section of a balance sheet. Intangible assets derive their value from the rights and privileges granted to the company using the assets and are discussed in this chapter.

SUMMARY OF LEARNING OBJECTIVES

1. **Describe the characteristics of intangible assets.** Intangible assets have two main characteristics: (1) They lack physical existence, and (2) they are not financial instruments. In most cases, intangible assets provide services over a period of years so they are normally classified as long-term assets.

2. **Identify the costs to include in the initial valuation of intangible assets.** Intangibles are recorded at cost. Cost includes all acquisition costs and expenditures necessary to make the intangible asset ready for its intended use. If intangibles are acquired in exchange for stock or other assets, the cost of the intangible is the fair value of the consideration given or the fair value of the intangible received, whichever is more clearly evident. When a company buys several intangibles, or a combination of intangibles and tangibles, in a "basket purchase," it should allocate the cost on the basis of relative fair values.

3. **Explain the procedure for amortizing intangible assets.** Intangibles have either a limited useful life or an indefinite useful life. Companies amortize limited-life intangible assets. They do not amortize indefinite life intangible assets. Limited-life intangibles should be amortized by systematic charges to expense over their useful life. The useful life should reflect the period over which these assets will contribute to cash flows. The amount to report for amortization expense should reflect the pattern in which a company consumes or uses up the asset, if it can reliably determine that pattern. Otherwise use a straight-line approach.

4. **Describe the types of intangible assets.** Major types of intangibles are: (1) *marketing-related intangibles,* used in the marketing or promotion of products or services; (2) *customer-related intangibles,* resulting from interactions with outside parties; (3) *artistic-related intangibles,* giving ownership rights to such items as plays and literary works; (4) *contract-related intangibles,* representing the value of rights that arise from contractual arrangements; (5) *technology-related intangibles,* relating to innovations or technological advances; and (6) *goodwill,* arising from business combinations.

5. **Explain the accounting issues for recording goodwill.** Unlike receivables, inventories, and patents that a company can sell or exchange individually in the marketplace, goodwill can be identified only with the business as a whole. Goodwill is a "going-concern" valuation and is recorded only when an entire business is purchased. A company should not capitalize (record in

no relationship to the costs incurred in the development of that goodwill. Goodwill may exist even in the absence of specific costs to develop it. Costs to maintain and restore goodwill are **not** capitalized. To record goodwill, a company compares the fair value of the net tangible and identifiable intangible assets with the purchase price of the acquired business. The difference is considered goodwill. Goodwill is the residual. Goodwill is often identified on the balance sheet as the excess of cost over the fair value of the net assets acquired.

6.   **Explain the accounting issues related to intangible-asset impairments.** Impairment of a long-lived asset occurs when the carrying amount of the asset is not recoverable. Companies use a recoverability test and a fair value test to determine impairments for limited-life intangible assets. They use only a fair value test for indefinite-life intangibles. Goodwill impairments require a two-step process: First, test the fair value of the reporting unit, then do the fair value test on implied goodwill.

7.   **Identify the conceptual issues related to research and development costs.** R & D costs are not in themselves intangible assets, but research and development activities frequently result in the development of something a company patents or copyrights. The difficulties in accounting for R & D expenditures are: (1) identifying the costs associated with particular activities, projects, or achievements, and (2) determining the magnitude of the future benefits and length of time over which a company may realize such benefits. Because of these latter uncertainties, companies are required to expense all research and development costs when incurred.

8.   **Describe the accounting for research and development costs and other similar costs.** The costs associated with R & D activities and the accounting treatment accorded them are as follows: (1) **Materials, equipment, and facilities:** Expense the entire costs, unless the items have alternative future uses (in R & D activities or otherwise), then carry materials as inventory (and allocate to R & D expense as consumed) and capitalize equipment and facilities (and depreciate as used). (2) **Personnel:** Salaries, wages, and other related costs of personnel engaged in R & D should be expensed as incurred. (3) **Purchased intangibles:** Expense the entire cost, unless the items have alternative future uses, then capitalize and amortize. (4) **Contract services:** The costs of services performed by others in connection with the reporting company's R & D should be expensed as incurred. (5) **Indirect costs:** A reasonable allocation of indirect costs (except for general and administrative costs, which must be related to be included) are included in R & D costs and expensed. Many costs have characteristics similar to R & D costs. Examples are start-up costs, initial operating losses, and advertising costs. For the most part, these costs are expensed as incurred, similar to the accounting for R & D costs.

9.   **Indicate the presentation of intangible assets and related items.** On the balance sheet all intangible assets other than goodwill can be reported as a single separate item. Contra accounts are not normally shown separately for intangibles. If goodwill is present, it should be reported as a separate item. On the income statement, companies should report amortization expense and impairment losses for intangible assets as part of continuing operations. Goodwill impairment losses should be presented as a separate line item in the continuing operations section, unless the goodwill impairment is associated with a discontinued operation. The notes to the financial statements have additional detailed information. Financial statements must disclose the total R & D costs charged to expense each period for which an income statement is presented.

TIPS ON CHAPTER TOPICS

TIP:	A corporation's intangible items such as quality of management, customer loyalty, information infrastructure, trade secrets, knowledge, intellectual capital, and computer programming know-how often provide more value to a corporation than its "hard" assets (like buildings and equipment), and yet they are normally not reported on the company's balance sheet. These "soft" assets are all part of goodwill if and when they are purchased by another corporation as a part of the whole business in a business combination.
TIP:	The costs incurred to create intangibles are generally expensed as incurred. The only internal costs capitalized are direct costs incurred in obtaining the intangible, such as legal costs. Thus, even though a company may incur substantial research and development costs to create a product for which they obtain a patent, these costs are expensed. Only the legal costs to obtain the patent, the fees charged by the government for obtaining the patent, and any other direct costs of obtaining the patent are capitalized and charged to the Patent account.
TIP:	The systematic allocation of the cost of intangible assets to expense over the periods benefited is called **amortization.** Usually the straight-line method is employed. Each intangible with a limited life should be amortized over its useful life. The greater the uncertainty regarding an asset's useful life, the shorter is the amortization period. If an intangible becomes impaired or worthless, the asset should be written down or written off immediately to expense (or loss).
TIP:	When an intangible asset is amortized, the charge (debit) should be reported as an expense and the credit is made to the appropriate asset account. A separate accumulated amortization account may be used but usually the asset account is credited directly.
TIP:	In the event that the estimated life of a limited-life intangible asset is revised, the remaining carrying amount should be amortized over the remaining useful life.
TIP:	If no legal, regulatory, contractual, competitive, or other factors limit the useful life of an intangible asset, a company considers its useful life to be indefinite. **Indefinite** means that there is no foreseeable limit on the period of time over which the asset is expected to provide cash flows.
TIP:	Research and development (R & D) costs are to be expensed in the period incurred. The FASB established this guideline after a study revealed that very few R & D projects ever culminate in a successfully marketed product. When great uncertainty exists, a conservative approach indicates that we choose the alternative with the **least** favorable effect on net income and on assets.
TIP:	To record goodwill when a business is acquired, the total fair market value of the net tangible and identifiable intangible assets is compared with the purchase price of the acquired business. The difference is considered goodwill, which is why goodwill is sometimes referred to as a "master valuation" account. Goodwill is the residual: the excess of cost over fair value of the identifiable net assets acquired.
TIP:	A manufacturing company has a patent on a manufacturing process and another patent on the finished product it is manufacturing. The periodic amortization of the patents will be classified as a cost of manufacturing and will become a part of the cost of the finished goods inventory. At the point of sale of the product, the cost of the product sold becomes cost of goods sold expense.

CASE 12-1

Purpose: (L.O. 1, 2, 3, 4)   This case will review the six major categories of intangible assets and will discuss the guidelines for determining the cost of an intangible asset.

A classified balance sheet will report a company's current assets followed by long-term investments, property, plant and equipment, and intangible assets.

Required:
(a)   Describe the two main characteristics of an asset to be classified as an intangible asset on the balance sheet.
(b)   List and describe the six major categories of intangible assets. Give examples of each.
(c)   Explain how the cost of an intangible asset is determined.
(d)   Explain how to determine whether an intangible asset is to be amortized or not amortized.

Solution to Case 12-1

(a)   Intangible assets have two main characteristics which are:
1.   **They lack physical existence.** Unlike tangible assets such as property, plant, and equipment, intangible assets derive their value from the rights and privileges granted to the company using them.
2.   **They are not a financial instrument.** Assets such as bank deposits, accounts receivable, and long-term investments in bonds and stocks lack physical substance, so they are intangible by nature; however, they are not classified as intangible assets for accounting purposes. These assets are financial instruments and derive their value from the right (claim) to receive cash or cash equivalents in the future.

(b)   There are many different types of intangibles, and they are often classified into the following six major categories.
1.   **Marketing-related intangible assets** are those assets primarily used in the marketing or promotion of products or services. Examples are trademarks or trade names, newsprint mastheads, Internet domain names, and noncompetition agreements.

A **trademark** or **trade name** is a word, phrase, or symbol that distinguishes or identifies a particular enterprise or product. Under common law, the right to use a trademark or trade name, whether it is registered or not, rests exclusively with the original user as long as the original user continues to use it. Registration with the U.S. Patent and Trademark Office provides legal protection for a number of renewals for periods of ten years each; therefore, you may properly consider the trademark or trade name to have an indefinite life (therefore, its cost is not amortized).

2.   **Customer-related intangible assets** occur as a result of interactions with outside parties.   Examples are customer lists, order or production backlogs, and both contractual and noncontractual customer relationships.

3.   **Artistic-related intangible assets** involve ownership rights to plays, literary works, musical works, pictures, photographs, and video and audiovisual material. These ownership rights are protected by copyrights.

A **copyright** is a federally granted right that all authors, painters, musicians, sculptors, and other artists have in their creations and expressions. A copyright is granted for the life of the creator plus 70 years. It gives the owner, or heirs, the exclusive right to reproduce and sell an artistic or published work. Copyrights are not renewable; thus they have a limited life and must be amortized.

4. **Contract-related intangible assets** represent the value of rights that arise from contractual arrangements. Examples are franchise and licensing agreements, construction permits, broadcast rights, and service or supply contracts.

   A **franchise** is a contractual arrangement under which the franchisor grants the franchisee the right to sell certain products or services, to use certain trademarks or trade names, or to perform certain functions, usually within a designated geographical area.

   Another type of franchise is the arrangement commonly entered into by a municipality (or other governmental body) and a business enterprise that uses public property. In such cases, a privately owned enterprise is permitted to use public property in performing its services. Examples are the use of public land for telephone or electric lines, the use of public waterways for a ferry service, or the use of the airwaves for radio or TV broadcasting. Such operating rights, obtained through agreement with governmental units or agencies, are frequently referred to as **licenses** or **permits.**

5. **Technology-related intangible assets** relate to innovations or technological advances. Examples are patented technology and trade secrets. Patents are granted by the U.S. Patent and Trademark Office. The two principal kinds of patents are **product patents** (which cover actual physical products) and **process patents** (which govern the process by which products are made). A **patent** gives the holder exclusive right to use, manufacture, and sell a product or process for a period of **20 years** without interference or infringement by others.

6. **Goodwill** is an excess of cost over the fair value of net identifiable assets acquired in a business combination. The cost (purchase price) of an acquired business is assigned where possible to the identifiable tangible and identifiable intangible net assets; the remainder is recorded in an unidentifiable intangible asset account called **Goodwill.** The only way goodwill can be sold is to sell the business. Goodwill acquired in a business combination is considered to have an indefinite life and therefore should **not** be amortized.

(c) The guidelines used in determining the cost of an intangible asset are similar to those you have already learned for determining the cost of inventory and property, plant, and equipment items. The cost of an intangible asset includes all costs of acquisition and expenditures necessary to make the intangible asset ready for its intended use—for example, purchase price, legal fees, and other incidental costs. The cost of the intangible is measured by the fair market value (cash equivalent value) of the consideration given or by the fair market value of the intangible asset received, whichever is more clearly evident. When several intangibles, or a combination of intangibles and tangibles are bought in a "basket purchase," the total cost should be allocated to the individual items on the basis of their fair market values or on the basis of the relative sales values of the items. Thus, essentially the accounting treatment for purchased intangibles closely parallels that followed for purchased tangible assets.

TIP:	If a patent or trademark (or trade name) is acquired from another entity, its capitalization cost is the purchase price. If the product for which a patent is obtained is developed by the enterprise itself or if a trademark or trade name is developed internally, the capitalizable cost includes attorney fees, registration fees, consulting fees, design costs (for the trademark or trade name); successful legal defense costs, and other expenditures directly related to securing it (excluding research and development costs). When the total cost of a trademark, trade name, patent or any other intangible is insignificant (immaterial), it can be expensed rather than capitalized.
TIP:	Legal fees and other costs incurred in successfully defending a patent lawsuit are debited to Patents, an asset account, because such a suit establishes the legal rights of the holder of the patent. Such costs should be amortized along with acquisition cost over the remaining useful life of the patent.

(d)   An intangible asset has either a limited (finite) useful life or an indefinite useful life. An intangible asset with a limited life is amortized; an intangible asset with an indefinite life is **not** amortized. Limited-life intangibles should be amortized by systematic charges to expense over their useful lives. The useful life of an intangible asset should reflect the periods over which the assets will contribute to cash flows.

TIP:	**Indefinite** means that there is no foreseeable limit on the period of time over which the intangible asset is expected to provide cash flows.
TIP:	If the estimate of the useful life of an intangible asset changes, the remaining carrying amount should be amortized over the remaining useful life.
TIP:	The life of a trademark or trade name is generally indefinite; therefore, its cost is **not** amortized.
TIP:	The useful life of a patent or copyright is often less than its legal life. The costs of the patent or copyright should be allocated to the years in which the benefits are expected to be received.
TIP:	Franchises and licenses may be for a definite period of time, for an indefinite period of time, or perpetual. The enterprise securing the franchise or license carries an intangible account titled Franchise or License on its books only when there are costs (such as a lump sum payment in advance or legal fees and other expenditures) that are identified with the acquisition of the operating right. The cost of a franchise (or license) with a limited life should be amortized as operating expense over the life of the franchise. A franchise with an indefinite life, or a perpetual franchise, should be carried at cost and not amortized. Annual payments made under a franchise agreement (sometimes called royalty payments) should be reported as operating expenses in the period in which they are incurred because they do not represent an asset since they do not relate to future rights to use property.

EXERCISE 12-1

Purpose: (L.O. 2, 8) This exercise will give you practice in identifying items that are to be classified as costs associated with various intangible assets.

The Redskins Corporation incurred the following costs during January 2014:
1. Attorneys' fees in connection with organization of the corporation
2. Meetings of incorporators, state filing fees, and other organization costs to begin corporation
3. Improvements to leased offices prior to occupancy
4. Costs to design and construct a prototype
5. Testing of prototype
6. Troubleshooting breakdowns during commercial production
7. Fees paid to engineers and lawyers to prepare patent application; patent granted January 22
8. Payment of six months rent on leased facilities
9. Stock issue costs
10. Payment for a copyright
11. Materials purchased for future research and development projects; materials have alternative future use
12. Costs to advertise new business
13. Costs for one-time activities to start a new operation.

Instructions
(a)   For each item above, identify what account should be debited to record the expenditure.
(b)   Indicate in which classification the related account will be reported in the financial statements.

Solution to Exercise 12-1

(a) Account Debited	(b) Classification
1. Organization Cost	Operating Expense
2. Organization Cost	Operating Expense
3. Leasehold Improvements	Property, Plant, and Equipment (or Intangible Asset)
4. Research and Development Expense	Operating Expense
5. Research and Development Expense	Operating Expense
6. Factory Overhead	Allocated to Inventory and Cost of Goods Sold
7. Patent	Intangible Asset
8. Prepaid Rent	Current Asset
9. Organization Cost	Operating Expense
10. Copyright	Intangible Asset
11. Raw Materials Inventory	Current Asset
12. Advertising Expense	Operating Expense
13. Start-up costs	Operating Expense

EXERCISE 12-2

Purpose: (L.O. 2, 3) This exercise will review the accounting guidelines related to three types of intangible assets—patent, franchise, and trademark.

Information concerning Linda Heckenmueller Corporation's intangible assets follows:

1.   Heckenmueller incurred $85,000 of experimental and development costs in its laboratory to develop a patent which was granted on January 2, 2014. Legal fees and other costs associated with registration of the patent totaled $16,000. Heckenmueller estimates that the useful life of the patent will be 8 years; the legal life of the patent is 20 years.

2.   On January 1, 2014, Heckenmueller signed an agreement to operate as a franchisee of Cluck-Cluck Fried Chicken, Inc. for an initial franchise fee of $117,400. The agreement provides that the fee is not refundable and no future services are required of the franchisor. The agreement also provides that 5% of the revenue from the franchise must be paid to the franchisor annually. Heckenmueller's revenue from the franchise for 2014 was $1,800,000. Heckenmueller estimates the useful life of the franchise to be 10 years.

3.   A trademark was purchased from Wolfe Company for $64,000 on July 1, 2011. Expenditures for successful litigation in defense of the trademark totaling $16,000 were paid on July 1, 2014. Heckenmueller estimates that the trademark will have an indefinite life.

Instructions

(a)   Prepare a schedule showing the intangible asset section of Heckenmueller's balance sheet at December 31, 2014. Show supporting computations in good form.

(b)   Prepare a schedule showing all expenses resulting from the transactions that would appear on Heckenmueller's income statement for the year ended December 31, 2014. Show supporting computations in good form.

(AICPA adapted)

Solution to Exercise 12-2

(a)
**Linda Heckenmueller Corporation
INTANGIBLE ASSETS
December 31, 2014**

Patent, net of accumulated amortization of $2,000 (Schedule 1)	$ 14,000
Franchise, net of accumulated amortization of $11,740 (Schedule 2)	105,660
Trademark (Schedule 3)	80,000
Total intangible assets	$ 199,660

Schedule 1: Patent

Cost of securing patent on 1/2/14	$ 16,000
2014 amortization ($16,000 x 1/8)	(2,000)
Cost of patent, net of amortization	$ 14,000

Schedule 2: Franchise

Cost of franchise on 1/1/14	$ 117,400
2014 amortization ($117,400 x 1/10)	(11,740)
Cost of franchise, net of amortization	$ 105,660

Schedule 3: Trademark

Cost of trademark on 7/1/11	$ 64,000
Cost of successful legal defense on 7/1/14	16,000
Cost of trademark	$ 80,000

(b)
**Linda Heckenmueller Corporation
EXPENSES RESULTING FROM SELECTED INTANGIBLES TRANSACTIONS
For the Year Ended December 31, 2014**

Patent amortization (Schedule 1)	$ 2,000
Franchise amortization (Schedule 2)	11,740
Franchise royalty fee ($1,800,000 x 5%)	90,000
Total expenses	$103,740

TIP: The $85,000 of research and development costs incurred in developing the patent would have been expensed prior to 2014 in accordance with GAAP.

Approach: The ideal approach would be to prepare the journal entries associated with the facts given and post them to T-accounts to determine the balances to be reported on the income statement for the year ending December 31, 2014 and on the balance sheet at December 31, 2014. Under some circumstances (such as exam conditions), time may not permit these additional steps. You should at least think about and visualize the flow of the information through the accounts. This will greatly aid the successful completion of the schedules required.

Explanation:
1. Research and development costs are to be expensed in the period incurred. Thus, the $85,000 of experimental and development costs incurred in developing the patent would have been expensed prior to 2014. Legal fees and other costs associated with obtaining the patent should be matched with each of the eight years estimated to be benefited; therefore, the $16,000 of legal fees and registration costs should be capitalized and amortized.

2.   The franchise rights will benefit future periods. Therefore, the costs associated with obtaining those rights should be capitalized and amortized over future periods. The acquisition cost is determined by the cash given ($117,400). The fact that "the fee is not refundable and no future services are required of the franchisor" has no impact on how the franchisee accounts for the franchise. The provision in the agreement which calls for the franchisee to pay 5% of the annual revenue from the franchise to the franchisor does not initially require any accounting treatment; an expense accrues as revenues are earned from use of the franchise. The capitalized franchise costs are to be amortized over the useful period of 10 years.

3.   The purchase price of the trademark ($64,000) was capitalized in mid-2011 when the trademark was acquired. Expenditures of $16,000 for successful litigation in defense of the trademark rights are to be charged to the Trademark account because such a suit establishes the legal rights of the holder of the trademark (which benefits future periods). The cost of the trademark is not being amortized becasue the trademark is estimated to have an indefinite life.

EXERCISE 12-3

Purpose: (L.O. 5) This exercise will review the procedure for determining the recorded value for purchased goodwill.

Sharon Gilkey, owner of Montana Designs, is negotiating with Chris Buffet for the purchase of Hospitality Galleries. The condensed balance sheet of Hospitality is given in abbreviated form below.

Hospitality Galleries
Balance Sheet
As of December 31, 2013

Assets		Liabilities and Stockholders' Equity		
Cash	$150,000	Accounts payable		$ 75,000
Land	100,000	Long-term notes payable		450,000
Building (net)	300,000	Total liabilities		525,000
Equipment (net)	275,000	Common stock	$300,000	
Copyright (net)	40,000	Retained earnings	40,000	340,000
Total assets	$865,000	Total liabilities and		
		stockholders' equity		$865,000

Sharon and Chris agree that:
1.   The fair value of the land exceeds its book value by $70,000.
2.   The fair value of the equipment is less than its book value by $15,000.

Chris agrees to sell Hospitality Galleries for $530,000.

Instructions
(a)   Prepare the entry to record the purchase of the gallery on Sharon's books.
(b)   Prepare the entry to record the amortization of goodwill for 2014.

Solution to Exercise 12-3

(a) Journal Entry:

Cash	150,000	
Land	170,000	
Building	300,000	
Equipment	260,000	
Copyright	40,000	
Goodwill	135,000	
Accounts Payable		75,000
Long-term Note Payable		450,000
Cash		530,000

Approach and Explanation: Goodwill is the excess of the purchase price ($530,000) over the fair market value of the net identifiable assets.   Net assets equal assets minus liabilities. Identifiable assets include all tangible and intangible assets other than goodwill.   Thus, to compute goodwill; sum the fair values of the assets being conveyed, deduct the fair value of the liabilities being assumed, and compare the fair value of the net identifiable assets with the purchase price. The fair value of an asset is assumed to be equal to its book value unless the parties agree otherwise.

Computation:

Cash	$150,000
Land	170,000
Building, net	300,000
Equipment, net	260,000
Copyright, net	40,000
Accounts payable	(75,000)
Long-term note payable	(450,000)
Fair market value of net identifiable assets	$395,000
Purchase price	530,000
Value assigned to goodwill	$135,000

(b) There is no journal entry to record the amortization of goodwill for 2014. Goodwill acquired in the acquisition of a business is considered to have an indefinite life; therefore, the goodwill should **not** be amortized.

TIP: In a few cases (e.g. a forced liquidation or distressed sale due to the death of a company founder), the purchaser in a business combination pays **less than** the fair value of the identifiable net assets. That is, assets are worth more if sold individually than as a total package. Such a situation is referred to as a **bargain purchase** and the excess amount of fair value of identifiable net assets over purchase price is recorded as a gain (**not** extraordinary) by the purchaser.

ILLUSTRATION 12-2
ACCOUNTING FOR IMPAIRMENTS OF PROPERTY, PLANT AND EQUIPMENT AND LIMITED LIFE INTANGIBLES (L.O. 6)

A summary of the key concepts in accounting for impairments is presented below:

A **recoverability test** is used to determine whether an impairment has occurred: If the sum of the expected future net undiscounted cash flows (from the use of the asset and its eventual disposition) is less than the carrying amount of the asset, the asset has been impaired.

If the recoverability test indicates that an impairment has occurred, a loss is computed. The **impairment loss** is the amount by which the carrying amount of the asset exceeds its fair value. The fair value of an asset is measured by its market value (if an active market exists) or by the present value of expected future net cash flows (if an active market does not exist). If an asset is to be disposed of instead of held for use, the asset's net realizable value (fair value less cost to sell) is used as a measure of the net cash flows that will be received from this asset.

Subsequent to recognizing the loss from impairment, the following guidelines are to be followed:
1. If the asset is to be held for use, it will be depreciated based on the new cost basis.
2. If the asset is to be sold, no more depreciation is taken once the asset is no longer used.
3. Restoration of the impairment loss is not permitted for an asset which is held for use.
4. Restoration of the impairment loss is allowed for an asset held for sale. Because assets held for disposal will be recovered through sale rather than through use in operations, they are continually revalued. Each period they are reported at the lower of cost or net realizable value. Thus, an asset held for disposal can be written up or down in future periods, as long as the write-up does not produce a new carrying value greater than the carrying amount of the asset before an adjustment was made to reflect a decision to dispose of the asset.

TIP: Losses or gains related to impaired assets should be reported as part of income from continuing operations (generally in the "other expenses and losses" section). Thus, they are **not** classified as extraordinary items.

TIP: The impairment rule for goodwill is a two-step process. First, the fair value of the reporting unit should be compared to its carrying amount including goodwill. If the fair value of the reporting unit is greater than the carrying amount, goodwill is considered not to be impaired. However, if the fair value of the reporting unit is less than the carrying amount of the net assets, then a second step must be performed to determine whether impairment has occurred. In the second step, the fair value of the goodwill must be determined (implied value of goodwill) and compared to its carrying amount to determine if an impairment has occurred.

TIP: Companies should test indefinite-life intangibles for impairment at least annually.

TIP: The impairment test for an indefinite-life asset other than goodwill is a fair value test. This test compares the fair value of the asset with the asset's carrying amount. If the fair value of the asset is less than the carrying amount, an impairment loss is recognized. Companies use this one-step test because many indefinite-life assets easily meet the recoverability test (because cash flows may extend many years into the future). As a result, the recoverability test is not used.

CASE 12-2

Purpose: (L.O. 6) This case will examine the accounting for impairments.

In some cases, the carrying amount of a long-lived asset (property, plant, and equipment or intangible asset) is not recoverable, and therefore a write-off is needed. This write-off is referred to as an impairment.

For each type of long-lived asset listed below, indicate the impairment test suitable for that kind of asset.

Type of Long-Lived Asset	Impairment Test
Property, plant, and equipment	_____
Limited-life intangible	_____
Indefinite-life intangible other than goodwill	_____
Goodwill	_____

Solution to Case 12-2

Type of Long-Lived Asset	Impairment Test
Property, plant, and equipment	Recoverability test, then fair value test
Limited-life intangible	Recoverability test, then fair value test
Indefinite-life intangible other than goodwill	Fair value test*
Goodwill	Fair value test on reporting unit, then fair value test on implied goodwill*

*An optional qualitative assessment may be performed to determine whether the fair value test needs to be performed.

EXERCISE 12-4

Purpose: (L.O. 6) This exercise will illustrate the accounting for impairment of an intangible asset with a limited-life.

The following information relates to a patent owned by Pulido Company:

Cost	$4,300,000
Carrying amount	2,100,000
Expected future net cash flow	1,900,000
Fair value	1,500,000

Instructions

(a) Prepare the journal entry (if any) to record the impairment of the asset at December 31, 2013, assuming Pulido will continue to use the asset in the future.

(b) Using the same assumption as part (a) above, prepare the journal entry to record amortization expense for 2014 assuming the asset has a remaining useful life of 4 years at the beginning of 2014.

(c) Using the same assumption as part (a) above, prepare the journal entry (if any) at December 31, 2014, assuming the fair value of the asset has increased to $2,400,000.

(d) Prepare the journal entry (if any) to record the impairment of the asset at December 31, 2013, assuming Pulido ceased using the patent at the end of 2013 and intends to dispose of the patent in the coming year. Pulido expects to incur a $12,000 cost of disposal.

(e) Using the same assumption as part (d) above, prepare the journal entry at December 31, 2014 for amortization for 2014, assuming the asset has not been sold at that time.

(f) Using the same assumption as part (d) above, prepare the journal entry at December 31, 2014 assuming the asset has not been sold at that time and the fair value of the asset has increased to $2,400,000.

(g) Indicate the income statement classification of the account, Loss on Impairment.

Solution to Exercise 12-4

(a)   Loss on Impairment.. 600,000
         Patent (or Accumulated Patent Amortization) 600,000

Approach and Explanation: Follow the guidelines in **Illustration 12-2:**

Recoverability test: The expected future net undiscounted cash flows from the use of the asset and its eventual disposition amount to $1,900,000 which is **less than** the carrying amount (book value) of the asset of $2,100,000; hence, the recoverability test indicates that an impairment has occurred.

Impairment loss: The impairment loss ($600,000) is the amount by which the carrying amount of the asset ($2,100,000) exceeds its fair value ($1,500,000).

(b)   Amortization of Patent Expense... 375,000
         Patent.. 375,000

Explanation: After an impairment is recognized, the reduced carrying amount of the patent is its new cost basis. The patent's new cost should be amortized over its remaining useful life (which may be shorter but not longer than its remaining legal life).

(c)   No journal entry is to be recorded at December 31, 2014 due to the increase in fair value of the patent. Restoration of a previously recognized impairment loss is not permitted when the asset is expected to be held and used by the company in the future.

(d)   Loss on Impairment.. 612,000
         Patent.. 612,000

Approach and Explanation: Follow the guidelines in **Illustration 12-2:**

Recoverability test: The expected future net undiscounted cash flows from the asset's expected disposition is measured by the asset's net realizable value (fair value less cost to sell) which is $1,500,000 less $12,000 equals $1,488,000. The expected future net cash flows of $1,488,000 is less than the carrying amount of the asset ($2,100,000); hence, the recoverability test indicates that an impairment has occurred.

Impairment loss: The impairment loss ($612,000) is the amount by which the carrying amount of the asset ($2,100,000) exceeds the asset's fair value ($1,500,000) reduced by the estimated disposal cost ($12,000).

(e)   There is no journal entry for amortization of the patent in 2014.

Explanation: No amortization is taken once an asset is no longer used in operations.

(f) Patent...	612,000	
Gain from Restoration of Impairment Loss.........		612,000

Explanation: Restoration of the impairment loss is allowed for an asset held for sale. An asset held for disposal can be written up or down in future periods, as long as the write-up does not produce a new carrying value greater than the carrying amount of the asset before an adjustment was made to reflect a decision to dispose of the asset.

(g)   Loss on Impairment is reported in the "other expense and loss" section of the income statement.

ILLUSTRATION 12-3
ACCOUNTING FOR R & D ACTIVITIES (L.O. 8)

To differentiate research and development costs from other similar costs, the FASB issued the following definitions:

> **Research** is planned search or critical investigation aimed at discovery of new knowledge with the hope that such knowledge will be useful in developing a new product or service ... or a new process or technique ... or in bringing about a significant improvement to an existing product or process.

> **Development** is the translation of research findings or other knowledge into a plan or design for a new product or process or for a significant improvement to an existing product or process whether intended for sale or use. It includes the conceptual formulation, design, and testing of product alternatives, construction of prototypes, and operation of pilot plants. It does not include routine or periodic alterations to existing products, production lines, manufacturing processes, and other on-going operations even though those alterations may represent improvements; it does not include market research or market testing activities.

Many costs have characteristics similar to those of research and development costs, for instance, costs of relocation and rearrangement of facilities, start-up costs for a new plant or new retail outlet, marketing research costs, promotion costs of a new product or service, and costs of training new personnel. To distinguish between R & D and those other similar costs, the following schedule provides (1) examples of activities that typically would be **included** in research and development, and (2) examples that typically would be **excluded** from research and development.

1. R & D Activities

(a) Laboratory research aimed at discovery of new knowledge.

(b) Searching for applications of new research findings.

(c) Conceptual formulation and design of possible product or process alternatives.

(d) Testing in search for or evaluation of product or process alternatives.

(e) Modification of the design of a product or process.

(f) Design, construction, and testing of preproduction prototypes and models.

(g) Design of tools, jigs, molds, and dies involving new technology.

(h) Design, construction, and operation of a pilot plant not useful for commercial production.

(i) Engineering activity required to advance the design of a product to the manufacturing stage.

2. Activities Not Considered R & D

(a) Engineering follow-through in an early phase of commercial production.

(b) Quality control during commercial production including routine testing.

(c) Trouble-shooting breakdowns during commercial production.

(d) Routine, on-going efforts to refine, enrich, or improve the qualities of an existing product.

(e) Adaptation of an existing capability to a particular requirement or customer's need.

(f) Periodic design changes to existing products.

(g) Routine design of tools, jigs, molds, and dies.

(h) Activity, including design and construction engineering related to the construction, relocation, rearrangement, or startup of facilities or equipment.

(i) Legal work on patent applications, sale, licensing, or litigation.

TIP: R & D activities do not include routine or periodic alterations to existing products, production lines, manufacturing processes, and other ongoing operations, even though these alterations may represent improvements. Routine ongoing efforts to refine, enrich, or improve the qualities of an existing product are not considered R & D activities.

TIP: Disclosure should be made in the financial statements (generally in the notes) of the total R & D costs charged to expense each period for which an income statement is presented.

The costs associated with R & D activities and the accounting treatment accorded them are as follows: (1) **Materials, equipment, and facilities:** Expense the entire costs, unless the items have alternative future uses (in R & D activities or otherwise), then carry materials as inventory (and allocate to R & D expense as consumed) and capitalize equipment and facilities (and depreciate as used). (2) **Personnel:** Salaries, wages, and other related costs of personnel engaged in R & D should be expensed as incurred. (3) **Purchased intangibles:** Recognize and measure acquisition cost at fair value. After initial recognition, account for in accordance with their nature (as either limited life or indefinite-life intangibles). (4) **Contract services:** The costs of services performed by others in connection with the reporting company's R & D should be expensed as incurred. (5) **Indirect costs:** A reasonable allocation of indirect costs (except for general and administrative costs, which must be related to be included) are included in R & D costs and expensed. Many costs have characteristics similar to R & D costs. Examples are start-up costs, initial operating losses, and advertising costs. For the most part, these costs are expensed as incurred, similar to the accounting for R & D costs.

EXERCISE 12-5

Purpose: (L.O. 7, 8) This exercise will give you practice in identifying activities that constitute R & D activities.

Listed below are four independent situations involving research and development costs:

1. During 2014 Bebe Co. incurred the following costs:

Research and development services performed by Way Co. for Bebe	$ 325,000
Testing for evaluation of new products	300,000
Laboratory research aimed at discovery of new knowledge	375,000
Research and development services performed by Bebe for Elway Co.	220,000

How much should Bebe report as research and development expense for the year ended December 31, 2014?

2. Holly Corp. incurred the following costs during the year ended December 31, 2014:

Design, construction, & testing of preproduction prototypes & models	$ 220,000
Routine, on-going efforts to refine, enrich, or otherwise improve upon the qualities of an existing product	250,000
Quality control during commercial production including routine testing of products	300,000
Laboratory research aimed at discovery of new knowledge	360,000
Conceptual formulation and design of possible product alternatives	100,000

What is the total amount to be classified and expensed as research and development for 2014?

3. Polanski Company incurred costs in 2014 as follows:

Equipment acquired for use in various R & D projects (current and future)	$ 890,000
Depreciation on the equipment above	135,000
Materials used in R & D	300,000
Compensation costs of personnel in R & D	400,000
Outside consulting fees for R & D work	150,000
Indirect costs appropriately allocated to R & D	260,000

What is the total amount of research and development expense that should be reported in Polanski's 2014 income statement?

4. Liverpool Inc. incurred the following costs during the year ended December 31, 2014:

Laboratory research aimed at discovery of new knowledge	$ 175,000
Routine design of tools, jigs, molds, and dies	60,000
Radical modification to the formulation of a chemical product	125,000
Research and development costs reimbursable under a contract to perform R & D for Johnathon King, Inc.	350,000
Testing for evaluation of new products	275,000

What is the total amount to be classified and expensed as research and development for 2014?

Instructions
Provide the correct answer to each of the four situations.

Solution to Exercise 12-5

1.
Research and development services performed by Way Co. for Bebe	$	325,000
Testing for evaluation of new products		300,000
Laboratory research aimed at discovery of new knowledge		375,000
Total R & D expense		$ 1,000,000

> **TIP:** R & D costs related to R & D activities conducted for other entities are classified as a receivable (because of the impending reimbursement).

2.
Design, construction & testing of preproduction prototypes & models	$ 220,000
Laboratory research aimed at discovery of new knowledge	360,000
Conceptual formulation & design of possible product alternatives	100,000
Total R & D expense	$ 680,000

3.
Depreciation on the equipment acquired for use in various R & D projects	$	135,000
Materials used in R & D		300,000
Compensation costs of personnel in R & D		400,000
Outside consulting fees for R & D work		150,000
Indirect costs appropriately allocated to R & D		260,000
Total R & D expense		$ 1,245,000

> **TIP:** Equipment, facilities, and purchased intangibles that have **alternative future uses** (in other R & D projects or otherwise) are to be **capitalized**; the **related depreciation and amortization are to be classified as R & D**.

4.
Laboratory research aimed at discovery of new knowledge	$ 175,000
Radical modification to the formulation of a chemical product	125,000
Testing for evaluation of new products	275,000
Total R & D expense	$ 575,000

Approach: Read the requirement of each situation before you begin detailed work on the first one. Notice that all four items deal with research and development costs. Therefore, review in your mind the definitions of the words "research" and "development." Recall what you can from the list of activities considered to be R & D. Think of why the items logically appear on the list. It is important to think about these items **before** you dig into the questions because details in the situations may mislead you. To minimize confusion, organize your thoughts and recall what you know about the subject before you begin to process the data at hand.

Explanation: Refer to **Illustration 12-3** for the definitions and examples of research and development activities.

CASE 12-3

Purpose: (L.O. 8) This case is designed to give you practice in differentiating expenditures which are classified as research and development costs and expenditures which are not included with R & D.

Instructions

Various types of expenditures are listed below. Indicate the accounting treatment appropriate for each type of expenditure listed.

Type of Expenditure	**Accounting Treatment**
1. Construction of long-range research facility for use in current and future projects (three story, 400,000-square-foot building).	
2. Acquisition of R & D equipment for use on current project only.	
3. Acquisition of machinery to be used on current and future R & D projects.	
4. Purchase of materials to be used on current and future R & D projects.	
5. Salaries of research staff designing new laser bone scanner.	
6. Research costs incurred under contract with another corporation and billable to that company monthly.	
7. Material, labor, and overhead costs of prototype laser scanner.	
8. Costs of testing prototype and design modifications.	
9. Legal fees to obtain patent on new laser scanner.	
10. Executive salaries.	
11. Cost of marketing to promote new laser scanner.	
12. Engineering costs incurred to advance the laser scanner to full production stage.	
13. Cost of successfully defending patent on laser scanner.	
14. Commissions to sales staff marketing new laser scanner.	

SOLUTION TO CASE 12-3

Type of Expenditure	Accounting Treatment
1. Construction of long-range research facility for use in current and future projects (three story, 400,000-square-foot building).	Capitalize and depreciate as R & D expense.
2. Acquisition of R & D equipment for use on current project only.	Expense immediately as R & D.
3. Acquisition of machinery to be used on current and future R & D projects.	Capitalize and depreciate as R & D expense.
4. Purchase of materials to be used on current and future R & D projects.	Inventory and allocate to R & D projects; expense as consumed.
5. Salaries of research staff designing new laser bone scanner.	Expense immediately as R & D.
6. Research costs incurred under contract with another corporation and billable to that company monthly.	Record as a receivable (reimbursable expenses).
7. Material, labor, and overhead costs of prototype laser scanner.	Expense immediately as R & D.
8. Costs of testing prototype and design modifications.	Expense immediately as R & D.
9. Legal fees to obtain patent on new laser scanner.	Capitalize as patent and amortize to overhead as part of cost of goods manufactured.
10. Executive salaries.	Expense as operating expense (general and administrative).
11. Cost of marketing to promote new laser scanner.	Expense as operating expense (selling).
12. Engineering costs incurred to advance the laser scanner to full production stage.	Expense immediately as R & D.
13. Cost of successfully defending patent on laser scanner.	Capitalize as patent and amortize to overhead as part of cost of goods manufactured.
14. Commissions to sales staff marketing new laser scanner.	Expense as operating expense (selling).

TIP: Refer to **Illustration 12-3** for an explanation of the types of costs associated with R & D activities and the accounting treatment accorded them.

TIP: Refer to **Item 6** above. Sometimes one enterprise conducts R & D activities for other entities under a contractual arrangement. In this case, the contract usually specifies that all direct costs, certain specific indirect costs, plus a profit element, should be reimbursed to the enterprise performing the R & D work. Because reimbursement is expected, such R & D costs should be recorded as a receivable. It is the company for whom the work has been performed that reports these costs as R & D and expenses them as incurred.

ANALYSIS OF MULTIPLE-CHOICE TYPE QUESTIONS

QUESTION

1. (L.O. 2) Innoventions Inc. acquired a patent from Whizkid Inc. on January 1, 2014, in exchange for $7,000 cash and an investment security that had been acquired in 2010. The following facts pertain:

Original cost of investment	$ 14,000
Carrying value of patent on books of Whizkid Inc.	4,500
Fair market value of the investment security on January 1, 2014	23,000

The cost of the patent to be recorded by Innoventions Inc. is:
   a. $7,000.
   b. $11,500.
   c. $21,000.
   d. $30,000.

Approach and Explanation: Recall the guideline for determining the cost of any intangible asset. The cost of an intangible asset includes all costs incurred to acquire the asset. The historical cost principle dictates that cost be measured by the fair market value (i.e., cash equivalent value) of the consideration given or by the fair market value of the consideration received, whichever is the more clearly evident. Innoventions Inc. gave $7,000 cash plus the investment security with a fair market value of $23,000 at the date of the exchange. The cost of the patent is, therefore, $30,000. (Solution = d.)

QUESTION

2. (L.O. 4) The adjusted trial balance of the Laventhal Corporation as of December 31, 2014 includes the following accounts:

Trademark	$ 30,000
Discount on bonds payable	37,500
Organization costs	12,500
Excess of cost over fair value of identifiable net assets of acquired business	175,000
Advertising costs (to promote goodwill)	20,000

What should be reported as total intangible assets on Laventhal's December 31, 2014 balance sheet?
   a. $205,000
   b. $230,000
   c. $237,500
   d. $275,000

Approach and Explanation: Identify the classification of each item listed. Sum the ones you identify as being intangible assets.

Trademark	$ 30,000
Excess of cost over fair value of identifiable net assets of acquired business	175,000
Total intangible assets	$ 205,000

Discount on bonds payable is to be classified as a contra liability. Organization costs are to be expensed as incurred. Advertising costs incurred are to be reported as an expense on the income statement. The costs to develop, maintain, or restore goodwill are **not** to be capitalized. Only the costs to acquire goodwill with a going business can be recorded as goodwill. The "excess of cost over fair value of net identifiable net assets of acquired business" is a technical term referring to goodwill. (Solution = a.)

QUESTION

3. (L.O. 3, 4) A patent with a remaining legal life of 12 years and an estimated useful life of 8 years was acquired for $288,000 by Bradley Corporation on January 2, 2010. In January 2014, Bradley paid $18,000 in legal fees in a successful defense of the patent. What should Bradley record as patent amortization for 2014?
    a. $24,000
    b. $36,000
    c. $38,250
    d. $40,500

Approach and Explanation: Analyze the Patent account. Use the data given to compute the amounts reflected therein and the resulting amortization for 2014.

Cost at beginning of 2010	$ 288,000	
Amortization for 2010-2013	(144,000)*	
Book value at beginning of 2014	144,000	
Legal fees capitalized	18,000	
Revised book value, beginning of 2014	162,000	
Remaining years of life	÷ 4	
Amortization for 2014	$ 40,500	(Solution = d.)
*Beginning of 2010, patent cost	$ 288,000	
Estimated years of service life	÷ 8	
Annual amortization for 2010-2013	36,000	
Number of years used	4	
Total amortization 2010-2013	$ 144,000	

QUESTION

4. (L.O. 3, 4) On January 1, 2014, Teeple Corporation acquired a patent for $30,000. Due to the quickly changing technology associated with the patent, Teeple is amortizing the cost of the patent over 5 years. What portion of the patent cost will Temple defer to years subsequent to 2014?
    a. $0
    b. $6,000
    c. $24,000
    d. $30,000

Explanation: $30,000 ÷ 5 yrs. = $6,000 amortization per year.
If $6,000 is amortized, then the amount to defer is computed as follows:

Total patent cost	$ 30,000	
Amount amortized in 2014	(6,000)	
Amount to defer to subsequent periods	$ 24,000	(Solution = c.)

> **TIP:**   Note the importance of reading the question carefully. An intermediate step—the computation of the $6,000 amortization amount for 2014—is one of the distracters. You should read the last sentence of the question stem first to understand the essence of the problem. It is wise to write down the essential computation to keep your focus:
> Total Patent Cost
> - Amount to Amortize in 2014
> = Amount to Defer

QUESTION

5. (L.O. 4) The legal life of a patent is:
    a.   17 years.
    b.   20 years.
    c.   40 years.
    d.   The life of the inventory plus 50 years.

Explanation: A patent offers its holder an exclusive right to use, manufacture, and sell a product or process over a period of 20 years without interference or infringement by others. It is not subject to renewal. (Solution = b.)

QUESTION

6.   (L.O. 4) The cost of permits and licenses are material to the entity for whom you are accounting. The cost of these items should be:
  a.   expensed in the period acquired.
  b.   expensed over the useful life of the items.
  c.   charged against paid-in capital.
  d.   capitalized but not amortized.

Explanation: Licenses and permits offer the holder certain rights. Like all other intangible assets, the cost of these items should be matched with the periods benefited. To comply with the expense recognition (matching) principle, the cost of an intangible asset is to be amortized over its useful life. (Solution = b.)

QUESTION

7.   (L.O. 2, 5) The costs of intangible assets which are internally created are typically:
  a.   capitalized but not amortized.
  b.   capitalized and amortized over a long period of time.
  c.   capitalized and amortized over a short period of time.
  d.   expensed as incurred.

Explanation: The following is helpful to keep in mind:

Type of Intangible	Manner Acquired Purchased	Internally Created	Amortization
Limited-life intangibles	Capitalize	Expense, except direct costs	Over useful life
Indefinite-life intangibles	Capitalize	Expense	Do not amortize

If you purchase a patent from an inventor or an owner, the cost of that patent is capitalized. If you develop (internally generate) a product yourself, the research and development costs related to the development of the product or idea that is subsequently patented must be expensed as incurred. However, other costs incurred in connection with securing a patent, as well as attorney's fees and other unrecovered costs of a successful legal suit to protect the patent, can be capitalized as a part of the patent cost. (Solution = d.)

QUESTION

8.   (L.O. 6) As the result of certain changes in circumstances indicating that the carrying amount of plant assets may not be recoverable, Timberlake Company reviewed the assets at the end of 2014 for impairment. The company estimates that it will receive net future cash inflows of $85,000 (undiscounted) as a result of continuing to hold and use these assets. The fair value of the assets at December 31, 2014 is estimated to be $75,000. The assets were acquired two years ago at a cost of $500,000 and have been depreciated using the straight-line method and a five-year service life. The loss from impairment to be reported at the end of 2014 is:
  a. $0.
  b. $215,000.
  c. $225,000.
  d. $300,000.

Explanation: The carrying amount of the asset at the end of 2014 is $300,000 [$500,000 cost less (2 years X $500,000 X 20%)], but the recoverable amount is only $85,000. Thus, the test for recognition of an impairment loss has been met. The impairment loss is measured by the excess of the carrying amount ($300,000) over the fair value ($75,000). Therefore, Timberlake should recognize a loss of $225,000 ($300,000 - $75,000 = $225,000). (Solution = c.)

QUESTION
9. (L.O. 6) The carrying amount of an intangible is:
    a.   the fair market value of the asset at a balance sheet date.
    b.   the asset's acquisition cost less the total related amortization recorded to date.
    c.   equal to the balance of the related accumulated amortization account.
    d.   the assessed value of the asset for intangible tax purposes.

Approach and Explanation: Write down the definition for the term book value: **book value** is the asset's original cost (acquisition cost) less accumulated amortization. Look for the answer selection that agrees with your definition. (Solution = b.)

QUESTION
10. (L.O. 6) Windsor Corporation is being organized in 2013 and will begin operations at the beginning of 2014. Prior to the start of operations, the following costs have been incurred in 2013:

Attorneys' fees for assistance in obtaining corporate charter and drafting related documents	$ 33,000
Meetings of incorporators	14,000
Improvements to leased office space prior to occupancy	48,000
Fees to promoters to help locate buyers for Windsor's common stock	21,000
	$116,000

Based on the above data, what amounts should be charged to the Organization Expense account in 2013?
    a. $21,000.
    b. $33,000.
    c. $68,000.
    d. $116,000.

Approach and Explanation: Before reading through the list of costs incurred, define "organization costs" and think of the most common examples. **Organization costs** are costs incurred in the formation of a corporation such as fees to promoters, legal fees, state fees of various sorts, and certain promotional expenditures. They are one type of startup costs and all startup costs are to be expensed in the period incurred. Windsor should charge the following to Organization Expense:

Attorneys' fees for incorporation	$ 33,000	
Meetings of incorporators	14,000	
Fees to promoters	21,000	
Total organization costs	$ 68,000	(Solution = c.)

TIP: The $48,000 of improvements to leased office space prior to occupancy should be recorded in the Leasehold Improvements account and depreciated (amortized) over future periods (the service life of the improvements or the remaining life of the lease, whichever is shorter).

QUESTION

11.   (L.O. 7) Motts Corporation purchased the following items at the beginning of 2014:

Materials to be used in R & D activities; these materials have alternative future uses and they remain unused at the end of 2014.	$ 50,000
Materials to be used in R & D activities; these materials do not have alternative future uses and $12,000 of them remain unused at the end of 2014	33,000
Equipment to be used in R & D activities; this equipment was used in one R & D project during 2014 and is expected to be used in other R & D projects to be undertaken over the next 5 years. It has no residual value. Motts normally uses the straight-line depreciation method for equipment.	100,000
Total	$ 183,000

Based on the above information, Motts should report R & D expenses for 2014 of:

a. $183,000.
b. $103,000.
c. $53,000.
d. $21,000.
e.   None of the above.

Approach and Explanation: Mentally review the proper accounting treatment for materials and equipment acquired for use in R & D activities. The cost of materials acquired for use in R & D activities should be expensed in the period acquired unless the items have alternative future uses (in R & D projects or otherwise); then they should be carried as inventory and allocated to R & D expense as used. The cost of equipment and facilities acquired for use in R & D activities should be expensed in the period acquired unless the items have alternative future uses (in R & D projects or otherwise); then they should be capitalized and depreciated as used (the resulting depreciation should be classified as R & D expense). Thus, Motts would have the following R & D expense for 2014: (Solution = c.)

Materials acquired, no future alternative use	$ 33,000
Depreciation on equipment used in R & D activities	
($100,000 ÷ 5 years)	20,000
Total R & D expense for 2014	$ 53,000

QUESTION

12.   (L.O. 7) In 2014, Barry Sanders Corporation incurred research and development costs as follows:

Equipment	$ 200,000
Personnel	300,000
Indirect costs	100,000
Total	$ 600,000

These costs relate to a product that will be marketed in 2015. It is estimated that these costs will be recouped by December 31, 2017. The equipment has no alternative future use. What is the amount of research and development costs that should be charged to income in 2014?

a. $0
b. $100,000
c. $400,000
d. $600,000

Explanation: All R & D costs are to be expensed in the period incurred. Equipment used in R & D activities that has alternative future use would be capitalized and depreciated. This equipment has no alternative use, so it is expensed immediately. A reasonable allocation of indirect costs should be included in R & D. Costs of personnel engaged in R & D activities are to be expensed in the period incurred. (Solution = d.)

QUESTION
13. (L.O. 8) The costs of organizing a corporation include legal fees, fees paid to the state of incorporation, fees paid to promoters, and the costs of meetings for organizing the promoters. These costs are said to benefit the corporation for the entity's entire life. These costs should be:
   a.   capitalized and never amortized.
   b.   capitalized and amortized over 40 years.
   c.   capitalized and amortized over 5 years.
   d.   expensed as incurred.

Explanation: Although the accounting profession recognizes that organization costs are incurred with the expectation that future revenues will occur or increased efficiencies will result, the determination of the amount and timing of future benefits is so difficult that a conservative approach is required. All start-up costs, which include organization costs, are to be expensed in the period incurred. The costs of issuing stock (such as the fees paid to underwriters in issuance of stock) are usually treated as a reduction of additional paid-in capital (see **Chapter 15**). (Solution = d.)

QUESTION
14. (L.O. 8) A development stage enterprise should use the same generally accepted accounting principles that apply to established operating enterprises for:

	Recognition of Revenue	Recognition of Expenses
a.	Yes	Yes
b.	No	No
c.	No	Yes
d.	Yes	No

Explanation: The FASB indicates that the accounting practices and reporting standards should be no different for an enterprise trying to establish a new business than they are for other enterprises. Thus, the "same generally accepted accounting principles that apply to established operating enterprises shall govern the recognition of revenue by a development stage enterprise (DSE) and shall determine whether a cost incurred by a DSE is to be charged to expense when incurred or is to be capitalized or deferred." This means that items constituting preoperating costs should be expensed unless the same costs would be deferred by an established business; the fact that the costs are incurred before the entity has any significant revenue earned is not by itself justification for deferral of such costs. Treating preoperating costs as expenses often results in the reporting of an operating loss in the year of start up of a new entity. (Solution = a.)

QUESTION
15. (L.O. 9) The total amount of patent cost amortized to date is usually:
   a.   shown in a separate Accumulated Patent Amortization account which is shown contra to the Patent account.
   b.   shown in the current income statement.
   c.   reflected as credits in the Patent account.
   d.   reflected as a contra property, plant and equipment item.

Explanation: In accounting for intangible assets, the amortization of an asset is usually credited directly to the intangible asset account rather than shown separately in a contra asset account. (Solution = c.)

IFRS Insights

- There are some significant differences between IFRS and GAAP in the accounting for both intangible assets and impairments.

- Like GAAP, under IFRS intangible assets (1) lack physical substance and (2) are not financial instruments. In addition, under IFRS an intangible asset is identifiable. To be identifiable, an intangible asset must either be separable from the company (can be sold or transferred) or it arises from a contractual or legal right from which economic benefits will flow to the company. Fair value is used as the measurement basis for intangible assets under IFRS, if it is more clearly evident.

- With issuance of a recent converged statement on business combinations, IFRS and GAAP are very similar for intangibles acquired in a business combination. That is, companies recognize an intangible asset separately from goodwill if the intangible represents contractual or legal rights or is capable of being separated or divided and sold, transferred, licensed, rented, or exchanged. In addition, under both GAAP and IFRS, companies recognize acquired in-process research and development (IPR&D) as a separate intangible asset if it meets the definition of an intangible asset and its fair value can be measured reliably.

- As in GAAP, under IFRS the costs associated with research and development are segregated into the two components. Costs in the research phase are always expensed under both IFRS and GAAP. Under IFRS, however, costs in the development phase are capitalized once technological feasibility (referred to as **economic viability**) is achieved.

- IFRS permits revaluation on limited-life intangible assets. Revaluations are **not** permitted for goodwill and other indefinite-life intangible assets.

- IFRS permits some capitalization of internally generated intangible assets (e.g., brand value) if it is probable there will be a future benefit and the amount can be reliably measured. GAAP requires expensing of all costs associated with internally generated intangibles.

- IFRS requires an impairment test at each reporting date for long-lived assets and intangibles and records an impairment if the asset's carrying amount exceeds its recoverable amount. The recoverable amount is the higher of the asset's fair value less costs to sell and its value-in-use. Value-in-use is the future cash flows to be derived from the particular assets, discounted to present value. Under GAAP, impairment loss is measured as the excess of the carrying amount over the asset's fair value.

- IFRS allows reversal of impairment losses when there has been a change in economic conditions or in the expected use of limited-life intangibles. Under GAAP, impairment losses **cannot** be reversed for assets to be held and used; the impairment loss results in a new cost basis for the asset. IFRS and GAAP are similar in the accounting for impairments of assets held for disposal.

TRUE/FALSE (Circle the correct answer for each).

T   F   1.   In considering research and development costs, costs in the research phase are always expensed under both IFRS and GAAP.

T   F   2.   Costs in the development phase of a new product are capitalized once technological feasibility (referred to as economic viability) is achieved. This pertains to both GAAP and IFRS.

T   F   3.   IFRS permits revaluation on limited-life intangible assets; revaluations are **not** permitted for goodwill and other indefinite-life intangible assets.

T   F   4.   IFRS permits some capitalization of internally generated intangibles whereas GAAP requires expensing of all costs associated with internally generated intangibles.

T   F   5.   Although both IFRS and GAAP require an impairment test for long-lived assets, they differ with respect to the recognition of an impairment loss and any subsequent reversal.

Solutions:

1.   T   4.   T
2.   F   5.   T
3.   T

CHAPTER 13

CURRENT LIABILITIES AND CONTINGENCIES

OVERVIEW

Initially, the resources (assets) of a business have to come from entities outside of the particular organization. Two main sources of resources are creditor sources (liabilities) and owners' sources (owners' equity). In this chapter, we begin our in-depth discussion of liabilities.

Due to the nature of some business activities, it is common to find some goods and services being received while payment for these items is made days or weeks later. Therefore, at a specific point in time, such as a balance sheet date, we may find that a business has obligations for merchandise received from suppliers (accounts payable), for money it has borrowed (notes payable), for interest incurred (interest payable), for sales tax charged to customers which has not yet been remitted to the government (sales taxes payable), for salaries and wages (salaries and wages payable), and for other amounts due to government agencies in connection with employee compensation. Such payables are reported as current (short-term) liabilities, because they will fall due within the next 12 months and will require the use of current assets (cash, in these cases) to liquidate them. Accounting for these and other current liabilities is discussed in this chapter.

SUMMARY OF LEARNING OBJECTIVES

1. **Describe the nature, type, and valuation of current liabilities.** Current liabilities are obligations whose liquidation a company reasonably expects to require the use of current assets or the creation of other current liabilities. Theoretically, liabilities should be measured by the present value of the future outlay of cash required to liquidate them. In practice, companies usually record and report current liabilities at their full maturity value. There are several types of current liabilities. The following list details the most common types: (1) accounts payable, (2) notes payable, (3) current maturities of long-term debts, (4) dividends payable, (5) customer advances and deposits, (6) unearned revenue, (7) taxes payable, and (8) employee-related liabilities.

2. **Explain the classification issues of short-term debt expected to be refinanced.** A short-term obligation is excluded from current liabilities if both of the following conditions are met: (1) the company must intend to refinance the obligation on a long-term basis, *and* (2) it must demonstrate an ability to consummate the refinancing.

3. **Identify types of employee-related liabilities.** The employee-related liabilities are: (1) payroll deductions, (2) compensated absences, and (3) bonus agreements.

4. **Identify the criteria used to account for and disclose gain and loss contingencies.** Gain contingencies are **not** recorded. They are disclosed in the notes only when the probability is high that a gain contingency will become a reality. A company should accrue an estimated loss from a loss contingency by charging expense and recording a liability only if **both** of the following conditions are met: (1) Information available prior to the issuance of the financial statements indicates that it is probable that a liability has been incurred at the date of the financial statements, and (2) the amount of the loss can be reasonably estimated.

5.   **Explain the accounting for different types of loss contingencies.** (1) **Litigation:** The following factors must be considered in determining whether a liability should be recorded with respect to pending or threatened litigation and actual or possible claims and assessments: (a) the time period in which the underlying cause for action occurred; (b) the probability of an unfavorable outcome; and, (c) the ability to make a reasonable estimate of the amount of loss. (2) **Warranties:** If it is probable that customers will make claims under warranties relating to goods or services that have been sold and it can reasonably estimate the costs involved, the company uses the accrual method. Under the accrual basis, it charges warranty costs to operating expense in the year of sale. (3) **Sales promotions:** Premiums, coupon offers, and rebates are made to stimulate sales. Companies should charge their costs to expense in the period of the sale that benefits from the promotion (premium) plan. (4) **Asset retirement obligations**: A company must recognize asset retirement obligations when it has an existing legal obligation related to the retirement of a long-lived asset and it can reasonably estimate the amount.

6.   **Indicate how to present and analyze current liabilities and contingencies.** The current liability accounts are commonly presented as the first classification in the liabilities and stockholders' equity section of the balance sheet. Within the current liabilities section, companies may list the accounts in order of maturity, in descending order of amount, or in order of liquidation preference. Detail and supplemental information concerning current liabilities should be sufficient to meet the requirement of full disclosure. If the loss is either probable or estimable but not both, and if there is at least a reasonable possibility that a company may have incurred a liability, it should disclose in the notes both the nature of the contingency and an estimate of the possible loss. Two ratios used to analyze liquidity are the current and acid-test ratios.

TIPS ON CHAPTER TOPICS

TIP: **Current liabilities** are often called **short-term liabilities** or **short-term debt**. **Noncurrent liabilities** are often called **long-term liabilities** or **long-term debt**.

TIP: **Current liabilities** are obligations whose liquidation is reasonably expected to require the use of existing resources properly classifiable as current assets, or the creation of other current liabilities. **Noncurrent liabilities** are obligations which do not meet the criteria to be classified as current.

TIP: An estimated loss from a loss contingency should be accrued by a charge to expense and a credit to a liability if **both** of the following conditions are met: (1) it is **probable** (likely) that a liability has been incurred at the date of the balance sheet, and (2) the amount of the loss can be **reasonably estimated**. If the loss is either probable or estimable but not both, or if there is at least a **reasonable possibility** that a liability has been incurred, the contingency must be disclosed in the notes (but not accrued). If it is only **remotely possible** (unlikely) that a liability has been incurred, no accrual or note disclosure is required (there are some exceptions to this guideline).

TIP: **Self-insurance** is not insurance; rather, it is **risk assumption.** Any company that assumes its own risks puts itself in the position of incurring expenses or losses as they occur. It is **not** generally acceptable to charge expense and report a liability prior to the occurrence of the event even if the amount of loss is reasonably estimable.

EXERCISE 13-1

Purpose: (L.O. 1) This exercise tests your ability to distinguish between current and noncurrent (long-term) liabilities.

Instructions
Indicate how each of the following items would be reported on a balance sheet being prepared at December 31, 2014.

1. Obligation to supplier for merchandise purchased on credit. (Terms 2/10, n/30)
2. Note payable to bank maturing 90 days after balance sheet date.
3. Bonds payable due January 1, 2017.
4. Utilities payable.
5. Interest payable on long-term bonds payable.
6. Income taxes payable.
7. Portion of lessee's lease obligations due in years 2016 through 2020.
8. Revenue received in advance, to be earned over the next six months.
9. Salaries payable.
10. Rent payable.
11. Short-term notes payable.
12. Pension obligations maturing in ten years.
13. Installment loan payment due three months after balance sheet date.
14. Installment loan payments due after one year.
15. Portion of lessee's lease obligations due within a year after the December 31, 2014 balance sheet date.
16. Bank overdraft.
17. Accrued officer bonus.
18. Coupon offers outstanding.
19. Cash dividends declared but not paid.
20. Deferred rent revenue.
21. Stock dividends payable.
22. Bonds payable due June 1, 2015
23. Bonds payable due July 1, 2015 for which a sinking fund will be used to pay off the debt. The sinking fund is classified as a long-term investment.
24. Discount to the bonds payable in item 3 above.
25. Current maturities of long-term debt.
26. Accrued interest on notes payable.
27. Customer deposits.
28. Sales taxes payable.
29. FICA withholdings.
30. Contingent liability (reasonable possibility of loss).
31. Contingent liability (probable and estimable).
32. Obligation for warranties.
33. Unearned warranty revenue.
34. Gift certificates outstanding.
35. Loan from stockholder.

Solution to Exercise 13-1

> **TIP:** Apply the definition of a current liability. Analyze each situation and determine if the liability will fall due within a year (or operating cycle) of the balance sheet date and whether it will require the use of current assets or the incurrence of another current liability to be liquidated. If so, it is current; if not, it is long-term. Recall that current assets include cash and assets expected to be converted to cash or sold or consumed within the next year or operating cycle, whichever is longer.

1. Current liability (called Accounts Payable).
2. Current liability.
3. Noncurrent liability.
4. Current liability.
5. Current liability; interest on bonds is usually due semi-annually or annually.
6. Current liability.
7. Noncurrent liability.
8. Current liability.
9. Current liability.
10. Current liability.
11. Current liability.
12. Noncurrent liability.
13. Current liability.
14. Noncurrent liability.
15. Current liability.
16. Current liability (assuming no other bank accounts with positive balances in the same bank).
17. Current liability.
18. Current liability; may also classify a portion as a noncurrent liability.
19. Current liability.
20. Current liability or noncurrent liability, depending on when the revenue is expected to be earned.
21. Paid-in capital; it does not meet the definition of a liability. ("Stock dividends payable" is a poor caption for "stock dividend distributable.")
22. Current liability.
23. Noncurrent liability; even though it is coming due within a year, it will not require the use of current assets to be liquidated.
24. Contra noncurrent liability (deducted from the related bonds payable).
25. Current liability.
26. Current liability, generally; in rare cases may be noncurrent.
27. Current liability or noncurrent liability, depending on the time left before they are to be returned or earned.
28. Current liability.
29. Current liability.
30. Note disclosure only.
31. Current liability or noncurrent liability, depending on the date settlement is expected.
32. Current liability and/or noncurrent liability, depending on term of warranty (this account title is used with the expense warranty method).
33. Current liability and/or noncurrent liability, depending on term of warranty (this account title is used with the sales warranty method).
34. Current liability, most likely; could have a portion as a noncurrent liability.
35. Current liability or noncurrent liability, depending on the due date of the loan; loans with related parties are required to be separately disclosed; if this loan is due on demand, the payable must be classified as a current liability.

EXERCISE 13-2

Purpose: (L.O. 1) This exercise will provide an example of the proper accounting for an obligation to an agency of the state government—unremitted sales taxes.

During the month of September, Chelsea's Boutique had cash sales of $702,000 and credit sales of $411,000, both of which include the 6% sales tax that must be remitted to the state by October 15. Sales taxes on September sales were lumped with the sales price and recorded as a credit to the Sales Revenue account.

Instructions

(a)   Prepare the adjusting entry that should be recorded to fairly present the financial statements at September 30.

(b)   Prepare the entry to record the remittance of the sales taxes on October 5 if a 2% discount is allowed for payments received by the State Revenue Department by October 10.

Solution to Exercise 13-2

(a)   9/30   Sales Revenue 63,000

           Sales Taxes Payable..   63,000

Computation:	
Sales plus sales tax	
($702,000 + $411,000)	$1,113,000
Sales exclusive of tax	
($1,113,000 ÷ 1.06)	1,050,000
Sales tax	$ 63,000

(b)   10/5   Sales Taxes Payable.. 63,000

           Cash (98% x $63,000)..   61,740

           Gain on Sales Tax Collections (2% x $63,000).............   1,260

Explanation: Sales taxes on transfers of tangible personal property and on certain services must be collected from customers and remitted to the proper government authority. A liability is set up to provide for taxes collected from customers but as yet unremitted to the tax authority. The Sales Taxes Payable account should reflect the liability for sales taxes due to the government.

When the sales tax collections credited to the liability account are not equal to the liability as computed by the governmental formula, an adjustment of the liability account may be made by recognizing a gain or a loss on sales tax collections.

EXERCISE 13-3

Purpose: (L.O. 2) This exercise will provide you with two unrelated examples of the proper treatment of short-term debt expected to be refinanced.

Situation 1

On December 31, 2013, Amy's Specialty Foods Company had $1,000,000 of short-term debt in the form of notes payable due February 4, 2014. On January 22, 2014, the company issued 20,000 shares of its common stock for $40 per share, receiving $800,000 proceeds after brokerage fees and other costs of issuance. On February 4, 2014, the proceeds from the stock sale, supplemented by an additional $200,000 cash, are used to liquidate the $1,000,000 debt. The December 31, 2013 balance sheet is issued on February 20, 2014.

Situation 2

Included in Hubbard Corporation's liability account balances on December 31, 2013 were the following:

14% note payable issued October 1, 2013, maturing September 30, 2014	$500,000
16% note payable issued April 1, 2007, payable in six annual installments of $200,000 beginning April 1, 2011	600,000

Hubbard's December 31, 2013 financial statements were issued on March 31, 2014. On January 13, 2014, the entire $600,000 balance of the 16% note was refinanced by issuance of a long-term obligation payable in a lump-sum. In addition, on March 8, 2014, Hubbard consummated a noncancelable agreement with the lender to refinance the 14%, $500,000 note on a long-term basis, with readily determinable terms that have not yet been implemented. Both parties are financially capable of honoring the agreement, and there have been no violations of the agreement's provisions.

Instructions

Situation 1:   Show how the $1,000,000 of short-term debt should be presented on the December 31, 2013 balance sheet, including note disclosure.

Situation 2:   Explain how the liabilities should be classified on the December 31, 2013 balance sheet. How much should be classified as a current liability?

Solution to Exercise 13-3

Situation 1

Amy's Specialty Foods Co.
PARTIAL BALANCE SHEET
December 31, 2013

Current liabilities:

    Notes payable (Note 1) $ 200,000

Long-term debt:

    Notes payable refinanced in February 2012 (Note 1)   800,000

    Note 1—Short-term debt refinanced

        As of December 31, 2013, the Company had notes payable totaling $1,000,000 due on February 4, 2014. These notes were refinanced on their due date to the extent of $800,000 received from the issuance of common stock on January 22, 2014. The balance of $200,000 was liquidated using current assets.

OR

Current liabilities:

    Notes payable (Note 1) $ 200,000

Short-term debt expected to be refinanced (Note 1)   800,000

Long-term debt   XXX,XXX

    (Same Note as above)

Situation 2

The entire $600,000 balance of the 16% note is properly excluded from short-term obligations since before the balance sheet was issued, Hubbard refinanced the note by issuance of a long-term obligation. The $500,000, 14% note is properly excluded from short-term obligations due to the fact that, before the balance sheet was issued, Hubbard entered into a financing agreement that clearly permits Hubbard to refinance the short-term obligation on a long-term basis with terms that are readily determinable.

Approach and Explanation: Review the criteria which will require an enterprise to exclude a short-term obligation from current liabilities and apply the criteria to the situation at hand.

In accordance with GAAP, an enterprise is allowed to exclude a short-term obligation from current liabilities only if both of the following conditions are met:

    1.   It must **intend to refinance** the obligation on a long-term basis, and

    2.   It must **demonstrate an ability** to consummate the refinancing.

Intention to refinance on a long-term basis means the enterprise intends to refinance the short-term obligation so that the use of working capital will not be required during the ensuing fiscal year or operating cycle, if longer. The **ability** to consummate the refinancing must be demonstrated by:

    (a)   **Actually refinancing** the short-term obligation by issuance of a long-term obligation or equity securities after the date of the balance sheet but before it is issued; or

    (b)   Entering into a **financing agreement** that clearly permits the enterprise to refinance the debt on a long-term basis with terms that are readily determinable.

If an actual refinancing occurs, the portion of the short-term obligation to be excluded from current liabilities may not exceed the proceeds from the new obligation or equity securities issued that are to be used to retire the short-term obligation. When a financing agreement is relied upon to demonstrate ability to refinance a short-term obligation on a long-term basis, the amount of short-term debt that can be excluded from current liabilities cannot exceed the amount available for refinancing under the agreement.

> **TIP:** By excluding short-term debt expected to be refinanced from the current liability classification, the company's working capital position and its current ratio are improved.

EXERCISE 13-4

Purpose: (L.O. 3) This exercise will review accounting for compensated absences.

Patricia McKiernan Company began operations on January 2, 2013. It employs 9 individuals who work 8-hour days and are paid hourly. Each employee earns 10 paid vacation days and 6 paid sick days annually. Vacation days may be taken after January 15 of the year following the year in which they are earned. Sick days may be taken as soon as they are earned; unused sick days accumulate but do not vest. Additional information is as follows:

Actual Hourly Wage Rate		Vacation Days Used by Each Employee		Sick Days Used By Each Employee	
2013	**2014**	**2013**	**2014**	**2013**	**2014**
$7.00	$8.00	0	9	4	5

Patricia McKiernan has chosen not to accrue paid sick leave until used, and has chosen to accrue paid vacation time at expected future rates of pay without discounting. The company used the following projected rates to accrue vacation time:

Year in Which Vacation Time Was Earned	Projected Future Pay Rates Used to Accrue Vacation Pay
2013	$7.90
2014	8.60

Instructions
(a)   Prepare journal entries to record transactions related to compensated absences during 2013 and 2014.

(b)   Compute the amounts of any liability for compensated absences that should be reported on the balance sheet at December 31, 2013 and 2014.

Solution to Exercise 13-4

(a)   **2013**

To accrue the expense and liability for vacations:	Salaries and Wages Expense Salaries and Wages Payable	5,688 (1)	5,688
To record sick time paid:	Salaries and Wages Expense Cash	2,016 (2)	2,016
To record vacation time paid:	No entry.		

2014

To accrue the expense and liability for vacations:	Salaries and Wages Expense Salaries and Wages Payable	6,192 (3)	6,192
To record sick time paid:	Salaries and Wages Expense Cash	2,880 (4)	2,880

To record vacation time paid:	Salaries and Wages Expense
	    Salaries and Wages Payable
	    Cash
		65
		5,119 (5)
			5,184 (6)

(1)   9 employees x $7.90/hr. x 8 hrs./day x 10 days = $5,688.
(2)   9 employees x $7.00/hr. x 8 hrs./day x 4 days = $2,016.
(3)   9 employees x $8.60/hr. x 8 hrs./day x 10 days = $6,192.
(4)   9 employees x $8.00/hr. x 8 hrs./day x 5 days = $2,880.
(5)   9 employees x $7.90/hr. x 8 hrs./day x 9 days = $5,119.
(6)   9 employees x $8.00/hr. x 8 hrs./day x 9 days = $5,184.

(b)   Accrued liability at year-end:

	2013 Vacation Wages Payable	**2014** Vacation Wages Payable
Jan. 1 balance	$ 0	$ 5,688.00
+ accrued	5,688.00	6,192.00
- paid	(0)	(5,119.20)
Dec. 31 balance	$ 5,688.00 (1)	$ 6,760.80 (2)

(1)   9 employees x $7.90/hr. x 8 hrs./day x 10 days   = $ 5,688.00

(2)   9 employees x $7.90/hr. x 8 hrs./day x 1 day   = $ 568.80
        9 employees x $8.60/hr. x 8 hrs./day x 10 days   =   6,192.00
                                                                                                    $ 6,760.80

TIP:	The expense and related liability for compensated absences should be recognized in the year in which the employees earn the rights to those absences. Vacation and holiday pay must be accrued if it vests or accumulates. Sick pay must be accrued only if it vests.

EXERCISE 13-5

Purpose: (L.O. 3) This exercise will provide an example of recording liabilities associated with payroll taxes.

The payroll of Lionshead Company for July 2014 is as follows:

1.   Total payroll was $620,000 of which $120,000 is exempt from FICA tax because it represents amounts paid in excess of $102,000 to certain employees.

2.   The amount paid to employees in excess of $7,000 was $540,000. The state unemployment tax is 5.7% on the first $7,000 of annual earnings for each employee. Lionshead is allowed a credit of 2.5% by the state for its unemployment experience.

3.   The current FICA tax is 6.2% on an employee's wages up to $102,000. The Hospital Insurance (Medicare) tax is 1.45% on the employee's total compensation.

4.   The federal unemployment tax rate (on the first $7,000 of each employee's earnings) is 0.8% after the state credit.

5.   Income tax withheld amounts to $117,000. Union dues of $11,000 was also withheld from employees.

Instructions
Prepare the necessary journal entries to record the salaries paid and the related payroll taxes. Record the employer payroll taxes in a separate entry.

SOLUTION TO EXERCISE 13-5

Salaries and Wages Expense	620,000	
Withholding Taxes Payable		117,000
FICA Taxes Payable		39,990
Union Dues Payable		11,000
Cash		452,010

Computations:
   $620,000 – 120,000 = $500,000 Subject to F.I.C.A. tax
   $500,000 X 6.2% = $31,000 F.I.C.A. taxes—employee portion
   $620,000 x 1.45% = $8,990 Medicare taxes—employee portion
   $31,000 + $8,990 = $39,990 Social Security taxes—employee portion

   $620,000 - $117,000 - $39,990 - $11,000 = $452,010 net cash paid to employees

Payroll Tax Expense	43,190	
FICA Taxes Payable		39,990
SUTA Taxes Payable		2,560
FUTA Taxes Payable		640

Computations:
$620,000 - $120,000 = $500,000 Subject to FICA tax
$500,000 X 6.2% = $31,000 FICA taxes—employer portion
$620,000 X 1.45% = $8,990 Medicare taxes—employer portion
$31,000 + $8,990 = $39,990 Social Security taxes—employer portion
(5.7% - 2.5%) X ($620,000 - $540,000) = $2,560 State Unemployment tax
.8% X ($620,000 - $540,000) = $640 Federal Unemployment tax
$39,990 + $2,560 + $640 = $43,190 Payroll tax expense

ILLUSTRATION 13-1
ACCOUNTING TREATMENT OF LOSS CONTINGENCIES (L.O. 4, 5)

Loss Related to	Usually Accrued	Not Accrued	May Be Accrued*
1. Collectibility of receivables	X		
2. Obligations related to product warranties and product defects	X		
3. Premiums offered to customers	X		
4. Risk of loss or damage of enterprise property by fire, explosion, or other hazards		X	
5. General or unspecified business risks		X	
6. Risk of loss from catastrophes assumed by property and casualty insurance companies including reinsurance companies		X	
7. Threat of expropriation of assets			X
8. Pending or threatened litigation			X
9. Actual or possible claims and assessments**			X
10. Guarantees of indebtedness of others***			X
11. Obligations of commercial banks under "standby letters of credit"***			X
12. Agreements to repurchase receivables (or the related property) that have been sold***			X

*Should be accrued when both criteria are met (probable and reasonably estimable).
**Estimated amounts of losses incurred prior to the balance sheet date but settled subsequently should be accrued as of the balance sheet date.
***Should be disclosed even though possibility of loss may be remote.

EXERCISE 13-6

Purpose: (L.O. 1, 4, 5) This exercise will enable you to practice analyzing situations to determine whether a liability should be reported, and if so, at what amount.

Clare Avery Inc., a publishing company, is preparing its December 31, 2014 financial statements and must determine the proper accounting treatment for each of the following situations:

1.   Avery sells subscriptions to several magazines for a two- or three-year period. Cash receipts from subscribers are credited to Unearned Subscription Revenue. This account had a balance of $5,300,000 at December 31, 2014, before adjustment. An analysis of outstanding subscriptions at December 31, 2014 shows that they expire as follows:

During 2015:	$ 800,000
During 2016:	900,000
During 2017:	1,200,000

2.   A suit for breach of contract seeking damages of $1,000,000 was filed by an author against Avery on June 1, 2014. The company's legal counsel believes that an unfavorable outcome is probable. A reasonable estimate of the court's award to the plaintiff is in the range between $200,000 and $800,000. The company's legal counsel believes the best estimate of potential damages is $350,000.

3.   On January 2, 2014, Avery discontinued collision, fire, and theft coverage on its delivery vehicles and became self-insured for these risks. Actual losses of $40,000 during 2014 were charged to Delivery Expense. The 2013 premium for the discontinued coverage amounted to $75,000, and the controller wants to set up a reserve for self-insurance by a debit to Delivery Expense of $35,000 and a credit to Liability for Self-insurance of $35,000.

4.   During December 2014, a competitor company filed suit against Avery for copyright infringement claiming $600,000 in damages. In the opinion of management and company counsel, it is reasonably possible that damages will be awarded to the plaintiff. The best estimate of potential damages is $175,000.

Instructions

For each of the situations above, prepare the journal entry that should be recorded as of December 31, 2014, or explain why an entry should not be recorded. Show supporting computations in good form.

Solution to Exercise 13-6

1. Unearned Subscription Revenue 2,400,000*
        Subscription Revenue 2,400,000
            (To adjust the unearned revenue account)

        *Liability account:
        Book balance at December 31, 2012 $ 5,300,000
        Adjusted balance ($800,000 +
            $900,000 + $1,200,000)   (2,900,000)
        Adjustment required $ 2,400,000

2. Estimated Loss from Pending Lawsuit 350,000
        Estimated Liability from Pending Lawsuit 350,000
            (To record estimated minimum damages on
            breach-of-contract litigation)

    This situation involves a contingent liability. Because it is **probable** that a liability has been incurred and the loss is reasonably estimable, the loss should be accrued. When the expected loss amount is in a range, the best estimate within the range is used for the accrual. When no amount within the range is a better estimate than any other amount, the dollar value at the low end is accrued and the dollar amount at the high end of the range is disclosed in the notes.

3. No entry should be made to accrue for an expense because the absence of insurance coverage does not mean that an asset has been impaired or a liability has been incurred as of the balance sheet date. Avery may, however, appropriate retained earnings for self-insurance as long as actual costs or losses are not charged against the appropriation of retained earnings and no part of the appropriation is transferred to income. Appropriation of retained earnings and/or disclosure in the notes to the financial statements are not required, but are recommended. Appropriation of retained earnings has no impact on the income statement.

4. No entry should be made for this loss contingency, because it is not probable that an asset has been impaired or a liability has been incurred as of the balance sheet date. The loss contingency (along with the best estimate of amount) should be disclosed in the notes to financial statements because the likelihood of loss is judged to be reasonably possible.

EXERCISE 13-7

Purpose: (L.O. 5) This exercise will provide an example of accounting for premium claims outstanding.

Shuck Company includes 1 coupon in each box of cereal that it packs and 10 coupons are redeemable for a premium (a toy). In 2014, Shuck Company purchased 9,000 premiums at 90 cents each and sold 100,000 boxes of cereal at $2.00 per box; 40,000 coupons were presented for redemption in 2014. It is estimated that 60% of the coupons will eventually be presented for redemption. This is the first year for this premium offering.

Instructions

Prepare all the entries that would be made relative to sales of cereal and to the premium plan in 2014.

Solution to Exercise 13-7

Inventory of Premiums (9,000 x $.90)	8,100	
Cash		8,100
Cash (100,000 x $2.00)	200,000	
Sales Revenue		200,000
Premium Expense	3,600	
Inventory of Premiums [(40,000 ÷ 10) x $.90]		3,600
Premium Expense	1,800*	
Premium Liability		1,800

*[(100,000 x 60%) - 40,000] ÷ 10 x $.90 = $1,800

Explanation: The first entry records the purchase of 9,000 toys which will be used as premiums. The second entry records the sales of cereal (100,000 boxes). The third entry records the redemption of 40,000 coupons with customers receiving one premium for every 10 coupons. The cost of the 4,000 toys distributed to these customers is recorded by a debit to expense. The fourth entry is an adjusting entry at the end of the accounting period to accrue the cost of additional premiums included in boxes of cereal sold this period that are likely to be redeemed in future periods. This is an application of the expense recognition (matching) principle. The expense of a premium should be recognized in the same period as the related revenue which, in this case, is from the sale of cereal boxes containing the coupons that customers will redeem for a premium.

EXERCISE 13-8

Purpose: (L.O. 5) This exercise will provide an example of the journal entries involved in accounting for a warranty that is included with the sale of a product (warranty is not sold separately). Two methods are examined—the cash basis and the expense warranty method (an accrual method).

Zacko Corporation sells laptop computers under a two-year warranty contract that requires the corporation to replace defective parts and to provide the necessary repair labor. During 2013 the corporation sells for cash 400 computers at a unit price of $2,000. On the basis of past experience, the two-year warranty costs are estimated to be $90 for parts and $100 for labor per unit. (For simplicity, assume that all sales occurred on December 31, 2013, rather than evenly throughout the year.)

Instructions
(a)   Record any necessary journal entries in 2013, applying the cash basis method.
(b)   Record any necessary journal entries in 2013, applying the expense warranty accrual method.
(c)   What liability relative to these transactions would appear on the December 31, 2013 balance sheet and how would it be classified if the cash basis method is applied?
(d)   What liability relative to these transactions would appear on the December 31, 2013 balance sheet and how would it be classified if the expense warranty accrual method is applied?

In 2014 the actual warranty costs to Zacko Corporation were $14,800 for parts and $18,200 for labor.
(e)   Record any necessary journal entries in 2014, applying the cash basis method.
(f)   Record any necessary journal entries in 2014, applying the expense warranty accrual method.
(g)   Under what conditions is it acceptable to use the cash basis method? Explain.

Solution to Exercise 13-8

(a)   Cash (400 x $2,000)... 800,000
           Sales Revenue   800,000

(b)   Cash (400 x $2,000)... 800,000
           Sales Revenue   800,000

        Warranty Expense [400 x ($90 + $100)] 76,000
           Warranty Liability...   76,000

(c)   No liability would be disclosed under the cash basis method relative to future costs due to warranties on past sales.

(d)   Current Liabilities:
          Warranty Liability $38,000

          Long-term Liabilities:
          Warranty Liability $38,000

(e)   Warranty Expense..   33,000
          Inventory (Parts)...   14,800
          Salaries and Wages Payable   18,200

(f)   Estimated Liability Under Warranties.....................................   33,000
          Inventory (Parts)...   14,800
          Salaries and Wages Payable   18,200

(g)   The cash basis is used for income tax purposes. Theoretically, the accrual basis
          (expense warranty method in this case) should be used for financial reporting purposes.
          However, the cash basis is often justifiably used for accounting purposes when warranty
          costs are immaterial or when the warranty period is relatively short.

EXERCISE 13-9

Purpose: (L.O. 6) This exercise will exemplify the journal entries involved in accounting for
          a warranty that is sold separately from the related product. The sales warranty
          accrual method is used for such situations.

The Contessa Company sells scanners for $800 each and offers to each customer a three-year
warranty contract for $90 that requires the company to perform periodic services and to replace
defective parts. During 2013, the company sold 500 scanners and 400 warranty contracts for
cash. It estimates the three-year warranty costs as $30 for parts and $50 for labor and accounts
for warranties on the sales warranty accrual method. Assume all sales occurred on December 31,
2013, and revenue from the sale of the warranties is to be recognized on a straight-line basis
over the life of the contract.

Instructions
(a)   Record any necessary journal entries in 2013.
(b)   What liability relative to these transactions would appear on the December 31, 2013
          balance sheet and how would it be classified?

In 2014, Terence Trent Company incurred actual costs relative to 2013 scanner warranty sales
of $3,800 for parts and $6,000 for labor.
(c)   Record any necessary journal entries in 2014 relative to 2013 scanner warranties.
(d)   What amounts relative to the 2013 scanner warranties would appear on the December 31,
          2014 balance sheet and how would they be classified?

Solution to Exercise 13-9

(a)   Cash ($400,000 + $36,000) 436,000

                Sales Revenue (500 x $800)... 400,000

                Unearned Warranty Revenue (400 x $90)..................... 36,000

(b)   Current Liabilities:

                Unearned Warranty Revenue $12,000

                  (Note: Warranty costs are assumed to be
                  incurred equally over the three-year period)

            Long-term Liabilities:

                Unearned Warranty Revenue $24,000

(c)   Warranty Expense... 9,800

                Inventory (Parts)... 3,800

                Salaries and Wages Payable 6,000

            Unearned Warranty Revenue 12,000

                Warranty Revenue.. 12,000

(d)   Current Liabilities:

                Unearned Warranty Revenue $12,000

             Long-term Liabilities:

                  Unearned Warranty Revenue $12,000

EXERCISE 13-10

Purpose: (L.O. 5) This exercise will review the accounting recognition for an asset retirement obligation.

Silverado Corp. purchased mining equipment with cash on January 1, 2014, at a cost of $3,000,000. Silverado expects to actively extract units from the mine for 5 years at which time it is legally required to perform certain steps to close the mine and remove the mining equipment. It is estimated that it will cost $500,000 to properly dismantle the equipment and close the mine at the end of its useful life. Using an interest rate of 8%, the present value of the asset retirement obligation on January 1, 2014, is $340,290. The estimated residual value of the equipment is zero.

Instructions

(a)   Prepare the journal entries to record the acquisition of the mining equipment and the asset retirement obligation for the mine on January 1, 2014.

(b)   Prepare any journal entries required for the equipment and the asset retirement obligation at December 31, 2014.

(c)   On January 5, 2019, Silverado Corp. pays $481,000 to close the mine and remove the equipment. Prepare the journal entry for the settlement of the asset retirement obligation.

Solution to Exercise 13-10

January 1, 2014

(a)   Mining Equipment 3,000,000
         Cash   3,000,000

       Mining Equipment 340,290
         Asset Retirement Obligation   340,290

Explanation: The equipment is recorded at a cost of $3,000,000. In addition, the company must recognize an asset retirement obligation (ARO) when it has an existing legal obligation associated with the retirement of a long-lived asset and when the amount of the liability can be reasonably estimated. The ARO is to be recorded at fair value; fair value can be estimated based on present value techniques.

An asset retirement cost is recorded as part of the related asset because these costs are considered to be a cost of operating the asset and are necessary to prepare the asset for its intended use.   The capitalized asset retirement costs should not be recorded in a separate account because there is no future economic benefit that can be associated with these costs alone. Therefore, the specific asset (the mine) should be debited because the future economic benefit comes from the use of this productive asset.

December 31, 2014

(b) Depreciation Expense.. 668,058
         Accumulated Depreciation   668,058
         ($3,340,290 ÷ 5 = $668,058)

     Interest Expense.. 27,223
         Asset Retirement Obligation....................................   27,223
         ($340,290 x 8% = $27,223)

Explanation: During the life of the asset, the asset cost ($3,000,000) and the asset retirement cost ($340,290) are allocated to expense. In addition, interest must be accrued each period.

TIP: The interest expense for the second year (2015) for the asset retirement obligation would be 8% of the ARO, so 0.08 X ($340,290 + $27,223) = $29,401.

(c)   **January 5, 2019**
     Asset Retirement Obligation 500,000
         Gain on Settlement of ARO...   19,000
         Cash...   481,000

By the end of the asset's 5-year service life, the interest accrued on the asset retirement obligation will have brought the balance of the Asset Retirement Obligation account to $500,000. That balance exceeds the actual cost of retiring the asset—hence, a gain results.

ANALYSIS OF MULTIPLE-CHOICE TYPE QUESTIONS

QUESTION
1. (L.O. 1) A current liability is an obligation that:
    a. was paid during the current period.
    b. will be reported as an expense within the year or operating cycle that follows the balance sheet date, whichever is longer.
    c. will be converted to a long-term liability within the next year.
    d. is expected to require the use of current assets or the creation of another current liability to liquidate it.

Approach and Explanation: Before you read the answer selections, write down the definition for "current liability." Compare each answer selection with your definition. A **current liability** is an obligation which will come due within one year and whose liquidation is reasonably expected to require the use of existing resources properly classifiable as current assets or the creation of other current liabilities. (Solution = d.)

QUESTION
2. (L.O. 1) Burt Reynolds Company borrowed money from Loni Anderson Company for nine months by issuing a zero-interest-bearing note payable with a face value of $106,000. The proceeds amounted to $100,000. In recording the issuance of this note, what account should Burt debit for $6,000?
    a. Interest Payable
    b. Interest Expense
    c. Prepaid Interest
    d. Discount on Note Payable

Approach and Explanation: The excess of the face value of a zero-interest-bearing note payable and the proceeds collected upon its issuance is the cost of borrowing. This cost of borrowing (interest expense) should be recognized over the months the loan is outstanding. Therefore, the total interest ($6,000) is initially debited to a Discount on Note Payable Account. The balance of that account is then amortized (allocated) to interest expense over the life of the note. (Solution = d.)

TIP: A **zero-interest-bearing note** is often called a **non-interest-bearing-note**.

QUESTION
3. (L.O. 1) Martha's Boutique sells gift certificates. These gift certificates have no expiration date. Data for the current year are as follows:

Gift certificates outstanding, January 1	$ 225,000
Gift certificates sold	750,000
Gift certificates redeemed	660,000
Gross profit expressed as percentage of sales	40%

At December 31, Martha should report unearned revenue of:
a. $90,000.
b. $126,000.
c. $261,000.
d. $315,000.

Approach and Explanation: Draw a T-account for the liability and enter the data given.

Unearned Revenue
(Gift Certificates Outstanding)

Redeemed	660,000	Beginning Balance	225,000
		Sold	750,000
		Ending Balance	315,000

(Solution = d.)

TIP: The gross profit percentage is not used in the solution for the balance of unearned revenue. Revenue and unearned revenue are gross amounts, not net amounts.

QUESTION
4. (L.O. 1) A local retailer is required to collect a 6% sales tax for the state's department of revenue and remit in the month that follows the sale. The retailer does not use a separate Sales Taxes Payable account; rather the sales price of products sold and the related sales tax is all credited to Sales Revenue. During the month of March, credits totaling $25,440 were made to the Sales Revenue account. The amount to be remitted to the state in April for sales taxes collected during the month of March:
a. is $1,526.
b. is $1,440.
c. is $2,697.
d. cannot be determined from the data given.

Approach and Explanation: Set up an algebraic expression to describe the relationships between the data given and solve.

$$Sales + .06\ Sales = \$25,440$$

$$1.06\ Sales = \$25,440$$

$$Sales = \frac{\$25,440}{1.06}$$

$$Sales = \$24,000$$

$25,440 Total - $24,000 Sales = $1,440 Sales Tax   (Solution = b.)

QUESTION

5. (L.O. 2) Included in Arnold Howell Company's liability accounts at December 31, 2014 was the following:

    12% Note payable issued in 2010 for cash and
    due in May 2015 $2,000,000

    On February 1, 2015 Arnold issued $5,000,000 of five-year bonds with the intention of using part of the bond proceeds to liquidate the $2,000,000 note payable maturing in May. On March 2, 2015, Arnold used $2,000,000 of the bond proceeds to liquidate the note payable. Arnold's December 31, 2014 balance sheet is being issued on March 15, 2015. How much of the $2,000,000 note payable should be classified as a current liability on the balance sheet?

    a. $0
    b. $800,000
    c. $1,000,000
    d. $2,000,000

Approach and Explanation: Mentally review the definition of a current liability and the guidelines for reporting short-term debt expected to be refinanced. At the date the balance sheet is issued, we have evidence of the intent and ability to refinance the debt on a long-term basis. That evidence is the post balance sheet issuance of long-term debt securities. The proceeds from the bond issuance exceed the reported amount of the note. Therefore, the entire $2,000,000 note payable should be classified as a long-term liability. (Solution = a.)

QUESTION

6. (L.O. 3) An employee's net (or take-home) pay is determined by gross earnings minus amounts for income tax withholdings and the employee's:
    a.   portion of Social Security taxes, and unemployment taxes.
    b.   and employer's portion of Social Security taxes, and unemployment taxes.
    c.   portion of Social Security taxes, unemployment taxes, and any voluntary deductions.
    d.   portion of Social Security taxes, and any voluntary deductions.

Approach and Explanation: Before you read the answer selections, write down the model for the net (take-home) pay computation. Then find the answer selection that agrees with your model.

    Employee's gross earnings for the current period
- Federal income tax withholdings
- Social Security tax withholdings
- Withholdings for voluntary deductions; such as for charitable contributions, group
    health and life insurance premiums, savings, retirement fund contributions, and
    loan repayments
= Net (or take-home) pay   (Solution = d.)

TIP:	The employer bears the burden of all unemployment taxes and its share of Social Security, FICA and Medicare taxes.

QUESTION
7.   (L.O. 4) An example of a contingent liability is:
     a.   sales taxes payable.
     b.   accrued salaries.
     c.   property taxes payable.
     d.   a pending lawsuit.

Approach and Explanation: Mentally define contingent liability and think of examples before you read the alternative answer selections. A contingent liability is a situation involving uncertainty as to possible loss or expense that will ultimately be resolved when one or more future events occur or fail to occur. Examples are pending or threatened lawsuits, pending IRS audits, and product warranties. Accrued salaries result in an actual liability. Sales taxes payable and property taxes payable are both actual liabilities if they exist at a balance sheet date. (Solution = d.)

QUESTION
8.   (L.O. 4, 5) A contingent loss which is judged to be reasonably possible and estimable should be:

	Accrued	Disclosed
a.	Yes	Yes
b.	Yes	No
c.	No	Yes
d.	No	No

Explanation: A contingent loss that is probable and estimable is to be accrued. A contingent loss that is reasonably possible should be disclosed, but it should not be accrued. A contingent loss that is remotely possible can be ignored (unless it is one of the items on a list of contingencies that must always be disclosed, regardless of the likelihood of loss occurrence, such as guarantees of indebtedness of others). (Solution = c.)

QUESTION
9.   (L.O. 4) Mayberry Co. has a loss contingency to accrue. The loss amount can only be reasonably estimated within a range of outcomes. No single amount within the range is a better estimate than any other amount. The amount of loss accrual should be:
     a.   zero.
     b.   the minimum of the range.
     c.   the mean of the range.
     d.   the maximum of the range.

Explanation: The FASB calls for the accrual of a loss contingency when it is probable and estimable and states that, when the reasonable estimate of loss is a range and some amount within the range appears at the time to be a better estimate than any other amount within the range, that amount shall be accrued. When no amount within the range is a better estimate then any other amount, however, the minimum amount in the range should be accrued. At first, you may think this does not go along with conservation; however, we are already being conservative by providing the charge to income for the estimated amount. (Solution = b.)

QUESTION
10. (L.O. 5) Scott Corporation began operations at the beginning of 2013. It provides a two-year warranty with the sale of its product. Scott estimates that warranty costs will equal 4% of the selling price the first year after sale and 6% of the selling price the second year after the sale. The following data are available:

	2013	2014
Sales	$400,000	$500,000
Actual warranty expenditures	10,000	38,000

The balance of the warranty liability at December 31, 2014 should be:
a. $12,000.
b. $42,000.
c. $44,000.
d. $50,000.

Approach and Explanation: Draw a T-account and enter the amounts that would be reflected in the account and determine its balance.

Warranty Liability

(2) Expenditures in 2013	10,000	(1) Expense for 2013	40,000
(4) Expenditures in 2014	38,000	(3) Expense for 2014	50,000
		12/31/14 Balance	42,000

(Solution = b.)

(1) $400,000 x (4% + 6%) = $40,000 expense for 2013.
   The total warranty cost related to the products sold during 2013 should be recognized in the period of sale (expense recognition principle).
(2) Given data. Actual expenditures during 2013.
(3) $500,000 x (4% + 6%) = $50,000 expense for 2014.
(4) Given data. Actual expenditures during 2014.

> **TIP:** Because some items are sold near the end of the year and the warranty is for two years, a portion of the warranty liability should be classified as a current liability (the amount pertaining to the actual expenditures estimated to occur in 2015) and the remainder as a long-term liability.

QUESTION
11. (L.O. 5) Crazy Pete Theme Park is self-insured. Premiums for insurance used to cost $100,000 per year before Crazy Pete discontinued coverage. During 2014, Crazy Pete suffered losses of $39,000 that used to be (but are no longer) covered by insurance. Crazy Pete thinks this was a "light" year and greater losses in future years will offset the lower amount sustained in 2014. In order to avoid volatility in earnings due to being self-insured, Crazy Pete wants to set up a Liability for Self-insurance. A reasonable estimate of losses to be incurred in 2015 is $120,000. The liability to be reported by Crazy Pete at December 31, 2014 due to this situation is:
a. $0.
b. $61,000.
c. $100,000.
d. $120,000.

Approach and Explanation: Even if the amount is estimable, the future losses from self-insurance do not result in liabilities at the December 31, 2014 balance sheet date because the losses in the future will result from future events, not from a past event. It is not generally acceptable to accrue future losses from self-insurance. Self-insurance is not insurance; it is risk assumption. (Solution = a.)

> **TIP:** Crazy Pete should report $39,000 of losses on its 2014 income statement.

QUESTION
12.   (L.O. 5) Powercell, a manufacturer of batteries, offers a cash rebate to buyers of its size D batteries. The rebate offer is good until June 30, 2015. At December 31, 2014, the balance sheet should include an estimated liability for unredeemed rebates in order to comply with the:
       a.   Revenue recognition principle.
       b.   Expense recognition principle.
       c.   Historical cost principle.
       d.   Time-period assumption.

Explanation: Premium, coupon, and rebate offers are made to stimulate sales, and their costs should be charged to expense in the period of the sale that benefits from the premium plan. At the end of the accounting period, many of these premium, coupon, and rebate offers may be outstanding and, when presented in subsequent periods, must be redeemed. The number of outstanding premium, coupon, and rebate offers that will be presented for redemption must be estimated in order to reflect the existing current liability and to match expenses with revenues. An adjusting entry is made with a debit to Rebate Expense and a credit to Estimated Liability for Rebates. (Solution = b.)

QUESTION
13.   (L.O. 5) The ratio of current assets to current liabilities is called the:
       a.   current ratio.
       b.   acid-test ratio.
       c.   current asset turnover ratio.
       d.   current liability turnover ratio.

Explanation: Two major ratios used to measure liquidity of an entity are the (1) current ratio and the (2) acid-test ratio. The current ratio is computed by dividing current assets by current liabilities. The acid-test ratio is computed by dividing quick assets (cash + marketable securities + net receivables) by current liabilities. Marketable securities in this context refer to short-term (temporary) investments. The current ratio is sometimes called the working capital ratio; the acid-test ratio is often called the quick ratio. (Solution = a.)

IFRS Insights

- Similar to U.S. practice, IFRS requires that companies present current and noncurrent liabilities on the face of the statement of financial position (balance sheet), with current liabilities generally presented in order of liquidity. However, many companies using IFRS present noncurrent liabilities before current liabilities on the statement of financial position.

- The basic definition of a liability under GAAP and IFRS is very similar. In a more technical way, liabilities are defined by the IASB as a present obligation of the entity arising from past events, the settlement of which is expected to result in an outflow from the entity of resources embodying economic benefits. Liabilities may be legally enforceable via a contract or law but need not be; that is, they can arise due to normal business practices or customs.

- IFRS requires that companies classify liabilities as current or noncurrent on the face of the statement of financial position (balance sheet), except industries where a *presentation* based on liquidity would be considered to provide more useful information (such as financial institutions).

- Under IFRS, the measurement of a provision related to a contingency is based on the best estimate of the expenditure required to settle the obligation. If a range of estimates is predicted and no amount in the range is more likely than any other amount in the range, the "midpoint" of the range is used to measure the liability. In GAAP, the minimum amount in a range is used.

- Both IFRS and GAAP prohibit the recognition of liabilities for future losses. However, IFRS permits recognition of a restructuring liability, once a company has committed to a restructuring plan. GAAP has additional criteria (i.e., related to communicating the plan to employees) before a restructuring liability can be established.

- IFRS and GAAP are similar in the treatment of asst retirement obligations (AROs). However, the recognition criteria for an ARO are more stringent under GAAP. The ARO is **not** recognized unless there is a present legal obligation and the fair value of the obligation can be reasonably estimated.

- Under IFRS, short-term obligations expected to be refinanced can be classified as noncurrent if the refinancing is completed by the financial statement date. GAAP uses the date the financial statements are issued.

- IFRS uses the term provisions to refer to estimated liabilities. Under IFRS, contingencies are not recorded but are often disclosed. The accounting for provisions under IFRS and estimated liabilities under GAAP are very similar.

- GAAP uses the term "contingency" in a different way than IFRS. Contingent liabilities are **not** recognized in the financial statements under IFRS, whereas under GAAP a contingent liability is sometimes recognized.

TRUE/FALSE (Circle the correct answer for each).

T   F   1.   Many companies using IFRS present noncurrent liabilities before current liabilities on the statement of financial position.

T   F   2.   To be classified as a liability, an amount must be legally enforceable via a contract or law.

T   F   3.   Both IFRS and GAAP prohibit the recognition of liabilities for future losses.

T   F   4.   Under IFRS, short-term obligations expected to be refinanced can be classified as noncurrent if the refinancing is completed by the date the financial statements are issued.

T   F   5.   IFRS uses the term provisions to refer to estimated liabilities.

Solutions:

1.   T   4.   F
2.   F   5.   T
3.   T

CHAPTER 14

LONG-TERM LIABILITIES

OVERVIEW

Sources of assets include current liabilities, long-term liabilities, and owners' equity. Liabilities are considered a "temporary" source of assets; whereas, owners' equity is a more "permanent" source of assets. When a company borrows money, it does so with the expectation of using the borrowed funds to acquire assets that can be used to generate more income. The objective is to generate an amount of additional income which exceeds the cost of borrowing the funds (interest).

Long-term debt consists of probable future sacrifices of economic benefits arising from present obligations that are not payable within a year or the operating cycle of the business, whichever is longer. Bonds payable, long-term notes payable, mortgages payable, pension liabilities, and lease obligations are examples of long-term liabilities. This chapter will focus on the first two of these.

Although the subject of accounting for bonds is included in the principles of accounting course, many intermediate students don't remember the details of the procedures and look upon this topic as one of the most difficult they have encountered. Perhaps they have problems with the material because they try to memorize their way through the topic. As a result, it is imperative that you think about the time value of money concepts introduced in **Chapter 6** and grasp how they are applied in the computations involved in accounting for long-term debt. When you see the logic and rationale of the accounting procedures, you will find it easier to recall these guidelines years from now.

SUMMARY OF LEARNING OBJECTIVES

1. **Describe the formal procedures associated with issuing long-term debt.** Incurring long-term debt is often a formal procedure. The bylaws of corporations usually require approval by the board of directors and the stockholders before corporations can issue bonds or can make other long-term debt arrangements. Generally, long-term debt has various covenants or restrictions. The covenants and other terms of the agreement between the borrower and the lender are stated in the bond indenture or note agreement.

2. **Identify various types of bond issues.** Various types of bond issues are: (1) *secured and unsecured bonds*; (2) *term, serial bonds, and callable bonds*; (3) *convertible, commodity-backed, and deep-discount bonds*; (4) *registered and bearer (coupon) bonds*; and (5) *income and revenue bonds*. The variety in the types of bonds results from attempts to attract capital from different investors and risk-takers and to satisfy the cash flow needs of the issuers.

3. **Describe the accounting valuation for bonds at the date of issuance.** The investment community values a bond at the present value of its future cash flows, which consist of interest and principal. The rate used to compute the present value of these cash flows is the interest rate ͏t ͏ ͏ ͏ ͏idee ͏ ͏ ͏ ͏ ͏ ͏nntoble return on an investment commensurate with the issuer's risk

appearing on the bond certificate is the stated, coupon, or nominal rate. The issuer of the bonds sets the rate and expresses it as a percentage of the face value (also called the par value, principal amount, or maturity value) of the bonds. If the rate employed by the buyers differs from the stated rate, the present value of the bonds computed by the buyers will differ from the face value of the bonds. The difference between the face value and the present value of the bonds is either a discount or premium.

4. **Apply the methods of bond discount and premium amortization.** The discount (premium) is amortized and charged (credited) to interest expense over the period of time that the bonds are outstanding. Amortization of a discount increases bond interest expense and amortization of a premium decreases bond interest expense. The profession's preferred procedure for amortization of a discount or premium is the effective interest method. Under the effective-interest method, (1) bond interest expense is computed by multiplying the carrying value of the bonds at the beginning of the period by the effective interest rate, and (2) the bond discount or premium amortization is then determined by comparing the bond interest expense with the interest to be paid for the same interest period.

5. **Describe the accounting procedures for the extinguishment of debt.** At the time of reacquisition, the unamortized premium or discount and any costs of issue applicable to the debt must be amortized up to the reacquisition date. The reacquisition price is the amount paid on extinguishment or redemption before maturity, including any call premium and expense of reacquisition. On any specified date, the net carrying amount of the debt is the amount payable at maturity, adjusted for unamortized premium or discount and issue costs. Any excess of the net carrying amount over the reacquisition price is a gain from extinguishment. The excess of the reacquisition price over the net carrying amount is a loss from extinguishment. Gains and losses on extinguishments are recognized currently in income and are reported in the Other Gains and Losses section of the income statement.

6. **Explain the accounting procedures for long-term notes payable.** Accounting procedures for notes and bonds are similar. Like a bond, a note is valued at the present value of its future interest and principal cash flows, with any discount or premium being similarly amortized over the life of the note. Whenever the face amount of the note does not reasonably represent the present value of the consideration received in the exchange, a company must evaluate the entire arrangement in order to properly record the exchange and the subsequent interest.

7. **Describe the accounting for the fair value option.** Companies have the option to record fair value in their accounts for most financial assets and liabilities, including noncurrent liabilities. Fair value measurement for financial instruments, including financial liabilities, provides more relevant and understandable information than amortized cost. If companies choose the fair value option, noncurrent liabilities, such as bonds and notes payable, are recorded at fair value, with unrealized holding gains or losses reported as part of net income. An unrealized holding gain or loss is the net change in the fair value of the liability from one period to another, exclusive of interest expense recognized but not recorded.

8. **Explain the reporting of off-balance-sheet financing arrangements.** Off-balance-sheet financing is an attempt to borrow funds in such a way to prevent recording obligations. Examples of off-balance-sheet arrangements are (1) non-consolidated subsidiaries, (2) special purpose entities, and (3) operating leases.

9. **Indicate how to present and analyze long-term debt.** Companies that have large amounts and numerous issues of long-term debt frequently report only one amount in the balance sheet and support this with comments and schedules in the accompanying notes. Any assets pledged as security for the debt should be shown in the assets section of the balance sheet. Long-term debt that matures within one year should be reported as a current liability, unless retirement is to be accomplished with other than current assets or the creation of a new liability other than a current liability. If a company plans to refinance the debt, convert it into stock, or retire it with a bond retirement fund, it should continue to report it as noncurrent, accompanied with a note explaining the method it will use in the debt's liquidation. Disclosure is required of future payments f

5 years. Debt to total assets and times interest earned are two ratios that provide information about debt-paying ability and long-run solvency.

*10.   Describe the accounting for a debt restructuring. There are two types of debt settlements: (1) transfer or noncash assets, and (2) granting of equity interest. Creditors and debtors record losses and gains on settlements based on fair values. For accounting purposes there are also two types of restructurings with continuation of debt with modified terms: (1) the carrying amount of debt is less than the future cash flows, and (2) the carrying amount of debt exceeds the total future cash flows. Creditors record losses on these restructurings based on the expected future cash flows discounted at the historical effective interest rate. The debtor determines its gain based on undiscounted cash flows.

*This material is covered in **Appendix 14A** in the text.

TIPS ON CHAPTER TOPICS

TIP:	The denomination of a bond is called the **face value**. Synonymous terms are **par value**, **principal amount**, **maturity value**, and **face amount**.
TIP:	Bond prices are quoted in terms of percentage of par. Thus, a bond with a par value of $4,000 and a price quote of 102 is currently selling for a price of $4,080 (102% of $4,000). A bond with a quote of 100 is selling for its par value.
TIP:	The bond contract is called an **indenture**. This term is often confused with the term "debenture." A **debenture** bond is an unsecured bond.
TIP:	The interest rate written in the bond indenture and ordinarily appearing on the bond certificate is known as the **stated rate**. Synonymous terms are **coupon rate**, **nominal rate**, and **contract rate**.
TIP:	The rate of interest actually earned by bondholders is called the **effective**, **yield**, or **market rate**.
TIP:	A bond's **issuance price** is determined by the present value of all of the future cash flows promised by the bond indenture. The future cash flows include the face value and interest payments. The bond's present value is determined by using the market rate of interest at the date of issuance. An excess of the issuance price over par is called a **premium**; an excess of par value over the issuance price is called a **discount**.
TIP:	In computing the present value of a bond's (1) maturity value and (2) interest payments, the **same** interest rate is used. That rate is the effective interest rate on a per interest period basis. As an example, if a ten-year bond has a stated rate of 10%, pays interest semiannually, and is issued to yield 12%, a 6% rate is used to perform **all** of the present value calculations.
TIP:	Bond prices vary inversely with changes in the market rate of interest. This means that as the market rate of interest goes down, bond prices go up; and as the market rate of interest goes up, bond prices go down. It also means that at the date of issuance, if the market rate of interest is below the stated rate, the price will be above par; likewise, if the market rate is above the stated rate, the issuance price will be below par. Hence, **a premium or a discount is an adjustment to interest via an adjustment to price**. The adjustment to interest is recorded by the process of amortizing the premium or discount over the periods the bond is outstanding.
TIP:	Interest payments on notes payable are generally made on a monthly or quarterly basis. Interest payments on bonds payable are usually made semiannually. Despite these common practices, interest rates generally are expressed on an annual basis. Therefore, care must be taken that the annual rate be converted to a "rate per period" before other computations are performed.

TIP: The **Discount on Bonds Payable account** is a contra liability account so its balance should be deducted from Bonds Payable on the balance sheet. The **Premium on Bonds Payable account** is an adjunct type valuation account so its balance should be added to the balance of Bonds Payable on the balance sheet. Unamortized Bond Issuance Costs are to be classified as a deferred charge in the "Other Assets" classification on the balance sheet; they should be amortized over the bond's life using the straight-line method.

TIP: The **effective interest method** of amortization is sometimes called the **interest method** or the **present value method** or the **effective method**. When the effective interest method is used, the bond's carrying value will equal its present value (assuming the amortization is up to date). The effective interest method is the only amortization method that qualifies as a generally accepted principle (method). However, when the results of applying the straight-line method of amortization are not materially different than the results of using the effective interest method, the straight-line method may be used without being considered a departure from (i.e., a violation of) GAAP.

TIP: When the accounting period ends on a date other than an interest date, the amortization schedule for a bond or a note payable is unaffected by this fact. That is, the schedule is prepared and computations are made according to the bond periods, ignoring the details of the accounting period. The interest expense amounts shown in the amortization schedule are then apportioned to the appropriate accounting period(s). As an example, if the interest expense for the six months ending April 30, 2015 is $120,000, then $40,000 (2/6) of that amount would go on the income statement for the 2014 calendar year and $80,000 (4/6) of it should be reflected on the income statement for the 2015 calendar year.

TIP: Accounting for loan impairments was discussed in **Appendix 7B** where loans were held as assets. The principles are the same when dealing with loan impairments where a loan is a liability from the viewpoint of the reporting entity. However, a reduction in the liability is viewed as a gain situation from the debtor's viewpoint while the reduction is a loss from the creditor's viewpoint.

ILLUSTRATION 14-1
COMPUTATION AND PROOF OF BOND ISSUANCE PRICE (L.O. 3, 4)

Guemple Company issues a 5-year bond on January 1, 2014 (maturity date is January 1, 2019, with a stated interest rate of 6%. The market rate of interest at the date of issuance is 5%, the par value is $1,000, and interest is due annually on January 1.

The bond is a promise to pay $1,000 on January 1, 2019 and $60 (6% x $1,000) every January 1 beginning January 1, 2015 and ending January 1, 2019. The price of the bond is determined by the present value of all future cash flows related to the bond. The present value of the bond is found by discounting all of the promised payments at the market rate of interest (5%). This process is illustrated by the following timeline and present value calculations:

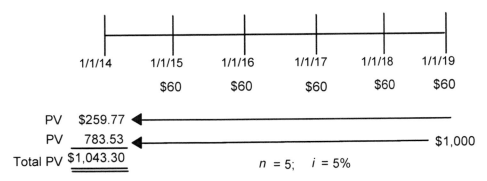

Present value of an ordinary annuity of $60 per period for 5 years at
    5% interest ($60 x 4.32948) $ 259.77
Present value of $1,000 due in 5 periods at 5% interest ($1,000 x .78353).   783.53
Total present value $1,043.30

TIP: The factor of .78353 was derived from the Present Value of 1 table and the factor of 4.32948 was derived from the Present Value of an Ordinary Annuity of 1 table.

Thus, the bond price would be $1,043.30. Theoretically, this is the sum that would be required to be invested now at 5% compounded annually (market rate) to allow for the periodic (annual in this case) withdrawal of $60 (stated amount of interest) at the end of each of 5 years and the withdrawal of $1,000 at the end of 5 years. The following is proof that $1,043.30 is the amount required in this case.

ILLUSTRATION 14-1 (Continued)

Jan. 1, 2014	$1,043.30 ————————▶	$1,043.30	
	+ 52.17 **interest at 5%**◀	× .05	**market rate**
	1,095.47	52.1650	**effective**
1st interest payment on 1/1/15	- 60.00		**interest**
	1,035.47 ————————▶	1,035.47	
	+ 51.77 ◀	× .05	
	1,087.24	51.7735	
2nd interest payment on 1/1/16	- 60.00		
	1,027.24 ————————▶	1,027.24	
	+ 51.36 ◀	× .05	
	1,078.60	51.3620	
3rd interest payment on 1/1/17	- 60.00		
	1,018.60 ————————▶	1,018.60	
	+ 50.93 ◀	× .05	
	1,069.53	50.9300	
4th interest payment on 1/1/18	- 60.00		
	1,009.53 ————————▶	1,009.53	
	+ 50.48 ◀	× .05	
	1,060.01	50.4765	
5th interest payment on 1/1/19	- 60.00		
	1,000.01		
Principal payment	- 1,000.00		
	$ .01 Rounding error		

An amortization schedule can be constructed using the computations above. It would appear as follows:

Date	Stated Interest	Effective Interest	Premium Amortization	Carrying Value
1/1/14				$ 1,043.30
1/1/15	$ 60.00	$ 52.17	$ 7.83	1,035.47
1/1/16	60.00	51.77	8.23	1,027.24
1/1/17	60.00	51.36	8.64	1,018.60
1/1/18	60.00	50.93	9.07	1,009.53
1/1/19	60.00	50.47*	9.53	1,000.00
	$300.00	$256.70	$ 43.30	

*The rounding error of $.01 is plugged to interest expense in the last interest period.

ILLUSTRATION 14-2
FORMATS FOR COMMON COMPUTATIONS INVOLVING
BONDS PAYABLE (L.O. 4)

1. Cash Interest Per Period.

       Par value

   x <u>Stated rate of interest per period</u>

   = Cash interest per period

Cash interest is always a constant amount each period.

2. Interest Expense Using Straight-line Amortization Method.

       Cash interest for the period

   + Discount amortization for the period

OR - <u>Premium amortization for the period</u>

   = Interest expense for the period

Interest expense is a constant amount each period using this method.

3. Amortization Amount Using Straight-line Method.

     Issuance premium or discount ÷ Periods in bonds life = Amortization per period

4. Interest Expense Using Effective Interest Method.

       Carrying value at the beginning of the period

   x <u>Effective rate of interest per interest period</u>

   = Interest expense for the interest period

The carrying value changes each interest period so the interest expense changes each period.

5. Amortization Amount Using Effective Interest Method.

       Interest expense for the interest period

   - <u>Cash interest for the interest period   </u>

   = Amortization of discount for the interest period

Interest expense is greater than cash interest for bonds issued at a discount.

                                  OR

       Cash interest for the interest period

   - <u>Interest expense for the interest period   </u>

   = Amortization of premium for the interest period

Cash interest is greater than interest expense for bonds issued at a premium.

6. Carrying Value and Net Carrying Value.

       Par value

   - Unamortized discount

OR + <u>Unamortized premium   </u>

   = Carrying value

   - <u>Unamortized debt issue costs</u>

   = Net carrying amount

The process of amortization decreases the unamortized amount of discount or premium; hence the carrying value moves toward the par value.

7. Gain or Loss on Redemption.

       Net carrying amount

   - <u>Redemption price   </u>

   = Gain if positive, that is, if net carrying value is the greater.

OR = Loss if negative, that is, if redemption price is the greater.

ILLUSTRATION 14-2 (Continued)

TIP: An **interest payment** promised by a bond is computed by multiplying the bond's par value by its stated interest rate. This amount is often referred to as the **cash interest** or **stated interest**.

TIP: Using the **straight-line method of amortization**, interest expense is determined by either adding the amount of discount amortization to the cash interest or deducting the amount of premium amortization from the cash interest. The periodic amount of amortization is determined by dividing the issuance premium or discount by the number of periods in the bond's life.

TIP: The **life** of a bond is measured by the time between the date of issuance and the date of maturity. The bond's life is shorter than the term of the bond if the bond is issued on a date later than it is dated.

TIP: The **effective interest expense** (interest expense using the effective interest method of amortization) is determined by multiplying the bond's carrying value at the beginning of the period by the effective interest rate. The difference between the interest payment (cash interest) and the effective interest expense for a period is the amount of premium or discount amortization for the period. The amount of amortization for a period causes a reduction in the balance of the unamortized premium or unamortized discount which in turn causes the carrying value to change.

TIP: A bond's **carrying value** (**book value**, **carrying amount**) is equal to the (1) par value plus any unamortized premium, or (2) par value minus any unamortized discount. When the effective interest method of amortization is used and the amortization is up to date, the bond's carrying value will equal its present value (determined by using the bond's effective interest rate to discount all remaining interest payments and par value). A bond's **net carrying value** is equal to its carrying value minus any related unamortized bond issuance costs.

TIP: The pattern of interest expense using the effective interest method may be compared to the pattern of interest expense using the straight-line method for both a bond issued at a discount and a bond issued at a premium by reference to the graph in **Illustration 14-3**. The relationship between interest expense and cash interest should also be noted. The difference between the cash interest and interest expense for a period is the amount of amortization for the period. The pattern of the periodic amount of amortization is also depicted by the graph.

TIP: If you use the effective interest rate (market rate at the date of a bond's issuance) to compute the (1) present value of the bond at the beginning of a given period, and (2) the present value of the same bond at the end of the given period, the difference between the two present value figures equals the amortization of the bond's premium or discount during that same period. This is true because the effective interest method results in reporting the present value of the liability (using the bond's effective interest rate for the discounting process) at a balance sheet date. That's why the effective interest method is the only method that is GAAP.

EXERCISE 14-1

Purpose: (L.O. 3, 4, 5) This exercise will illustrate (1) the computations and journal entries throughout a bond's life for a bond issued at a discount and (2) the accounting required when bonds are called prior to their maturity date.

Arnold Howell Company issued bonds with the following details:

Face value	$100,000
Stated interest rate	7%
Market interest rate	10%
Maturity date	January 1, 2017
Date of issuance	January 1, 2014
Bond issue costs	$8,000
Call price	102
Interest payments due	Annually on January 1
Method of amortization	Effective interest

Instructions

(a)   Compute the amount of issuance premium or discount.
(b)   Prepare the journal entry for the issuance of bonds.
(c)   Prepare the amortization schedule for these bonds.
(d)   Prepare all of the journal entries (subsequent to the issuance date) for 2014 and 2015 that relate to these bonds. Assume the accounting period coincides with the calendar year.
(e)   Prepare the journal entry to record the retirement of bonds assuming they are called on January 1, 2016.

Solution to Exercise 14-1

(a) $100,000 par x 7% stated rate = $7,000 annual cash interest
Factor for present value of a single sum, $i = 10\%$, $n = 3$ .75132
Factor for present value of an ordinary annuity, $i = 10\%$, $n = 3$ 2.48685

$100,000 x .75132 =	$ 75,132.00	
$7,000 x 2.48685 =	17,407.95	
Issuance price	$ 92,539.95	

Face value	$ 100,000.00
Issuance price	92,539.95
Discount on bonds payable	$ 7,460.05

(b)

Cash ($92,539.95 - $8,000.00)	84,539.95	
Discount on Bonds Payable	7,460.05	
Unamortized Bond Issue Costs.................................	8,000.00	
Bonds Payable		100,000.00

Approach and Explanation: Always start with the easiest part of a journal entry. The issuance of a bond is **always** recorded by a credit to the Bonds Payable account for the par value of the bonds ($100,000 in this case). Because the issuance price is less than par, a contra type valuation account must be established; it is titled Discount on Bonds Payable and is debited for the issuance discount of $7,460.05. The $8,000.00 issuance costs are to be amortized over the periods benefited by the loan in order to comply with the matching principle; hence they are initially charged to an asset account. Cash was received for the issuance price less the issuance costs (fees to attorneys, accountants, printers, and underwriters) so debit Cash for the net proceeds of $84,539.95.

> **TIP:** The Unamortized Bond Issue Costs account can be titled Bond Issue Costs. The Discount on Bonds Payable account is sometimes called Unamortized Bond Discount. Regardless of whether the word unamortized appears in the account titles or not, the balances of these accounts at a balance sheet date (after adjustments) represent the unamortized amounts.

(c)

Date	7% Stated Interest	10% Interest Expense	Discount Amortization	Carrying Value
1/1/14				$ 92,539.95
1/1/15	$ 7,000.00	$ 9,254.00	$ 2,254.00	94,793.95
1/1/16	7,000.00	9,479.40	2,479.40	97,273.35
1/1/17	7,000.00	9,726.65[a]	2,726.65	100,000.00
	$ 21,000.00	$ 28,460.05	$ 7,460.05	

[a]Includes rounding error of $.69.

Explanation: Stated interest is determined by multiplying the par value ($100,000) by the contract rate of interest (7%). Interest expense is computed by multiplying the carrying value at the beginning of the interest period by the effective interest rate (10%). The amount of discount amortization for the period is the excess of the interest expense over the stated interest (cash interest) amount. The carrying value at an interest payment date is the carrying value at the beginning of the interest period plus the discount amortization for the period.

> **TIP:** The amount of interest expense of $9,479.40 appearing on the "1/1/16" payment line is the amount of interest expense for the interest period ending on that date. Thus, in this case, $9,479.40 is the interest expense for the twelve months preceding the date 1/1/16, which would be the calendar year of 2015.
>
> **TIP:** Any rounding error should be plugged to (included in) the interest expense amount for the last interest period. Otherwise, there would forever be a small balance left in the Discount on Bonds Payable account long after the bonds were extinguished.
>
> **TIP:** Notice that the total interest expense ($28,460.05) over the three-year period equals the total cash interest ($21,000.00) plus the total issuance discount ($7,460.05). Thus, you can see that the issuance discount represents an additional amount of interest to be recognized over the life of the bonds.

(d)   **December 31, 2014**

Interest Expense	9,254.00	
Interest Payable		7,000.00
Discount on Bonds Payable		2,254.00
Bond Issue Expense	2,666.67	
Unamortized Bond Issue Costs		2,666.67

     ($8,000.00 ÷ 3 = $2,666.67)

January 1, 2015

Interest Payable	7,000.00	
Cash		7,000.00

December 31, 2015

Interest Expense	9,479.40	
Interest Payable		7,000.00
Discount on Bonds Payable		2,479.40
Bond Issue Expense	2,666.67	
Unamortized Bond Issue Costs		2,666.67

(e)   **January 1, 2016**

Interest Payable	7,000.00	
Bonds Payable	100,000.00	
Loss on Redemption of Bonds	7,393.31	
Discount on Bonds Payable		2,726.65
Unamortized Bond Issue Costs		2,666.66
Cash ($102,000 + $7,000)		109,000.00

     ($7,460.05 - $2,254.00 - $2,479.40 = $2,726.65 unamortized discount)
     ($8,000.00 - $2,666.67 - $2,666.67 = $2,666.66 unamortized issue costs)
     ($100,000.00 x 102% = $102,000.00 price to retire)
     ($100,000.00 - $2,726.65 = $97,273.35 carrying value)
     ($97,273.35 - $2,666.66 = $94,606.69 net carrying value)
     ($102,000.00 - $94,606.69 = $7,393.31 loss)

TIP: There was a **call premium** (amount in excess of par required) of $2,000.00 in this situation which is included in the loss computation.

TIP: Gains or losses on extinguishment of debt are to be classified as Other Gains and Losses on the income statement.

TIP: The debit to interest payable (for interest accrued last period) assumes that reversing entries are **not** made. Reversing entries were discussed in **Appendix 3B**.

ILLUSTRATION 14-3
GRAPH TO DEPICT INTEREST PATTERNS FOR BONDS (L.O. 4)

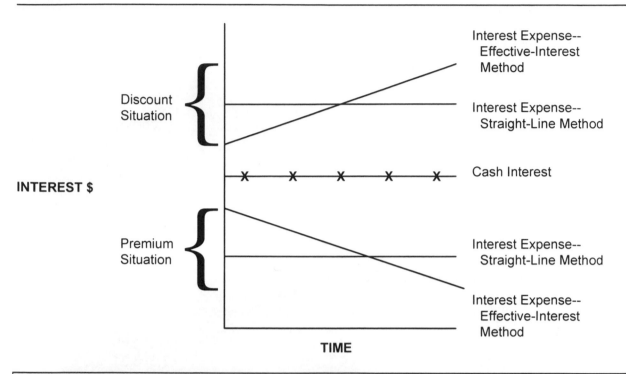

TIP:	Regardless of whether the straight-line method of amortization or the effective interest method of amortization is used, the following will occur:
1.	The amount of cash interest (stated interest) is a constant amount each period.
2.	The bond's carrying amount increases over the bond's life if it is issued at a discount, due to the amortization of the discount.
3.	The bond's carrying amount decreases over the bond's life if it is issued at a premium, due to the amortization of the premium.

TIP:	If the straight-line method of amortization is used, the following relationships will exist:
1.	The amount of amortization is a constant amount each period.
2.	The amount of interest expense is a constant amount each period.

TIP:	If the effective interest method of amortization is used, the following relationships will exist:
1.	The effective interest rate is constant each period.
2.	The interest expense is an increasing amount each period if the bond is issued at a discount (because a constant rate is applied to an increasing carrying amount each period).
3.	The interest expense is a decreasing amount each period if the bond is issued at a premium (because a constant rate is applied to a decreasing carrying amount each period).
4.	The amount of amortization **increases** each period because the difference between the effective interest expense and the cash interest widens each period.

EXERCISE 14-2

Purpose: (L.O. 4) This exercise will serve as an example for both the issuance of bonds between interest payment dates and the use of the straight-line method of amortization.

On May 1, 2014, Peter Pan Tools Corporation issued bonds payable with a face value of $1,400,000 at 104 plus accrued interest. They are registered bonds dated January 1, 2014, bear interest at 9% payable semiannually on January 1 and July 1, and mature January 1, 2024. The company uses the straight-line method of amortization.

Instructions

(a)   Compute the amount of bond interest expense to be reported on Peter Pan's income statement for the year ended December 31, 2014. (Round computations to the nearest dollar.)

(b)   Compute the amount of bond interest payable to be reported on Peter Pan's balance sheet at December 31, 2014.

(c)   Compute the amount of bond interest expense to be reported on Peter Pan's income statement for the year ended December 31, 2015.

Solution to Exercise 14-2

(a)		
	Interest paid on July 1, 2014 ($1,400,000 x 9% x 6/12)	$ 63,000
	Premium amortized on July 1, 2014 ($56,000 x 2/116)	(966)
	Accrued interest collected on May 1, 2014 ($1,400,000 x 9% x 4/12)	(42,000)
	Interest accrued on December 31, 2014 ($1,400,000 x 9% x 6/12)	63,000
	Premium amortized on December 31, 2014 ($56,000 x 6/116)	(2,897)
	Total bond interest expense for the year ending December 31, 2014	$ 80,137

Approach and Explanation: Prepare the journal entries to record the issuance of the bonds, the payment of interest and amortization of premium on July 1, 2014, and the year-end adjusting entry. Post the entries to the Interest Expense account and determine its balance at December 31, 2014.

May 1, 2014

Cash....	1,498,000^c	
Bonds Payable		1,400,000
Premium on Bonds Payable		56,000^a
Interest Expense		42,000^b
(To record sale of bonds at a premium plus accrued interest)		

^{a}(104% x $1,400,000) - $1,400,000 = $56,000 issuance premium.

^{b}9% x $1,400,000 x 4 months/12 months = $42,000 accrued interest (for January through April 2014).

^{c}$1,400,000 face value x 104% = $1,456,000 issuance price. $1,456,000 issuance price + $42,000 accrued interest = $1,498,000 cash proceeds.

July 1, 2014

Interest Expense ($63,000 - $966)	62,034	
Premium on Bonds Payable ($56,000 x 2/116)	966	
Cash ($1,400,000 x 9% x 6/12)		63,000

(To record semiannual payment of interest
and amortization of premium for two months)

> **TIP:** A premium or discount is to be amortized over the period the bonds are outstanding (from the date of issuance to the date of maturity). In this case, May 1, 2014 to January 1, 2024 is 4 months shy of 10 years (which is 116 months).

December 31, 2014

Interest Expense ($63,000 - $2,897)	60,103	
Premium on Bond Payable ($56,000 x 6/116)	2,897	
Interest Payable		63,000

($1,400,000 x 9% x 6/12)
(To record accrual of interest since last payment
date and amortization of premium for 6 months)

Interest Expense				Interest Payable		
7/1/14	62,034	5/1/14	42,000		12/31/14	63,000
12/31/14	60,103					
Balance					Balance	
12/31/14	80,137				12/31/14	63,000

> **TIP:** Bonds are often issued between interest payment dates. When this occurs, the issuer requires the investor to pay the market price for the bonds plus accrued interest since the last interest date. At the next interest payment date, the corporation will return the accrued interest to the investor by paying the full amount of interest due on outstanding bonds. In the situation at hand, the issuer collects from the investor interest from the date the bonds are dated to the date of issuance (from January 1, 2014 to May 1, 2014 is 4 months). When the next interest date rolls around (July 1, 2014), a full interest payment is made to the investor. Thus, the investor receives the two months' interest earned from May 1, 2014 to June 30, 2014, plus the accrued interest for four months that the investor paid in at the purchase date. Accrued interest at the date bonds are sold by an issuer is handled in this manner to expedite the issuer's payment procedures. At any interest payment date, interest for a full interest period is paid to each bondholder, there is no need to compute the actual time the bond investment was held by a particular bondholder and to prorate the interest because the investor has already paid in any portion of the full interest payment not earned by them during that interest period.
>
> **TIP:** The journal entry to record the second interest payment on January 1, 2015 would be as follows (assuming reversing entries are not used):
> | | | |
> |---|---|---|
> | Interest Payable | 63,000 | |
> | Cash | | 63,000 |
>
> (To record a full interest payment)

> **TIP:** Refer to the journal entry made at the date of issuance (May 1, 2014). Rather than credit Interest Expense for $42,000, you may credit Interest Payable for the accrued interest of $42,000. This procedure will then require a modification to the entry on July 1, 2014. That entry would then include a debit to Interest Payable for $42,000 and a debit to Interest Expense for $20,034 rather than a debit to Interest Expense for $62,034.
>
> **TIP:** Refer to the journal entry made at December 31, 2014. You may wish to make two separate entries rather than the one compound entry. The equivalent single entries would be as follows:
>
> **December 31, 2014**
>
> | | | |
> |---|---|---|
> | Interest Expense | 63,000 | |
> | Interest Payable | | 63,000 |
> | (To record accrued interest for the 6 months) | | |
> | ($1,400,000 x 9% x 6/12 = $63,000) | | |
> | | | |
> | Premium on Bonds Payable | 2,897 | |
> | Interest Expense | | 2,897 |
> | (To record premium amortization for 6 months) | | |
> | ($56,000 x 6/116 = $2,897) | | |

(b) Accrued interest payable at December 31, 2014:
    $1,400,000 x 9% x 6/12 = $63,000

> **TIP:** Refer to explanation of part (a) above and balance of T-account for Interest Payable.

(c)

Interest paid on July 1, 2015 ($1,400,000 x 9% x 6/12)	$ 63,000
Premium amortized on July 1, 2015 ($56,000 x 6/116)	(2,897)
Interest accrued on December 31, 2015 ($1,400,000 x 9% x 6/12)	63,000
Premium amortized on December 31, 2015 ($56,000 x 6/116)	(2,897)
Total bond interest expense for the year ending December 31, 2015	$ 120,206

EXERCISE 14-3

Purpose: (L.O. 4) This exercise will illustrate the computation of the bond price when interest is due semiannually. Additionally, it will present the accounting for bonds where the effective-interest method of amortization is used and the end of the accounting period does not coincide with the end of an interest period.

P & J Chase Company sells $500,000 of 10% bonds on November 1, 2014. The bonds pay interest on May 1 and November 1 and are to yield 12%. The due date of the bonds is May 1, 2018. The accounting period is the calendar year. No reversing entries are made. Bond premium or discount is to be amortized at interest dates and at year-end.

Instructions

(a)   Compute the price of the bonds at the issuance date.

(b)   Prepare the amortization schedule for this issue.

(c)   Prepare all of the relevant journal entries for this bond issue from the date of issuance through May 2016.

Solution to Exercise 14-3

(a)   Time diagram:

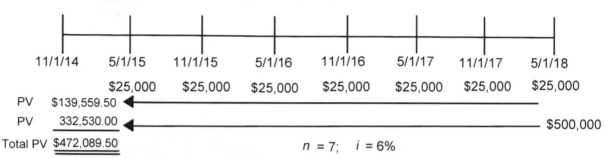

Factor for present value of a single sum, $i = 6\%$, $n = 7$ .66506
Factor for present value of an ordinary annuity, $i = 6\%$, $n = 7$ 5.58238
$500,000 x 5% = $25,000 interest per period
$500,000 x .66506 = $ 332,530.00
$25,000 x 5.58238 =   139,559.50
Issuance price $ 472,089.50

(b)

Date	5% Stated Interest	6% Interest Expense	Discount Amortization	Carrying Value
11/1/14				$ 472,089.50
5/1/15	$ 25,000.00	$ 28,325.37	$ 3,325.37	475,414.87
11/1/15	25,000.00	28,524.89	3,524.89	478,939.76
5/1/16	25,000.00	28,736.39	3,736.39	482,676.15
11/1/16	25,000.00	28,960.57	3,960.57	486,636.72
5/1/17	25,000.00	29,198.20	4,198.20	490,834.92
11/1/17	25,000.00	29,450.10	4,450.10	495,285.02
5/1/18	25,000.00	29,714.98*	4,714.98	500,000.00
	$175,000.00	$202,910.50	$27,910.50	

*Includes a rounding error of $2.12.

TIP: There are two interest periods per year; therefore, the stated interest rate per interest period is the annual rate (10%) divided by 2, which is 5%.

TIP: If you round all of your computations to the nearest cent, your rounding error will be small. A small (less than $5.00) rounding error provides some comfort that the amortization schedule is largely correct. A large rounding error (more than $10.00) indicates that one or more mistakes are likely included in the computation within the schedule or in the determination of the starting point (issuance price of the debt).

> **TIP:** The amortization schedule displays amounts according to bond periods. If one interest period overlaps two different accounting periods, the amount of expense and amortization for that interest period must be appropriately allocated to the respective accounting periods.
>
> **TIP:** Instead of just memorizing what goes on an amortization schedule, think about the reason the amounts have been included. That will help you to construct a schedule without much effort. In the date column, start with the issuance date, followed by each interest date. The stated interest amount is computed by multiplying the face value of the instrument by the stated rate of interest per interest period. Interest expense is computed by multiplying the carrying value at the beginning of the period (end of the prior line on the amortization schedule) by the market rate of interest per period. The difference between the stated interest and the interest expense for the period is the amount of the amortization for the period. Discount amortization is added to the previous carrying value (or premium amortization is deducted from the previous carrying value) to arrive at the carrying value at the end of the interest period (interest payment date).

(c)

November 1, 2014

Cash	472,089.50	
Discount on Bonds Payable	27,910.50	
Bonds Payable		500,000.00

December 31, 2014

Interest Expense	9,441.79	
Discount on Bonds Payable		1,108.46
Interest Payable		8,333.33

($28,325.37 x 2/6 = $9,441.79)
($3,325.37 x 2/6 = $1,108.46)
($25,000.00 x 2/6 = $8,333.33)

May 1, 2015

Interest Payable	8,333.33	
Interest Expense	18,883.58	
Discount on Bonds Payable		2,216.91
Cash		25,000.00

($28,325.37 - $9,441.79 = $18,883.58)
($3,325.37 - $1,108.46 = $2,216.91)

November 1, 2015

Interest Expense	28,524.89	
Discount on Bonds Payable		3,524.89
Cash		25,000.00

December 31, 2015

Interest Expense	9,578.80	
Discount on Bond Payable		1,245.47
Interest Payable		8,333.33

($28,736.39 x 2/6 = $9,578.80)
($3,736.39 x 2/6 = $1,245.46 + $.01 to balance)
($25,000.00 x 2/6 = $8,333.33)

May 1, 2016

Interest Expense	19,157.59	
Interest Payable	8,333.33	
Discount on Bonds Payable		2,490.92
Cash.		25,000.00

($28,736.39 - $9,578.80 = $19,157.59)
($3,736.39 - $1,245.47 = $2,490.92)

EXERCISE 14-4

Purpose: (L.O. 3, 4, 8) This exercise will enable you to practice identifying data required to perform computations involving bonds payable and applying the terminology associated with bonds.

On January 1, 2014, Tuna Fishery sold $100,000 (face value) worth of bonds. The bonds are dated January 1, 2014 and will mature on January 1, 2019. Interest is to be paid annually on January 1. Issue costs related to these bonds amounted to $2,000, and these costs are being amortized by the straight-line method. The following amortization schedule was prepared by the accountant for the first 2 years of the life of the bonds:

Date	Stated Interest	Effective Interest	Amortization	Carrying Value of Bonds
1/1/14				$ 104,212.37
1/1/15	$ 7,000.00	$ 6,252.74	$ 747.26	103,465.11
1/1/16	7,000.00	6,207.91	792.09	102,673.02

Instructions
On the basis of the information above, answer the following questions (round your answers to the nearest cent or percent) and explain the reasoning or computations, as appropriate.
(a)   What is the nominal or stated rate of interest for this bond issue?
(b)   What is the effective or market rate of interest for this bond issue?
(c)   Prepare the journal entry to record the sale of the bond issue on January 1, 2014, including the issue costs.
(d)   Prepare the appropriate entry(ies) at December 31, 2016, the end of the accounting year.
(e)   Identify the amount of bond issue costs and the amount of interest expense to be reported on the income statement for the year ended December 31, 2016.
(f)   Show how the account balances related to the bond issue will be presented on the December 31, 2016 balance sheet. Indicate the major classification(s) involved.
(g)   What is the book value of the bonds at December 31, 2016?
(h)   What is the net book value of the bonds at December 31, 2016?
(i)   If the bonds are retired for $100,500 (excluding interest) at January 1, 2017, will the bonds be retired at a gain or a loss? What is the amount of that gain or loss? Where will it be reported on the income statement for the year ending December 31, 2017?

Solution to Exercise 14-4

(a)   Stated interest = Stated rate of interest x Par
$7,000 = Stated rate of interest x $100,000
$7,000 ÷ $100,000 = Stated rate of interest
7% = Stated rate of interest

(b)   Effective interest = Market rate x Carrying value at beginning of period
$6,252.74 = Market rate x $104,212.37
$6,252.74 ÷ $104,212.37 = Market rate
6% = Market rate

(c)
Cash	102,212.37	
Unamortized Bond Issue Costs	2,000.00	
Bonds Payable		100,000.00
Premium on Bonds Payable		4,212.37

(d)
Bond Interest Expense	6,160.38	
Premium on Bonds Payable	839.62	
Interest Payable		7,000.00

($102,673.02 x 6% = $6,160.38)

Bond Issue Expense	400	
Unamortized Bond Issue Costs		400

(e)   Bond issue expense[1] $400
Bond interest expense[2] $6,160.38
[1]$2,000 ÷ 5 years = $400
[2]$102,673.02 X 6% = $6,160.38

(f)
Other assets
Unamortized bond issue costs $ 800
Current liabilities
Interest payable $7,000
Long-term liabilities
Bonds payable, 7%, due 1/1/19 $100,000.00
Unamortized premium[1]   1,833.40
                                       $101,833.40

[1]$4,212.37 - $747.26 - $792.09 - $839.62 = $1,833.40

(g) $101,833.40 [See solution for part (f).]
Book value is another name for carrying value or carrying amount.

The amount, $101,833.40, can also be computed by:
Carrying value at 1/1/16 per schedule $ 102,673.02
Amortization for 2016 [part (d)]   (839.62)
Carrying value at 12/31/16 $ 101,833.40

(h)		
	Bonds payable balance	$100,000.00
	Premium on bonds payable balance	1,833.40
	Book value at 12/31/16	101,833.40
	Unamortized bond issue costs	(800.00)*
	Net book value at 12/31/16	$101,033.40

*[$2,000 - 3($400) = $800]

(i)   Gain. A gain will result because the retirement price is less than the net carrying value at the date of retirement.

Net carrying value at 1/1/17 [part (g)]	$101,033.40
Retirement price	100,500.00
Gain on retirement of debt	$ 533.40

This gain from retirement of debt should be classified in the Other Gains and Losses section on the income statement.

EXERCISE 14-5

Purpose: (L.O. 3) This exercise will illustrate how to account for the redemption of bonds by cash payment prior to maturity.

The balance sheet for Waisman Corporation reports the following information on December 31, 2013:

Long-term liabilities	
9% Bonds payable, due December 31, 2017	$ 1,000,000
Less: Discount on bonds payable	60,000
	$ 940,000

Interest is payable annually on December 31. The straight-line method of amortization is used. Interest rates have declined in the market place since the above mentioned bonds were issued. Waisman decides to borrow money from another source at a lower interest rate to lower its annual interest charges. Therefore, on July 1, 2014, Waisman redeems all of the old outstanding bonds at 102 (recall that bond prices vary inversely with changes in the market rate of interest).

Instructions
Prepare the journal entry(ies) to record the redemption of these bonds on July 1, 2014.

Solution to Exercise 14-5

Interest Expense..	45,000	
Cash...		45,000
(To record the payment of accrued interest at		
July 1, 2014)		
($1,000,000 x 9% x 6/12 = $45,000)		

Interest Expense..	7,500	
Discount on Bonds Payable...		7,500
(To record the amortization of discount for six months)		
[($60,000 ÷ 4) x 6/12]		

Bonds Payable..	1,000,000	
Loss on Bond Redemption...	72,500[3]	
Discount on Bonds Payable...		52,500[2]
Cash...		1,020,000[1]
(To record the redemption of the bonds		
payable at 102)		

       [1]$1,000,000 face value x 1.02 = $1,020,000 redemption price.
       [2]$60,000 - $7,500 = $52,500 balance at July 1, 2014.
       [3]$1,020,000 redemption price - $947,500 carrying value = $72,500
        loss on redemption.

Approach and Explanation: Break the required entries into three simple parts— payment of accrued interest, update of discount amortization, and extinguishment of the liability. The bond holder is entitled to interest for the months between the last interest payment date and the redemption date, which is six months in this case. The amortization of the discount must be updated to arrive at the carrying value of the debt at the redemption date. In this case, six months of amortization must be recorded. The straight-line amortization method is being used so the $60,000 balance in the discount account at December 31, 2014 applies evenly to the remaining four years of the bond's term. The amortization for six months would, therefore, be one-half of the $15,000 annual amount.

For the entry to record the redemption, do the following: (1) Begin with the easiest part of the journal entry. Credit Cash to record the payment of the redemption price which is 102% of the face value of the bonds. (2) Remove the carrying value of the bonds from the accounts by debiting Bonds Payable for the face value of the bonds and crediting Discount on Bonds Payable for the balance of the related unamortized discount ($60,000 balance at December 31, 2013 less the $7,500 amortization for the first six months of 2014 = $52,500). (3) Record the difference between the redemption (retirement) price and the carrying value of the bonds as a gain or loss on redemption. An excess of carrying value over redemption price results in a gain. In the case at hand, the redemption price ($1,020,000) exceeds the carrying value of the bonds ($1,000,000 - $52,500 = $947,500). Since it cost $1,020,000 to eliminate a debt that appears on the books at only $947,500, a loss results.

EXERCISE 14-6

Purpose: (L.O. 6, 8) This exercise will illustrate the accounting for the issuance of a note payable to acquire land when the note bears an interest rate that is unreasonably low in relation to the market rate of interest.

On December 31, 2013, Jason Weiss, Inc. purchased land by giving $40,000 in cash and a 3% interest-bearing note with a face value of $500,000. There was no established exchange price for the land, nor a ready market for the note. The land had an assessed value of $320,000 for purposes of taxation by the county. The note is due December 31, 2017. Interest is payable each December 31. Jason's incremental borrowing rate is 10%.

Instructions
(a)   Draw a time line for the note and determine the amount to record as the cost of the land.
(b)   Prepare the amortization schedule for the note payable.
(c)   Determine the amount to report as interest expense on the income statement for the fiscal year ending March 31, 2015.
(d)   Determine the amount to report as interest paid on the statement of cash flows for the fiscal year ending March 31, 2015.
(e)   Determine the amounts to appear (with respect to the above information) on the balance sheet at March 31, 2015, and indicate the proper classification for each item.

Solution to Exercise 14-6

(a)   Time line:

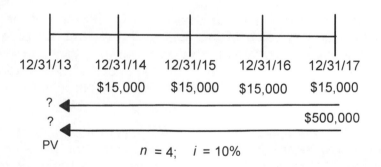

12/31/13	Land	429,052.90	
	Discount on Note Payable	110,947.10	
	Note Payable		500,000.00
	Cash		40,000.00

The market rate of interest is used to compute the present value of the note which is then used to establish the exchange price for the land. The cash down payment of $40,000.00 plus the present value of the note of $389,052.90 equals the $429,052.90 cost of the land. The market rate of interest should be the rate the borrower normally would have to pay to borrow money for similar activities.

Computation of the present value of the note:

Maturity value		$500,000.00
Present value of $500,000 due in 4 years at 10% ($500,000 x .68301)	$341,505.00	
Present value of $15,000 payable annually for 4 years at 10% ($15,000 x 3.16986)	47,547.90	
Present value of the note and interest		389,052.90
Discount on note receivable		$110,947.10

(b)

Amortization Schedule for Note Payable

Date	3% Stated Interest	10% Effective Interest	Amortization of Discount	PV Balance
12/31/13				$ 389,052.90
12/31/14	$15,000.00[a]	$ 38,905.29[b]	$ 23,905.29[c]	412,958.19[d]
12/31/15	15,000.00	41,295.82	26,295.82	439,254.01
12/31/16	15,000.00	43,925.40	28,925.40	468,179.41
12/31/17	15,000.00	46,820.59[e]	31,820.59	500,000.00
Totals	$60,000.00	$170,947.10	$110,947.10	

[a]$500,000.00 face value x 3% stated interest rate = $15,000.00 stated interest.
[b]$389,052.90 present value x 10% effective interest rate = $38,905.29 effective interest.
[c]$38,905.29 effective interest - $15,000.00 stated interest = $23,905.29 discount amortization.
[d]$389,052.90 PV balance 12/31/13 + $23,905.29 discount amortization for 12 months = $412,958.19 PV balance 12/31/14.
[e]Includes rounding difference of $2.65.

Explanation: When a note is given in exchange for property, goods, or services in a bargained transaction entered into at arms length, the stated interest rate is assumed to be fair and is thus used to compute interest revenue unless:

1.   No interest rate is stated, or
2.   The stated interest rate is unreasonable, or
3.   The face amount of the note is materially different from the current cash sales price for the same or similar items or from the current market value of the debt instrument.

In these circumstances, the present value of the note is measured by the fair value of the property, goods, or services. If the fair value of the property, goods, or services is not readily determinable, the market value of the note is used to establish the present value of the note. If the note has no ready market, the present value of the note is approximated by discounting all of the related future cash payments (for interest and principal) on the note at the market rate of interest. This rate is referred to as an imputed rate and should be equal to the borrower's incremental borrowing rate (that is, the rate of interest the maker of the note would currently have to pay if it borrowed money from another source for this same purpose). Jason Weiss, Inc. issued a note in exchange for land. No information was given about the fair value of the services or the market value of the note. Thus, the debtor company's incremental borrowing rate of 10% was used to impute interest and determine the note's present value.

(c)   Interest from April 1, 2014 thru December 31, 2014:

$38,905.29 x 9/12	$29,178.97
Interest from January 1, 2015 thru March 31, 2015:	
$41,295.82 x 3/12	10,323.96
Interest for the fiscal year ending March 31, 2015:	$39,502.93

TIP: The amount of interest shown on the 12/31/14 line in the amortization schedule is the amount of interest that pertains to the interest period that is just ending on that date (12/31/14 in this case). When interest is payable annually, an interest period is twelve months in length. When interest is payable semi-annually, each interest period is six months long.

TIP: When the end of an accounting period does not coincide with an interest payment date, interest must be apportioned to the proper periods. For example, we will use the amortization schedule above and assume that the accounting period ends on March 31, 2014. The effective interest of $38,905.29 for the calendar year ending December 31, 2014 must be apportioned between two fiscal years: the one ending March 31, 2014 and the one ending March 31, 2015. 3/12 X $38,905.29 = $9,726.32 would be allocated to the fiscal year ending March 31, 2014 and 9/12 X $38,905.29 = $29,178.97 would be allocated to the fiscal year ending March 31, 2015. The twelve months ending March 31, 2015 would include the 9/12 X $38,905.29 plus three months of the $41,295.82 interest amount shown on the 12/31/15 payment line.

Entering the interest amounts from the amortization schedule into the proper places on a time line should greatly help your comprehension of these computations. The following pictoral will aid you in following the logic of the computations.

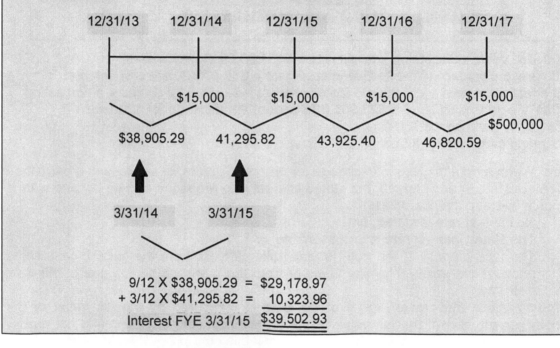

(d) A payment of cash of $15,000 was made for interest on December 31, 2014. Thus, a cash outflow of $15,000 would be reflected in the operating activity section of the statement of cash flows for the fiscal year ending March 31, 2015.

(e)
                                    Balance Sheet
                                    March 31, 2015

Property, Plant & Equipment   Current Liabilities
Land $429,052.90   Interest Payable $3,750.00[a]

                                               Long-term Liabilities
                                               Note Payable $500,000.00
                                               Less: Discount on
                                                     Note   80,467.85[b]
                                                                    $419,532.15

[a]$3/12 \times \$15,000 = \$3,750.00$
[b]$3/12 \times \$26,295.82 = 6,573.96$ amortization of discount for 01/01/15 - 03/31/15

$110,947.10	Balance of Discount on Note Payable on 12/31/13
(23,905.29)	Amortization for 01/01/14 thru 12/31/14
(6,573.96)	Amortization for 01/01/15 thru 3/31/15
$ 80,467.85	Balance of Discount on Note Payable on 03/31/15

EXERCISE 14-7

Purpose: (L.O. 6) This exercise will illustrate the accounting entries for a long-term note payable.

The Weiss Corporation issued a $400,000, 10%, 10-year mortgage note on December 31, 2013. The terms provide for semiannual installment payments of $32,097.03 on June 30 and December 31. The note along with $80,000 cash was given in exchange for a new building. The accounting period is the calendar year.

Instructions
Prepare the journal entries to record:
(a) The acquisition of the building and inception of the mortgage loan payable.
(b) The first mortgage payment on June 30, 2014.
(c) The second mortgage payment on December 31, 2014.

SOLUTION TO EXERCISE 14-7

December 31, 2013

(a) Building.. 480,000.00

     Cash...   80,000.00

     Mortgage Note Payable..   400,000.00

June 30, 2014

(b) Interest Expense.. 20,000.00*

    Mortgage Note Payable... 12,097.03**

     Cash..   32,097.03

*Principal balance at December 31, 2013	$400,000.00
Semiannual interest rate	X .05
Interest expense for first 6 months	$ 20,000.00
**First payment	$32,097.03
Interest portion of first payment	(20,000.00)
Reduction in principal - first installment payment	$12,097.03

December 31, 2014

(c) Interest Expense.. 19,395.15*

    Mortgage Note Payable... 12,701.88**

     Cash..   32,097.03

*Principal balance at December 31, 2013	$400,000.00
Reduction in principal - first installment payment	(12,097.03)
Principal balance at June 30, 2014	387,902.97
Semiannual interest rate	.05
Interest expense for second 6 months	$ 19,395.15
**Second payment	$32,097.03
Interest portion of second payment	(19,395.15)
Reduction in principal - second installment payment	$12,701.88

Explanation to part (a): The cost of the building is determined by the fair market value of the consideration given which is the $80,000 cash plus the $400,000 present value of the note payable.

Explanation to parts (b) and (c): The mortgage note payable is recorded initially at its face value ($400,000), which is often referred to as the note's beginning principal, and each installment payment reduces the outstanding principal amount. The installment payments are an equal amount each interest period; however, the portion of the payment going to cover interest charges and the portion going to reduce the outstanding principal varies each period. In this exercise, the installment payments are due semiannually; thus, the length of an interest period is six months and the annual interest rate (10%) must be expressed on a semiannual basis (5%) to perform the interest computation. Interest is a function of outstanding balance, interest rate, and time. Thus, the interest sustained for the first six months is determined by the note's initial carrying value (the face value of $400,000), the annual rate of 10%, and a six-month time period. The interest sustained for the second six months cannot be determined until the outstanding principal balance is updated for the portion of the first installment payment that is to be applied to the principal balance. The updated principal balance (carrying value) is used

require a complete payment schedule (often called an amortization schedule) for this note, one is presented below for your observation and study. Notice that as subsequent installment payments are made, a decreasing portion of each payment goes to cover interest and an increasing portion is applied to the principal balance. The reason for this is the fact that interest is computed by a constant interest rate (5% each interest period) multiplied by a decreasing principal balance (carrying value).

TIP:	The stated rate of interest (10% in this case) is assumed to be equal to the market rate of interest; therefore, the present value of the note at its inception is the same as the face value ($400,000) and there is no discount or premium related to this mortgage note payable.
TIP:	A mortgage note will usually require the borrower to make monthly payments, and interest is then compounded monthly. In this exercise, semiannual payments are assumed (thus interest is compounded twice a year) in order to simplify the amortization schedule but yet allow you an opportunity to view a situation involving the compounding of interest more than once a year.

Mortgage Installment Payment Schedule

Semiannual Interest Period	(A) Cash Payment	(B) Interest Expense (D) X 5%	(C) Reduction of Principal (A) - (B)	(D) Principal Balance (D) - (C)
12/31/13				$400,000.00
6/30/14	$ 32,097.03	$ 20,000.00	$ 12,097.03	387,902.97
12/31/14	32,097.03	19,395.15	12,701.88	375,201.09
6/30/15	32,097.03	18,760.05	13,336.98	361,864.11
12/31/15	32,097.03	18,093.21	14,003.82	347,860.29
6/30/16	32,097.03	17,393.01	14,704.02	333,156.27
12/31/16	32,097.03	16,657.81	15,439.22	317.717.05
6/30/17	32,097.03	15,885.85	16,211.18	301,505.87
12/31/17	32,097.03	15,075.29	17,021.74	284,484.13
6/30/18	32,097.03	14,224.21	17,872.82	266,611.31
12/31/18	32,097.03	13,330.57	18,766.46	247,844.85
6/30/19	32,097.03	12,392.24	19,704.79	228,140.06
12/31/19	32,097.03	11,407.00	20,690.03	207,450.03
6/30/20	32,097.03	10,372.50	21,724.53	185,725.50
12/31/20	32,097.03	9,286.28	22,810.75	162,914.75
6/30/21	32,097.03	8,145.74	23,951.29	138,963.46
12/31/21	32,097.03	6,948.17	25,148.86	113,814.60
6/30/22	32,097.03	5,690.73	26,406.30	87,408.30
12/31/22	32,097.93	4,370.42	27,726.61	59,681.69
6/30/23	32,097.03	2,984.08	29,112.95	30,568.74
12/31/23	32,097.03	1,528.29[a]	30,568.74	0.00
Totals	$641,940.60	$241,940.60	$400,000.00	

[a]Includes rounding difference of 15¢.

TIP:	Notice that the total interest to be incurred over the ten-year period is $241,940.60 on the loan of $400,000.00. The pattern of interest charges is one of a decreasing amount each interest period because interest is a function of present value balance, constant rate, and time.

EXERCISE 14-8

Purpose: (L.O. 6, 8) This exercise will illustrate how an installment note payable affects the financial statements.

The use of a mortgage note is a common vehicle to finance the acquisition of long-lived tangible assets. A mortgage note usually requires the borrower to repay the loan by equal periodic payments over the life of the loan. Each payment goes to cover the interest accrued during the time segment since the previous payment and to reduce the principal balance.

Instructions

Using the amortization schedule from **Exercise 14-7**, answer the following questions:
(a)   How much interest expense would be reported on the income statement for the year ending December 31, 2014?
(b)   How would the two payments during the year 2014 of $32,097.05 each be reflected in the statement of cash flows for the year ending December 31, 2014?
(c)   How would the balance of $375,201.09 at December 31, 2014 be reported on a balance sheet as of that date?

SOLUTION TO EXERCISE 14-8

(a) $20,000.00   Interest expense 1/01/14 - 6/30/14
      <u>19,395.15</u>   Interest expense 7/01/14 - 12/31/14
      <u>$39,395.15</u>   Total interest expense for the year ending 12/31/14

(b)   The amounts paid during year 2014 for interest ($20,000.00 + $19,395.15 = **$39,395.15**) should be reported as a cash outflow due to operating activities. The amounts paid during year 2014 for principal reduction ($12,097.03 + 12,701.88 = **$24,798.91**) would be reported as payments on debt which are classified as cash outflows from financing activities on a statement of cash flows for the year ended December 31, 2014.

(c)   The balance of the Mortgage Note Payable account is reported as a liability in the balance sheet. The portion of the installment payments scheduled to be due and paid within the next year (that is, the year that follows the balance sheet date) that represents the reduction of the principal balance is to be reported in the current liability section of the balance sheet; the remaining unpaid principal balance is classified in the long-term liability section.

      $ 13,336.98   Amount due June 30, 2015
        <u>14,003.82</u>   Amount due December 31, 2015
      <u>$ 27,340.80</u>   Current liability as of December 31, 2014

      <u>$347,860.29</u>   Long-term liability as of December 31, 2014

TIP: If Weiss Corporation (**Exercise 14-7**) had its accounting period end on March 31, 2015 rather than December 31, 2014, the answers to parts "a"., "b"., and "c". of **Exercise 14-8** would be as follows:

a.
$10,000.00	$20,000.00 X 3/6 = Interest expense 3/31/14 to 6/30/14
19,395.15	$19,395.15 X 6/6 = Interest expense 7/01/14 to 12/31/14
9,380.03	$18,760.05 X 3/6 = Interest expense 01/01/15 to 03/31/15
$38,775.18	Total interest expense for the year ending 03/31/15

b. The payments on 6/30/14 and 12/31/14 fall in the year ending March 31, 2015. Therefore, this answer would be the same as in **Exercise 14-8**:

$20,000 + $19,395.15 = $39,395.15 cash outflow due to operating activities (interest paid)

$12,097.03 + $12,701.88 = $24,789.91 cash outflow due to financing activity (payment on debt)

c. For the balance sheet:

$ 13,336.98	Amount due June 30, 2015
14,003.82	Amount due December 31, 2015
$ 27,340.80	Current liability as of March 31, 2014
$347,860.29	Long-term liability as of March 31, 2014

Notice that answers "b" and "c" above are the same as answers "b" and "c" in the **Solution to Exercise 14-8**. This is because the cash payments are made at a point in time and a principal reduction applies at a point in time when a cash payment is made. Fractions (such as 3/12 and 9/12) are applied to interest amounts (which are for a period of time) to apportion interest to the appropriate accounting periods. However, fractions are **never** applied to principal reduction figures.

EXERCISE 14-9

Purpose: (L.O. 7) This exercise will give an example of using the fair value option for reporting a long-term note payable.

On April 1, 2014, Halbmann Company issued a long-term note payable for cash. The note had a face value of $200,000 and a stated interest rate of 8%. The market rate of interest was also 8% on April 1. Interest is paid at the end of each month.

Halbmann chooses to use the fair value option for this note. At December 31, 2014, the fair value of the bonds was $185,000 because interest rates in the market place had increased. At December 31, 2015, the fair value of the bonds was $202,000 because the market rate of interest for this type of note had decreased.

Instructions:

a.   Prepare the adjusting journal entry at December 31, 2014 required to report the note payable at fair value.
b.   Indicate the amounts to be reported on the balance sheet at the end of 2014 and the income statement for 2014 that relate to this note payable.
c.   Prepare the adjusting journal entry at December 31, 2015 required to reflect the note payable at fair value.
d.   Indicate the amounts to be reported on the balance sheet at the end of 2015 and the income statement for 2015 that relate to this note payable.

Solution to Exercise 14-9

a.   Note Payable   15,000
         Unrealized Holding Gain or Loss—Income.....................   15,000
         ($200,000 - $185,000 = $15,000)

b.   On the balance sheet under long-term liabilities:
         Note payable $185,000
      On the income statement under expenses:
         Interest expense $12,000
         ($200,000 x 8% x 9/12 = $12,000)
      On the income statement under Other Gains:
         Holding gain from change in market interest rate $15,000

c.   Unrealized Holding Gain or Loss—Income   17,000
         Note Payable   17,000
         ($202,000 - $185,000 = $17,000)

d. On the balance sheet under long-term liabilities:
        Note payable $202,000
    On the income statement under expenses:
        Interest expense $ 16,000
        ($200,000 x 8% x 12/12 = $16,000)
    On the income statement under Other Losses:
        Holding loss from change in market
        interest rate $ 17,000

Explanation: Noncurrent liabilities such as bonds and notes payable are generally measured at amortized cost (face value of the payable, adjusted for any payments and amortization of any premium or discount). However, as previously indicated, companies have the option to use fair value for reporting most financial assets and liabilities, including bonds and notes payable. As mentioned in **Chapter 7,** the FASB believes that fair value measurement for financial instruments, including financial liabilities, provides more relevant information because fair value reflects the current cash equivalent value of financial instruments.

If a company chooses to use fair value to report an item (such as a financial asset or liability) the net change in the fair value of the item from one period to another (exclusive of interest recognized but not recorded) is accounted for as an unrealized holding gain or loss and reported on the income statement.

*ILLUSTRATION 14-5
SUMMARY OF ACCOUNTING FOR IMPAIRMENT AND TROUBLED DEBT RESTRUCTURINGS (L.O. 10)

Event	Accounting Procedure
1. Impairment	**Creditor:** Loss based upon difference between present value of future cash flows discounted at historical effective interest rate and carrying amount of note. Recognize interest revenue (or bad debt expense reduction) based upon new carrying amount and original effective rate. **Debtor:** No recognition.
2. Restructuring—Settlement of Debt a. Transfer of noncash assets.	**Creditor:** Recognize ordinary loss on restructure. **Debtor:** Recognize gain on restructure and recognize gain or loss on asset transfer.
b. Granting of equity interest.	**Creditor:** Recognize loss on restructure. **Debtor:** Recognize gain on restructure.
3. Restructurings—Continuation of Debt with Modified Terms a. Carrying amount of debt is less than future cash flows (no gain for debtor).	**Creditor:** Recognize ordinary loss based upon present value of restructured cash flows. Use the historical effective rate of the loan to compute this present value amount. Recognize interest revenue based upon new recorded value and original effective rate. **Debtor:** Recognize no gain on restructure. Determine new effective interest rate to be used in recording interest expense.
b. Carrying amount of debt is greater than total future cash flows (gain for debtor)	**Creditor:** Recognize loss based upon present value of restructured cash flows. Recognize interest revenue based upon new recorded value and original effective rate. **Debtor:** Recognize gain on restructure and reduce carrying amount to the sum of the undiscounted cash flows. Recognize no interest expense over the remaining life of the debt.

TIP: When there is a restructuring that involves the continuation of debt with modification of terms, the computations made by the creditor to assess impairment are based on discounted future cash flows (at the original effective interest rate). However, the debtor's gain is calculated based upon undiscounted amounts. As a consequence, the gain recorded by the debtor will not equal the loss recorded by the creditor under many circumstances.

TIP: When there is a restructuring that involves a settlement of debt by transfer of noncash assets, the debtor has the following gain-loss computations:
(1) The excess of the carrying amount of the debt over the fair market value of the assets is recorded as a gain on restructuring; this gain is reported as an other item on the income statement.
(2) The difference between the fair market value of the assets and their recorded value (book value) is recorded as a gain or loss on disposition of assets; this gain or loss is reported in the other gains or other losses section of a multiple-step income statement.
    (a) If the fair market value of the assets exceeds their book value, a gain results.
    (b) If the book value of the assets exceeds their fair market value, a loss results.

*EXERCISE 14-10

Purpose: (L.O. 10) This exercise will illustrate the accounting for a transfer of noncash assets to settle a debt obligation in a troubled debt situation.

Boston Co. owes $194,400 to San Diego Trust Co. The debt is a 10-year, 8% note. Because Boston Co. is in financial trouble, San Diego agrees to accept some property and cancel the entire debt. The property has a cost of $150,000, accumulated depreciation of $80,000, and a fair market value of $110,000.

Instructions
(a) Prepare the journal entry on Boston's books for the debt restructure.
(b) Prepare the journal entry on San Diego's books for the debt restructure.

Solution to Exercise 14-10

(a) **BOSTON'S ENTRY:**

Notes Payable	194,400	
Accumulated Depreciation	80,000	
Property		150,000
Gain on Property Disposition (Not extraordinary)		40,000*
Gain on Restructuring of Debt (Extraordinary)		84,400**

*$110,000 - ($150,000 - $80,000) = $40,000
**$194,400 - $110,000 = $84,400

Approach and Explanation: (1) Begin with the easiest part of the journal entry. Remove the debt amount by a debit to Notes Payable for $194,400. (2) Remove the carrying value of the property by a debit to Accumulated Depreciation for $80,000 and a credit to Property for the $150,000 cost. (3) Compute and record the gain from settlement ($84,400 credit) and, (4) compute and record the gain from disposition of assets ($40,000). (5) Double check the entry to make sure it balances.

The debtor is required to determine the excess of the carrying amount of the payable ($194,400) over the fair value of the assets transferred ($110,000) and report that difference as an extraordinary gain ($84,400). The difference between the fair value of those assets and their carrying amounts is to be recognized as a gain or loss on disposition of assets. In this case, the fair value of $110,000 exceeds the carrying amount of $70,000; therefore, an gain of $40,000 is to be recognized.

(b) **SAN DIEGO'S ENTRY:**

Property	110,000	
Allowance for Doubtful Accounts (or Loss on Restructuring)	84,400	
Notes Receivable		194,400

Approach and Explanation: (1) Remove the carrying amount of the receivable from the accounts by a credit to Notes Receivable for $194,400. (2) Record the acquisition of the property by a debit to Property for its fair value of $110,000. (3) Record the loss on settlement of $84,400 by a debit to Allowance for Doubtful Accounts or to a loss account. (4) Double check the entry to make sure it balances.

The creditor is required to determine the excess of the carrying amount of the receivable over the fair value of the assets being transferred to the creditor and record it as a charge against the Allowance for Doubtful Accounts account or to a loss account (such a loss is **not** to be classified as an extraordinary item).

ANALYSIS OF MULTIPLE-CHOICE TYPE QUESTIONS

QUESTION
1.   (L.O. 2) Bonds for which the owners' names are **not** registered with the issuing corporation are called:
   a.   bearer bonds.
   b.   term bonds.
   c.   debenture bonds.
   d.   secured bonds.

Approach and Explanation: Briefly define each answer selection. Choose the one that is described in the question's stem. **Bearer** (or **coupon**) **bonds** are bonds for which the name of the owner is not registered with the issuer; bondholders are required to send in coupons to receive interest payments and the bonds may be transferred directly to another party. **Registered bonds** are bonds registered in the name of the owner. **Term bonds** are bonds that mature (become due for payment) at a single specified future date. **Debenture bonds** are unsecured bonds. **Secured bonds** are bonds having specific assets pledged as collateral by the issuer. (Solution = a.)

QUESTION
2.   (L.O. 3) The periodic amortization of a premium on bonds payable will:
   a.   cause the carrying value of the bonds to increase each period.
   b.   cause the carrying value of the bonds to decrease each period.
   c.   have no effect on the carrying value of the bonds.
   d.   cause the carrying value always to be less than the par value of the bonds.

Approach and Explanation: Think about the process of amortizing a premium on bonds payable and how it affects the carrying value of the bonds. The Premium on Bonds Payable account has a normal credit balance. A premium is an adjustment to interest via an adjustment to price. Therefore, the entry to amortize the premium involves a debit to Premium on Bonds Payable and a credit to Interest Expense. The amortization process reduces the balance of the unamortized premium. The carrying value of a bond issued at a premium is calculated by adding the premium balance to the face value of the bond. Thus, the carrying value of bonds payable issued at a premium will decrease each period until the maturity date (at which time the carrying value will equal the face value). (Solution = b.)

QUESTION
3. (L.O.3) A large department store issues bonds with a maturity date that is 20 years after the issuance date. If the bonds are issued at a discount, this indicates that at the date of issuance, the:
    a.   nominal rate of interest and the stated rate of interest coincide.
    b.   nominal rate of interest exceeds the yield rate.
    c.   yield rate of interest exceeds the coupon rate.
    d.   stated rate of interest exceeds the effective rate.

Approach and Explanation: Before reading the answer selections, write down the relationship that causes a bond to be issued at a discount: market rate of interest exceeds the stated rate of interest. Then list the synonymous terms for market rate and for stated rate: (1) market rate, effective rate, and yield rate; (2) stated rate, coupon rate, nominal rate, and contract rate. Selection "a" is incorrect because the nominal rate and the stated rate are just different names for the same thing. Selections "b" and "d" are incorrect because an excess of nominal rate (stated rate) over the yield rate (effective rate) will result in a premium, not a discount. Selection "c" is correct because when the yield rate (market rate) exceeds the coupon rate (stated rate), an issuance discount will result. (Solution = c.)

QUESTION
4. (L.O. 3) The amount of cash to be paid for interest on bonds payable for any given year is calculated by multiplying the:
    a.   face value of the stated interest rate.
    b.   face value by the market interest rate at the date of issuance.
    c.   carrying value at the beginning of the year by the market interest rate in existence at the date of issuance.
    d.   carrying value at the beginning of the year by the stated interest rate.

Explanation: The amount of cash interest to be paid is the amount promised by the bond contract (indenture) which is the contractual (stated) interest rate multiplied by the face value of the bond. (Solution = a.)

QUESTION
5. (L.O. 4) The amortization of a discount on bonds payable results in reporting an amount of interest expense for the period which:
    a.   exceeds the amount of cash interest for the period.
    b.   equals the amount of cash interest for the period.
    c.   is less than the amount of cash interest for the period.
    d.   bears no predictable relationship to the amount of cash interest for the period.

Approach and Explanation: Think about the process of amortizing a discount on bonds payable and how it affects interest expense. The Discount of Bonds Payable has a normal debit balance. Thus, to amortize it, you credit Discount on Bonds Payable and debit Interest Expense. A debit to the expense account increases its balance. Thus, interest expense is comprised of the amount to be paid in cash for interest for the period plus the amount of discount amortization for the period. Another way of viewing this situation is as follows: a discount is an additional amount of interest to be paid at maturity but is recognized (charged to expense) over the periods benefited (which would be the periods the bonds are to be outstanding). (Solution = a.)

QUESTION
6. (L.O. 4) If bonds are initially sold at a discount and the straight-line method of amortization is used, interest expense in the earlier years of the bond's life will:
   a. be less than the amount of interest actually paid.
   b. be less than it will be in the latter years of the bond's life.
   c. be the same as what it would have been had the effective interest method of amortization been used.
   d. exceed what it would have been had the effective interest method of amortization been used.

Approach and Explanation: Quickly sketch the graph that shows the patterns of and relationships between interest paid, interest expense using the straight-line method, and interest expense using the effective interest method. The graph appears in **Illustration 14-3**. Treat each of the possible answer selections as a True-False question. Look at the graph after reading each of the answer selections to determine if it is a correct answer.

Selection "a" is False because interest expense for a bond issued at a discount will be greater than interest actually paid throughout the bond's entire life, regardless of the amortization method used. Selection "b" is False because interest expense is a constant amount each period when the straight-line method is used; hence interest expense will be the same amount in the latter years as it is in the earlier years. Selection "c" is False because in the earlier years of life for a bond issued at a discount, interest expense computed using the straight-line method is greater than interest expense computed using the effective interest method. Selection "d" is True. The interest expense will increase over a bond's life when the bond is issued at a discount and the effective interest method of amortization is used. In the earlier years of life, that expense amount is less than interest expense using the straight-line method; and, in the latter years of life, that expense amount is more than interest expense computed using the straight-line method. (Solution = d.)

QUESTION
7. (L.O. 4) At the beginning of 2014, the Alston Corporation issued 10% bonds with a face value of $400,000. These bonds mature in five years, and interest is paid semiannually on June 30 and December 31. The bonds were sold for $370,560 to yield 12%. Alston uses a calendar-year reporting period. Using the preferable method of amortization, what amount of interest expense should be reported for 2014? (Round your answer to the nearest dollar.)
   a. $44,333
   b. $44,467
   c. $44,601
   d. $45,888

Approach and Explanation: Write down the formula for computing interest using the effective method of amortization. Use the data in the question to work through the formula.

	Carrying value at the beginning of the period	$370,560.00
x	Effective rate of interest per interest period	6%
=	Interest expense for the first interest period	22,233.60
-	Cash interest for the interest period	20,000.00*
=	Amortization of discount for the first interest period	2,233.60
+	Carrying value at the beginning of the first period	370,560.00
=	Carrying value at the beginning of the second period	372,793.60
x	Effective rate of interest per interest period	6%
=	Interest expense for the second interest period	22,367.62
+	Interest expense for the first interest period	22,233.60
=	Interest expense for the calendar year of 2014	$ 44,601.22

*$400,000 x (10% ÷ 2) = $20,000 (Solution = c.)

TIP: The interest must be computed on a per interest period basis. In this question, the interest period is six months. The interest for 2014 is comprised of the interest for the

QUESTION

8. (L.O. 5) At December 31, 2014 the following balances existed on the books of the Malloy Corporation:

Bonds Payable	$ 500,000
Discount on Bonds Payable	40,000
Interest Payable	12,500
Unamortized Bonds Issue Costs	30,000

If the bonds are retired on January 1, 2015, at 102, what will Malloy report as a loss on redemption?
a. $92,500
b. $80,000
c. $67,500
d. $50,000

Approach and Explanation: Write down the format for the computation of the gain or loss on redemption and plug in the amounts from this question.

	Par value	$ 500,000
-	Unamortized discount	40,000
=	Carrying amount	460,000
-	Unamortized debt issue costs	30,000
=	Net carrying amount	430,000
-	Redemption price	510,000*
=	Gain (Loss) on redemption	$ (80,000)

*$500,000 x 102% = $510,000.

(Solution = b.)

QUESTION

9. (L.O. 5) "In-substance defeasance" is a term used to refer to an arrangement whereby:
a. a company gets another company to cover its payments due on long-term debt.
b. a governmental unit issues debt instruments to corporations.
c. a company provides for the future repayment of a long-term debt by placing purchased securities in an irrevocable trust.
d. a company legally extinguishes debt before its due date.

Explanation: In-substance defeasance is an arrangement whereby a company provides for the future repayment of one or more of its long-term debt issues by placing purchased securities in an irrevocable trust, the principal and interest of which are pledged to pay off the principal and interest of its own debt securities as they mature. The company, however, is not legally released from being the primary obligor under the debt that is still outstanding. (Solution = c.)

QUESTION

10. (L.O. 6) Bandy Rentals borrowed money from a local savings and loan to build new mini-warehouses. Bandy gave a 20-year mortgage note in the amount of $100,000 with a stated rate of 10.75%. The lender charged 4 points to close the financing. Based on this information:
a. Bandy should debit Interest Expense in recording the points at the date the money is borrowed.
b. Bandy's effective interest rate is now less than the 10.75% stated rate.
c. Bandy should record the Mortgage Note Payable for only $96,000 since only $96,000 cash was received.
d. Bandy should amortize the points to interest expense over the life of the loan.

Explanation: Bandy will receive $96,000 cash but will have to repay $100,000 plus interest at 10.75% on the $100,000. Thus, the points raise the effective interest rate above the stated rate and should be accounted for as interest expense over the life of the loan. (Solution = d.)

QUESTION
11.   (L.O. 6) A corporation borrowed money from a bank to build a building. The long-term note signed by the corporation is secured by a mortgage that pledges title to the building as security for the loan. The corporation is to pay the bank $80,000 each year for 10 years to repay the loan. Which of the following relationships can you expect to apply to the situation?

   a.   The balance of mortgage payable at a given balance sheet date will be reported as a long-term liability.
   b.   The balance of mortgage payable will remain a constant amount over the 10-year period.
   c.   The amount of interest expense will decrease each period the loan is outstanding, while the portion of the annual payment applied to the loan principal will increase each period.
   d.   The amount of interest expense will remain constant over the 10-year period.

Explanation: Mortgage notes payable are recorded initially at face value, and entries are required subsequently for each installment payment. Each payment consists of (1) interest on the unpaid principal balance of the loan, and (2) a reduction of loan principal. Because a portion of each payment is applied to the principal, the principal balance decreases each period. Interest for a period of time is computed by multiplying the stated (contract) rate of interest by the principal balance outstanding at the beginning of the period. Thus, the amount of each payment required to cover interest decreases while the portion of the payment applied to the loan principal balance will increase each period. (Solution = c.)

QUESTION
12.   (L.O. 9) The debt to total assets ratio measures the:
   a.   relationship between interest expense and income.
   b.   portion of assets financed through creditor sources.
   c.   portion of debt used to acquire assets.
   d.   relationship between debt and interest expense.

Approach and Explanation: Write down the computation for the debt to total assets ratio and think about is components and their relationship. The debt to total assets ratio is computed by dividing total debt by total assets. This ratio measures the percentage of the total assets provided by creditors. The higher the percentage of debt to total assets, the greater the risk that the company may be unable to meet its maturing obligations. (Solution = b.)

QUESTION
13.   (L.O. 9) The times interest earned ratio provides an indication of the:
   a.   company's ability to meet interest payments as they become due.
   b.   relationship between current liabilities and current assets.
   c.   percentage of assets financed by debt.
   d.   relationship between debt and interest expense.

Approach and Explanation: Write down the computation for the interest earned ratio and think about the relationship of the components of the ratio. The interest earned ratio is computed by dividing interest before income taxes and interest expense by interest expense. This ratio provides an indication of the relationship between income (before taxes and interest expense have deducted) and the amount of interest expense for the period. It is an indication of the company's ability to meet interest payments as they become due. (Solution = a.)